Serial Killers

Serial Killers

The Growing Menace

Joel Norris

arrow books

Serial Killers

Previously published in 1990 by Arrow Books Ltd

This paperback edition published in 1997 by Senate,
an imprint of Random House UK Ltd, Random House,
20 Vauxhall Bridge Road, London SW1V 2SA

ISBN 0 09971 750 6

Printed and bound in Great Britain by
Cox & Wyman Ltd, Reading, Berkshire

For all of the victims and my steadfast supporters:
Joel Jones, Margurite McKinney, Judy Lawrence Mahoney,
and David Maurer.

Contents

The Unifying Patterns of a Serial Killer

Preface

You are about to read a book which takes you into the bizarre and distorted mind of the serial killer. A relative rarity, the serial killer occupies the darkest side of human nature, fusing the most regressive regions of sexual and aggressive conflicts into his criminal behavior. This is the ultimate perversion, and, as such, stimulates our most intense interest and horror. Joel Norris captures, in this fascinating portrayal, the essence of the serial killer and those factors which have created him.

This is an important book. America is in the midst of an increasing crescendo of violence, affecting every element of our society. With few exceptions, we have responded to this with traditional American solutions: outcries for 'law and order,' stiffer sentences for offenders, and escalating demands for capital punishment. Our jails and prisons are literally bursting with inmates, in spite of frantic building programs. We have abandoned any ideas of rehabilitation. Our prisons are little more than warehouses, providing only token educational and vocational programs. Recidivism rates are high and showing no tendency to fall. The costs of building and maintaining our penal institutions is approaching the level where the taxpaying public will be forced to find other, more innovative solutions for the problem of criminal justice. Our 'out of sight, out of mind' approach is simply becoming too expensive.

As Dr. Norris so eloquently describes in this book, criminal behavior is no simple matter. It is an exceedingly complex 'common final pathway' for disorders of the biological, psychological, and social aspects of human existence. I am in complete agreement with Dr. Norris when he defines serial killers as a public health problem. Unlike many other public health problems, however, we have not put resources into research into the causes of criminality and its prevention. Unfortunately, the field of criminology has little prestige within the scientific community. There appears to be apprehension on the part of many professionals who might otherwise consider working with criminals. Some express a fear of being victimized themselves, while others, perhaps less forthrightly, attribute the fear to their spouses. Statistics, however, consistently indicate that the risk of assault upon staff is far greater in mental hospitals than it is in prisons. Psychiatrists, like myself, who have chosen to work in penal institutions, find them full of the most fascinating examples of psychopathology. We see our inmate patients as the products of complex, yet understandable, interactions between nature and nurture. The majority are personality disordered individuals, true developmental disorders, with features which are traceable to inherited and environmental influences. Some are even amenable to psychotherapy. Most have some association between their offense and alcohol or drug use, while some have demonstrable brain damage. Of the latter group, a very high percentage have never been diagnosed, in spite of medical screening before their trials or during incarceration. Of these, a significant number have neurological impairments which are clearly related to their criminal offenses. It has been my experience that organic brain pathology is vastly underdiagnosed in the prison population and plays a much larger role in criminal behavior than we have previously thought. It is gratifying to note Dr. Norris' awareness and sensitivity to this generally neglected area.

Reading *Serial Killers* has been, for me, a true 'busman's holiday.' The author has, in his literary research, discovered those elements in the serial killer which constitute his tragic uniqueness and has shared with us these important insights. If these insights were to stimulate a greater awareness in the public of the need for research into the causes and treatment of criminal behavior, his work would, indeed, be historic as well as informative, stimulating, and entertaining.

–Philip S. Hicks, M.D.
Chief Psychiatrist
California State Prison
San Quentin, California

Acknowledgments

Many people are to be thanked for assisting in this effort. First and foremost are the three victims' families, who readily shared with me their grief and outrage. Rather than becoming vengeful people who only sought the executions of the murderers, these families were eager to understand the factors that motivated the killers. And today they are actively supportive in seeking ways to prevent future serial murderers from preying upon defenseless victims. I would also like to thank the families of the killers, as well as the killers themselves, who have shared their particular kind of pain.

Recognition and appreciation must extend to the medical and scientific experts who read the first drafts of this manuscript, and contributed their efforts to making sure that all the information was accurate and up-to-date. I also thank scientists such as Vernon Mark, Paul New, Jan Brunner, Sarnoff Mednick, Jonathan Indik, Robert Thatcher, and William Walsh, who have contributed to the medical and scientific opinions of the serial killers that we studied in the course of this book.

Thanks also go to the following friends and assistants, who, in the process, have learned more about serial murderers than they ever wanted to know: Connie and Jeff Ichihashi, Michael Eisenbach, Peter Corsi, Jeffery Robbins, Tom Pacheco, Judy Hanson, Susan and Roland Moussa, Linda Monez, and Gerry Vics.

I acknowledge also the help of other writers and editors along the road to completing this book. I was fortunate to first share this task with Brad Darrach, and Richard Burgheim of *Life* magazine. Special gratitude goes to Texas journalist Nan Cuba, Sheriff Jim Boutwell, Captain Bob Prince of the Texas Rangers, Clementine Schroeder, and the doctors and the hospitals in Dallas who performed the neurological testing on Henry Lucas.

Also to be thanked are my New York literary agent Carol Mann and her assistant Nancy Hogan and Jim Fitzgerald and Laura Nixon of Doubleday.

Finally, I would like to thank Bill Birnes, the coauthor of *Serial Killers: The Growing Menace*. Besides being an expert with words, Bill was chosen as coauthor because of his many years of experience working with the National Endowment for the Humanities in Washington, D.C., first as a Fellow, and then as a Judge. The NEH, by promoting the development of new pedagogies and funding the testing of new ideas outside the bell jar of the undergraduate classroom, has become known as a bipartisan model of social change that encourages interdisciplinarian approaches to traditional problems. I knew that Bill Birnes would appreciate the growth, and the subtle roadblocks that prevent government, mental health, and criminal justice professionals from understanding the nature of the problem that is confronting all of us.

It is my hope that the efforts of all my colleagues, during this task, will stimulate new research into the study of prevention of extraordinary violence and serial murder.

–J.N.

Introduction

I am a trained counseling psychologist. I have worked as an educator to the defense and appeals teams of several convicted killers in Georgia, some of whom were multiple killers. I taught supportive counseling techniques to inmates and prison guards at the Atlanta Federal Penitentiary, was a consultant to the University of Georgia on prevention of violence, and addressed the members of the Georgia State legislature on juvenile justice reform. And after years of working within the criminal justice and corrections systems and within the professional milieu of mental health and academia I have been witness to a vast chasm of misunderstanding between the most violent people in our country and those mandated by their chosen professions to understand and control them. I was fascinated by this fact. How could people who were responsible for dealing with the most violent elements of our population so completely misunderstand the people they were trying to control? There were no easy answers. Finally, after several years of intense community work, I took a sabbatical leave to reorganize my thoughts, regroup my energies, and undertake further research into the issues. This book is the result of that research.

The misunderstanding between those who commit violent acts and those who are supposed to apprehend, try, and institutionalize them manifests itself in a variety of ways. First, the justice system does not concern itself with the underlying motivations of the killers. Prevention of crime is not the issue here; punishment is. The trials of the multiple killers on whose cases I worked had more to do with calming the public's appropriate, but misplaced, rage; with the style, personality, charisma, drive, motivation, and financial and political strength of the attorneys involved; with the agenda of the court; and with the pervasive influence of the media. Chance and the legal technicalities of state statutes and judicial precedent were more beneficial to the attorneys on both sides than were any of the psychiatric explanations of the defendants' motivations. And the juries in these cases were simply ill equipped to understand the complex issues that formed the underlying structure of the killers' aberrant psyches. Simply stated, all the evidence wasn't in the courtroom when the cases were presented to the juries, only the evidence that floated on the surface of the arguments.

At the University of Georgia, while helping to devise a core curriculum for the development of creative therapy programs to study the prevention of violence and some forms of mental illness, I had the opportunity to discuss my observations with faculty members in a variety of academic fields. These professors were in a critical position to formulate policy for research, demonstration, and training projects both at universities and at state facilities. They were also able to select target populations for research and could influence the way violence would be studied for generations to come. Yet almost none of them had ever been inside a prison or interviewed a killer face to face. They were fascinated by my death row stories and would talk for hours about the subject of multiple and violent homicide, theorizing and speculating about motives and causality. But unfortunately their natural curiosity and their almost intuitive understanding of this unique prison population did not translate into the public and competitive arena of academia. To voice an intuitive theory about convicted killers or to present a member of this deviant group to an elitist board of regents or other academic policymaking groups, or even to suggest that convicted killers be used as target subjects for research, demonstration, or training projects, was risky to the professional future of the individual expert as well as to the program he or she wanted to develop. Consequently those who were in the best position to inform professional opinion about the true causes of multiple killings and other episodically violent offenses were too afraid for their reputations to get involved with the real issues of the problem.

At the same time the general public was enraged by society's growing vulnerability to violence. They wanted protection from criminals, and they wanted to see justice done in the courtroom. However, in the glare of media publicity that made multiple killers larger-than-life characters, the issues of prevention and motivation got lost and were replaced by demands for vengeance and retribution. It was easy to see why no academic or political figure would stake his professional livelihood on a program that might be perceived as 'coddling killers.'

Yet with each killer I met I saw a growing number of ill individuals, albeit people with no obvious disease. As a group, they all looked spent, drained but calm, as if ·hey had recently experienced an internal storm. In the cages of the institutions where they were housed the inmates looked at peace, even though they were on trial for their lives, were serving life sentences, or were waiting on death row for their appointment with the executioner. Obviously they were physically and psychologically damaged people, some more than others. Almost all of them had scars on their bodies, missing fingers, evidence of previous contusions and multiple abrasions on and around the head and neck area. And they had permanent scars from accidents, fights, knifings, bullet and shotgun wounds, and burns; many of which had been inflicted by the killers' own family members while the killers were still at a young age. All of the killers talked about the desire for freedom even while they seemed to be 'at home' in their prison environments. More than once, after a particularly grueling interview with a killer, the attending guard would put his arm around the inmate in a knowing and fatherly way and say, as he was taking the killer back to his cell, 'Come on, son, let's go home.'

Almost all the killers I met were repeat offenders, and some were serial killers. They all spoke about how offensive prison life was, but through their behavior they had yielded to and embraced a particular lifestyle that ensured that an institution would become their permanent environment. It intrigued me that intelligent individuals would repeatedly make choices in their lives that would lead them to such an environment. Had they lost their free will in making such a choice? One such killer said to me: 'As soon as I leave the prison and breathe the air of freedom, I am like a parakeet out of its cage – out of control – and will do anything to get back in the cage.'

Some of the killers had been psychotic, but few had been judged legally insane because they had passed the litmus test, known as the McNaghten rules, which are used to determine whether one was capable of differentiating between right and wrong. The McNaghten rules came to American jurisprudence from England in the 1800s. Basically they state that if a person can intellectually understand the difference between right and wrong and the consequences of his behavior, then the person is not insane. This definition is the cornerstone of the concept of legal insanity and therefore informs all perspectives and theories about violence in our country. It causes me great concern that the most progressive society ever known to humankind, with all of the medical and scientific advances it has made since the turn of the century, continues to rely on such an antiquated and completely inaccurate definition of human behavior. To premise a legal definition of insanity on the McNaghten rules is just like applying nineteenth-century medicine to treating cancer or AIDS.

I also found that the media were interested not in the generally violent person but in the 'superstar killers' such as Jean Harris, Charles Manson, and Ted Bundy or in murder stories with a hero who had escaped or a detective or a parental victim who had saved the day. Because I was from Georgia and the Atlanta Child Murders case was still on everyone's mind, I proceeded with preliminary research into that case and the evidence against convicted murderer Wayne Williams. To my surprise, I discovered six additional serial murder cases in Georgia that took place in the same four-year span as the Atlanta tragedy. Upon further investigation, I discovered that the syndrome was not only indigenous to Georgia but was nationwide. It was at that point that I decided to focus my research on the most ultimately malevolent group of people on the spectrum of violence in American society: the serial murderers. In January 1984 the FBI announced that there was an epidemic of serial murder in America. And this coincided with my observations that serial murder and other severe forms of episodic aggression was a form of disease that had to be identified and diagnosed before it engulfed all of our social institutions. Accordingly, in August 1984, I published my first article on the subject in *Life* magazine.

During the next couple of years I had the opportunity to interview several accused and convicted serial killers face to face and to learn their own personal stories of violence and pain. I began my odyssey in my own hometown and eventually became a consultant to the defense team of Carlton Gary, the 'Stocking Strangler' of Columbus, Georgia, and the convicted killer of elderly women in my own childhood neighbourhood. I saw Ted Bundy and interviewed Bobby Joe Long on Florida's death row and Henry Lee Lucas in Georgetown, Texas. Kneeling in Lucas' jail cell and participating in prayer sessions with Henry and his confidante, Sister Clemmie, became as routine as hearing the killer's grandiose confessions and his recantations of those confessions just one year later. We learned to expect the unexpected.

I interviewed Joseph Kallinger at Farview Prison in eastern Pennsylvania and worked with his biographer Flora Schreiber, the author of *Sybil* and *The Shoemaker*. I witnessed the unique bond that had formed between Schreiber and Kallinger even though they came from different backgrounds and had led vastly different lives. I spoke to the relatives of victims of serial murderers as well, including Doris Tate, mother of Sharon Tate, and RoseAlyce and Charles Thayer, and the Fentons whose daughter was raped and murdered by Gary Schaefer in Springfield, Vermont. Experiencing their pain and understanding the ramifications of their irreversible trauma was an important step in evaluating the effects that serial murders have on their communities. Then in Quantico, Virginia, I met the 'supersleuth' agents of the Behavioral Science Unit of the FBI and was impressed by their fierce dedication to their task and fascinated by their skill in identifying the emerging patterns of commonality from murder case to murder case which allowed them to develop skillful techniques of apprehension. Yet I was also concerned because they did not understand how the patterns they had developed could be used by other professionals for the purposes of preventing serial murder.

Although the stories of the individual killers were

different, the patterns of parental abuse, violence, neglect, childhood cognitive disabilities, and alcohol and drug abuse were virtually identical. Now, four years later, after more than five hundred interviews, many hours spent in libraries and on the telephone collecting anecdotes and symptoms from the histories of serial killers, I am releasing my initial findings with *Serial Killers*. The highlight of the research that I hope will encourage others to examine new evidence in this field has been the overwhelming interest of the individuals I have met along the way. Other writers, experts from a wide range of related medical and psychiatric disciplines, serial killers themselves, families of victims, and both prosecution and defense attorneys have contributed more information and recommendations than a single book can contain.

What you are about to read will shock, terrify, sadden, and sometimes repel and enrage you. This is not the story of one serial killer, nor is it only the documentation of the disease of the serial killer. It is an investigation of a disease that is running rampant in society and threatens to overwhelm our juvenile justice, criminal justice, and correctional institutions. As you will find, this book acts as a mirror of the fine line that separates each one of us from yielding to the primal, instinctual, animal behavior that lurks beneath the veneer of psychological self-control and social convention. But as the conditions of society become more stressful, those social conventions will break down even further and the controls will give way. This is why the Surgeon General of the United States has called domestic and social violence one of the newest public health risks to the future of society. And as long as we treat violence – and especially serial murder – with an eye-for-an-eye attitude of personal vengeance, our body counts of victims of serial killers will expand exponentially with every passing decade.

The Nature of a Serial Killer

1

The Serial Killer in Our Midst

At first it was concern that rippled through the Wynnton section of Columbus, Georgia, in the unseasonably warm autumn of 1977. Ferne Jackson, a sixty-year-old white widow, popular and from a socially important family, a public health teacher in the Columbus schools who had lived alone for years in this most exclusive neighborhood of Columbus, had been found dead in the bedroom of her house. She had been beaten violently about the face and head, sexually assaulted, and finally strangled to death with her own nylon stocking, which the police found still wound tightly around her neck. Finally, her attacker had pulled the covers up over her bleeding and half-naked body. The detectives from forensics at the crime scene noted that the killer entered the house through the rear sliding glass doors, surprised Mrs. Jackson in her bedroom, struck her until she could offer no resistance, twisted the stocking around her neck, raped her, and then strangled her. The killer then took her keys, stole her car, and left it abandoned in the Carver Heights section of the city, a black neighborhood in the flat lowland that separates Wynnton from downtown and the Chattahoochee River. It was a violent and ugly crime, and it broke on the evening news like a summer thunderstorm. That was on September 16.

On Saturday, the twenty-fourth, Jean Dimenstein, a seventy-one-year-old white spinster, was found beaten, sexually assaulted, and strangled with a stocking in her bedroom just four blocks away from where Ferne Jackson lived. Her car had been stolen and driven to Carver Heights, and it was parked just a hundred yards away from where the police had found Ferne Jackson's car four days earlier. One killing in the white-brick, well-manicured suburb of Wynnton was tragic enough, but two killings within days of one another, both stranglings of older women who lived alone, were enough to echo a pattern to the people of Columbus. They had seen this type of killing pattern on the evening news: body counts after the Richard Speck killings of student nurses, the continuing news of the violent deaths of young girls in the Seattle area, and the persistence of murders and rapes that were the hallmark of cities like Atlanta, Los Angeles, and New York. But now it was happening in the quiet city of Columbus.

Under pressure to find the murderer quickly, the police first arrested Jerome 'Duck' Livas, a mentally deficient who was a convenient suspect in another murder, and quickly announced that he was confessing to the murders of the Wynnton victims. But just as Wynnton had begun to relax from the tension, eighty-nine-year-old Florence Scheible, legally blind and confined to a walker, was also found strangled to death in her bedroom. Like the other victims, she was a white woman who lived alone and, like the others, she had been attacked by an intruder who broke in, bludgeoned her with his fists, raped her, and then strangled her to death with one of her own stockings and, prior to leaving, covered up her body.

Four days later sixty-nine-year-old Martha Thurmond was found dead in her home, strangled as well. Ironically, the throwbolt locks she had installed to protect her after the Scheible murder were put in backward, and the murderer had picked them with ease. This time, however, the killer didn't even touch her car. The police and Columbus residents then realized that robbery had clearly not been the motive for the crime.

The continuing pattern of identical murders that persisted even after the arrest of the police's only suspect weakened the case against Livas. The district attorney, however, refused to release him until two weeks later when, in an exclusive interview with Carl Cannon, a reporter from the Columbus *Ledger*, Livas confessed to the murders of both Presidents John F. Kennedy and William McKinley. The story broke in the paper the next day, and a red-faced Ronnie Jones, the director of the robbery and homicide division of the Columbus police, who had announced on morning television weeks earlier that the police had caught the suspect, admitted that the hunt for the real killer was still on.

By the end of 1977, after another murder victim – seventy-four-year-old Kathleen Woodruff, widow of George 'Kid' Woodruff, a member of the Woodruff Coca-Cola family – had been found raped and strangled with her scarf in the parlor of her house on exclusive Buena Vista Road, the panic about a killer on the loose began to change the community. There was now the realization that the crimes were not burglaries first and murders second; they were, in fact, violent, sexual attacks with murder as a primary motive. Secondly, after the killer had changed his pattern by not stealing the cars of his victims, it became obvious to the entire city that he was monitoring the news reports of his crimes and had altered his course of actions only to confuse the police.

In a once aristocratic neighborhood the stately white-columned mansions, built by Wynnton's founders before the Civil War, now became fortresses protected by deadbolts and elaborate burglar alarms. In the daytime police dogs sniffed for clues among the blossoming azaleas and along the tree-shaded streets while patrol cars became the sentries of the night, their whirling blue lights a blur as they crisscrossed through the dark neighborhood streets. Little old ladies carried revolvers neatly tucked into their purses on their way to church on Sundays, and an entire community had become fearful, suspicious of any new face.

Gradually the local Columbus police, the prosecutor's office, and the newspaper and television reporters who were tracking the case came to realize that the elusive phantom who was seemingly striking down these old women at will was not a traditional murderer as most people have come to understand murderers. Now the local police, the Georgia Bureau of Investigation, and the FBI were beginning to assemble a profile of such killers based on similar evidence patterns in Seattle, where college student Ted Bundy was in the midst of his career as a serial killer of young coeds; in Chicago, where John Gacy, a $200,000-a-year building contractor, had been killing young boys and burying them in his basement for five years; in California, where Ed Kemper had engaged in a killing spree of eight women; or even in the neighboring city of Atlanta where Wayne Williams was serving out his sentence for the kidnapping, sexual abuse, and murder of more than twenty-five young boys, the investigators now were coming to believe that they had a different type of murderer on their hands.

The dead women in Wynnton were part of a larger national pattern – victims of apparently motiveless killers whose methods and activities make them almost undetectable. Not really a traditional form of murder, as most police and criminologists understand it, this crime is actually a form of disease. Its carriers are serial killers who suffer from a variety of crippling and eventually fatal symptoms, and its immediate victims are the people struck down seemingly at random by the disease carriers.

It is the disease of serial murder that is rapidly becoming an epidemic in American society today and one of the patterns of violence that the office of the U.S. Surgeon General has called one of the top-priority issues of public health.

Wynnton was not accustomed to being a community of victims. The residents here were descendants of the planters and textile mill owners who rebuilt Georgia out of the ruins of the Civil War. The women who had been killed were Southern archetypes, matriarchs, and wealthy and influential standard-bearers of the city of Columbus who for years had funded charities and community service events. More importantly, they had been the domestic employers of the Columbus working-class and black populations. Striking out against the Wynnton matrons was to strike out against a symbol of the old South, the heart and soul of the community itself. As the Columbus residents read of the Atlanta Child Murders taking place just over a hundred miles away, they agonized over the strangling murders of their own mothers and waited for news of the next victim.

The murders continued. A short time after Ruth Schwob had successfully fought off her attacker in the early morning of February 12 and triggered a burglar alarm in her home, only two hundred yards away seventy-eight-year-old Mildred Borom was being beaten, sexually assaulted, and strangled with a window blind cord in her bedroom on Forest Avenue. The murderer, only minutes ahead of the local police who had responded to the burglar alarm, had not only eluded capture but in the midst of his interrupted frenzy had walked just a few doors down the street to attack his next victim. This boldness, the sheer audacity of a killer who could enter, rape, and murder while the police were up the street questioning one of his victims, raised the level of general panic to the point where an exodus of older women from the community had begun.

Three days later Don Kilgore, the county coroner, announced that 'negroid' pubic hairs were found at the scenes of the crimes. With the announcement, an ensuing public debate pitted the coroner and the police department against the local chapter of the NAACP. Racial tensions in the Columbus area began to flare and the Ku Klux Klan announced that it would patrol the streets of Wynnton to protect the women. The racial implications were considered all the more serious because what the police had suggested – a killer who crossed racial lines – conflicted starkly with a profile that the FBI had already begun to create. The coroner's announcement was at variance with Ruth Schwob's tentative identification of her attacker as Lyle Gingel, a young white man, the emotionally disturbed son of a popular radio personality.

At the end of March the police received a letter from a copycat killer threatening revenge on black women if the killer of the white women was not caught. The writer, who called himself the Chairman of the Forces of Evil, implied that he was a white man avenging the deaths of the Wynnton matriarchs. The police feared that he would become a copycat killer who reacted to the news of the serial murderer by committing his own homicides. One day later their fears proved to be valid. The bodies of two black prostitutes, Gail Faison and Irene Thirkild, were found on the grounds of the military reservation adjoining the Army's Fort Benning, and the Columbus chief of police agreed to negotiate the killer's $10,000 ransom demand on the lives of future victims. When the police and the Army's Criminal Investigation Division at Benning arrested Private First Class Henry Hance, a black man who would later be convicted of another murder and implicated in a third, the police knew that the pattern of secondary violence had already begun.

It wasn't until after another murder and after the cost of the investigation had exceeded a million dollars that the murders finally stopped. The Columbus police in desperation had even interrogated Wayne Williams, the suspect in the Atlanta Child Murders, but he had no connections to the crimes. It wasn't until six years later, when Carlton Gary was finally arrested in Albany, Georgia, on robbery charges and fugitive warrants, that the Stocking Strangler was found. After confessing to being present at the murder scenes, Gary was charged with rape, burglary, and murder in three of the Wynnton stranglings, and three years later he was convicted and sentenced to death.

Now, more than ten years after the first murder, Carlton Gary is still in jail, awaiting his appeal and subsequent trials that will cost the state in excess of another two to three million dollars to finance. Bud Siemen, his defense counsel, has told the court that Gary will readily admit to all the charges if he is allowed to plead insanity and remain institutionalized for the rest of his life. However, because of the sensitivity of the community and the nature of the murder victims, Siemen charges, the state will be happy only after Carlton Gary has been executed in the electric chair. The appeals process alone may take another three to five years and cost Georgia an additional million dollars if it has to go to the United States Supreme Court. This, I might add, the case of the Columbus Stocking Strangler, is only one serial killer at work in one community.

Other communities besides Columbus have known the panic that washes over people when a murderer moves into the area and victims first disappear and then are discovered in shallow graves, one after the other. In Texas and the neighboring panhandle states, more than three hundred people died, allegedly at the hands of Henry Lee Lucas. Even though questions still remain about the truth and accuracy of Lucas' early confessions, which he later recanted, some of them are so graphic and lurid that even the police refused to believe them. It was reported by the Texas Rangers and law enforcement officials nationwide that he killed hundreds of men, women, and children whom he did not know except for the few brief hours when he had stalked, tortured, put them to death, mutilated their bodies, dismembered them, and buried their remains. In Atlanta an entire community was frozen with terror as each week more and more bodies of its children were found sexually assaulted and buried in the area around the Chattahoochee River. The police in Seattle were baffled for years while they searched for the killer of a score of young, attractive women who had seemed to offer no resistance to the person who took their lives. It wasn't until Ted Bundy was finally arrested in another community that the Seattle killings stopped. It took another series of murders in Utah and then later in Florida, to which Bundy had escaped, to finally bring him to sentencing. Even after their convictions and sentencing, questions still remain about the full extent of their crimes, and families wonder whether their children who have been missing for years will ever be listed among the killers' victims.

Currently among the group of serial killers who are most prominently in the public eye and under police and FBI investigation are Richard Ramirez, also known as the 'Nightstalker,' a cat burglar by trade who indiscriminately killed anyone who happened to cross his path and discover him while he was in the act of robbing a house; an unknown killer on the loose in southern Los Angeles who has already murdered at least twenty prostitutes and is the object of an intense manhunt by the LAPD, and the 'Green River Killer' in Seattle, who has also murdered more than twenty prostitutes and buried their bodies along the banks of the Green River, which runs just outside of the city limits. When one adds to this list the 'Tylenol Killers' and a multitude of copycat killers who strike whenever a serial killer enters an area, the list grows seemingly without limit.

These killers belong to a newly identified class of criminals called serial murderers, motiveless killers, recreational killers, spree killers, or lust murderers whose numbers are increasing at an alarming rate every year. In 1983 alone, according to the FBI, approximately five thousand Americans of both sexes and all ages – fifteen people a day and fully twenty-five percent of all murder victims – were struck down by murderers who did not know them and killed them for the sheer 'high' of the experience. The FBI calls this class of homicides serial murders and their perpetrators recreational or lust killers. The FBI describes them as the most cunning and sinister of all violent people. Almost impossible to capture, diagnose, or predict using ordinary investigative methods and perversely attracted to the police who are pursuing them, serial murderers dance just beyond their pursuers' reach from state to state, retreating into the background, then springing up again in a different part of the country to begin another series of seemingly motiveless killings.

Addicted to the act of murder as if it were a drug, serial killers compulsively and silently troll for their victims amid shopping malls at twilight, darkened city streets, or country roads in isolated rural communities. They are motivated by a force that even they don't understand. Once they have sighted a potential victim, they begin to stalk with a dogged relentlessness that does not cease until the victim is cornered and the trap is sprung. Like tormented beasts of prey, serial murderers do not commit simple homicides. They often torture their victims, taking delight in the victims' agonies, expressions of terror, cries of despair, and reactions to pain. Then, in a period of marked depression that follows the high of the murder, the killers plead for help from the police or newspapers as did Richard Herrins, a serial killer in Chicago in the early

1960s, who wrote in lipstick on a dressing-room mirror above his victim's head: 'Catch me before I kill again.' Always hidden in plain sight, the killers ask to be caught, promise to turn themselves in so that they can receive therapy, but vanish again only to emerge after the next murder.

What makes a serial killer? What are the roots of this extraordinary violence? Why was a murderer like Ted Bundy so difficult to catch? What enabled Henry Lee Lucas to elude the police for more than ten years as he moved from state to state, leaving in his wake scores of his victims buried in mass unmarked graves. Why does Carlton Gary, the Columbus Stocking Strangler, even today admit to being present at every Wynnton murder but cling to the story that it was someone else – one of his known aliases – in the house with him every time who actually committed the crime? Are these individuals supercriminals who are able to outsmart the police at every turn or is the nature of their crime fundamentally so different from other types of crimes that local police forces are unable to control it?

Unfortunately for all of us, serial murder is different in kind from any other type of crime. Only recently have the police, the FBI, the courts, the medical profession, or any agency of government fundamentally accepted this fact. Most murders are committed for specific, identifiable motives. A fight between two people suddenly turns into a homicide when one of them draws a lethal weapon; lovers in the midst of a violent confrontation strike out at one another until one of them lies dead; a burglar suddenly freezes as the lights in an apartment or store are turned on and fires his weapon at the first person he sees; or the passions in a family confrontation suddenly explode into violence. Police can solve any one of these homicides within days or even hours. The motives are straightforward. The victims have a clearly traceable relationship with the murderer, and the murderer himself is so filled with remorse and guilt that he makes it easy for the police to find him. Moreover, the overwhelming majority of murders are committed by individuals who are 'novice' killers. They have little or no evasive skills, and their only reaction is to run away in panic after leaving a crime scene littered, with clues and witnesses. If they run fast enough and long enough, they believe, they will eventually be safe. It is only the weight of the crime itself that undoes them in the end. Were they the least bit practiced in the crime of murder or had they planned their escape route in advance and prepared a safe hiding place, they might elude capture just long enough for the trail to turn cold and for other murder cases to occupy the attention of the overworked homicide squad. Armed robbers who commit murder are also relatively easy to track down. Those who flee from state to state still leave clues that make their capture a certainty once the FBI joins the chase. And in cases of contract murder – gangland slayings and political assassinations – the motives are clear and the police need only find the killer to close the books.

Even mass murderers differ fundamentally from serial killers. First, mass murderers are almost always caught by the police. Some examples are: James Huberty, who killed more than twenty-five people at a Los Angeles McDonald's; Richard Speck, who killed seven nurses in Chicago; Charles Whitman, who killed more than ten people from the University of Texas tower almost twenty years ago; and most recently Juan Gonzales, the Staten Island ferry slasher who hacked his way through a crowd of Fourth of July celebrants. They differ from the serial killer in that they have a more tenuous camouflage of normalcy. Some experts say these mass murderers are more apt to have obvious psychotic neurological symptoms that are very easy to diagnose than the serial murderers. In fact several lawsuits are currently pending in cities around the country by victims who claim that the hospitals who released these individuals before their final acts of violence are liable for the damage the killers inflicted.

The serial murderer is an entirely different criminal. First, the serial killer is practiced and accomplished at what he does and can cloak himself with a mantle of normal, acceptable behavior. After all, most fully emerged serial murderers have been engaged in the crime for years. Even newly emerged serial murderers have been fantasizing for lifetimes about committing their crimes. The actual event itself has been rehearsed over and over again, just like an escalating masturbatory fantasy. Literally hundreds of potential victims have crossed the killer's path and have been the unwary actors in an internal psychological drama.

Second, the victim may be missing for months or even years before being discovered. It is only after the victim's discovery that the police begin the homicide investigation. The sheer volume of missing persons in a given jurisdiction might be so great that the police spend more time defending the community against a siege than tracking whatever clues might still linger in the area. Then it is only by chance, a random encounter between a police officer on patrol and a killer caught at the scene of the crime, that a suspect is apprehended. The relationship between the victim and the murderer, when the victim finally turns up, might be so fragile that the police are unable to comprehend it. Carlton Gary was convicted for killing only those white elderly women who reminded him of the type of person his mother had to work for when he was growing up, and Ted Bundy bludgeoned only those attractive and confident young women who reminded him of the fiancée who had rebuffed him. Not even the most farsighted of police investigators can put together these types of clues until after the killer has been caught and profiled.

Most traditional killers flee to avoid capture. Professional and contract killers know how to fade into the background quickly and have planned their escape routes beforehand. Those killers who strike down a family member, a child or a spouse, out of uncontrollable violence are more afraid of what they've done than of the police and quickly turn themselves in. Serial killers, however, are like wild animals. They are fascinated with the remains of their crime. They visit the graves of their victims and attend their funerals. They lurk in the shadows, camouflage themselves with all of the trappings of normalcy, and dog the heels of the police as they relive the crime through the efforts of the investigators. The Green River Killer in Seattle telephoned a homicide detective's wife and taunted her about her husband's ineffectiveness, and Ted Bundy often confronted the police officers who followed him and asked them about the progress of their investigation. More often than not the killer has been in the custody of the police or a mental health professional prior to the discovery of his crimes. The enormity of his confession in those earlier situations, however, is usually so unbelievable that the authorities simply let him go, preferring to investigate a more traditional type of criminal.

After running out of vulnerable or archetypal prospects in a given area – young children, elderly people living alone, young women without escorts, prostitutes of both sexes, derelicts, gays – the killer moves away, trolling for victims in another city or state where fear has not yet gripped the populace. Often, in this new area, reports of missing persons or identifiable traits of the murder victims are not relevant to the police who suddenly find themselves confronted with a series of disappearances or bodies turning up in unmarked graves. Few homicide investigators will check the unsolved murder reports from localities two or three states away, and only recently has there been a national network of unsolved homicides. Even the FBI, unless specifically authorized to investigate, will respect the territoriality of the local police department. Thus a killer like Henry Lee Lucas who does not have the kind of public involvement with his victim that can be tracked by the authorities can strike in Texas, Oklahoma, New Mexico, and Arkansas without fear of being trapped by converging police departments. By the time the pattern of his crimes has become clear, he usually has long since left the area or is in custody on another charge.

Killing his victims at the rate of two or more a month, year after year and often for decades, the serial murderer commits his crimes in numbers vastly disproportionate to those of the traditional murderer. Since 1960 not only have the number of individual serial killers increased but so have the number of victims per killer and the level of savagery of the individual crimes themselves. The FBI has estimated that there are at least five hundred serial killers currently at large and unidentified in this country. Their toll on the rest of society is enormous.

However, as if this statistic were not bad enough, consider the fact that the epidemic of serial murderers is spreading. Passed on from generation to generation in the form of child abuse, patterns of chronic childhood malnutrition, drug abuse, and alcoholism, serial murder is actually a disease that is thriving in American society. In the last twenty years the United States, with only five percent of the world's population, has produced seventy-five percent of the world's serial murderers. Of the 160 serial killers who have been captured or singled out by law enforcement authorities over this period, at least 120 were found in the United States. As the influence of American culture spreads to less developed countries, the fear is that, unless checked somehow, the disease of serial murder will spread as well.

The serial murderer in an episodic frenzy can strike without warning. He often preys on the most vulnerable victims in his area and then moves on, leaving the police to find the missing persons and search for traces of the scant clues he has left behind. Because his killing is not a passion of the moment but a compelling urge that has been growing within him sometimes for years, he has completely amalgamated this practice into his lifestyle. It is as though he lives to kill, surviving from one murder to the next, stringing out his existence by connecting the deaths to his victims. Without this string of murders, he feels he will fall apart, that he will disintegrate psychologically. The remainder of his life is devoted to maintaining the mask of normalcy and sanity.

Between crimes, he quietly slips back into the fabric of society. He lives and exists in plain sight from day to day, but on the sly he is observing the police who are busily trying to assemble clues but never seeing the larger picture. The serial killer meantime is waiting until the next convenient stranger crosses his path. The new victim may have a particular way of smiling, a certain style of hair, a familiar perfume or cologne, an air of confidence, or even the style of their house may trigger the murderer and move him quickly into his stalking phase. Whatever it may be, it only takes an instant for the killer to size up his prey and begin stalking. He may follow his unwary victim for days in an internal, one-sided foreplay to murder, memorizing their licence plate, waiting for them to cross an intersection where he is waiting for them, watching them in the rear-view mirror of his car as they leave from work every evening. He waits until they are alone or until he can introduce himself, lure them into his confidence, and spring the trap.

The serial murderer, unlike the traditional criminal, is addicted to his passion. He is suffering from a disease that is terminal, not only for his numerous victims but also for himself. He is his ultimate victim. On his own initiative, the serial killer can no more stop his killing than a heroin addict can kick his habit. Suffering from waves of primal pain and fear of the deepest nature after his most recent killing, an unusual set of defence mechanisms emerges. He simply forgets his crime as well as the victim. Soon thereafter, the urge to murder comes upon him again. He may loathe what he does and despise his own weakness, but he can do nothing on his own to control it. Perversely, he wishes for death, and the threat of the gas chamber, the electric chair, or the lethal injection is only an inducement to keep committing murders until he is caught and put to death. This is why, upon apprehension, so many serial killers readily confess to their crimes and beg for punishment. In retrospect, many police investigations reveal that a serial killer had been in custody one or more times, confessed indirectly to the crimes under investigation, and warned their interrogators that they would kill again. They were not believed by the authorities and released. Most serial killers are only partially aware of what they are doing, and because they have reduced their victims to totemic objects their recollections of the actual murders are very sketchy and vague. Most police investigators dismiss the pleas for help and the inexact descriptions of the crimes as the ramblings of attention-seeking cranks who are incapable of committing murders on a mass scale.

Like John Wayne Gacy and Ted Bundy, the overwhelming majority of serial killers seem on the surface to be normal-looking individuals who go to work or school, come home, and blend into their environments. They might even be married and lead routine lives in their communities. But in reality they are walking time bombs ready to ignite at just the right combination of events. For Bobby Joe Long in Florida, it was the sight of a barfly looking to be picked up by one of the men who frequented the singles clubs along the North Tampa 'strip'; for Ed

Kemper, it was the sound of a voice that reminded him of his mother; and for John Gacy it was the threat of any young man who challenged his authority.

An individual who is on the verge of becoming a serial killer may seem like a dormant volcano. No one knows that beneath the usually bland exterior is a psyche in turmoil, reliving the years of physical and emotional abuse heaped upon him by his closest relatives. He may be an epileptic or someone with serious brain damage who has been able to cover up his impairment for most of his life. But at some point all of the elements that combine to form the active serial killer reach a critical mass, and at just the right stimulation – a sight, a sound, or a smell – the individual slides into his trolling phase and the search for a victim begins.

2

The Phases of Serial Murder

A serial killer's addiction to his crime is also an addiction to a specific pattern of violence that becomes the killer's way of life. Each serial murderer has incorporated the act of killing into a ritual of psychological survival in which the particular victims, the preparations for their capture and torture, the moment of death, and the disposition of the remains each have an element of perverted significance to the criminal's behavior. This reliance on ritual is an across-the-board identifier of the serial murderer and sets him apart from his traditional counterparts. The sequence of ritualistic acts is the killer's way of building up to the 'murder high' and the emotional and sexual orgasm, the explosion of power, he experiences at the moment of the murder itself.

Criminologists who have studied serial murderers have broken the ritual into seven key phases:

1. The Aura Phase

This is some form of withdrawal from everyday reality that indicates the beginnings of a behavior change. First, time seems to slow down. Sounds and colors become more vivid. Odors become more intense, and the killer's skin now becomes sensitive to even the slightest pressure.

What now replaces the reality of day-to-day existence is a compulsion to find a companion, at first in fantasy, who will act out a role in the killer's primal ritual. The aura phase can last only for a moment or two, or it can last for months. In such a hallucinatory state, the killer is completely cut off from any stimuli until the aura phase has passed and he begins the search for his victim. Serial killers who experience such types of hallucination exist only in a world of their own creation and react to the invisible stimuli that only they individually can experience.

At the very beginning of the aura phase some serial killers can still verbalize their feelings and report that they are losing their grip on reality. At this point they can be treated by a therapist, and the murder cycle can be short-circuited. However, the vast majority of serial killers cannot verbalize this sensation, and once they enter the aura phase they do not reemerge until after the crime has been committed.

The aura phase can also begin as a prolonged fantasy. In this mode, the killer acts out the thrill of the crime in his own mind. He progresses from one step to another step, exciting himself as the vision reaches its climax. In this mode, the fantasy can play itself over and over again in the killer's mind for weeks or even years at a time. Every stranger who crosses his path can become a performer in that fantasy until an emotional trip wire is snapped, the fantasy becomes real, and the trolling begins. If the aura phase begins as a fantasy such as this, the killer is possibly reachable through intervention. He is able to describe what is happening around him, and through expressing his fantasy he can defuse his compulsion.

The aura phase once entered, however, is like a portal between two realities. On the one side is the reality that all of us, even the most neurotic, react to and inhabit all of our lives. This is a world of normalcy, of social convention in which laws are obeyed and rules observed. However, on the other side of the portal is the killer's reality. It is a world of compulsion, a world dominated by the replaying of the fantasy of violence in which there is no social convention or obedience to rules. It is a world in which everyday choices no longer exist because on this side of the portal the killer is simply a biological engine driven by a primal instinct to satisfy a compelling lust. The ritual of killing has become bound up with an automatic survival mechanism, almost as if the murderer had become a single-celled creature reacting to an overpowering chemical stimulus.

Passing through the aura phase, the serial murderer is translated into a different kind of creature. Whatever is human in him recedes for a while, and he enters into a shadowy existence, a death in life in which law and threats of death or punishment, morality, mores, taboos, or the importance of life itself hold no meaning. Although prosecutors, jurors, and society may eventually hold him accountable for whatever he does, he has in fact lost all power of reason, inhibition, and control. He attempts to medicate himself with large quantities of alcohol or drugs, but, like pouring gasoline on a fire, these create an opposite reaction and only feed his lust. He will not reemerge into the world of the living until after the hallucination has broken or the ritual has been acted out.

2. The Trolling Phase

Having entered into a compulsive stage, the killer now actively begins searching for his next victim. His earlier observations, fantasies, and perverted needs direct him to the likeliest spots where the fatal stranger will cross his path. Each serial killer has different favorite spots. He only has to troll like a fisherman spreading his net, plying back and forth across likely areas for abduction: the parking lots of suburban shopping malls; darkened city streets where single people are apt to travel at night; the student centres and coed dormitories of a large university campus; the playgrounds of elementary schools, schools for the deaf or retarded, or the rural roads where he has noticed that young children or coeds sometimes walk home from school.

Trolling does not consist of random or accidental patterns. It is an unconscious compulsion, a deliberate form of cruising for the likeliest prey. Some killers find themselves staking out certain territories where the most vulnerable victims are to be found. John Gacy looked for a certain type of teenage boy in the demimonde of male hustlers. Ted Bundy searched for pretty coeds on the Seattle University campus where he was a law student. Once he had made his escape from Utah to Florida, he quickly sought out new victims on the college campuses in Tallahassee. Carlton Gary preyed upon elderly women. He chose the Wynnton section of Columbus in his fantasy of robbing from the rich and giving to the poor and trolled the streets until he spied the right kind of house where his wealthy potential victim lived. Then he would stake out a house for days before he gained entry.

The trolling phase is a series of compulsive, frenzied, and paranoiac behavior patterns in which the serial killer becomes very alert and focused. Although at this point he is no longer functioning as an individual in the real world, he is nevertheless instinctively reacting to everday stimuli. It is as if, once the serial killer has passed through the aura phase and into the trolling phase, there begins to operate a new level of behavior programming which directs his every move. Ted Bundy, for example, although compelled by a lust to have a momentary intense relationship with his victim before he killed her, was able to appear charming and ingratiating. His arm strapped up in a false sling, he lured his victim into his car by asking for help with books, packages, or even the hull of a sailboat. Those victims who escaped reported that Bundy never seemed to be out of control until he actually struck. Similarly, Henry Lee Lucas often managed to strike up casual conversations with his victims, sizing them up for the kill.

The latter part of the trolling phase involves the identification and stalking of the victim. Once he has identified his intended prey, the killer begins his pattern of stalking from a distance. Carlton Gary kept watch on his victims' houses for weeks, stalking these elderly women as he travelled through their neighborhood delivering drugs and meeting young women for sexual encounters. He memorized his victims' schedules and habits. So when he did finally strike, he was able to move through the area silently, knowing what entrances could be penetrated without much trouble, and knowing how to leave the scene quickly after the victim lay beaten and strangled upon her bed. He knew which women in Wynnton lived alone. He attacked only widows or spinsters, women who reminded him of the mother he never had and the rich white women who employed his aunt and grandmother as domestic servants. At the same time, Gary believed that these lonely old women's absences would not be noticed until they were found in their houses, hours or days after he had left the crime scene.

Henry Lee Lucas trolled together with companion Ottis Toole along the desolate interstates that crisscross Texas. He found his victims in bars, standing by their cars at gas stations or rest areas, and alongside the roads, hitching a ride. Once he caught sight of a woman in a solo circumstance he would follow her until she was isolated. Then he would abduct her at gunpoint and take her to the spot where she would be humiliated, tortured, mutilated, and finally killed. Lucas revealed that he let a lot of potential victims go without harm. However, if a woman challenged him, resisted him, insulted him, or if her looks, voice, or body movements reminded him of his mother in any way, he would feel an involuntary chill and 'she was as good as dead.' Lucas claims that there are still scores of victims he has murdered who have never turned up and never will until he shows the police where the bodies are buried.

Richard Begenwald, another recently convicted serial killer, stalked his victims along the country roads of affluent New Jersey suburbs. Spotting pretty high school cheerleaders as they walked home from school, Begenwald tracked them day after day until he knew which ones would be alone in isolated spots and which ones had to walk the last stretch of road with no companions. It was then that he would strike, freezing his victims at first in the glare of his headlights. Then he lured them into his car with offers of rides. His next step was to spring the trap, overpowering them quickly and violently, finally savoring the moment of death and his moment of triumph. He then would either bury their bodies in a remote section near the murder scene or transport them in his trunk to his mother's house on Staten Island. There they would be buried in her backyard.

Most homicide cops report that it is the killer's stalking phase that most unnerves a police department once a pattern of serial murders has been established in an area. While the killer is stalking victim after victim, the police have to sit back and trace the few if any clues they have. The problem is compounded by the sensational nature of the news of each murder that appears on television every evening. This sometimes inspires the serial killer who is tracking both the police investigation, as Carlton Gary did, and the media reporting, as Ted Bundy did, to change the pattern of his crimes to throw both the police and the media off the trail. In the process the killings just keep on happening, bodies keep on turning up, and the police wind up looking as though they are completely ineffective and their investigations are getting nowhere.

For example, in Atlanta during the child murders investigation, the official criticism of the police department became so intense that a special task force of 'superdetectives' had to be assembled from the nation's largest cities to help. Even then there were jurisdictional fights among the neighboring city, county, and sheriff's departments. There was friction among the local and federal officers on the case, and the hunt for the killer went on for months before an agent from the Georgia Bureau of Investigation on special stakeout detail happened to notice Wayne Williams on the Chattahoochee River bridge.

Bob Keppel, one of the Seattle homicide detectives who investigated the Ted Bundy murders before Bundy relocated to Utah, complained that it was the knowledge that a killer was out there, actively pursuing his next victim, that was the most disturbing thing about the case. The police were always two giant steps behind the killer – first searching for the missing person, then identifying the dismembered and partially decomposed body – always following a trail that had turned cold long before they uncovered it. It was Keppel's experience tracking Bundy that convinced him that the police couldn't be reactive when trying to solve a serial murder case. They have to be preemptive. They have to be able to predict the killer's probable next moves from a behavior profile that they develop. The types of victims he chooses and the condition of the bodies after the murder are two important factors they must evaluate. Once they know what type of victim is most likely to be stalked, they can mass their resources in a specific area. It was Keppel who helped form the Behavioral Science Unit at the FBI. This unit assembles a character profile of a potential serial killer from the gathered information and assists local police forces through their interrogations of likely suspects.

3. The Wooing Phase

Most serial killers disarm their suspects by winning their confidence and luring them into a trap. Ruth Schwob, for example, the only victim to have survived the Columbus Stocking Strangler, remembered a feeling of erotic pleasure as Gary raped her and began to strangle her while she was in a twilight state between life and death. John Gacy, the Chicago building contractor who killed scores of young boys and buried them in his basement, accomplished this by promising his victims jobs in his company, cash for sexual favors, and even fatherly warmth and understanding. Once they had agreed to accompany him to his home office or to a job site, Gacy had them in his power. If the boy seemed to be just looking for money to tide him over, Gacy usually gave him money, had sex, and let him go. However, if the boy challenged him or tried to con him, Gacy then overpowered the victim with a blow to the head, bound him, raped and sodomized him, tortured him, and then killed him. Serial killers such as Ottis Toole who prey on young children routinely lure them away from shopping malls, their own backyards, or schoolyards to remote locations. Most young children do not fear strangers who offer them candy or promise to take them to their parents, and they readily follow such a person. Ted Bundy, who was a part-time law student in Seattle, had an ingratiating, boyish manner that charmed his female victims into thinking they were helping a friendly stranger with a broken arm. Bundy was adept at insinuating himself into the confidence of his victims by reversing the typical courtship pattern. It was the victim who was strong, healthy, and almost patronizing toward the good-looking stranger who approached her in the parking lot or on the beach. The murderer was injured, self-effacing, and embarrassed in his request for assistance. In fact one of the most startling aspects of most serial killers is that they are neither repulsive or even merely off-putting. They do not terrorize their victims into submission, they actually seduce them before turning on them.

When homicide detectives finally begin to uncover a pattern of serial murder, one of the first things they notice is that the victims rarely seem to have struggled against their killers. As Seattle's Bob Keppel realized from the few clues he was able to assemble and from the statements of those coeds who escaped from Ted Bundy, the victims willingly placed themselves in Bundy's power without realizing that they were in danger. The serial killer is often very selective about the type of victim he chooses and is able to relate to that person with little difficulty. As a result the victims are either taken in by the killer's charm and manners, or they believe his story, or they don't listen to their own instincts. It is only those who resist from the outset who have any chance of escape.

4. Capture

This event can be as sudden as the locking of a car door, a sudden break-in through a window, or a quick, well-timed blow that renders the victim dazed and helpless at the killer's feet. It can also be as gradual and terrifying as a conversational monologue fraught with innuendos about the violence that is about to happen. The killer waits until he has the victim alone and then he begins his ascent to a psychological high. The trolling and stalking phases served to heighten his expectation of the event itself, and the capture, when the victim has finally been ensnared in the trap, is the penultimate moment. This is the moment he savors because he believes that he has closed off all possibility of the victim's escape and can take all the time he wants to prepare the victim for the ritual that will follow.

The way the capture is effected differs widely from serial killer to serial killer. Carlton Gary struck quickly at his defenseless victims once he had broken into their houses. He threatened them, raped them, and then strangled them with one of their own nylon stockings, the slick cord from a window blind, or a silk scarf, and then covered their exposed bodies. Ted Bundy kept charming his victims, maintaining the veneer of the courtship, until he reached one of his 'safe places,' killing fields where he was completely isolated. Then he bludgeoned his victims to death and bit into their flesh. Henry Lee Lucas talked to his victims once the capture was completed. He went into detail describing what was about to happen and took delight in the terror he was inflicting, even before he began the regimen of physical abuse.

5. The Murder

Until the day she died Ruth Schwob, the only victim to have fought off the Columbus Stocking Strangler, believed that her assailant behind the ski mask was not Carlton Gary but someone else. Even when confronted with the evidence of the killer the police had accused, Ruth Schwob did not identify him but incriminated Lyle Gingel instead. That was how effective Carlton Gary's camouflage was, even during the moments when he should have been the most exposed. Ruth Schwob's description of being surprised in the intimacy of her own bedroom and of the sexual assault by her businesslike attacker is one of the few descriptions police have of what it is like to be the victim of a serial murderer.

To Ruth Schwob, the killer behind the ski mask was invisible, a faceless man who raped and abused his victims as if wreaking a terrible vengeance upon them for sins of omission they had practiced in the course of their daily living. These older women, the matrons of Columbus society, had looked through their black domestic employees as if they were invisible. They omitted them from their catalogue of human beings, and in Carlton

Gary's fantasy he was repaying them for that. Mrs. Schwob described the sexual violence to the police as an almost tantalizing torture that evoked memories of distant pleasures. Yet she knew, as she fought off the man tightening the stocking around her neck and struggled to reach the emergency trip buttons of the burglar alarm, that she was meant to be the next victim of the man the newspapers had called the Columbus Stocking Strangler. Although she did not realize it, Ruth Schwob was playing a role in the killer's private vision of his own hell. She was the matron Gary's family had to serve in order to eat. And now she was the focus of his revenge. Yet she never realized who the man was behind the ski mask.

For Carlton Gary, Ruth Schwob's failure to identify him was just as it should have been. He was meant to be invisible to his victims because it was invisibility itself that was at the core of his pathological addiction to murder. As his lawyers are quick to point out, the violent sexual assaults and strangling murders of the six elderly white women in the oldest and most exclusive neighborhood of Columbus point to a pattern of crime that goes well beyond the typical murder. It is a ritual in which Carlton Gary is reenacting an event over and over again. The murders are secondary in Gary's mind; the event being reenacted is primary. Gary can't even admit remembering the actual killings, insisting instead that he watched while someone else committed the crimes. By bringing the defendant's biopsychosocial case history into court as evidence of his incompetence to stand trial, his defense counsel had hoped to show that in Carlton Gary's consciousness he was never really there. They will argue that, in much the same way that he was never really visible throughout his childhood years when he watched his grandmother and his aunt carry out domestic chores for the very women he killed, he was just as invisible when he broke into their homes and raped them.

To these matrons of Wynnton, as were most blacks in the 1950s, Carlton Gary was invisible. From the narrow windows of his own existence, plagued by physical abuse and rejection by his father, malnutrition, and a destructively negative self-image that was reinforced by everything around him, he watched while most of his female relatives trudged up the long hill from the center of Columbus to Wynnton to work for women he would later kill. Their power in the community was unchallengeable, and in Carlton Gary's view they comprised their own pantheon, making the economic and social decisions that translated the lives of Gary's relatives into hope or hopelessness. But most frustrating of all to an abused but intellectually gifted black child growing up in Columbus was that he was absolutely invisible to the matrons of Wynnton. Not that they weren't kindly, churchgoing, charitable women; they were all that and more. They were the epitome of what a Southern lady should be, but the antithesis of what Carlton Gary's mother actually had been. They simply looked right through Gary and other black males as if they weren't there at all. Thus when, after twenty years, Carlton Gary emerged as a full-blown serial killer, he struck from behind a mask of invisibility, ripping away at the very sex of the women who dominated his childhood but who looked right through him, and strangling them with their own articles of clothing.

Carlton Gary's example illustrates the fundamental similarities that unite all serial killers: the murder phase is a ritual reenactment of the disastrous experiences of the killer's childhood. Only, this time, the killer tries to reverse the roles occupied in his childhood experiences. In this way he can almost magically cancel out his earlier suffering and reestablish his own power and identity. A Carlton Gary can strike while invisible, but this time he is the initiator who wreaks the revenge and rights all perceived wrongs.

Similarly, John Wayne Gacy, who was a sickly and effeminate child and who was also abused as a child by his violent, alcoholic, and castrating father, struck at the genitalia of the boys he had trapped in his basement. While strangling them slowly, he recited the Twenty-third Psalm and urged them to be brave in the face of torture and death. It was not the immediate death of the young boys that Gacy sought, it was the prolonging of the process of death. Through this ritual Gacy sought to reassert his own vision of a masculine identity that had been squashed down by his father.

Joseph Kallinger, in an almost identical ritual, had his cokiller son, sixteen-year-old Michael, cut the penises off their two male victims while they were still alive. Joseph's later confessions revealed that his mother had ordered him to hold his open palm over a flame until the skin began to smolder. If the young Kallinger cried, he was savagely beaten. This, his mother told him, would make him strong. Men shouldn't cry; they should be able to bear extremes of pain, and in bearing their sufferings silently they will become strong. This perversion of the ideal of the laconic male hero motivated Kallinger throughout his career as a serial murderer. The more his victims, one of whom was his son, screamed in terror and pleaded for their lives, the more delight Kallinger took. The death of the victim was almost anticlimactic to the process of torture and slow death. The moment one of his last victims, Kallinger's own thirteen-year-old son Joey, took his last breath and said, 'Daddy, please help me,' Kallinger had an orgasm and the hallucination broke.

Other stories of serial murders exceed even the wildest violence of the drive-in movie bloodbath. Henry Lee Lucas and Ottis Toole burned their struggling victims with cigarettes and white-hot metal. Lucas confessed that he burned and cut into the most private parts of his female victims and forced them to watch as he sawed off their fingers and toes. The act of mutilation was the high point of the ritual for Lucas, who himself had been burned and scarred by his mother when he was a child. He had been forced to watch his mother have sex with multitudes of strange men who had turned upon him with violence after abusing his mother. Thus Lucas, when he emerged, turned that same violence on women who reminded him of his mother. Ottis Toole, the homosexual who had been abused by his father and raised as 'the Devil's child' by his Satanist grandmother, turned that abuse on children and homosexual men. The confessed murderer of Adam Walsh, whose story has been documented on national television, Toole assaulted his helpless victims sexually, killed them, dismembered them, and ate parts of their bodies.

The moment of murder itself is the emotional high for most confessed serial killers. At this instant, when the victims were dying at their hands, many serial killers report an insight so intense that it is like an emotional quasar, blinding in its revelation of truth. In those seconds of acting out the absolute pinnacle of their own anguish, some report spontaneous orgasms, a sexual release so complete that it is clearly their moment of triumph, a powerful statement of their own existence when they can face the collective demons of their past without the least trace of fear.

6. The Totem Phase

As do most moments of intense insight, the serial killer's triumphant vision of truth fades rapidly after the victim is finally dead. The murderer's fantasy has been so all-consuming that he is drained after the crime and begins to slide quickly into depression. Some serial killers try to preserve the intensity of the murder, to prolong the feeling of power and triumph over their pasts, by attempting to preserve the body through a ritualistic dismemberment of the dead victim. Either the victim's genitals are cut off and carried away, or the limbs are severed, or the head is removed. Serial killers have eaten parts of the victims' remains, carried off parts of the body with them for later preservation in jars or scrapbooks, buried parts of their victims' bodies in isolated 'sacred' spots, or shown them to their subsequent victims. This is the totemic phase in which the dead victim has become a symbol of what the murderer had hoped would have been an emotional triumph. The victim has been transformed from symbolic creature to symbolic trophy, an object which, the murderer hopes, can transmit to him the fleeting feelings of power and glory at the moment when his private ritual reached its climax.

Many of the killers hold onto the moment of vision by taking Polaroid snapshots of the murder. Leonard Lake shot a series of video tapes of the moments leading to his victims' deaths. In California serial killer Edmund Kemper killed his mother, the woman whose voice had dominated his every thought throughout his life, as his final act of murder; to symbolize his victory, he cut out her vocal cords, burned them, and threw the remains in the garbage disposal, and brought her head back to his apartment where he used it as a dart board for several days. However, these parts of victims' bodies or photographs of the murder have no magical qualities that can be transferred, and the emotional high of the murder quickly fades.

7. The Depression Phase

Ted Bundy confessed that he never really had got what he had hoped for out of the murders. In fact, he reported, they had actually left him with a feeling of emptiness and hopelessness, as if he could never ultimately achieve the emotional release he was trying to reach. Kallinger reported the same type of depression, as did Henry Lee

Lucas and others. The reasons for this lie in the emotional premises of the murder itself: the killer is simply acting out a ritualistic fantasy. There is no more healing salve of reality in the ritual than there is in the false identity of the victim in the killer's mind. The tragedy is that a helpless individual had to be slaughtered as a form of sacrifice to the killer's own past. But, once sacrificed, the victim's identity within the murderer's fantasy is lost. The victim no longer represents what the killer thought he or she represented. The image of a fiancée who had rejected the killer, the echo of the voice of the hated mother, or the taunting of the distant father: all remain vividly in the killer's mind after the crime. Murder has not erased or changed the past because the killer hates himself as much as he did before the climax of emotion. And even during the course of the murder the killer finds out that it is only his own past that is acted out. He has failed again. No real power is ever achieved, and the killer is left feeling as empty, forlorn, and damned as he had throughout the entirety of his life. Instead of reversing the roles of his childhood, the killer has just reinforced them, and by torturing and killing a defenseless victim, the killer has restated his most intimate tragedies. He becomes the victim and remains unfulfilled and unsatisfied. And in this depression phase not even the newspaper headlines announcing the discovery of another one of his victims is enough to help him recapture the power he had experienced.

For days or weeks after the most recent murder the killer will inhabit a shadowy world of gloom in which he feeds on his own sorrow. All the while he is going about the business of life as if he were normal. Then, sick of the crimes he has committed, he may send a confessional note to the police or he may even call the local newspaper to ask for help. He may even be lucid about his own affliction. But soon the fantasies begin to assemble in his mind; his uncontrollable urges begin to overtake him again, and, driven by a lust for murder, he starts up the car again and drives off into the night to seek out the trolling grounds where his next victims will unwittingly congregate. Again, an unwary stranger will cross his vision, enter his corridor of death, and the killing ritual will once more be carried out to its inevitable conclusion.

3

The Disease of Serial Murder

To understand the enormity that the problem of serial murder poses for society's institutions, multiply the Carlton Gary killings in Columbus, the Ted Bundy killings in Seattle, Utah, and Tallahassee, and the Richard Ramirez Nightstalker killings in Los Angeles and San Francisco five hundred times. Add to this the more than three hundred confessed killings by Henry Lee Lucas, the crime sprees of John Gacy and Ed Kemper, and the revelations of child sex abuse cases that are turning up in cities all over the country and the scope of the problem seems endless. However, it doesn't stop there: the problem is spreading and has escalated every year since 1959. At present the FBI estimates there are at least thirty-five serial killers on the loose and under investigation by the Bureau. Moreover, local police are still trying to solve ongoing serial murder cases in the Green River area of Seattle, a string of prostitute murders in Los Angeles, murders of elderly black women in Atlanta, murders of redheaded women throughout Florida, and a series of slayings of male derelicts in San Francisco who have been found with the sign of the pentangle etched into their flesh.

Only in the past few years have professionals begun to

understand the process through which such ultimately malevolent individuals have been created in each generation. After these professionals come to understand how the episodic killers have been shaped by patterns of child abuse, pathologically negative parenting, brain injuries resulting from physical traumas, inherited neurological disorders, chronic malnutrition, chronic drug and alcohol abuse, and toxic poisoning from environmental pollutants, the true nature of the medical/social epidemic will become clearer. What public health officials now know is that the cycles of violence in all of its forms that have been spawned from the previous generation feed upon themselves in each successive generation. Parents who abuse their children, physically as well as psychologically, instill in them an almost instinctive reliance upon violence as a first resort to any challenge. As each generation teaches the next generation to react with violence and as this is reinforced and compounded by the media, the patterns of violent behavior spread, consuming increasingly greater numbers of victims.

Until only recently, the linkage among violence in the background of an offender, a pattern of substance abuse, forms of psychomotor epilepsy that seem to debilitate – even momentarily – a person with a record of sex abuse or child abuse, and a pervasive self-destructive type of personality has gone unrecognized by criminologists and doctors as a form of medical syndrome. People who display this syndrome have historically been categorized as either sociopaths or psychopaths and have been relegated to the care of the criminal justice system. Under this system, they are treated as though they have volition and were capable of managing their own behavior. They are treated as though they were within the range of normal human existence, yet had willingly become deviant. This is not the case. Serial murderers are nonpersonality types who seem to come alive only during the episodic cycle of murder. However, because the criminal justice system concentrates on apprehension and punishment rather than on discovering the causality of violence and preventing its spread, individuals who display this type of medical syndrome have slid through the system untreated. And as a consequence the infection has been allowed to spread through society like a plague: the emerging serial killers are the carriers, transmitting the syndrome from one generation to the next, and six thousand Americans per year are their primary victims and the syndrome's most visible casualties.

Our evaluations of serial killers show that each of them has an amalgamation of symptoms that point to a type of disease that can actually shape their behavior patterns. It is a disease that some experts say can be prevented ninety percent of the time. During the period when they are experiencing episodic explosions of violence, these serial murderers are out of control. They are unable to own any sense of right and wrong and have a significantly diminished ability to judge objectively their own activities. They have lost their free will. They are in the grip of a form of episodic frenzy that does not fit traditional legal descriptions and cannot be evaluated by traditional criminological or psychoanalytical techniques. Their condition lies beyond insanity. When placed in the custody of an institution, however, be it prison or a hospital for the criminally insane, a medical treatment facility, or any place where systematic rules govern the daily activities of the inmates, there is a marked improvement in their behavior. It is as if, having no internal structure to their lives, the killers amalgamate the rules system of the institution as a form of external skeleton. Thriving in this controlled environment and sustained by any improvement in their diets and receiving frequent counseling, the killers become mercurial or placid, bonding closely with male or female authority figures, jail ministers, lawyers, and biographers, and they tailor their confessions to fit the needs of their interrogators and the requirements of the moment. By then, however, they tend to lose their sense of the past and to confuse the events of their lives. It is almost as if the murders never took place, as if a part of their consciousness has been shut down, and they begin to function like other institutionalized patients who rely on their external environments for all sensient activity. And almost all of them are markedly guiltless, as if the moral responsibility for the crimes they committed had been borne by someone else. However, when the appropriate feelings of remorse return, the grief and sadness have more to do with the tragedies of their own lives than with the lives of their victims.

The prevalence of these repeated patterns in all of the case histories of the serial murderers we have studied, the overwhelming similarities of their modus operandi, the primal qualities of their violent behavior, the similar patterns of brain dysfunction and learning disabilities that each of them evidences, the similarities in the results of the biochemical tests that many of them have taken once in prison, and finally the remarkable consistency of their reactions to institutionalization lead to the conclusion that serial murder is a form of disease. To be sure, this is not an illness that fits into traditional medical categories, but, until the work of Breuer, Freud, and Jung, neither were psychoses or neuroses. Serial murder is an illness that has eluded detection because it very conveniently slipped between the cracks of most diagnostic schema. Because many cases of minimal brain damage and lesioning due to forms of psychomotor epilepsy are not confirmed conclusively until after the brain is examined in an autopsy, a diagnosis could not be made. Also, because the murderers themselves seemed to be fully aware of the nature of the charges against them and even admitted their guilt, traditional insanity defenses could not be mounted. And because the episodes of truly psychotic hallucinatory behavior by some were controllable in an institutional setting – often the first stable living environment many of the killers ever experienced – the actual playing out of the murderers' dream visions never took place. Finally, and most importantly, many murderers wish for death and several have attempted suicide. They welcome it as a final solution to their agony. Therefore, rather than defend themselves against the murder charges, they embrace the death sentence as the ultimate murder episode in which their fantasies of self-destruction – fantasies that have driven them throughout their lives – are consummated.

Serial murderers share a significant number of common medical-psychological patterns that include evidence of possible genetic defect, soft signs of brain damage resulting from injuries or other physical trauma, severe chemical imbalances brought about by chronic malnutrition and substance abuse, an absence of a sense of self which is the result of consistently negative parenting or nonparenting, and an almost hair-trigger violent response to external stimuli with no regard for the physical or social consequences. One of the most significant common behavior patterns is a failure to perceive punishment as a deterrent to their actions and a fascination with police procedures and the officers who are pursuing them. Carlton Gary even dated a female deputy sheriff while he was actually committing the Wynnton murders. He led a double life as her lover and she was unaware of his actions. The psychophysiological mechanisms that keep most people from immediately acting on violent or negative impulses is simply absent in them. Once the killing begins, they are unable to control their behavior no matter what the circumstances are. However, in the specific instance of serial murder, this period of loss of control is episodic. During these episodes the criminal's behavior repeats a ritualistic pattern of trolling, stalking, wooing, capture, torture, murder, recapture, and postmortem depression.

Between the episodes, the absence of a sense of self allows the criminal to fade back into society as a common individual. Some killers are actually hypervigilant do-gooders. For example, during his killing spree John Gacy entertained children in hospitals. Ted Bundy worked on a suicide hotline and wrote a manual for rape crisis intervention.

This loss of control – the lack of rational behavior with regard to appreciating the consequences of personal violence, and the compulsive premeditation with regard to each successive victim – is what sets the serial murderer apart from other killers. As a result of scientific studies conducted by numerous institutions and individuals across the country on the causality of violence, we have developed the hypothesis that episodic aggression, which involves child and family abuse, rape, and serial murder, is inherently a disease and therefore treatable and preventable.

The key to detecting this disease in individuals is a recognition of the key behavioral patterns common to all episodic violent offenders in general and to convicted serial murderers in particular. First and most obvious is the subject's animallike, primal approach to the act of murder. The range can vary from a simple rape murder to ritualistic torture and dismemberment of the victim. In addition, many serial killers evidence a reliance upon hair-trigger violence as a first response to conflict or challenge. In the cases of both Henry Lee Lucas and John Gacy, encounters with strangers turned into murder when the serial killers felt challenged by the potential victim. Bobby Joe Long reported that after a serious motorcycle accident had left him permanently disabled and damaged a significant part of his brain he was unable to control his temper. Even the slightest annoyance, such as the tapping of a hammer or a sudden noise, would be enough to send him into a fury. Years later Long emerged first as a rapist and then as a serial killer who raped and tortured his victims before murdering them. John Gacy's story is very similar. Years before he killed his first victim, but always after a bout of heavy drinking, Gacy routinely sought encounters with young men in bus stations and other public places, offering them money and drugs, having sex with them, and going out to dinner. It was only years later, as a fully emerged serial killer, when any of his male sexual encounters offered him a direct challenge or confronted him in any way, that he lured the victim back to his house, where he tortured him and buried the body under his house.

This tendency to resort spontaneously to violence often turns up in abused or battered children. They, in turn, pass it along to their children in the succeeding generation. In fact, as Marvin Wolfgang has shown in a study of a cohort of males born in 1945, those people with violent criminal backgrounds often experienced violence in their households when they were growing up and were themselves victims of violent parents. A first resort to violence can also be indicative of a form of minimal brain damage, especially to the limbic region or the frontal lobe – the inhibitors of judgmental and primitive animal defensive reactions. Many serial killers who have undergone CAT or PET scans evidenced some form of significant damage to the limbic region of the brain.

Juvenile offenders who have committed violent crimes and homicidally aggressive children are particularly important in deciphering the developmental nature of this disease. For many of the most violent, this is not their first offense. An examination of their criminal records reveals a tendency toward violence that manifested itself from their first brushes with any authority. Often one or more parents have engaged in some form of criminal activity, and that violence has been a part of their backgrounds as well. Medical examinations of violent juvenile offenders tend to reveal a variety of physiological and neurological problems ranging from degrees of brain damage or dysfunction to nutritional deficiencies to forms of toxic poisoning.

Even at an early developmental stage, potential serial murderers show signs of pathology and grandiosity. Some experts say that the deficit occurs prior to age five. This is where skilled diagnosis is important and the most meaningful research has yet to be done. As full-blown sociopaths, they evidence no guilt nor do they see any necessary consequences of their actions. At their most violent and uncontrollable, serial murderers simply claim to block out any memory of their crimes and change their confessions to fit the needs of their interrogators and the moment. They have convenient but nonetheless real loss of memory and are able to lie with complete freedom about their previous crimes. This is what makes serial killers so difficult to interrogate and diagnose. It also makes them infuriating to their investigators. They can manipulate and even confuse the most skilled interrogator or diagnostician, even the lie detector operator. Everything they say must be documented by objective evidence because they will change the truth to conform to any situation. They are not plagued by a gnawing guilt that forces them into a confession. Their sufferings are internal and have little or nothing to do with any specific crime. For this reason, early intervention in the life of an evolving serial killer – while his pain and fury are still relatively close to the surface – is important. Once the entire architecture of violence has been digested by the emerging criminal, it will only objectify itself in its victims, and that is what sustains the murderer until the architecture collapses from its own weight and the murderer attempts suicide to end his own torment.

If primal displays of violence and a family background of violence are the most identifiable behavioral characteristics of the serial killer syndrome, history of head trauma, degrees of brain or neurological dysfunction, or forms of psychomotor epilepsy are important medical characteristics. Genetic factors can also play a role in the evolution of the serial killer syndrome. Because certain forms of epilepsy and brain dysfunctions can be inherited, the serial killer need not necessarily have received an injury or be a victim of a birth defect in order to have impaired brain activity. These physiological impairments directly affect outward behavior and the social controls the individual is able to exert over behavior. Even minor brain dysfunctions or minor damage resulting from injuries can result in a significant loss of control of violent tendencies. When this condition is brought about because of beatings received in childhood or exists in a highly unstable family background, the normal social conditioning that should have taken place doesn't, and the individual has no basis for controlling his emotions. His behavioral reference points are all internal rather than external, and he has no personality map to help him negotiate through the world. He is already losing control.

The final pathology components of this syndrome involve behavioral reactions to chemical imbalances resulting from malnutrition, substance abuse, and toxic poisoning. The first, malnutrition, results not only from an unstable family background in which the child's physiological development was impaired, but from continuing nutritional disorders and the resulting vitamin and mineral deficiencies. A diet that is severely lacking in any nutrients deprives the brain of fuel it needs to function. Deficiencies in iron weaken the system and deprive it of resiliency; deficiencies in mineral zinc and potassium can affect the hormonal system and place the individual in a chronic state of emotional turmoil; and deficiencies in vitamins B and C leave the body vulnerable to low levels of infection. In these situations, behavioral disorders such as hair-trigger reactions to outside stimuli are almost normal occurrences. These disorders can also result as reactions to an overabundance or deprivation of sugar and starch or to a serious deficiency in trace minerals other than zinc or iron. They can also result from physiological reactions to lead or cobalt poisoning, two environmental pollutants that have regularly turned up in laboratory analyses of blood taken from serial killers. This is why the clinical testing for a predisposition to commit violent acts should include laboratory analysis of the patient's blood and serum chemicals.

Substance abuse, either alcohol or drugs, also forms a major behavioral component of the serial killer's makeup. Most convicted serial killers are chronically heavy drinkers and narcotics addicts who are either drunk or high at the time they commit their crimes. The problem, however, goes well beyond a claim of temporary drunkenness. Alcohol has a residual effect on the brain and neurological system. Prolonged use of alcohol actually destroys brain tissue, rendering portions of the brain moderately impaired. During a prolonged drunken state, when the entire brain function is inhibited and social controls are lowered in general, there is simply no form of normal control exerted by the predisposed individual to prevent antisocial activity. During periods of episodic violence, alcohol only increases the level of the serial killer's disorientation and further separates him from reality. Much the same can be said for narcotics. They contribute to the serial killer's hallucinatory state and markedly diminish all brain functions. Henry Lee Lucas revealed that all of his murders were committed while he was drunk. Ted Bundy is a chronic alcoholic and had joined AA while in prison, and John Gacy became so violent while given alcohol in prison that he had to be placed in a straitjacket to prevent him from injuring himself. Most serial killings are committed while the murderer is under the influence of alcohol or drugs.

As a form of violence that is spreading in epidemic proportions and whose pathology is demonstrable medically, serial murder truly belongs to the areas of physical abuse that U.S. Surgeon General Dr. C. Everett Koop has designated as a critical issue of public health. The Surgeon General cited family violence, child abuse, sex abuse, substance abuse, and any crimes or homicides – all of which are components of the serial murderer's syndrome – resulting from these causes as public health issues that require a level of intervention from health care and social work professionals beyond the obvious involvement of criminal justice professionals. Rather than simply 'medicalizing' the problem of child abuse or rape, the U.S. Public Health Service is seeking a new form of prevention. By recognizing that violence is a form of disease, the Public Health Service can extend the responsibility for preventing these special types of crimes beyond the immediate level of the police and the courts and into parole boards, doctors' offices, hospital emergency rooms, school nurses' offices, and guidance departments in school districts around the country. By focusing the attention of the hospital or school social worker and even the local police juvenile officer on the case of a particular victim and examining the events surrounding the crime, the Surgeon General has suggested, the career of that perpetrator can be short-circuited before he can commit any more crimes or emerge fully as a serial or mass murderer.

Like physical diseases, most forms of family and personal violence are preventable. One of the first signs of the acceptance of this point of view is the Surgeon General's suggestion that violence is a disease that calls for medical intervention. Heart disease falls into this category as do many forms of progressive neurological diseases. Serial murder and many forms of violent behavior are similarly preventable if the person is identified and diagnosed in time. In many cases that diagnosis can be initiated by an emergency room physician or a school nurse who notices the patterns of bruises on a patient, the attitude of a woman who has been sexually assaulted, or even the behavior of an adolescent offender who has been apprehended by a school guard or a police officer. However, most professionals at an early possible point of intervention are so repelled by what they see, they simply turn away as if their own primal instincts were dictating their fear.

That fear and revulsion have to be addressed and overcome. Then, by making a preliminary investigation of the person's background and family environment, evaluating a subject's medical history, running a series of autonomic reflex and psychological recognition tests, checking a pupillary response to light, or even conducting a perfunctory medical examination, a doctor, nurse, or trained paraprofessional can see whether there is any reason to probe deeper. These tests and simple medical interviews can be performed in the space of an hour or two and require only that a health care professional evaluate whether the patient or subject is displaying any signs of uncontrollable hostility, psychological disorientation bordering on explosive violence or actual brain damage.

Further tests are always necessary to confirm any diagnosis. In the case of diagnosing a predisposition to episodic violence, the evaluation and appropriate clinical follow-through should be conducted by neurological specialists and clinical psychologists who have a knowledge of causes of violence and the applicable criminal law as well as court procedures for determining either insanity or functional incompetence during hallucinatory or fantasy cycles. This evaluation should include a thorough medical and psychological examination of the subject. Ultimately, new diagnostic tools will have to be developed from what we understand about the nature of episodic violent behavior to predict that form of violence in individuals. New training procedures will have to be developed as well to help physicians and other health care professionals to recognize the signs of an episodically violent person.

The premise of this activity is to provide a meaningful medical causality for the instances of episodic violence in any particular individual, determine the course of treatment, and, ultimately, save the lives of the victims of any crimes he would have committted. This level of intervention also presupposes that the causality of uncontrollable and episodic violent behavior is not only a lapse in volition but also a definable set of organic malfunctions – some genetic over three generations, some chronic, and some environmental – that, when combined with a history of violent upbringing and negative parenting in which the traditional polarities of reward and punishment and love and hate are reversed, results in a nonpersonality type – a nosferatu – an individual with no means of controlling violent impulses, who is incapable of functioning within a normal social framework. Everett Koop and his colleagues in the field of public health recognize that prosecuting individuals who commit extraordinary violent crimes solves only a minute portion of the problem. The issue is to recognize this form of violence as a disease and bring the full structure of the medical and legal establishment to bear on preventing its spread.

The biosocial case histories of recent serial murderers in the following chapters will validate this hypothesis and show how the disease manifests itself in specific individuals and how the system as it now exists prevents significant investigation and intervention in these individuals.

4

Serial Killers Today

The serial murder syndrome is not a new phenomenon historically, even though it has dramatically increased in American society since 1958 and is only just coming to the attention of the courts, the police, and the medical profession. In fact, throughout history, societies have recorded the crimes of individuals which look suspiciously like the crimes committed by serial murderers today. The stories of Caligula, Vlad Tepes, Giles de Reis, and Jack the Ripper are among the many legends about individuals who seemed to kill out of a blood lust for the act of murder itself and not from any other motivation. And certainly the many legends of vampires and werewolves that have circulated throughout Europe from the Middle Ages to the present seem to reflect a fear that some individuals lurk beyond the walls of society, preying on victims out of a necessity to kill. Where records have been kept, they often show that serial murderers seem to appear within the same extended family and that outbreaks of the pathology take place in each generation. Often the evidence of this pathology is manifested by an obvious physical abnormality such as an elongated middle toe, webbed skin between the fingers, or epileptic tremors. Many of these serial murderers belonged to families that held power within their societies, allowing the criminals to seek their prey at will until the family had the person shut away or the criminal eventually died.

Today, however, in the light of modern crime reporting statistics and the records of police investigations, a truer picture of the work of the serial killer has emerged, and the growing magnitude of the crimes and the extent of the violence of each individual crime now seems clear. The capsule descriptions in this chapter of some of the most active serial killers and their crimes since 1961 demonstrate how the level of violence continues to grow and how the murderers we are profiling fit into the general class of serial killers.

1961 – *Melvin D. Rees, Jr.*, was a jazz musician convicted of slaying a family in Maryland whom he had kidnapped from their car in a highway ambush. The mother, who was found with her dress pulled up over her head, had been strangled with one of her nylon stockings. Her little daughter had been beaten to death, and her husband was found a distance away from the car, his hands tied together with his tie. He had been shot through the head and the year-and-a-half-old child he was cradling in his arms when he was shot was suffocated when the weight of his body fell over hers. Rees was also a primary suspect in other killings in Maryland. After his conviction he asked for the death penalty but received life imprisonment instead.

1964 – *Albert DeSalvo*. Better known as the 'Boston Strangler,' DeSalvo held Boston in a grip of terror during his murder spree. A master of disguise, he gained entrance to his victims' apartments by pretending he was a plumber or a handyman. His compulsion to kill drove him to take greater and greater risks, even while he was living a normal life with his own family.

1966 – *Michael Lee Herrington.* In Milwaukee this twenty-three-year old tool and die maker confessed to the mutilation slayings of two women and another attempted murder over a period of three months. Herrington was married but had no children.

Suspect Unknown. In Cincinnati an eighty-one-year-old woman was one of five victims who were discovered in their homes with lamp cords tied around their necks. All of them had been raped. After ten months the murders stopped, and the suspect was never identified.

1967 – *Dr. Ronald E. Clark,* of Detroit, a former mental patient himself, killed his own patients by injecting them with lethal doses of sodium pentothal. He was also brought up on charges of sexual attacks on his patients and on children.

1969 – *Antone Costa* of Cape Cod was convicted of murdering three women whose bodies were found dismembered, mutilated, and buried in the sand dunes. The police are still officially searching for more bodies.

1971 – *William Pierce,* a Georgia prison parolee in Beaufort, South Carolina, was charged with his eighth and ninth slayings: a twenty-year-old housewife and a gas station attendant. Despite a report from a prison psychologist that said 'he may be dangerous to himself and others,' Pierce was placed on parole in 1970.

Edmund J. Cody was a truck driver who married nine times. He was charged with killing Letha Gay, his ninth wife, whose body was found strangled and decomposing in the trunk of his car. He is suspected of killing at least another four of his wives while the remaining four are still listed as missing. Cody is currently serving a life sentence.

1972 – *Benjamin Franklin Miller* of Stamford, Connecticut, was a self-ordained minister who preached on street corners. Charged with the slaying of five black women over a four-year period, he was known as the 'Bra Killer,' because he strangled the victims with their own bras. Miller believed himself to be another Billy Graham and was frequently invited to neighborhood churches to preach. It was there, police assume, that he met his five victims.

Charles Schmid, Jr., was called the 'Pied Piper of Tucson' by the police, who charged him with the murder of three teenage girls in 1965. Schmid admitted to strangling the teenagers and burying their bodies in the desert because it made him 'feel good.'

1973 – *Girard John Schaefer,* called the 'Sex Beast,' was connected to more than twenty murders in the Oakland Park area of Florida. Schaefer, who himself was an ex-police officer, was linked to the killings because jewelry, teeth, and articles of clothing belonging to the victims were found in the trunk of his car.

Herbert Mullin in Santa Cruz, California, was convicted of ten serial murders. This came as a shock to the community because in high school the killer was an outgoing, socially adept individual who was voted 'most likely to succeed.'

Edmund Emil Kemper, also from Santa Cruz, was charged with the murder of his mother and at least seven female hitchhikers. He had dismembered all of the bodies and preserved limbs and organs in a variety of ways. Kemper had a long history of mental illness and had been in and out of mental institutions throughout his life. After killing his mother, Kemper turned himself in to the police because he knew that he would keep on killing until he was finally stopped or killed.

Bruce Henderson Shreeves, an AWOL sailor, was linked to three murders in Spencerville, Maryland. Police said that the bodies were disposed of in a ritualistic way that connected the murders to one another and pointed to the work of the same killer.

Dean Corll, the 'Man with the Candy,' and *Elmer Wayne Henly* in Houston, Texas, together performed more than twenty-seven torture slayings of young boys. Corll lured the boys to his candy store, where he would have 'parties' during which he forced the victims to perform sodomy and other sexual acts. He would then kill them, sprinkle their bodies with crushed lime rock, and bury them. Corll himself was killed by Henly. According to Henly's story, Corll tied him up along with two other people. When Henly offered to torture the other victims if he were untied, Corll released him, whereupon he grabbed Corll's gun and shot him.

Julian Kennedy, thirty, of Lake City, Florida, was formally charged with the murder of a woman. During his confession to the police he admitted to thirteen other murders over a fifteen-year span.

His first murder, he explained, was part of an initiation rite into a motorcycle gang: he was told to beat a man to death with a chair and an axe handle.

1974 – *Larry C. Green, J. D. Simpson, Manuel Moore,* and *Jesse Cooks* claim to be members of a cult called the 'Death Angels.' Charged with committing the 'Zebra Killings,' a series of murders in which blacks killed whites, the cult boasted more than two thousand members and announced that its mission was to torture, mutilate, and kill white victims.

Joseph Kallinger, the 'Shoemaker,' along with his son Michael killed three people in New York. Kallinger claimed a mandate from God to torture his victims before killing them.

The '*Zodiac Killer*' murdered and sexually assaulted several children in San Francisco. Given his name by the police because he carved the sign of the zodiac into the bodies of his victims, the killer was never apprehended and the murder cases remain unsolved. The killer is believed either to have been killed himself or been confined to a mental institution. The murders stopped after a few months as mysteriously as they had begun.

Calvin Jackson, a former drug addict and ex-convict, admitted to raping and then strangling eleven elderly women in their New York City apartments.

1975 – *Thomas E. Creech,* in Wallace, Idaho, admitted to having killed forty-two persons over the previous eight years as a 'contract executioner' for a national motorcycle gang involved in drug trafficking or during cult worship. He also said he ranked eighth in the amount of victims killed by contract killers for the gang.

1976 – *Vaughn Greenwood,* also in Los Angeles, was indicted for murdering eleven skid row derelicts over a two-year period. He slashed the victims' throats and left a cup of blood on each of their bodies. He also sprinkled salt in a hoodlike design around the heads of the dead victims.

1977 – *Dr. Mario E. Jascalevich,* in the 'Dr. X' killings in Hackensack, New Jersey, murdered five of his hospital patients by injecting them with lethal does of curare, the African dart poison.

Patrick Kearny, who was a former aerospace engineer, and *David Hill* were convicted in the Southern California 'Trash Bag Murders.' The two killed more than twenty-eight homosexuals, wrapped up the remains, and dumped their bodies in the trash.

1978 – *Kenneth Bianchi,* the 'Hillside Strangler,' was convicted along with *Angelo Buono, Jr.,* of killing nine young women in an exclusive Los Angeles neighborhood.

Gary Gene Tison, in Florence, Arizona, broke out of prison, where he was serving a life sentence for murder, by his three sons. The four went on a three-week killing spree, murdering a two-year-old boy and his parents, a teenage girl, and a honeymooning couple. At a roadblock, two of the sons were captured, a third was killed by police, and Tison escaped into the desert. He was found dead of exposure a few weeks later.

Mary Rose Robatzynski, in Baltimore, was indicted

for killing four of her patients in the hospital's ICU by unhooking their life-support systems.

1979 – *Joseph Fischer*, was arrested in California for killing his wife, admitted to police that he'd killed nineteen other people at random in New Mexico, Arizona, Maine, Connecticut, and New York since being paroled from a California prison in June of 1978.

Suspect Unknown. In Houston, Joann Huffman and Robert Spangenberger were found dead in a park. She had been shot to death and he was discovered, decapitated, in the trunk of a car. The work was presumably done by the same murderer, and it was the second such murder in Houston in the same year.

Paul Bateson, an X-ray technician at New York University Medical Center in Manhattan, was convicted of murdering Addison Verill, a New York writer. Bateson claimed that he had killed a number of other men, dismembering their bodies and wrapping them in trash bags which he then dumped in the Hudson River.

John Wayne Gacy, a highly respected member of his community who owned a construction and building development company in Chicago, was arrested for the murders of thirty-three boys. In one of the most famous serial murder cases of all time, Gacy was accused of picking up the boys at bus stations or along the road, having sex with them, torturing and murdering some of them, and burying the bodies in the basement of his suburban home. His crime was finally reported by his wife, who complained of the putrid odors arising from beneath the house.

Theodore Bundy, in another famous murder case, was convicted of murdering two coeds in a Florida college dormitory and a twelve-year-old girl. He was also connected to numerous other murders in Seattle and Salt Lake City and was the object of a country-wide manhunt on a fugitive warrant. He was sentenced to death, but the sentence was delayed while his appeals are progressing through the courts.

Gerald Eugene Stano killed eighteen waitresses in Florida over a five-year period, and is currently on death row in San Quentin.

1980 – *Roy Lewis Norris* and *Lawrence S. Bittiker* were convicted of killing five teenage girls in the Los Angeles area, and are currently on death row in San Quentin.

Suspect Unknown in the case of a cult killer of seven hitchhikers in Point Reyes Station, California. The killer is still at large.

Carlton Gary commited nine murders of prominent women in the Wynnton section of Columbus, Georgia. Known as the 'Stocking Strangler,' Gary was able to elude the police until 1984. He was convicted and sentenced to death in 1986. The conviction and sentence are still on appeal.

1981 – *Suspect Unknown.* Termed the 'Skid Row Slasher' by the NYPD, this killer murdered eight derelicts and street people by stabbing them while they slept in alleys and doorways. The case is still open.

Suspect Unknown. In a related set of killings, a person called the 'Midtown Slasher' by the

NYPD murdered six Hispanic victims in the Times Square/midtown area of Manhattan. The case is still open.

Wayne B. Williams was arrested for the Atlanta Child Murders. These killings of young children in Atlanta kept the city in the grip of terror for more than a year, set local and state law enforcement agencies at odds with one another, and captured the front pages of newspapers around the country. Williams was convicted for the murder of one victim on purely circumstantial evidence, but his case has been reopened because new evidence has been introduced. The killings stopped after Williams' arrest, but many Atlanta residents feel that Williams is not the Atlanta 'Child Murderer' and that the real killer is still at large.

Carl Eugene Roberts of Houston, Texas, is the confessed killer of at least thirteen women. He was sentenced to sixty years in prison after a plea bargain with the county prosecutor.

Suspect Unknown in the deaths of seven black women in Atlanta. As the city prepared for the worst, many residents believed that the 'Child Murderer' was striking again at a new set of victims or that the Columbus murders of 1977 had spawned another killer of older women. The case is still open.

Suspect Unknown in the Richland, Georgia, slayings of three teenage girls who were found brutally beaten, sexually assaulted, and bound with twisted metal coat hangers to trees, where they eventually died of their wounds. The case is still open.

Suspect Unknown in the 'Sunday Morning Slashings' in Houston, where a serial killer murdered more than forty black women by stabbing them with a large knife. The case is still open.

Juan Corona, a contractor for migrant labor on California fruit farms, was convicted for the murder of scores of migrant workers and sentenced to twenty-five years in prison. He buried busloads of victims in mass graves after performing cultlike ritual murders.

David Bullock killed at least six people, including his business partner and an actor, on a Manhattan street corner. He told the New York state criminal court judge that 'killing makes me happy.'

Dale Robert Henderson, a drifter in Tavares, Florida, confessed to killing ten or more people in five states.

Joseph John Sullivan was arraigned in Syracuse, New York, for the murders of twelve people.

William Bonnin, the 'Freeway Murderer,' was convicted of killing ten young boys and men and abandoning their bodies along Southern California's freeways.

Bernard Burton Hunwick was arrested in Dade County, Florida, for a series of murders and confessed to being the head of a 'hit squad' responsible for at least a hundred additional murders.

Christine Falling was convicted in Florida of killing from two to five children by strangulation or suffocation while baby-sitting for them. She was a diagnosed epileptic who believed her victims were epileptic as well.

1983 – *Suspect Unknown* in the killing of four White Plains, New York, women within seven months. The killings suddenly stopped and the case is still open.

Henry Lee Lucas and *Ottis Toole,* both ex-convicts with histories of mental problems, were indicted in Galveston, Texas, for the murders of twenty-eight women.

Angelo Buono, Jr., an auto upholsterer, is convicted along with Kenneth Bianchi, the 'Hillside Strangler,' for killing nine young women in an exclusive neighborhood in Los Angeles.

Henry Brison was convicted in Chicago of the murders of three people during highway robberies. He is on death row along with John Gacy, whom he has sworn to kill as well.

Richard Begenwald killed four women and one man in New Jersey and buried them in shallow graves.

Charles Hatcher, charged with the murder of a four-year-old boy, admitted to the murders of sixteen other people.

Douglas David Clark, the 'Sunset Slayer,' killed six women in Los Angeles.

Suspect Unknown. The Galveston police and the Austin Hills Nursing Home Convalescent Center are investigating the deaths of twenty-eight geriatric patients. A nursing home employee is suspected.

Suspect Unknown. The 'Green River Killer' in Seattle murdered thirteen to twenty-one young girls and women and dumped their bodies along the banks of the Green River. The women were either runaways or prostitutes.

Suspect Unknown in the 'Dune Case' in Provincetown, Massachusetts, where police are investigating the serial killer who left the bodies of twelve young women in sand dunes. The case is still open at the insistence of the county prosecutor's office.

Genene Jones was convicted for three murders but is also suspected in the murders of sixty-one infants at the Bexar County Administrative Medical Center in San Antonio, Texas.

1984 – *Gerald Gallego,* a truck driver and bartender, was convicted of the kidnapping of a college couple, shooting the man in the head and raping and then murdering the girl. He was also convicted of killing four others in Utah and is suspected of another murder in Oregon and three in California. Gallego's father was also convicted of murder and sent to the electric chair in 1955. Gallego is currently on death row.

Debra Sue Tuggle killed her own five children and one of her boyfriend's children in Camden, New Jersey.

Joseph Paul Franklin, an avowed racist, was convicted of killing two black men in Utah. He is a suspect in the random slayings of eight other black men and four white women in seven states from 1977 to 1980. Franklin was a former member of the Ku Klux Klan and the American Nazi Party and usually ambushed his victims with a long-range rifle.

Robert Hanson in Anchorage, Alaska, confessed to killing seventeen women. He is a married man but told police that throughout his life he had a feeling of 'rejection by women.'

Calvin Perry, an eighteen-year-old inmate in Fort Wayne, Indiana, was found hanging in his cell after he admitted killing Dan Osborne, his wife, and their eleven-year-old son. He also raped and beat their two-year-old daughter and even clubbed their dog to death. Before his death Perry also admitted killing other people. Prison authorities suspect that Perry himself was murdered.

Christopher Wilder, in West Palm Beach, Florida, millionaire, was killed in a gun battle with state troopers. Wilder was linked to eleven sex slayings of women, four of whom are still missing.

Robert R. Diaz, a night nurse in Los Angeles, was charged with twelve counts of murder in the hospital in whose coronary care unit he was stationed. He injected his victims with ten times the normal dose of Lidocaine. He is now on San Quentin's death row.

Despite the apparent differences in the backgrounds of these individuals, overwhelming patterns of similarity do emerge. The most apparent similarity is the ability of the majority of the killers to lead relatively normal lives while pursuing their homicidal compulsions. Edward Paisnal, John Gacy, Juan Corona, Albert DeSalvo, and Ted Bundy all held legitimate positions within their communities that allowed them to navigate freely from place to place. Some used their camouflage to get in a better position to locate new victims. DeSalvo gained access to his victims by claiming that he had been hired by the landlord to check the plumbing. Once admitted to an apartment, he sprung his trap and strangled his victim to death. Both Paisnal and John Gacy lured people to their houses with promises of jobs, and both had rooms prepared for the torture and interment of their victims. And Ted Bundy, as a college student, had unlimited access to the lounges, dormitories, and other places where attractive coeds gathered.

Almost all of these killers chose their victims completely at random. In other words, there was no relationship between the victim and the killer other than the one that was established at the moment the victim entered the killer's sight. This is a pattern of critical importance because law enforcement authorities and homicide investigators rely on the relationship between killer and victim as the basis for solving murder cases. When a relationship is absent, as it is in most serial murder cases, the police are left without one of the most important clues in their examination of the crime.

Finally, there is growing evidence that each one of the killers on this list was 'sick' in one way or another. Our research shows that 88% have one or more symptoms. While not legally insane, according to the McNaghten test, each killer distorted reality so completely that he or she was able to keep on killing, for months or even years at a time, by amalgamating the act of killing into his or her personality. Eventually, many serial killers if not apprehended or killed, would commit suicide as a way of ending the pain and self-loathing. And, indeed, most serial killers do report that they have attempted suicide in the past or are actively contemplating suicide. To a person, each killer would readily admit that he or she is sick, and a large majority of the serial killers on this list have sought help for their feelings of homicidal sexuality at some point during their lives. Usually they reach out right before they begin their careers as fully emerged serial murderers.

The similarities among the different killers suggest that they share a common illness, a common syndrome whose origins are not defined by social class, race, or environment. An understanding of the nature of that illness and the ability to detect the appearance of this syndrome in children are the first steps in preventing the spread of serial murder.

5

The Anatomy of a Serial Murder Case:

The Murderer, the Victims, and the Community

April 9 was the first really warm day of spring, Judy Zeitz remembered. It was a Saturday. Her ten-year-old daughter Rachel and Rachel's twelve-year-old friend Caty Richards had just come back from dance rehearsal at the Park Street school. Mrs. Zeitz had offered to let Caty stay over at the Zeitz house so Caty's mother, RoseAlyce Thayer, an artist and teacher, could have the afternoon free to paint. Rachel and Caty came downstairs from Rachel's room and asked for money to play arcade games at Athens Pizza just down the road. Mrs. Zeitz refused. She really didn't want them to go back out now, so late in the afternoon and so close to dinner. The girls bargained: Could they go if they found money on their own? 'It's okay with me,' Judy said. But she told herself that when they couldn't find any money they wouldn't be able to go.

The girls surprised her by managing to scrape together enough spare change to play a game. Mrs. Zeitz kept her part of the bargain and let the girls go. At first Rachel wanted to walk over on her friend's old crutches. 'No way,' Caty screamed at her, and Rachel put the crutches back in her room. Giggling, the two girls raced across the front lawn while Mrs. Zeitz watched from the living room window. 'They look so happy and well pleased with themselves,' she thought, probably because they had thwarted her lazy attempts to prevent them from going.

Caty Richards had been born to RoseAlyce Thayer late in life, her fourth child and first daughter. Her mother had divorced Caty's father and married Charles Thayer, a retired mechanical engineer who made toy sleds and cradles that RoseAlyce painted; they were sold at the quaint country stores that dot the Vermont countryside. Caty had a learning disability and, although she had an average IQ, she was emotionally much younger than her peers. As a result she was easily intimidated. Caty had also been the victim of harassment by an adult male neighbor for nineteen months prior to her death, and her own natural father had threatened to kidnap her. In fact Caty was so terrorized by male strangers that her mother requested that the school assign her only to classes taught by women. What neither Caty nor her mother nor anyone else knew was that she and her friend Tina Cross had also been followed for the past six months by a man named Gary Schaefer who was a member of a local fundamentalist sect.

Caty followed her friend Rachel over to the pizza parlour. But it was too crowded, and the lines in front of the arcade games were too long. The girls decided to walk back to Rachel's house along Route 106. It was four-thirty in the afternoon.

Gary Schaefer was driving his brand-new blue and white Pontiac J2000 along Route 106 north out of Springfield on Saturday afternoon, listening to his tapes and enjoying the first warm day of the new season. He passed two young girls walking along the side of the road. He thought he recognized one of them as his step-daughter, his ex-wife's child by her former husband.

'I wasn't really paying attention to where I was going or what I was doing 'cause I was thinking, just driving and listening to good music,' he remembered, 'when in my rear-view mirror I thought I saw Jodie. So I turned the car around and headed back towards Springfield and I went by the girls again. They were heading up Pedden Acres Road. So I drove into Pedden Acres and turned my car around and stopped and waited for who I thought was Jodie to come up to the car and she did. She walked right up to my car.

'I wasn't even paying attention to the other girl at this time. Not at all. I mean I know she was there, but I wasn't even thinking about anything about her at all. I was in the car, I had the window down and we talked about something, I don't know what we said. I don't even remember the conversation that went on. I know what they say that I said. I said, they said, I asked something about Joe Cerniglia or something like that. I don't remember saying anything like that. I could have, but probably did. I just don't recall. Then I remember opening the door and telling Jodie to get in the car or she was going to be in trouble.'

It was around 5 P.M. when Judy Zeitz, who had lost track of the time, was getting the girls' dinner ready. Rachel appeared at the sliding door with Linda Noyes, the Zeitzes' neighbor from down the hill. Rachel was crying and red in the face. 'Caty was kidnapped,' she kept repeating. 'She was kidnapped by a man in a blue car.' Vernon Zeitz jumped in his car and went back down the road to look for the blue car and Caty. His wife phoned RoseAlyce Thayer. Linda's husband had already called the police. 'I told Rose I'd come for her and for her to get some pictures of Caty.'

RoseAlyce was already on the phone by the time Judy Zeitz arrived. She placed a call to her son Ed but he was out. She left a message. She also called Charlie Thayer, her husband, who was at a meeting in Cuttingsville. She left a message there too. It was five-thirty. The two women drove to the police station, racing through a red light on the way, and began what was to be hours of interviews with the police. How did Caty get along with her stepfather? they asked RoseAlyce Thayer. What was her home life like? Where was Caty's natural father? Did she ever sneak out at night? Did she go out with older men? Was she sexually active?

RoseAlyce sat through the interviews while in a part of her mind she could see the image of her terrified daughter waiting, praying, and expecting to be rescued. 'I still have nightmares of Caty reaching out,' she said years later, 'crying for the police and for help.'

Rachel Zeitz leafed through police mug shots and gave a description of the kidnapper to the police artist for a composite Identikit sketch. 'The man drove a blue compact car like my mother's,' she said. He was wearing a red sweat shirt with kangaroo pockets and the numbers 1983 in white down the sleeve. He had orange-tinted glasses with oval lenses. Having driven past them a couple of times, he finally stopped the car on an S-curve, out of sight of the rest of the road and of the Noyes house only a hundred yards away. First he asked directions. Then he got out of the car, leaving the door on the driver's side open, put his hand in the pocket of his sweat shirt, and said, 'What if I tell you if you don't get in the car I'll shoot and kill you?' Caty bent forward and gasped. She made an 'uhhh' sound and started crying. The man spoke in a monotone, looking only at Caty as if he were trying to hypnotize her. Rachel ran toward the hill, and when she looked back Caty was already in the driver's seat of the car. There was something else about the sweat shirt, Rachel said. Joel DeLorenzo, one of her classmates, had worn the exact same one to school only the week before.

'I guess you know from what the other girl said and everything, I threatened to kill 'em if she didn't get in the car, but I don't remember saying anything like that. I'm not saying that I didn't say it,' Gary Schaefer told the police in his confession a year later. 'I just drove off. I didn't squeal tyres or nothing. I could have, I don't remember doing that. I don't think I would have. I just drove off. And I went back down the road and headed north, I rode out up Gassetts Road and got on 103 and headed towards Rutland. I was talking to her like she was my daughter. She must have been very scared and that's why she got in the car. I mean, I'm saying that she must have been because that's how she must have reacted. I don't know how she reacted. I would have reacted that way if I was a twelve-year-old girl or however old she was.'

Gary Schaefer asked the girl about school, about her friends, about how she had spent her day. They stopped for hamburgers, stopped at a gas station where she went to the bathroom, and finally stopped at a remote place where Schaefer used to visit when he himself was a kid. 'Used to hike up there, but I think I remember that's where I stopped. There was a garbage can and that's where we had our sexual encounter. It was the same thing that I always did with other girls. It wasn't anything different than any other time. It was oral, and then I rubbed myself between her legs. Never had any intercourse or anything like that. It never was Caty. I mean it never was Caty. Never saw her as Caty, never heard her as Caty, or talked to her as Caty, or anything like that. I mean I know it was now, but at the time it wasn't. It was Jodie, and it was the same kind of encounter, sexual encounter, that Jodie and I had all the time.'

Rachel Zeitz became annoyed when the police suggested that Caty Richards wanted to run away from home or that she had wanted to go with the man wearing the red sweat shirt. RoseAlyce was more than annoyed. She kept repeating: Caty was still a little girl; she still played with dolls; she was naive; she was always trying to be helpful; she trusted the law and the police, and she trusted her parents to come to her aid. RoseAlyce told Police Chief Peter Herdt that she and her friends wanted to start an immediate search. Her husband Charlie was a pilot, she said, and they had friends with planes. 'Please do an air search before dark,' she implored.

'Searchers will destroy evidence,' Herdt responded. 'We're already starting a search.' The harder RoseAlyce pressed, the more vehemently the police chief denied her requests. And, as night came, winter returned to Springfield in the form of a thirty-degree drop in temperature and a steady fall of icy rain. At ten that night, RoseAlyce remembers, she lost all hope of ever seeing Caty alive again. She knew that Theresa Fenton, the victim of an earlier and almost identical kidnapping in the Springfield area, had been found barely alive, abandoned by the side of the road. She died in the hospital the next morning. But RoseAlyce knew that Caty had been dressed in summer clothing and could not survive a night of freezing rain and snow.

The next morning Rachel was interviewed by the police again and by the state police and an investigator from the prosecutor's office. The police drove her to a number of parking lots, asking her if she recognized any of the cars or if she could find one that was the same color as the kidnapper's. Finally they drove her over to the DeLorenzo house. The police chief was already there, holding up a sweat shirt which Rachel had described to the police on the evening of the kidnapping. That was the one, Rachel said. That was just like the sweat shirt the man in the blue car was wearing when he told Caty to get into the car.

'I stopped the car. Got out and went to the bathroom. It seems to me that she followed me. I went to the bathroom, and I know she came up behind me, and that's when I lose all control. Changed it to be Dorothy, and it just changes to the cemetery and just changes to the – I get very scared that she is going to hurt me again and that I'm not going to let that happen and then I do the things to her that Dorothy did to me. It's – it's more than just that – it's not – it's just – everything. I lose control over everything. I mean everything just changes. It's not that I can start to breathe real fast and I get a rush or anything like that. It's just the whole scene changes and everything is different. I see myself getting hurt by my sister. I see that whole thing happening to me again, and this time I'm not going to let it happen like that.

'I make her lay down. I think she's on her belly. And I just do the same things to her that she – my sister – that she did to me. You see, it's not – it's not the little girl waiting there, I mean it's actually my sister that's there and that, I'm gonna, and I'm forcing her to do those things to me, just like she forced me to do 'em to her. And then I spanked her. It was all over and I spanked her.'

Schaefer forced Caty Richards to perform oral sex while they hid in a secluded spot just two miles from where he had originally forced her into the car with him. It was close to 8 P.M., just three hours after he had seen the two girls in his rear-view mirror. Schaefer confessed that in his mind he was spanking his victim, just like his sister Dorothy, he alleges, used to spank him after forcing him to perform oral sex with her. However, Schaefer wasn't actually spanking Caty Richards. 'I mean, it was, I was hitting her on the head with a rock, I didn't know that till – I mean I just didn't know that at the time. At the time I thought I was just spanking her. I hit her on the head with a rock and a lot of times. I don't know how many times. I know it was a lot.'

By nine-thirty in the morning on April 11, Caty Richards had become Autopsy #A4762, 'a lean white female wearing a bloodied, striped T-shirt with cerebral tissue around the back of the neck and on the shoulder portion. The shirt is pulled up above the breasts. There is a pair of mud-stained but new blue jeans on the lower legs turned down around the calves. There is a pair of blue on blue sneakers, the right sneaker of which appears to have been unlaced. The left sneaker is loosely tied. There is no sock on the right foot. There is a blue and white striped tennis sock on the left foot. There are five safety pins with various colored beads secured around the toe lacing of the right sneaker and a pin: I LOVE MAINE.' Caty Richards died at eight-thirty on the evening of her capture from severe brain injuries resulting from multiple blows to her skull with a blunt instrument.

She was so disfigured that no reconstruction was possible. Her coffin was closed at the funeral, and the only person to have seen her after she died was her brother Tom.

Gary Schaefer was sick on the morning after the murder. Thinking he had caught the flu, he had breakfast, threw it back up, shaved and showered, shined his shoes, and started off to church, where he was one of the leaders of the congregation. He still had no recollection of what had taken place the night before. 'Sunday. Sunday morning, I always pick my aunt up, my mother, and take 'em to Sunday school. I use my mother's car always and when I was going in – I was sick – I wasn't feeling good and I was headed towards the bathroom to upchuck.'

Beth DeLorenzo, Joel's mother and Gary Schaefer's cousin, had told the police that at about three in the afternoon on the day of the kidnapping Gary had stopped by on his way into Rutland to pick up some cars for the Springfield dealership where he worked. He was upset, she remembered, because he couldn't see his adopted daughter's baby, and he was also upset about his father's death, which had taken place just the year before.

'My cousin Beth stopped me, and told me that there was a little girl missing and that the police had been up to her father's house and they were looking for some guy with a red sweat shirt, and it was then that I knew that I had to have – I was somehow responsible for it.'

Beth DeLorenzo told the police that she had seen her cousin at church on the Sunday following the reported kidnapping. She noticed nothing different about Gary's behavior. He had asked her to go out with him. Suddenly she asked if the police had been over to see him yet. The police had already been to her house, she explained, questioning her family about the red hooded sweat shirts and telling her that the guy who had kidnapped the girl in Springfield had been wearing one of the shirts. Gary ran back into the church and vomited, DeLorenzo told the police later, and had to go home.

Schaefer drove the car directly into his garage, something he never did, and closed the doors. He cleaned the car so thoroughly that not a fingerprint, bloodstain, or any trace of Caty Richards remained in it when the police impounded it at two that afternoon.

'I always wear a red sweat shirt. I wore it a lot after I had gotten it. I knew somehow or other that I was involved in what was going on. I just – couldn't put nothing together in my mind that you know said that well you did this, and you did that, and you did this. It's just nothing – nothing clicked, nothing made no sense at all for me at all. I knew that somehow or another that I was involved. It's just – it's just a feeling that I had, and it was a bad feeling. You know I had my cousin drive me home.

'Then I went in the house, when I got back home. I know I went upstairs and sat at my desk for a long time trying to figure out what was going on. And I knew, I just knew that I was involved. I just didn't know what. I just knew that somehow or another I was involved in that little girl missing. That's all Beth told me, that there was a girl missing, and I knew that somehow or another, I was involved in it, but I just didn't know what.'

Caty Richards was found at noon on Sunday at the first location the police searched, an isolated stretch along Baltimore Road about two miles from where Schaefer had picked her up. People in Springfield who had scanners in their houses picked up the police call, and the news started to circulate through town even while Rachel Zeitz and her mother was still in church. 'When we arrived home, Rachel rushed up the stairs past Vernon who was coming down,' Mrs. Zeitz recalled in her statement to the prosecutor's office. 'He told me that Caty's body had been found. We didn't realize Rachel remained at the top of the stairs and heard us. She screamed, "No, no. It can't be. She can't be dead." '

The Thayers had not yet been informed. Finally, at two in the afternoon, still anxious that the family had heard nothing from the police chief, RoseAlyce called the station house. Indeed, she was told, Caty's body had been found. Now her daughter was the third young girl in Springfield to die after having been kidnapped.

Rachel Zeitz felt guilty about her friend's death. According to her mother, she felt bad that Caty had been alone when she died. Rachel felt she should have stayed with her friend, that she could have saved her, that she could have grabbed her hand and dragged her away, or that she could have yelled at Caty to run. She remembered that, even though it seemed as if she were trying to run away from the stranger as quickly as possible, she was going too slowly. She wanted to open her mouth and yell, but she couldn't. She blamed herself, and the blaming continues to this day.

Even four and a half years after Caty's funeral, Rachel still suffers from guilt. In June of 1986, her parents took her to see Caty's grave for the first time. She planted some flowers.

The abduction and murder of Caty Richards occurred against a background of the murder of another Springfield girl, Theresa Fenton, in 1981 and the abduction of seventeen-year-old Deana Buxton from Brattleboro the previous year. Even then, the police were pursuing leads to Gary Schaefer involving several abductions and rapes and including the murder of thirteen-year-old Sherry Nastasia, who lived in Schaefer's brother's garden apartment complex. However, the leads to Schaefer were tenuous, and police were proceeding slowly rather than have the case unravel in court for lack of a chain of evidence, although Deana Buxton had told the police about the kidnapper's blue car and the fact that he had driven her through the main streets of town in broad daylight after forcing her into the car. The Identikit composite made by Deana was almost interchangeable with the one made by Rachel. This was what led police directly to Gary Schaefer.

Five months later, in September, under pressure from a public letter written by RoseAlyce Thayer challenging him to stand by the precepts of his fundamentalist religion, Schaefer confessed to the murders of Catherine Richards and Theresa Fenton and to the rape and abduction of Deana Buxton. 'I am responsible for the deaths of Caty Richards, and Teresa Fenton. I do not feel that it is necessary to go into the details that caused their deaths, as I am sure you are or soon will be made aware of the circumstances concerning my state of mind,' he scrawled in a letter to William Bos, the state's attorney for Windsor County, Vermont. In December, Schaefer agreed to plead no contest to the sexual assault, abduction, and second-degree murder of Catherine Richards. In return for Schaefer's confession to the Fenton murder, charges in that case were dropped, although Theresa Fenton's parents were allowed to visit with Schaefer in his cell and hear his own confession of guilt until he requested the authorities not to have the Fentons visit again. Schaefer was sentenced to a term of from thirty years to life in January 1984 and is currently serving his time at the federal penitentiary at Leavenworth, Kansas.

RoseAlyce Thayer subsequently filed a complaint

against Peter Herdt and the Springfield Police Department for violating her and Caty's civil rights. She has charged, in a suit in federal court, that there was no search for the victim of this witnessed abduction for more than nineteen hours after the report of the crime and that she and her husband were physically prevented from initiating a search on their own or from the air. Mrs. Thayer testified before the Vermont legislature that the state needed a law that would mandate a centralized record-keeping facility for all missing children, so that a search for any missing children could begin immediately. The bill was passed by the Vermont state legislature in May 1985. RoseAlyce Thayer now travels throughout the nation speaking on behalf of missing children and their families; Mrs. Fenton has opened a bakery in her kitchen, and Mrs. Schaefer, Gary's mother, disowned him. The Christadelphian sect excommunicated Schaefer from the group.

The Springfield police department, although criticized by the state for its handling of the Caty Richards kidnapping, was publicly exonerated of any wrongdoing by the town officials. And RoseAlyce and Charles Thayer adopted a child, fifteen-year-old Cyndi, in August 1987.

The Caty Richards murder is like a microcosm. In it, we can see how murderer and victim came together, how each brought an individual past directly to the moment of encounter and the ensuing tragedy, and how those pasts helped create and shape the tragedy, and how the shock waves from the murder overwhelmed the lives of the families and friends that were involved, the police investigators, the courts, and even the state legislature itself. Unfortunately, Caty Richards was a prime victim. As a learning-disabled child, she was naive and emotionally immature for her age, and she relied on adults for direction and support. As a child who had been followed by an adult male neighbor for the year and a half previous to her encounter with Schaefer, she was already fearful. It was the act of confronting Schaefer after he had driven by her a number of times that put her at risk and meshed with Schaefer's own perceptions of her on the road.

By her own admission, Judy Zeitz had misgivings about letting the girls go back outside so late in the day. They were free-floating misgivings, to be sure, but misgivings nevertheless. However, like most parents, she didn't want to say no unless she had a concrete reason for saying no, and simply listening to her own instincts wasn't strong enough to take a firmer stand. Perhaps the presence of a visitor in the house and the combined impact of both girls' wants made Mrs. Zeitz more acquiescent than she would have been normally. And she was expending additional energy by watching Caty so that Caty's mother, RoseAlyce, could have the afternoon free to paint. She didn't know that a male neighbor had been chasing Caty near her mother's home. It was as if there just wasn't enough energy there to make the protest. Even she characterized her attempts at keeping the girls in the house as 'lazy.'

In the background, and seemingly out of mind, was the fact that over the past four years, in the immediate area two adolescent girls had been abducted, raped, and murdered, and one seventeen-year-old had been abducted and raped. She had the presence of mind to escape when her captor stopped for beer. Those other cases were not out of Chief Herdt's mind, however. When Judy Zeitz and RoseAlyce Thayer reached the police department after Rachel reported the kidnapping, the Theresa Fenton case file was upright in a holder on Police Lieutenant Chadbourne's desk. Also, aerial photos of the route that Schaefer had taken with Theresa Fenton lined the walls of the squad room. Judy Zeitz noticed that immediately and made the connection in her own mind between the Fenton murder and Caty Richards' abduction. RoseAlyce had made the same connection while riding to the police station in the car but tried to put it out of her mind. Unknown to both Judy and RoseAlyce at the time were the two other cases that remained unsolved: Sherry Nastasia in 1979, and Deana Buxton in 1982. The police had another opportunity to find the child murderer who had been eluding them for four years.

From the outset the police were aware of Schaefer as a potential suspect. They had a description of the car and had made a connection between the Deana Buxton case and Schaefer even though they had not positively identified him as the assailant. The police also knew that Caty Richards was a potential victim. Herdt had interviewed Caty Richards for one and a half hours after Theresa Fenton's death at the time when Caty was being harassed by the neighbor. The police chief knew what Caty was like.

RoseAlyce Thayer has also charged that the chief didn't want family members participating in the search. According to Judy Zeitz, the chief said that he didn't want 'amateurs' destroying evidence. If, indeed, the police had got a break in the three child abductions and two murders that had baffled them for the past few years, they didn't want to throw it away along with any chance of finding Caty Richards because someone had disturbed a vital clue at the crime scene. As in the Atlanta Child Murders, the Stocking Strangler murders, and many of the other serial murder cases around the country, the police are so desperate to find the killer and, once found, not lose him through the legal process that they might even compromise the safety of the victim so as not to compromise the integrity of the search, arrest, and eventual prosecution of the killer.

Once a suspect in the Richards case had been arrested and charged, another set of political and legal considerations were brought into play, for which the county prosecutor's office and the local police would later be criticized. William Bos found himself with a ten-year-old witness who positively identified Schaefer from a lineup as the man who forced Caty Richards into his car. Semen smears from Caty's body did not exclude Schaefer as the murderer, and Schaefer's alibi that he was in Rutland with his boss fell apart almost immediately. Bos knew that he had his man. However, he also knew that the links to the still open Theresa Fenton case were identical to those in the Richards case, and he wanted to make a further connection between Schaefer and the Nastasia murder and the Buxton kidnapping. And Donald Graham, Schaefer's public defender, was already moving in the direction of an insanity defense which would, at the very least, leave these cases pending for years during the appeals process, even if the state got its conviction in the Richards case alone. The public defender would have used Schaefer's insanity plea in a drug/arson case that the Navy had brought against him when he was in the service years earlier, even though the Navy psychiatrists found that Schaefer was sane at the time. Thus, with a drawn-out insanity trial in the offing, Bos felt that he had to move very deliberately and quickly to get a confession on all the open cases.

Then RoseAlyce Thayer went public with an open letter that baited Schaefer into his handwritten confession. Accusing him of being a 'series killer,' Mrs. Thayer charged him with the murders of eleven victims that he performed according to an established ritual. 'Mr. Schaefer follows this pattern laid down by so many others; he had a cleansing ritual, prior to the kidnapping, he had certain words he spoke to his victims, he had a particular type of weapon, a certain type of place to dispose of the body and he also took the traditional souvenirs of the victim.' She accused him of living a lie and being a member of a group of criminals who have become 'scorned rejects of society.'

She then turned to an attack upon his religious beliefs: 'Mr. Schaefer's self-justification is hidden behind an altogether transparent religious facade. His religion is a warped thing of his own decision, not truly related to the sincere beliefs of many members of the Christadelphian Church of whom I knew. It looks as though he has become flattered by the publicity which he has received. He is an egocentric person who has little regard for the pain being suffered by the members of his family church.

'Men like Schaefer are cowards who prey upon children who are too young, too innocent, and too weak to protect themselves; they are not real men, any man who will cause, or permit the death of a child to happen is not a real man. He is not a religious man, one who lives by the Holy Bible.'

Gary Schaefer responded quickly in a letter to William Bos by confessing to the murders of Theresa Fenton and Caty Richards and to the rape of Deana Buxton. He admitted that what he had been about to write was contrary to the advice he had received from his defense counsel but stated that he was more concerned about his religious beliefs than his legal defense. 'Contrary to what Mr. LeClair said about me not being a religious person, I am. And it is necessary for me to confess my sins in order that I may have any hope for God's mercy, even though I don't deserve it.' He concluded his confession by saying that, his legal defense notwithstanding, 'The only possible way that I can have any hope of having my sins forgiven me is to make this public confession of my sins and to follow what God commands me to do. I hope in doing so it clears up any questions Mr. Bos has concerning the three incidents in question.'

William Bos now had on his hands a public baiting of his suspect by the victim's mother and a confession so tainted that any competent defense attorney could have got it thrown out of court and have tied up the entire case in an appeals process for years. He might also have had a real fear that the forced confession could have been used as the basis for a mistrial. And, moreover, Donald Graham, the public defender, was a competent attorney. Graham believed initially that his client was insane when he murdered Caty Richards and that he was innocent of the Buxton rape. The crimes were dissimilar enough, he thought, that Bos wouldn't be able to use the Richards case as a pattern for convicting Schaefer of raping Buxton. Graham believed that there was no evidence to link Schaefer to the Nastasia murder or to the Fenton murder.

Whatever William Bos might have thought about the other crimes, he did not want to lose a conviction in the Richards case, especially because there was no doubt about Schaefer's guilt, only about his sanity. Bos was able to prove subsequently that Schaefer was competent enough to stand trial for the Caty Richards murder, and he negotiated a plea-bargaining arrangement with the defendant that allowed the state to close the books on the Fenton and Buxton cases as well as the Richards case. Bos came to believe, like Graham, that the links between Schaefer and Nastasia would never result in a murder conviction, although the case is still hanging over Schaefer's head many years later.

Schaefer agreed to plead no contest to sexually assaulting Catherine Richards and to murder in the second degree. He further agreed to plead guilty to the kidnapping of Deana Buxton and to provide full confessions to the Richards and Fenton murders. Lastly he was to admit his guilt to the parents of Theresa Fenton. In return, the state did not bring charges against him for the murder of Theresa Fenton. Even though Donald Graham argued that advances in the field of psychotherapy might eventually result in a complete cure for his client, the judge sentenced him to a term of from thirty years to life with the possibility of parole after nineteen years. Bos was confident, however, and predicted that, given Schaefer's record, 'he will spend the rest of his natural life in prison.' The prosecutor claimed that, with Schaefer safely convicted, 'parents in Windsor County should be able to sleep better.' In May 1986, after Governor Kunin signed a 'life with no parole' bill into law in Vermont, the chances of Schaefer's being granted parole in 2003 were greatly diminished.

What about Gary Schaefer? His sister Dorothy has conclusively refuted any accusations that she sexually abused her brother or struck him in any way. While rumours abound regarding the cultlike practices of the Christadelphian sect, the familial relationships among the members, and the charges of incest among family members that have arisen from time to time, there is no independent corroboration of anything that Schaefer described in his January 1985 confession. Schaefer's stepdaughter has also refused to comment.

If his revelations are true, and no one in Springfield doubts their veracity, then it is clear that Schaefer was insane at the time of the murders of both Theresa Fenton and Caty Richards. In both instances, he was perhaps acting out a hallucination of a ritual he claims he performed with his stepdaughter and which he claims was performed upon him by his sister. In his own mind, he was not committing a murder, he was spanking his sister in retaliation for the spanking he claims she had given him. Maybe his vision of a spanking was his way of blocking the ritualistic murder of his sister over and over again.

Schaefer's descriptions of cruising along back roads until he spotted someone in the mirror who resembled his stepdaughter is a valuable firsthand description of the onset of the hallucination and the switching from the trolling to the wooing phase of a serial murderer's cycle. Rachel Zeitz's description of the murderer's luring of Caty Richards, complete with his almost hypnotic stare as he ordered the girl he thought was his daughter into his car, is a frightening image of the intimate first encounter between the killer and his victim. In Caty Richards' case, it is all the more poignant, because she was the daughter of a man who had abandoned her when she was very young, plus the victim of a man who had followed her around in his car for nineteen months. Caty was also an emotionally immature, learning-disabled child who was more apt to freeze in terror than actively flee for her life. For Schaefer, she was the perfect victim.

Among the many tragedies of the Springfield child murders was the fact that everybody acted out his or her part with ballet-like precision. There were no false moves. Schaefer was afflicted with all of the symptoms of the prototypical serial killer. He was a loner, a man who was abused by and afraid of women, a hyperreligious individual who belonged to a cultlike Christian sect in which a strict, literal adherence to the Bible was its major precept. He admitted to having a drinking problem, and, furthermore, during the Deana Buxton rape, to which he confessed in 1983, he was under the influence of alcohol. Schaefer also had severe memory impairment to the point of blocking out the murders completely until months after incarceration, discussion with police and court officers, and different forms of counseling.

Gary Schaefer, like Henry Lee Lucas, Carlton Gary, and Wayne Williams in Atlanta, has become a symbol of the system and the local politics surrounding the serial murder crime and its impact upon the community. The serial murderer, once caught, becomes an important symbol of the way justice operates. A death sentence for serial killer Carlton Gary, for example, and the millions of dollars that the state of Georgia will spend arguing the sentence over the next eight to ten years throughout the appellate system, are far more important to the voters of Georgia than a summary guilty plea and a sentence of life imprisonment. For the prosecutor and the judge, the crimes against the matrons of Wynnton, though admittedly brutal, were far too heinous for them to come up with anything less than the strictest form of retribution under the law, even if that retribution might not be enacted for the next decade. The sentence itself was all that mattered because it was a political necessity. In this way, the murderer becomes a form of totem.

Wayne Williams was a similar gold mine for harried families of the victims of Atlanta. Although he was convicted only on circumstantial evidence in a case that involved the murder not of a child but of a young adult, Williams served as the focus for the fear and rage of an entire community. For the whites who administered the state's criminal justice system, Williams was conveniently black. For the black political establishment of Atlanta, Williams' conviction spared them from the specter of racially motivated violence had the perpetrator been a white. However, the Williams case may soon be re-opened. He was too convenient, and at least one of the state's witnesses has recanted an important part of his testimony. The hunt for the Atlanta Child Murderer might have to begin all over again.

Perhaps the biggest firestorm of all has arisen over the revelations that Henry Lee Lucas has provided the Texas Rangers and state police from hundreds of jurisdictions across the country. Lucas' many confessions gave prosecutors the opportunity to close missing person cases that had been unsolved for years. Members of missing people's families were able, through Lucas' confessions to lay to rest their fears that a spouse or child might still be wandering in an unknown city. When the fears that Lucas had been prompted to confess to crimes that he had not committed surfaced, Lucas willingly admitted that he hadn't killed anyone except his mother. In other words, he became the person his interrogators wanted him to be. His reliability dropped commensurately.

Similarly, Gary Schaefer's case allowed the state to close the files on one additional murder and a rape. It solved the problem of the serial murders that had been threatening the Springfield area for five years. Gary Schaefer is off the street, and although he might be released sixteen years from now, after having undergone more than a decade of therapy at Leavenworth, for the present he represents a murderer who has been caught and convicted and cases that have been solved.

Schaefer, Lucas, Williams, Bundy, and Carlton Gary are all politically important to their respective jurisdictions because they all represent disproportionate threats to their communities. They have killed randomly; they have killed out of a compulsion that could make anyone into a victim. Consequently, the way the community adjudicates their cases is of vital importance to the sense of justice that keeps communities in balance. The serial murderer remains a threat to the community even after he is caught. His trial and sentence have to satisfy the victims' and the community's collective hunger for justice or neither the sense of loss nor the feeling of resolution will ever be satisfied.

The greater tragedy is that, because the serial murderer kills in such disproportionate numbers and because the community is paralyzed with fear throughout his reign of terror, the damage goes far beyond the families of the victims. Entire cities are traumatized when everyone becomes a potential victim. Even though the capture and conviction of the serial killer offers a resolution, people must come to realize that, for every serial killer who is finally caught, there are probably three more waiting to emerge.

6

The Police and the Serial Killer

Police homicide units are becoming increasingly more sophisticated in their investigations and tracking of serial murders. At first, detectives were strictly reactive. When a murder was reported, detectives gathered whatever evidence they could, traced the victim's identity, and tried to reconstruct the crime from what they could determine about the victim's movements during his or her final hours. If there were witnesses, they were interviewed also. Although this procedure works seven out of ten times in solving other types of homicide, it doesn't work so well in solving serial murder cases. The reason for this is simple: the serial murderer doesn't behave like other killers. His motive for murder is not dependent upon the particular situation or upon the individual victim; it is a chronic compulsion that drives him through an ever repeating pattern of violence.

The reactive homicide investigation depends upon the following to provide solutions to the crime: the weight of evidence, clues at the crime scene, the relationship between the victim and the murderer, involved witnesses or passersby, and finally the fear and guilt of the killer himself. In felony murder cases – in which the murder was committed as a secondary act – solving the first crime usually solves the murder case. Thus if someone were discovered during a breaking and entering, panicked, and killed the robbery victim, the clues that led the police to the burglar would also lead them to the murderer. The police in these cases will use informants to help them locate the stolen items. A large number of felony murders take place as adjuncts to drug deals that turned sour. These murders are also very traceable through informants or the network of street dealers in the neighborhood. Cases of family homicide or those in which the victims are related through friendship – these compose the largest single number of murders – usually rely on witnesses. Felony murders and family homicides also have well-defined motives that can be used to locate potential suspects. Once the police begin interrogating a suspect, a confession or arrest usually follows quickly.

Since 1980, however, almost twenty-five percent of all murders have been 'stranger' homicides in which the killer is not driven by any apparent rational motive and has no apparent connection with the victim. These serial murders are the ones in which the killer is compelled by forces beyond his control, and unless those forces are understood the killer eludes detection. Such cases are frustrating because the killer may be in the area for only a short time, run up a skein of victims, and move on. Worse, in rural areas that are not under the jurisdiction of a single municipal police department, many different jurisdictions might not routinely share information about unsolved homicides in their areas. The problems of one county sheriff are not the problems of the local police force in a different town. Hence, a killer might be seeking victims in three different counties in the same part of the country and never be the target of a combined task force investigation, until all of the homicide squads agree to pool their information.

Sometimes the connection between murders in different

locations is brought to the attention of homicide detectives not by the police but by outside concerned parties. In the Ted Bundy investigation, for example, the Seattle police had investigated and cleared Bundy on at least two separate occasions. Even after Elizabeth Kendall, his own fiancée, reported her suspicions to the police, the Seattle homicide detectives decided that Bundy was not a likely suspect. It was only after she informed them about a similar pattern of crimes taking place in the Salt Lake City area, where Bundy had relocated to attend law school, that they reopened the inquiry. Finally, after Bundy was charged in Salt Lake City with trying to elude police and being in possession of burglar's tools, the Seattle detectives began seriously to reconsider him as a suspect in the thirty-five murders of young women that had been unsolved for years.

It was through Elizabeth Kendall's assistance that Bob Keppel of the Seattle homicide squad was finally able to identify Bundy as the prime suspect in the area's unsolved murder cases. But Keppel never got his conviction. Bundy was convicted in Utah of the attempted kidnap of Carol DaRonch and was on trial for murder in Colorado when he escaped and fled to Florida. After Elizabeth Kendall read a news item about a rape murder in a sorority house on the University of Tallahassee campus, she notified the FBI that she thought the murderer might be Ted Bundy. They still didn't believe her and continued to doubt that he had gone to Florida until he was arrested there for the rape murder of a twelve-year-old girl.

In another case, the police and sheriffs' detectives in rural Texas were baffled by a string of murders along Route 35 until Henry Lee Lucas confessed to the crimes. His desire to conform to the wishes of the Texas authorities was so strong that he kept on confessing to murders he could not possibly have committed until, confronted with his own inconsistencies, Lucas recanted all of his confessions, even to the murders for which the police had corroborating evidence.

In felony murders, family homicides, and street crimes, the victim is often not isolated by the killer before the murder, nor is there usually any planned entrapment. The almost coincidental nature of the homicide is usually one of the factors that help the investigation along. This is especially true in felony murders when the killer never intended to kill the victim in the first place. In family murders that are committed out of passion or rage with little thought to the consequences, the abundance of clues, clarity of motive, presence of witnesses, and panic on the part of the murderer usually lead to a solution of the crime within twenty-four hours. The actual apprehension of the fleeing fugitive may take longer, but the weight of guilt acts as a ball and chain and usually forces the killer to turn himself in.

Getting confessions out of felony murderers and coincidental killers of friends or family members is also easier for the police to accomplish. Contrary to popular belief, most murderers do ultimately want to confess. It is only the hardened sociopath who is incapable of experiencing guilt and feels no need to express his remorse. The sociopathic serial killer falls into the twenty-five percent of all cases in which there is no prior personal connection between murderer and victim. The psychological basis for applying pressure on a potential murder suspect is not readily apparent. Even if the police have questioned the actual murderer during the course of the investigation, there is no immediate impetus for the murderer to reveal himself.

The crime scene itself is also a large issue in the success or failure of a murder investigation. Most crime scenes of typical homicide are not under the killer's control. Because he killed out of passion, fear, rage, or by accident, he was unable to isolate his victim or to make sure that there were no coincidental witnesses or passersby. In other words, he didn't consider clues. In most homicides, the medical examiner's autopsy on the recent victim provides invaluable clues that either help the police find the killer or at the very least shorten the list of potential suspects. As the former Los Angeles county coroner, Thomas Noguchi, has shown, the medical examiner's report indicates the probable cause of death, the probable time the death took place, whether that death was a homicide or the result of natural causes, and what weapons were most likely used. Medical examiners often advise police about the size and strength of the murder suspect, whether he or she is right- or left-handed, and whether the homicide was accidental, the result of a fit of passion, or premeditated. As Noguchi's examinations of the cases of Jean Harris, Claus Von Bulow, and Jeffery MacDonald have shown, a detailed and exacting medical examiner's report can provide the types of clues that can almost determine the outcome of the investigation right at the outset. However, the longer a body remains hidden, the harder it is for the medical examiner to find any clues that will identify a suspect. Also, if the body has been mutilated, cut into pieces, and/or buried for any length of time, it makes the investigator's job seemingly impossible.

Organized serial killers always maintain a high degree of control over their crime scenes. First, they familiarize themselves with the locale during the trolling phrase. They choose isolated spots where they can act out their fantasies in private. Second, they choose the likeliest spots for encountering potential victims. Side exits of shopping centres, streets that are particularly deserted during the night, bus stations where strangers tend not to be noticed, or lonely stretches of road adjoining populated sections of a town are the most common sites for serial killers. Third, they usually transport the victim or the victim's body to a different location for burial. This creates two crime scenes and often confuses the investigators until they either discover the common burial ground or establish a relationship between the scene of the abduction or murder and the burial site.

Leonard Lake and John Gacy maintained particularly strong control over their crime scenes. In Lake's case, the police weren't even aware of the existence of his crimes until they traced Lake's address through documents relating his ex-wife, Cricket Balazs, to her property in rural Calaveras County. There they found the bodies of persons who had previously been reported by their relatives as missing. John Gacy actually led a double life – a builder, happily married man, and member of many civic organizations, and a serial murderer – while he used the crawl space under his house as a burial ground. Henry Lee Lucas' murders were so random and committed in areas so rural that he often buried the bodies near where the crimes were committed. With the exception of Granny Rich, Lucas' final murder victim, the bodies were turning up as Jane Does ten years before he confessed to the crimes. In fact, until recently, Lucas had maintained that there were far more victims than have been discovered by the police, but that he had forgotten their descriptions or the locations of the crimes.

The serial killer's two most effective weapons are his mobility and his mask of normalcy. Essential to the serial killer's pathology is his compulsion to roam. He is a traveller who, although in his everyday life a resident of a particular city or town, during his episodes of limbic psychosis, seeks out places where the types of victims he preys on are available. John Gacy sought transient young boys with no connections to family or friends; thus the bus and train stations became his favourite haunts. Even if a serial murderer is killing in his own community, the number of murders that are committed within a specific time frame usually overwhelm the ability of the police to investigate each homicide properly. The amount of press coverage that a crime receives puts the police department's investigation squarely in the spotlight. Thus exposure actually helps a serial murderer to avoid detection. He simply changes his modus operandi for every crime. Finally, the fear that the murders arouse in the community has such a chilling effect on the public that the murderer is almost free to roam while the police spend their time calming fears, responding to crank confessions, and solving copycat murders. While the police are occupied in a particular community, the killer, who is never confined to a specific location, simply moves on to a neighboring municipality or state and continues his spree. He can always move back later. All the while, he monitors the police department's movements through reading the newspapers or listening to TV and radio news.

Because serial killers are sociopaths, they never develop empathic ties to their communities. For example, among Elizabeth Kendall's most shocking discoveries about Ted Bundy was the seemingly endless number of intimate girl friends and even fiancées who kept on turning up in Bundy's life, even though she and Bundy had been almost living together during their years in Seattle. Despite Bundy's repeated assurances, both verbally and in writing and both before and after his arrests in Utah and Florida, that he cared for Liz Kendall, he couldn't explain away the other women and continued to have relationships with them. Bundy was incapable of experiencing empathy for other people, especially those closest to him. This lack of empathy for individuals translates into a lack of empathy for the whole community as well. That is why a killer like Carlton Gary can be on the prowl in the neighborhoods of his own youth, committing murders, and yet not feel any guilt or remorse for the terror those murders are inflicting on the community at large. The same is true for the Atlanta Child Murderer, whether or not he is Wayne Williams, who witnessed the paralysis and confusion of Atlanta's black community while homicide investigators from more than half a dozen jurisdictions tried to solve the crimes.

Having no sympathies for the community means that the serial killer can easily live and work in any neighborhood, participate in community functions, and even, like John Gacy and Ted Bundy, be a community leader. This is an especially frightening aspect of the serial murderer syndrome because without any feelings of sympathy for the people he sees every day he is freed from the guilt that would eventually force the more traditional killer into giving himself up. A serial killer has no family and no friends. He perceives himself as a solitary stalker among his prey, fading into normalcy during the periods between his killing episodes, and emerging as a killer in response to electrochemical impulses deep in his limbic brain.

This same lack of sympathy enables him to wear a mask of normalcy as a camouflage. Gary Schaefer not only lived and worked among religious and family-oriented people in rural Vermont, he was a member of the Christadelphians. The members of this sect lived according to the fundamentalist interpretation of the Bible. Yet Gary Schaefer, whose family belonged to this church as well, lived the double life of a rapist and serial killer of young girls and a member of the church brotherhood. He lived this way until the very day he was arrested.

To most people, it is appalling that a person who was most trusted as a normal, civic-minded individual can turn out to be a serial killer. This aspect of the syndrome always baffles the police. Detective Keppel had Ted Bundy under investigation on at least two occasions and dismissed him from consideration twice – once after a Seattle girl reported that on the very day a murder had taken place she had been requested by a man named Ted who drove a VW Beetle and had a cast on his arm to help him load his boat onto a luggage rack and drive it back to his residence. She thought him just a bit 'strange,' she told homicide detectives later, and begged off. It was only after she read of the discovery of the body that she telephoned the police to tell them that it was likely she had been accosted by the murderer. One of Bundy's professors actually reported him to the police. The faculty member told the Seattle homicide detectives that he drove a VW. The police noted that Bundy was a prelaw student, had no prior police record, had been active in local politics and worked for some Republican candidates. He had also worked for local community and student groups. As a member of the community, he was a student whose schedules were highly structured, he had a steady long-term heterosexual relationship with a young woman whose daughter from a previous marriage lived with her, and he was well liked. He was too normal, they thought, clearly not the type of person who would go on a murder spree. Yet again and again his name was brought up, and this time by the very person he had been dating. The police questioned her but found that Bundy had not threatened her or her daughter and, in fact, had been the person who was more 'in control' than she was. Liz Kendall didn't take no for an answer. After she found plaster cast material in Bundy's closet she called the police again. But again the police refused to consider him as a suspect. He was just too normal.

A serial killer is a roamer. He eludes police detection and is always ten steps ahead of any pursuit. Or, when a serial killer is an upstanding normal member of the community whose comings and goings are on public exhibit, the police often don't waste their time investigating him. Almost all of the serial killers fit into one or the other category or even both at the same time. Carlton Gary, for example, was a roamer, dropping in, then out of society, and yet he was dating a female uniformed officer from the sheriff's department who was unaware of his activities while he was committing the Wynnton murders. Even though Gary had a police record, was a fugitive from other jurisdictions, and was dealing in cocaine and heroin, he was still able to maintain the semblance of a relatively normal heterosexual relationship.

Bobby Joe Long's description of the final days before his arrest exemplify the serial killer's well-tuned sense of survival. Long knew that because of the growing public clamor over the North Tampa murders the police were patrolling the area in greater numbers. He also knew that his own pattern of crimes, the places where he found his victims, and the types of victims he chose were a matter of public record. He had read about them in the newspaper. He also heard on the news that local and state authorities had formed a task force to catch him. 'At that point, I could have gone to Miami or even back to California,' he later explained from his cell on death row. 'I could have gone back to West Virginia for a visit. I could simply have walked away from Tampa and stopped picking up girls there, and I'd still be a free man today because the police had no idea who or where I was until I let McVay go and she went to the police.' Even then, he explains, he could have fled the area, but he didn't. He was steps ahead of the police. He was caught because he wanted to get caught. He wanted the murder spree that was killing him as well as his victims to stop, but he couldn't stop it himself. What is most important, however, is that the police couldn't stop him until he revealed his whereabouts to the task force by releasing his next to last victim. Then and only then did the police have the clues to establish his identity.

The critical factor that most police investigators fail to understand is that a serial killer is not an individual who has reached an equilibrium or who is in any type of stasis. He is a person with a disease in a process of development whose symptoms are changing. The skein of serial murders is just the penultimate stage of that disease. The final stage is his own suicide. Like a caterpillar that transforms into a moth that transforms into a butterfly, the serial killer also transforms. As a child, he is a mere victim. Like Charles Manson and Henry Lee Lucas, he is rejected by parents, deprived of any intimacy and sensory stimulation, beaten, malnourished, and abused. In extreme cases the child's own sense of self is so distorted that it is never established until much later in his adult life, if at all. It is interesting, for example, to see that two of the most infamous serial murderers in our study, Henry Lee Lucas and Charles Manson, were both forced to attend the first day of school dressed as girls because their parents or guardians felt it would be for their own ultimate good.

In his childhood, the serial killer acquires many of the scars he will later inflict on his future victims. If his deepest fears are aroused by a hatred of his father and a hatred of his own masculinity, he most likely will be a killer of young boys. Like John Wayne Gacy, he will act out an endless ritual of killing the boy that he was and torturing that source of weakness within himself. If it is his hatred of his mother and the fear of femininity within him that are aroused, he will most likely be a woman killer. Bobby Joe Long killed women he characterized as whores and sluts, women who, he said, manipulated men with their bodies. Although she has consistently denied that, Long claims that his mother had had sex with other men in the room where he as a child was sleeping and that she even forced him to sleep in the same bed with her until he was twelve. Or, like Gary Schaefer, if there was a little girl who aroused him, during torture he will become a killer of little girls and act out a ritual that was a part of his childhood fantasy of violent revenge.

Sometimes, as a child, the serial killer experiences physical injuries like concussions, fractures of the skull, and other forms of head trauma. He may have a genetic defect or a birth defect as a result of an accident during the pregnancy. Whatever the cause of the problem, this is a child who can have a disorder of the limbic region of the brain. It is serious enough that it will impair the way the primal neurological circuit functions for the rest of his life. It may result in a dyslexia, a reasoning or cognitive disorder, a form of deep psychomotor epilepsy, or a lesion in the hypothalamus that affects the body's hormone system. The child will not be able to control his rage. He will display extraordinary or inappropriate violence with almost no regard for those around him. He might be antisocial and extremely unhappy. He often will be accident prone, with an especially high risk of head injuries as he gets older. Finally, he will experience difficulties in perception and learning that will make his elementary school years a period of unbearable torture. In the schoolyard pecking order, he will be near the bottom, living in his own private hell.

This child will also be at high risk of confrontations with the juvenile justice system. He will display extreme cruelty to animals, excessive violence toward younger children and his younger siblings. He may be a fire starter who has no regard for the personal property of others. He will always be at the centre of accidents, collisions in the halls, or falls in the gym or schoolyard. This is the first emergence of the syndrome that may later claim the lives of five, ten, or three hundred victims before it claims the life of its carrier.

It is easy to lose track of a serial killer-as-child because he will have developed an uncanny knack for becoming invisible and fading into the background. Once he becomes aware of his own accident proneness, he will overcorrect for it and learn how to appear and disappear with as little fanfare as possible. However, the physiological forces set in motion during fetal, newborn, and early childhood periods will continue to develop. The malformation of his limbic brain, the disorder in the hypothalamus, or the discharges of electricity from his temporal lobe will continue to alter his behaviour. It will seem to him as if he is living out certain fantasies, he will find himself talking out loud to persons who exist only within his own mind, or he will find himself strangely unable to react to certain situations. He might not be able to make directional decisions and literally go in circles while deciding which way he wants to go. If he makes a choice, it will invariably be the wrong choice, and he will ultimately shrink from making any choices. But he will have his greatest difficulties when he tries to relate to other people. He may grow to hate girls because they are threats, and he may hate members of his own sex because he can't express the sexual feelings he has for them. While other preadolescents begin to explore relationships with one another, this preadolescent will retreat. Henry Lee Lucas was routinely killing animals and having sex with their carcasses by the time he was ten, and he had sex with his brother shortly thereafter. He committed his first rape murder when he was only fifteen. As a ten-year-old, Carlton Gary was already on the run, seeking out his mother and turning up unannounced at his uncle's Army base hundreds of miles away from Columbus, Georgia. He was already a street hoodlum by the time he was ten, robbing stores and starting fires. He had been tagged by the local police as a 'bad kid' before he reached his teens.

Charles Manson was in and out of reformatories before he reached his teens. He spent most of his life in jails and reform schools. He was beaten by guards, assaulted by other prisoners, and humiliated by every institution society could bring to bear. When one considers that Manson never had a father figure even remotely present except in jail, and that his mother was more often in jail for hustling sex than with her child, it is no wonder that Manson was at an extremely high risk of confrontations with the criminal justice system even before he turned thirteen. Like Henry Lee Lucas, Manson claims that he was punished, abused, and made to do things that no human being should ever be made to do. With no external structure that they could internalize, these two cult figures of modern murder were beyond anybody's definition of insanity by the time they were adults.

As Bobby Joe Long was reaching puberty, his body began to transform before his very eyes from that of a young boy into that of a young girl. Long, like many other members of his family, suffered from a chromosomal disorder, similar to Klinefelter's syndrome, that caused his glands to produce excessive amounts of estrogens that resulted in an enlargement of his breasts. Associated with an extra X chromosome on the male gene, disorders like Klinefelter's syndrome are also associated with different forms of psychological gender reversal, perceptual difficulties, and learning disorders. Long had an operation to remove the six pounds of extra tissue from his breasts, but his sexual disorientation continued, supported by his mother's manipulative behaviour and her sharing the same bed with her son. It wasn't until Long was thirteen and reaching masculine puberty that he no longer shared a bed with his mother. However, at thirteen, Long met the woman who would later become his wife. Thus, Bobby Joe long was nurtured by two women: his mother and his wife-to-be; and at age thirteen his mother handed her son off to his wife-to-be. Eleven years later Long became known as the 'Classified Ad Rapist' and assaulted more than fifty women in the Miami-Dade area. Less than ten years after that he would commit nine rape murders, bludgeoning his victims to death after raping them, driving around with the corpses still in his car, and burying them in shallow graves.

Almost all serial murderers have had a conflict with the juvenile or criminal justice authorities during their teenage years. After a period of incarceration or psychological hibernation during which the sexual and violent fantasies of the teenager often become full-blown hallucinatory experiences, the sexually aroused serial murderer emerges. He may begin by committing a series of rapes, as Bobby Joe Long did, or by tiptoeing up to the crime as Bundy did at first. Yet, ultimately, he will cross the line and commit his first murder. From that point on, driven by fear of what is within him as well as fear of the police who are pursuing the crime, the serial murderer eludes detection until the weight of his own morbidity causes him to collapse from within. For some serial killers, the fantasy itself must break, as it did for Henry Lee Lucas after the murder of his common-law wife, for Kallinger after the murder of his younger son, or for Long after the assault on Karen McVay. For some, like Charles Manson, the fantasy still hasn't broken.

What is important about this developmental process of the serial murderer from the police investigator's point of view is that it is impossible to see a complete picture of the criminal's motivation until well after he has been apprehended and diagnosed. The police might well have had this individual in custody once, twice, or perhaps twenty times over the course of his life, but they have failed to see the connection. Certainly Carlton Gary was well known to the Columbus police as Carlton Gary but not as the Stocking Strangler. The present police training focuses on the traditional murderer who is not compelled to murder, and who flees because he fears the police and prosecution. The serial murderer often seeks the very form of capital punishment that is being held over his head as a deterrent. He goes on committing enough crimes to ensure his own destruction.

The police have only the facts surrounding a murder on which to build their investigation. If it is an isolated murder, the case may go unsolved for years because the police won't be able to connect it with the ten or fifteen murders that have preceded it in other locations. If it is the first of a series of murders within a particular jurisdiction, the police often have to wait for a break in the case before they can solve anything. The breaks usually come only by chance. For example, even though the similarities between the murders in Seattle and the murders in Salt Lake City had prompted Bob Keppel to begin working with his homicide department counterparts in Utah on investigating Ted Bundy, this was the only common thread in both sets of murders. It wasn't until Bundy was arrested for trying to elude police and searched that he finally became implicated in both sets of murders. Keppel put all of the pieces together at that point, but he never arrested Bundy or got a confession. If the state of Florida has its way and executes Bundy for the murder of a twelve-year-old girl, Keppel will never prosecute him for the Seattle murders and neither will the homicide detectives who pursued him in Utah.

A homicide investigator looking over a crime scene must make a quick evaluation of the type of murderer he is dealing with. First, he must determine whether or not the murderer felt sufficiently in control of the scene to spend time there or whether he felt he had to flee immediately after committing the crime. A good detective will try to determine whether the scene had been arranged in anticipation of the victim or whether it was coincidental. If there are multiple crime scenes, an investigator looks for similarities among them. Both of Gary Schaefer's rape murders, for example, took place along similar stretches of deserted highway near where the victims lived. The victims of the Green River murders outside Seattle were all buried along the banks of the riverside, and the victims of the Hillside Strangler were all from the same Los Angeles suburb and buried in the hills just outside the city.

The police want to know if the murderer felt confident enough to spend time at the crime scene or whether he felt he had to hit and run. Most serial killers, police have found, are in complete control of the murder scene and spend the necessary time there to perform whatever rituals they must both before the victim's death and afterward. If the body has been placed in strange positions, either spreadeagled on the ground or propped upright – all of this can be determined from an autopsy and a thorough examination of the corpse – then the killer was confident enough that he would not be discovered. If the victim did not seem to have put up a struggle, then it is likely that she either knew the killer or that the killer gained her trust before the murder. If the victim has been mutilated, it is important to determine just when the mutilation took place. If the killer had to murder the victim first, then he was afraid to face her alive. If the multilation took place as a death ritual, then the ritual was an attempt to gain power over the victim.

Did the killer rape the victim before murdering her or afterward? This is one of the most crucial questions for the police because it helps them profile the killer. The killer who rapes his victims first and then murders them can maintain more control over them than the killer who has sex with victims only after they are dead. In the former cases, investigators surmise, once the thrill of the rape has passed, the killer is disgusted with himself more than with the victim. He tries to eradicate this revulsion by killing the victims, burying them, and erasing the crime. This is a killer who is perhaps a charmer, an individual who might woo his female victims into accompanying him somewhere before subduing them or tying them up. This most closely approximates the ways Ted Bundy, Carlton Gary, and Bobby Joe Long killed their victims. On the other hand, the killer who strikes first, takes the bodies to a remote location, and then has sex with the victims is less in control. He can face neither his victims nor the act of having sex with them. Therefore he kills first and performs whatever rituals he must after his victims' deaths.

If victims seem to be missing without a trace, then it is likely that the killer is exercising such control over the crime that the bodies might not be found for months. A news report of a discovered grave might be the event that triggers a flight reaction in the killer, sending him to a different location. On the other hand, the serial killer might like to keep the crime alive in his memory by reading about the dead victim in the newspapers and even visiting the site where he first found his victim. When many murders have been committed at the same site, it is likely that the killer periodically returns there even when he has no victim to kill. These are the types of clues police investigators must look for when searching for a serial killer.

If the killings took place quickly and without much ritual before the event, police surmise that the murderer is young, perhaps in his twenties, and that he wants to get the crime over with quickly. The murder itself is equated with a sudden orgasm so that the killer can experience it in reflection. Killers who take a long time with their victims are usually older, perhaps in their thirties or even early forties. They know what they are doing and have done it many times before.

How tentative was the murderer with the female corpse? Did the autopsy reveal semen inside the vagina or was it on the insides of the victim's thighs and around her pubic area? Did the killer achieve orgasm by actually having sex with the victim either before or after death, or did he simply ejaculate out of anticipation and then proceed to kill his victim in rage? By examining whether there were any signs of a struggle, investigators can determine whether the killer achieved his orgasm on the body after the murder or whether the act of struggling jolted the criminal into orgasm. These are two vital clues in creating the profile of the killer that will be used in interviews with witnesses and friends of the victim.

It is now clear to homicide specialists that most serial killers come from broken homes, that they were abused as children, and that the abuse came primarily from one parent. The degree of the intimidation and the type of destructive feelings the killer has for himself are usually manifested in some similar physical abuse of their victims. Ed Kemper was so intimidated by the sound of his mother's voice that after he killed her he cut off her head, removed her vocal cords, burned them, and put the remains down the garbage disposal.

If the killings and crime scene are all in the same area, it is likely that the killer is also from the same area. Police interrogators might have already interviewed the killer or might have had him in custody at one time and released him. Armed with a preliminary profile of the killer's personality, the police will fan out and interview all the residents in the area for descriptions of any strangers people might have noticed. They also look for anyone whose reactions conform to the profile they have developed. If the killer has been profiled as a white male in his twenties who seems to attack his victims and have sex with them after they are dead, the police will be looking for a shy person, perhaps someone who lives with his mother, who cannot easily confront them. If they find such a person they will direct the questioning toward his background, asking him where he was on the nights the murders were committed, asking for the names of people who can corroborate his whereabouts, and eventually try to shake a confession out of him. They understand what he must be going through, especially if he is going to kill again. They suggest that, by coming to the police, he will prevent himself from killing again and will get help. Police expect that that line of questioning will eventually pull a confession out of a suspect. However, when dealing with a fully emerged serial killer, the police are usually mistaken. Even the shyest and most disturbed serial killer would tend not to confess unless he was ready to end his own torment. He would instead become invisible, and if probed too hard he would leave the area.

The best weapon the police have against a serial murderer's sprees is their behavior profile. The psychological or behavioral profile, inaccurate as it may be, gives investigators the following basis from which to begin: it tells them whether to look for a younger man or an older one, a charmer who manipulates women or a withdrawn individual who kills almost immediately, a white man or a black man, a heterosexual or a bisexual, and finally whether it is a person who lives nearby or a transient who has just turned up in the community. Some profiles are so accurate that they lead police directly to a person they've already interrogated. Many times, as in the case of Albert DeSalvo, the Boston Strangler, they're not. Items such as body parts or specific articles of clothing that are missing from the victims are other key pieces to the puzzle. The killer may collect memorabilia from his victims, or he may have kept detailed records of each one of his murders in diary form. A serial killer is likely to have some perceptual disorder or learning dysfunction as well. The behavior profile might include the fact that the person is unable to spell or may routinely reverse letters. A sample of handwriting or any indication that the person has a learning disorder, a body tic or jerky movement, or a propensity to become easily rattled and short-tempered is noted in the profile. If the killer is especially savage with respect to the bodies of his female victims, police should look for evidence of feminine physical traits on the suspect. Does he have especially fine hair? Does he have an elongated or disproportionate body shape for a man? Are his features disproportionately delicate? This kind of hatred of the killer's own physical traits usually translates itself into the most horrific forms of mutilation of the dead victim.

With these behavior profiles in hand, homicide detectives can begin looking back over the people they've already interrogated in connection with other murders and as potential witnesses to this crime. If that proves unsuccessful, they can circulate their profile of the killer to other neighbouring jurisdictions and, of course, to the FBI to see whether unsolved murders by a person with a similar profile have been committed elsewhere.

The special task force is another administrative weapon police routinely use. If the crime is gruesome enough and if no leads to the crime turn up quickly, the police will assemble a special homicide task force. They might also assemble such a force immediately if the type of victim chosen, such as a child who has been sexually assaulted and mutilated as well as murdered, leads police to believe that this person will strike again in the community. The task force usually consists of detectives assigned to specific tasks: interviewing witnesses, fanning out and gathering information from people who live nearby or who knew the victim, responding to tips on the special phone number, gathering information from other jurisdictions, working with the FBI or other federal authorities, securing the crime scenes and going over the results with the forensics specialists, releasing information to the press, and coordinating with the district attorney's office. By combining the efficiency and maximum effort of a mobilized task force with the advantages of the psychobehavioral profile of the probable suspect, police are better able to marshal their resources against a killer who is psychotically motivated and protected only by his animal instincts of survival.

Finally, it is vital that police routinely utilize the power of electronic information gathering and retrieval. By computerizing modi operandi and establishing a national on-line network of missing persons and unsolved murder cases, police are able to compare similar cases not only among neighboring jurisdictions but across the entire country. A killer like Henry Lee Lucas, who thrived on the inability of police forces to cooperate on investigations from state to state, would be effectively thwarted because his possible whereabouts would be indicated by the similar types of crimes he committed. In fact, some criminologists have suggested that, if a national homicide task force were provided with the computerized reports of unsolved murders around the country, at least two thirds of those cases would be solved within the month. It took the kidnapping and murder of nine-year-old Adam Walsh and the efforts of his parents to create a national information hot line for missing children. Before that time, tracking missing children was a painstaking hit-or-miss process. Now there is at least some attempt to maintain an on-line information service similar to the services that track stolen vehicles and other property By expanding this same kind of data management and retrieval operation to unsolved murder cases, the police will be able to perceive patterns in the movements of possible suspects.

One of the most important recent developments in the battle against the spread of serial murder has been the formation of the FBI's Behavioral Science Unit in Quantico, Virginia. This is largely an information-gathering, processing, and dissemination facility that profiles probable suspects in murder cases. The unit was established with police officer Pierce Brooks, an LAPD homicide detective expert in the formation of special task forces, and Seattle detective Bob Keppel, who had spent four years in an unsuccessful pursuit of Ted Bundy. After having solved a serial murder case involving an American Indian torture ritual, Brooks realized that homicide squads needed a national information clearing house of unsolved homicides stored on a large central computer that could be accessed by local police departments. Such a database, he felt, would serve two purposes: it would help police find patterns to homicides they couldn't solve locally and it would alert them to serial killers who might be headed toward their jurisdictions. Although he tried to sell this idea to police chiefs around the country and to the federal government in 1967, he had no luck until he met Bob Keppel during the investigation of the Atlanta Child Murders in the 1970s.

At that time both Brooks and Keppel had been called in as consultants to the Atlanta Police Department to help form a task force to investigate the current wave of killings. The two detectives realized that their experiences as well as their work in Atlanta indicated a need for some type of national organization to manage information regarding serial killers and to get this data to the homicide detectives who were acting as front-line investigators. In 1981 the FBI agreed with Brooks and Keppel that the epidemic of serial murders showed no signs of abating, and the two detectives were hired as consultants to the Behavioral Science Unit it had established.

The Unit's first assignment was to begin developing behavioral profiles of killers. Special agents trained in social and behavioral sciences interviewed scores of apprehended serial killers to learn their methods and motivations and to establish the common patterns that appeared from criminal to criminal. They matched these to a killer's own confessions and revelations after he had been convicted and was serving time in prison. What the Unit learned about serial killings was enough to alert them to a far greater danger than either Brooks, Keppel, or the investigators imagined when they first started collecting data. First, they determined that, in order to profile the killer, they needed to profile the victim. As in the cases of Bobby Long and Ted Bundy, the first rape/murder victim usually sets the pattern for the entire series of crimes.

Long attacked only women who seemed to be prostitutes or hustlers. He used their preying on him to lure them into his car. In many ways they reminded him of his mother and his ex-wife, both manipulative women who dominated Long and his father. Bundy killed pretty coeds who reminded him of the fiancée who had rejected him years earlier. She, in turn, represented his mother, who had rejected him by giving him up for adoption, a fact that he never came to accept. Both of these men fit a pattern of serial rape/murderers: they did not emerge full-blown as killers, all of their crimes had discernible patterns, the clues that were present in their personalities and their pasts were readily observable to the trained eye, and they both had clearly reached out for help earlier in their lives before they began their killing sprees. And in an interesting footnote to these two cases, both of them changed their modi operandi toward the end of their killing sprees, possibly in an attempt to get caught and end their respective miseries.

It was this Behavioral Science Unit that first revealed how serial killers are compulsive trollers who travel in ever widening patterns to locate their victims. This trolling pattern appears very early in their careers, well before their first rapes or murders are committed, and is usually an indicator of escalating violence in the future. Neurologists have since established that the trolling pattern is actually a physiological mechanism within the limbic part of the brain that sets the individual in motion. He may be hallucinating during the trolling process, feeding himself with delusions of his own grandeur or hatred of others, or fantasizing about the sexual encounters he is seeking. The need to be on the move is one of the most important early indicators of a person predisposed to episodic violence. This fact alone was very important to the Unit.

The Unit also discovered that the serial killer has a clear history of abuse and that he was the victim of considerable abuse as a child, usually by his mother. Kenneth Bianchi (the Hillside Strangler), Ed Kemper, Henry Lee Lucas, Charles Manson, and Ed Gein – the model for Alfred Hitchcock's *Psycho* – all received extraordinary abuse from the dominant female figures in their lives with no male figure to exercise control or to whom they could turn. The male figure, especially in the case of Henry Lee Lucas, was so weak that the mother might have routinely abused him as well. In Carlton Gary's and Charles Manson's cases, the father was completely absent.

The Unit also detailed the types of sadism and brutality that serial killers, or 'lust murderers,' as they call them, display toward their victims. Because they themselves are afraid of the sex they want to engage in, they have sex with their victims only after they are bound, unconscious, or dead. Like Carlton Gary and Bobby Long, who strangled their victims into submission first, most lust killers can't confront the act of sex with a live, functioning person. Henry Lee Lucas routinely killed his victims first and had sex with different parts he had cut off their bodies. These killers don't see their victims as real or complete human beings, they are only carcasses, body parts that arouse the killers to an erotic fury. Whether it be the victim's breast, buttocks, genitalia, or other part of the body, it is what the victim represents that matters and not who the victim is.

And finally, the Unit's data revealed that serial killings are only one point in the life of a criminal who has been escalating toward this level of violence for many years. They stressed that individuals who may start off as voyeurs or peeping Toms and eventually break into women's homes to steal undergarments or similar artifacts can be considered candidates for serial killers in the future. Because the thrill of one level of arousal is too minimal to continue the stimulation, the individual requires an even greater 'high.' The theft of an article of clothing may be subordinated to a ritual in which the thief becomes an assailant and fondles the victim before stealing the garment. His fear of discovery or capture, however, may be too great, and he finds he must subdue his victim first before making sexual contact. When that fails to arouse him to his previous level, he will actually assault the victim before raping her, strangling her into submission or knocking her unconscious and then escaping. Finally, the full-blown serial killer will emerge, and his victims will be doomed by the random nature of their appearance during his violent episodes.

The Unit also found that a serial killer's cycles are much like a menstrual cycle. He drifted between episodes based upon his arousal and the need he felt to satisfy it. Actually, what the Unit still hasn't discovered is that the cycles are not *like* menstrual cycles, they are *forms* of a menstrual cycle in which the hormones responsible for arousal, violence, fear, and anxiety are generated according to a rhythm established in the hypothalamus. For those individuals who experience forms of psychomotor epilepsy or limbic psychosis, the cycles of behavior are akin to deep brain seizures that alter perception and behavior without physically incapacitating the individual. Bobby Joe Long reported that because of his actually growing woman's breasts when he was reaching puberty he was able to tell when the moon was full without looking at the night sky or consulting a calendar. He went on to explain that even on death row in the Florida state penitentiary the killers who cannot see the sky know when the moon is full because they begin to howl and fight among themselves. Since the menstrual cycle itself is controlled by hormones, it is natural that, if the area of the brain that controls normal hormonal function in the ductless glands is malfunctioning, the body's normal hormonal control system will malfunction as well.

To date the Behavioral Science Unit has consulted on hundreds of heretofore unsolvable murder cases and has provided police with accurate profiles of the potential suspects. It is still gathering information from interviews of apprehended serial killers and is computerizing their profiles and MOs. By disseminating these profiles and MOs to local departments and homicide squads, the FBI will begin to make a significant contribution to the tracking down of serial killers. However, until the juvenile justice system is brought into the same arena, and schools and emergency room doctors are made aware of the types of symptoms that show up early in a potential serial killer's life, law enforcement will only be playing a never ending game of catch-up with the problem instead of actually preventing it from spreading. This is why the Surgeon General cited the escalating levels of violent crime as one of the major issues of public health confronting American society. When the FBI and other government agencies that routinely deal with serial murderers and other forms of episodic violence turn their attention to preventing the violence before it becomes a crime, the corner will have been turned.

The Personal Statements of Five Serial Killers:

Stories of Their Lives and Crimes in Their Own Words

Henry Lee Lucas, Carlton Gary, Bobby Joe Long, Leonard Lake, and Charles Manson were all prolific killers during their careers. Each of their life stories typifies the basic constellation of physiological, psychological, chemical, and social patterns that point to the disease of serial murder. Each of their backgrounds illustrates a history of some degree of physical and emotional child abuse or negative parenting. Each personal statement reveals a medical history of varying degrees of head injury or diagnosed damage to the critical areas of the brain that control primal behavior responses or reasoning ability. With the exception of Leonard Lake, each serial killer on this list has a documented history of alcohol or drug dependence, with Lucas and Manson virtually living on chemical substances throughout most of their adult lives. Lake was a child of an adult alcoholic.

Tragically, each serial killer's life is out of his control. Lucas and Manson were so thoroughly abused during their early years that it is a wonder they even survived. And Lucas, Manson, and Gary spent the majority of their years in some form of juvenile or correctional institution. These men remember very little of a happy home life or family bliss whatsoever. When at home they were subjected alternately to severe beatings or absolute neglect. Their parents inverted the normal meanings of good and bad so that the children were told that all the evil things they were experiencing at home or in institutions were ultimately for their own good. Even Bobby Joe Long, who was not severely beaten as a child, was emotionally manipulated by his mother, who forced him to share a bed with her until he was thirteen. When Bobby wasn't in bed with her, one of her many lovers was, he claims, and Bobby was forced to compete with him.

Each of the killers on our list has manifested some form of congenital damage. Both Lucas and Long suffer from some form of gender misidentification. Lucas was made to dress up like a girl by his mother, who was a prostitute, and Long's hormone imbalance actually caused him to grow breast tissue, which had to be removed surgically, and to experience the emotional swings typical of a menstrual cycle. Even in prison, Long reports that his personality changes according to the lunar cycle each month.

Carlton Gary, Leonard Lake, Henry Lucas, and Charles Manson all evidence some form of learning dysfunction associated with congenital neurological defects. And Carlton Gary's webbed fingers and elongated middle toe are additional examples of the type of congenital disorder that can, given the other physiological, psychological, and social factors, result in a life of episodically violent behavior.

Each killer whose statement appears in this section has experienced the phases of the serial murderer in his own unique way. Lucas reveals that he had a long period of hallucinations during which he lost touch with reality while he was in prison in Michigan. He heard his dead mother's voice telling him to commit suicide and to commit murder, and when he asked for help from the prison medical authorities his request was turned down. Lucas, who claims that he was transformed into a lust killer in prison, spent periods during the next two decades constantly trolling for new victims. Always on the edge of violence, he explains that his killing episodes were always preceded by periods of heavy drinking after which he became almost stuporous. It was in this semistupor that he committed the vast majority of his homicides.

Lucas sought out hitchhikers, travelers, or other people who had become isolated by virtue of their being on the road. By offering them rides or striking up conversations at roadside service stations, he would make his first contact. Then, under the guise of offering a ride or giving directions, Lucas was able to lure his victim into his power. Once in his car, the victim was helpless. Lucas struck quickly, usually with his knife, killing his victim and having sex with the corpse. Then he buried the person in a shallow grave or jammed the body into a roadside culvert.

In those instances when Lucas had some attachment to the victim, he often tried to preserve a part of the body as a totem and visited the grave after the murder. However, his memory between episodes was affected by alcohol as well as by the extensive damage to his brain. During his recantation phase he alternated between amnesia and hyperamnesia – the memory of specific, tiny details that are dissociated from the larger event, which has always been forgotten.

Lucas claims his murders were always followed by periods of depression. He was never able to sustain the murder high, and, lapsing into subsequent alcoholic stupors, he trolled for his victims from Georgia to California. The depression finally became unbearable after he murdered Becky Powell, his common-law wife. He resolved never to murder again, but the next Sunday he killed Kate Rich, an old woman he had worked for as a day laborer. After he was arrested on a weapons charge in Texas months later, Lucas confessed to the Powell and Rich murders and to more than three hundred additional homicides in more than twenty-five states. He has since recanted his confessions and then recanted his recantation, but authorities still suspect him of more than a hundred murders. Lucas is on death row in Huntsville prison in Texas.

Bobby Joe Long's personal statement reveals that, although he was dominated by women throughout his life, he never struck back until after receiving severe head injuries in a motorcycle accident. He became hypersexual and fantasized about having continuous intercourse with every woman he encountered. Although he reported this symptom to his Army doctors, they dismissed it, and Long was not given any treatment. His newly discovered sexual dependence on women dovetailed with his lifelong emotional dependence on mother figures. Shortly after his divorce he became a rapist who lured victims into his trap by answering ads in the classified section of the local newspaper. This was his particular method of trolling. He would call the phone number in the listing, and if a woman's voice answered the phone, his sexual fantasies were aroused. He made an appointment to visit the seller. Once his victim was isolated with him in her house, he sprung his trap. He was not excessively violent at first. He threatened the victim with a knife, then simply tied her up, told her that he wouldn't have used the knife even if she had screamed. Long explains that he never consciously wanted to hurt his victims but that he felt compelled to commit the rapes by a force inside of him. He never understood it but was greatly afraid that the crimes would escalate unless he was able to muster the power to control his sexual urges.

As Miami's 'Classified Ad Rapist,' Long committed more than fifty assaults. During this period he also dated and lived with different women. Yet his sexual fantasies only became worse, and he found himself having delusions of violence as well. Finally he began a spree of murders in North Tampa's red-light district.

Feeling compelled to begin driving along the strip of singles bars outside of North Tampa in a hunt for a sexual companion, Long did not realize at first that he would be committing a murder. He was trolling, looking for girls who would be easy pickups for one night. His first murder even took him by surprise, he claims. He was picked up at one of the bars by a young Oriental woman who had actually lured him into a liaison. Once he had her isolated in his car, he turned on her and strangled her until she lost consciousness. The trap was sprung. Then he tied her up, took her to a deserted area outside the city, raped her, strangled her to death, and buried her. He fantasized about raping her for a short period after the crime, then the fantasies grew to a fever pitch once again and he went out trolling for another victim.

With each subsequent victim, picked up in exactly the same way in one of the singles bars, he became more and more depressed. He knew he was sick and needed help, yet he claims that he could not stop himself. When he tried to prevent himself from going out, he became so aroused that when he surrendered to the urgings he was more violent than he had been previously. And after each crime he felt depressed because he could not recover the feelings of sexual passion that had driven him to commit the crime. Finally, like Henry Lee Lucas, he left enough clues to allow the police to find him, and he began confessing to his crimes as soon as he was in custody.

Bobby Long kept a detailed newspaper clipping file about each of his crimes. These were his totems: by reliving the event through the news reports, he tried to recapture the feeling of passion and arousal that had almost, but never quite, satisfied his lust. When the totems and fantasies lost their power he would begin trolling along the same strip of bars for young women. With each crime, however, his depression over his own situation became more intense. When he was finally arrested, he explained, he felt a great relief that his life as a serial murderer had come to an end. He explained that he knew exactly what he was but that he had no control over the feelings that came upon him. He still believes that, had he received the help he needed when he requested it, the murders and the rapes might never have taken place. Bobby Joe Long received the death penalty and is on death row in Stark, Florida.

Carlton Gary experienced the phases of a serial murderer through phantom figures that he generated in his own mind. Like the other killers in this section, he was a severely abused and malnourished child who exhibited homicidally violent tendencies very early in his life. His pattern of trolling for victims, first as a mugger, then as a rapist, and finally as a killer, emerged very early. Like Long and Lucas, Gary complained to prison or medical authorities that he had visions of violent sex which he knew would soon drive him to a series of killings. His pleas for help were ignored. When he returned to his hometown of Columbus, a fugitive from New York, he plotted what he termed a series of robberies at the homes of elderly white women in the Wynnton section of the city.

Gary's confessions reveal that he was at the scene of every crime. However, he claims that he witnessed the crimes as they were committed by another person. Therefore, while never actually confessing to the homicides, Carlton Gary was able to reveal the details of the crimes as a witness and to provide the police with the facts they needed to charge him as the Stocking Strangler. Gary admitted to having mental blackouts and to using drugs. His statements to the Columbus police, however, reveal a person who has abstracted himself from the crimes so as to avoid the immediacy of the act.

Gary trolled for victims by 'casing' houses that would offer the least resistance to a break-in. He never remembered physically encountering one of his victims, but he remembered their being raped and killed. He watched from another room or from the street, but he was never there. When confronted with physical evidence such as pubic hairs that were at the crime scenes, Gary restated his admission that he was present at the crimes but claimed that he did not actually commit the murders. He was found guilty, sentenced to death by lethal injection, and is now on death row in Jackson, Georgia.

Leonard Lake's life is still shrouded in mystery because he committed suicide while in the custody of the San Francisco police on an illegal weapons charge. Most of what is known about Lake's crimes has been sealed by the courts in California because of extradition hearings against Charles Ng, Lake's suspected partner in the murders he is alleged to have committed. However, newspaper accounts of Lake's life, his career in the Marines, and accounts of his dungeon and torture compound in the rural Calaveras County hill country and interviews with his family reveal that Lake adhered to the basic pattern of the serial murderer.

Like Bobby Joe Long, Lake made contact with his victims through classified ads. He attracted Harvey and Debbie Dubs with an ad for the sale or exchange of video equipment. When they visited him in his isolated cabin, Lake sprung his trap, imprisoned them in an underground bunker, tortured them, executed them, and buried them in a troughlike grave on his property. Similarly, he lured Paul Cosner, an automobile dealer, to his property with the promise of buying a Honda if it were delivered. When Cosner delivered the car Lake killed him and took his driver's license and credit cards. Cosner's body was found in the same grave as the bodies of the Dubs family and Lake's other victims.

Lake's personal diary reveals that he was fantasizing heavily about the violence he was about to commit as he fled from Humboldt County to Calaveras County. His delusions of grandeur and his vision of a survivalist compound in which only the strongest and bravest would survive the coming onslaught shed light on his siege mentality that was isolating him from the rest of the world. His aura phase began with his flight from Humboldt and his setting up the compound on Blue Mountain Road in the small town of Wisleyville. He stockpiled guns and supported himself by making snuff videos and selling drugs. His trolling nets were the classified ads he placed and those he read in the newspapers. He expanded his net by contacting the friends and relatives of people he had previously killed and drawing them to his cabin, where he captured them. His male victims were summarily killed for their possessions. His female victims became the star players in the videos he made. The police uncovered many of these tapes, which contained torture sequences in which Lake and his partner Ng encouraged the women to scream for their lives and beg for mercy.

The videos were Lake's and Ng's totems. However, they did not stop at murdering their victims. They carefully dissected them and boiled the skin off the bones and encased them in plastic bags which they buried in troughs near the bunker. In this way Lake and Ng lived on the grave site with their triumphs, constantly spreading their nets wider and wider as more victims passed by.

Leonard Lake swallowed poison while he was being interrogated by San Francisco police detectives in connection with a stolen car, stolen property, and illegal weapons that were in the trunk of that car. Charles Ng, who was with Lake at the time a hardware store owner called the police to charge Ng with shoplifting, escaped while the detectives were questioning Lake. Ng was later apprehended in Canada and is being held there awaiting extradition for kidnapping and murder. Leonard Lake died in the hospital the day after he took poison.

Charles Manson and his family are perhaps the most infamous killers since the 1950s. His 'helter-skelter' murders of the Tate and LaBianca families and his commune family's involvement with scores of other murders throughout California in the late 1960s as well as with the attempted assassination of President Gerald Ford raised them to cult figure status. Yet clinically, Manson is very much like the other serial killers whose lives are reviewed in this book in that he suffered from the same patterns of abuse and head injury, had virtually no childhood bliss whatsoever, was institutionalized from the time he was twelve, was brutalized and raped by prison guards and inmates, and abused every type of psychedelic drug he could get hold of. He was also a drug dealer and contract killer. Manson's background differs from the other serial killers', however, in that he did not actually do any of the killings himself. His homicidal patterns were actuated by the other members of his group whom he inspired to commit the specific crimes.

Nevertheless, Manson reveals that he experienced the same types of phases that the other serial killers did. During his extended aura phase, which began under the influence of drugs in San Francisco's Haight-Ashbury section after his release from federal prison, Manson was constantly on the move. He joined a number of religious and Satanic cults to heighten the other-worldly sensations he was experiencing, gathered other rootless young men and women to join his family commune, curried favour with children of entertainers in order to get his music produced, and performed whatever tasks he could in order to make money.

As his hallucinatory experiences became more intense and his relationships with cults and pseudoreligious groups more extensive, Manson began to act upon his apocalyptic visions. His fantasies became reality, and he sent his family members out on missions to bring about chaos through demonstrations of brutal homicides. As Susan Atkins, Tex Watson, and Patricia Kenwinckle returned from each mission they brought vivid stories as totems to allow Manson to experience the violence vicariously. New evidence reveals that Manson revisited the murder scene at the Tate house the same night of the murders. All of the episodes merged into one long murder spree that didn't end even with the arrest and conviction of the leader of the family. Years later 'Squeaky' Fromme was arrested for the attempted assassination of President Ford, the last of the serial murder assaults committed by the Manson family. Manson's death sentence in 1971 for the Tate/LaBianca murders was overturned by the Supreme Court. He is currently serving a life term at San Quentin. He is up for parole every five years.

The personal statements in the five chapters that comprise this section represent the attempts of five individuals to reconstruct periods of their lives during which they were often beset by hallucinations and delusions and suffered from mental blackouts. Much of their reality was distorted by alcohol and drugs and their constant need to hide or stay on the move. Each of these killers was compelled to find new victims, and this explains their constant motion as they set out at the beginning of each episode of violence to seek victims.

What surfaces in each of the statements is the extreme hatred each person feels for the society around him and the isolation of having to cope with the violence and turmoil raging within. Henry Lee Lucas expressed it best when he claimed that he hated each and every day of his life. Each of these killers hated, and each sought the means to control the hate, to extinguish the fires that were consuming them, or to prevent themselves from inflicting violence upon those around him. None of them were successful, and each lived out his career as a serial murderer, destroying families and striking terror into communities as a consequence of his crimes.

There is no external logic in any of the following personal statements. No killer will explain what he did in any way that reveals a causality or a motive for his actions. Henry Lee Lucas kills Kate Rich partly as a consequence of having gone out drinking with her and partly out of a misplaced feeling of unhappiness after having killed Becky Powell the day before. There is no logic or motive to Lucas' action. Bobby Joe Long will feel no remorse for any of his victims.

Carlton Gary explains his actions to the police as if he were walking in a dream. The figures in Gary's confessions aren't real people, they are phantoms. There is the phantom killer who accompanies Gary to the hotel in Albany, New York, where he murders his first victim, and there is the phantom who accompanies Gary on each of his robberies in Wynnton, where each of the victims is raped and strangled. Gary feels no remorse for his crimes because, in his mind, he never committed the crimes. He is not lying; his mind does not accept the murders as something he committed.

All we have of Lake's personal statements are the videos and the snippets from his diary that the California courts have released. The real Leonard Lake will never emerge until after Ng has been brought to trial in California and the evidence is finally presented. From what we know about the individual who slaughtered animals and boiled them down into soup, Lake lived a life of fantasy. His delusional episodes were strung together to form one continuum. His world was populated by demons and warlocks – characters out of a dungeons-and-dragons game – and he was the warrior with an unlimited license to kill all those around him. Thus, Lake's tale is the most difficult to comprehend because he isn't alive to assist with the research.

The personal statement of Charles Manson reveals some of the darkest elements of human existence. He, like Lucas, fed upon his own hate of the world around him. His vision of the apocalypse was a violent bloodbath in which his victims were gutted and left to die like animals. Manson's statements, more than those of any of the other serial killers, express the feelings of a dead man. By the time Manson was interviewed in San Quentin in 1987, there is no single pattern of causality that emerges in his life. He is the ultimate victim, the bastard with no birthright, the emblem of his mother's shame, and her affliction. In the Bible-reading family into which Charles Manson was thrust like a curse, he was a focus of evil. Bartered away by his mother for a pitcher of beer when he was six, influenced by a rigid and militaristic uncle, sent away to reform school where his runt size made him the plaything of the guards and older boys, Manson could only absorb punishment. In the venom of his own words, he was raped, sodomized, beaten, and tortured by everyone who came in contact with him while he was in prison.

The statements of these killers have been placed within the biographical context of their lives. However any narrative that imposes a causality or reason for the crimes these killers have committed falls far short of the real horror of their separate truths. There is no rationale for their crimes and certainly no justification. And just as there is no rationale, there is nothing that society will gain from their executions. The threat of the electric chair or the hangman's noose did not stop Lucas from hating nor did the image of a needle of lethal poison being injected into his veins stop Bobby Joe Long's violent sexual fantasies.

The narratives place the killers' lives within a frame of

reality, but it is what the killers say about themselves that creates the greater reality. If to understand the implications of serial murder one has to hear about it in the killers' own words, then what these five murderers have to say must be said without prejudgemental interpretation.

7

Henry Lee Lucas

1.	Also known as:	none
2.	Date of birth:	8/16/32
3.	Place of birth:	Blacksburg, Virginia
4.	Place of arrest:	Montgomery County, Texas
5.	Date of arrest:	9/5/83
6.	Charge:	Illegal weapons, murder
7.	Convictions:	Murder, rape, kidnapping
8.	Sentence:	Eleven murder convictions, one death penalty, serving six life sentences, two seventy-five-year sentences, one sixty-year sentence
9.	Current status:	Death row, Huntsville, Texas

'I hated all of my life. I hated everybody. When I first grew up and can remember, I was dressed as a girl by Mother. And I stayed that way for two or three years. And after that I was treated like what I call the dog of the family. I was beaten; I was made to do things that no human bein' would want to do. I've had to steal, make bootleg liquor; I've had to eat out of a garbage can. I grew up and watched prostitution like that with my mother till

I was fourteen years old. Then I started to steal, do anything else I could do to get away from home . . . but I couldn't get away from it. I even went to Tecumseh, Michigan, got married, and I started livin' up there, and my mother came up there and we got into an argument in a beer tavern . . . that's when I killed her.'

Henry Lee Lucas remembers very little of the actual killing. Both he and his mother had been drinking heavily that night. He remembers that during the fight with his mother, Viola, she accused him of having sex with his sister, ridiculed him in the presence of his new wife, and he began slapping her until she fell to the floor. When he went to pick her up, he found his knife in his hand and saw his mother stabbed through the chest. He took off and left her alone in the house, and she died in a hospital the next day. That fight with his mother was the culmination of a twenty-three-year nightmare during which Lucas was repeatedly beaten with sticks and, on at least one occasion, with pieces of a two-by-four timber, deprived of food until he was near starvation, and forced to watch his mother, a sometimes prostitute, have sex with scores of men. A neighbor's report confirmed Lucas' stories about his early years.

She had also beaten Lucas' father, Anderson Lucas, an alcoholic who lost both his legs when in a drunken stupor he fell under the wheels of a slowly moving freight train. He was a double amputee called 'No Legs' by the locals of Blacksburg, Virginia. This occurred before he met and married Viola, the daughter of a Chippewa Indian. Anderson Lucas made moonshine liquor, skinned minks, and sold pencils for a living. But he drank most of the moonshine himself and taught his son Henry how to mind his still. Henry Lucas' own taste for alcohol developed by the time he was ten. 'He hopped around on his ass all his life,' Lucas says of his father, who was also coerced into watching his wife have sex with a variety of men. He would watch until it made him sick; then he would crawl out of the dirt-floored cabin and lie in the snow. Finally one night in 1950, after he had taken all he could take, he went out the door and stayed in the snow all night. He caught pneumonia a few days later and died, leaving his youngest son, Henry, alone to face the mother's brutality. Henry even recalls being beaten by Bernie, his mother's live-in-boyfriend who lived with them in the three-room cabin.

Lucas' childhood was a mixture of horror and pathos, a virtual breeding ground for the type of violence that turned Texas Interstate Highway 35 into a mass burial ground for Lucas' future victims. Viola beat the child mercilessly with broom handles, sticks, pieces of timber, and any other weapons she could find. Her cruelty was such that she would not even let him cry. After beating him and telling him that what she had done was for his own good, she would prophesy that he was born evil. She went on to predict that he would someday die in prison. Her continuing violence began to infect every level of his existence. Henry Lucas' earliest memory, he claimed, is of his mother finishing up with a customer, then pulling out a shotgun and shooting the man in the leg. The blood spattered all over him in the process. This traumatic scene may very well have set the stage for his own fascination with spilling blood and the fragility of the human body later in his life.

Viola Lucas also liked to outfit her young son in girls' clothing. Lucas remembers that on his first day at school his mother curled his long blond hair and made him go to school in a dress. The teacher, one of few people in official positions of authority who came in contact with Henry Lee Lucas during his youth, was shocked. She took the responsibility for cutting his curls and dressing him in pants. Later this same teacher fed the malnourished youth sandwiches during school lunchtimes and took him home to her house, where he would receive the only hot meals he ever ate as a child. 'I think she was responsible for my first pair of shoes,' Lucas remembers. Years later, in a rare interview, his teacher described Lucas as one of the many impoverished and desperate West Virginia hill children in her classes. But, she revealed, he was especially dirty, smelled very bad, and was constantly tormented as an outcast by the other children.

As he grew older, the injuries he sustained from his mother grew in seriousness. One day, when he was too slow to fetch wood for the cabin stove, his mother hit him especially hard across the back of the head with a two-by-four. In his own account, Lucas claims to have remained in a semiconscious state for about three days before Bernie got scared and took him to a hospital. As an excuse, he claimed the child had fallen from a high ladder. After that incident, Lucas reports, he had frequent bouts of dizziness, blackouts, and at times felt as though he were floating in the air. Neurological examinations and X rays conducted years later confirmed that Lucas had sustained serious head traumas resulting in damage to those areas of the brain that control violent behavior and the ability to manage emotions.

Lucas claims that, as a child, anything that he liked or played with his mother destroyed. He remembers a pet mule that he kept. His mother, seeing him take pleasure in the animal, asked him whether he liked it or not. When he replied that he did, she went into the house, reappeared with a shotgun, and killed the mule. Then she beat him because of the expense she had just incurred in needing to have the mule carcass carted away. Incidents like this were responsible for Lucas' inability to love or admit to love and for his perverted emotions toward other living creatures. He became accustomed to the fact that there was little or no value to life and that people were no different from any of thousands of inanimate objects that populated his world.

After Henry's first serious head trauma, he received another injury about a year later. His brother accidentally sliced into his left eye with a knife. The wound punctured the eye, and for months Lucas could only see shadows and phantom images. His peripheral vision was seriously impaired as well, causing him to walk sideways so that he could see what was on his left. He was eventually returned to school where the teacher who had shown him so much kindness when he was younger, purchased special readers with large type so that Lucas could continue learning to read. Even this level of progress was interrupted when another teacher at the school, while striking out at another student, missed, accidentally hit Henry instead, reopened his wound, and caused him to lose the impaired eye completely. It was replaced with a glass eye that he still wears.

As a young teenager Henry Lee Lucas reported having sex with his half brother and with the animals whose throats the two would cut open before performing bestiality. He often caught small animals and skinned them alive for pleasure. He began stealing for food and money. 'I started stealing, I guess, as soon as I was old enough to run fast,' Lucas remembers, ' 'cause I didn't want to stay at home. I figured if I could steal, I could get away from home and stuff.'

He claims to have committed his first murder at fifteen. He cornered a seventeen-year-old girl at a bus stop, carried her up an embankment, and attempted to rape her. When she struggled and screamed, Lucas began strangling her. 'I had no intention of killing her,' he said thirty-three years later in an interview about his life. 'I don't know whether I was just being afraid somebody was going to catch me or what. That killing was my first, my worst, and the hardest to get over. . . . I would go out sometimes for days, and just every time I turned around I'd see police behind me. Then I'd be always looking behind me and watching. Everywhere I'd go I'd have to be watching for police and be afraid they were going to stop me and pick me up. But they never did bother with me.'

It was also at age fifteen that Lucas was first convicted for breaking and entering and committed to a reformatory as a delinquent. This began a pattern for the remainder of his life that stretched from state prison to federal prison to death row in Huntsville, Texas. He was discharged from the reformatory a year after having made what the prison report calls 'a good adjustment.' A year after his release he was again convicted of breaking and entering and sentenced to the Virginia State Penitentiary for four years. He escaped in 1956 and with a male companion stole a series of cars from Virginia to Michigan. Later in 1956 he was arrested on a federal charge of transporting stolen property across state lines and sentenced to a federal reformatory in Ohio. He was transferred back to Virginia to serve out his original sentence with time added for the escape. He was finally discharged in September 1959 and made his way back to Michigan to join his sister. It was in Michigan, just four months later, that he wounded his mother fatally with his knife. He fled the crime scene, leaving her bleeding on the floor. By the time Henry's sister found Viola Lucas fourteen hours later and took her to the hospital, it was too late. She died from complications resulting from the wounds her son had inflicted. Henry Lee Lucas was convicted and sentenced to forty years for second-degree murder.

In prison in Michigan and eventually in the Ionia State Psychiatric Hospital to which he was transferred on the recommendation of the prison psychiatrists, Lucas was diagnosed as a psychopath, a sadist, and a sex deviate. He was cooperative, though, telling his doctors that he sometimes heard voices telling him to do 'bad things.' He felt from time to time as if he were floating in the air, and claimed that he was sorry for the murder and rapes he had committed. The reports describing the inmate Henry Lee Lucas document a personality completely turned in upon itself. Incapacitated by an inferiority complex, Lucas was 'grossly lacking in self-confidence, self-reliance, will power, and general stamina.' There was also evidence of a 'general preoccupation with sexual impotence, the same which is believed to exist as only another reflection of his deflated impression of personal qualities in general.'

The person the prison psychiatrists described in July 1961, the schizophrenic Henry Lee Lucas who had been so brutalized by his mother that he eventually could achieve sexual potency only after he had killed his victim, attempted suicide several times in the Michigan State Penitentiary. First, he cut open his stomach with a razor blade. After that proved unsuccessful, he tried slashing his wrists. It was while serving time in the Michigan State Penitentiary in 1961, he claims, that he heard his mother's voice burning inside his head. 'I kept hearing her talking to me and telling me to do things. And I couldn't do it. I had one voice that was tryin' to make me commit suicide, and I wouldn't do it. I had another one telling me not to do anything they told me to do. That's what got me in the hospital, was not doing what they told me to do.' Lucas claims that he became a changed person in the Michigan prison. Where before he had killed only out of instant rage, he now became blatantly determined to kill as many people as possible. He was filled with hate and tormented by the sound of his mother's voice echoing inside his brain.

His multiple suicide attempts and his refusal to abide by prison routines prompted his transfer to Ionia State Hospital, where he remained for almost five years. He was eventually returned to the prison and his hallucinations continued. He used the prison records room to study the criminal cases of the other inmates. He immersed himself in the details of their crimes. During this time he studied the techniques the police employed in pursuing their investigations and developing leads. He learned how they used their suspects' mistakes to track them down. He studied police procedures so aggressively that upon his release he was able to commit crimes and escape the authorities with much greater ease. His new knowledge enabled him to predict the authorities' next moves. According to his own later statements, he had learned how to be a career criminal. 'I learned every way there is in law enforcement. I learned every way there is in different crimes; I studied it. After I got out of that hospital, they put me in the records room. And every record that jumped through there, I would read it, study it, and see how what got who caught.'

Lucas was recommended for parole in 1970 even though he warned the prison officials and the staff psychologist that if he were released he would kill again. He told them he was sick, that he was hearing a voice from the dead, and that the forces that had compelled him to attempt suicide while he was in prison would now compel him to kill strangers if he were let loose. The state of Michigan, however, was facing a prison overcrowding problem in 1970. The parole board released him even though he claimed not to have been rehabilitated. 'I knew I was going to do it!' he proclaimed years later in his Texas jail cell. 'I even told 'em I was going to do it! I told the warden, the psychologist, everybody. When they come in and put me out on parole, I said, "I'm not ready to go; I'm not going." They said, "You're going if we have to throw you out." They threw me out of the prison because it was too crowded. So I said, "I'll leave you a present on the doorstep on the way out." And I did it, the same day, down the road a bit. It wasn't too far away from it. But they never proved it.' Lucas found his first murder victim in Jackson, only a few miles away from the Michigan penitentiary. He killed her and left her within walking distance of the prison gate. The case wasn't solved until Lucas confessed to it in Texas.

In 1970 he began a killing spree that took him across much of the Southwest and into Florida, abducting children, raping young girls, and killing whoever was convenient. 'I was bitter at the world,' he claimed years later. 'I hated everything. There wasn't nothin' I liked. I was bitter as bitter could be.'

It was for the murder of his common-law wife, Frieda 'Becky' Powell, the niece of his companion Ottis Toole, that Lucas was finally apprehended and convicted again. Becky had first met Henry when she was nine and he was forty. He cared for her as if he were her father, providing her with food and clothing and generally raising her. He made sure that she went to school. In a ludicrous parody of normal parenthood, he even introduced her to his own skills and taught her the rudimentary techniques of his profession, including thievery, breaking and entering, and random murder. Soon the pair were no longer surrogate parent and child but common-law husband and wife and partners in crime. In December 1981, Becky was caught and sent to a juvenile detention home in Florida. Soon thereafter Henry and Ottis Toole helped her escape and all three of them began another killing spree across the Southwest to California where they eventually settled.

Henry used some of his prison-acquired skills as a laborer, carpenter, and roofer to earn money doing odd jobs. He worked often for the owners of an antique refinishing store in California in exchange for room and board for him and Becky Powell. In early March 1982 the owners of the antique store, Mr. and Mrs. Jack Smart, talked about going down to Texas, where Henry and Becky were to be paid to care for Mrs. Smart's eighty-year-old mother, Kate Rich. Henry and Becky and the Smarts bought tickets and left for Texas on what was

.o become the final chapter in Becky's life and the beginning of the end of Henry's freedom.

They were welcomed by Kate Rich, whose idea it had been to invite them to live with her, doing odd jobs around the house in return. The rest of the family in Texas quickly became suspicious of the two drifters and eventually forced them to leave. On the road while hitching a ride the pair met Ruben Moore, a preacher who led a small fundamentalist sect called the House of Prayer in an old converted chicken farm in Stoneberg, Texas. He also had a small roofing company and invited Henry Lucas and Becky Powell to join his group, live in one of the communal shacks, and have access to the group's kitchen in exchange for Henry's services as a roofer and day laborer. The same day that Henry and Becky met Moore they moved in.

Becky Powell quickly found a meaning in the group's religious practices. She attended Sunday services, made friends in the community, enjoyed the communal atmosphere, and even visited Kate Rich, who lived only ten miles north of there, whenever she could. The following August she decided that she wanted to start her life over again and return to Florida and the reformatory. After arguing with Henry, who wanted her to stay with him, she convinced him to take her back to Florida. The two left the House of Prayer in August 1982 and started hitchhiking back east.

A few days after they had set out the two drifters reached Denton County, where they could neither hitch a ride nor find a room in the local motel. Though it was a hot and muggy night, there was no rain so they decided to spread out their blankets and sleep in an open field. Henry started drinking heavily. Their bedtime conversation soon became an argument: Henry didn't want to go to Florida. For one of the first times in his life he was happy living at the House of Prayer. He liked Moore, he had friends in the religious community, and he also had legitimate work. Becky was adamant: she was tired of being a fugitive, always in danger of being caught and returned. Back at the reformatory in Florida she would be able to make a new start, clean her slate, and begin life all over again. She didn't want to leave Henry, but she didn't want to be on the run for the rest of her life either. Their voices got louder and their tempers rose. Each pushed the other closer to the edge until Becky slapped Henry hard across the face. That was his trigger: still there after his years at the Michigan penitentiary and the Ionia State Hospital and still just as fragile as the night in Tecumseh when his mother slapped him. Without thinking, he later confessed, he reached for his knife in his bedroll and plunged it deep into her chest. The blade penetrated her heart, and she died immediately. Henry Lucas said that he just looked at the little twelve-year-old girl twisted on the ground before him and wept.

Later, he remembers, he thought he should try to bury the body, so he removed her ring from her finger and then cut Becky into pieces. He put all but the legs in two pillowcases and placed her remains in a shallow grave. Then he tied a belt around Becky's legs and dragged them into the brush where he buried them. For the rest of that night and on several subsequent trips to the grave site he talked to Becky's remains. He wept, telling her that he was sorry for having killed her, and promised her that someday he would join her. His remorse over his reflex murder seemed to throw a switch somewhere in the psyche of Henry Lee Lucas. He was no longer interested in covering up his tracks with the same cunning as before. From that moment, his criminal career began to unravel. It was another nine months before he was finally apprehended. It was then that he would confess to the murder of Becky Powell and hundreds of other nameless victims.

After killing Becky, Lucas returned to Ruben Moore's

House of Prayer and casually reported that she had run off with a trucker on her way back to Florida. He then visited the widow Kate Rich one more time to take her to church services one Sunday evening in early September. Before church, they drove into Oklahoma for a couple of six-packs of beer. They drove around and drank and talked for hours until it was too late to catch the services, and then they decided to go home. On the way back to Ringgold, Texas, where Kate lived, they turned off the highway to a remote old pumped-out oil patch. In a sudden fit of rage, Henry stabbed Granny Rich to death there. Had she asked about Becky just one too many times? Had she argued with Henry about missing church services? Had she confronted the drifter about something he could not answer? Not even Henry is sure about what triggered him to kill her, but he did. He only remembers cutting an upside-down cross between the old woman's breasts, having sex with the dead body, and afterward dragging it into a culvert where he lodged it there with a two-by-four.

Granny Rich's children reported her disappearance to Montague County sheriff William Conway. He sought Lucas, who was the last person to have seen her alive. On and off throughout the next nine months Sheriff Conway questioned Lucas, pursuing him vigorously until Lucas fled the area. He traveled to California to visit Kate Rich's daughter. The police in California held him for questioning because of the bloodstains on his car seat. This, too, aroused suspicions, and the Smarts reported their fears to Sheriff Conway back in Texas. Lucas then traveled to Illinois, where he spent the remainder of the year unsuccessfully looking for legitimate work. Finally he returned to Texas where William Conway, having received the reports filed by the Smarts, wanted him arrested for Kate Rich's disappearance. It was at the House of Prayer that he was finally turned in by his friend

Ruben Moore for possessing a gun: a felony for an ex-convict. Henry was arrested in June 1983 on the weapons charge, and within weeks, after experiencing what he called a religious conversion in the cold and darkness of his jail cell, he began confessing to the murders of Becky Powell, Kate Rich, and hundreds of other victims.

Many of his confessions were found to be false, the police later concluded. Henry was a practiced liar and had been simply testing his interrogators. But also, because his own sense of self was so throughly absent, he would become a chameleon and conform reality to the perceived wants and needs of others. Many of the details that Lucas remembered and the descriptions of the burial locations proved to be right on target. From his jail cell in Texas, where he unwound a tale that would spread across the center of the country, his testimony began clearing up unsolved crimes in states throughout the South and Midwest. The deepest fears of hundreds of parents whose children had been listed as missing for years came to the surface. A large portion of these confirmed crimes involved the series of slayings along Texas Interstate 35 and in particular the lingering investigation into the grisly murder of a nameless victim known as 'Orange Socks.'

A motorist driving on I-35 on Hallowe'en had found the strangled, nude body sprawled face down and hugging the concrete along the side of the road. She was a pretty, reddish-brown-haired girl in her mid-twenties who had little scars around her ankles where she had evidently infected insect bits in childhood by scratching at them too much. She also had venereal disease. She was difficult to identify because not only did she have a set of flawless teeth, making a dental records trace all but impossible, but there was no evidence of surgery or of previously healed fractures. She wore a silver abalone-inlaid ring but had no pocketbook, no credit cards, and no driver's license. The identifying features were bunched-up remains of paper towels she had fashioned into a tampon and her stretched, dusty, pumpkin-coloured socks that had been pulled down around her ankles as if the person undressing her had left them on by mistake. She had also eaten just before she died. The sheriff dubbed the Jane Doe Orange Socks. She was just one of the scores of unsolved homicides along I-35, an area that by 1981 had become a dumping ground for the corpses of hundreds of murder victims. It stretched for five hundred miles from Laredo to Gainesville.

These random murders included an assortment of victims who had been sexually assaulted, sodomized, shot, strangled, beaten, and dismembered. No single pattern of murder emerged that investigators could use to group the victims together. The victims themselves puzzled the investigators. Some of them were women, some men, some teenagers, some middle-aged businessmen; some were obviously hitchhikers, others were elderly women found in homes near the road, some were single women who might have had car trouble, and others were obviously vagrants bumming toward the Mexican border. There were no apparent similarities. The authorities had always assumed that the bodies were the victims of different murderers who had easy access to the area because it was wide open and not well patrolled. The murders were committed in a variety of ways, some by strangulation, some by gunshot wounds, but there was no unifying pattern that tied the crimes together except for the common burial ground. The police had no solution and no suspects. Many thought that none of the cases would ever be solved. That was until Henry Lee Lucas was taken into custody in 1983.

'Yeah, that one, she was a hitchhiker, and she would have been a strangle,' Lucas said after looking at the picture of Orange Socks's face. She was lying on her back at the edge of the macadam. 'I picked her up in Oklahoma

City,' he said into the videotape camera after having been read his Miranda rights by Sheriff Boutwell, who had interrogated the mysterious, glass-eyed ex-convict on Sheriff William Conway's wild hunch. 'Then we drove around awhile; we stopped and had sex . . . voluntarily. We had sex one time, and I wasn't satisfied. She put her clothes back on, and we stopped and ate at a truck stop. . . . We started to head back south, so we took 35. And after we got on 35, why, I asked her to have sex with me. Then she said no.' Even though Lucas' court-appointed lawyer stepped in at this point to advise his client that he was confessing to a capital crime under Texas law, Lucas wanted to continue. He had already attempted suicide himself numerous times, he claimed, now he might just as well let the state do it. That way he could pay for his crime and keep his promise to the dead Becky Powell.

'Well, we were talking about sex, and she told me, "not right now," ' he continued, remembering the scene with a vivid attention to detail. 'She tried to jump out of the car, when I grabbed her and pulled her back. We drove for a little piece further than that, and I pulled off the road because she was fighting so hard that I almost lost control of the car and wrecked. After I pulled her over to me, why, I choked her until she died, I had sex with her again . . . then I pulled her out of my car, and I dropped her into a culvert.' It was a wrap. The police felt satisfied they had their murderer. The camera and tape machine were turned off, the room lights were turned back on, and the book was closed on Orange Socks.

The following spring a San Angelo jury found Lucas guilty of the rape/murder of the Jane Doe female nicknamed Orange Socks and sentenced him to die by lethal injection. Although Lucas' partner, Ottis Toole, later admitted to the murder himself and the whole case is undergoing a reexamination in light of some of the obvious lies that Lucas told in many of his other confessions, the Orange Socks murder and the hundreds of other stories that Lucas told about finding his victims and killing them shed light on the behavior of a serial murderer. Whether or not Lucas killed the hundreds of victims described in his confessions, he has become the center of a political firestorm in the Texas criminal justice system.

There is no doubt that Henry Lee Lucas murdered his mother, Becky Powell, and Kate Rich. It is also highly probable that he murdered scores, if not hundreds, of strangers along Interstate 35 in Texas and in a number of neighboring states. His descriptions of the victims, his drawings of their faces, and his hyperamnesia – an ability to remember even the slightest of specific details while forgetting entire blocks of time – point to a knowledge of the crimes that only someone at the murder scene could possibly recall. However, like most perpetrators of seemingly random or motiveless killings, Lucas has become the centre of the conflicting ambitions of state and country prosecutors, police departments from different jurisdictions, and politicians from opposing parties.

For Sheriff Boutwell and the Texas Rangers who have followed the case since Lucas' first confession to the Orange Socks murder, the prisoner has become the key to scores of unsolved murders. To the families of missing children and young girls, Lucas has been a source of peace, a criminal whose confessions have allowed families to release their lives from doubt and let grief and mourning finally fill the void left by the missing person. To local prosecutors, however, whose cases are based entirely upon Lucas' statements – confessions of a man already sentenced to die – he has been a source of embarrassment. They have to hope that his confessions are true so that they can close the books on their missing person cases and allay their fears that the real kidnapper may be still at large. In other words, the police and the prosecutors each legitimately need Lucas to be either a monstrous serial killer or a man lying to buy time for himself by fending off the executioner's needle until there are no more crimes left to confess to. And the prisoner at the centre of it all feeds upon the attention and thrives in its glow.

Lucas was tranferrred from his own private cell at a Texas jailhouse, where he had been confined since 1983, to death row at the federal prison in Huntsville. He has almost run out of appeals on his original convictions. While at Georgetown he had a heavy appointment schedule, made appearances on national television, held interviews for national magazines and posed for photographers, and was the subject of a series of detailed physical and neurological examinations. Yet he is still an enigma who has led police officers on wild goose chases across three or more states only to find that the murder victim Lucas so carefully described was still alive and well.

Henry Lee Lucas exemplified the type of deviant we have categorized as a serial murderer. According to his confessions which police have been able to verify, he committed at least three murders of unrelated victims within the space of six months. His actual victim count is probably much higher. Described as a sociopath with a debilitating character disorder, his real actions have defied traditional psychological labels and he has functioned at close to normal levels within certain types of highly structured communities such as prisons and hospitals. He was able to look back upon his own crimes with such a convincing sense of remorse that even the most experienced police officers and psychologists have been unable to explain it. At times they felt that they were manipulated. In reality Lucas' remorse was the result of his being confined to a stable environment. Completely

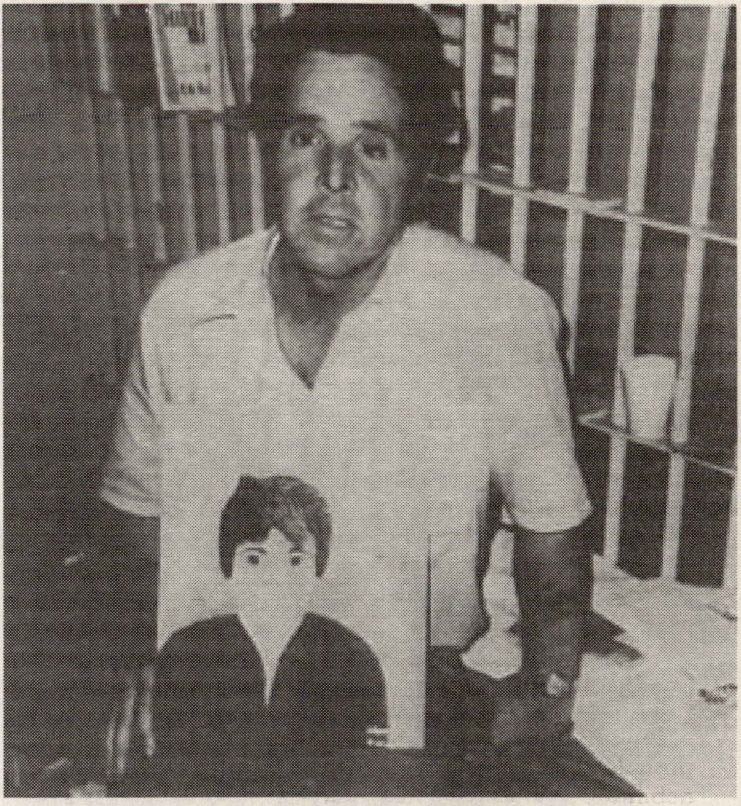

Henry Lee Lucas in the county jail in Georgetown, Texas. He is posing here for a picture taken for *Life* magazine with a portrait he drew of his beloved 'sister' Clemmie. (Cuba)

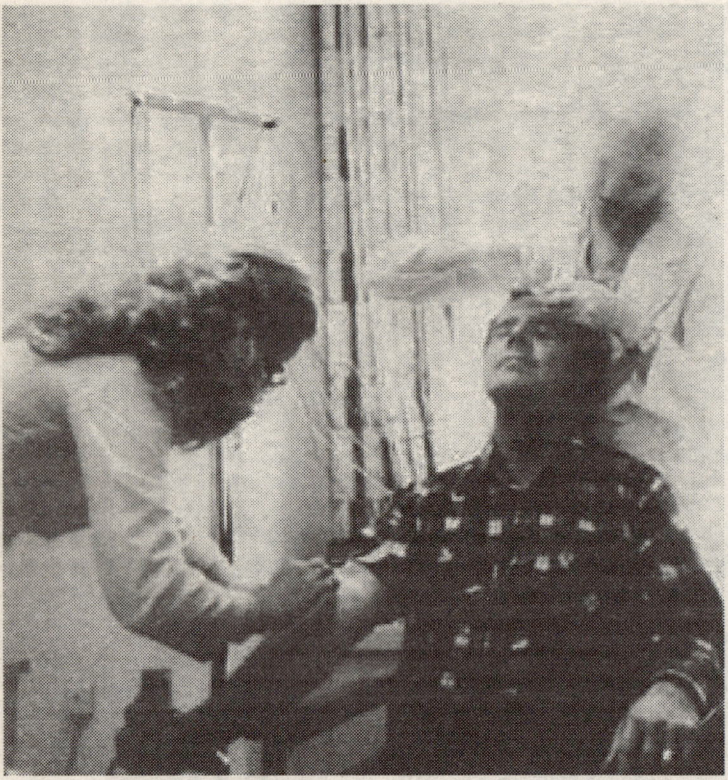

Lucas undergoing EEG testing. (Cuba)

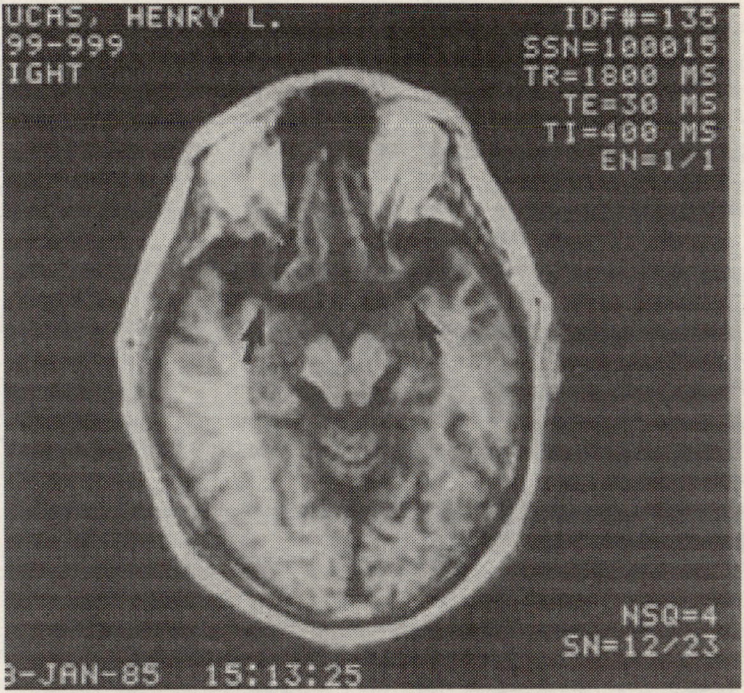

This photograph is the result of a magnetic resonance scan of Henry Lee Lucas' brain. The arrows, which are in the temporal lobe, point to a black area of spinal fluid accumulations. Some accumulation in this area is normally present, but the spinal fluid channels are widened at the expense of the surrounding brain, more on the left side than on the right. This may be a result from a past injury. (Norris/Cuba)

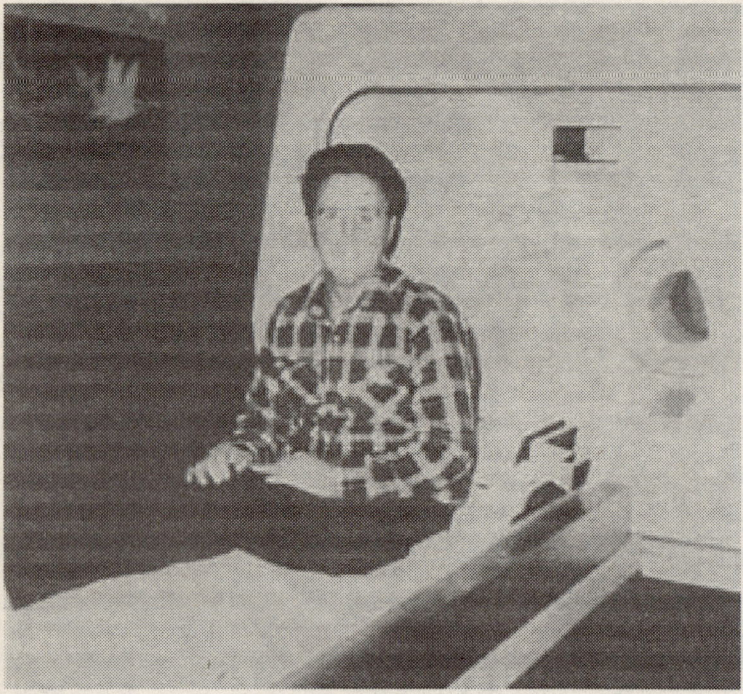

Henry Lee Lucas prior to a CAT scan at Baylor University Hospital in Dallas, Texas. (Cuba)

Defense attorney August 'Bud' Siemen and accused murderer Carlton Gary hearing the guilty verdict being read in the Atlanta courtroom. (Allen Horne/Columbus *Ledger-Inquirer* newspapers)

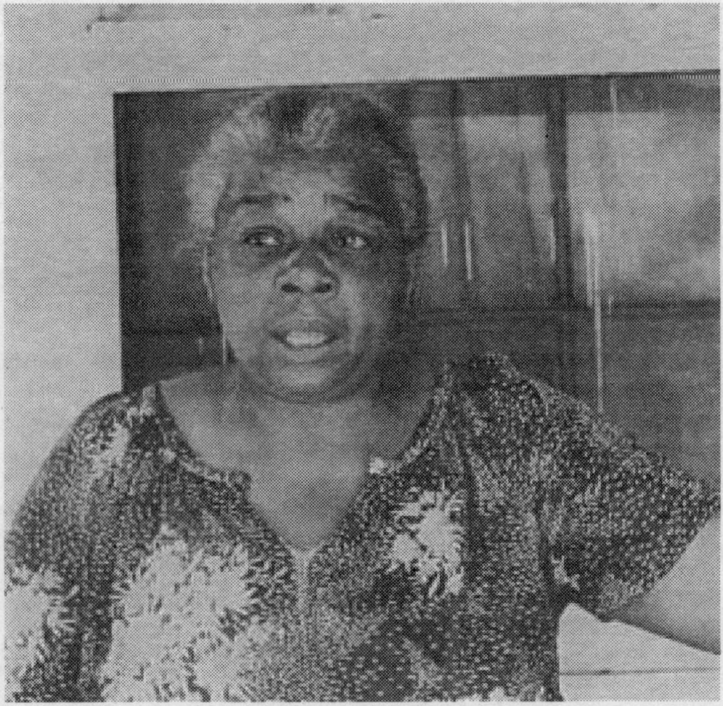

Carolyn David, Carlton Gary's mother. She had emotional and drinking problems all of her adult life and is the antithesis of the gentile white matriarchs that her son killed. (Allen Horne/Columbus *Ledger-Inquirer* newspapers)

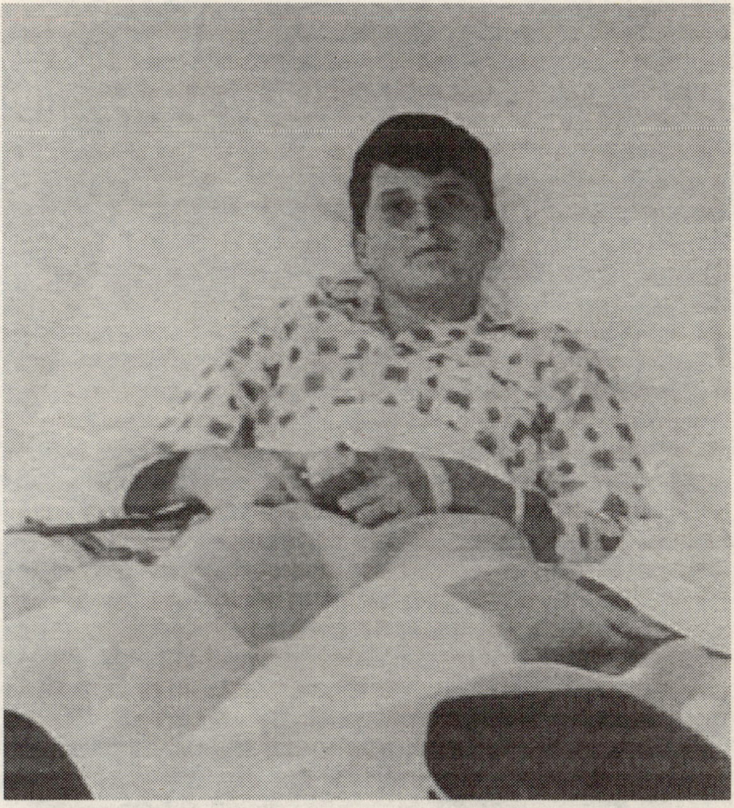

Bobby Joe Long at the age of twelve, recuperating in the hospital after having six pounds of breast tissue removed. Long remembers being terrified that he was becoming a woman. (Long)

Louella long, Bobby Joe Long's mother; Bobby Joe Long; his wife Cindy. These are the two women that Long blames for his untempered hatred of women. (Long)

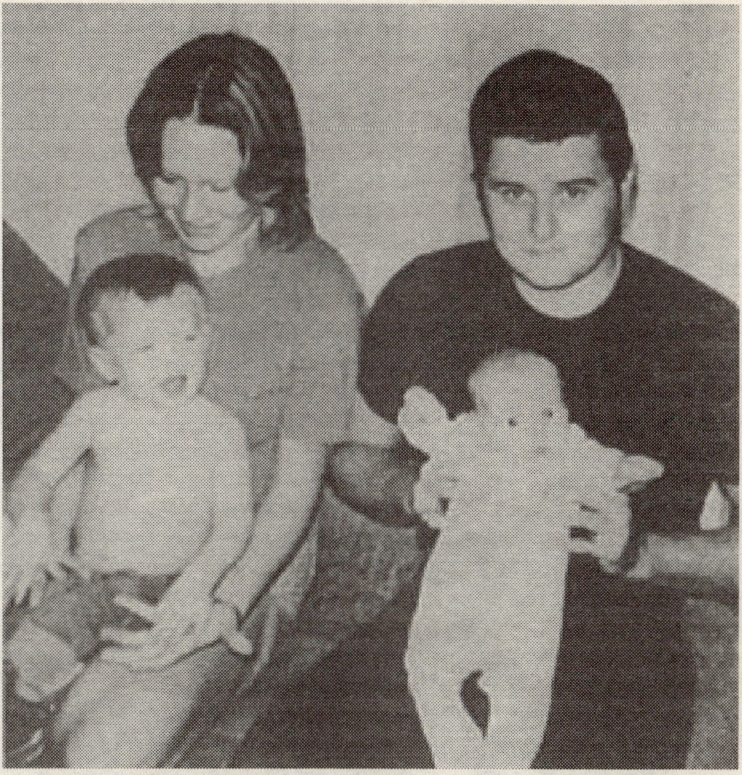

Bobby Joe Long pictured with his wife Cindy and their two children during the time that Long was raping women. (Long)

Charles Manson, age thirty four, being led into court in Independence, California, for a preliminary hearing on a charge of possessing stolen property. At this time it was only speculation that Manson was involved with the Sharon Tate and LaBianca murders. (Wide World Photos)

Left: Leonard Lake as a young boy wearing an ROTC uniform. As an adult, when he became a murderer, he also began practicing staunch survivalists' techniques and preparing for America's holocaust. (Norris)

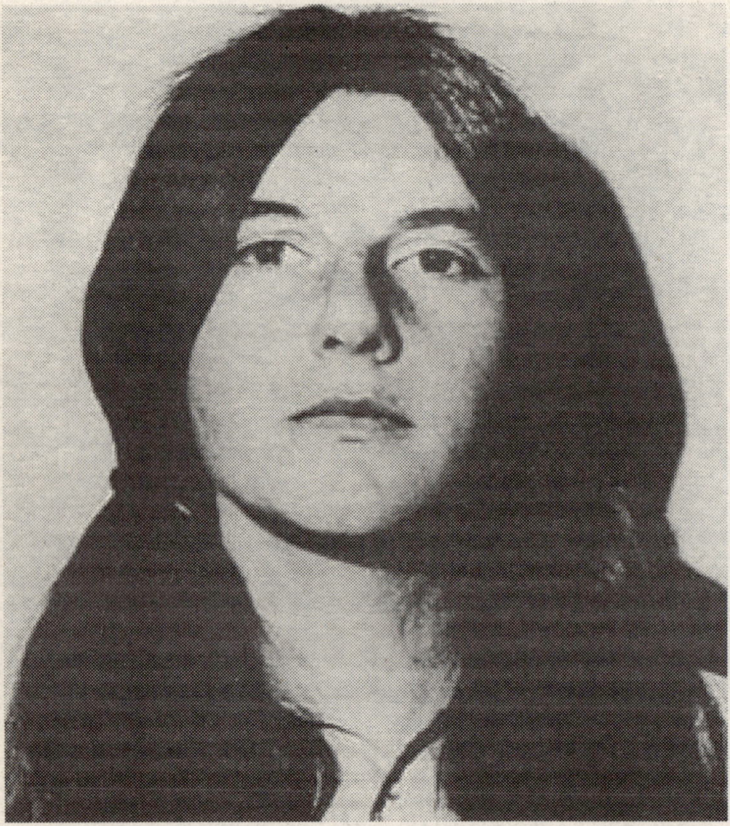

Patricia Krenwinkle (Wide World Photos)

Right: Leslie Van Houten and Susan Atkins (Wide World Photos)

Tex Watson (Wide World Photos)

Steve Grogan (Wide World Photos)

Lerotha Harris, ex-wife of Carlton Gary, testifies of Gary's increasing abuse of her when they were married. (Allen Horne/Columbus *Ledger-Inquirer* newspapers)

institutionalized, Lucas is now on a stable diet, he has undergone psychotherapy in which his hallucinations and confessions of crimes were taken seriously for the first time, and he has claimed to have experienced several religious conversions. It is as if at Georgetown he had started to mature emotionally as a result of the forced structure of his prison environment. This is not a paradox. It is what typically happens when a serial murderer is finally incarcerated and begins to adjust to prison and his captors.

The complexity of Lucas' behavior and the layering of his different medical and psychological problems are the results of the years of abuse he suffered as a child and his severe brain damage. CAT scans and nuclear magnetic resonance tests done on Lucas reveal that the repeated head traumas he received during childhood damaged those sectors of his brain that control primal emotions such as love, hate and fear. Lucas' chronic drug and alcohol abuse also contributed to his criminal behavior by diminishing his voluntary control over his emotions and increasing the length and depth of his mental blackout period. He claims that he always drank heavily immediately preceding every murder. Furthermore, the high levels of lead and cadmium content in his blood indicate a nonresilient personality, one that is unable to cope with any negative stimulus. However, all of these factors – the brain damage, his savagely violent childhood, his substance abuse, and his nonresiliency – fused and automatically have turned Lucas into a serial murderer. Each aspect of his life would have contributed independently to a psychologically crippled adult were it not for the negative parenting that taught Lucas that life was without value and that he was a person of no worth in a hostile world. It was as if his mother's negative parenting, the constant reinforcement that Lucas was 'the child who would come to no good,' was a self-fulfilling prophecy. It was the single factor that acted as a catalyst, combining all of the other negative factors in Lucas' deviant childhood into the violent individual who could only relate to creatures who had died.

Lucas came alive only in the death of another being. He gained sexual potency after he had bludgeoned and strangled his sex partner into a coma or to death, and he then had intercourse with the victim's remains. He existed in the world of the living by subterfuge and camouflage and by trusting no one. He even turned on those who had been his companions, killing Becky Powell because she confronted him as his mother had. He killed Kate Rich for probably the same type of confrontation. He failed at everything positive in life, succeeding only at murder.

Clinical evaluations we conducted on Henry Lee Lucas after his murder conviction revealed extensive neurological damage to his brain. There were small contusions to the frontal poles that indicated a frontal lobe injury. There was damage to his temporal lobe and pools of spinal fluid at the base of his brain. There was an enlargement of the right and left Sylvian fissure at the expense of the surrounding brain tissue that indicated significant loss of judgmental functions and was the result of head traumas received after birth. Neurologists, commenting on the results of both the CAT scan and the nuclear magnetic resonance test, confirmed that the extent of brain abnormality indicated an individual who was not able to control violence with the same degree of success that people with more normal brains were able to do.

The neurological diagnoses are also supported by symptoms of hypergraphia, the inability to control one's self-expression through writing, painting, and speaking, and by periods of either blackout or grey-out in which the person experiences long periods of floating sensations and the inability to perceive different objects around him. The experience of floating sensations also indicates a form of deep sensory motor epilepsy that requires constant EEG monitoring for periods of from thirty-six to forty-eight hours to diagnose. The length of the test is necessary for the machine to pick up the telltale deep spikes of the seizures. In addition, Lucas' hypergrandiosity and hyper-religiosity are traits common to people who have incurred damage to their temporal lobes. The loss of judgmental ability, the loss of the ability to balance feelings against logic and sensory input, leads to a form of internal feedback in which the brain acts directly upon its own delusions. In other words, what the brain thinks it sees becomes reality. Lucas' extreme dealings with Satanic cults in Florida and Texas and his sudden conversion to born-again Christianity in jail only a few years later are examples of this symptom. Even after his conversion to Christianity, Lucas continues to lie and to manipulate those around him with an almost uncanny ability to sense what he thought they want him to say.

Toxicological tests also reveal that the high levels of lead and cadmium found in his nerve tissue, combined with the years of chronic alcohol and drug poisoning, destroyed a significant amount of cerebral capacity and left him with no physical or psychological resiliency. The three indicators of active cadmium poisoning – loss of dream recall, excessively strong body odor, and loss of sense of smell – are all well documented in Lucas' medical tests. In fact, the killer still does not remember most of his dreams and allegedly rode in a car for three days with the decapitated head of one of his victims without noticing the acrid odor of decomposing flesh.

Like all serial killers and most multiple murderers, Henry Lee Lucas demonstrated bizarre and violent sexual activity combined with a confusion regarding his sexual identity even before he committed his first serious crime. He claimed that he had sex with relatives, committed bestiality, and engaged in forms of necrophilia with parts of his victims' bodies. He has killed, he has said, in order to gain sexual potency because he was unable to have sex with a living person who, just by being alive, challenged Lucas' superiority and posed a life threat to him. Any ability to rely on his own sense of being was so completely destroyed by Lucas' mother that even today he realizes that in order to have any relationship with a person he must kill that person. And after he has killed his sex partner, if the relationship has been positive in his own mind, he mourns for the victim and for himself. If the relationship was only sexual, he had coitus with the remains and left them in a shallow grave or in a roadside culvert.

'Sex is one of my downfalls,' Henry has said. 'I get sex any way I can get it. If I have to force somebody to do it, I do. If I don't, I don't. I rape them; I've done that. I've killed animals to have sex with them and I've had sex while they're alive.' Forced to watch his mother have sex with her clients, and forced to wear girl's clothing to school and to wear his hair in curls, Lucas developed a hatred of women that has contaminated his entire life. Even Becky Powell had only to argue with her up-to-then protector, and in the next moment she lay dead from a knife wound through her chest. And with the memory of Becky's murder still playing back in his mind, Lucas turned his attention to Granny Rich and killed her only a few weeks later. Thus, he put to death the only two women with whom he had any close relationship because he did not have the personal resiliency to sustain those relations in moments of confrontation.

For all of his childhood years and until his imprisonment, Lucas was chronically malnourished. His mother forced both Henry and his father to scavenge for food on the streets or in garbage cans while cooking for herself, her customers, and her pimp. As a schoolboy, his teacher used to provide him with sandwiches and an occasional hot meal. Lucas' diet during the years immediately preceding his arrest for murder included a daily consumption of alcohol and drugs, five packs of cigarettes a day, and peanut butter and cheese. These years of malnutrition, especially during childhood, resulted in stunted development of the cerebral tissue as well as in impaired judgment and cognitive performance. It was only during his incarceration that his diet was stabilized to the point where he no longer suffered from elevated levels of blood sugar and severe vitamin and mineral deficiencies.

Throughout his life Lucas has demonstrated an escalating propensity toward violence, another important trait of the emerging serial murderer. As a very young child, he was a fire starter and was maliciously cruel to animals. As an older child, he practiced bestiality, rape as an adolescent, and single murder as a young adult. As a fully emerged serial killer, he has committed multiple murders, necrophilia, torture, mutilation, dismemberment, and totemic preservation of the remains of his victims. He has even admitted that, despite his conversion, he recognizes that he can exercise no control over himself, was grateful for the intervention of the criminal justice system for that control, and admitted on more than one occasion that if released through some quirk of justice he would probably kill again. He recognizes society's laws but maintains that punishment has no meaning for him because he has been through what no human being should ever have to endure. Even though he has been diagnosed as sane, Lucas knows that within him there is a darkness that nothing can reach.

'When I'm around people,' he explains, 'I feel tense, nervous. I guess it's because I haven't been around people. Most of the life I've lived has been alone. I have trouble talkin' to them; I always have. I don't think there's a doctor in the world that's going to go against another doctor's word. They say there's nothing wrong with me, so that's the way it is. I don't feel there's something wrong with me, I *know* it! People don't do the things they do unless there's something wrong with them. I just thought there's no way I could kill somebody, so it's not that. Something pushes me into doin' it. What other choice is there?'

Thus Lucas has lived his years in a kind of phantom world, in part because his brain was never able to process information in the same ways that healthy brains do, and in part because the normal conditioning that takes place when parents raise their children was twisted by his mother into an aberration in which evil became her version of good. The successive head injuries, the starvation of his brain through prolonged malnutrition, and the poisoning of the cerebral tissue from alcohol – which Lucas began consuming in large quantities by the age of ten – and drugs all combined to cause a progressive degeneration of Lucas' neurological system. The physical connections between the different areas of the brain, the hundreds of thousands of electrochemical switches that balance primal feelings of violence with logical, socially ordered behavior, simply didn't work properly. As a result, when pushed to a certain point, Lucas was incapable of controlling his own actions. When asked how he perceived his victim at the time of the murder, he explained: 'It's more of a shadow than anything else. You know it's a human being, but yet you can't accept it. The killin' itself, it's like say, you're walkin' down the road. Half of me will go this way and the other half goes that way. The right-hand side didn't know what the left-hand side was going to do.' But even more important, the combination of physiological, chemical, and psychological events resulted in a type of nonperson, an individual who was so far beyond the bounds of normalcy that the traditional categories used to describe deviant behavior no longer applied. Henry Lee Lucas, like the other serial killers in this section, belongs to the walking dead. He is a man who died emotionally and socially before the age of ten and for whom existence had become only a hunt to satisfy his primal urges from each moment to the next.

Typical of an individual who has never internalized any coherent patterns of social and emotional behaviour, Henry Lee Lucas dwelt in a world of shadows when not under the care of an institution. Once in prison or in a state psychiatric hospital he became docile, identifiable as a schizophrenic with a severe character disorder but certainly within the pale of human experience. He even attempted suicide on many occasions to end his own misery and to stop the voices that were reverberating in his brain. Finally, on death row in Huntsville, Texas, and living on an institutional diet, Lucas has responded. The structure of the institution has become an exterior emotional skeleton, a shell that supports discrete elements of his personality. Supported by the structure of this shell, some personality development can take place in Lucas. He senses the early feelings of grief, and he mourns for himself and for the person he will never become. But he probably will never honestly mourn for his victims. 'I feel each one of these victims I go back to; I got to go and relive each victim. It's like going back and completely doing the crime all over again. . . . I find myself many a time breakin' down and cryin'. Before I didn't have that. I didn't have feelings for nobody – a person was a blank.'

8

Carlton Gary

1. Also known as:	Carl Michaels, Mike Gary, Michael Davis, Michael Anthony David
2. Date of birth:	12/15/52
3. Place of birth:	Columbus, Georgia
4. Place of arrest:	Columbus, Georgia
5. Date of arrest:	9/12/83
6. Charge:	Murder, rape, assault, robbery
7. Convictions:	Murder, rape, assault
	8. Sentence:Death
9. Current status:	Death row, Jackson, Georgia

'There was a cigarette stand and an elevator where John was standing. Then this white dude came down and asked us what we wanted. I told this white dude that we were looking for a Mrs. Polite, as we were looking for a dishwasher's job that was advertised in the newspaper. This white dude said it was too late to find anybody in the housekeeping department. The white dude went back to the desk and John and I got in the elevator. John worked the self-service elevator. I didn't pay any attention to what floor we got off but John pushed the button. The elevator stopped, John and I got off and we walked down the hallway with John leading the way.

'While walking down the hallway, John put on his rubber gloves. He told me not to worry about my fingerprints as I had no record and they couldn't be traced. We came to this hotel room door. I notice that when John or Pop came to this door he had some kind of material jammed in the door lock. John went in first. I followed him. John turned to me and said, "Check out the bathroom." The bathroom was dark. I recall now that at this time all John had on were his Converse black All Star sneakers. I was in the bathroom. I looked around. I could see John in the other room and he was holding a flashlight and going through papers. Outside of the bathroom there was a door. I opened this door and it was a closet. I looked in the room where this closet was and John was holding a flashlight and he was looking through the dresser drawers. I noticed the bed was all messed up. I heard some people coming down the hall. I got scared. Now after the sounds stopped I seen John with his flashlight go over toward a door and I seen John direct the flashlight to this door at the bottom of which was a low, big trunk. John asked me to help him move this trunk. When the flashlight that John was holding shined on the trunk I noticed the head of a human being up against this trunk. The head of this human being was stretched out on the floor. There was a lot of papers thrown over the rest of the body to which this head was attached. I could tell this was the body of a woman, a white woman. I seen John reach down and grab this human head by the hair and throw it to one side. I did not step over the body but John asked me to help him put this trunk on the bed. I reached down and with my hands I picked up the trunk and with John helping me we put the trunk on the messed-up bed. John started to work on the lock of the trunk. There were some pots and pans and some household stuff in the trunk. Some of the stuff in the trunk was wrapped up in papers. We searched through the stuff in the trunk. I picked up John or Pop's snow boots and I walked out of the hotel room. I walked around the hallway and down to the elevator. John was still in the room. I walked out of the Wellington Hotel and up to the corner of State and Eagle streets outside of the DeWitt Clinton Hotel. I waited there about twenty-five or thirty minutes and then John or Pop came up State Street and he joined me. We walked down Eagle Street to the Gulf gas station at Eagle and Howard streets in Albany, New York.'

In this confession to the Albany police department in July 1970, Carlton Gary under the alias of his alter ego Carl Michaels, described the murder of eighty-five-year-old Nellie Farmer, a prototype of the murders he would be convicted for sixteen years later in Georgia. Gary was never prosecuted for this, one of a string of robbery murders committed in Albany that even today are still open cases although the crimes were used to establish a pattern of behavior similar to the Columbus stranglings that helped a county jury convict him in 1986.

In his confessions to the Albany police and later to the Columbus police in the Wynnton murders, Gary admitted to being at the crime scene and participating in the burglary, but he implicated an accomplice who he said had actually committed the murders. In Albany, John Lee Williams, the man Gary incriminated while he was being held in the county jail, was convicted on his testimony and sentenced to Dannemora. The conviction was later overturned when Gary withdrew his testimony, and John Williams was deemed innocent and released. In Columbus, the jury found that there was no accomplice in the Wynnton murders and that Gary had acted alone, robbing the old women, bludgeoning them, raping them, and finally strangling them with a stocking or a scarf.

'He's always been a crook,' former Gainsville, Florida,

detective Homer McGilvray said about the young Carlton Gary, whose name seemed to turn up every time a crime was committed in the area. Gary himself told the New York State prison authorities that he never had a home and never had any parents. That was partially true. Having lived with his mother as she moved from place to place, later with his aunt, with his grandmother, or completely on his own when he tried to find his mother, Carlton Gary had never had a home. Before his first arrest as a juvenile, he listed fifteen different residences. From the time neighbors spotted him rummaging in garbage cans in Columbus for food while he was a very young child to his first arrest for arson at age sixteen, his life reads like a blueprint for violence and crime.

Carlton Gary had a gifted-level IQ and creative abilities that were overshadowed by probable developmental disabilities and the lack of any childhood bliss. His congenital disorders are evidenced by several minor physical anomalies, the obvious webbing of skin between his fingers and an elongated middle toe. While still in elementary school he was afflicted with at least one severe head trauma which left him unconscious and comatose on the schoolyard ball field. Rejected by his father, chronically malnourished as a child, and a heavy drug user through his teens, Gary had been charged with robbery, assault, and arson before he turned eighteen.

Carlton Gary became a person who combined opposites: a husband and a pimp, a killer of older women and a care giver for his older aunt, a thief and a benefactor. While committing the Wynnton murders and pushing drugs in the black neighborhoods of Columbus and modeling on local television, he was living with a female deputy sheriff who had no idea that Gary was leading a double life.

Gary never confessed to the murders. In fact, publicly he still maintains that he worked with an accomplice named

Michael Crittendon who cased the houses of intended burglary victims and who actually committed the murders while Gary hid outside in the bushes. The prosecution produced no witnesses to the murders, although a victim of one of the sexual assaults identified Gary as her attacker after undergoing a session with a hypnotist months after the crime. Even then her angry testimony, according to Gary's lawyer, Bud Siemen, was inconsistent and not strong enough to serve as the basis for charging Gary with rape and attempted murder.

What was the basis of the prosecution that was able to win a death sentence without even producing a single eyewitness to the crime? And what was the path itself that led Carlton Gary full circle back to Columbus after twenty years of guerrilla warfare with police and prisons in Florida, South Carolina, and New York? First, the case against Gary rested upon a repeated pattern of behavior that the prosecution was able to connect with the rest of the stocking stranglings and with the robbery murder in New York. Although the state only charged Gary with the murders of Florence Scheible, Martha Thurmond, and Kathleen Woodruff – largely on the basis of fingerprints left at the scene – they used the murders of Ferne Jackson and Jean Dimenstein to create a larger pattern of related crime. And they used the murder of Nellie Farmer in Albany to establish a lifetime pattern of similar criminal activity that stretched back seventeen years.

Carlton Gary had confessed to being at the three crime scenes. In a midnight ride, he accompanied the Columbus police to the victims' houses and demonstrated how he had gained entrance and where the victims were at the time of the murders. Although he blamed the actual murders on Michael Crittendon, who was later cleared by the police, Gary described how the murders were committed and how Crittendon had raped and beaten the women. The prosecution used these robbery confessions to place Gary at the scenes and at the times of the murders and used the results of semen tests to show that Gary could have been the attacker who had raped the women. Further laboratory tests indicated that 'negroid' pubic hairs found on the victims also did not exclude Gary as the assailant. Finally, the prosecutor was able to use Gertrude Miller's testimony as positive identification of the man who beat, raped, and choked her with a knotted nylon stocking in 1977, only four days before the first of the Columbus stranglings was discovered. Carlton Gary was found guilty by the nine men and three women on the county jury and sentenced to the electric chair.

'I don't have any parents,' Carlton Gary once said. And by most people's standards that was true. He never knew his father, a construction worker who eventually died in an accident, saw him only once when the boy was twelve. And his mother was always on the move each time she met another man. The young Carlton Gary moved with her sometimes and sometimes he was left with his great-aunt Alma Williams or with his father's sister, Lillian Nesbit. Soon Gary was moving from place to place, often without the knowledge of his mother, aunt, or great-aunt. He became an orphan of the streets, developing a keen instinct for survival that enabled him to ingratiate himself with women and adults or anyone else who could help him. His uncle on his mother's side, William David, remembered that he was once notified by the MP at the main gate at the Fort Lee Army post in Virginia – four days before Christmas – that there was a visitor for him. Eight-year-old Carlton was put on the phone. 'Unk, it's Gary. Come get me.' To this day, David cannot understand how his nephew got to Virginia by himself. William David enrolled him in school, but by the following spring he was shipped out to another uncle in North Carolina.

Without a real home or any parents to assume legal responsibility, a teenage Carlton Gary gravitated between his aunts Alma and Lillian in Columbus and his mother in Florida. In Fort Myers, Florida, after he had finally established a residence with his mother, he returned home from school one day to find that she and her new man had moved out of the apartment. And he was on the road again, a sixteen-year-old with no home, seeking his mother, who had moved to Gainesville. It was in Gainesville that he met his first wife, Sheila, and was convicted for fire-bombing a white-owned grocery store whose owner had prosecuted Gary's mother for refusing to make good on a bad cheque.

That wasn't the first time Gary had been charged with a crime. Six months earlier, he was charged with breaking and entering an automobile in Gainesville, and two months after that he was charged with another breaking and entering. Gary escaped from custody in Gainesville, and made his way north to Connecticut. He sent for his wife and the two lived and worked in Old Saybrook, New London, Hartford, and Bridgeport, cities and towns along the southern Connecticut shore. Then, after being charged with assaulting a Bridgeport cop, Gary and his wife fled across the state line to Albany, New York, where he began playing music in nightclubs and was finally arrested for taking part in the robbery and murder of Nellie Farmer.

In a deal with the Albany county prosecutor's office, Gary admitted to burglary and testified that John Williams murdered Nellie Farmer, a rape/robbery/murder that occurred just two months after Marion Brewer, another retired worker from the welfare department, was raped and strangled with a pillowcase in a hotel nearby. Gary was sentenced to ten years at Dannemora on the burglary charge, even after the state's case against John Williams fell apart for lack of corroborating evidence, and murder charges against Gary were never filed. He was released on parole after serving five years.

Four months later he was rearrested for breaking parole. A year later he was reinstated on parole.

Finally, after escaping from Onondaga County prison in New York in August 1977, Gary returned to Columbus, where he committed the stocking stranglings throughout the fall and winter of 1977 and into 1978. By April of that year he had stopped the skein of murders and begun a series of robberies of fast food restaurants in Columbus and South Carolina, where he was finally caught and convicted in February 1979, almost a year after the last of the stranglings was committed. And it was there in South Carolina that he confessed to the restaurant robberies in Georgia and to escaping from the Onondaga prison. Five years later Gary escaped again and was arrested in Georgia, where he was indicted one day later for the Stocking Strangler murders. He was sentenced to death in August 1986.

Carlton Gary's trial was almost a pro forma exercise to invoke the death penalty on the killer nine years after the crimes were committed and almost two and a half years after the suspect was arrested. The appeals process will take at least another six to eight years. And Carlton Gary may never face the electric chair and the state of Georgia may never get what it wanted from the moment the first Stocking Strangler victim was discovered. The real tragedy is that these murders need never have taken place had someone in either Onondaga or Syracuse taken Carlton Gary seriously when he warned that he was embarking on a path of episodic violence fifteen years earlier. He asked for help from a parole officer even then. His pleas were ignored.

In much the same way the road signs of Gary's potential for future violence were evident when he was a schoolchild rummaging through the neighborhood garbage cans for food or when he turned up unannounced at the front gate of the Fort Lee Army post. Like Henry

Lee Lucas, Carlton Gary was born into an unstable and violent home environment. His father was never present, and his mother drifted from new address to new address as easily as she moved from relationship to relationship. Gary was abused as a child not only by his mother but by the men she lived with. He was malnourished while growing up, and, as evidenced by significant signs and symptoms observed from preliminary medical and psychological interviews, he suffers from a minimal brain dysfunction.

Gary has had a history of severe brain trauma on more than one occasion, he has been a chronic drug abuser, and he has been treated for psychological problems as well. Throughout his youth he displayed a propensity toward violence and antisocial behavior. He has been convicted of arson, robbery, assault, sexual abuse, and multiple murder. And this pattern of violence and crime has continued unabated throughout most of his life. In fact he has spent most of his thirty-five years either in jail or as a fugitive from the police. However, unlike more traditional criminals, his murder victims have not been people he has known, they have been complete strangers whom he first raped and bludgeoned before finally strangling them with a scarf or stocking. And his skein of murders seems to have run in patterns: two or more elderly white women in Albany and then five elderly white women in Columbus. In other words, even without the extensive battery of physiological tests that were used to establish the benchmark symptoms for Henry Lee Lucas, Carlton Gary has displayed all of the outward manifestations of a serial murderer who mixed freely among people while he was committing his reign of terror.

The book on Carlton Gary is far from being closed. Throughout the course of the appeals process, and until his condition is diagnosed, his lawyers will seek to have the death sentence overturned on the grounds that a proper defense was prevented from being presented. If, in the process of these appeals, deep brain EEGs and CAT scans reveal organic abnormalities and skin and hair tests reveal high levels of mood-altering toxins, it will come as no surprise. The combination of physiological, psychological, and social abnormalities set against the pattern of his criminal behavior will reveal that he was an individual who was not in control of his behavior during the cycles of the Wynnton murders, and the missing puzzle pieces of Carlton Gary's life will finally come together.

9

Bobby Joe Long

1.	Also known as:	None
2.	Date of birth:	10/14/53
3.	Place of birth:	Kenova, West Virginia
4.	Place of arrest:	Tampa, Florida
5.	Date of arrest:	7/14/83
6.	Charge:	Murder, rape
7.	Convictions:	Murder, rape
8.	Sentence:	Death
9.	No. of victims:	Fifty (plus) rapes, nine murders
10.	Current status:	Death row, Stark, Florida

When Bobby Joe Long spotted the pretty young woman bicycling home from work in North Tampa, he had already decided he'd had enough. For seven months he had been on a wild spree of rape and murder that loosely followed the cycle of the full moon. He picked up 'loose women' in bars or on the street, drove them to a deserted stretch of road in the rural countryside around Tampa, overpowered them and tied them up, raped them, strangled them to death, and left their bodies along the side of the road. The local homicide detectives were stymied and assembled a task force of state police and special agents from the Behavioral Science Unit of the FBI.

'I knew when I let her go that it would only be a matter of time,' Long remembers from his cell on Florida's death row. 'I didn't even tell her not to talk to the police or anything. And before her, when I first read about the task force in Tampa, I could have gone to Fort Lauderdale or somewhere else and they would have never found me. I just didn't care any more, and I wanted to stop. I was sick inside. Doesn't the fact that I could have run and didn't count for something?'

During this entire period, Bobby Long lived and worked among the residents of Tampa, dated girls, worked at whatever jobs he could, and obtained a degree as an X-ray technician. He tried as best he could to satisfy a sex drive that had reached a level of compulsion. He knew that a part of his personality was no longer working. He knew that ever since the massive head injuries he had received in a motorcycle accident ten years earlier things just weren't the same inside him. He lost his temper easily. Loud or sudden noises sent him into a fury. He became violent with little or no provocation. He had lost all resiliency and couldn't roll with the punches the way he had before the accident. And he had an insatiable drive for sex. While he was still married, he had sex with his wife two or three times a day and masturbated at least five more times a day. He had fantasies of making love to his wife's sister and her friends. He had fantasies of group sex and of overpowering women. These fantasies started while he was still in the hospital recovering from the accident.

After each murder, in the solitude of his apartment in North Tampa in 1983, Bobby Long would sleep deeply for sometimes more than twelve hours, and upon awakening he would wonder whether he had only dreamed the murder or had actually performed it. He would walk across the street to the nearby Magic Market to get a newspaper to read whether he had only dreamed the murder or whether it was real. He read about the growing panic in Tampa with the discovery of each new body. He read about each girl's background, the mysterious victims who had worked the streets and bars in North Tampa, and their grieving families. If he could have had any emotions about his victims, he would have hated them. Ngeon Thi Long, a dancer in the strip bars along North Nebraska Avenue in Tampa, was the first. He knew she was a prostitute, and he detested women who were whores, who were aggressive, who had no allegiance to any man. In reality, he claims, he was sympathetic toward women. When he was the Classified Ad Rapist in Ford Lauderdale and Ocala eight years earlier and had assaulted housewives who placed 'for sale' ads in the newspaper, he felt pity for them. He explained that he didn't want to hurt them, and wouldn't have hurt them even if they tried to scream for help. More often than not Long would try to apologize to them during the assault. 'Many times we would just talk. You would be surprised what some of them told me.'

But by November 1983 it was different. Bobby Joe Long was getting progressively worse. He had already committed eight murders. He was disgusted with what he was doing, but he couldn't stop. Then he saw the girl on the bike. She had got off her late shift at the doughnut shop after midnight and was riding home. Bobby Long's reaction was almost instinctive. Any pretty girl out this late had to be trouble. She seemed too aggressive, focused as she was on pedaling her bike along the dark road. Long hid in the bushes and waited until she passed. Then he sprang out from hiding and knocked her off her bike. He overpowered her at once and tied her up.

But this victim wasn't aggressive. Long blindfolded her, put her in his car, and then began a twenty-six-hour odyssey with her that eventually led to her release. She was a true victim. Her family had no money and her stepfather was out of work and confined to a wheelchair. She told Bobby that he, too, had abused her when she was younger. Now she had to work the late night shift in a doughnut shop just to help support her family. And she was also a student. Long knew that she didn't deserve to die; she wasn't like the other girls. She wasn't a prostitute or a woman who used her body to manipulate men. He drove her around blindfolded for many hours and tried to talk to her the way he had spoken to his first rape victims eight years before. He explained that he didn't want to hurt her. He drove to a bank machine for cash, and she was able to peek at the dashboard and around the car from under her blindfold. Then he took her back to his apartment where she again was able to sneak looks at the interior and later give police an exact description of where she had been and what the place looked like. He raped her, but it wasn't the same for him as it had been before. Finally he drove her back to where he had first picked her up and set her free.

He knew that she would lead the police back to him as soon as she was released. He had also known it was near the end when the first police task force was assembled. But there was still a living part of his brain that couldn't continue the violence any longer, and it closed him down. His fantasy had exploded, and his skein of rapes and murders was coming to an end.

Two days later his compulsion came over him again. As he was driving along the outskirts of North Tampa late in the evening, he spotted a car swerving back and forth in front of him. He thought it was being driven by a woman and that she was drunk. He followed her. She almost swerved off the road, but then she noticed she was being followed. She pulled over to the side. Bobby Long stopped his car directly behind hers, got out, walked over to her car, and the two of them began a conversation. In a few moments she agreed to ride around with him, believing that he would drive her back to her car in the morning. Bobby noticed how big she was. He described her later as a hard-looking girl in cowboy boots. Not fat, but she had a large frame. He disliked her from the moment he saw her.

As soon as she got in beside him he attacked her. She screamed and fought back, kicking him in the shins and putting her boots through his dashboard. The two struggled until Long overpowered her and tied her hands. She kept on screaming, however, until he forced her to stop by squeezing her windpipe. She became quiet, and he began cruising with her. Every time she started to scream he squeezed her throat until she stopped. Finally he strangled her until she lost consciousness. She came to shortly thereafter and began screaming again. And again he strangled her until she lost consciousness. Bobby undressed her but found, as he looked at the stirring figure, that what had been a raging desire for sex had simply dried up. Finally she came to again and began to scream for help, and this time he strangled her until she died. He rode through North Tampa with the naked body of the dead Kim Swann beside him for hours. Nobody stopped him even after he'd pulled into a local gas station to fill up. Finally he drove the body to a secluded area outside of the city and pushed it out of the car. He had never even bothered to rape her. Four days later he was arrested for the rape and kidnapping of the seventeen-year-old, and the violent career of thirty-one-year-old Bobby Joe Long was now in the courts.

When the eleven-year-old Bobby Long was reaching puberty, he realized that his breasts were growing. It was embarrassing for him to look down and see his enlarged breasts filling out his shirt as if he were a young girl. All of his clothing became tight, and his figure started to change shape as well. Other members of his family had experienced this congenital dysfunction of the endocrine system and his doctor prescribed surgery. Long's mother recalls that the surgeon removed more than six pounds of tissue from her son's chest. That seemed to remedy the problem, but it didn't keep Bobby Long from experiencing a lunar protomenstrual cycle for the rest of his life.

'Even now,' he recalls, 'I can always tell when it's the full moon. I get crazy when the moon is full; I can't sit still; I have to pace; even the smallest thing sets me off. And I'm not the only one. All over the row, you can tell when it's the full moon, even if you can't see it from this hole. People start screaming and carrying on, you just know that it's a full moon.'

Long's fear of being transformed into a woman when he was reaching puberty paralleled the many problems he had relating to women throughout his life. When he was still a very young child his mother divorced his father and took the boy to Florida. They were very poor, Long recalls. They rented single rooms in boardinghouses where they both had to sleep in the same bed. Bob's perception and his mother Louella's memory vary greatly. His mother worked nights and dated a lot of different men, some of whom Bob claimed regularly visited her at the boardinghouse. Even though Louella Long, Bobby's mother, denies this, they both agree that she changed jobs frequently and kept them on the move from place to place wherever she could pick up new work. Therefore he was never in one community long enough to make any lasting friendships. He was always the new kid in the neighborhood and was forced to rely on his mother for most of his companionship. For Bobby Joe Long, this situation aroused extreme rage in him, especially when the attractive and seductive Louella Long had relationships with grown men.

When his mother wasn't working nights, Long remembers, he asked her to spend time with him at home.

Instead, 'she would never stay home. She would always go out. I used to ask her why she couldn't spend her nights off with me. Take me out once in a while. But she would go out and leave me with one of the neighbors.' Worse than the loneliness, however, was the fact that Long and his mother shared the same bed until he was twelve, at which time she married her second husband. For Long, it was awkward and embarrassing; for his mother, it was an economic necessity.

'I never undressed in front of him or did anything anyone would consider indecent,' his mother explains. 'We just didn't have the money to rent two bedrooms.' She also remembers that, because she worked nights and didn't get home until five or six in the morning, 'by the time I was getting undressed to go to bed, Bobby was getting up to go to school.' According to her, the two were actually using the same room in shifts: he would sleep at night and she during the day. She also denies ever bringing men over to where the two lived. 'We were very poor and had to live on the tips I could make waitressing or carhopping. There were times when I didn't even know where I would get the money for the next meal, not to mention the rent, and I was afraid we'd be living in the street. But no matter what Bobby Joe or anyone says, I was never a prostitute, and I tried to be a good mother.'

Bobby's father saw his son only rarely between 1956, when Louella left West Virginia with their son, and 1968, when she divorced her second husband. 'They would come back to Kenova on Christmas or some other times, and I would see them. But for the most part, I didn't see Bobby Joe at all when he was growing up.' During Bobby's trial, it was disclosed that during his young life, on several occasions, Bob Long, Sr., while visiting the family in Florida, would become violent and sexually attack Louella, sometimes using a knife. Even today, he speaks of his son from a state of severe grief. But it was

Bobby's mother who raised him and who became the dominant influence in his life. She remembers him as the 'perfect, cute little boy. He made good grades at school. Then he met Cindy.'

When he was thirteen, Bobby Joe began dating Cindy Jean Guthrie, the girl who lived with her aunt just a few blocks away from Bobby and his mother and the person he would marry seven years later. She became the other woman who exercised control over his life. 'Cindy and I were inseparable from the first times we began dating,' Bobby recalls. 'She would be over at our house, or I would be at hers. We were always together.' From time to time they would break up, date other people, but get back together again. Five years and two children later they were divorced.

Cindy behaved like Bobby Joe's mother. She was forceful and told him what to do. The two women also look very much alike. Both are thin and fair, they have similar voices, and both are aggressive and able to manipulate the men they want. And Bobby Joe had found Cindy at just the time his mother had married her second husband. In his own mind, it was a natural transition from one mother-son relationship to the next. Louella had established herself with a new partner, and so did her son. His romance with Cindy would last throughout the stormy times in Louella's second marriage, the trips back to West Virginia to visit her first husband, and constant fights the two teenagers had. It lasted through Bobby's first brush with the law on a breaking and entering charge that was eventually dropped and throughout high school and his enlistment in the Army.

Louella didn't like the attention Bobby gave Cindy, and even today the two women are bitter about one another. 'She was manipulative,' Louella Long says of Cindy. 'She was one of the cruellest people I ever knew. She never really had a mother or a family for that matter and was jealous of the family that Bobby had. I tried to be a mother to her and to help her with the children, but she never liked me.' She remembers that her son's performance in school, which had always been affected by his changing residences every few months, had still been above average until he met Cindy. Then his grades fell apart completely, and he never finished high school. In fact Louella even blames Cindy in part for her son's crimes. 'You have no idea how she changed him and how what she did ruined his whole life.'

Bobby Joe Long married Cindy after he had enlisted in the Army, where he was training to become an electrician. He had worked as an apprentice electrician while he was in school and he saw the Army as a way to get enough experience to become a licensed professional. However, all that changed six months into his enlistment when he was almost killed in a motorcycle accident on the way to cash a cheque. 'I must have been doing at least sixty-five or seventy when I broadsided a car. My Bell motorcycle helmet was shattered. That's what kind of force my head hit the car with. I don't remember a thing about it until I woke up in the hospital.'

Bobby Joe severely fractured his skull in the accident and remained in a semiconscious state for weeks. He had severe headaches, which continue to this day, and was unable to focus his vision. He reports that his pupils remained dilated for a short period after the accident, and that his right pupil continued to be larger than his left for many months. His medical records indicate that he had sustained a serious head trauma, but neither his X rays nor his EEG were evaluated by a skilled neurologist at the time. During his trial, more than ten years after the accident, Dr. Dorothy Otnow Lewis of the psychiatry department at NYU's Medical Center has reevaluated Long and found that the brain damage he sustained was serious enough to warrant a thorough neurological examination.

The injuries to Long's brain from the motorcycle accident compounded possible damage received from four previous documented head traumas he sustained before he was ten. At the age of five he fell from a swing, lost consciousness, and awoke to find that a stick had punctured his eye and was embedded in the medial portion of his left eyelid. A year later he injured his head when he was thrown from his bike, and a year after that he was knocked unconscious when hit by a car bumper. He lost several teeth and was diagnosed as having received a severe concussion. A year after that he was thrown by a pony and was dizzy and nauseous for the next several weeks. 'That was the sickest I had ever been in my entire life,' Long says about the event. 'I couldn't even stand up straight without getting dizzy.' Dr. Lewis reported to Long's defense attorney that the aggregate result of these injuries was a significant level of damage to the left temporal lobe of Long's brain, with damage to the surrounding areas of the central nervous system as well, and loss of those neurological functions generally commensurate with that type of damage. She also noted that Long had a lesion on his left temporal lobe, indicated by the results of an EEG, and irregularities in the muscular ability on his right knee and ankle. The left side of Long's face is still numb as a result of the accident, and he still walks with a limp.

The motorcycle accident, more than any other single event, transformed Long's life. 'Anybody who knew me before the accident and knows me now would say that it's like I was two different people,' Long explains. 'I knew there was something wrong with my head when I was in the hospital after the accident. I was just out of it for months and then, while still in the hospital, I started thinking about sex. That's all I could think about day and night. I thought about it with my wife, with her friends, with people I knew from before. It started driving me crazy.'

Bobby and Cindy had their first child a few months later, after his release from the hospital, but Bobby Joe's troubles were only just beginning. First there were the physical and emotional repercussions from the accident. 'I tried to tell the doctors at the hospital that there was something still wrong with me. I couldn't get these thoughts of sex out of my mind, and Cindy and I had gone from having sex two or three times a week to at least two times a day. And I was still masturbating to get relief. I thought about having sex with just about every girl I met or got to know. Then there were the headaches that wouldn't go away, and the feeling that the side of my face was dead. And there were the noises. The slightest sound would seem like an explosion. I would scream at my son to be quiet, when he wasn't really making much noise at all. It only sounded like a lot of noise to me. To this day, I can't take loud noises – they make me get mad and crazy.' Besides his insatiable appetite for sex, the most disturbing change to Long's personality was his violent reaction to anything that didn't go his way. 'Before the accident, I was pretty much laid back. I would get mad, but I never really got crazy even when I was pushed. After the accident, though – and I noticed this as soon as I got home – the least little thing would make me furious. I mean, I really got so violent that I couldn't control myself sometimes, and that made me worried. I was never like that before.'

Often violence would come over him like a thunderstorm, with little or no provocation, and leave just as suddenly. When a violent outburst of temper had passed, Long would have no memory of it whatsoever. His mother remembers one such incident when she had borrowed his car to go shopping. When she passed by where he was sitting to pick up the keys, he reached out and grabbed her, put her over his knees, and spanked her very hard on the buttocks for several minutes. He had raised several painful bruises. He then stormed out of the house. When he returned, he could not remember the incident. Even today, Long claims not to remember spanking his mother, and she has never confronted him directly about it since it happened.

Over the next few months severe character disorders emerged in Bobby Long's personality. He was contentious, overreacted to any negative situation, and suffered from constant headaches and dizziness. After two years of difficult recovery from his motorcycle accident, his career in the Army came to an end when he claimed the Army violated his enlistment contract by not providing complete medical diagnosis of his injuries. He worked sporadically as an X-ray technician but was fired from job after job for making advances toward the female patients and, in one instance, for showing obscene material to a young girl. He served two days in jail on that charge and lost his job as well. After returning to West Virginia to work at a hospital there, he lost his job because he made the female patients undress before taking their X rays. Long was never hostile or overtly threatening, but there was something menacing about him nevertheless.

From 1980 to 1983, Long committed more than fifty rapes in Florida as the Classified Ad Rapist and terrorized the communities around Fort Lauderdale, Ocala, Miami, and Dade County. He called the numbers listed in classified ads for the sale of furniture and other household articles and made appointments to meet the sellers during the day when he was most likely to encounter housewives. Once inside the house, he would pull out his knife, tie up the victim, rape her, and rob the house. He never committed any murders and was rarely violent. 'I felt sorry for them, and I told them that I didn't want to hurt anybody. I didn't even like tying them up. I think they knew that I wasn't violent because many of them victims talked to me not like I was a criminal but like I was a person. They were pretty sad too because of the lives they had. If conditions had been different, we might have had a relationship.'

The classified ad rapes continued for more than two years despite the fact that the local police had assembled task forces to catch the rapist and had brought in the FBI. During this time Long was trying to lead as normal a life as possible: coping with a divorce and his ex-wife's remarriage, changing jobs, communicating with his parents, who had since got back together and were planning to remarry, and carrying on an active social life. It was also during this period that Long was falsely charged with rape by a former girl friend. The entire incident involved changing relationships in a love triangle from which Long had tried consistently to extricate himself. He admits that the woman was able to manipulate him because he wanted and needed to have sex. However, out of jealousy of her former boyfriend's new relationship and anger at Bobby Joe Long's intervention, a woman charged Long with raping her after she had invited him back to her apartment. 'This showed me what a real bitch could do when she didn't get her way,' Long explained. 'I've committed rapes and I've murdered women. I know what happens inside of me when I get violent. I know how I feel. I can tell you that I did not rape that girl. We had sex, but she was drunk, she invited me back to her place, and she announced in front of my friends that she wanted to have sex. Then, the next day, she told the police that I raped her.'

Long was formally charged in November 1981 with rape, and the case went to trial. However, even after having been convicted, he wrote a letter to the court asking for a new trial, and the judge granted it. 'The judge took it as a motion,' Long said, 'and he granted it. The charges were later dropped because I had witnesses who told the police that the woman had asked me to take her back home and had come over in the first place looking for sex. She was a whore anyway, and once that came out, the whole charge was thrown out of court.'

Ironically, it was at this time that Long was still committing rapes and robberies through the classified ads. He claims, however, that he tried to stop. 'I was dating a nurse, and I explained my problems to her – I didn't tell her that I was a rapist – but I explained part of what was wrong. She told me that I had a medical problem, and I came very close to seeing a doctor about it. I walked out of the doctor's office, though, because I knew that once I told him what I was doing he would tell the police. If I had any idea then that my behavior might have been neurological, I would have gone to a neurologist, but I didn't know.'

For all the years after the accident and during the period of the two series of rapes, Long was fully aware of the moral implications of what he was feeling and doing. Indeed, the psychological evaluation of Long in February 1985 found him to be competent to stand trial and to be punished for what he did despite evidence of psychomotor dysfunction, impaired cerebral function, and lesions on the left and right hemispheres of his brain. The EEG evaluations that the court-appointed doctors performed were superficial because they did not cover the full thirty-six-hour period necessary to document a deep brain dysfunction, and the neurological reflex tests were compromised because Long was bound in shackles at the time. The clinical experts made no mention of the hormonal imbalance that had caused Long to grow breasts, experience a form of menstrual cycle, and had resulted in serious impairments to socialization, gender confusion, behavior alterations, and physiological deformities. The state's experts did not see the significance of Long's reported hypersexuality, nor did they relate it to the motorcycle accident. Relying on the medical reports written in 1974, the state's witnesses, like the Army doctors years earlier, determined that Long had recovered from the accident sufficiently that there was no permanent cerebral impairment. Dorothy Lewis, however, noted that Long's hypersexuality and hair-trigger violence conformed to a pattern of behavior disorders associated with neurological damage to the limbic region of the brain.

The implicit tragedy in the deaths of the women and the more than fifty rapes committed two years earlier was that, had Long known at the time that he was suffering from a medical problem, he would have had it treated. 'If there was a place I could have gone for treatment, I would have gone. I knew I was sick, but there was nothing I could do about it. I was afraid that the first thing a doctor would do would be to call the police, and they would stick me in jail. Finally I got so sick of what I was doing, I got myself turned in.'

Long recalls feeling an escalating sense of revulsion with each ensuring rape murder. He had no feelings of remorse for the victims at first because he thought they were women who used men. 'I know what I did. I raped them and murdered them. But they were the ones who offered the invitation.' He remembers that the first murder began when the victim picked him up in one of the strip bars on Nebraska Avenue in Tampa. 'She picked me up really, I didn't go after her. She was a whore. She manipulated men, and she wanted to manipulate me. Once I had her in the car, I tied her up and raped her. Then I strangled her and dumped her body alongside the highway. I knew what I was doing, but I just couldn't stop myself. I hated her. I hated her from the time she picked me up, but I didn't plan to murder her. I don't even think that I planned to rape her either. She was just sitting there in the front seat of the car, and I grabbed her, covered her mouth, and tied her up. I couldn't believe what I'd done the next morning. I was sick, and I knew I was in real trouble. Then a few days later I met the Simms girl, and it was the same thing all over again. She was a barfly. She really picked me up, and I just turned on her in the car.'

In a regular procession, the next six victims invited themselves into Long's presence and unknowingly placed their lives in jeopardy. Even after the third rape in only two months, the girls along Nebraska Avenue continued to be attracted to Bobby Long. 'I knew when the police task force was announced that I was running out of time. I should have gotten out of the area, but I wanted to get caught. I could have gone anywhere in Florida, kept on raping and murdering, and the police would never have found me. I could have gone back to California and done the same thing. Then, right before I was caught, the cops stopped me just to check on some report of a robbery in the area. But they took my license and looked over the car and then let me go. I knew they were following me then. I'm not completely stupid not to know what the cops were doing. It was just a matter of days, so I made myself visible and gave them all the time they needed to arrest me. Even Cindy called me and asked me if I'd heard about all the rapes in my area. As if she wasn't giving me a clue that the cops were on to me and that they'd already called her. But I wanted to be stopped because I couldn't stop myself.'

Then he met his seventeen-year-old rape victim. 'When I started talking to her I knew it was all over. Her own stepfather had raped her and she had to work to support him. She was the first girl that I stopped who didn't come over to me first. I knocked her off her bike. That was a first. I tied her up and blindfolded her and brought her back to my apartment, and I knew that if I let her go she would tell the police. I talked to her and asked her not to, but she hates me. When they tried me, she was among the people who wanted to see me fried the most.'

Long and his attorney, Ellis Rubin, believe that he will

get a new trial because his first confession was forced by the police. 'Once they had me in custody, I couldn't stop talking. Then I realized that I could be fried for what I was saying, so I asked for a lawyer. But they wouldn't let me see a lawyer until I finished what I was saying because they said that I already knew my rights. I know now that they had to let me see a lawyer when I asked for one.' Long's behavior when he was taken into custody fits the pattern of other serial killers who feel the immediate need to confess when they are arrested.

It was after he was put on trial, however, that he realized that his case had become a political issue. 'What kills me the most is that the girls I raped were all dope addicts and whores. Not that anybody really deserves to get killed, but they weren't saints. I'm sick. I know there's something wrong with my brain. I knew it from the first times in the hospital when I felt what I felt. I told doctor after doctor what I felt, but it made no difference. I'm no killer, not like the other guys here on the row. But it made no difference to the court or to the governor. Bloody Bob Graham needs me to die because he has to get reelected, just like he needed Ted Bundy to die to get reelected. He kept on signing death warrants for Bundy and putting him on death watch even though he knew that the court was going to step in. Everybody knew it. But it made no difference because we're here just to die so that people can get elected back into office. As far as I'm concerned, they're the real killers because they're not sick and are using the state to kill so that they can get ahead in their careers. I'm sick and I'm going to be fried alive. After I'm dead, they're going to open up my head and find that just like we've been saying a part of my brain is black and dry and dead. But they're not going to give a fuck.'

10

Leonard Lake

1. Also known as:	Charles Gunnar, Paul Cosner, Scott Stapley
2. Date of birth:	7/20/46
3. Place of birth:	San Francisco, California
4. Place of arrest:	San Francisco, California
5. Date of arrest:	6/2/85
6. Charge:	Illegal weapons, fugitive warrant
7. Convictions:	None
8. Sentence:	None
9. Current status:	Committed suicide while in the custody of the San Francisco police department

Sergeant Ronald L. McFall, a detective in the San Francisco police department, is reviewing a videotape labeled 'M Ladies Kathy/Brenda' that was found by a squad of police and Calaveras County Sheriff's Department officers at an abandoned cabin off Blue Mountain Road in Wisleyville, a rural, densely wooded section of northern California. The scratchy video depicts a young white woman with her hands cuffed behind her sitting in a chair in the living room of the mountain cabin. A voice off camera tells her: 'Mike owes us and unfortunately he can't pay. We're going to give you a choice, Kathy. It's probably the last choice we're going to give you. You can go along with us. You're going to cooperate and in approximately thirty days – if you want a date, you can write in your calendar the fifteenth of May. We will either drug you, blindfold you, or in some way or other make sure you don't know where you are and where you're going, and take you back to the city and let you go. And what you say at that time, I don't care. My name you don't know. His name is Charlie, but screw it. By then, hopefully, Mike will have disappeared gracefully. If you don't cooperate with us, we'll probably put a round through your head and take you out and bury you someplace. No witnesses. You will give us information on Mike. Basically Mike will move off in the horizon.

'While you're here you'll wash for us, you'll clean for us, you'll fuck for us. That's your choice in a nutshell. It's not much of a choice unless you have a death wish. You'll probably think worse things in the next few weeks.'

A balding, powerful-looking man with a black beard enters the frame. His name is Leonard Lake. He puts leg irons on the woman's feet and then takes her handcuffs off. He has her undress. She is very reluctant to take her pants off. An Asian male enters the frame and says: 'The piece is on the table.'

'Don't make it hard for her, Charlie,' the bearded man says.

The woman named Kathy Allen undresses and goes to shower with the Asian male. The tape cuts to a bedroom and shows the black-haired man on a bed with a woman sitting on his back. There is another cut in the tape and the black-bearded man appears, again in the bedroom with Kathy Allen, indicating that it is four days later and that he is upset with her for bending the hasps on a lock in her cell. She is strapped to the bed while he threatens her and takes still photos of her naked body. He tells her that they killed Mike and buried him. It will soon be her turn to join him.

Now the tape cuts to a second female named Brenda O'Connor. She, like Kathy Allen, is sitting fully clothed in a chair with her hands cuffed behind her back. Standing beside her, holding a knife in his hand, is an Asian male named Charles Ng. He uses the knife point to cut Brenda's shirt off and then slowly cuts her brassiere in two. In a voice-over, the sergeant hears Leonard Lake giving her the same instructions he gave to Kathy Allen. 'If you don't do what we tell you, we will tie you to the bed, rape you, shoot you in the head, and take you out and bury you.' Lake informs Brenda that he has taken her baby and placed it with a family in Fresno, and even though Brenda becomes hysterical and pleads with Lake and Ng for the return of her baby, the two of them only repeat their original instructions. The tape ends.

Sergeant McFall is horrified at what he sees: snuff videos that combine violent sex with vivid scenes of actual murders committed on camera, photo portraits of women in chains, snapshots of dead victims moments before their burial, and bags of human bones that had been boiled down into soup. The police found the scattered teeth of Lonnie Bond, Jr., the two-year-old child Brenda O'Connor pleaded with her captives to spare, and the remains of Kathy Allen and at least nineteen other people in shallow graves off Blue Mountain Road. The task force of San Francisco detectives and Calaveras County sheriff's officers also discovered a concrete bunker that served as a torture chamber and film studio for Lake's and Ng's videos. Police also found a 100-page personal journal entitled 'The Diary of Leonard Lake – 1984.'

'Leonard Lake,' the book begins, 'a name not seen or used much these days in my second year as a fugitive.

Mostly dull day-to-day routine – still with death in my pocket and fantasy my goal.' Among the fantasies and visions described in the 1984 journal and other diaries that were found in the Wisleyville cabin is Lake's plan for Operation Miranda. Hatched in the isolated hamlet of Miranda in the hills of northern California's Humboldt County, Operation Miranda was a plan for stockpiling bunkers with food and guns to survive a nuclear holocaust. Among the provisions Lake had planned for was a cadre of 'sex slaves' who would act out the fantasies of the survivalists and be kept locked in isolated chambers.

Lake viewed other people, particularly women, as if they were property. Human beings and inanimate objects were treated as one and the same. They existed to be placed at his disposal, his for the taking, used and then discarded. He was described by the police as a man who was without morality, who preyed primarily upon transient victims without a purpose to their own lives who were drawn into his vision by the promise of a better life. Some of his other victims responded to classified ads for the sale of video equipment, and still others came to his cabin to deliver cars that he had offered to buy. He would build a shelter, he promised himself in his diary, that would 'provide a facility for my sexual fantasies. It will provide physical security for myself and my passions. It will protect me from nuclear fallout. Tapes, photographs, and weapons will be hidden away.'

Lake's existence was a stringing together of private fantasies of earlier violent times when killing was a reflection of one's personal code of justice. 'He was interested in paganism and the Vikings,' said Cricket Balazs, his former wife. 'He could quote the Bible upside down, but he didn't believe in God. He was into Odin and Valhalla.' His interest in medieval legends and fascination with the folklore of early civilization and his own study of genetics led him to become a 'co-creator of the unicorns' at the Renaissance Pleasure Faire. He worked for the people who grafted the single horn onto the head of a goat that in 1984 became a part of the Barnum & Bailey circus, and he was the barker for the attraction at the West Coast Renaissance Faire. However, another employer of his at the Philo Motel remembers entering Lake's room and seeing a large pot boiling on the stove. When Lake lifted the pot, the employer saw the head of a single-horned goat cooking into a soup.

Leonard Lake died in a San Francisco hospital in 1985 after taking a cyanide capsule while in police custody. He was arrested on a weapons charge after interceding for Charles Ng, who was caught shoplifting a vise at South City Lumber in San Francsico. While the police were questioning Lake, who offered to pay for the vise, Ng disappeared. After a search of Lake's car revealed a handgun with a silencer, the police arrested him and began a search of the car's registration and the driver's license Lake was carrying. In the police station Lake asked for a glass of water and for paper and pencil so that he could write out a statement. While left alone, he took the cyanide, swallowed it with the water that the police brought him, and scribbled a note to Cricket Balazs, his ex-wife, that read, 'I love you. Please forgive me. I forgive you. Please tell Mama, Fern, and Patty I'm sorry.' Then he blurted out his true name to the police and slumped forward. He died four days later without ever regaining consciousness; during those four days the police had traced the car Lake was driving to missing car salesman Paul Cosner. Following leads found in the car and information from a records check on Lake's background, the police uncovered a warrant for his arrest on bail jumping and information about a rural cabin in Calaveras County. A search of that property on the day Lake died revealed the remains of eight people in unmarked graves, an underground bunker with prison cells, videotapes of torture and murder, and Leonard Lake's journals.

Who was Leonard Lake? the San Francisco newspapers asked. How did he manage to lure his victims into his power at his survivalist retreat in the mountains? And what drove him to butcher not only men and women but tiny children as well, leaving bags of their remains in a long trench just beyond the bunker? Lake's grandmother, the strict disciplinarian who raised him when he was younger, refused to provide any answers to the police or for this study. To this day she maintains that Lake was a good boy misled by his friends. Lake's mother, Gloria Ebeling, revealed that the Lake family was frightened that mental illness ran in every generation. Hers was a family of alcoholics, and she had married into Lake's father's family, also plagued by alcoholism in every generation.

When he was six, Lake's parents discovered they could no longer raise him. Out of money and with mounting debts, Lake's father sent the oldest boy to live with his grandparents. The old man, also an alcoholic, subjected the boy to a militaristic upbringing, teaching him unquestioning discipline and a fear of punishment. However, Lake still maintained contact with his parents, who were raising a younger son, Donald. Lake's father was extremely cold toward the children and disciplined Leonard whenever he could. Yet Donald, who became sickly and accident prone, was taken under his mother's wing. With every accident, every fall from a swing, and every concussion he received while a child, Donald was protected more and more. He himself became a type of victim and from the age of twelve, after experiencing a serious head trauma, he became an epileptic and suffered from severe seizures and body tremors. At the same time he developed an unusual cruelty to animals, began setting fires, and sexually assaulted both his sisters. Had he not eventually become one of Leonard Lake's murder victims, he might have developed into a serial murderer like his older brother.

Although Leonard Lake displayed early signs of compulsivity and obsession, his most violent tendencies didn't emerge until after his tours of duty as a Marine in Vietnam. As a child and later as an adolescent, he protected his grandmother and mother from his father's and grandfather's violence even though his mother showed a greater fondness for her younger child, Donald. Leonard also showed early signs of hypergraphia and obsessive attention to minute detail in his experiments as a youth with rats and mice. He traced the life cycle of mice from conception to death and kept detailed notes on the various stages of their development. He kept records of which pairs of mice bred from which litters, and was able to track genetic features through many successive generations of offspring. From these early experiments as a child, he became a self-taught geneticist.

Lake was also a compulsively clean person as a child. Perhaps because this commitment to inspection status was inculcated by his grandparents or perhaps, as in most obsessively clean people, cleaning and bathing are immediately self-gratifying, he took several showers a day, often washing his hands before beginning any new activity. The tapes found in his Wisleyville cabin also show that, before beginning the sex torture ritual with any of his victims, Lake forced them to take a shower.

Lake's fascination with photographs of nude women began while he was still a child. His mother explained that their family had always encouraged Lake to be proud of the nude body and to take pictures of girls, even his sisters and cousins. 'He took pictures of pretty young girls all of his life and kept them in picture albums like a hunter keeps a trophy.' His mother was not surprised that Lake made underground porno films and kept video records of his torture rituals. Even his wife, Cricket Balazs, served as a model for some of the custom sadomasochistic tapes he shot for clients. Balazs would use the customer's first name in the tapes as she acted out his sexual fantasies. Lake scripted, directed, and filmed these while, his ex-wife explains, he was probably making even weirder violence and pornography videos on the side.

Lake believed that he was the ultimate victim of women, and in his vision of a post-nuclear-holocaust civilization, women would live to serve him. In his survivalist compound he had elaborate shackling devices that he forced his female victims to wear while they submitted to his fantasies. He made them perform slave rituals just before having sex with them, and tortured them to increase the urgency of their submission. In his videos he portrays his victims as chained prisoners, struggling against their bonds and tortured by sadomasochistic devices that force them to scream out in pain, even when there is no pain at all.

His younger half sisters explained that Lake's delusions regarding the submission of women began while he was still an adolescent, even before he joined the Marines. His younger sister looked to Leonard to protect her from the violence and aggressiveness of Donald, Lake's younger brother, who by this time was periodically losing control of his behavior. Leonard solicited and received sexual favors. Lake began to equate success with domination over women and asserting himself against a world he believed to be hostile toward him. His expectations were high, but his accomplishments never measured up to those expectations. Finally, at age thirty-nine, after having been discharged from the Marines for emotional difficulties, he told his brother-in-law that he had only one final chance for financial success.

In his final years Lake drifted from community to community, always keeping in touch with his ex-wife, who acted as a sometime fence for the goods and credit cards he stole. Police believe that even before he settled in Wisleyville he had committed a series of murders in a similar survivalist compound at a place called the Mother Lode in Humboldt County, California. He had been arrested on weapons charges there, jumped bail, and fled to Calaveras County, where he was caught. At the Mother Lode, Lake had murdered his best friend from his Vietnam years, Charles Gunnar, and assumed his identity. It was also in Humboldt County that Leonard murdered his younger brother, Donald, who had visited him there in quest of money.

Lake lived in the Blue Mountain Road cabin under the identity of Charles Gunnar but frequently assumed the identities of his victims. His cache of documentation, found by the police in their search of the cabin and bunker, revealed stolen credit cards, drivers' licenses, and vehicle registrations for the cars Lake had taken from his victims. Even when he was arrested in the lumber store parking lot after Ng had tried to shoplift a bench vise, he maintained that he was Paul Cosner until just before he swallowed the cyanide capsule. He had also assumed the identities of victims Scott Stapley, who had tried to help Brenda O'Connor and her child, Lonnie Bond, Jr., flee Calaveras County, and Michael Carrol, whom Ng had befriended in a federal penitentiary, as he sold drugs and pornographic videos in the last months of his life.

In his final journal he described the unraveling of his life after he moved to the Blue Mountain road. His dreams of success had eluded him, he admitted to himself that his boasts about heroic deeds in Vietnam were all delusions, and the increasing number of victims he was burying in the trench behind his bunker only added to his unhappiness. By the time he was arrested in San Francisco, Lake had reached the final stage of the serial murderer syndrome: he realized that he had come to a dead end with nothing but his own misery to show for it. And he performed his final act of execution upon himself. He had prepared for it in advance by carrying the cyanide pill with him, and his final confession revealed to the police his true identity and his status as a fugitive on a weapons charge.

What Sergeant Ronald McFall couldn't see after he switched off Lake's final videotape was the support systems that had helped Lake survive during his last years. Even though he had espoused a survivalist creed and fantasized himself as an ancient warrior alone in a hostile world, he had been living off stolen property, money sent to him by his ex-wife and his mother, and money he made from pushing drugs, selling stolen goods, and producing porno films. Never had Lake been confronted with his own shortcomings, even though he was painfully aware of them. His mother, a licensed nurse who worked in a mental ward, had simply looked the other way, believing that her son was incapable of violence. His ex-wife participated in his pornographic movie business and delayed in revealing that Lake had been systematically murdering the people he was doing business with. And his grandmother to this day refuses to release any documents that will incriminate Lake in any way. His sister Fern, a registered nurse and the family member who was closest to Leonard, grieves because she too failed to intervene. Lake's life, therefore, was a series of missed opportunities for intervention, any one of which might have short-circuited the career of a killer who claimed people from all walks of everyday life as his victims of chance. Paul Cosner and the Dubs family were unfortunate enough to have done business with him. Brenda O'Connor, Lonnie Bond, and Scott Stapley were unfortunate enough to have been his neighbors in rural Wisleyville. And Kathy Allen was unfortunate enough to have been Mike Carrol's girlfriend. Each of these victims, and numerous others who had crossed Lake's path years earlier, was a sacrifice to the refusal of those who knew of Lake's propensity toward violence to intervene in his life.

As is consistently the case with the overwhelming majority of serial murderers, the people who knew Lake simply turned away and refused to acknowledge that he was a sick person preying on other people. He was allowed to go underground, to delude himself into living a survivalist's creed of independence in a hostile society, and to kill his own brother and later his best friend. To the police, who were amazed at the extent of Lake's destruction, the cases were closed when the victims were identified and evidence was collected against Charles Ng for extradition from Canada on a charge of murder in the first degree. However, what the videotapes retrieved from Calaveras County also showed was the dark side of a man who had taught grade school children in a local California 4-H Club, who donated his time as a volunteer firefighter in nearby Philo, and who worked for a company that provided free insulation to elderly people who couldn't afford to maintain their homes. He wrote that he had become increasingly sullen, withdrawn, and angry during the last years of his life and that, despite any attempts to integrate with society, there was a part of him that kept him on the outside until killing was his only response mechanism.

In Leonard Lake's case, we will never completely know what organic problems upset the fragile balance of his existence because his brain was destroyed after he was cremated. We are only left to guess and to extrapolate about Lake's problems from the problems of his brother Donald and of his father. The mystery of Leonard Lake has been best expressed by one of his neighbors at a commune he lived in a few years before the murders who called him 'the most pleasant unpleasant man I have ever known.'

11

Charles Manson and Serial Killers in Groups

1. Also known as: None
2. Date of birth: 11/12/34
3. Place of birth: Ashland, Kentucky
4. Place of arrest: Los Angeles County, California
5. Date of arrest: 10/12/70
6. Charge: Murder, conspiracy to commit murder
7. Convictions: Murder
8. Sentence: Death, commuted to life
9. Current status: San Quentin, awaiting parole

Although most serial killers are solitary individuals incapable of forming normal relationships with other people, many of them bond with one another from time to time and become 'killing pairs' or 'families.' Some, like Charles Manson, can attract many other people and form killing groups or cults in which the individual members feed one another's fantasies, sharing the episodic madness, and provide the group with most victims from the outside. While the Manson family is the most infamous of the serial or spree murder cults in the United States, killing pairs such as Leonard Lake and Charles Ng, the father/son team of Joseph and Michael Kallinger, the Kenneth Bianchi/Angelo Buono team of Hillside Stranglers, and the homosexual companions Henry Lee Lucas and Ottis Toole have also emerged as subjects of study in the 1980s. In each of these cases the fantasies of one killer were fed on the fantasies of the other: Toole killed when he became jealous of Lucas' liaisons with women; Joseph Kallinger convinced his son to accompany him on a killing spree that was ordered by God Himself; and Manson ordered the members of his family to dissolve the oppressive social order into a chaos within which frightened people ran helter-skelter amid their confusion.

No one killing group has captured the imagination of contemporary society more than the Manson family. Sociologists argued that the time was right for Manson. He was the product of all that was wrong in American society. An illegitimate child, he was passed like a football from relative to relative and finally to his mother, who brought him up in bars and on street corners where she hustled. Any sense of self-worth had long been beaten out of him by adults even before his early confrontations with the juvenile justice system. By the time he was twelve jails, courtrooms, and prisons had been his entire life. And after he had reached sixteen, he brags, there was nothing that the criminal justice system could do to him that he couldn't take. He had lost all fear. In his own words, he had been 'raped and savaged by society . . . fucked by attorneys and friends . . . beaten by guards.' There was no more pain left for Manson to bear. He had entered into his own twilight zone.

Enough books have been written about Manson and the family – both by observers and by family members themselves – that the Charles Manson story has become almost mythic in America. The cult status has reached the point where fourteen- and fifteen-year-old European adolescents who weren't even born when the Tate/ LaBianca murders were committed have turned Manson into a folk hero. His original music and lyrics were smuggled out of Vaca Ville Hospital for the criminally insane and turned up in an underground album published in France, and internationally children form their own counterculture families in imitation of the way Manson and the family lived in the late sixties and early seventies.

'I'm a mechanical man,' the lyrics of one of Manson's underground songs complain. He says that he has been used by society's institutions in thousands of ways. He has become a recreation of society, an entity that only fulfills the expectations and fears of others. In prison he complains that he is constantly on exhibit but thrives on the attention. To the psychologists who have diagnosed him, he was a subject, and to the press he was the living symbol of a culture gone wild. To the district attorney who prosecuted him and later wrote about him, Manson was an example of how justice was served. For others, he was the incarnation of the Devil at a time when some in our society needed a devil to be the magnet for their sins.

To his relatives who took him from his mother, he was the physical embodiment of their charity. They were fanatical in their religious practices and fulfilled their Christian duty by taking care of him. His grandmother dominated the household: she was stern and unwavering in her interpretation of God's plan, Manson says, and demanded that those under her roof abide by her practices. Drinking and smoking were forbidden in the house; the display of emotion toward the opposite sex was sinful. Facial makeup was evil and only used by women of the streets, and cursing or using the Lord's name in vain in front of her brought instant condemnation. As a child, Manson never saw any affectionate displays between his grandparents. His grandfather, who worked on the

Baltimore & Ohio Railroad for his entire life, was rebuked as a sinner every time he tried to comfort his wife with any warmth. He maintained harmony at home by acquiescing, letting his wife rule the house, and he became psychotic and died in an asylum from kidney failure brought on by alcoholism.

This was the family that Manson's mother, Kathy Maddox, fled from when she was fifteen and became, in Manson's words, a flower child of the thirties. She lived on the streets for a year before giving birth to her son, who was listed in the Cincinnati records as 'No Name Maddox.' He was, he claims, an outlaw from birth. The name Manson came from Bill Manson, the person Kathy Maddox lived with shortly after Charles's birth. 'He was not my real father,' Manson explains, but he did give him a name.

The parent/child bond between Charles Manson and his mother was tenuous at best. He was often handed off to relatives while his mother worked, and usually his grandmother would have to rescue the baby-sitter when Kathy Maddox failed to return from work on time to pick up the child. Once – and Manson admitted to his biographer Neal Emmons that this may be an apocryphal story – he was sold to a bar waitress for a pitcher of beer. As it was told to him, Kathy Maddox was out of cash and nursing her last beer at a local bar with her infant son on her lap. The waitress told Kathy that she envied her the child because she had always wanted a baby of her own. 'A pitcher of beer and he's yours,' Kathy reportedly said to the waitress, who disappeared and returned with the next pitcher. Kathy stayed in the bar long enough to finish off the pitcher, and two days later Manson's uncle, searching for the missing child, found him at the waitress' house. Manson doesn't vilify his mother for this incident but uses it to explain why he never conformed to any rules: he always felt he was an outsider being retrieved from strangers' homes at the last minute, left to wait with relatives, or traded for beer at a local bar. Whatever benefits the normal family provided to other children growing up at the tail end of the Depression were not benefits that Manson ever received. He was an outcast who grew up in emotional isolation even though he was surrounded by people.

Like Carlton Gary and Leonard Lake, Charles Manson was taken from his mother and placed with her relatives when he was still very young. After Kathy Maddox was arrested for armed robbery, convicted, and sentenced to the women's ward at Moundsville State Prison in West Virginia, six-year-old Charles was sent to his grandmother's house to live. He recalls that this was a time of strict discipline, thanking the Lord at mealtimes, long prayer sessions each night before bedtime, and of turning the other cheek to every aggressive act from another child. After a few weeks of being taught to be meek, he was sent to his aunt and uncle in Maychem, Virginia. There his uncle rebuked him for being a sissy and for turning the other cheek instead of standing his ground. Promising him that he would either learn to be a man or be treated like a girl, his uncle punished him for crying about being removed from his grandmother's house or about missing his mother. Finally, to bring his point to a conclusion, the uncle sent him to his first day of school dressed in girl's clothing. In a situation ironically identical to that of Henry Lee Lucas, Manson was teased by the other children until he flew into a rage and fought a violent series of battles with the other boys in the schoolyard. He remembers in his biography that dressing like a girl didn't really teach him how to become a man, but it taught him to fight hard and not give up.

Two years later Manson was back with his mother again. She was released from Moundsville at age twenty-three, and the two of them were reunited in an erratic relationship that took the pair around the Southeast. Kathy, who had now become a bisexual after her experiences in prison, fell into a variety of sexual relationships with both men and women, and Manson was a firsthand witness to all of them. He explains that he was routinely jealous of her male lovers and felt he was in competition with them. He liked it better when she had other lesbians sleeping with her because it made him feel less threatened. Years later Manson's feeling of security among lesbians would be translated to his support of sexual relationships among his own female family members in California.

Kathy Maddox soon found that she could not raise a growing boy. She would place him with moonshiner uncle Jess in Kentucky from time to time, where he acquired a taste for corn whiskey and any other type of alcohol, but was too often forced to take him back again. Finally, in desperation, Kathy placed him with the Order of Catholic Brothers, a stern, tightly disciplined monastic institution known as the Gibault Home for Boys in Terre Haute. Kathy had never told her son that this was to be his new home. It was only on the second day that the eight-year-old Charlie Manson realized that his mother was not coming back and that this was his new home.

Manson claims that infractions of the rules at Gibault were punished by severe beatings with a leather strap or wooden paddle. The few privileges that the brothers allowed the children were quickly suspended if a child violated any disciplinary rule. In Manson's case, because he was a bedwetter, he was often whipped while being promised that he was being taught how to control himself. In a phrase that echoes psychiatrist Alice Miller's description of an especially cruel form of parenting, the Christian brothers explained that they beat the children 'for their own good,' to make them mindful of their responsibilities, and to turn them into men. Manson rebelled against the rules at Gibault and was consistently whipped. He claims that he escaped twice to reunite himself with his mother, but she turned him over to the police, who brought him back to Gibault. Each time he was returned, his punishments became harsher. Finally Manson escaped again, but this time he headed for the city.

By the time he was twelve, he was living alone in a single-room-occupancy boardinghouse in Indianapolis, stealing money to live on, and scraping food out of garbage cans. He hustled money wherever he could, until the police caught him and discovered he was a minor. His landlord had also reported to the police that he believed a minor was living in the rooming house, and Manson was sent to Father Flanagan's Boys' Town. Manson remembers this as an environment that brought swift punishment for any disciplinary infraction. Manson's psychosis manifested itself yet again, and he escaped to avoid the incessant punishment. He stole a car, was convicted as a juvenile, and was sentenced to a city juvenile institution. When he proved too difficult for the city to manage, he was transferred to a state institution, the Indiana School for Boys at Plainfield.

He had made it to the big time by the age of fifteen. The inmates at the Indiana School were not wards of the state but real inmates who had been convicted of violent crimes. Again Manson claims that these guards maintained a level of brutality associated with many of the snake-pit institutions that were outlawed in the 1960s. However, this was 1949, and Manson was a fourteen-year-old inmate at the mercy of guards who today would be convicted as sexual offenders and child molesters. Manson first ran foul of a guard who used to incite the older boys to beat up the younger ones. He beat Manson on a regular basis and was fond of having the older inmates hold Manson down and beat him while the guard masturbated. He forced the boys to torture Manson until he cried out in pain, and at that point the guard was able to achieve orgasm. The same guard also incited the older inmates to gang-rape Manson on a regular basis, and he routinely forced Manson to drop his pants in the reform school yard while he asked him, 'Who's fucking you today, Manson?'

Manson claimed that there was yet another guard who singled him out for particular brutality. The guard had a penchant for a gauntlet-type game in which the inmates would line up in two rows about four feet apart. The inmate being punished was forced to run the gauntlet between the rows while the inmates on both sides hit him as hard as they could. If the boy was knocked down he would have to get up and run the gauntlet again. If one of the inmates in the rows didn't swing hard enough, *he* was forced to run the gauntlet. In this way the seeds of a love/hate ambivalence were sown in Manson and he learned never to trust anyone, particularly those closest to him. Also the head traumas he received from the almost daily beatings began to be manifested in body tics and facial spasms: the outward symptoms of temporal lobe damage and epileptic behavior that typifies episodically violent individuals.

The years at the Indiana School brutalized Manson far more than he realized until years later when he recalled his days there. He explains that, while most teenage children were living with their parents and going to high school, he was cleaning human excrement out of cells. While teenagers in the 1950s were dating and learning how to be successful, he was getting whipped by the sadistic guards and made to sit in raw effluent while his wounds were still bleeding. Deep brown scars like canals cut into his back are evident almost forty years later and bear witness to the state-sanctioned violence from which one of the most infamous of modern murderers emerged.

At sixteen, Charles Manson was finally successful in an escape attempt and made it all the way to California. There he stole cars, robbed grocery stores, and terrorized victims. He was arrested again and sentenced to the National Training School for Boys in Washington, D.C. It was there that he became institutionally hardened at last. He recalls that even the worst criminals at that federal penitentiary for juveniles had at least some family who visited them on a regular basis. Manson had no one. He was totally alone in the world and now a hardened institutionally trained criminal. He was living with older, tougher inmates who themselves were fully developed sociopaths, and he learned to survive. He developed sexual relationships with the other prisoners, and he performed the sexual acts that kept them satisfied.

In his cell at San Quentin where he is currently serving out the life sentence for instigating and masterminding the Tate/LaBianca killings, Manson is reflective about his experiences at the National Training School. It was here, he believes, that he finally accepted what it meant to be a lifetime criminal. The other boys he was serving time with knew no other way of life. They depended on the institution for a sense of identity and a sense of being. Manson grew to develop that dependence also. He grew to accept the brutality of the guards and the demeaning and dehumanizing nature of the prison system in general. And he came to understand that in the eyes of the institution human life meant very little. What mattered was that institutions thrived on order, and the maintenance of that order at the expense of the individual was the force that kept institutions functioning. Replace order with chaos, Manson discovered, and the institutions would crumble.

Manson spent more than three years in federal penal institutions where he learned to emulate not Joe DiMaggio or other celebrated sports heroes of the fifties establishment, but the mobsters and criminals who were getting away with committing crimes under the same system that had kept Manson in custody since he was twelve. Manson explains that since he was first placed in reform school he has been a victim of the system. If a guard didn't like the way he looked, Manson was beaten or tortured. If a guard wanted sexual favors from one of the juvenile inmates, he would threaten him with abuse by older inmates. It was a world of brutality ruled by the whim of the reform school guards and the older inmates who had kept Manson as a victim for seven years. Now, at nineteen, Manson was about to be set free legitimately for the first time in seven years.

In the very short time that Manson tasted freedom, he married and had a child, tried to go straight but was busted again for passing a bad cheque, was sent back to prison but was released again only to become a pimp. He was finally sent back to federal prison for seven more years for running an interstate vice ring and was released from the reformatory at Terminal Island in California in 1967. Like Henry Lee Lucas, Manson begged the authorities at Terminal Island not to release him. He said that he still needed help and required the structure of the institution in order to live. He was, in fact, terrified after his release. He refused to leave the island but sat on the dock until a passing truck driver talked him into accepting his own freedom. It was March 21, 1967, and Charles Manson had thirty-five dollars release money in his pocket, his parole officer's telephone number, an ex-wife who had taken his son Charlie and run away with a truck driver, and absolutely no vocational training that would have allowed him to survive on the outside for any appreciable period of time. He was thirty-two years old and had been in and out of prison or reform school continually for the past twenty years. The only skills he had developed were the survival skills of the functionally institutionalized, mechanisms that enabled him to navigate through the violence and capricious brutality that characterized the reform schools and juvenile institutions in the 1940s and '50s. But now it was the late 1960s, and for a newly emerged Charles Manson it was truly a brave new world.

Twenty-four hours after his release from Terminal Island, Manson found himself in the Haight-Ashbury section of San Francisco observing the free sex scene for the first time and taking a variety of drugs, including the powerful hallucinogen LSD. At a Grateful Dead concert at the Avalon Ballroom where Manson used the drug for the first time, he experienced what he later called a catharsis. In fact, the wildly colored strobe lights, the driving hard rock beat, the hallucinogen's effect on his central nervous system, and the press of hundreds of teenagers and young adults engaging in what had been for Manson a forbidden fruit sent him into a frenzy. Before he realized what was happening to him he had run out onto the dance floor and begun 'innovating' to the music of the Dead. He became the centre of attention, drawing applause from the other dancers as he spun out of control and with a complete loss of inhibition. He described it as a rebirth, as a complete transformation of his spirit, after which he collapsed and blacked out.

Whether this incident was a direct seizure or just a 'rumbling neurology,' as some neurologists call it, it was a reaction of Manson's central nervous system to the impact of the seizure-inducing strobes and the LSD. Several other epileptoid symptoms or indicators of limbic psychosis were also emerging at this time. They included wanderlust or incessant cruising from place to place, hypersexuality, hypervigilance, obsessive behaviour, and an extreme interest in religious or cult ceremony and quasi-religious totems. These are all symptoms of individuals who have sustained damage to the temporal lobe or suffer from a limbic brain psychosis. Ironically, these symptoms helped Manson integrate completely with the social groups he had found.

These were peripatetic individuals whom Manson had discovered: hippies, drug dealers, musicians, college students dropping in and out of courses on campuses across California, high-school-age runaways, and draft dodgers who had gone underground. There were also protesters and student activists among the groups at Haight-Ashbury who were traveling to keep one step ahead of the police or FBI. Manson quickly became a fixture in these groups. He could understand such people because many of them were social outcasts just like him. They were lawbreakers, fugitives, young people with neither homes nor families, and artists trying to live on the edge of society. Manson's need to cruise from place to place, to troll for new experiences, fitted into the wanderlust lifestyle his new friends had adopted. He was constantly on the move from the park to individual apartments to sleeping on the floor in strange rooms. He travelled among the cities of San Francisco, Reno, Los Angeles, and Sacramento, but always wound up back at Haight-Ashbury.

Manson was a paradox to many of the street people at the Haight. He was over thirty, yet he was like a child. His instincts were keenly survival oriented, and he had much to teach those he met about staying alive on the streets by hustling and stealing. He was a paranoid – his rejection by his mother and subsequent years in prison had taught him that much – who was able to function by reflecting what he thought other people wanted from him. He was skilled at interpreting the key elements of other people's personalities and determining what responses would put them at ease and make them allies, friends, or sexual partners. At the same time, many of the people he was meeting were not sophisticated, having only just run away from home or dropped out of school. Consequently,

Manson's skills found easy targets, and he was able to manipulate and control many of the people he met, especially the young girls. Psychologists have pointed out in their studies of empathy that this skill, when used by a trained therapist, can be quite useful in relating to a troubled patient. Yet in the hands of a person without integrity – and Manson was a sociopath – it can be a highly dangerous instrument. Manson was dangerous, and he used his abilities to assemble around him a family group he could control by changing his personality to reflect the needs of each individual member of the group. He was like a father figure to many of the girls who had run away from home, but he was also a sexual figure who seemed to know exactly what they wanted. Most importantly, Manson was not judgmental. He encouraged the street people to find their own meaning out of existence and not to accept the judgments of other people. This was a time of manic behavior for Manson; a time that he called 'helter-skelter.'

Yet he was pursuing a musical career and within a matter of months after his release he was making money by playing his music in San Francisco's tawdry bars, in the Tenderloin, and by playing his music on street corners for quarters. He also made some money by panhandling for loose change, hustling some of the young girls he'd met, and through dealing drugs. He was also engaged in outright burglary and in running con schemes on people who visited the Haight-Ashbury section to see the local color.

Soon his need to cruise had taken him beyond the Haight. Within six months after his release he had begun acquiring vans and school buses, trading up for larger and larger vehicles to support the increasingly larger groups that were assembling around him. In doing this, however, he was just like many other leaders of hippie groups and musical bands that were forming up in San Francisco in the late sixties. Many of the homeless had actually run away from privileged lifestyles and were able to drop back into their biological families to get money or items that could later be sold for cash on the outside. Manson was able to find these types of people and get them to finance his lifestyle.

Thus, by early 1969, he was considered a chic, strange figure among the dropout street people in San Francisco and Los Angeles. During the next year he lived with hundreds of different people and had sex with both young girls and boys: making them family members by becoming the reflection of their individual needs. He also became involved with several occult and Satanic groups, forming his own subgroups within them and seeking out new relationships and sexual partners. During this manic stage he kept pursuing his dream of a musical career and sought out those relationships that would help him achieve his dream.

His many faces and kinds of behavior quickly evolved into the chameleon-like demeanor of a traditional serial killer. Like a Bundy or a Long, he could blend into any group quickly so as not to appear the odd man out. Manson, however, raised it to a high art. He could actually become the significant other of any person he met by ferreting out those personality attributes the other person was seeking. As Susan Atkins, one of the members of his killing family, once described him, he was constantly changing from second to second, becoming anybody he wanted to be and putting on any face he had to put on at any given moment.

He was involved with at least three different occult groups during this period, which were heavily based on ritual bondage, sacrifice, and also murder. Manson moved easily from group to group. His contacts with movie personalities, rock musicians, and hangers-on at the major studios gained him entrance to a world of money, sex, power, and drugs. It was a world in which California money was able to buy any experience and pay handsomely those individuals who were able to provide it. At a time when people who were on the outside were thought to have more answers than those on the inside, Manson was clearly at his manic peak. It was as if he suddenly found himself in a position of power over all those who had been his abusers for the previous twenty years. And he used it to his advantage. He used his celebrity connections to circulate his music among movie studios; he was one of the religious consultants for a movie about Jesus Christ that was produced at Universal and he extracted a promise from the director to use his music in the motion picture's sound track; he became friends with Dennis Wilson of the Beach Boys and tried to get the group to play his music; and he became intimate with the children of the rich and famous who had fled from San Francisco to Los Angeles to drop out.

By 1969, Manson and his growing family were occupying the Spahn Movie Ranch from where the family began to act out Manson's dream of violence and helter-skelter. This former movie set with its ramshackle buildings reminiscent of a frontier town in the 1880s was owned by eighty-one-year-old George Spahn, who let the family live there. He was unaware of the murders they had committed. After the Tate/LaBianca murders, the family relocated to the Barker Ranch in Death Valley where they hid in anticipation of a police raid. The Tate/LaBianca murders and the subsequent murders and attempts on the lives of witnesses and people whom the prosecution brought forward to testify against the family were the final acts of rage that Manson inspired his family to commit. Throughout the ensuing trial of Manson, Tex Watson, Bruce Davis, Leslie Van Houten, Patricia Krenwinkle, Susan Atkins, and the rest of the family the media revealed that the pent-up rage that had been building in

Manson for twenty years was still far from having expended itself. In fact, 'the most dangerous man in America' had more rage than a lifetime could store.

Even before the final murders new evidence shows that Manson had become involved in underworld crime, murder-for-hire rings, and child pornography in his attempts to get his music published and to become a rock superstar. During the year preceding Tate/LaBianca, he was becoming more and more out of control and grandiose. He was taking drugs on a regular basis, having hallucinations, and participating in ceremonial rituals simulating human sacrifice and torture. And as these visions spilled over into his everyday life it became harder and harder for him to control his rage. As one of his acquaintances reported, one day Manson saw a father and daughter walking down a street in San Francisco. Uncontrollably, Manson lunged after them, knife in hand, and threatened to cut their throats. He later told a friend that he had a homicidal rage caused by an inflamed tooth that had secreted poison into his brain. This is only one example of the explosiveness of his behavior. California jurisdictions cite many more instances in which Manson and his family might be responsible for more than thirty-five murders throughout the northern part of the state.

In prison now and still applying for parole at every chance he gets, Manson exhibits much of the paranoia and frenetic behavior that characterized him twenty years ago. He paces like a trapped animal and constantly shifts his personality according to what he believes the interviewer wants to see. He maintains that he has been the ultimate victim of society and that his helter-skelter vision of Armageddon was an almost natural response to the life that was forced upon him. Even though most of his medical records are officially sealed, it is clear that he has suffered some brain damage from the repeated head traumas. His history of hallucinations and episodic delusions points to a form of limbic psychosis, and his history of drug and alcohol abuse indicates another pattern of brain dysfunction. Analysis of his hair documents a lifelong chemical imbalance. An examination of Manson's letters shows that he is dyslexic and more than likely learning disabled as well. Yet the power he derived from being at the centre of his family and his hypersexuality with partners of both sexes are evidence of his mastery of some form of socialization, even if it is only to control others. And at only fifty-two years of age, it is also clear that his story is not yet finished.

The Unifying Patterns of a Serial Killer

12

The New Criminologists

When Dr. Dorothy Otnow Lewis evaluated convicted serial killer Bobby Joe Long she was most influenced by his reports of hypersexuality immediately following his motorcycle accident in 1974. While still in his cast, Long began suffering from an overwhelming sex drive and was masturbating at least five times a day. His compulsion to have intercourse with women escalated, and within a few years after the accident he had become the notorious Classified Ads Rapist who preyed on housewives he had contacted through 'for sale' ads they placed in the local Fort Lauderdale papers. Just a few years later Long had become a rapist murderer who preyed on the barflies along the strip just outside North Tampa.

Although Long had reported significant neurological symptoms to his doctors at the time of the accident, his symptoms had gone undiagnosed until Dr. Lewis suggested that Long had probably incurred serious damage to the limbic region of the brain as a result of his motorcycle accident. That damage, in addition to damage from at least three previous head traumas, the severe hypogonadal condition in childhood when he grew breasts, and Long's deep hatred of women that had started with his mother and continued with his wife, all combined to push

Bobby Joe Long, almost like a watermelon seed, into committing murders that repelled him and that he now claims he never wanted to commit.

Was any one aspect of Long's particular syndrome the trigger that unleashed the hatred that had been building in him for thirty years? Do all people who sustain head traumas become murderers? Do all people who hate women become murderers? Do all people who sustain chronic physical abuse as children become murderers? As Long's attorney, Ellis Rubin, and the Florida state prosecutor argued the issues of culpability and mental competence, these questions bobbed to the surface of the debate. And if a biopsychosocial syndrome exists that compels individuals against their conscious will to commit series of murders, both Bobby Long's and Carlton Gary's lawyers have asked the state courts, who is competent to evaluate the medical history of the defendants?

Most traditional psychiatric evaluations only evaluate whether the defendant was competent to judge his own actions at the time of the murder and whether the defendant is competent to stand trial, knowingly participate in his own legal defense, and knowingly exercise his constitutional rights. And therefore most traditional psychiatrists and psychologists are limited in the types of evaluations they submit to the court. They determine whether the defendant knew what he was doing at the time and whether the defendant understands the nature and seriousness of the charges against him. Furthermore, they try to determine whether the defendant understands that he is being tried for a crime. Simply put, in most cases if the defendant knows where he is and what he has done, the court psychiatrists report that he is competent to stand trial and it is up to the defense to provide their own evaluation, proving that the defendant is not competent. For most defendants, who cannot afford to hire sophisticated psychiatric consultants, an insanity defense is just too expensive. For most indigent defendants, it is out of the question. It is also difficult to convince the average jury of the technical aspects required to prove an insanity defense, and as a result there is a higher probability that defendants pleading insanity will be convicted and receive the death penalty.

But traditional insanity defenses notwithstanding, because a typical psychological evaluation for the court only deals with mental competency at the time of the crime and the time of the trial, the symptoms that underlie the serial murderer syndrome usually fall outside of a traditional psychiatrist's expertise. This is why, in Dorothy Lewis' evaluation of Bobby Joe Long, she was careful to incorporate a neurological and organic as well as a psychiatric basis for her recommendation that a full workup be completed on the subject as quickly as possible.

Dorothy Lewis, a research psychiatrist at New York University, belongs to a new category of neuropsychiatric specialists who go much further in linking organic, psychiatric, and social symptoms with one another than other specialists have gone in the past. Their approach takes into account the organic, psychological, social, and environmental factors that combine to shape an individual's behavior. Ultimately, the theories they have developed through working with convicted serial murderers will become the basis for a methodology of predicting the propensity for violence in individuals. In fact, even now, according to Vernon Mark of Harvard, scientists using theories that link organic, psychological, social, and environmental factors of criminal behavior are able to predict dangerousness in individuals with an accuracy rate of ninety percent.

The type of research conducted by the new criminologists has isolated whole new areas of discovery in which seemingly insignificant symptoms and soft signs points to chemical imbalances, brain traumas, epileptoid behaviour, and other neurological dysfunctions that can result in extraordinary levels of violence. Foremost among the new researchers has been Dr. Vernon Mark, retired chief of neurosurgery at Boston General Hospital, who has demonstrated a positive relationship between episodic aggressive behavior and certain forms of psychomotor epilepsy – a form of temporal lobe epilepsy in which sufferers can act in a confused, bewildered, and fugue state for hours or even days. Damage to the temporal lobe can cause hair-trigger violent reactions against persons perceived as threats, and people with or without temporal lobe damage resulting in repeated epileptic seizures are often suicidal. This form of epileptoid behavior, although rare in the general population, is common among serial killers and criminals who commit violence according to a definable cycle.

Most forms of epileptic attacks begin with an aura phase in which the subject experiences a form of hyperstimulation. Among serial killers, this aura phase immediately precedes the onset of hallucinations or fantasies in which the murderer acts out the complete crime in his mind with a victim of his own creation. It is then, during the trolling phase, that he seeks to replace the victim of his own creation with a real person. Vernon Mark's investigations have revealed that the relationship between psychomotor or limbic epilepsy and severe mental disorders is profound and has a long history in the literature of psychology. In fact, during the seizure state, the limbic epileptic may have symptoms that are virtually indistinguishable from those of paranoid psychosis. Between seizures, however, the person can be completely camouflaged by a cloak of normalcy. Hence the nature of episodic fantasies, delusions, hallucinations, and violence. As in the case of Henry Lee Lucas, specifically, irritative lesions in or near the limbic cortex give rise to epileptoid discharges accompanied by emotional feelings of terror, fear, strangeness, and unreality (the aura phase), sadness, the need for emotional isolation, and feelings of a paranoid nature. As in the cases of Gary Schaefer and Carlton Gary, distortions of actual perception also occur.

Dorothy Lewis' evaluation of Bobby Joe Long focused particularly on the large number of successive head traumas he suffered as indicators of extensive damage to his temporal lobe. This portion of the brain is peculiarly vulnerable to injury despite its seemingly well-protected site low in the skull. The skull bone at this point is thinnest and puncture wounds can penetrate the brain with relatively little force. Even in the more common traumas from blunt injuries in which large areas of the brain are affected, the temporal lobe usually suffers the worst damage. Alternatively, permanent lesions on the temporal lobe can result from impact contusions to the side of the head – such as the type usually received from blows to the head – and can cause forms of amnesia and epileptic seizures. Damage can also result from internal pressure and from respiratory obstruction associated with other injuries or accidents, or from other forms of epilepsy in which the air passageway is blocked.

In Bobby Joe Long's case, physiological, behavioral, and experiential factors contributed to his extreme violence. The type of glandular disorder that produces gender misidentification puts Long in a possible high-risk group for confrontation with the criminal justice system. That risk was compounded exponentially by Long's head injuries, resulting in lesions to his temporal lobe and a loss of control over his violent impulses. His upbringing, in which he was dominated by his mother, who moved him from place to place and who shared a bed with him, made him more than distrustful of women and lit a flame of hostility that has continued to burn. His marriage to Cindy, based as it was on her manipulativeness, only fueled the fire and created a personality disorder in which manipulative women became Long's enemies. Finally, his near fatal motorcycle accident, which caused extensive brain damage, removed the last vestiges of neurological control over his behavior. Although he was aware of what he was doing and was consciously opposed to his actions, he was unable to stop himself from committing more than fifty rapes and nine murders. Fear of punishment kept him from seeking professional help during the course of his career, although he realized that he was unable to control his almost reflex impulses. In the end he finally put a stop to his career by letting one of his victims go free and simply waiting for the police to catch him.

Dr. Lewis' studies are still in their infancy and need to be replicated before any definitive predictions can be made regarding delinquent children in general. The early results do suggest, however, the existence of a critical constellation of factors that may result in an adult whose life is at risk of being marked by episodes of aggressive and violent criminal acts. Perhaps in doing so Dr. Lewis and these experts will reduce this constellation of factors to a prescription for violence. First, having a seriously psychiatrically impaired mother – as had Henry Lee Lucas – is likely to contribute to a child's violent behavior in several ways. The fact that the mother has been hospitalized for a psychiatric disorder from time to time suggests that the child has experienced a sense of loss, a pervasively inconsistent home life, and erratic nurturing. Moreover, a seriously disturbed mother is likely to have been emotionally unavailable even when physically present. And in addition to their own psychopathology, more than sixty percent of the mothers of homicidally aggressive children in Dorothy Lewis' study had married violent, physically assaultive men. Thus the households in which the children were raised were filled with violence. In Henry Lee Lucas' own biosocial history, even though his father had been incapacitated by the loss of his legs, Viola Lucas' pimp, Bernie, abused Henry and beat him regularly.

Thus, homicidally aggressive children had mothers who were either psychotic or who were hospitalized for psychotic behavior, aggressive and assaultive fathers who themselves behaved homicidally toward the child, some form of neurological dysfunction that caused at least one seizure or other neurological dysfunction and suicidal feelings brought on by their perception of the hopelessness of their own plight. The neurological dysfunction more often than not was the result of physical injury either sustained accidentally, as in the case of Bobby Joe Long, or deliberately, as in the case of Henry Lee Lucas.

There are other types of head trauma that influence behavior as well, and these result from events that can affect the developing fetus. The fetus may be malnourished, resulting in inadequate or incomplete development of the brain; it may be injured as a result of trauma to the mother; and it may suffer from oxygen deprivation as a result of a difficult birth. Any of these events may so affect the fetal brain that the child's development is compromised. Antisocial or even episodically violent behavior is certainly possible in cases such as these.

Pointers to this critical mass of symptoms are more obvious indicators that might readily come to the attention of juvenile investigators, court officers, doctors, or school guidance counselors. Among these are visual or auditory hallucinations, loose or illogical thought patterns, forms of paranoid or hypergrandiose delusions, profound feelings of isolation or withdrawal, episodic periods of deep sadness and crying, bedwetting, sleepwalking, suicidal fantasies or even attempts at jumping from windows or trying to stab oneself, series of life-threatening assaults on other children either with deadly objects or by choking, extreme cruelty to animals, deviant sexual behavior such as exposure of genitalia or molestation of younger family members, and fire starting in an attempt to inflict injury. These signs in children establish the prima facie criteria for several kinds of diagnosis of mental disorder, and if remedial measures are instituted when the behavior first becomes apparent, the development of a criminal personality in adult life may be short-circuited by intensive psychiatric and physiological treatment and by the intervention of state agencies to stabilize the child's environment.

Research suggests that these criteria are more than just a grab bag of random behavioral abnormalities: they point to an amalgamation of physiological, social, and emotional disorders that can only be diagnosed by a specialist capable of interpreting firsthand complex neurological data, conducting an in-depth psychological evaluation of the child and the child's immediate family, and interpreting the social conditions that comprise the child's environment. Most court-appointed diagnosticians, however, tend to assume that juvenile criminals are simply bad rather than sick, even though the medical, social, and psychological conditions point to other explanations. When the court-appointed diagnostician works with an adult serial killer, rarely does empathy between the accused and the diagnostician emerge because the diagnosis is tainted by the legal responsibility to declare the person either competent or incompetent to stand trial. This is a quick and dirty diagnosis that relates only to the patient's ability to remember the date, the name of the current President of the United States, his remembrance of the crime, and his ability to judge whether he committed a wrongful act. Many adult serial killers compulsively admit their guilt and admit that they have committed a wrongful act. Thus research into the paradigm of physiological, psychological, social and experiential causes of adult episodically violent behavior will have far-reaching consequences not only for the way juvenile criminals are treated by the justice system but also for the way serial killers are diagnosed by the court.

Dr. Jan Volavka of the New York University Medical Center is another researcher who is examining the importance of diagnosing psychomotor epilepsy in episodically violent criminals. Volavka has shown that the telltale vertical spike that interrupts the EEG brain-wave patterns of violent felons indicates a spontaneous and powerful uncontrollable discharge of electricity deep within the limbic brain. In many of his patients, the high-voltage spike is so great that it makes the stylus of the EEG shoot across the chart as if it were recording the impact of a bullet. These seizures originate in the most primitive area of the brain and are so deep that routine EEGs don't pick them up. The damaged limbic area where control over the primary emotions of fear and rage is exercised is repeatedly damaged by these discharges and becomes dysfunctional, unable to curtail displays of violence before they reach the surface. Volavka believes that the deep EEG spikes which indicate this type of epilepsy can be used as a litmus test for potentially violent individuals who have previously displayed extreme antisocial behavior or have regular episodes of inappropriate responses to external stimuli.

The only psychiatrist to exclusively study the serial killer, Dr. Helen Morrison of Chicago, attributes significant importance to the role played by an organic dysfunction deep within the primitive brain. In her work with serial murderers John Gacy, Ted Bundy, Richard Macik, and the 'Yorkshire Ripper' in Great Britain, Dr. Morrison has focused her attention on the activity of the hypothalamus – the emotional voltage regulator of the brain –

as an indicator of a person's inability to control primitive, violent impulses. Experiments with monkeys and lower animals over the past fifty years have shown that the hypothalamic region forms the major component of an emotional circuit that helps sustain life functions and automatically regulates the animal's defence systems through the emotions of fear and rage. Because the hypothalamus regulates the hormonal system, including the functions of the vital adrenal and thyroid glands, it is the fulcrum point of the body's basic emotional responses to all kinds of stimuli.

Damage to the hypothalamus, whether as a result of repeated head traumas or as a birth defect, can destabilize the hormonal system and short-circuit the brain's ability to measure emotional and physical responses to real or perceived threats. And because the hormonal system is largely cybernetic, requiring little direct conscious intervention on the part of the individual to monitor its emotional fluctuations, and also because critical hormonal responses to life-threatening situations are channeled through the autonomic nervous system, the higher brain has only limited control over the hypothalamic-hormonal functions. And whatever control it can exercise can be brought about only through training. An example of this emotional short-circuiting is a person's reaction when startled by the sudden or unexpected appearance of a family member or friend. Although the startled person recognizes the familiar face and has consciously turned off any emotion of fear, the unexpectedness of the appearance has sent a primary message along the neural pathways of the hypothalamus. The response – a scream or a jump – is primal and never reaches the level of conscious recognition. The startled person can be as startled by the response as he or she is by the appearance of the other person. Suddenly, the startled person screams, even after he has recognized the face of a friend.

Dr. Morrison carries this basic stimulus-response model to a much more complex level in her description of what takes place within the primitive neural circuits of the serial murderer. First, she suggests, the hypothalamus gradually asserts control over the primal emotions as the individual matures. Thus children and adolescents often have marked emotional swings resulting from their perceptions of the outside world and the presence or absence of certain hormones in the bloodstream. As the individual grows and his brain develops, the higher cerebral functions impose a fixed order over the raw perceptions based on experience and the emotional swings are not nearly so great. In homes where there is a strong family structure and both parents deal with the child in a mature and supportive environment, the maturing individual learns from his parents how to react to a variety of situations and that helps him develop the initial patterns he will build on throughout his life. In homes where one parent is particularly strong, that parent's patterns will be used as either a positive or negative model for the growing child, depending upon the sex of the parent and child and the child's relationship with the parent. In homes where both parents are weak or there is no parent support, the child can be left largely to his own devices and may or may not be able to exercise control over his primal emotions.

Similarly, if the child is beaten or chronically malnourished or if the fetus is injured in some way, the hypothalamus may become damaged or may never develop to maturity. In this scenario, the emotional regulator itself is flawed and never functions as properly as it should. The individual may always react as a child does to threats and strike out violently at any perceived challenge, or the hypothalamus itself may be starved because of inadequate nutrition. Measuring the electrical discharges within the hypothalamus and the chemistry of the hormonal system is one indicator of organic dysfunction deep within the brain. Outward signs such as chemical imbalances or severe sleep disorders that produce confusional behavior and hallucinations are other indicators.

Many of the serial killers whom Dr. Morrison has studied have evidenced disorders of the hypothalamus that range from distorted sleep patterns to critical hormone imbalances. In our triad of the key factors of organic dysfunctions, psychopathological behavior, and social deprivation that underlie the syndrome of serial murderers, disorders of the hypothalamus, the temporal lobe, or the limbic brain have been at the crux of the symptoms. And depending upon the individual's upbringing and the way he led his adult life, the person eventually reached a level of dangerousness that translated itself into episodic crime. At the very least, individuals with damaged hypothalamuses are mortally sad to the point of suicide, and usually become their own worst enemies. Many of these people sink deeper into an irretrievable depression, even though they may never actually assault another person. These are the other victims of hypothalamic disorders whose stories never reach the front pages because they have succumbed to their own grief privately and silently.

Dr. James Prescott, a neuropsychologist, has also developed a 'deep brain dysfunction' theory to explain violent antisocial behavior in people. In comparative studies of chronically and episodically psychotic individuals, Prescott claims to have isolated the septal region of the midbrain, adjacent to the hypthalamus, as one of the controlling centres of emotion and awareness of the external world. Schizophrenics, he points out, and psychotics who suffer only from episodic hallucinations are unable to integrate feelings of pleasure and other emotions into their senses of self. He argues that, because of a dysfunction in the deep primitive brain, the individual is unable to perceive the boundaries of the self: the border between the person and the rest of the world. The person seems to meander in a semidream state, experiencing hallucinations or delusions as if he were a healthy person on the very edge of sleep. Because the psychotic has little or no self-image and is completely devoid of a sense of himself as a separate entity, his own thoughts seem to be coming from outside. As a result, feelings and sensations seem to come from outside rather than from his own mind. This leaves him deficient in emotional expression and he is characterized by a proneness to violence, rage, and excessive fear. In a healthy, integrated person, these primitive fear reactions are controlled by an ability to experience pleasurable sensations. In the psychotic person, no such balance exists, and the person is tossed about by the external pressures of fear and violence.

Prescott's experiments have shown that in psychotic individuals this syndrome is directly related to lesions in the septal region of the brain which are indicated by septal 'deep spikes' on an EEG – another litmus test for a predisposition to violent behavior. Tests on both humans and monkeys have shown that electrical stimulation of the septal region can both remedy and induce septal deep spiking and consequent violent or hallucinatory behavior. Moreover, because the episodically psychotic human subject has no basis on which to form judgments about the nature of his hallucinatory experiences, they become another level of reality, as if they were a consciousness within a consciousness. Thus, Carlton Gary's claims that another person committed the Wynnton murders might be real experiences for him and not just a story that he told to the police to exonerate himself from guilt.

Prescott and his colleagues have suggested that a

combination of early sensory deprivation in the form of tactile stimulation from the parents and maternal intimacy may be one cause of the dysfunction of the septal region. The types of visceral responses in newborns to the sound of the human voice and to human touch indicate that the infant is 'stimulus ready,' and this extreme receptivity to touch and voice is critical for the development of parts of the neurological system. Many neurological theoreticians argue that early vocal and tactile stimuli establish the border line between 'self' and 'nonself' for the infant. Without this distinction, they claim, the child never adequately makes the self and nonself distinction, which results in a severe psychosis. If Prescott is correct, a physiological correlation to this early developmental progress point is found in the brain's septal region, a portion of the emotional regulation circuitry. The psychological symptoms have physiological correlates in the midbrain which can be stimulated and measured.

Prescott's experiments on chimps have reinforced his theory that sensory deprivation retards the development in the midbrain and results in chronic or episodic psychosis-like symptoms. At first both the sensory-deprived human and the simian newborns go into states of deep, almost autistic, withdrawal. Subsequently they become violent and strike out at those around them. The violence is inappropriate in that it has no relationship to the nature of the actual stimulation. Chimps who have been living in a state of sensory isolation will begin attacking other members of their troop savagely while they are still very young. Ultimately they will turn their violence upon themselves, nip and scratch at their own flesh, beat themselves, and later they will bludgeon their heads against the walls of their cages in a final act of self-destruction. Unless sedated or restrained, they will actually commit suicide.

Most of the serial killers whose careers have been documented reported that they were either separated from one or both parents at an early age or otherwise deprived of the mother's direct emotional involvement. Even when the mother was in very close proximity, as in the case of Bobby Joe Long where both mother and son slept in the same bed until he was twelve years old, because she was working at night and usually never around even on her days off, Long felt deprived of maternal affection. He reported that he often felt in competition with his mother's boyfriends for her attention and often begged her to stay home with him on her nights off. Bobby Joe Long's claimed distant cousin, Henry Lee Lucas, was also deprived of his mother's attention and affection as a young child. In Lucas' case, he received negative attention from his mother, who habitually beat him with lethal weapons, inducing a coma on at least one occasion. Lucas eventually killed his mother with a knife years later. The same pattern of maternal deprivation or control was a factor in Carlton Gary's upbringing as it was for cult murderer Charles Manson and killers Richard Ramirez and Ted Bundy.

Much to the chagrin of behavioral psychologists, a growing number of researchers believe that the predisposition to criminal violence is largely congenital. Whether or not the individual in fact actually becomes a serial murderer in adult life may be a factor of his upbringing and later socialization, but the predisposition to violence and crime, some researchers believe, is already determined at conception or in utero. Among these researchers is C. Robert Cloninger, a psychiatrist at the University of Washington School of Medicine whose research on adoptees has shown that individuals whose biological parents are criminals are four times more likely to become criminals than individuals whose biological parents are not criminals. Although Cloninger has not definitively isolated the actual genes that predispose one to criminal tendencies, he believes that certain types of brain dysfunctions are congenital, as are birth defects in the neurological or hormonal systems. Scientists now know that thyroid dysfunctions tend to run in families as do heart disease, diabetes, and predispositions to cancer. Parents with congenital learning disabilities tend to have children who are predisposed to those disabilities as well.

Cloninger's research has been supported by the results of a major study on twins at the University of Minnesota in which siblings who were raised apart and had never met were found to have similar personality traits, intelligence levels, allergies, and levels of ambition. They shared these traits despite the fact that they were reared in entirely different family environments. Even traits such as reactions to stress and leadership seem to be influenced primarily by inheritance rather than by social conditioning, though conditioning can either reinforce or undermine those traits. What is emerging from the Minnesota study is an understanding that heredity and not environment plays the most important role in determining those basic traits that define an individual's personality, even among normal nonneurotic individuals. In cases where parents had criminally deviant personalities and serious psychophysiological disorders, the children manifested similar if not identical characteristics.

Dr. Sarnoff Mednick at USC also supports these findings with his own independent research on Danish male adoptees. He found that among those adoptees twenty percent of those whose parents were property criminals also became criminals. If both the biological and adoptive parents were criminals, the figure rose to twenty-four percent. Other researchers such as Philip Firestone and Susan Peters found that obvious physical and congenital defects such as webbed fingers, attached ear lobes, elongated limbs, and other abnormalities are significant in the etiology of schizophrenic behavior. It is suggested that in instances where an individual displays ten to fifteen obvious physical abnormalities there is a strong likelihood that he or she has experienced birth defects and neurological damage. When there are five or more physical abnormalities, an individual should strongly consider neuropsychiatric and neurological testing. Among the features that Mednick points to – and which are displayed by Carlton Gary – are:

1. Long second or small toe
2. Pterodactyloid fingers that are long and clawlike
3. Webbed fingers
4. Ear lobes that are connected to the side of the head
5. Bulbous or ball-like extensions on the tips of the fingers

Abnormal EEG readings are especially important indicators of genetic abnormality because they point to progressively more critical symptoms as the individual develops. Mednick discovered that boys who later became delinquents registered alpha waves on their EEGs at a lower frequency, eight or nine per second, than the higher normal frequency of from ten to twelve per second. In this case, the alpha wave deviation, although an indicator of serious organic dysfunction in the brain, only resulted in a violent personality when reinforced by events in the environment. Among serial murderers, this type of dysfunction can be triggered by the highly unstable situation that results when there is tension between the child and his difficult parents. Because many serial murderers were raised by adoptive parents or caretakers both within and outside of their biological parents' families, the stage for this type of tension was set while the individual was still a very young child. In the case of Carlton Gary, who probably was already at high risk because of the significant number of congenital defects, the inherent tension between him and his grandmother who raised him caused him to leave the home environment while still a young child to search for other relatives who could care for him. His trip to his uncle's military base is just one of the sojourns the young Carlton Gary took. Others involved trips to visit his mother in Florida and other relatives. He became self-sufficient as a child to a point well beyond criminal deviance. And as an adult his inability to form permanent relationships with people combined with his instinctive distrust of society and its institutions turned him into a sociopath long before he began his skein of serial murders in Wynnton.

Sarnoff Mednick suggests that, once the congenital predisposition toward episodic violence is established, the home environment can act as a matrix, which would explain why every person with congenital defects doesn't automatically become a violent criminal. Mednick looks for a combination of genetic and environmental factors in the individual, such as the institutionalization of one or both parents or the conviction of one or both parents for criminally violent acts. He has found that, in homes where the predisposed child had a mother who was institutionalized for alcoholism or for psychotic behavior, it was likely that the child would become withdrawn as well as violent, unable to relate to other people socially. In homes where the father was criminally violent, the child himself became a criminally violent individual, even if there had been no genetic predisposition to violent behavior. Finally, in those homes where the child had a congenital neurological defect and was raised by parents who were either criminals themselves or who committed violent acts, especially upon the child, it is logical to assume that the child could emerge as an episodically violent criminal, and possibly a serial murderer.

Environmental factors also have an impact upon the physiology of the neurological system, especially the development of the brain in growing children. The backgrounds of Henry Lee Lucas and Bobby Joe Long demonstrate that head traumas can cause severe damage to areas of the brain that control behavior and emotion. Much the same can be said for prolonged malnutrition and exposure to environmental toxins. Pioneering this research are Diane Fishbein and Robert Thatcher, both of whom are at the Unversity of Maryland School of Medicine. In their study of the environmental backgrounds of maladaptive behavior they have focused specifically on the types of factors that place the individual at high risk of eventual contact with the criminal justice system. In other words, they are evaluating those factors that disrupt behavior in such a way that the individual, most often a juvenile, commits a criminal antisocial act. They suggest that combinations of biological factors such as head traumas, exposure to environmental toxins, the abuse of alcohol or drugs, the lack of prenatal care, and the adequacy of nutrition all affect the behavior of the individual. And what is most interesting for our purposes is that the most common site for the interaction of all these variables is the brain.

Thatcher and Fishbein cite several reports that suggest that diets high in refined carbohydrates such as white flour and white sugar, cakes, candies, potato chips, and the like can create or aggravate behavioral·abnormalities and learning disabilities. Among the types of antisocial behaviour that are stimulated by inadequate nutrition are mood swings from depression to euphoria, violence, irrationality, hyperactivity, inappropriate aggressiveness, and impaired cognitive function. The chronic ingestion of refined carbohydrates, in many instances, can also precipitate a condition known as hypoglycemia or low blood glucose, resulting in seriously impaired mental functions. Because glucose serves as the brain's primary source of fuel, any diet that causes wide swings in the blood glucose level affects the brain's ability to function. Therefore, the scientists suggest, aggressive or even criminally antisocial behavior in children can be treated by diet if the child is diagnosed to be chronically malnourished or hypoglycemic.

Fishbein and Thatcher also identify trace mineral elements as another aspect of the nutritional status that can influence brain functioning and behavior. These trace elements include minerals essential for the functioning of the body such as zinc, calcium, magnesium, selenium, chromium, iron, and potassium. Zinc and iron are especially important in this category because, if they are sufficiently lacking in the diet, severe behavior problems may occur and emotional stability is compromised. Iron plays a role in the ability of the blood to carry oxygen and glucose to the brain and affects the individual's overall resiliency. Zinc is directly related to the function of the hormonal system and plays a role in the stabilization of emotions and the brain's rational control over the drives of sex and rage.

The researchers from Maryland also focus their studies on other trace elements that are not nutritional but are toxic in certain concentrations and that impair brain functioning and cognitive ability and impede socially adaptive behavior. These trace substances are lead, cadmium, arsenic, aluminum, and mercury and they regularly occur in the environment. Human beings don't have a mechanism for directly excreting these substances in large amounts, and when exposure to them is significant, they can build up large concentrations in the body tissue and directly influence behavior. When they accumulate in larger concentrations, they begin to impair other neurological functions such as memory and cognition. If the individual is exposed to toxins in the foods he ingests daily, his behavior can become chronically maladaptive until the toxins are removed from his environment. His behavior will abruptly begin to shift back to a more normal state.

One significant study conducted by Thatcher revealed an important relationship between the amount of lead and cadmium concentrations in the hair of children from a school in eastern Maryland and their intelligence levels and school achievement. The higher the concentrations of lead or cadmium, the lower the performance of the individual in any cognitive exercises. What was most interesting about these studies was that, even before the loss of muscular control and the impairment of motor functions, the individual who had higher than average concentrations of lead or cadmium experienced a significant degree of cognitive impairment as the only symptom of poisoning. And what is true for the schoolchildren in the Maryland study is also true for the serial killers whom Dr. William Walsh has studied for this book.

Walsh, a chemist at the Health Research Institute near Chicago, has been doing research on chemical imbalances in violent individuals for ten years. He has developed a novel classification method for violent criminals based on distinctive patterns of certain elements in hair tissue. These patterns were first discovered during a controlled sibling experiment involving extremely delinquent, violent children and brothers who were 'all-American boys' with no history of behavioral problems. The violent siblings were found to possess abnormal trace element patterns that fell into two major categories. The Type A pattern involved an elevated copper/zinc ratio, depressed sodium, potassium, and manganese, and elevated lead, cadmium, and iron. The Type B subjects had a somewhat opposite chemical pattern, with extremely low levels of copper and sky-high values of sodium and potassium. Both groups exhibited elevated levels of lead and cadmium, previously found by other researchers to be associated with violence.

The Type A subjects exhibited episodic dyscontrol, whereas the Type B children evidenced consistent violence associated with an antisocial personality. These chemical imbalances have been the subject of three large controlled studies involving mixed violent and nonviolent subjects. In a test of 198 extremely violent children, prison residents, and ex-convicts with matched nonviolent controls, Walsh and coworkers again found the distinctive chemical patterns to be present in the majority of violent subjects and absent in most of the controls. Walsh's ability to distinguish between violent and nonviolent subjects based on chemistry alone was confirmed in two 'double-blind' experiments supervised by the University of California.

Clinical tests of 18 Type B (sociopathic) persons revealed abnormalities in blood and urine chemistry. All 18 Type B subjects were found to exhibit elevated blood histamine, depressed blood zinc and spermidine, and elevated kryptopyrroles in urine. In addition, a high incidence of hypoglycemia and toxic overload (lead and cadmium) were observed. These tests are significant not only because of the specific trace chemicals that turned up in sociopathic individuals but because they correlated a type of behavior with a distinct chemical pattern. The trace chemicals themselves may lead scientists to a 'fingerprinting' method of determining behavioral predisposition through chemical trace testing.

Follow-on testing of general delinquent populations revealed two additional chemical patterns (Types C and D) which are common to persons exhibiting low to intermediate violence. Type C individuals exhibit very low levels of all elements (except lead and cadmium) and are believed to suffer from malabsorption. Type D pattern is identical to Type C except for extremely elevated calcium and magnesium levels. Walsh believes that the Type D persons suffer from hypoglycemia.

Walsh and the Health Research Institute have been studying changes that occur in violent persons when their chemical imbalances are corrected. More than 80 Type A, B, C, and D subjects have been treated for chemical imbalances at the Princeton Brain Bio center in Skillman, New Jersey. The anecdotal results are very encouraging, according to Walsh. He reports that eighty percent of the treated subjects report a major improvement that lasts for more than two years. Most striking has been the improvement in antisocial-personality children following treatment. A double-blind experiment to measure the behavioral improvement associated with correcting chemical imbalances is in the planning stages.

Walsh has tested ten serial killers and found that nine exhibited the Type B chemical imbalances, usually with extraordinary elevations of toxins lead and cadmium. The Type B subjects included Henry Lee Lucas, Leonard Lake, and Charles Manson. The only exception was Bobby Joe Long, whose chemical levels were quite normal. Walsh concludes that Long's violence stems from brain damage resulting from his motorcycle accident and not from a chemical imbalance or as a result of poor fetal development. He believes that individuals possessing these imbalances are usually sensitive to their environment, especially with respect to parental influences, stress, alcohol, toxic exposures, and poor nutrition. Walsh's conclusions regarding Long coincide with the onset of Long's symptoms while still in the hospital recovering from the accident. Long did not evidence any overt hostility or violent behavior when he was younger, even though the other factors such as negative parenting and interrupted child bliss were present.

Fishbein and Thatcher argue that in the overwhelming majority of instances children receive adequate prenatal care, adequate diet, are not exposed to environmental toxins, and do not sustain repeated head traumas. The overwhelming majority of children develop adaptive behaviors that allow them to navigate through the challenges of life, learn from those mistakes they make, and become productive adults. However, when the majority of these upbringing factors are negative, when children have sustained repeated head traumas and have suffered from poor nutrition and exposure to different forms of toxins and dangerous substances, there is a much greater likelihood that as adults they will eventually adopt a criminal form of behavior as a response. The challenge to the criminologist that Fishbein and Thatcher have emphasized is to be able to isolate key predictors that indicate whether an individual will confront the criminal justice system as a result of his exposure to these factors.

One of their indicators is the presence of some kinds of learning disabilities in the child or in the biosocial history of the adult. They caution that learning disabilities in themselves do not constitute an indicator of antisocial or criminal behavior. Many people with learning disabilities and different types of dysfunction such as dyslexia overcome them and make valuable contributions to their respective professions. However, some forms of learning disabilities as a part of a pattern of physical abuse or severe head trauma, poor nutrition, and exposure to environmental toxins can frequently be traced to organic abnormalities in the brain. Environmental factors such as exposure to lead or lead fumes, for example, can have adverse effects on the development of the brain and result in learning or cognitive impairment. The same is true for the other factors we have cited. To compound the problem, the risk factors that impair brain functioning and result in a cognitive disability may also affect the brain's ability to regulate adaptive behavioral responses to life situations, thus placing the individual at an additional social disadvantage. And individuals who have such social disadvantages resulting from brain abnormalities are among the highest-risk groups with respect to confrontations with the criminal justice system. In summary, Fishbein and Thatcher have shown that learning disabilities are clear indicators of individuals who have physiological abnormalities in their neurological systems and who are at high risk of developing maladaptive and even criminal behavior.

Fishbein and Thatcher go even further and argue that, because the learning disabilities in question should have a physiological rather than a purely psychological basis in fact, they require diagnosis through an electrophysiological tool such as a computer-enhanced EEG. Nonobjective analyses such as evaluations of the individual's social and psychological backgrounds can be culturally biased and open to different interpretations depending upon who is conducting the evaluation. EEGs, however, tend to minimize any subjective intervention and are a direct measure of the neuroelectrical activity in the brain. Accordingly, the researchers suggest that computer-enhanced EEG evaluations be conducted on children with known learning disabilities or abnormal reactions at an early age to determine whether the disability is the result of a neurological disorder or of a psychological disorder. Either way, the early diagnosis of the disorder could lead to therapy and remediation.

In the fields of social psychology and Jungian psychoanalysis, respectively, Marvin Wolfgang of Pennsylvania and Swiss psychoanalyst Alice Miller have developed their own sets of predictors of violence and dangerousness. Wolfgang, who studied an entire cohort of males born in Philadelphia in 1945, found that encounters with the criminal justice system were organized according to family patterns. Where a father had had criminal careers, it was overwhelmingly likely that the sons would have criminal careers as well. Where mothers were institutionalized for criminal behavior, it was equally likely that the sons would commit criminal acts during their lifetimes. However, where both parents had criminal backgrounds, it was a virtual certainty that their sons would have extensive criminal careers. And the more criminal violence in the family unit, the greater the likelihood that the son would become a violent criminal. As if the statistics weren't proof enough of the importance of family patterning on the development of children, Wolfgang could point to other factors that supported his findings.

He cited evidence of alcoholism and drug abuse that predominated in families and of children who were raised in foster homes or institutions where they were neglected and deprived of any parental supervision whatsoever. In these instances, the children developed in an almost feral state with no moral training or discipline. Their encounters with the juvenile justice system began very early and continued well into adolescence. In the absence of any intervention, the children became career criminals in their adult lives. In other instances, learning disabilities and other organic neurological disorders were passed on from generation to generation and often laterally through families. These organic disabilities were indicators of other neurological factors that ultimately caused maladaptive behaviors, put the individuals at a disadvantage with respect to the rest of society, and resulted in their later encounters with the criminal justice system. In other words, the deck was stacked in one generation and every succeeding hand was dealt out according to that genetic deck. Medical intervention would have helped identify the problem and retraining or therapy might have helped remove specific individuals from their high-risk groups. However, Wolfgang learned, the institutions of society are simply not attuned to the medical and social backgrounds of violent crime. And as a result the problem that he began tracing in the male cohort of 1945 has got far worse over the intervening forty-two years despite the billions of dollars that have been spent to solve it and the ancillary problems it has created.

Alice Miller, who examined the childhood of German dictator Adolf Hitler, child murderer Jurgen Bartsch, and heroin addict 'Christiane F.,' has uncovered what seem to be two unmistakable clues that account for the vertical transmission of violence from one generation to the next and the lateral spread of that violence, including serial and mass murder, with each succeeding generation since the early part of the twentieth century. It also accounts for the epidemic rise in episodic violence in America since the 1950s. Dr. Miller explains that the roots of violent behavior in adulthood are to be found in a level of cruelty in child rearing that is invisible to the untrained eye. In her book *For Your Own Good* she explains that parents who commit implicit acts of cruelty toward their children by explaining to them that it is all for their own good are guilty of a 'poisonous pedagogy,' a perversion of the concepts of good and evil. In other words, the parents or caretakers teach the child that what is physically and emotionally painful to bear and cannot be expressed is in the child's best interests. In some cases the insanity of this reversal is evident, as in the example of Joseph Kallinger's mother and father, who forced the boy to hold his hand over an open flame until the skin blistered and charred from the intense heat. If he cried out in pain, he was brutally beaten. His mother explained that it was for his own good – he was being trained to bear pain. His most critical developmental years were spent experiencing this level of frustration. This severely damaged his own sense of his self-worth – a vital component to individual emotional development and the ability to accept a socially ordered external world – and left him permanently scarred.

In essence, poisonous pedagogy is a splitting off of feeling, sympathy, tenderness, intimacy, and pain from the individual in order to make that individual tough and hard. It is to experience brutality and not flinch – not acknowledge the terror and pain – so as to become stronger and invulnerable to weakness of feeling or remorse of conscience. These are the very emotions that serial killers first experience once they have admitted to themselves what they have done and have been placed within a stable environment. It is the force that once compelled Henry Lee Lucas to keep on confessing to crimes, not only to expurgate his own soul, but to deepen and broaden the feelings of remorse that he has, first in mourning his own lost life and then in mourning for the people he has killed. It was the emotions that Viola Lucas sought to destroy in her son when she asked him whether he loved his pet mule and then shot it, subsequently beating him for the expense it would entail to have the animal carcass removed from the property.

Miller explains that training children not to experience any feelings of love or sympathy need not be a brutal or overtly cruel or violent act. Indeed, in modern society much of this training is implicit because it is a 'right' and 'wrong' based on the parents' needs and not on the needs of the child. Parents who stress that imposing their own values on children is done for the child's own benefit commit, in Miller's words, a form of 'gentle violence,' suppressing completely the child's emerging personality and lighting a fuse of aggressiveness that will explode decades later. It is as if they are beating their children with velvet clubs that cause no overt scars, draw no public blood, inflict no visible pain, but do massive amounts of damage beneath the surface. These parents instill in their children a sense of helplessness and frustration because they are never allowed to acknowledge feelings of rage and rebellion. These naturally violent childhood emotions are, again, split off from the child's personality and never develop to a harmless stage of acceptance. By short-circuiting them, parents confine their children to reliving the frustration and rage over and over again until they can either accept it or break out in uncontrolled violence against the larger parent figure of society itself.

If Alice Miller is correct, there must be hundreds of thousands of emotional time bombs camouflaged by society who can explode at any minute. Why don't they simply explode? And isn't there a 'defusing' process that can remedy the ills brought about by Miller's poisonous pedagogy? If there is no defusing process, why has not society already consumed itself in generational violence to the point of extinction? The answer to all these questions is: yes, there are hundreds of thousands of potential aberrant violent criminals who have the critical number of symptoms. They have not yet exploded into violence because for many of them the event that is the critical trigger has not taken place. Still, the number of people who do explode into apocalyptic mass violence or serial violence increases exponentially every year.

We also know that there was once a set of natural defusing processes that kept much violence in check, but those social controls are evolving out of our social structure as the nature of the family continues to change. And unfortunately generational violence is also bringing certain aspects of our social order to a form of extinction. That is the point of the Surgeon General's warning to the American people that violence has become an issue of public health, and that is the point of most of the current research into domestic, generational, and episodic violence.

Miller's theory of generational violence – both explicit and implicit or 'gentle' – also accounts for its spreading so rapidly through post-World War II American society. She explains that in earlier social cultures, even though one parent might assume the role of authoritarian figure and suppress the child's own development, other family members, present in the same household, would support the child. In other words, the child had other adult family figures – including siblings – to whom he or she could turn for emotional relief from an overly domineering parent. The extended family structure living within the same household, the social order of the village parish, or the formally ordered structure of the family clan with its well-defined architecture of authoritarian responsibilities gave the child a multitude of support figures and outlets for rebellion and rage. The child also had cousins and siblings who shared the burden of parental abuse so that it was not heaped upon the single child of a small family. However, over the course of the twentieth century, families have been getting smaller, they have become highly unstable, with children going through serial families of pseudo fathers as a result of multiple marriages. Now, in the middle of the final quarter of the century, families are in danger of breaking down and the very concept of parental responsibilities is undergoing redefinition in the courts as a result of surrogate parenting and *ex utero* conception. Children are routinely placed in child-care enrichment programmes at age two – often under intense pressure to 'qualify' – and the parents themselves are more often than not involved in serial sexual relationships with multiple partners even while they are married. There are now more children living in homes with divorced parents than there are children living in the same home with both biological parents. In other words, the family structure is undergoing a massive restructuring, especially in the postwar period, and this has removed what Miller has called the critical family member or members who served as the parent figures who supported the child's development and counterbalanced the terrorizing parent.

In single-parent homes or 'no-parent' homes, the situation can be even more devastating for the child. An entire generation of children will shortly emerge for whom there are no normal, supportive parental relationships.

This generation, to which New York Senator Pat Moynihan has been pointing since the early 1980s, will have grown up in complete poverty, reared by the administrations of the states' welfare systems, and chronically malnourished, so that their entire adult lives will be spent requiring medical care to repair the damage done to their bodies and spirits during the development stages. They represent the largest area of population growth of our society, and they will in turn give birth to a succeeding generation of children out of control, who will carry the disease of generational violence well into the next century and well beyond the borders of the United States.

What Alice Miller and the other experts in the rapidly growing field of new criminology have shown, however, is that the individual symptoms of this disease and certain types of its carriers can be identified and diagnosed. However, the challenge is far greater than that. Scientists and doctors must understand that they are themselves impaired by a 'linkage blindness,' an inability to relate causalities in disparate professional disciplines to one another. Consequently, sociologists look for social causalities and find them; psychologists look for psychological and developmental causalities and find them; and neurologists look for organic causalities and identify them as well. The police and prosecutors simply brand criminals as 'bad,' track them down, and bring the few they find before the courts. However, each of the different professions is merely groping like a blindfolded person around the body of an elephant. Nobody can see the elephant and nobody recognizes that anybody else is there. As a result, the problem is not solved and its magnitude isn't even comprehended. It is this battle against linkage blindness that must be won first before fundamental solutions to the problems of episodic violence and serial murder can be attempted.

13

Inside the Brain of a Serial Killer

'Around fifteen years of age, God came to me with both a voice and visual presence and ordered me to undertake orthopedic experiments to heal myself and save mankind. This was the time when I was having the strange movements, and my parents had put a lock on their bedroom door and a bat behind their door, so I felt hopeless,' Joseph Kallinger explained in an interview a few years ago.

'I kept hearing her talking to me,' Henry Lee Lucas said about the mother he had killed only a few years earlier. 'And telling me to do things. And I couldn't do it. Had one voice that was tryin' to make me commit suicide, and I wouldn't do it. I had one tell me not to do anything they told me to do. And that's what got me in the hospital, was not doing what they told me to do,' Lucas explained about the decision of the Michigan prison officials to send him to the Ionia State Hospital for the criminally insane.

'There is something the matter with me,' Ted Bundy told his former girl friend, Liz Kendall, after his arrest in Florida. He admitted to a force within him that had begun sucking in his living personality just as the supergravitational pull of a black hole sucks in all light and then the matter from the neighboring stars. He tried to suppress this force that was building in him, but it was too strong. The more energy he applied against it to keep normal, the more the force grew in him. It destroyed his ability to function in school, it continued to warp his relationship with Liz Kendall, and finally it consumed him. He was unable to lead a normal life, although he presented the appearance of someone who could exert complete control over any situation. Bundy knew when the dark feelings were upon him. He tried to stay off the streets when he felt the urgings start, so that he wouldn't encounter any women who might cross his path. However, as it became increasingly difficult, Bundy felt himself slipping under its control again and again. And the feelings escalated to the point where, if he were on the street and a pretty young woman crossed his path, he would follow her. He tried to fight to remain in control many times by just following down the street until she disappeared into a dormitory or sorority house, but many times he couldn't. Weeks later the girl would be discovered in a shallow grave.

It wasn't as though he had a split personality, he explained to Kendall, because he knew what he was doing and where he was. He didn't have real blackouts. However, he also knew that what was inside him wasn't a figment of his imagination, it was real. It was a part of him that he couldn't understand but that exercised a control so powerful that he found himself committing murder for the sheer sexual thrill of it. He also knew that whatever was inside of him prevented him from truly loving a woman. He professed love to Kendall, and to other girls he had known, but he couldn't experience love. And when he had been cold toward Kendall or what she had called cruelly selfish, he begged forgiveness with tears. But they were the tears of someone too frightened of being abandoned and not tears of remorse. Years later Kendall found out that when Bundy was acting his most withdrawn from her, as if he were protecting a part of him that she could never know, it was out of self-protection and fear. To know him, Bundy finally said about himself, was to know something despicable and inhuman. In the end he asked Kendall not even to ask about it because even he couldn't face the truth within him even though he knew he was very, very sick.

While he was still a schoolboy, just a few years after he had fallen on the back of his head from a jungle gym and had begun to have epileptic seizures, Kenneth Bianchi molded a sculpture of a head that had two faces: one in front, and one in back. The one in front is the face of a sensitive, delicate human being. The one in back is the face of a killer ape. Kenneth had been diagnosed as having temporal lobe epilepsy by a psychologist. Another psychologist wrote about him that he expended a great amount of energy keeping his hostility under control and under cover.

After his accidental fall young Bianchi routinely wet his pants. His adoptive mother used to spank him before he went into the bathroom to punish him in advance for not emptying his bladder completely at the toilet. And when he stole money from her room, she would burn his hand over a gas flame, telling him that it was for his own good and making him profess that he loved her despite the pain of the torture.

Bianchi's mother had violent tantrums, and one day when he was nine he hid under a table to escape her temper. It was there that he claims he saw, beside him under the table, another little boy whose name was Steve. Steven hated Kenneth's mother and urged him to run away from her. But Kenneth was afraid, and for the next four years, despite the fact that they were inseparable friends, Steve told Kenneth that he hated him also. When Kenneth Bianchi's father died, Steve disappeared as well.

However, for the next fifteen years the psychologically damaged Bianchi led a double life. As Kenneth, he was a handsome man who was able to form relationships with women, fall in love with a young girl named Laura, survive the pain when she left him, and fall in love with another woman named Kelli. He had a son named Sean, and he worked as a security guard at Washington State. As Steve, a person Kenneth hadn't seen for years, he collected magazines and films that featured violent pornography, and he masturbated compulsively into a piece of rabbit's fur.

While he lived in Los Angeles, Bianchi as 'Steve' and his uncle Angelo Buono became a killing pair. They trolled the streets for women whom they captured, raped, strangled, and dumped along the hillsides surrounding Los Angeles. Steve flourished as Buono's partner and took delight in the slaughter of scores of young women. However, after Kenneth moved to Washington with Kelli, Steve disappeared: but still there, still hating Kenneth for his dependence on women, and still looking for the opportunity to strike. The pent-up frustration and rage became so strong that one night Steve emerged, killed two young girls, and deliberately left enough evidence in the area to incriminate Kenneth Bianchi.

It wasn't until Bianchi was evaluated by the court to establish his mental capacity to stand trial that a psychiatrist examined him again. And under hypnosis Steve came out and told the grizzly stories about Bianchi's mother, his uncle Angelo Buono, and the women they had buried outside of Los Angeles. The story was too far-fetched for the jury, who convicted him and his uncle of murder. Steve has disappeared again while Bianchi serves out his life sentence, but a panel of five other psychiatrists believed that Steve's appearance was a real occurrence of a multiple criminal personality.

Whether a form of multiple personality or not, Lucas, Bundy, Kallinger, Bianchi, and many of the other serial murderers have all reported feelings they could not control, voices whose urgings forced them into criminal acts, or sensations from deep within their minds that seemed to take over their bodies and hold them hostage. Some killers report that what began in childhood as strange voices or sexual urgings that were different from what other children talked about escalated into rituals within which these individuals would assault other people, rape women, achieve orgasm only when the victim lay helpless before them, and even commit murder and mutilation to hide the evidence and prevent their being caught. The more violent the crime, the more the feelings of violence escalated until the crimes themselves were no longer enough to blot out the disgust and revulsion the killers felt about themselves. Never able to show remorse, never able to experience the feelings of empathy and love other people seemed to experience, these killers lived in their own dark universes until a part of them gave up, attempted suicide, or left a telltale set of clues that led the police to make the arrest.

Where did those voices and feelings originate? Were the head traumas or birth defects ultimately responsible for the obvious neurological disorders or was there a critical mass of organic, psychological, and social causes that pushed each killer into his dark world? Did the killer-to-be while still a child recognize that there was something fundamentally different about him or was this a revelation that sprang upon him at puberty or only before each murder? Where is the point at which the damaged psyche can no longer exercise control over itself and looses a primal force of destruction upon the rest of society?

To answer these questions, psychiatrists Dorothy Lewis and Jonathan Pincus examined all fifteen inmates on Florida's death row and found that they all had a remarkable similarity of neurological impairments. One of those inmates, Bobby Joe Long, also commented that there were people on death row 'so far gone that it's like they're not even there when you talk to 'em.' He admits that he thinks a part of his brain, damaged in the motorcycle accident, 'has already dried up and died. . . . But there are people here who are just plain crazy and don't even know what's goin' on around 'em.'

To understand how someone can be neurologically impaired and still function or how someone like Bundy can lead an apparently normal life, live with a woman and her young daughter, and still have episodes during which he will rape and kill other young women, one has to understand the complex of symptoms that serial killers seem to have. And to understand how that damage controls their behavior, we have to look at how what we call consciousness or sentience is the product of a biological mechanism.

There is nothing magic or mystical about how the brain operates, although it is at the center of the miracle of life. What we call consciousness or awareness is actually the high-speed overlap of millions of electrochemically communicated messages between the senses, areas of recognition, memory banks, and nerves that control muscular movement. The brain is both a parallel processor, accomplishing many things at the same time along the same pathways, and a subordinating processor that prioritizes tasks and loads them into different job queues for completion as necessary. Based on the physical state of the body at any given moment, on the nature of the external world that the brain perceives, the urgency of messages that are stored in different memory stacks, and the emotional level of the organism, the brain allocates an importance factor to each job that it must process and organizes them accordingly. In the unconflicted person, this allocation process is as routine as setting up a 'things to do' list and ticking them off as they are accomplished, only on a vastly more complicated scale. In the conflicted person, and this describes ninety-nine percent of all of us, the brain makes millions of compromises. Do we have the next cup of coffee or make the difficult phone call; do we avoid the task or jump on it; do we face a fear or run away from it? The brain makes these types of decisions every nano-second in response to the millions of messages it receives from the external world and from its own memory banks.

But this machine model of the human brain still oversimplifies the complexity of the organ and the neurological system it manages. Because the system is driven electrochemically instead of only electrically, different types of communication can take place at the same time and actually alter the mind's interpretation of the messages. If a person is tired and hungry, his body is overworked, and his mind is overstressed with concerns about the day's problems and fears not only about tomorrow but about his family and financial situations as well, he will react to the same types of stimuli differently than someone who is unstressed, not hungry or tired, and more confident. On more specific levels, a person who has not eaten all morning will tend to snap at others and be extremely more irritable than the person who has had a nutritious breakfast. The former may not actually feel hungry, but his brain feels the need for chemical nourishment. It wants to be fed, and the chemical messages it receives inhibit its ability to respond logically to negative stimuli. We may not know this is happening, as in the case when someone drinks too much and his judgment and reflexes are compromised, but it is a measurable physiological phenomenon. Sexual arousal, fear, anger, and pain elicit similar chemical messages through the hormonal system that override the dominant logic that most brains exercise over their visceral emotions. And among serial killers whose body chemistry is drastically impaired, the brain can scarcely function normally at all.

Most people have seen diagrams that indicate what area of the brain controls what body function. Carl Broca in the nineteenth century isolated one of the areas that controls speech, the scientists mapped the areas that control muscular functions, receive messages from the optic nerve, intercept auditory signals, and discriminate among tastes or smells. The early twentieth-century perception of the brain assumed it to be a set of pigeonholes or compartments, each one controlling a specific part of the body. This has been largely shown to be false. It has been supplanted by the realization that the brain is a signal-switching device whose main function is to relay messages back and forth among different areas and in so doing establish what we commonly call 'awareness.' In this, human beings are just like any lower animals who see, hear, smell, touch, feel pain, experience hunger, feel the need to eliminate wastes, fear, have sexual arousals, and experience a form of vicious rage. However, because human beings have higher brain functions, use language, and exist in a metaphysical world in which they can make judgments about the nature of reality, their brains have an awareness of their own activity. We can understand statements such as: 'I'm trying to think' or 'My mind just isn't working today,' or 'It's on the tip of my tongue.'

Thus the human brain is a complicated but elegant communication device wherein the instantaneous nature of the signal switching within the different areas of the brain between what is reported by the senses and what is stored in the memory banks provides a base level of consciousness. Deprive a person completely of his sensory input and his entire sense of consciousness will be painfully distorted. Depriving a newborn baby of fundamental sensory input – especially tactile stimulation – some think is tantamount to condemning that newborn to a life of psychological pain and violence. Experiments on monkeys and other primates show that in the absence of sensory stimulation the animals become destructive and violent, and they eventually attempt forms of suicide by banging their heads against the sides of their cages.

In the normal brain sensory information from the outside world is relayed electrically to specific centres along pathways of nerve cells. What the nerves transmit to the brain is compared with similar information the brain has stored and the information is recognized and identified. Part of this information process is used to keep the individual oriented spatially and temporally. In other words, to establish what we sense as a continuum from one moment to the next, the brain constantly 'flashes' pictures of the outside world. These hundreds of billions of flash cards comprise a conscious reality. Change a major aspect of the outside world in between the flash cards so that it no longer conforms to what the brain expects and the individual can lose the ability to orient himself. In other words, if it is twelve noon, we don't expect it to be as dark as night in the next moment. And until the ancients understood and predicted solar eclipses, they had no basis for orienting themselves to what was happening. Change an aspect of gravity, as in a rapidly descending elevator, alter sound or suddenly thrust a new person into a place where he is not expected to be, and primal brain circuits override moment-to-moment cognitive activity, throwing the person into a form of defensive reaction. We call that reaction momentary panic, and we most commonly experience it when someone unexpectedly jumps out at us into our plane of vision. Children frighten one another like this all the time.

What really happens neurologically when we are frightened in this way is that the suddenness of the appearance is transmitted along a different neural pathway to the autonomic nervous system. This is controlled in the primal area of the brain: the temporal lobe, the limbic region, and the hypothalamus. These areas control the body's prime emotions and hormonal systems. They can and do override any cognitive functions because they maintain the body's metabolic balance. It is in these regions that the biological algorithm is translated from a cellular level to the level of the organism. These areas control fear and rage, the sexual drive, the sense of pleasure or well-being, and the basic sense of self that differentiates one individual from the rest of reality. The autonomic message that someone has appeared unexpectedly triggers a reaction in the hypothalamus of fear and the need for flight. We may scream and jump, the heart will pound, and we will break out into a sweat. Our first reactions – and the untrained person has absolutely no control over them – are to run or fight back. We may recognize the person with our cognitive minds as he registers in memory, but the threat presented by the sudden instrusion has gone down a different pathway and, from somewhere within the brain, we react. We are aware of this reaction. We are aware of it at almost the exact same time that we recognize the person who caused us to jump in terror, and we are embarrassed by it. But we know that something inside of us has this reaction. It is as if there is another person within us who forces us to react even though we consciously do not want to. This type of sensation – magnified hundreds of times – is much like what the serial killer feels when a part of his brain takes over from its 'normal' activity.

Under routine circumstances, the brain quickly identifies abnormal sensory experiences and signals a type of alert status until the abnormality is resolved. The logical control exercised by the usually dominant left hemisphere provides a matrix of order and consistency and imposes a structure upon the raw sensory data the brain receives. It serves as a filter, establishing a continuum from one reality flash card to the next, and it judges the validity and content of the information it receives through the sensory receptors. Our ability to discriminate between real and nonreal or true and false is governed to a large extent by the judgmental, logical controls resident in the left hemisphere. This is what keeps even the most emotional person functioning within the social order and behaving according to a consistent set of rules. In dreams, however, the dominance of the governing cerebral hemisphere recedes and along with it the judgmental functions that we rely upon in a waking state. When that happens the logical structure of everyday existence is no longer present and the results are illogical, fanciful dreams that we accept at face value without dismissing them.

In dreams the continuum of reality is often shattered by abrupt changes of scene from one split second to the next. Loved ones or relatives who have died can populate our dreams and interact with people alive and well in the present. In dreams we can see ourselves as children acting within the present and even acting in the present with our adult selves. Dreams can come upon us instantly, it seems, especially when we are very tired, and the dream-stimulating chemicals begin to flow, carrying us off to sleep. At these half-dream/half-waking moments, there is a complete intermix between dream reality and symbology and waking reality. The waking brain exercises some control, but we feel an irresistible force pulling us into the dream state. If nothing jars us out of it, like oncoming headlights or the sound of a horn, we might drift into sleep without even realizing it until we've awakened moments or hours later.

Dreams also have their own symbology, which protects the waking mind from the terror of some of the deepest memories and fears that are stored there. For example, people who appear in our dreams often stand for other people who elicit similar emotional reactions. Siblings sometimes replace one's children, and upon waking the dreamer has a brief moment of insight regarding his or her relationship with the child of today. Parents, relatives, and friends may be interchangeable in one's dreams, and this, too, can be a source of revelation to the dreamer or to a therapist about the person's assumptions and deeper emotions. However, these moments of insight about dreams are made not by the dreaming mind but by the waking mind or with the help of the therapist. The subordinate hemisphere has no such judgmental capability in the typical adult brain and must be analyzed by some logical entity. During the killing sprees, in the mind of the serial murderer, no such logical entity exists for any extended period of time.

The half-dream/half-waking state that mixes memories and terrors with reality is a true episodic state for the serial killer with a limbic dysfunction or with other symptoms. The aspects of dreams intrude themselves upon waking reality without warning, and the killer finds himself in a world of his own terror-filled fantasies with no basis for determining whether he is dreaming or waking. It is all the same to him. And as in dreams in which people replace people and identities become confused, the delusional or hallucinatory state of the serial killer confuses individuals from the killer's past, such as parents or siblings, with the victim who has just crossed his path or entered his car. As the killer's frenzy silently builds before he springs the trap, he has locked himself firmly into a dream world and the victim before him has no identity whatsoever, except for the identity his mind has already imposed.

The physiological reaction that trips the dream/delusion mechanism can be triggered by an event in the real world just as in Gary Schaefer's case when his mind was already troubled over his stepdaughter just as he drove by Caty Richards and her friend. Or it can be purely episodic, like the emotional menstrual-like cycle that Bobby Long experiences. His severely damaged brain, which has been battered by successive head traumas, no longer has a functioning regulator to control the flow of emotions that are stimulated by hormones. As a result, Long found himself acting out of a waking dream, unable to suppress the rage and violence that had become associated with sex during the years with his mother and his domineering wife.

For Ted Bundy, it was the sight of a pretty coed who aroused a frenzy of sexual feelings. However, Bundy had been rejected by just such a woman. Her confidence in her good looks, and her demeanor, which exuded a belief in her own self-worth, terrified Bundy at the very moment it aroused him. He hated her and lusted after her at the same time, and the two feelings intertwined and became one. He needed to dominate such a woman and destroy the power that had rejected him. To do so excited him sexually and stimulated his entire body. That became the trip wire for the part of Ted Bundy's brain that was out of control. Already trolling for victims, his arm in a cast in a feigned demonstration of weakness, he played upon the very aspects of the woman's self-confidence to entrap her. And as a dialogue between Bundy and his victim was established and he felt the woman being lured into his web, he became more and more aroused. The emotional force that was surging in his brain became more powerful and spiralled him to the next phase of the crime. And at the moment of triumph, when she was beside him in the car, he had her. A quick succession of blows to render her helpless, and Bundy was at the penultimate stage of the crime. Now that she was unconscious and near death, he would rape her – sex and his hatred of this woman had become one and the same – and then he killed her. Now, at the post-mortem of the crime, he was filled with self-loathing. His acts of violence had proved nothing, and he had a body to dispose of. He buried her and placed a late phone call to Liz Kendall in a desperate effort to lurch back to reality and to establish himself as a living being. And this pattern continued through the lives of more than thirty victims in Seattle, more in Colorado, another set of victims in Utah, and a final set of murders in Florida.

For John Gacy the impetus was that he had to destroy something he felt was active and cancerous inside himself. The ritual of slaughtering the young men he encountered was a reenactment of a terrible dream in which his father was slaughtering the boy John Gacy that he had grown to despise for his own weakness and perceived lack of masculinity. Gacy assumed both his father's role and his own role at one and the same time. And, as in a waking dream, his damaged brain allowed the physical playing out of the self-torture and hatred that had been stored in memory since Gacy was a young child. The feelings of helplessness and rage and the childhood need to destroy what was most painful came to the surface when Gacy brought his victims back to his house. But in his own despondence after the failure to achieve a true release from the pain, he buried his victims in the soft mud under his house.

Although Gacy, Bundy, Manson, Lucas, Kallinger, Bianchi, Long and the others all evidence at least one trip mechanism in each of their particular behaviors, the truth is that there is usually more than one set of causes at work in the individual. If that were not the case, anyone with damage to his limbic brain or to his hypothalamus would automatically become a serial murderer. We know that the brain is a far more resilient organ than that and has a compensating mechanism that tries to correct for deficiencies. If a person has gone for many hours without eating and begins to react with inappropriate violence toward those around him, his normal sense of social order, though diminished, will respond to a direct query such as 'Don't you know what you're doing?' or 'Why did you do that?' The fear of disturbing the equilibrium of one's family or of losing one's job also serves to counterbalance temper tantrums or violent outbursts. Even alcoholics who are pushed to the brink, if their upbringing has been supportive, can still rebound and benefit from treatment or therapy.

The brain can also sustain repeated damage and continue to function because it is still a 'plastic' organ that reforms neural pathways to compensate for those that have been damaged. People who have experienced strokes on the left side of the brain and have lost muscular control on the right side, as well as the power of speech, can be retrained to function. Neurologists know that there is an *ur* speech area on the right side of the brain that to a large extent mirrors Broca's area on the left side. That area can be taught to take over from the left hemisphere in many cases of stroke and resulting speech impairment. We also know that neural pathways that control other motor functions can likewise be compensated for in a physical therapy programme after a stroke. And brain tissue can also rejuvenate itself after the destructive effects of alcohol abuse. Once the source of the toxin is removed and the tissue is allowed to recover, many cerebral functions that had been lost during the period of greatest abuse gradually return. A person may never recover one hundred percent of his previous cognitive abilities or long-term memory capacity, but he will recover enough to allow him to function without obvious impairment.

Paradoxically, it is the brain's gyroscopic capacity to right itself and compensate for damage and error that constructs the matrix out of which serial killers are produced. It is a form of defense mechanism which is so complex that when fully operational has turned the individual into a violent predator of other living creatures. To appreciate how a defense mechanism can evolve into a destructively aggressive behavior, one has to appreciate that the prime directive of any living organism is to survive. This is a type of biological algorithm, a biochemical reaction that is basic to the distinction between living and nonliving matter. Reproduction is a manifestation of the biological need to survive: the reproduction of genetic material mirror-like fashion to guarantee the development of another living host for it. Thus, sexual arousal is a primal chemical reaction.

Self-defense in all of its forms is also a manifestation of the need to survive. Therefore fear, violence, rage, flight, terror, and panic are all chemically induced reactions that exist in almost all living creatures in one form or another. They are a part of the compensation process that keeps living entities from simply blundering into death. In human beings, the primal self-defense reactions were socialized very early in the evolution of the species – at about the same time verbal language was developed – so that humans could function in groups and survive the elements and their natural predators in nature. This social evolution of the species is mirrored in the psychological and social development of each individual. In other words: ontogeny, the development of the individual, follows philogeny, the evolution of the species. If that development process in the individual is impaired in any way so that the brain or neurological system has to compensate in order to regain an internal balance, the individual no longer mirrors the rest of society. He becomes a psychophysiological mutation. This is what happens in the development of a serial murderer.

The behaviors that serial killers display, although they are ultimately self-destructive, are the behaviors that their brains have developed to compensate for the levels of physiological and emotional damage they have incurred. If the child has not received the sensory stimulation he requires and therefore has not established a boundary between himself and the outside world, the brain will compensate, but a vital component will be missing. A portion of the infant's brain never develops to the point where it can exercise regulatory control over primal emotions. The individual may become all-encompassing and see only himself and nothing else. He recognizes no physical limitations to himself and seems literally to 'walk over everyone around him.' He has no sense of hurting anyone else, feels no remorse, and shows no sympathy. When the behavior is at its most extreme, the individual exists in his own universe, isolated from the rest of humanity. He may perform violent acts upon small animals at first and ultimately upon people. His own rage is an extension of himself, not capable of being held in check by the part of his brain that never developed properly. To a lesser extent, the individual displays sociopathic tendencies. He may be selfish and demanding and simply unresponsive to the needs of other people. He still exists in his own universe, but perhaps because his brain functions are not seriously impaired, or because of a more cohesive upbringing, or by having learned how to function in a socially ordered environment with great difficulty, he has trained himself to control violence.

In the cases of a Kenneth Bianchi, a Charles Manson, or a Henry Lee Lucas, in which the levels of childhood physical abuse were so extreme that each day was a challenge to survive, the developing psyche was simply crushed. It was taught that it was unloved and adrift within a hostile universe where it could find no solace except in self-gratification. To survive, it became a predator of others and, like a wild animal, it took what it could while avoiding contact with creatures that would destroy it. The physical damage impaired these killers' brain functions while the emotional damage resulted in elaborate defence mechanisms to enable them to withstand the constant torture. Paradoxically, in order to survive, the child had to be dead. Thus, figuratively speaking, the psyche died so that the physical entity could live on. Had there not been physical damage to the brain, perhaps the psychotic individual who emerged would not have lacked control over primal brain functions. But, given the physical damage, there was no control. Consequently, all of Lucas' and Bianchi's primal urgings were given free rein by an impaired brain, they lost control, and they became serial killers.

A close examination of the histories of each of the serial killers researched shows that what society called criminal behavior was in reality a type of defense mechanism against what was confronting him. And this amalgamation of psychological devastation, physiological brain damage, and a history of either substance abuse or crippling chemical imbalances, resulted in each case in an individual who is beyond our normal definition of insanity. The biological algorithm that was at work in this person kept him in a form of equilibrium. However, the forces that were at work both without and within him so skewed that equilibrium away from the mainstream that the individual is no longer recognizable in human terms. We perceive him to be a monster, and of course he perceives himself to be almost nonhuman when measured against the normal people he sees around him. Yet, tragically, what he has developed into was not entirely of his own choosing. In order to survive, as Charles Manson has described himself, he had to make a virtue of a necessity and embrace the creature he had become. Thus, in Manson's violent world of chaos, where bad was good and good was bad, his psyche's response was 'helter-skelter,' the absolute devastation of the external world in a mirror image of the devastation of his own internal universe.

If there is any hope in the description of how serial killers develop and what internal and external forces cause this particular form of mutation, it still lies in the resiliency of the human mind. Bundy, Long, Lucas, Kallinger all realize that they are sick. Even Manson recognizes that his behavior is well beyond the bounds of normalcy. He blames society and his upbringing for the pain that was inflicted upon him, but within the structured environment of prison he recognizes what he did. Susan Atkins, Tex Watson, Henry Lee Lucas, and other serial killers have embraced the revelation of fundamentalist Christianity as their structure for recreating their personalities. With the institutional structure of prison imposed upon their lives, having been detoxified from the residual effects of drug and alcohol abuse, and receiving a relatively stable diet of institutional food, the bodies of incarcerated serial killers begin to restabilize. Most of them realize that they might kill were they to be summarily released, but all of them now know that proper intervention would have kept them from killing in the first place or at least helped them understand what was happening even after their killing sprees had started. And one killer, Bobby Joe Long, was at the point of turning himself over to psychiatric care, but he became afraid of the consequences of prosecution at the last minute and walked away from the therapist's office building.

Most of the serial killers knew what was happening to them and either tried to suppress it themselves, as Bundy explained, or pleaded with authorities to help them. Lucas, Long, Gary, and Ed Kemper all told prison or medical authorities that they were sick and needed help. Lucas frankly told the prison doctors that, if released, he would go on killing sprees. The officials released him anyway. Bobby Joe Long tried for years to tell his Army doctors that he was severely injured and was experiencing symptoms that worried him, but the doctors rejected his claims as an attempt to increase his veteran's benefits. And when Carlton Gary explained to doctors and parole officers in New York's Ossining penitentiary that he was experiencing homicidal feelings and needed treatment, they claimed that he was looking to do easier time.

Clearly more research is needed, not only in the area of

episodic violence specifically, but also in the area of brain development and operation. Recent studies that have linked the organic growth of new neurons and neural pathways in response to the stimuli of learning new items promises new fields of research. The work of Drs. Lewis, Mark, Mednick, Walsh, Fishbein, and Thatcher will indicate new directions that criminology will take. And in the area of public policy, now that even the Surgeon General himself has recognized that violent crime is an issue of public health, the only course of action is to develop programmes that will identify victims of abuse and family violence before they retreat into their twilight worlds. Otherwise some of them will only emerge ten to fifteen years later as grisly headlines in local newspapers.

14

The Serial Killer Profile

On the basis of substantive interviews with more than a dozen serial killers and their immediate families and extensive casework interviews with neurologists, surgeons, psychiatrists, social workers, medical examiners, and research chemists, we have developed biological and social profiles of the potential serial killer. With the help of attorneys who have defended serial murderers, homicide detectives who have pursued them, and members of the Behavioral Science Unit of the FBI, we have been able to refine these profiles to include relevant details about the serial killer's habits and predilections. As our understanding of the serial killer syndrome deepened, we realized that these profiles could lead to the development of a diagnostic or prediction instrument that would identify individuals who might be at risk or whose backgrounds might require an extensive investigation or a biopsychosocial evaluation.

Unlike the phrenologists of the late nineteenth century, who examined the shapes of people's heads and bumps on their skulls, or even some of the behaviorists of the early 1940s, we are not looking specifically for 'criminal types.' Most police investigators will argue that anybody can become a criminal type simply by committing a crime and being processed through the justice system. We are hypothesizing, however, that serial murdering is a form of disease rather than simply a lifestyle, a syndrome that has specific hard and soft signs that are symptoms and identifiable long before the potential murderer commits his first homicide. The disease is the most ultimate form of episodic aggression. This we have learned from interviews with killers who revealed that they had experienced violent fantasies for many years before they stalked their first victims. And the subsequent murders they committed were, in most cases, reenactments of those fantasies and a response to the mounting dyscontrol.

We have learned that the disease has some of its origins in diagnosable organic disorders within the subject's neurological and central nervous systems. Injuries to the brain, prolonged and chronic biochemical imbalances, genetic disorders, and severe cases of epilepsy of the limbic brain all leave traces of the tissue damage and soft signs. These organic disorders are directly related to behavioral disorders, schizophrenic-like reactions, learning disorders, aggressive behavior and sometimes criminally antisocial activities. The afflicted person seems to have epileptic-like seizures that take the form of hallucinations, intruding themselves upon his consciousness, distorting time and reality and leaving only vague afterimages in their wake like the phantom traces of nightmares against the morning. The only signs that doctors may have as indicators are the long spikes on a deep-probe EEG or a series of soft neurological signs such as dyslexia, obsession with fires, memory gaps, and so on.

What indicators prompt diagnosticians and neurologists to order such an extensive test as a deep-probe EEG? How does a doctor determine when to send a hair sample to a toxicologist for chemical analysis? Do all children with learning disabilities have the types of dysfunctions that could eventually lead them to careers as murderers of women and children? And what of the killer who has committed his first homicide? Is there a way to intervene before he paralyzes an entire community like the Atlanta Child Murderer or the Son of Sam? And how many future Charles Mansons are developing in the darkness of our institutions and in their own miseries? Are their fears and desperations the catalysts translating them into nosferati? What are the signs that will alert those with whom they come into contact? What will it take to stimulate urgently needed research?

The behavioral and biological patterns and psychological profiles set forth in this chapter are the signs that indicate a probability that an individual may be predisposed to episodic violence and criminal activity. A critical number of signs point to the potential of dangerousness without actually labelling anyone a criminal. They can only be considered red flags. This is an important distinction. It may be that many individuals are able to navigate through life on the border between incipient violence and normal behavior and without ever treading over the line. They may live in fear of their own potential for destruction and in terror of what they know lies beneath the surface of their own social demeanor, but they have not been pushed into violence by some critical combination of forces. Their upbringing may have given them a structure of behavior that allows them to look upon themselves critically. They may be so aware of nutritional deficiencies that they use diet as a means of behavioral self-control. And most likely they will have found a spouse or a significant other who provides them with an objective sense of reality. Although these people may demonstrate some of the biological and psychological symptoms of the serial killer syndrome, they will spend their lives as carriers of the disease and may never emerge as violent criminals. The patterns developed in this chapter will apply to these people only incidentally, but can be used as directional guides for research.

The purpose of defining a set of patterns and predictors is to help identify afflicted people at an early stage in their careers or lives. Children who inflict extraordinary violence upon their peers or upon animals, who repeatedly start fires and become entranced by the sight of flames, who have themselves been the victims of family violence or abuse and have suffered contusions or head injuries, and who exhibit chronic learning disabilities or other forms of organic neurological dysfunction are among the likeliest candidates for further evaluation. Similarly, juvenile offenders in institutions who seem incorrigible for reasons other than simply their home environments or those whose home environments are so tragically violent that they have become scared are also candidates for further evaluation. In any case, the patterns that follow are not intended to be a primary tool in predicting or labeling individuals as serial murderers or potential serial murderers but only as a guide or model for gathering further information about such people who are suspected of suffering from those or similar symptoms.

Essentially, the profile should serve as a diagnostic tool, for both medical professionals and officers of criminal and juvenile courts, indicating that the offender is actually himself a victim and requires intervention and not only punishment. It is not meant to exonerate individuals of the crimes they have committed but to suggest that the crime may have its origins in the serial killer syndrome, identified by some as dyscontrol syndrome or limbic brain psychosis, and that certain forms of medical help, therapy, and positive correction may prevent him from embarking on a life of chronic homicidal violence. In other words, skilled use of these patterns may save the lives of many thousands of potential victims by short-circuiting the careers of their murderers-to-be. The profile can be of significant benefit to people belonging to the following groups:

1. Individuals who are afraid they are experiencing symptoms and are losing control of their violent tendencies. This is not meant to scare anyone into thinking he is a potential serial killer but to alert people who are truly suffering from delusions of violence, hallucinatory fantasies of ritualistic violence, and violent hypersexuality to the presence of a real disease. Ideally people, such as other episodically violent people like rapists, wife beaters, and repeated assaulters, so alerted will seek some form of medical help before they succumb to their increasingly perverted and more violent fantasies.

2. People or groups who act as advocates for individuals they suspect of being at risk. Friends, relatives, children, or spouses who fear abuse from an individual yet realize that he may be acting out a behavior pattern not entirely of his own making. Especially important in this group are people who live with individuals who experience episodic behavioral disorders. The more regular these episodes become and the more bizarre the behavior aberrations associated with these episodes, the more important it is that the spouse or relative seek intervention. Potential victims can protect themselves first by recognizing the likelihood of violence and then obtaining intervention to help the potential offender, even if that person is a spouse, parent, or intimate friend. In all the killers researched, a relative or a significant other missed opportunities to intervene prior to or during a killing spree.

3. Judges, prosecutors, defense attorneys, police investigators, and other law enforcement personnel who confront potential serial murderers often through the criminal justice system. By approaching the phenomenon as an illness and recognizing the behavioral symptoms,

criminal justice professionals will be better equipped to investigate the crimes, protect potential victims, and apprehend the killer before he has a chance to elude detection and leave the area.

4. Members of parole boards, pardon committees, and professionals in the corrections professions who must understand the complexity of the disease that drives serial murderers. Often episodically violent persons are released prematurely or, like Henry Lee Lucas, Charles Manson, and Carlton Gary, they are released despite their own threats that they might act out asocially or violently again or that they will not be able to function outside of the institution. If members of parole boards understood more about the dynamics of the serial murderer's personality they would know better what symptoms to look for and would better recognize the danger signs in the people whose cases they must evaluate and the critical signs therein.

5. Doctors, nurses, hospital emergency room personnel, neurologists, psychiatrists and other therapists, social workers, and teachers who may frequently come in contact with individuals who display symptoms of this syndrome. These professionals, victims notwithstanding, are the primary contact groups because the early and subsequent confrontations between serial murderers and society's institutions take place in elementary schools, hospital emergency rooms, and psychiatric wards as well as in juvenile courts and police stations. These institutions are society's early warning system, and the records they keep often unknowingly track the developments of potential serial murderers as they make their first passes at society. An emergency room doctor who treats the same child for repeated head injuries or homicidally aggressive behavior on many subsequent occasions might be in a unique position to call that child's case to the attention of

a social worker or a juvenile officer at a local police department. At least by being brought to the attention of the emergency room's supervising physician, the case might make its way into the official records. A school nurse who sees the same child on numerous occasions for headaches, blurred vision, aberrant social behavior, unexplained bouts of crying, temper tantrums, unexplained but chronic bruises, symptoms of malnutrition, or just because the child is always at the centre of trouble might be watching the child's first clashes with social authority. Is the child secretly emotionally or learning-disabled? Does the child have an undetected neurological dysfunction that makes him incapable of following instructions in the same way as the other children? Does the child's antisocial behavior result in fights with the other children every day after school? Does the child look as though he has been abused physically, emotionally, or sexually in his home environment? Does the child exhibit other nonresilient qualities? These are the types of questions that should prompt school officials to consider the predictors developed in this chapter, always being careful not to label someone as a potential murderer but to suggest diagnosis and follow-up.

6. Researchers in medicine, education, law enforcement, and the social sciences who are in a position to pursue definitive studies into serial murder and other forms of episodic aggression as a form of public health issue can use these patterns to establish early parameters for their models. These patterns are meant to stimulate research by defining areas of need that require further investigation.

The following list of behavior patterns is a result of all the data that has been compiled on the very nature of a person suffering from the symptoms of episodic aggressive behavior.

THE SERIAL KILLER PROFILE

Twenty-one Patterns of Episodic Aggressive Behavior

1. Ritualistic behavior
2. Masks of sanity
3. Compulsivity
4. Search for help
5. Severe memory disorders and a chronic inability to tell the truth
6. Suicidal tendencies
7. History of serious assault
8. Deviate sexual behavior and hypersexuality
9. Head injuries or injuries incurred at birth
10. History of chronic drug or alcohol abuse
11. Alcohol- or drug-abusing parents
12. Victim of physical or emotional abuse or of cruel parenting
13. Result of an unwanted pregnancy
14. Products of a difficult gestation period for the mother
15. Interrupted bliss or no bliss of childhood
16. Extraordinary cruelty to animals
17. Arsonal tendencies without obvious homicidal interest
18. Symptoms of neurological impairment
19. Evidence of genetic disorders
20. Biochemical symptoms
21. Feelings of powerlessness or inadequacy

Pattern 1 – Ritualistic Behavior

The ritual that is always a part of the serial murderer's modus operandi is either explicit at the scene of the crime or made explicit by the murderer when he confesses to the police. This ritual is a repeated observable pattern, so that there is a fundamental sameness from crime to crime that even the killer can't alter. It forms the basis of the serial killer's personality and is evident, perhaps even in outline form, long before the first crime is ever committed. Serial killers use ritual as a kind of behavioral skeleton – much like an insect – to provide an architecture for their fantasies and a structure to the violence that informs their conscious existence.

Many times the first investigators to arrive at the crime site become aware that the victims were treated in a ritualistic way, either by decapitation, forms of mutilation or sexual molestation, or burial after the crime. Many times the killings seem random until the killer makes a confession and the police see the edges of ritual that tied the crimes together. Killers may take photographs or shoot videotapes of their victim's suffering, they may make audio tapes of their cries of pain or pleas for mercy, or they may incarcerate their victims for days before killing them. The ritual may be present in the way the victims are caught or in the poses the killer uses. Ted Bundy usually feigned weakness or injury, for example, preying on an innocent girl's desire to help out an obviously charming, good-looking, and ingratiating man. Leonard Lake, who committed suicide in a police interrogation room in San Francisco, made videos of the ritualistic torture of his victims. Bobby Joe Long would ride with his victims sitting next to him in his car for hours, as if he were on a date with them, before killing them and dumping their bodies. And Gary Schaefer reenacted the same ritual of killing his older sister with a rock with each of his victims.

What investigators discover is that the ritual is primal; it is the behavior of a human being that lacks civilized humanness and now acts as though a deeply primitive neuropsychological circuit were continally firing and stimulating itself over and over again. This is the behavioral model of psychomotor epilepsy or the episodic cycles of electrochemical turbulence within the limbic brain and hypothalamus regions. There is a primal identity that the serial killer seems to adopt during these episodes that is part of his normal social personality but is mostly fixated on the desperate need to satisfy an almost feral instinct. Unfortunately, that instinct manifests itself in forms of violence toward other people.

In essence, ritual killings are a part of a developing downward spiral, a metastasizing loss of control which may have started when the individual was only eight, nine, or ten. When the complete ritual is analyzed and traced, which can only happen after many hours spent in gaining the trust of the killer and dealing with his inconsistencies and memory gaps, the ritual appears to be a sum total of the perceived childhood horrors and his chronic damaged physical condition. It turns out to be the survival pattern of a person who has never developed the channels for emotions such as fear, lust, and rage and is driven by them as if he lives within a primordial neurological soup, an unstructured conscious dream world in which there is no logic and no social order. These are the interictal episodes of behavior during which the crimes are committed and the ritual of the crimes is an outward depiction of the fears and rage that are exploding deep within the most primitive parts of the killer's badly damaged brain, psyche, and spirit.

To the killer during the act of the crime, the rituals are a form of morality play. They have an internal purpose and methodology that can be interpreted after society's external structure has been imposed upon the killer. They have a theme and the victims are archetypal symbols to the killer. Henry Lee Lucas killed his mother over and over again. Each time a woman confronted him, or baited or challenged him, she became a victim. Charles Manson was convinced that society needed to hear his paranoid message, and in a recent interview disclosed that most of the killers on death row in San Quentin believe that they are incarnations of Jesus Christ or the Antichrist. They claim to be carrying out divinely inspired instructions to wage war on society. Charles Manson's primary concession today is that he has not killed enough people. He has not made his message plain enough. He dogmatically reminds anyone who will listen that he is a reflection of society and that his crimes are the crimes society has created. He instructed Tex Watson, the surrogate leader of the Manson family, to make the Tate and LaBianca killings as 'messy' as possible so as to bring home to society the message that 'helter-skelter,' the apocalypse of Manson's obsession, had already begun.

The structure of ritual with its reliance on totemic objects, can be observed in most normal, healthy children. Toddlers have their special 'thumb-sucking' blankets or even pieces of cloth without which they cannot go to sleep. Gradually they lose their interest in these objects and replace them with others. As adults, normal people have favorite articles of clothing, robes, pajamas, or other items of comfort, but the pleasure derived from them has been intellectualized. There is nothing inherently magic about them, and they have no abnormal powers as objects. Although people may have 'lucky' pens without which they will not sign a contract or an agreement, these, too, have become intellectualized.

The serial killer, however, is a different animal. For him, the objects involved in his ritual do have a power over him. They are the tangible embodiments of forces that drive and sustain him, objective forms of the hallucinatory metaphors that structure his ritual. And the reliance on this ritual and its associated totems is evident in his penultimate killer state, and persist long after the normal adult has lost the need for personal ritual and private totems.

The presence of these ritualistic fantasies and the preservation of totemic objects taken from would-be victims or potential crime scenes indicates that even a person who has not committed a murder is involved in a ritual that could someday be acted out. Inherent in his dark scenarios are always themes of perverted meaning known only to himself. There are interwoven patterns of lust, rage, judgment enacted upon the enemy, punishment of the demons who haunt them, dominance over friend and foe, submission by the innocent, perversion of good into evil, a damaged creative spirit, androgyny, and a final concession of the powerlessness of the individual. Then there is a lapse into a postvision depression in which the morbid fears of the serial killer dominate him and force him into conformity with the rest of society. In a symbolic and kinesthetic way, the killer is acting out a montage of primal impulses, perceived racial memories, the hormonal messages of a damaged or perverted libido, and in so doing is using the immediate victim helpless before him as a way to hold the entire community at bay.

Pattern 2 – Masks of Sanity

As if he had a split personality, the very dark behavior of the serial killer is often masked by a veneer of very good and socially rewarded behavior. This is his mask of sanity and it is manifested through grandiosity or a belief in his own superhuman importance, hypervigilance or an extraordinary concern about acting morally and properly, and social adeptness to the point of extreme manipulative ability. Serial killers, like most mass murderers, have extremely well-honed manipulative skills. Charles Manson, Ted Bundy, John Gacy, Carlton Gary, Ed Kemper, and even Henry Lee Lucas all demonstrated one of the basic attributes of the effective manager: the ability to get other people to do what you want them to do. Manson, like a bomb-sniffing police dog, was able to sense the inferiority in others, the need to be dominated and told what to do, and the desperate need for approval. Although Susan Atkins and Leslie Van Houton might have seemed like normal, upstanding young people, albeit with free spirits, they were actually deeply scarred people who actively sought domination as a missing component in their own personalities. They derived strength from Manson as did Tex Watson, who offered his life to Manson as proof of his fidelity.

By having a keen sense of what is required to conform to the outward trappings of society, serial killers are able to exhibit acceptable, indeed often exemplary behavior in their communities. Their need for approval and their ability to second-guess confrontation is so great that they go undetected by the public at large and until they are confronted by family members, spouses, friends, or primary sexual partners as their conditions worsen. The qualities that compel serial killers to behave as they do are eerily like the qualities of achievement that American society expects from successful individuals. Manson, Leonard Lake, Carlton Gary, and Bundy were all involved with their communities during their murder sprees and 'doing good' in their own eyes, having penetrated the very society they hated so much.

There is a part of the personality of the serial killer, as there is in all of us, that needs acceptance and requires achievement. However, the more acceptance and achievement that come their way, the greater the need itself becomes. There is no satisfying or satiating it, whereas normally developed people can decide when to be 'selfish' and preserve quality time for themselves. The compulsive needs of serial killers are such that they have no self-esteem – psychobiologically, many of them can't even determine the boundaries of their own selves and thus can't conceive of themselves as having separate identities – and this factor is critical to their later explosions of violence. They have spent a lifetime repressing the cancerous rage at the core of their personalities. They have been experiencing a progressive and escalating loss of control and sense of madness from the time they first became aware of their own dark primal urgings. They have learned to fear and hate the dark sides of themselves yet succumb to them in moments of pure reactive violence. But they have developed a chameleon-like mask of sanity or normalcy whose purpose is to protect them from the turbulent and hostile violent central element of their psyches. This mask of sanity also camouflages them from the society they have learned to fear and hate.

During this period of development a unique set of defense mechanisms emerges, composed of the same elements that make for sociopathy or sociopathic and multiple personalities, and these interact with the neurological impairments that cause significant but convenient losses of memory and gaps in reality: the episodes during which the serial murders are committed. The drive to live within society, the ability to hope and dream about the possibilities the future holds for them, and the sense of self that allows them to benefit from personal and vocational achievements have all been physically or emotionally beaten away from them in their earlier years. Many have success, but they cannot feel successful. Manson, although quite capable as a classical guitarist and composer, failed at being a songwriter. And recent evidence shows that he killed for a music contract that had been based on a verbal promise that was not fulfilled. Leonard Lake was making his one last try at success when he ran afoul of the law after his companion Charles Ng was caught shoplifting. He told his brother-in-law that he would rather die than not be financially successful. And Carlton Gary was selling cocaine, robbing homes, even while dating a variety of women, including a policewoman and psychiatric nurse, while he was raping and murdering the matrons of Wynnton. Simultaneously he was providing emotional support for his beloved aunt Alma, who was in a nursing home. He would regularly visit her and walk the grounds with her, she on her walker and he holding steady, until she died. He was also a male fashion model and appeared on local television at the same time that he was robbing, raping, and killing his victims.

The killer who best personified the mask of sanity was the homophobic murderer John Wayne Gacy. At eighteen, Gacy began his involvement with Chicago politics by working as an assistant precinct captain on behalf of the Democratic candidate Philip Elderman. At long last he felt pride in himself of the same type that he'd felt when he ran the Chi Rho social club in high school. Although his father had constantly abused him by verbally castrating him as a child, and berated him for his involvement in community activities, as an adult he remained active in local Democratic politics. He would also become a member of the JCs and would be known to many as the hardest-working community volunteer in town. He was the grand marshal of the Polish Day Parade in Chicago for several years during which he directed the efforts of more than seven hundred people. During the same period that he ritualistically killed at least thirty-three young boys and buried their bodies in a muddy crawl space beneath his house, he began a construction business, tried to keep his marriage alive, and had many legitimate and illegitimate business deals all going on the side with a variety of young men who were working for him in his construction business. The deals ranged from getting better prices for lumber to arranging for robberies and the sales of drugs. And all the while Gacy was fighting a compulsive battle within himself to keep his composure and maintain his ability to navigate within a social reality. It was a battle that he eventually lost.

Dressed in sad-faced clown makeup and known as Pogo the Clown, Gacy would go with other JCs on a legitimate mission of mercy, namely, the entertainment of young children at hospitals in the Chicago metropolitan area. One of his favorite methods to lure laughter out of bedridden children was to trick them into handcuffing themselves. The surprise at being handcuffed was quickly mitigated by the clown's laughter and the release of the magician's young assistant. It was a favourite trick for the children who saw his act. He later used this same paraphernalia as part of his seduction ritual of the young males he killed. He would lure them into the handcuff trick at his moment of springing the trap. They would later be tortured and killed. During this period he was named the best JC chaplain for the state of Iowa. When the police searched his house they found pictures of Gacy shaking hands with Mayor Richard Daly and with Rosalyn Carter, the wife of President Jimmy Carter.

It was not enough that Gacy earned more than two hundred thousand dollars a year from his new business, nor was it enough that he was named the best JC of Waterloo, Iowa, or that he perceived that the mayor of Chicago depended upon him to deliver his precinct's votes. The more he accomplished, the more he needed to achieve and the more his grip upon normalcy was challenged by the drive to commit more murders. He would wash old ladies' windows, funnel complaints by people in his political precinct to the Democratic district leaders, and he was even assigned to escort Rosalyn Carter through Chicago on one of her campaign visits in 1976. And all the while he was a killer of young boys, lapsing into episodes of violence, the disclosure of which would rock an entire community and outrage a nation.

The other star performer who led a double life was Ted Bundy, who is still awaiting execution on Florida's death row. During the time he was killing more than thirty-five college coeds in Seattle he was doing course work for a prelaw degree, volunteering on a suicide prevention hotline, and working in local politics. Although a rapist, he wrote a rape prevention guidebook for the state of Washington and even obtained a mail-order Ph.D. in psychology from a degree mill in Washington which enabled him to open a private practice as a psychotherapist. What was most astounding about Bundy's double existence was that Bob Keppel of the Seattle police was investigating Bundy at the time. Bundy managed to elude him, flee the state, and finally get arrested in Florida after murdering young women in a college sorority house.

Bundy had been courted by local politicians and administrators at the university who sought his help in ministering to the needs of the large student community in the campus area. Bundy was chivalrous and handsome, and although his fiancée was aware of the dark side of his personality that would make him withdrawn, sullen, and smoldering on the precipice of a violent explosion of temper, she never spoke to the police until close to the very end. She confided her suspicions to a friend, but it was only when a girl referred to the guy who tried to pick her up as Ted that Bundy's fiancée called homicide detective Bob Keppel. By that time Bundy had made plans to flee the state, and his friends still couldn't believe that he was really implicated in a series of unsolved rape-murder cases stretching back for several years.

And finally even Henry Lee Lucas, although of a significantly lower socioeconomic level, managed to fit into the societies he tried to enter. 'He is one of the gentlest and most loving Christian persons I have ever known,' says Clementine Schroeder, confidante, jail minister, and Lucas' lover. Sister Clemmie, as she is known, is a naive country woman from rural Texas who became acquainted with Lucas and his case during her frequent visits to the Georgetown jail where he was held and where she was the ad hoc minister and religious counselor to the inmates. Since converting Lucas to Christianity – he had already claimed a religious vision in his cell after being arrested for the murder of Granny Rich – and becoming convinced that God sent Lucas, the most evil man in the world, into her ken for her to convert and nurture, their friendship has evolved into a lovers' relationship. Their stated dream is for Lucas to become free so that they can open a halfway house for prisoners. Lucas was also well loved by the family of Ottis Toole in Jacksonville, Florida, to the point where they allowed him to raise two of their youngest children, Becky and Frank Powell. Little did they know at the time that Lucas would train them both in the ways of murder, teach them the religious ministrations of Satanism, and become the common-law husband of Becky, whom he would ultimately stab to death, dismember, and bury. Frank Powell is confined to a mental institution in Florida to this day.

Lucas was able to ingratiate himself with the Powells and with the Riches because he was self-effacing, humble, and bore all the marks of a victim himself. Because he never had to work himself into a fury to kill those people he knew – it was a split-second, hair-trigger reaction – he never posed a threat. Granny Rich's children in Texas recognized that something was wrong with Lucas and pressured their mother to ask Lucas and Powell to move out, but to the members of the House of Prayer community, Lucas was just another drifter who signed on to do day work for the roofing company. He was able to camouflage himself amid the group until the very end when he no longer cared about evading the sheriff.

Pattern 3 – Compulsivity

Serial killers and potential serial killers have deeply compulsive personalities, and the compulsivity is manifested in more than one or two ways at a time. Several of the killers researched for this book had compulsivity concerning their physical appearance. Bobby Joe Long took several showers a day, sometimes as many as six, during most of his adult life even before the motorcycle accident. Carlton Gary was also a compulsive showerer.

He interrupted the court proceedings on several occasions because of self-criticism he had about the way he was dressed or the way he thought his physical appearance seemed to onlookers in the courtroom. Leonard Lake also had a compulsivity about being neat and clean around the home, according to his ex-wife Cricket Balazs, who reported that the two often argued about her cleanliness. As part of his murder ritual, he forced his victims to take showers prior to their rape and eventual murder.

Many serial killers are also compulsive record keepers. They maintain scrapbooks and organized memorabilia concerning the killings as well as preserving parts of their victims' bodies or clothing. This pattern is so common among the killers that some homicide detectives feel that the discovery of souvenirs is a high-priority piece of evidence during the investigation. Among the items of memorabilia catalogued by the serial killers in our study were scrapbooks with press clippings of the murders, press clippings of other or similar serial killings, books on psychology and deviant behavior, books on people who suffered from multiple personalities and manifested violent criminal behavior, biographies of Hitler and other mass murderers, personal items or body parts of the victims. These are especially indicative of the serial murderer syndrome because the taking of a victim's body part is associated with the ritualistic fantasy and it becomes a totem. Among the items catalogued were teeth, fingers, toes, nipples, breasts, and penises. Clothing and underwear were also collected as were snippets of hair, barrettes, and articles of decoration that the victims wore.

In some cases, killers have preserved whole sections of their victims' bodies, such as legs, trunks, and torsos. Edmund Kemper, for example, murdered his mother and kept her head in his possession for weeks after the killing. He also preserved the heads of some of his other victims. He would use the decaying heads as masturbatory objects as well as dart boards. He went so far after killing his verbally manipulative and cruel mother as to remove her vocal cords and run them through the garbage disposal unit.

Ed Gein kept his mother's cadaver, which he had amateurishly embalmed, on the property for many years. Gein masturbated with his mother's cadaver on frequent occasions during his killing sprees. He also made lampshades out of the skins of his victims and wove bracelets out of their hair.

A third pattern of compulsivity is the taking and cataloguing of photographs of victims by many of the killers. Leonard Lake kept an elaborate set of photographic records of his crimes. He attracted victims to his rural northern California encampment with classified ads in the San Francisco papers offering different types of equipment for sale. Records now in police custody include home videotapes of the torture of his victims, photographs of nude young girls, and photo scrapbooks of his victims. In some cases Lake murdered entire families whose only legacies are the photographs of their final agonies.

As a child, Lake was also a compulsive record keeper and maintained active studies about the life cycles of rats. From these recorded observations, the gifted child became a self-taught geneticist. His record keeping and neurotically compulsive attention to repeating the same patterns of behavior formed one of the basic patterns of his life.

Obsessive attention to detail and compulsivity regarding the performance of ritualistic daily activities are two behavioral symptoms that might indicate a violently unstable personality. These forms of personal emotional rigidity appear very early in afflicted persons and do not disappear as the persons grow older. And while it is natural for some children to develop rigid personalities in response to a difficult home environment or to social difficulties, this rigidity subsides after adolescence. Shades of it may linger into adult life, where it forms a cushion against an uncertain world, but the compulsive person tends to be neurotic and shrinks from violence. In the sociopath, interference with one's compulsivity can be punished by violence, especially when the compulsivity points to a deeper ritualistic behavior. This becomes the psychological no man's land for the emerging serial killer and often forms the trigger that launches his career. The more persistently compulsive the adult becomes, and the more habits are involved in the compulsion, the greater the probability that there is a severe underlying instability that could be a time bomb waiting for a skein of victims.

Compulsion and obsession manifest themselves further in the trolling or cruising activity associated with a search for a victim. Like the relentless animal hunt for food, the killers patrol their areas with little attention to the time of day or season of the year. If they sense the nearby presence of potential victims – the lounges and sorority houses of college campuses for Ted Bundy, the strip bars just north of Tampa for Bobby Joe Long, or the Chicago bus station for John Gacy – the killers weave through an area for a vulnerable victim as a fisherman trolls with his net for the catch.

Many killers have extraordinarily high mileage on their cars, and this can lead to their identification and arrest. Pierce Brooks and other FBI theorists have developed a component of the VICAP that can trace killers during their compulsive driving patterns from state to state. The best known and most successful of these FBI manhunts was the search for Christopher Wilder, a serial murderer who preyed on beauty contestants at pageants.

The serial killer's trolling pattern seems to have a biological correlative in the aura state preceding a seizure-like episode in the limbic brain. The trolling pattern, a relentless and obsessive weaving from place to place as if laying out a net, possibly being enacted out of a rhythm of electrical activity. It mirrors the activation of a primal self-stimulation circuit just below the conscious awareness of the killer. Possibly the killer is becoming hyperstimulated in the aura phase as neurons deep in the primitive brain begin to fire and cause a turbulence of early memories and primal emotions to mingle with live sensory data. The delusions and fantasies take over the killer's consciousness and the compulsion to kill drives him in search of his next victim.

Pattern 4 – Search for Help

Each killing or set of killings has a gestation period in that a killer reaches an unconscious point of no return. At this point he loses the conscious ability to control his actions. Prior to this, the serial murderer reaches out in various ways to ask for help. He can sense the primal rumblings of the violence fomenting in a part of his brain. He may, especially if he suffers from psychomotor epilepsy, experience an aura immediately preceding the seizure. Or the first images of his delusions may intrude upon his sleep and fill his dreams with his most primal fears from early childhood. It is at these moments, when he feels reality slipping away again, that he is most vulnerable and apt to cry out for help. Unfortunately, these moments can be fleeting, and once he becomes trapped in his own fantasies he is out of control.

However, long before the serial killer fully emerges, sometimes even in late childhood, the conscious brain tries to seek help to prevent the damaged primitive brain from exercising control. Edmund Kemper's career was marked by this reaching out as were the careers of Henry Lee Lucas and Bobby Joe Long. Kemper, who was in the hospital as a teenager after killing his grandparents, had been receiving psychotherapy with fair results. He asked for help and revealed the hatred that he had for his mother and the fear of manipulation and control that she aroused in him. The staff psychologist agreed with the patient and recommended to the parole board that he should not be released into her custody. 'This young man's mother has had her pound of flesh from Kemper,' the psychologist reported. He suggested that the boy be 'set free from the mother.' Kemper felt the same way, but the parole board intervened and rejected the recommendation of the psychologist and of Kemper's own testimony. They appointed the mother custodian of the vulnerable boy and returned him directly to the environment that had helped nurture his feelings of hatred and violence. This deadly pairing at the time that Kemper had pleaded for intervention and help culminated in Kemper's finally killing his mother and decapitating her.

Carlton Gary also revealed his violent tendencies when he was serving time in Ossining, New York, for the robberies of welfare recipients in Albany almost five years before he began his killing spree in Columbus, Georgia. He reported that he told the prison psychiatrists that he was a killer and was compelled to commit crimes at regular intervals by forces inside him that he could not control. The prison psychiatrists rejected his sensational claim and returned him to the cell block.

Similarly, Bobby Joe Long spent years after his motorcycle accident and resulting severe head injury trying to convince Army and civilian doctors that he was suffering from an injury-induced behavioral disorder. He reported to doctors that after he awoke in the hospital he felt that his sexual needs and his whole life were out of control. This frightened him because he had never felt that way before and because he realized that there was something seriously wrong with the way he was feeling. The Army doctors argued that he was simply trying to get more medical benefits or a medical discharge from the service and did not conduct further examinations. Other neurologists in Florida also failed to pursue the issue. Even in prison today the examinations he received were cursory until Dorothy Lewis began her neuropsychiatric evaluation.

Long also felt the need to seek medical attention even while he was committing the classified ad rapes. He was dating a nurse who suggested that he visit a psychiatrist and explain the strange forces that seemed to be driving him. While standing outside the doctor's office building, Long became afraid that he would be summarily turned over to the police and that his problems would remain unsolved. Hence he did not keep the appointment, and the rape/burglaries escalated into rape/murders within a few short years.

And finally Long's probable cousin, Henry Lee Lucas, reported that when he was about to be paroled after serving six years for the murder of his mother he tried to warn the personnel at the hospital that he was not ready to leave and still needed help in learning to cope with life. 'I tried marriage, and that didn't work. I tried religion, and that didn't work. And I tried to make friends, and I tried to reunite myself with my sisters, and none of that worked.' All his attempts to find an anchor in life that would keep him from drifting into the control of the destructive forces within him failed. No other people bonded with him to help him exert control over those forces. It was only in the prison environment that Lucas could find the necessary structure that would keep the forces in check and in which he could maintain a homeostasis concerning his most violent tendencies. He warned the prison officials in Ionia that he would kill again if released. However, they had severe overcrowding at the prison and released him on parole. Lucas reports that he raped and killed a woman near the prison and deposited her body just outside the gate. The body of another Jane Doe turned up five miles away from the prison just a few days later, and Lucas confessed to that murder as well.

Pattern 5 – Severe Memory Disorders and a Chronic Inability to Tell the Truth

Often individuals predisposed to episodic violence become pathological liars. On the one hand, lying is simply an extension of their chameleon-like ability to blend in with their background. They sense the information that people around them want to hear and provide it. Truth is not an issue for them, survival is. On the other hand, the concept of living according to a standard of honor and truth is a higher, intellectual virtue that can only be maintained by a person who is not a sociopath and does not have fundamental character disorders. The types of physiological damage to the hypothalamus and to the limbic region of the brain or the temporal lobe that helps the developing infant individuate himself from the rest of the world so distort the person's behavior that the concepts of truth and honesty are meaningless. Truth demands that the person perceive a modicum of self-worth. Because most episodically violent individuals perceive themselves as having no worth and no meaning for life, they are honest neither with themselves nor with others.

On a practical level, lying is a form of manipulaton. If one can lie successfully one can get others to believe what one wants them to. It can also be argued that, in politics and business, people lie as a rule and are not serial killers. Institutions routinely lie to protect themselves and their officers, and different cultural groups routinely lie to one another out of self-protection and the need to manipulate. Therefore, lying is also a practiced skill that the serial killer practices better than most.

When lying becomes chronic in the schoolchild or in the person whose recapitulation of basic facts may change from day to day, it is an indicator of other serious behavioral disorders. However, the clinical distinction must be made between lying out of practice and lying out of the brain's need to survive. Most serial killers sincerely believe the stories they are telling when they are telling them. Henry Lee Lucas, for example, confessed to more than three hundred murders. Some of those confessions were true, others were deliberate lies, and others were lies because police presented him with facts and he confessed to them because he thought it would please the authorities. Lucas might have truly believed he committed many of the crimes he confessed to. He might have felt that, if the police had evidence against him and his memory of the events was obscure, he would confess and save them the trouble of keeping the case open on the books. Besides, there was a behavioral pattern at work. When Lucas confessed to a crime he was rewarded and praised. It was easy to obtain rewards and praise from the police by confessing to all the crimes they asked him about.

Soon after some of his confessions proved to be inaccurate, Lucas recanted. Ultimately he recanted all of his murder confessions, including the killings of Becky Powell and Granny Rich. He changed his story because other prison authorities suggested that Lucas had done a bad thing by confessing to crimes he really hadn't committed. Now he had a new set of authorities to please, and he promptly changed his story to earn praise and rewards from them. His strategy has succeeded, and he changed the details of his past to conform to the wishes of the person who was conducting the interrogation.

Some experts feel that the memory disorders that afflict episodically violent people result from the periods of epileptic-like seizures, loss of conscious awareness during hallucinatory periods, and the dreamlike states that could even result from organically induced delusions from within the limbic brain. Similarly, killers who are chronic drug or alcohol abusers have lapses of memory during stupors and walking coma-like states. This loss of memory is counterbalanced by a pattern of hyperamnesia, or an extraordinary ability to remember the tiniest details of an event, that is also manifested in serial killers. The two patterns can coexist because the brain is unable to impose a structural management upon the neurological memory banks. Hence there are severe lapses of memory punctuated by reminiscences of small events like islands in the middle of an ocean of darkness.

Pattern 6 – Suicidal Tendencies

Often serial killers who are not caught eventually kill themselves. This is the final act in a life of utter despair and hopelessness. The suicide of such a serial killer is an active thought that has probably been with him since childhood. He learns to live with it as a daily option, choosing to act upon it only when his revulsion at what he is doing is too great to bear any longer. Most serial killers find ways to turn themselves in before they choose to commit suicide. They accomplish this by becoming too despondent to take the care to conceal their latest crime. In Bobby Joe Long's case he simply let a young woman, his next to last victim, free without killing her. She alerted the police within hours and provided a description of Long, his apartment, and his car. Unfortunately, the police were unable to place him under surveillance until after he had committed his next murder, and he committed that murder in the open. He also drove around Tampa with the body still in his car, hoping to get caught.

Long didn't flee the city after he let her go even though he realized that the police would soon catch up with him. When his wife called him to ask him about the sequence of rapes taking place in his area, he realized that the police had been in contact with her as well, and still he didn't leave the area. He began his confession the moment he was placed in police custody.

Lucas' story is similar. After he killed Becky Powell he grieved over the body. Then he promised her that he would find a way to end his career. He later revealed that after Becky's death all the energy seemed to flow out of him and he no longer had the need to protect himself. He wanted his career to end and made himself available to the police until they had the evidence to arrest him. He, too, began confessing his crimes shortly after he was arrested.

Pattern 7 – History of Serious Assault

Serial killers do not emerge in a vacuum. All of the killers in our study had a history of serious assault long before they committed their first murders. Often these assaults began in elementary school and took the form of attacks upon peers with lethal weapons or heavy objects. This indicator, readily apparent to teachers, school nurses, and guidance officers, is an early sign that the individual has a severe behavior disorder which can only be expressed through an inappropriate level of violence. The histories of Lucas, Kemper, and Carlton Gary serve as examples of the early background of criminal assault which occurred long before they committed their first homicides.

Pattern 8 – Deviate Sexual Behavior and Hypersexuality

Most of the serial killers on our list had long histories of deviate sexual behavior in their childhoods. Many, like Henry Lee Lucas, frequently exposed their genitalia to their peers when they were very young and escalated very quickly to forms of sexual assault upon their peers and younger siblings. In Lucas' case, he claimed he committed sex with relatives while still very young, and later testified to bestiality with animals he had killed. Lucas committed his first rape and murder when he was fifteen and then had sex with the dead body before he buried it.

Although his sister denies this, Gary Schaefer claimed in his confession to the Caty Richards murder that he was forced to have sex with his sister, who beat him afterwards to frighten him into keeping silent about the event. Joseph Kallinger and Charles Manson also reported histories of deviant sexual behavior in their early lives.

Pattern 9 – Head Injuries or Injuries Incurred at Birth

A history of head trauma or head injuries from birth is one of the common patterns uniting most of the serial murderers. When Dorothy Lewis begins her evaluations of convicted killers, she looks for a history of head injury first, because the damage that can be sustained to the temporal lobe, limbic region, or hypothalamus can severely alter behavior to the point where the individual is no longer responsible for his actions during episodic electrical discharges. The electrobiological pattern of aura-seizure activity-postactivity stupor mirrors the actual behavior pattern of delusions or hallucinations that precede a trolling period, discrete periods of criminal violence, depression and sleep, and memory loss or memory confusion of the entire sequence of events. When this pattern is present in the criminal behavior of the individual, it is likely that it is the result of damage to the areas of the primitive brain.

Henry Lee Lucas, Bobby Joe Long, Carlton Gary, Ted Bundy, Charles Manson, Leonard Lake, and John Gacy have all had either severe head injuries, repeated head traumas, or damage that occurred during birth. Almost all of them suffered signs which resemble some form of psychomotor epilepsy or severe hormonal imbalance which can be the result of a disorder in the hypothalamus. Because the primitive brain is the most vulnerable to injuries occurring on the side of the head – because of the thinness of the skull at that point and the lack of internal fluid protection – individuals who have received sustained blows to the side of the head are often at risk. Therefore it is incumbent upon medical personnel, especially school medical personnel, who are aware of children who have a history of head injuries, even if those injuries seem minor at the time, to identify those cases for possible follow-up. One of the similarities in all serial murder histories is that the individuals seem particularly vulnerable to repeated head traumas after they have received the first one. Lucas, for example, sustained so many head traumas and invasive eye injuries during his childhood that he lost his eye and experienced a coma on more than one occasion. Bobby Joe Long also had at least three severe head injuries before the massive concussion in the motorcycle accident that sent him into a coma. Repeated head injuries are one of the most important patterns for identification of individuals who are at risk of becoming episodically violent, even if there is no diagnosed brain malfunction.

Pattern 10 – History of Chronic Drug or Alcohol Abuse

Most multiple killers whom we have studied, serial killers as well as mass murderers, are consistently addicted to or dependent upon drugs or alcohol or both. These drugs include both prescription medications, such as psychotropics and barbiturates, and recreational drugs, such as amphetamines, psychedelics, cocaine, and heavy narcotics. Henry Lee Lucas reported that he was drunk every time he killed someone. John Gacy reported that he would start drinking before he went out cruising for a new encounter in the gay hustler bars and bus stations. Bob Long was, for a long time, a very heavy user of LSD and marijuana in the 1970s and routinely consumed large amounts of alcohol in the strip bars where he was searching for new victims. Nightstalker (Richard Ramirez) was addicted to cocaine during the year that he committed his murders in Los Angeles, and Carlton Gary was a cocaine addict as well as a pusher during the period in which he committed the murders in Wynnton.

Both narcotics and alcohol have similar effects on the brain and neurological system: they depress general body function while they suppress the normal social controls that keep aberrant behavior impulses in check. If the individual already has a damaged social control mechanism, the narcotic effects of alcohol or drugs, especially during periods of episodic delusions or hallucinations, can unleash a Hyde-like character capable of extraordinary violence. All human beings have this type of neurological entity within them. However, the overlying structures of the higher brain, the hormonal control mechanisms in the normally functioning hypothalamus, and the learned behavior to which people adapt within the typical family and social structure teach them how to subordinate their most primitive feelings and keep them in check.

Even with normal adults, if those social controls fail, the individual may find himself losing the ability to temper his anger or restrain his violent impulses. If a person has had even a little alcohol, he may find that his judgmental abilities have become impaired; recreational drugs such as marijuana in small amounts also allow people's more primitive feelings to come out; and during periods of dieting and reduced nutritional intake people are normally short-tempered and unable to cope with minor adversities. The episodically violent individual must live with these feelings of rage, fear, hopelessness, and incipient violence on a daily basis, even when he is not hallucinating or in the throes of a deep brain seizure. The critical combination of brain damage, child abuse, inability to secrete toxins, and the use of alcohol or drugs is already considered by some experts as a predictor of dangerousness.

Pattern 11 – Alcohol- or Drug-abusing Parents

A large segment of the criminal population in American prisons come from families in which one or both parents were chronic substance abusers. Some of these criminals were born with congenital drug dependencies and have lived the lives of junkies or alcoholics without ever having the ability to detoxify their systems. Other criminals were introduced to alcohol or drugs before adolescence and indulged in the substances as a matter of course. Henry Lee Lucas' mother was an alcoholic and his father was a bootlegger. Lucas was drinking regularly before the age of ten and by his teenage years had himself become an abuser.

The presence of alcohol or drugs in the family situation also influences the family life to a large degree and is symptomatic of other types of disorders. Therefore children who grow up in homes where a chronic substance abuse is present are at risk because the substance abuser cannot make an effective parent and will introduce the child, either passively or actively, to either alcohol or drugs, and if the substance abuse problem is congenital it is possible that the child may have inherited it.

Pattern 12 – Victim of Physical or Emotional Abuse or of Cruel Parenting

Marvin Wolfgang and others have shown conclusively that child abuse begets abuse. In his study of males born in the Philadelphia area in 1945, those individuals who were abused as children were very likely to become abusive adults. This finding is borne out by the serial killers in our study. Every one of them was abused in some way as a child, either physically or emotionally. Henry Lee Lucas is the extreme example. He was beaten, knocked unconscious, and repeatedly injured by his mother and her pimp. He grew up with absolutely no sense of self-worth and routinely inflicted abuse on animate and inanimate objects alike. In his confessions he described human beings as pieces of flesh to be cut up, burned, and used as masturbatory articles. He referred to his victims not as people but as 'strangles' or 'stabbings,' nameless entities that had the misfortune to encounter him during his periods of episodic violence. It was only after he had actually nurtured Becky Powell and felt love for her that he was able to feel remorse and guilt at having stabbed her. That broke his skein of murders.

Alice Miller has written that parents need not necessarily be physically abusive to the child. The passively cruel parent who imposes a rigid set of conflicting beliefs upon the child can create a monster. Bobby Joe Long describes his mother as cruel in her disregard for his needs. After he had reached adolescence he claims he was manipulated into conflict with one of her boyfriends on at least one occasion during which he had to beat the man up just to protect himself. On another occasion he was so angry at the attention his mother showered upon her little dog, in contrast to the neglect that he received, that he shoved a .22-caliber bullet into the dog's vagina.

Pattern 13 – Result of an Unwanted Pregnancy

Although many children are not actually planned, and a significant number might not be wanted at first, most parents accept the fact that they are going to have a child and do not deliberately inflict the inconvenience of the child's existence upon him. When that does occur, the child will grow up to be a scarred adult, but, again, most healthy people can live with those scars and not become emotionally disabled. Serial killers, however, belong to the extreme category of children who were not only unwanted but were punished for having been born. Children in this category are invariably at a high risk of confrontation with the criminal justice system at some point before they reach adulthood. Their socioeconomic status, the quality of their home life, the amount of physical or emotional abuse they receive, and the violence present in their environment will, in large measure, determine the extent of that risk. Senator Patrick Moynihan has suggested that the lack of sex education among young people today, especially children who have grown up in families on welfare or below the poverty level, is creating an entire generation of unwanted children who will become almost permanent wards of society. They will tax the ability of the social services system to provide for them and will ultimately enter the criminal justice system, where they will create an additional burden. These are unwanted children, children whose very existence is perceived by their parents as a form of retribution. As they reach childbearing age, they will also spawn another generation of children who are unplanned and unwanted. Unless this public health issue is addressed, society will simply be creating more generations of potentially violent offenders.

Pattern 14 – Products of a Difficult Gestation Period for the Mother

Almost all of the serial killers studied were born to mothers who had a difficult time during the pregnancy. In some cases the difficulties were self-inflicted because of alcohol or drug addiction. In other cases the extreme poverty of the family made the pregnancy difficult to sustain, and medical attention was almost nonexistent. And, in still other situations, because the mother did not want to be pregnant in the first place she was emotionally conflicted throughout the term and the child suffered accordingly.

Just what role a happy pregnancy plays in the development of the child has not been adequately documented. Researchers know, for example, that anxiety and tension in the mother are translated into the secretion of hormones that can affect the developing fetus. If the anxiety occurs immediately after the first quarter of the pregnancy, when the fetus' brain and autonomic nervous systems are developing, some form of brain malformation can result. At the very least, the brain may be dysfunctional in one or more ways. The area of the dysfunction and the seriousness of the damage determine how likely the child will be to have severe developmental problems and become a violence-prone individual. Even if the child is not damaged at birth, the mother's anxieties may result in a colicky, unhappy baby who becomes the object of mistreatment and abuse by a mother who was unhappy about being pregnant. Such mistreatment is also a factor in the development of a violence-prone individual.

Pattern 15 – Interrupted Bliss or No Bliss of Childhood

Serial killers are deeply sad people who can take no joy whatsoever in anything they derive from life. A major component of their sadness is that they never learned how to be happy, they were incapable of allowing themselves any pleasure as children. For most normal people, childhood is a pleasurable experience in which the developing individual learns how to be happy and how to derive happiness from as many situations as possible. We learn how to be optimists or pessimists as children and where to find happiness and pleasure. Because serial killers were deprived of this bliss of childhood, they do not have the emotional mechanism that allows them to feel pleasure as adults. As simple neurotics, they are condemned to look at the underside of life, seeing only the unhappiness that reflects their own unhappy state. As psychotics and sociopaths, they completely lack the ability to understand happiness or joy. These are foreign emotions. As brain-damaged or dysfunctional individuals, their organic pleasure centers in the primitive brain do not operate, and they are physically incapable of sensing pleasure.

Pattern 16 – Extraordinary Cruelty to Animals

It is not abnormal for a child to become fascinated with how ants can still walk after they've lost two or three of their legs or with the dance of a dying fly or spider. It is, however, quite abnormal for a child to torture household pets and larger animals for the pure delight of watching them suffer. Children who beat dogs and inflict injuries on cats out of a sheer lust for watching the animal suffer are children in crisis, and most of the serial killers in our study have taken just such delight in the pain of other creatures.

Henry Lee Lucas used to torture animals until they died, and then have sex with their remains. Bob Long, as we mention above, was so jealous of the attention and love that his mother showered upon her little dog that he shoved a .22-caliber bullet into the dog's vagina. He still remembers the incident and recalls that his frustration at not being able to receive any attention from his mother drove him into a fury. 'She wouldn't even bother to feed me,' he explains. 'But she would cook steaks and stews for that dog to eat. I had to make my own dinner.'

Pattern 17 – Arsonal Tendencies Without Obvious Homicidal Interest

Fire-starting is one early warning sign of psychotic or sociopathic dangerousness. The interest in fires is more than the passing fascination with the movement of the flames, it is the delight in the destruction that fire itself can cause and it is the interest in the indirect damage that one can inflict by igniting a fire. Carlton Gary was a fire-starter before adolescence as was Henry Lucas. But both individuals set fires as means of destruction without seeking the death of another person. The interest in setting fires usually disappears shortly after the individual reaches adolescence and begins committing violence with his own hands.

Pattern 18 – Symptoms of Neurological Impairment

Almost all serial killers display symptoms of neurological impairment, both soft and hard signs. These can be as straightforward as a consistent confusion between right and left, a reversal of letters of numbers, or more profound reading and learning disabilities with associated behavioral disorders. Depending upon the degree of damage to the underlying neurological structure, the individual may experience a complete distortion of sensory experience even during periods of nonviolence. During seizure-like violent episodes, the delusions or hallucinations might involve significantly greater distortions. The following impairments should be considered high-risk factors if they still appear in individuals after adolescence:

1. Dyslexia
2. Reading, mathematics, or directional problems
3. Hypergraphia
4. Grandiosity
5. Hypervigilance
6. Hypersexuality
7. Hyposexuality
8. Hyperreligiosity
9. Visual or auditory hallucinations
10. Loose, rambling, or illogical thought processes
11. Paranoid feelings or chronic feelings of persecution
12. Chronic feelings of isolation, alienation, or withdrawal
13. Prolonged and profound chronic depression and crying
14. Incontinence
15. Sleep disorders
16. Difficulty with spatial coordination and perception
17. Poor muscular coordination
18. History of seizures or seizurelike episodes

19. Reading or mathematical disabilities that resist remediation
20. Chronic headaches or migraine headaches
21. Lability of moods
22. Choreaform body movements or animallike body movements

Pattern 19 – Evidence of Genetic Disorders

Researchers have suggested that if an individual has at least three to five physical anomalies, such as webbed skin between his fingers or earlobes that are connected to the sides of his head, it is likely that he also has a genetic disorder of the primal brain. Because the development of the fetal brain takes place at the same time that the skin develops, any skin or cartilage abnormalities are usually indicators that the brain, too, has not completely developed. When such abnormalities prevail in families – for instance, the similarity of long toes in the Long and Lucas families – then it is likely that a congenital defect is causing the damage. The following abnormalities are representative indicators of genetic damage:

1. Bulbous fingertips
2. Fine or electric wire hair that will not comb down
3. Very fine hair that is soon awry after combing
4. Hair whorls
5. Head circumference outside a normal range of 1.5 cm or less than 1.5 cm
6. Epicanthus – upper and lower eyelids join the nose (the point of union is either deeply covered or partially covered)
7. Hyperteliorism – larger than normal distance between tear ducts or lower than normal distance between tear ducts
8. Low-seated ears – the point where the ear joins the head is not in line with the corner of the eye and the

nose bridge; it is either lower by .5 cm or greater than .5 cm

9. Adherent earlobes – lower edge of ear is extended upward and backward toward the crown of the head
10. Malformed ears
11. Asymmetrical ears
12. Very soft or very pliable ears
13. High-steepled palate
14. Roof of mouth is definitely steepled or flat and narrow
15. Forward tongue with deep ridges
16. Speckled tongue with either smooth or rough spots
17. Curved fifth finger – marked curve toward the other fingers or slightly curved inward toward other fingers
18. Singular transverse palmar crease
19. Third toe is longer than second toe or equal in length to second toe
20. Partial syndactyly of two middle toes
21. Larger than normal gap between first and second toes
22. Abnormalities in teeth
23. Abnormalities in dermatoglyphics

Pattern 20 – Biochemical Symptoms

Episodically violent individuals are often victims of toxic poisoning either through the inability of their systems to throw off toxins or because their environments have high levels of toxins. William Walsh's experiments on Lucas and other serial murderers have shown that episodically violent people have extraordinarily high levels of lead and cadmium present in strands of their hair. Other trace minerals appear in large concentrations in the chronically violent individual.

Pattern 21 – Feelings of Powerlessness or Inadequacy

Part of the tragedy of the serial killer's predatory behavior is that each killing only proves to him that he is powerless. The ritualistic murder that is an enactment of his power turns out to be only further proof that he is powerless to deal with the living and can only assume life-size proportions over the dead. The serial killer thrives among the dead; they rather than living people are his companions. And because of this he is truly dead inside.

This sense of powerlessness is an important indicator of future behavior because representations of it will appear in young people, particularly adolescents. One of the early signs that a child is reaching emotional adolescence is that he begins to exercise power. Sometimes that power takes the form of a direct confrontation or challenge to adult authority, but this challenge is normal. When the authority responds to the challenge in a supportive fashion and does not seek to crush the adolescent, the adolescent grows to accept an adult interpretation of authority and the social order and can deal with it. The powerless adolescent, however, will not seek to challenge authority directly. Nor will he seek confrontations. His behavior will be abnormal, even criminal, and will avoid direct confrontation whenever possible. The powerless adolescent will adopt a demeanor of camouflage but will cross swords with authorities in oblique ways. Eventually he will seek invisibility and will finally express himself in bizarre or abnormal behavior.

The sense of powerlessness will soon begin to express itself in the form of deviant sexual behavior, attacks on physically weaker members of the same or opposite sex, petty crimes, extreme cruelty to animals, and even attempted suicide. A large proportion of teenage rapes are actually committed by boys who have a sense of powerlessness so overwhelming that they are actually afraid of young girls. These individuals may also prey on preadolescent girls or young children. If these attacks seem episodic rather than strictly random, the person has a high probability of emerging as a serial killer within ten to fifteen years.

It would be easy to misinterpret these patterns as absolute predictors of future criminal behavior or to measure individuals against these patterns in order to label them as criminal types. This is not the intent of the patterns. The patterns are simply the synthesis of the combined symptomatology of hundreds of serial killers. The overwhelming similarities between them and the identical patterns of injuries that they have suffered; the similarities in their EEG charts and in their lack of physical and emotional resiliency; and the common bond of cruel or bizarre parenting that unites them – all are obvious indications that certain forces shape potential serial murderers. When these forces can be detected individually, especially in children who have not yet confronted the juvenile justice system, it is likely that any potential criminal or antisocial behavior can be short-circuited at the start. In any event, the patterns provide the direction and structure for future research by criminologists, neurologists, and chemists into the organic or physiological basis of criminal behavior.

15

Conclusion

What can society do about the growing menace of serial killers? Simply putting more police on the street and building more jails won't end the violence because the normal forms of deterrents don't work for serial killers. Executing convicted serial killers faster and closing down their avenues of appeal won't work either because most serial killers have a death wish to begin with. In other words, society's reactive attempts to deal with the problem will always fall short. There are too many episodically violent serial murderers emerging too quickly and attacking too many victims for the criminal justice system to keep up. For every one serial killer who is apprehended and brought to trial, three more are emerging and beginning their careers.

The current knowledge of experts in the fields of neurology, internal medicine, psychology, and criminal justice shows that the disease of serial murder is generational. It is passed on through child abuse, negative parenting, and genetic damage. It is activated by the environment through injuries to the person's head, heavy drinking, heavy use of drugs, and prolonged malnutrition. Even after it is activated, it normally requires a combination of serious traumatic events to pull the trigger. In the case of Henry Lee Lucas it was the confrontation with his mother in a bar in Tecumseh, Michigan. For Bobby Joe Long it was the motorcycle accident that left him in a state of hypersexuality. For Charles Manson it was a combination of drugs and the accessibility to all the forbidden fruits of his youth. In the cases of other serial killers, we might never know.

What we do know is that, because normal methods of criminal justice and current medical psychiatric diagnosis don't work, we have to treat serial murder in a different way. If we look at it as a symptom of the type of social violence that Surgeon General C. Everett Koop has described as an issue of public health, then we can treat serial murder as an infectious disease and adopt preventive measures. There is ample evidence to support treating violence as a public health issue. First, homicide is among the ten leading causes of death for all Americans. However, for black males between the ages of fifteen and twenty-four, homicide is currently the leading cause of death, according to the United States Department of Justice.

Second, in addition to the rise in the number of homicides since 1980, the number of aggravated assaults and occurrences of domestic violence have risen sharply as well. The National Crime Survey reports that almost twenty percent of the entire population is involved in spousal abuse, that more than fifty percent of the incidents of abuse against wives occurs on a regular basis at least three or four times a year, and that domestic violence is the foremost cause of injury to women.

Finally, almost two million children and adolescents are the victims of physical violence each year, much of it in the form of sexual abuse committed by a relative or family member. This physical abuse directed against children is called multigenerational domestic violence, and it is one of the core causes of the epidemic of serial murder. It is logical to suppose that as child abuse and domestic violence grow, so does the aggregate number of serial murder victims. The 260 serial killers researched for this book claimed a total of 10,360 victims during the course of their respective careers. This averages out to just under 40 victims per serial killer, a highly disproportionate number of homicides.

Many experts are just beginning to realize that within the next ten years most forms of episodic aggression – including serial murder – could be prevented through an organized programme of testing and diagnosis and intervention. Many of the new testing techniques rely on recent developments in the fields of psychopharmacology, psychosurgery, and nutritional therapies as well as on new diagnostic procedures and 'dangerousness' predictor scales. However, just because the techniques are available, it doesn't mean that the public will be able to set aside its perceptions of some of the most violent criminals in society and see them as truly diseased people.

In order to change political and public opinion about serial murder, the public health service must develop an information campaign about violence and the underlying causes of violent crime. Information about the causes of violence will itself help prevent its spread. Public health labeling that has been so successful with regard to cigarette packaging should be extended to alcohol and violent pornographic and sadistic and demonic materials as well. Warnings that state, 'The chronic consumption of alcoholic beverages can produce violence in some individuals,' or 'The chronic exposure to violent pornography can produce violence in some individuals,' are necessary so that high-risk people will become aware of the dangerous nature of the products they are using.

Rapists, child abusers, sex offenders and individuals convicted of having committed acts of domestic violence against spouses and children should be assigned to rehabilitative therapy groups as a part of their sentences or requirements for parole. These high-risk groups are one of the primal seedbeds out of which serial killers emerge because they usually begin their careers with chronic abuse and sexual assault crimes. While the vast majority of sexual offenders do not go on to become serial murderers, the vast majority of serial murderers were sexual offenders or were fantasizing heavily before they committed their first murders.

Hospitals, emergency trauma centers, clinics, medical offices, schools, and the juvenile departments of local police forces should be expected to investigate the background of any suspected child abuse victim. If the child seems to be a chronic victim, the backgrounds of the child's parents or guardians should be investigated as well. If the child is a victim of abuse, then the court must intervene to protect the individual within the limits of the law. This type of vigorous action might serve as a firebreak by preventing the routine spread of this kind of violence from one generation to the next.

Much research needs to be done on the development of a scale to predict dangerousness in high-risk individuals. The basis for such a scale already exists, but the implementation of a workable set of predictors on a broad basis is still years away and requires the financial support of government and private agencies. It is to everyone's advantage to see this research carried out because state and local governments are already spending hundreds of millions of dollars on apprehending and trying serial murderers and are not even making a dent in preventing new serial murderers from emerging. The private sector is ultimately paying the bill, both in tax dollars and in human lives. And because the number of serial killers and serial murder cases keeps increasing every year, it is clear that present methods of apprehension and adjudication just aren't working. Society needs to aim toward preventing the crimes from happening in the first place, and the only way to accomplish that is to stop the disease in individuals before it claims any victims. This is the reason for the predictor scale and for the financial commitment to developing one that can be used by doctors, school officials, and juvenile justice officials within their respective offices.

The predictor scale should be the result of interdisciplinary projects, especially in the fields of biochemistry, neurology, genetics, social psychology, and criminal justice. And researchers should share knowledge among their respective disciplines, thus avoiding the problem of linkage blindness. The research should also include first-hand and verified information gleaned from stabilized serial killers, rapists, sexual offenders, and other episodically violent individuals. Their observations about their own behavior are invaluable because they offer scientists insight into the workings of the darkest side of the human psyche. Too often, research into the causes and motivations of criminals is conducted by individuals who have never seen the inside of a prison or spoken to convicted felons. More experts simply need hands-on experience.

The public health and criminal justice institutions that come into direct contact with potentially dangerous individuals are already in a position to prevent these people from becoming threats to themselves and to others in the future. First, prisoners who ask for psychological counseling should receive it. Sex offenders who claim that they are subject to hallucinatory experiences or delusions of violence should be taken seriously and given some form of treatment. Had prison psychologists listened to Lucas or to Gary, for example, they might have short-circuited their careers before they began their serial murder sprees. Had Army doctors listened to Bobby Joe Long's complaints about his neurological symptoms, he might have received the treatment he needed. There are convicted rapists in jail at this moment who are asking for medical attention, but they are not receiving it. Some of these people, all of whom will sooner or later be released from prison, are human time bombs who will eventually become tomorrow's lurid newspaper headlines. Even Gary Heidnick, a suspect in a recent torture and serial murder case in Philadelphia, repeatedly asked for but was denied psychological treatment while in prison.

Similarly, schools, which routinely encounter cases of child abuse and extraordinary violence in children, should follow up when the person seems to be potentially dangerous to himself or to others. Had Lucas' schoolteacher, Annie Hall, been able to help Henry without fear of reprisal, he might have become a different person. However, current school procedures prevent most schoolteachers, administrators, and medical personnel from even raising suspicions about child abuse.

The many state laws requiring suppression of police and court records of juveniles further impair the abilities of justice authorities to intervene when a child is at risk. Because so many of the children who appear before the courts are themselves victims of chronic abuse or have already become abusers, they are in dire need of some form of crisis intervention. By the time many of them have reached the adult courts their juvenile criminal records, which are indicative of a life of violent crime, have been suppressed and the criminal courts are forced to start from scratch. If police were allowed to view juvenile records in cases of extraordinary violent crime or when chronic child abuse was noted, they would be better able to prevent this individual's becoming a potential killer.

The entire concept of criminal insanity must be updated and redefined so as to bring it out of the nineteenth century. What scientists now know about the chemical and biological causality of behaviorality has long since overturned traditional concepts of sane and insane behavior. From what we have learned about Henry Lucas, Bobby Joe Long, Albert DeSalvo, and other killers we know that it is possible for a person with severe damage to areas of his primitive brain to act within the guidelines of normalcy during periods between his violent episodes. During their episodes, however, they are acting as if under a different set of programming instructions. They lose touch with reality, experience blackouts, and feel as if something inside of them is directing their actions. Most serial killers can name the President of the United States and can tell their interrogators what year it is and where they are at the moment of their interrogation. However, they cannot account for the forces that compelled them to commit their crimes. These people need medical attention. By redefining insanity to account for episodically violent behavior, a whole new class of criminals will be admitted to state-administered therapy programs. In so doing, states will routinely be preventing potential serial killers from committing their first homicides.

The fear among defense lawyers, some doctors, schools, and civil liberties organizations is that any attempt to identify people, especially children, as potentially violent individuals would inevitably lead to a Draconian system of cataloguing people and identifying them as criminals in the making. The resulting tracking and identification procedures would leave individuals so catalogued with invisible tags that would be attached to them for the rest of their lives. These fears are justified. Without question, if an irresponsible society began tagging individuals as predisposed to criminal behavior, the potential for abuse of civil rights would be enormous. That is one of the reasons why, when Richard Nixon's personal physician, Arnold Hutsnecker, suggested a similar program eighteen years ago, he was widely criticized by civil rights groups.

The programme that we're suggesting is not a labeling

mechanism for identifying a potentially violent murderer but a crisis intervention plan designed to protect all children from abuse or from an illness. If a pediatrician recognizes that a child's tendencies go well beyond normal aggressiveness into the realm of extraordinary violence or homicidal aggression, he or she should have a method of reporting it to the parents or to the local juvenile authorities without fear of reprisal. Similarly, an emergency room physician or a school nurse who treats a child for what he or she believes to be physical abuse should be able to forward information to the police without fear of being sued by the parents, even if the suspicions prove to be untrue. If the report is made in good faith, neither the nurse, the doctor, the school, nor the hospital should be held liable, and the utmost integrity is required.

Such a program for identifying educational underachievers or children with chronic learning disabilities already exists as an entitlement program of the federal government. Procedures that provide for diagnosing these children, establishing independent educational plans for them, while at the same time safeguarding their rights as they progress through school can easily serve as the basis for establishing a program for identifying the abused or extraordinarily violent child. In other words, if a school nurse or physician recognizes a 'homicidally aggressive' child, the child should not be labeled as a potentially violent murderer but should be seen as an individual suffering from an illness akin to chronic depression or a childhood psychosis. The focus should be on finding out what is causing the extraordinary aggressiveness in the child's environment and then channeling the feelings of aggression positively.

We must ask ourselves what the proper limits of intervention are. At what point may a health professional, educator, or officer of the court legally enter a domestic setting to make a decision regarding the environment of the child? When might such an entry constitute an unlawful intrusion and a violation of rights that outweighs a clear and present danger to the child? These are the questions that society has to answer if its institutions are not to be overwhelmed by an epidemic of serial murder and other forms of episodic violence. But decisions have to be made soon because time is quickly running out. If the present generation is allowed to spawn another generation of serial killers and mass murderers, the legal and social institutions won't be able to handle them. At that point the society we know can be consumed in its own violence and repressiveness.

HELTER SKELTER

9:05 A.M., August 9. Three LAPD officers arrive at the Sharon Tate residence in response to a Code 2. They find the first bloody victim in a white Rambler parked in the driveway. Victims two and three—male, Caucasian, probably in his thirties; female, Caucasian, probably in her twenties—are on the lawn. The officers enter the house. In the living room is a long couch. Draped over the back is an American flag. In front of the fireplace is a scene so savage that it will sicken you—a scene that horrifies even the most case-hardened detectives...

November 18, 1969. Deputy district attorney Vincent Bugliosi is assigned the Tate case and the related homicides of supermarket owner Leno LaBianca and his wife Rosemary. For months, Bugliosi collects and sifts through the grisly evidence, listens to the chilling testimony of murderers and accomplices. Slowly, he puts the puzzle pieces together—and emerges with a complete and horrifying picture of the man who ordered the killings, the girls and young men who carried them out, the motive for the seemingly incomprehensible crimes.

Now Vincent Bugliosi tells the whole story —including the never-before-revealed "retaliation" slayings—of the most baffling mass murder case in the annals of American crime...

HELTER SKELTER

THE TRUE STORY OF THE MANSON MURDERS

VINCENT BUGLIOSI
PROSECUTOR OF THE TATE-LA BIANCA TRIALS
WITH CURT GENTRY

arrow books

First published in Arrow 1992

15 17 19 20 18 16 14

First published by W. W. Norton in 1974

Arrow Books
The Random House Group Limited
20 Vauxhall Bridge Road, London SW1V 2SA

Random House Australia (Pty) Limited
20 Alfred Street, Milsons Point, Sydney,
New South Wales 2061, Australia

Random House New Zealand Limited
18 Poland Road, Glenfield
Auckland 10, New Zealand

Random House (Pty) Limited
Endulini, 5a Jubilee Road, Parktown 2193, South Africa

The Random House Group Limited Reg. No. 954009

randomhouse.co.uk

A CIP catalogue record for this book
is available from the British Library

Papers used by Random House are natural, recyclable products made from wood grown in sustainable forests. The manufacturing processes conform to the environmental regulations of the country of origin.

ISBN 0 09 97500 9

Printed and bound in Great Britain by
Cox & Wyman Ltd, Reading, Berkshire

To Gail and Blanche

Contents

Cast of Characters

Los Angeles Police Department (LAPD)

TATE CASE DETECTIVES:

Helder, Robert J., Lieutenant, Supervisor of Investigations. Headed Tate investigation.

Buckles, Jess, Sergeant.

Calkins, Robert, Sergeant.

McGann, Michael J., Sergeant.

ASSISTED IN TATE INVESTIGATION:

Boen, Jerrome, Latent Prints Section, SID.

Burbridge, Robert, Officer.

Burdick, A. H., Lieutenant. Polygraph examiner, SID.

Clements, Wendell. Civilian fingerprint expert.

Deemer, Earl, Lieutenant.

DeRosa, Jerry Joe, Officer.

Dorman, D. E., Officer.

Galindo, Danny, Sergeant. Also assisted in LaBianca investigation.

Girt, D. L. Latent Prints Section, SID.

Granado, Joe. Forensic chemist, SID. Also assisted in LaBianca investigation.

Henderson, Ed, Sergeant.

Kamadoi, Gene, Sergeant.

Lee, William, Sergeant. Ballistics expert, SID.

Madlock, Robert C., Lieutenant.

Varney, Dudley, Sergeant.

Whisenhunt, William T., Officer.

Wolfer, DeWayne. Criminalist, SID.

LABIANCA CASE DETECTIVES:

LePage, Paul, Lieutenant. Headed LaBianca investigation.

Broda, Gary, Sergeant.
Gutierrez, Manuel "Chick," Sergeant.
Nielsen, Michael, Sergeant.
Patchett, Frank, Sergeant.
Sartuchi, Philip, Sergeant.

ASSISTED IN LABIANCA INVESTIGATION:

Claborn, J., Sergeant. Latent Prints Section, SID.
Cline, Edward L., Sergeant.
Dolan, Harold, Sergeant. Latent Prints Section, SID.
Rodriquez, W. C., Officer.
Toney, J. C., Officer.

Los Angeles County Sheriff's Office (LASO)

ASSIGNED TO THE HINMAN INVESTIGATION:

Guenther, Charles, Sergeant.
Whiteley, Paul, Sergeant.

Los Angeles County District Attorney's Office

Bugliosi, Vincent T., Deputy District Attorney. Prosecuted the Tate-LaBianca killers.

Kay, Steven, and Musich, Donald, Deputy District Attorneys. Brought in to assist Bugliosi after Stovitz was taken off the case.

Stovitz, Aaron, head of the Trials Division. Co-prosecutor of Manson and the three female defendants until taken off the case shortly after the start of the trial.

Inyo County District Attorney's Office

Fowles, Frank, Inyo County District Attorney.
Gardiner, Jack, Investigator.
Gibbens, Buck, Deputy District Attorney.

Defense Attorneys

Ball, Joseph. Interviewed Charles Manson and found him competent to represent himself.

Barnett, Donald. Leslie Van Houten's first attorney was replaced by Marvin Part.

Boyd, Bill. Charles Watson's Texas attorney.

Bubrick, Sam. With Maxwell Keith, defended Charles "Tex" Watson.

Caballero, Richard. Susan Atkins' attorney from November 1969 to March 1970.

Fitzgerald, Paul. First Charles Manson's lawyer, he later quit the Public Defender's Office to represent Patricia Krenwinkel.

Fleischman, Gary. Linda Kasabian's attorney.

Hollopeter, Charles. Charles Manson's attorney for a very brief period.

Hughes, Ronald. Once Charles Manson's "hippie lawyer," he later defended Leslie Van Houten, up until the time he was murdered by the Family.

Kanarek, Irving. Replaced Ronald Hughes as Charles Manson's lawyer.

Keith, Maxwell. Assigned by the Court to represent Leslie Van Houten after the disappearance of Ronald Hughes; also, with Sam Bubrick, defended Charles "Tex" Watson.

Part, Marvin. Leslie Van Houten's attorney for a brief period; was replaced by Ira Reiner.

Reiner, Ira. Replaced Marvin Part as Leslie Van Houten's attorney; was replaced by Ronald Hughes.

Salter, Leon. Robert "Bobby" Beausoleil's attorney.

Shinn, Daye. Replaced Richard Caballero as Susan Atkins' attorney.

Manson Family Members and Associates

Manson, Charles Milles, aka Jesus Christ, God, Soul, the Devil, Charles Willis Manson. Leader of the Family and mass murderer.

Alonzo, Maria, aka Crystal. Released after the murder of Lauren Willett, she was later arrested in connection with an alleged plot to kidnap a foreign diplomat.

Atkins, Susan Denise, aka Sadie Mae Glutz, Sexy Sadie, Sharon King, Donna Kay Powell. Involved in the Hinman, Tate, and LaBianca murders.

Bailey, Edward Arthur. Associated with the Family. May have seen Manson kill a man in Death Valley.

Bailey, Ella Jo, aka Yellerstone. Left Family after learning of the Hinman murder.

Bailey, Lawrence Edward, aka Larry Jones. Present when Tate killers left Spahn Ranch; involved in the Hawthorne shootout.

Baldwin, Linda. Alias used by Family member Madaline Joan Cottage.

Bartell, Susan Phyllis, aka Country Sue. Present when Zero allegedly "committed suicide while playing Russian roulette."

Beausoleil, Robert Kenneth "Bobby," aka Cupid, Jasper, Cherub, Robert Lee Hardy, Jason Lee Daniels. Involved in the Hinman murder.

Big Patty. Alias used by Family member Patricia Krenwinkel.

Brown, Kenneth Richard, aka Scott Bell Davis. Associated with the Family; friend of Zero.

Brunner, Mary Theresa, aka Marioche, Och, Mother Mary, Mary Manson, Linda Dee Moser, Christine Marie Euchts. First girl to join the Manson Family; had a son by Manson; involved in the Hinman murder and the Hawthorne shootout.

Capistrano. Alias used by Family member Catherine Gillies.

Clem. Alias used by Family member Steve Grogan.

Como, Kenneth, aka Jesse James. Escaped convict; associated with Manson Family; involved in Hawthorne shootout.

Cooper, Priscilla. Pleaded guilty to being an accessory after the fact in the murder of Lauren Willett.

Cooper, Sherry Ann, aka Simi Valley Sherri. Fled Barker Ranch with Barbara Hoyt.

Cottage, Madaline Joan, aka Little Patty, Linda Baldwin. Present when Zero died.

Country Sue. Alias used by Family member Susan Bartell.

Craig, James. State prison escapee; associated with Manson Family; pleaded guilty to being an accessory after the fact in the murders of both James and Lauren Willett.

Cravens, Larry. Family member.

Crystal. Alias used by Family member Maria Alonzo.

Cupid. Alias used by Family member Robert "Bobby" Beausoleil.

Davis, Bruce McGregor, aka Bruce McMillan. Involved in the Hinman and Shea murders; present when Zero died; suspect in three other deaths.

DeCarlo, Daniel Thomas, aka Donkey Dan, Daniel Romeo, Richard Allen Smith. Straight Satan motorcycle gang member; associated with the Family; later became a reluctant, but important, prosecution witness.

Donkey Dan. Name given to Daniel DeCarlo by Manson Family girls.

Flynn, John Leo "Juan." Spahn ranch hand; associated with the Family; testified to an extremely incriminating admission by Manson.

Fromme, Lynette Alice, aka Squeaky, Elizabeth Elaine Williamson. One of the earliest Manson Family members; became the Family's ex-officio leader after Manson was arrested.

Gillies, Catherine Irene, aka Capistrano, Cappy, Catherine Myers, Patricia Anne Burke, Patti Sue Jardin. Family member; granddaughter of the owner of Myers Ranch; wanted to go along the night of the LaBianca murders but wasn't needed; present when Zero died.

Glutz, Sadie Mae. Alias used by Family member Susan Atkins.

Good, Sandra Collins, aka Sandy. Married name Mrs. Joel Pugh. Family member.

Goucher, William. Associated with the Manson Family; involved in the murder of James Willett.

Grogan, Steven Dennis, aka Clem Tufts. Involved in the Hinman and Shea murders; was with the killers the night the LaBiancas were killed; involved in the attempted murder of prosecution witness Barbara Hoyt.

Gypsy. Alias used by Family member Catherine Share.

Haught, John Philip, aka Zero, Christopher Jesus. Officially "committed suicide while playing Russian roulette"; was probably murdered.

Hinman, Gary. Befriended the Manson Family; was murdered by them.

Hoyt, Barbara, aka Barbara Rosenburg. Fled the Family before the Barker Ranch raid; became prosecution witness; Family attempted to murder her with an LSD-laden hamburger.

Jones, Larry. Alias used by Family member Lawrence Bailey.

Kasabian, Linda Drouin. Accompanied the killers on the nights of the Tate and LaBianca murders; star witness for the prosecution.

Katie. Alias used by Family member Patricia Krenwinkel.

Knoll, George, aka 86 George. President Straight Satans motorcycle gang. Gave Manson the club sword which was later used in the Hinman slaying and taken along the night the LaBiancas were killed.

Krenwinkel, Patricia Dianne, aka Katie, Marnie Reeves, Big Patty, Mary Ann Scott. Involved in the Tate and LaBianca murders.

Lake, Dianne Elizabeth, aka Snake, Dianne Bluestein. Joined Manson at age 13; became a witness for the prosecution.

Lane, Robert, aka Soupspoon. Arrested in Barker Ranch raid.

Little Patty. Alias used by Family member Madaline Joan Cottage.

Lovett, Charles Allen. Family member involved in the Hawthorne shootout.

Lutesinger, Kitty. Robert "Bobby" Beausoleil's girl friend; fled the Family, then returned to it.

McCann, Brenda. Alias used by Family member Nancy Laura Pitman.

Marioche. Alias used by Family member Mary Brunner.

Minette, Manon. Alias used by Family member Catherine Share.

Monfort, Michael. State prison escapee; associated with the Manson Family; involved in the murders of both James and Lauren Willett.

Montgomery, Charles. Alias used by Family member Charles "Tex" Watson.

Moorehouse, Dean. Father of Family member Ruth Ann Moorehouse; sometime Manson follower.

Moorehouse, Ruth Ann, aka Ouisch, Rachel Susan Morse. Involved in the attempted murder of prosecution witness Barbara Hoyt.

Ouisch. Alias used by Family member Ruth Ann Moorehouse.

Pitman, Nancy Laura, aka Brenda McCann, Brindle, Cydette Perell. Pleaded guilty to being an accessory after the fact in the murder of Lauren Willett.

Poston, Brooks. Former Family member; supplied the prosecution with important evidence regarding Manson's bizarre motive for the murders.

Pugh, Joel. Husband of Family member Sandra Good. Though officially listed as a suicide, he is among the "possible" Manson Family murder victims.

Rice, Dennis. Involved in the attempted murder of prosecution witness Barbara Hoyt; also involved in the Hawthorne shootout.

Ross, Mark. Associated with the Family; Zero's death occurred in his apartment while he was away.

Sadie. Alias used by Family member Susan Atkins.

Sankston, Leslie. Alias used by Family member Leslie Van Houten.

Schram, Stephanie. Fled Barker Ranch with Kitty Lutesinger; testified for the prosecution that Manson was not with her on the nights of the Tate and LaBianca murders.

Scott, Suzanne, aka Stephanie Rowe. Family member.

Share, Catherine, aka Gypsy, Manon Minette. Participated in the "cleanup" following the Shea murder; involved in the Hawthorne shootout.

Simi Valley Sherri. Alias used by Family member Sherry Ann Cooper.

Sinclair, Collie, aka Beth Tracy. Family member arrested in Barker raid.

Smith, Claudia Leigh, aka Sherry Andrews. Family member arrested in Barker raid.

Snake. Alias used by Family member Dianne Lake.

Springer, Alan LeRoy. Member Straight Satans motorcycle gang. Manson admitted the Tate murders to him but his statement could not be used as evidence.

Squeaky. Alias used by Family member Lynette Fromme.

T. J. the Terrible. Alias used by sometime Family member Thomas Walleman.

Todd, Hugh Rocky, aka Randy Morglea. Family member arrested in Barker raid.

True, Harold. Lived at 3267 Waverly Drive, the house next to the LaBianca residence; Manson and other Family members visited him there four or five times.

Tufts, Clem. Alias used by Family member Steve Grogan.

Vance, William Joseph "Bill." Alias of ex-convict David Lee Hamic; associated with the Manson Family.

Van Houten, Leslie Sue, aka LuLu, Leslie Marie Sankston, Louella Alexandria, Leslie Owens. Involved in the LaBianca murders.

Walleman, Thomas, aka T. J. the Terrible. Sometime Family member; was present when Manson shot Bernard Crowe.

Walts, Mark. Hung out at Spahn Ranch; his brother accused Manson of his murder.

Watkins, Paul Alan. Manson's second in command and his chief procurer of young girls; provided Bugliosi with the missing link in Manson's bizarre motive for the murders.

Watson, Charles Denton, aka Tex, Charles Montgomery, Texas Charlie. Involved in the Tate and LaBianca murders.

Wildebush, Joan, aka Juanita. Was with Manson advance group at Barker Ranch; left Family and eloped with Bob Berry, Paul Crockett's partner.

Willett, Lauren. Associated with the Family; murdered on November 10 or 11, 1972, a few days after the body of her husband was discovered; several Manson Family members were linked to her death.

Willett, James. Murdered sometime prior to November 8, 1972; three associates of the Manson Family were charged with the slaying.

Zero. Alias used by Family member John Philip Haught.

HELTER SKELTER

Part 1

THE MURDERS

"How does it feel
To be
One of the
Beautiful People?"

The Beatles,
"Baby You're a Rich Man,"
Magical Mystery Tour album

Saturday, August 9, 1969

It was so quiet, one of the killers would later say, you could almost hear the sound of ice rattling in cocktail shakers in the homes way down the canyon.

The canyons above Hollywood and Beverly Hills play tricks with sounds. A noise clearly audible a mile away may be indistinguishable at a few hundred feet.

It was hot that night, but not as hot as the night before, when the temperature hadn't dropped below 92 degrees. The three-day heat wave had begun to break a couple of hours before, about 10 P.M. on Friday—to the psychological as well as the physical relief of those Angelenos who recalled that on such a night, just four years ago, Watts had exploded in violence. Though the coastal fog was now rolling in from the Pacific Ocean, Los Angeles itself remained hot and muggy, sweltering in its own emissions, but here, high above most of the city, and usually even above the smog, it was at least 10 degrees cooler. Still, it remained warm enough so that many residents of the area slept with their windows open, in hopes of catching a vagrant breeze.

All things considered, it's surprising that more people didn't hear something.

But then it was late, just after midnight, and 10050 Cielo Drive was secluded.

Being secluded, it was also vulnerable.

Cielo Drive is a narrow street that abruptly winds upward from Benedict Canyon Road. One of its cul-de-sacs, easily missed though directly opposite Bella Drive, comes to a dead end at the high gate of 10050. Looking through the gate, you could see neither the main residence nor the guest house some distance beyond it, but you could see, toward the end of the paved parking area, a corner of the garage and, a little farther on, a split-rail fence which, though it was only August, was strung with Christmas-tree lights.

The lights, which could be seen most of the way from the Sunset Strip, had been put up by actress Candice Bergen when she was living with the previous tenant of 10050 Cielo Drive, TV and record producer Terry Melcher. When Melcher, the son of Doris Day, moved to his mother's beach house in Malibu, the new tenants left the lights up. They were on this night, as they were every night, adding a year-round holiday touch to Benedict Canyon.

From the front door of the main house to the gate was over a hundred feet. From the gate to the nearest neighbor on Cielo, 10070, was almost a hundred yards.

At 10070 Cielo, Mr. and Mrs. Seymour Kott had already gone to bed, their dinner guests having left about midnight, when Mrs. Kott heard, in close sequence, what sounded like three or four gunshots. They seemed to have come from the direction of the gate of 10050. She did not check the time but later guessed it to be between 12:30 and 1 A.M. Hearing nothing further, Mrs. Kott went to sleep.

About three-quarters of a mile directly south and downhill from 10050 Cielo Drive, Tim Ireland was one of five counselors supervising an overnight camp-out for some thirty-five children at the Westlake School for Girls. The other counselors had gone to sleep, but Ireland had volunteered to stay up through the night. At approximately 12:40 A.M. he heard from what seemed a long distance away, to the north or northeast, a solitary male voice. The man was screaming, *"Oh, God, no, please don't! Oh, God, no, don't, don't, don't . . ."*

The scream lasted ten to fifteen seconds, then stopped, the abrupt silence almost as chilling as the cry itself. Ireland quickly checked the camp, but all the children were asleep. He awoke his supervisor, Rich Sparks, who had bedded down inside the school, and, telling him what he had heard, got his permission to drive around the area to see if anyone needed help. Ireland took a circuitous route from North Faring Road, where the school was located, south on Benedict Canyon Road to Sunset Boulevard, west to Beverly Glen, and northward back to the school. He observed nothing unusual, though he did hear a number of dogs barking.

There were other sounds in the hours before dawn that Saturday.

Emmett Steele, 9951 Beverly Grove Drive, was awakened by the barking of his two hunting dogs. The pair usually ignored ordinary sounds but went wild when they heard gunshots. Steele went out to look around but, finding nothing out of place, returned to bed. He estimated the time as between 2 and 3 A.M.

Robert Bullington, an employee of the Bel Air Patrol, a private security force used by many of the homeowners in the affluent area, was parked in front of 2175 Summit Ridge Drive, with his window down, when he heard what sounded like three shots, spaced a few seconds apart. Bullington called in; Eric Karlson, who was working the desk at patrol headquarters, logged the call at 4:11 A.M. Karlson in turn called the West Los Angeles Division of the Los Angeles Police Department (LAPD), and passed on the report. The officer who took the call remarked, "I hope we don't have a murder; we just had a woman-screaming call in that area."

Los Angeles *Times* delivery boy Steve Shannon heard nothing unusual when he pedaled his bike up Cielo Drive between 4:30 and 4:45 A.M. But as he put the paper in the mailbox of 10050, he did notice what looked like a telephone wire hanging over the gate. He also observed, through the gate and some distance away, that the yellow bug light on the side of the garage was still on.

Seymour Kott also noticed the light and the fallen wire when he went out to get his paper about 7:30 A.M.

About 8 A.M., Winifred Chapman got off the bus at the intersection of Santa Monica and Canyon Drive. A light-skinned black in her mid-fifties, Mrs. Chapman was the housekeeper at 10050 Cielo, and she was upset because, thanks to L.A.'s terrible bus service, she was going to be late to work. Luck seemed with her, however; just as she was about to look for a taxi, she saw a man she had once worked with, and he gave her a ride almost to the gate.

She noticed the wire immediately, and it worried her.

In front and to the left of the gate, not hidden but not conspicuous either, was a metal pole on the top of which was the gate-control mechanism. When the button was pushed, the gate swung open. There was a similar mechanism inside the grounds, both being positioned so a driver could reach the button without having to get out of the car.

Because of the wire, Mrs. Chapman thought the electricity might be off, but when she pushed the button, the gate swung open. Taking the *Times* out of the mailbox, she walked hurriedly onto the property, noticing an unfamiliar automobile in the driveway, a white Rambler, parked at an odd angle. But she passed it, and several other cars nearer the garage, without much thought. Overnight guests weren't that uncommon. Someone had left the outside light on all night, and she went to the switch at the corner of the garage and turned it off.

At the end of the paved parking area was a flagstone walkway that made a half circle to the front door of the main house. She turned right before coming to the walk, however, going to the service porch entrance at the back of the residence. The key was secreted on a rafter above the door. Taking it down, she unlocked the door and went inside, walking directly to the kitchen, where she picked up the extension phone. It was dead.

Thinking that she should alert someone that the line was down, she proceeded through the dining room toward the living room. Then she stopped suddenly, her progress impeded by two large blue steamer trunks, which hadn't been there when she had left the previous afternoon—and by what she saw.

There appeared to be blood on the trunks, on the floor next to them, and on two towels in the entryway. She couldn't see the entire living room—a long couch cut off the area in front of the fireplace—but everywhere she could see she saw the red splashes. The front door was ajar. Looking out, she saw several pools of blood on the flagstone porch. And, farther on, on the lawn, she saw a body.

Screaming, she turned and ran back through the house,

leaving the same way she had come in but, on running down the driveway, changing her course so as to reach the gate-control button. In so doing, she passed on the opposite side of the white Rambler, seeing for the first time that there was a body inside the car too.

Once outside the gate, she ran down the hill to the first house, 10070, ringing the bell and pounding on the door. When the Kotts didn't answer, she ran to the next house, 10090, banging on that door and screaming, "*Murder, death, bodies, blood!*"

Fifteen-year-old Jim Asin was outside, warming up the family car. It was Saturday and, a member of Law Enforcement Unit 800 of the Boy Scouts of America, he was waiting for his father, Ray Asin, to drive him to the West Los Angeles Division of LAPD, where he was scheduled to work on the desk. By the time he got to the porch, his parents had opened the door. While they were trying to calm the hysterical Mrs. Chapman, Jim dialed the police emergency number. Trained by the Scouts to be exact, he noted the time: 8:33.

While waiting for the police, the father and son walked as far as the gate. The white Rambler was some thirty feet inside the property, too far away to make out anything inside it, but they did see that not one but several wires were down. They appeared to have been cut.

Returning home, Jim called the police a second time and, some minutes later, a third.

There is some confusion as to exactly what happened to the calls. The official police report only states, "At 0914 hours, West Los Angeles Units 8L5 and 8L62 were given a radio call, 'Code 2, possible homicide, 10050 Cielo Drive.' "

The units were one-man patrol cars. Officer Jerry Joe DeRosa, driving 8L5, arrived first, light flashing and siren blaring.* DeRosa began interviewing Mrs. Chapman, but

*The confusion extends to the arrival times of the units. Officer DeRosa would later testify he arrived about 9:05 A.M., which was before he supposedly received the Code 2. Officer Whisenhunt, who came next, set the time of his arrival at between 9:15 and 9:25, while officer Burbridge, who arrived *after* both men, testified he was there at 8:40.

had a difficult time of it. Not only was she still hysterical, she was vague as to what she had seen—"blood, bodies everyplace"—and it was hard to get the names and relationships straight. Polanski. Altobelli. Frykowski.

Ray Asin, who knew the residents of 10050 Cielo, stepped in. The house was owned by Rudi Altobelli. He was in Europe, but had hired a caretaker, a young man named William Garretson, to look after the place. Garretson lived in the guest house to the back of the property. Altobelli had rented the main residence to Roman Polanski, the movie director, and his wife. The Polanskis had gone to Europe, however, in March, and while they were away, two of their friends, Abigail Folger and Voytek Frykowski, had moved in. Mrs. Polanski had returned less than a month ago, and Frykowski and Folger were staying on with her until her husband returned. Mrs. Polanski was a movie actress. Her name was Sharon Tate.

Questioned by DeRosa, Mrs. Chapman was unable to say which, if any, of these people were the two bodies she had seen. To the names she added still another, that of Jay Sebring, a noted men's hair stylist and a friend of Mrs. Polanski's. She mentioned him because she remembered seeing his black Porsche with the other automobiles parked next to the garage.

Getting a rifle from his squad car, DeRosa had Mrs. Chapman show him how to open the gate. Walking cautiously up the driveway to the Rambler, he looked in the open window. There *was* a body inside, in the driver's seat but slumped toward the passenger side. Male, Caucasian, reddish hair, plaid shirt, blue denim pants, both shirt and pants drenched with blood. He appeared to be young, probably in his teens.

About this time Unit 8L62, driven by Officer William T. Whisenhunt, pulled up outside the gate. DeRosa walked back and told him he had a possible homicide. DeRosa also showed him how to open the gate, and the two officers proceeded up the driveway, DeRosa still carrying his rifle, Whisenhunt a shotgun. As Whisenhunt passed the Rambler, he looked in, noting that the window on the driver's side was down and both lights and ignition were off. The pair then checked out the other automobiles and, finding them empty, searched both the garage and the room above it. Still no one.

A third officer, Robert Burbridge, caught up with them. As the three men reached the end of the parking area, they saw not one but two inert forms on the lawn. From a distance they looked like mannequins that had been dipped in red paint, then tossed haphazardly on the grass.

They seemed grotesquely out of place on the well-cared-for lawn, with its landscaped shrubbery, flowers, and trees. To the right was the residence itself, long, rambling, looking more comfortable than ostentatious, the carriage light outside the main door shining brightly. Farther on, past the south end of the house, they could see a corner of the swimming pool, shimmering blue green in the morning light. Off to the side was a rustic wishing well. To the left was a split-rail fence, intertwined with Christmas-tree lights, still on. And beyond the fence was a sweeping, panoramic view that stretched all the way from downtown Los Angeles to the beach. Out there life was still going on. Here it had stopped.

The first body was eighteen to twenty feet past the front door of the residence. The closer they came, the worse it looked. Male, Caucasian, probably in his thirties, about five feet ten, wearing short boots, multicolored bell bottoms, purple shirt, casual vest. He was lying on his side, his head resting on his right arm, his left hand clutching the grass. His head and face were horribly battered, his torso and limbs punctured by literally dozens of wounds. It seemed inconceivable that so much savagery could be inflicted on one human being.

The second body was about twenty-five feet beyond the first. Female, Caucasian, long dark hair, probably in her late twenties. She was lying supine, her arms thrown out. Barefoot, she was wearing a full-length nightgown, which, before the many stab wounds, had probably been white.

The stillness now got to the officers. Everything was quiet, too quiet. The serenity itself became menacing. Those windows along the front of the house: behind any a killer could be waiting, watching.

Leaving DeRosa on the lawn, Whisenhunt and Burbridge went back toward the north end of the residence, looking for another way to get in. They'd be open targets if they entered the front door. They noticed that a screen had been removed from one of the front windows and was leaning up against the side of the building. Whisenhunt also observed a horizontal slit along the bottom of the screen. Suspecting this might have been where the killer or killers entered, they looked for another means of entry. They found a window open on the side. Looking in, they saw what appeared to be a newly painted room, devoid of furniture. They climbed in.

DeRosa waited until he saw them inside the house, then approached the front door. There was a patch of blood on the walk, between the hedges; several more on the right-hand corner of the porch; with still others just outside and to the left of the door and on the doorjamb itself. He didn't see, or later didn't recall, any footprints, though there were a number. The door being open, inward, DeRosa was on the porch before he noticed that something had been scrawled on its lower half.

Printed in what appeared to be blood were three letters: PIG.

Whisenhunt and Burbridge had finished checking out the kitchen and dining room when DeRosa entered the hallway. Turning left into the living room, he found his way partly blocked by the two blue steamer trunks. It appeared that they had been standing on end, then knocked over, as one was leaning against the other. DeRosa also observed, next to the trunks and on the floor, a pair of horn-rimmed glasses. Burbridge, who followed him into the room, noticed something else: on the carpet, to the left of the entrance, were two small pieces of wood. They looked like pieces of a broken gun grip.

They had arrived expecting two bodies, but had found three. They were now looking not for more death, but some explanation. A suspect. Clues.

The room was light and airy. Desk, chair, piano. Then something odd. In the center of the room, facing the fireplace, was a long couch. Draped over the back was a huge American flag.

Not until they were almost to the couch did they see what was on the other side.

She was young, blond, very pregnant. She lay on her left side, directly in front of the couch, her legs tucked up toward her stomach in a fetal position. She wore a flowered bra and matching bikini panties, but the pattern was almost indistinguishable because of the blood, which looked as if it had been smeared over her entire body. A white nylon rope was looped around her neck twice, one end extending over a rafter in the ceiling, the other leading across the floor to still another body, that of a man, which was about four feet away.

The rope was also looped twice around the man's neck, the loose end going under his body, then extending several feet beyond. A bloody towel covered his face, hiding his features. He was short, about five feet six, and was lying on his right side, his hands bunched up near his head as if still warding off blows. His clothing—blue shirt, white pants with black vertical stripes, wide modish belt, black boots—was blood-drenched.

None of the officers thought about checking either body for pulse. As with the body in the car and the pair on the lawn, it was so obviously unnecessary.

Although DeRosa, Whisenhunt, and Burbridge were patrolmen, not homicide detectives, each, at some time in the course of his duties, had seen death. But nothing like this. 10050 Cielo Drive was a human slaughterhouse.

Shaken, the officers fanned out to search the rest of the house. There was a loft above the living room. DeRosa climbed up the wooden ladder and nervously peeked over the top, but saw no one. A hallway connected the living room with the south end of the residence. There was blood in the hall in two places. To the left, just past one of the spots, was a bedroom, the door of which was open. The blankets and pillows were rumpled and clothing strewn about, as if someone—possibly the nightgown-clad woman on the lawn—had already undressed and gone to bed before the killer or killers appeared. Sitting atop the headboard of the bed, his legs hanging down, was a toy rabbit, ears cocked as if quizzically surveying the scene. There was no blood in this room, nor any evidence of a struggle.

Across the hall was the master bedroom. Its door was also open, as were the louvered doors at the far end of the room, beyond which could be seen the swimming pool.

This bed was larger and neater, the white spread turned back to reveal a gaily flowered top sheet and a white bottom sheet with a gold geometric pattern. In the center of the bed, rather than across the top, were two pillows, dividing the side that had been slept on from the side that hadn't. Across the room, facing the bed, was a TV set, on each side of which was a handsome armoire. On top of one was a white bassinet.

Cautiously, adjoining doors were opened: dressing room, closet, bath, closet. Again no signs of a struggle. The telephone on the nightstand next to the bed was on the hook. Nothing overturned or upset.

However, there was blood on the inside left side of the louvered French door, suggesting that someone, again possibly the woman on the lawn, had run out this way, attempting to escape.

Stepping outside, the officers were momentarily blinded by the glare from the pool. Asin had mentioned a guest house behind the main residence. They spotted it now, or rather the corner of it, some sixty feet to the southeast, through the shrubbery.

Approaching it quietly, they heard the first sounds they had heard since coming onto the premises: the barking of a dog, and a male voice saying, "Shhh, be quiet."

Whisenhunt went to the right, around the back of the house. DeRosa turned left, proceeding around the front, Burbridge following as backup. Stepping onto the screened-in porch, DeRosa could see, in the living room, on a couch facing the front door, a youth of about eighteen. He was wearing pants but no shirt, and though he did not appear to be armed, this did not mean, DeRosa would later explain, that he didn't have a weapon nearby.

Yelling *"Freeze!,"* DeRosa kicked in the front door.

Startled, the boy looked up to see one, then, moments later, three guns pointing directly at him. Christopher, Altobelli's large Weimaraner, charged Whisenhunt, chomping the end of his shotgun. Whisenhunt slammed the porch door on his head, then held him trapped there until the youth called him off.

As to what then happened, there are contrary versions.

The youth, who identified himself as William Garretson, the caretaker, would later state that the officers knocked him down, handcuffed him, yanked him to his feet, dragged him outside onto the lawn, then knocked him down again.

DeRosa would later be asked, re Garretson:

Q. "Did he fall or stumble to the floor at any time?"

A. "He may have; I don't recall whether he did or not."

Q. "Did you direct him to lay on the ground outside?"

A. "I directed him, yes, to lay on the ground, yes."

Q. "Did you help him to the ground?"

A. "No, he went down on his own."

Garretson kept asking, "What's the matter? What's the matter?" One of the officers replied, "We'll show you!" and, pulling him to his feet, DeRosa and Burbridge escorted him back along the path toward the main house.

Whisenhunt remained behind, looking for weapons and blood-stained clothing. Though he found neither, he did notice many small details of the scene. One at the time seemed so insignificant that he forgot it until later questioning brought it back to mind. There was a stereo next to the couch. It had been off when they entered the room. Looking at the controls, Whisenhunt noticed that the volume setting was between 4 and 5.

Garretson, meantime, had been led past the two bodies on the lawn. It was indicative of the condition of the first, the young woman, that he mistakenly identified her as Mrs. Chapman, the Negro maid. As for the man, he identified him as "the young Polanski." If, as Chapman and Asin had said, Polanski was in Europe, this made no sense. What the officers couldn't know was that Garretson believed Voytek Frykowski to be Roman Polanski's younger brother. Garretson failed completely when it came to identifying the young man in the Rambler.*

At some point, no one recalls exactly when, Garretson was informed of his rights and told that he was under arrest for murder. Asked about his activities the previous night, he said that although he had remained up all night, writing letters and listening to records, he had neither heard nor seen anything. His highly unlikely alibi, his "vague, unrealistic" replies, and his confused identification of the bodies led the arresting officers to conclude that the suspect was lying.

Five murders—four of them probably occurring less than a hundred feet away—and he had heard nothing?

Escorting Garretson down the driveway, DeRosa located the gate-control mechanism on the pole inside the gate. He noticed that there was blood on the button.

The logical inference was that someone, quite possibly the killer, had pressed the button to get out, in so doing very likely leaving a fingerprint.

Officer DeRosa, who was charged with securing and protecting the scene until investigating officers arrived, now pressed the button himself, successfully opening the gate but also creating a superimposure that obliterated any print that may have been there.

Later DeRosa would be questioned regarding this:

Q. "Was there some reason why you placed your finger on the bloody button that operated the gate?"

A. "So that I could go through the gate."

Q. "And that was intentionally done?"

A. "I had to get out of there."

It was 9:40. DeRosa called in, reporting five deaths and a suspect in custody. While Burbridge remained behind at the residence, awaiting the arrival of the investigating officers, DeRosa and Whisenhunt drove Garretson to the

*Why he failed to identify the youth, whom he did know, is unknown. A good guess would be that Garretson was in shock. Also, adding to his confusion, it was about this time that, in looking toward the gate, he saw Winifred Chapman, whom he presumed dead, alive and talking to a police officer.

West Los Angeles police station for questioning. Another officer took Mrs. Chapman there also, but she was so hysterical she had to be driven to the UCLA Medical Center and given sedation.

In response to DeRosa's call, four West Los Angeles detectives were dispatched to the scene. Lieutenant R. C. Madlock, Lieutenant J. J. Gregoire, Sergeant F. Gravante, and Sergeant T. L. Rogers would all arrive within the next hour. By the time the last pulled up, the first reporters were already outside the gate.

Monitoring the police radio bands, they had picked up the report of five deaths. It was hot and dry in Los Angeles, and fire was a constant concern, especially in the hills, where within minutes lives and property could vanish in an inferno. Someone apparently presumed the five people had been killed in a fire. Jay Sebring's name must have been mentioned in one of the police calls, because a reporter phoned his residence and asked his butler, Amos Russell, if he knew anything about "the deaths by fire." Russell called John Madden, president of Sebring International, and told him about the call. Madden was concerned: neither he nor Sebring's secretary had heard from the hair stylist since late the previous afternoon. Madden placed a call to Sharon Tate's mother in San Francisco. Sharon's father, a colonel in Army Intelligence, was stationed at nearby Fort Baker and Mrs. Tate was visiting him. No, she hadn't heard from Sharon. Or Jay, who was due in San Francisco sometime that same day.

Prior to her marriage to Roman Polanski, Sharon Tate had lived with Jay Sebring. Though thrown over for the Polish film director, Sebring had remained friends with Sharon's parents, as well as Sharon and Roman, and whenever he was in San Francisco he usually called Colonel Tate.

When Madden hung up, Mrs. Tate called Sharon's number. The phone rang and rang, but there was no answer.

It was quiet inside the house. Though anyone who called got a ringing signal, the phones were still out. Officer Joe Granado, a forensic chemist with SID, the Scientific

Investigation Division of LAPD, was already at work, having arrived about 10 A.M. It was Granado's job to take samples from wherever there appeared to be blood. Usually, on a murder case, Granado would be done in an hour or two. Not today. Not at 10050 Cielo Drive.

Mrs. Tate called Sandy Tennant, a close friend of Sharon's and the wife of William Tennant, Roman Polanski's business manager. No, neither she nor Bill had heard from Sharon since late the previous afternoon. At that time Sharon had said that she, Gibby (Abigail Folger), and Voytek (Frykowski) were staying in that night. Jay had said he'd be dropping over later, and she invited Sandy to join them. No party was planned, just a quiet evening at home. Sandy, just over the chicken pox, had declined. Like Mrs. Tate, she had tried to call Sharon that morning but had received no answer.

Sandy assured Mrs. Tate that there was probably no connection between the report of the fire and 10050 Cielo Drive. However, just as soon as Mrs. Tate hung up, Sandy put in a call to her husband's tennis club and had him paged. It was important, she said.

Sometime between 10 and 11 A.M., Raymond Kilgrow, a telephone company representative, climbed the pole outside the gate to 10050 Cielo Drive and found that four phone wires had been cut. The cuts were close to the attachment on the pole, indicating that the person responsible had probably climbed the pole too. Kilgrow repaired two of the wires, leaving the others for the detectives to examine.

Police cars were arriving every few minutes now. And as more officers visited the scene, that scene changed.

The horn-rimmed glasses, first observed by DeRosa, Whisenhunt, and Burbridge near the two trunks, had somehow moved six feet away, to the top of the desk.

Two pieces of gun grip, first seen near the entryway, were now under a chair in the living room. As stated in the official LAPD report: "They were apparently kicked under the chair by one of the original officers on the scene; however, no one is copping out."*

A third piece of gun grip, smaller than the others, was later found on the front porch.

And one or more officers tracked blood from inside the residence onto the front porch and walk, adding several more bloody footprints to those already there. In an attempt to identify and eliminate the later additions, it would be necessary to interview all the personnel who had visited the scene, asking each if he had been wearing boots, shoes with smooth or rippled soles, and so on.

Granado was still taking blood samples. Later, in the police lab, he would give them the Ouchterlony test, to determine if the blood was animal or human. If human, other tests would be applied to determine the blood type—A, B, AB, or O—and the subtype. There are some thirty blood subtypes; however, if the blood is already dry when the sample is taken, it is only possible to determine whether it is one of three—M, N, or MN. It had been a warm night, and it was already turning into another hot day. By the time Granado got to work, most of the blood, except for the pools near the bodies inside, had already dried.

Within the next several days Granado would obtain from the Coroner's Office a blood sample from each of the victims, and would attempt to match these with the samples he'd already collected. In an ordinary murder case the presence of two blood types at the crime scene might indicate that the killer, as well as the victim, had been wounded, information which could be an important clue to the killer's identity.

But this was no ordinary murder. Instead of one body, there were five.

There was so much blood, in fact, that Granado overlooked some spots. On the right side of the front porch, as approached from the walk, there were several large pools of blood. Granado took a sample from only one spot, presuming, he later said, all were the same. Just to the right

*Since Granado, who arrived after DeRosa, Whisenhunt, and Burbridge, also saw them near the entryway, it would appear that the original officers weren't responsible.

of the porch, the shrubbery appeared broken, as if someone had fallen into the bushes. Blood splatters there seemed to bear this out. Granado missed these. Nor did he take samples from the pools of blood in the immediate vicinity of the two bodies in the living room, or from the stains near the two bodies on the lawn, presuming, he'd later testify, that they belonged to the nearest victims, and he'd be getting samples from the coroner anyway.

Granado took a total of forty-five blood samples. However, for some reason never explained, he didn't run subtypes on twenty-one of them. If this is not done a week or two after collection, the components of the blood break down.

Later, when an attempt was made to re-create the murders, these omissions would cause many problems.

Just before noon William Tennant arrived, still dressed in tennis clothes, and was escorted through the gate by the police. It was like being led through a nightmare, as he was taken first to one body, then another. He didn't recognize the young man in the automobile. But he identified the man on the lawn as Voytek Frykowski, the woman as Abigail Folger, and the two bodies in the living room as Sharon Tate Polanski and, tentatively, Jay Sebring. When the police lifted the bloody towel, the man's face was so badly contused Tennant couldn't be sure. Then he went outside and was sick.

When the police photographer finished his work, another officer got sheets from the linen closet and covered the bodies.

Beyond the gate the reporters and photographers now numbered in the dozens, with more arriving every few minutes. Police and press cars so hopelessly jammed Cielo Drive that several officers were detailed to try and untangle them. As Tennant pushed through the crowd, clutching his stomach and sobbing, the reporters hurled questions at him: "Is Sharon dead?" "Were they murdered?" "Has anyone informed Roman Polanski?" He ignored them, but they read the answers on his face.

Not everyone who visited the scene was as reluctant to talk. "It's like a battlefield up there," police sergeant Stanley Klorman told reporters, his features grim with the shock of what he had seen. Another officer, unidentified, said, "It looked ritualistic," this single remark providing the basis for an incredible amount of bizarre speculation.

Like the shock waves from an earthquake, news of the murders spread.

"FIVE SLAIN IN BEL AIR," read the headline on the first AP wire story. Though sent out before the identity of the victims had become known, it correctly reported the location of the bodies; that the telephone lines had been cut; and the arrest of an unnamed suspect. There were errors: one, to be much repeated, that "one victim had a hood over his head . . ."

LAPD notified the Tates, John Madden, who in turn notified Sebring's parents, and Peter Folger, Abigail's father. Abigail's socially prominent parents were divorced. Her father, chairman of the board of the A. J. Folger Coffee Company, lived in Woodside, her mother, Inez Mijia Folger, in San Francisco. However, Mrs. Folger was not at home but in Connecticut, visiting friends following a Mediterranean cruise, and Mr. Folger reached her there. She couldn't believe it; she had talked to Abigail at about ten the previous night. Both mother and daughter had planned to fly to San Francisco today, for a reunion, Abigail having made a reservation on the 10 A.M. United flight.

On reaching home, William Tennant made what was, for him, the most difficult call. He was not only Polanski's business manager but a close friend. Tennant checked his watch, automatically adding nine hours to get London time. Though it would be late in the evening, he guessed that Polanski might still be working, trying to tie up his various film projects before returning home the following Tuesday, and he tried the number of his town house. He guessed right. Polanski and several associates were going over a scene in the script of *The Day of the Dolphin* when the telephone rang.

Polanski would remember the conversation as follows:

"Roman, there's been a disaster in a house."

"Which house?"

"Your house." Then, in a rush, "Sharon is dead, and Voytek and Gibby and Jay."

"No, no, no, no!" Surely there was a mistake. Both men now crying, Tennant reiterated that it was true; he had gone to the house himself.

"How?" Polanski asked. He was thinking, he later said, not of fire but a landslide, a not uncommon thing in the Los Angeles hills, especially after heavy rains; sometimes whole houses were buried, which meant that perhaps they could still be alive. Only then did Tennant tell him that they had been murdered.

Voytek Frykowski, LAPD learned, had a son in Poland but no relatives in the United States. The youth in the Rambler remained unidentified, but was no longer nameless; he had been designated John Doe 85.

The news spread quickly—and with it the rumors. Rudi Altobelli, owner of the Cielo property and business manager for a number of show-business personalities, was in Rome. One of his clients, a young actress, called and told him that Sharon and four others had been murdered in his house and that Garretson, the caretaker he had hired, had confessed.

Garretson hadn't, but Altobelli would not learn this until after he returned to the United States.

The specialists had begun arriving about noon.

Officers Jerrome A. Boen and D. L. Girt, Latent Prints Section, Scientific Investigation Division, LAPD, dusted the main residence and the guest house for prints.

After dusting a print with powder ("developing the print"), a clear adhesive tape was placed over it; the tape, with the print showing, would then be "lifted" and placed on a card with a contrasting background. Location, date, time, officer's initials were noted on the back.

One such "lift" card, prepared by Boen, read: "8–9–69/10050 Cielo/1400/JAB/ Inside door frame of left French door/ from master bedroom to pool area/ handle side."

Another lift, taken about the same time, was from the "Outside front door/ handle side/above handle."

It took six hours to cover both residences. Later that

afternoon the pair were joined by officer D. E. Dorman and Wendell Clements, the latter a civilian fingerprint expert, who concentrated on the four vehicles.

Contrary to popular opinion, a readable print is more rare than common. Many surfaces, such as clothing and fabrics, do not lend themselves to impressions. Even when the surface is such that it will take a print, one usually touches it with only a portion of the finger, leaving a fragmentary ridge, which is useless for comparison. If the finger is moved, the result is an unreadable smudge. And, as officer DeRosa demonstrated with the gate button, one print placed atop another creates a superimposure, also useless for identification purposes. Thus, at any crime scene, the number of clear, readable prints, with enough points for comparison, is usually surprisingly small.

Not counting those prints later eliminated as belonging to LAPD personnel at the scene, a total of fifty lifts were taken from the residence, guest house, and vehicles at 10050 Cielo Drive. Of these, seven were eliminated as belonging to William Garretson (all were from the guest house; none of Garretson's prints were found in the main house or on the vehicles); an additional fifteen were eliminated as belonging to the victims; and three were not clear enough for comparison. This left a total of twenty-five unmatched latent prints, any of which might—or might not—belong to the killer or killers.

It was 1:30 P.M. before the first homicide detectives arrived. On verifying that the deaths were not accidental or self-inflicted, Lieutenant Madlock had requested that the investigation be reassigned to the Robbery-Homicide Division. Lieutenant Robert J. Helder, supervisor of investigations, was placed in charge. He in turn assigned Sergeants Michael J. McGann and Jess Buckles to the case. (McGann's regular partner, Sergeant Robert Calkins, was on vacation and would replace Buckles when he returned.) Three additional officers, Sergeants E. Henderson, Dudley Varney, and Danny Galindo, were to assist them.

On being notified of the homicides, Los Angeles County Coroner Thomas Noguchi asked the police not to touch the bodies until a representative of his office had examined them. Deputy Coroner John Finken arrived about 1:45, later to be joined by Noguchi himself. Finken made the official determination of death; took liver and environmental temperatures (by 2 P.M. it was 94 degrees on the lawn, 83 degrees inside the house); and severed the rope connecting Tate and Sebring, portions of which were given to the detectives so that they could try to determine where it had been manufactured and sold. It was white, three-strand nylon, its total length 43 feet 8 inches. Granado took blood samples from the rope, but didn't take subtypes, again presuming. Finken also removed the personal property from the bodies of the victims. Sharon Tate Polanski: yellow metal wedding band, earrings. Jay Sebring: Cartier wristwatch, later determined to be worth in excess of $1,500. John Doe 85: Lucerne wristwatch, wallet with various papers but no ID. Abigail Folger and Voytek Frykowski: no property on persons. After plastic bags had been placed over the hands of the victims, to preserve any hair or skin that might have become lodged under the nails during a struggle, Finken assisted in covering and placing the bodies on stretcher carts, to be wheeled to ambulances and taken to the Coroner's Office, Hall of Justice, downtown Los Angeles.

Besieged by reporters at the gate, Dr. Noguchi announced he would have no comment until making public the autopsy results at noon the following day.

Both Noguchi and Finken, however, privately had already given the detectives their initial findings.

There was no evidence of sexual molestation or mutilation.

Three of the victims—the John Doe, Sebring, and Frykowski—had been shot. Aside from a defensive slash wound on his left hand, which also severed the band of his wristwatch, John Doe had not been stabbed. But the other four had—many, many times. In addition, Sebring had been hit in the face at least once, and Frykowski had been struck over the head repeatedly with a blunt object.

Though exact findings would have to await the autopsies, the coroners concluded from the size of the bullet holes that the gun used had probably been .22 caliber. The police had already suspected this. In searching the Rambler, Sergeant Varney had found four bullet fragments between the upholstery and the exterior metal of the door on the passenger side. Also found, on the cushion of the rear seat, was part of a slug. Though all were too small for comparison purposes, they appeared to be .22 caliber.

As for the stab wounds, someone suggested that the wound pattern was not dissimilar to that made by a bayonet. In their official report the detectives carried this a step further, concluding, "the knife that inflicted the stab wounds was probably a bayonet." This not only eliminated a number of other possibilities, it also presumed that only one knife had been used.

The depth of the wounds (many in excess of 5 inches), their width (between 1 and 1½ inches), and their thickness (⅛ to ¼ inch) ruled out either a kitchen or a regular pocketknife.

Coincidentally, the only two knives found in the house *were* a kitchen knife and a pocketknife.

A steak knife had been found in the kitchen sink. Granado got a positive benzidine reaction, indicating blood, but a negative Ouchterlony, indicating it was animal, not human. Boen dusted it for prints, but got only fragmentary ridges. Mrs. Chapman later identified the knife as one of a set of steak knifes that belonged to the Polanskis, and she located all the others in a drawer. But even before this, the police had eliminated it because of its dimensions, in particular its thinness. The stabbings were so savage that such a blade would have broken.

Granado found the second knife in the living room, less than three feet from Sharon Tate's body. It was wedged behind the cushion in one of the chairs, with the blade sticking up. A Buck brand clasp-type pocketknife, its blade was 3/4 inch in diameter, 3 13/16 inches in length, making it too small to have caused most of the wounds. Noticing a spot on the side of the blade, Granado tested it for blood: negative. Girt dusted it for prints: an unreadable smudge.

Mrs. Chapman could not recall ever having seen this particular knife. This, plus the odd place where it was found, indicated that it might have been left by the killer(s).

In literature a murder scene is often likened to a picture puzzle. If one is patient and keeps trying, eventually all the pieces will fit into place.

Veteran policemen know otherwise. A much better analogy would be two picture puzzles, or three, or more, no one of which is in itself complete. Even after a solution emerges—if one does—there will be leftover pieces, evidence that just doesn't fit. And some pieces will always be missing.

There was the American flag, its presence adding still another bizarre touch to a scene already horribly macabre. The possibilities it suggested ranged from one end of the political spectrum to the other—until Winifred Chapman told the police that it had been in the residence several weeks.

Few pieces of evidence were so easily eliminated. There were the bloody letters on the front door. In recent years the word "pig" had taken on a new meaning, one all too familiar to the police. But what did it mean printed here?

There was the rope. Mrs. Chapman flatly stated that she had never seen such a rope anywhere on the premises. Had the killer(s) brought it? If so, why?

What significance was there in the fact that the two victims bound together by the rope, Sharon Tate and Jay Sebring, were former lovers? Or was "former" the right word? What was Sebring doing there, with Polanski away? It was a question that many of the newspapers would also ask.

The horn-rimmed glasses—negative for both prints and blood—did they belong to a victim, a killer, or someone totally unconnected with the crime? Or—with each question the possibilities proliferated—had they been left behind as a false clue?

The two trunks in the entryway. The maid said they hadn't been there when she left at 4:30 the previous afternoon. Who delivered them, and when, and had this person seen anything?

Why would the killer(s) go to the trouble of slitting and

removing a screen when other windows, those in the newly painted room that was to be the nursery for the Polanskis' unborn child, were open and screenless?

John Doe 85, the youth in the Rambler. Chapman, Garretson, and Tennant had failed to identify him. Who was he and what was he doing at 10050 Cielo Drive? Had he witnessed the other murders, or had he been killed before they took place? If before, wouldn't the others have heard the shots? On the seat next to him was a Sony AM-FM Digimatic clock radio. The time at which it had stopped was 12:15 A.M. Coincidence or significant?

As for the time of the murders, the reports of gunshots and other sounds ranged from shortly after midnight to 4:10 A.M.

Not all of the evidence was as inconclusive. Some of the pieces fitted. No shell casings were found anywhere on the property, indicating that the gun was probably a revolver, which does not eject its spent shells, as contrasted to an automatic, which does.

Placed together, the three pieces of black wood formed the right-hand side of a gun grip. The police therefore knew the gun they were looking for was probably a .22 caliber revolver that was minus a right grip. From the pieces it might be possible to determine both make and model. Though there was human blood on all three pieces, only one had enough for analysis. It tested O-MN. Of the five victims, only Sebring had O-MN, indicating that the butt of the revolver could have been the blunt object used to strike him in the face.

The bloody letters on the front door tested O-M. Again, only one of the victims had this type and subtype. The word PIG had been printed in Sharon Tate's blood.

There were four vehicles in the driveway, but one which should have been there wasn't—Sharon Tate's red Ferrari. It was possible that the killer(s) had used the sports car to escape, and a "want" was broadcast for it.

Long after the bodies had been removed, the detectives remained on the scene, looking for meaningful patterns.

They found several which appeared significant.

There were no indications of ransacking or robbery.

McGann found Sebring's wallet in his jacket, which was hanging over the back of a chair in the living room. It contained $80. John Doe had $9 in his wallet, Frykowski $2.44 in his wallet and pants pocket, Folger $9.64 in her purse. On the nightstand next to Sharon Tate's bed, in plain view, were a ten, a five, and three ones. Obviously expensive items—a videotape machine, TV sets, stereo, Sebring's wristwatch, his Porsche—had not been taken. Several days later the police would bring Winifred Chapman back to 10050 Cielo to see if she could determine if anything was missing. The only item she couldn't locate was a camera tripod, which had been kept in the hall closet. These five incredibly savage murders were obviously not committed for a camera tripod. In all probability it had been lent to someone or lost.

While this didn't completely eliminate the possibility that the murders had occurred during a residential burglary—the victims surprising the burglar(s) while at work—it certainly put it way down the list.

Other discoveries provided a much more likely direction.

A gram of cocaine was found in Sebring's Porsche, plus 6.3 grams of marijuana and a two-inch "roach," slang for a partially smoked marijuana cigarette.

There were 6.9 grams of marijuana in a plastic bag in a cabinet in the living room of the main residence. In the nightstand in the bedroom used by Frykowski and Folger were 30 grams of hashish, plus ten capsules which, later analyzed, proved to be a relatively new drug known as MDA. There was also marijuana residue in the ashtray on the stand next to Sharon Tate's bed, a marijuana cigarette on the desk near the front door,* and two more in the guest house.

Had a drug party been in progress, one of the participants "freaking out" and slaying everyone there? The police put this at the top of their list of possible reasons for the murders, though well aware this theory had several weaknesses, chief among them the presumption that there

*Apparently overlooked by LAPD, this was discovered by Roman Polanski when he visited the residence on August 17.

was a single killer, wielding a gun in one hand, a bayonet in the other, at the same time carrying 43 feet of rope, all of which, conveniently, he just happened to bring along. Also, there were the wires. If they had been cut *before* the murders, this indicated premeditation, not a spontaneous flare-up. If cut *after*, why?

Or could the murders have been the result of a drug "burn," the killer(s) arriving to make a delivery or buy, an argument over money or bad drugs erupting into violence? This was the second, and in many ways the most likely, of the five theories the detectives would list in their first investigative report.

The third theory was a variation of the second, the killer(s) deciding to keep both the money and the drugs.

The fourth was the residential burglary theory.

The fifth, that these were "deaths by hire," the killer(s) being sent to the house to eliminate one or more of the victims, then, in order to escape identification, finding it necessary to kill all. But would a hired killer choose as one of his weapons something as large, conspicuous, and unwieldy as a bayonet? And would he keep stabbing and stabbing and stabbing in a mad frenzy, as so obviously had been done in this case?

The drug theories seemed to make the most sense. In the investigation that followed, as the police interviewed acquaintances of the victims, and the victims' habits and life styles emerged into clearer focus, the possibility that drugs were in some way linked to the motive became in some minds such a certainty that when given a clue which could have solved the case, they refused even to consider it.

The police were not the only ones to think of drugs.

On hearing of the deaths, actor Steve McQueen, longtime friend of Jay Sebring, suggested that the hair stylist's home should be rid of narcotics to protect his family and business. Though McQueen did not himself participate in the "housecleaning," by the time LAPD got around to searching Sebring's residence, anything embarrassing had been removed.

Others developed instant paranoia. No one was sure who the police would question, or when. An unidentified film figure told a *Life* reporter: "Toilets are flushing all over Beverly Hills; the entire Los Angeles sewer system is stoned."

FILM STAR, 4 OTHERS
DEAD IN BLOOD ORGY

Sharon Tate Victim
In "Ritual" Murders

The headlines dominated the front pages of the afternoon papers, became the big news on radio and TV. The bizarre nature of the crime, the number of victims, and their prominence—a beautiful movie star, the heiress to a coffee fortune, her jet-set playboy paramour, an internationally known hair stylist—would combine to make this probably the most publicized murder case in history, excepting only the assassination of President John F. Kennedy. Even the staid New York *Times*, which rarely reports crime on its front page, did so the next day, and many days thereafter.

The accounts that day and the next were notable for the unusual amount of detail they contained. So much information had been given out, in fact, that the detectives would have difficulty finding "polygraph keys" for questioning suspects.

In any homicide, it is standard practice to withhold certain information which presumably only the police and the killer(s) know. If a suspect confesses, or agrees to a polygraph examination, these keys can then be used to determine if he is telling the truth.

Owing to the many leaks, the detectives assigned to the "Tate case," as the press was already calling the murders, could only come up with five: (1) That the knife used was probably a bayonet. (2) That the gun was probably a .22 caliber revolver. (3) The exact dimensions of the rope, as well as the way it was looped and tied. And (4) and (5), that a pair of horn-rimmed glasses and a Buck knife had been found.

The amount of information unofficially released so bothered LAPD brass that a tight lid was clamped on further disclosures. This didn't please the reporters; also, lacking hard news, many turned to conjecture and speculation. In the days that followed a monumental amount of false information was published. It was widely reported, for example, that Sharon Tate's unborn child had been ripped from her womb; that one or both of her breasts had been slashed off; that several of the victims had been sexually mutilated. The towel over Sebring's face became a white hood (KKK?) or a black hood (satanists?), depending on which paper or magazine you read.

When it came to the man charged with the murders, however, there was a paucity of information. It was presumed, initially, that the police were maintaining silence to protect Garretson's rights. It was also presumed that LAPD had to have a strong case against him or they wouldn't have arrested him.

A Pasadena paper, picking up bits and pieces of information, sought to fill the gap. It stated that when the officers found Garretson, he asked, "When are the detectives going to see me?" The implication was obvious: Garretson knew what had happened. Garretson did ask this, but it was as he was being taken through the gate, long after his arrest, and the question was in response to an earlier comment by DeRosa. Quoting unidentified policemen, the paper also noted: "They said the slender youth had a rip in one knee of his pants and his living quarters in the guest cottage showed signs of a struggle." Damning evidence, unless one were aware that all this happened *during*, not before, Garretson's arrest.

During the first few days a total of forty-three officers would visit the crime scene, looking for weapons and other evidence. In searching the loft above the living room, Sergeant Mike McGann found a film can containing a roll of videotape. Sergeant Ed Henderson took it to the Police Academy, which had screening facilities. The film showed Sharon and Roman Polanski making love. With a certain delicacy, the tape was not booked into evidence but was returned to the loft where it had been found.*

In addition to searching the premises, detectives interviewed neighbors, asking if they had seen any strange people in the area.

Ray Asin recalled that two or three months before there had been a large party at 10050 Cielo Drive, the guests arriving in "hippie garb." He got the impression, however, that they weren't actually hippies, as most arrived in Rolls-Royces and Cadillacs.

Emmett Steele, who had been awakened by the barking of his hunting dogs the previous night, remembered that in recent weeks someone had been racing a dune buggy up and down the hills late at night, but he never got a close look at the driver and passengers.

Most of those interviewed, however, claimed they had neither seen nor heard anything out of the ordinary.

The detectives were left with far more questions than answers. However, they were hopeful one person could put the puzzle together for them: William Garretson.

The detectives downtown were less optimistic. Following his arrest, the nineteen-year-old had been taken to West Los Angeles jail and interrogated. The officers found his answers "stuporous and non-responsive," and were of the opinion that he was under the residual effect of some drug. It was also possible, as Garretson himself claimed, that he had slept little the previous night, just a few hours in the morning, and that he was exhausted, and very scared.

Shortly after this, Garretson retained the services of at-

*One writer would later claim that the police found a vast collection of pornography in the residence, including numerous films and still shots of famous Hollywood stars engaged in various sexual acts. Aside from the above, and several unexposed rolls of videotape, the only photographs found anywhere on the property were a set of wedding pictures and a large number of publicity shots of Sharon Tate.

The same writer also claimed that a number of black hoods were found in the loft. Apparently he created them out of the same material as his photos, for nothing even resembling a hood was found.

torney Barry Tarlow. A second interview, with Tarlow present, took place at Parker Center, headquarters of the Los Angeles Police Department. As far as the police were concerned, it too was unproductive. Garretson claimed that although he lived on the property, he had little contact with the people in the main house. He said that he'd only had one visitor the previous night, a boy named Steve Parent, who showed up about 11:45 and left about a half hour later. Questioned about Parent, Garretson said he didn't know him well. He'd hitched a ride up the canyon with him one night a couple of weeks ago and, on getting out of the car at the gate, had told Steve if he was ever in the neighborhood to drop in. Garretson, who lived by himself in the back house, except for the dogs, said he'd extended similar invitations to others. When Steve showed up, he was surprised: no one else ever had. But Steve didn't stay long, leaving after learning that Garretson wasn't interested in buying a clock radio Steve had for sale.

The police did not at this time connect Garretson's visitor with the youth in the Rambler, possibly because Garretson had earlier failed to identify him.

After conferring with Tarlow, Garretson agreed to take a polygraph examination, and one was scheduled for the following afternoon.

Twelve hours had passed since the discovery of the bodies. John Doe 85 remained unidentified.

Police lieutenant Robert Madlock, who had been in charge of the investigation during the several hours before it was assigned to homicide, would later state: "At the time we first found the [victim's] car at the scene, we were going fourteen different directions at once. So many things had to be done, I guess we just didn't have time to follow up on the car registration."

All day Wilfred and Juanita Parent had waited, and worried. Their eighteen-year-old son Steven hadn't come home the previous night. "He didn't call, didn't leave word. He'd never done anything like that before," Juanita Parent said.

About 8 P.M., aware that his wife was too distraught to cook dinner, Wilfred Parent took her and their three other children to a restaurant. Maybe when we get back, he told his wife, Steve will be there.

From outside the gate of 10050 Cielo it was possible to make out the license number on the white Rambler: ZLR 694. A reporter wrote it down, then ran his own check through the Department of Motor Vehicles, learning that the registered owner was "Wilfred E. or Juanita D. Parent, 11214 Bryant Drive, El Monte, California."

By the time he arrived in El Monte, a Los Angeles suburb some twenty-five miles from Cielo Drive, he found no one at home. Questioning the neighbors, he learned that the family did have a boy in his late teens; he also learned the name of the family priest, Father Robert Byrne, of the Church of the Nativity, and called on him. Byrne knew the youth and his family well. Though the priest was sure Steve didn't know any movie stars and that all this was some mistake, he agreed to accompany the reporter to the county morgue. On the way he talked about Steve. He was a stereo "bug," Father Byrne said; if you ever wanted to know anything about phonographs or radios, Steve had the answers. Father Byrne held great hopes for his future.

In the interim, LAPD discovered the identity of the youth through a print and license check. Shortly after the Parents returned home, an El Monte policeman appeared at the door and handed Wilfred Parent a card with a number on it and told him to call it. He left without saying anything else.

Parent dialed the number.

"County Coroner's Office," a man answered.

Confused, Parent identified himself and explained about the policeman and the card.

The call was transferred to a deputy coroner, who told him, "Your son has apparently been involved in a shooting."

"Is he dead?" Parent asked, stunned. His wife, hearing the question, became hysterical.

"We have a body down here," the deputy coroner replied, "and we believe it's your son." He then went on to describe physical characteristics. They matched.

Parent hung up the phone and began sobbing. Later, understandably bitter, he'd remark, "All I can say is that it was a hell of a way to tell somebody that their boy was dead."

About this same time, Father Byrne viewed the body and made the identification. John Doe 85 became Steven Earl Parent, an eighteen-year-old hi-fi enthusiast from El Monte.

It was 5 A.M. before the Parents went to bed. "The wife and I finally just put the kids in bed with us and the five of us just held on to each other and cried until we went to sleep."

About nine that same Saturday night, August 9, 1969, Leno and Rosemary LaBianca and Susan Struthers, Rosemary's twenty-one-year-old daughter by a previous marriage, left Lake Isabella for the long drive back to Los Angeles. The lake, a popular resort area, was some 150 miles from L.A.

Susan's brother, Frank Struthers, Jr., fifteen, had been vacationing at the lake with a friend, Jim Saffie, whose family had a cabin there. Rosemary and Leno had driven up the previous Tuesday, to leave their speedboat for the boys to use, then returned Saturday morning to pick up Frank and the boat. However, the boys were having such a good time the LaBiancas agreed to let Frank stay over another day, and they were returning now, without him, driving their 1968 green Thunderbird, towing the speedboat on a trailer behind.

Leno, the president of a chain of Los Angeles supermarkets, was forty-four, Italian, and, at 220 pounds, somewhat overweight. Rosemary, a trim, attractive brunette of thirty-eight, was a former carhop who, after a series of waitress jobs and a bad marriage, had opened her own dress shop, the Boutique Carriage, on North Figueroa in Los Angeles, and made a big success of it. She and Leno had been married since 1959.

Because of the boat, they couldn't drive at the speed Leno preferred, and fell behind most of the Saturday night freeway traffic that was speeding toward Los Angeles and environs. Like many others that night, they had the radio on and heard the news of the Tate murders. According to Susan, it seemed particularly to disturb Rosemary, who, a few weeks earlier, had told a close friend, "Someone is coming in our house while we're away. Things have been gone through and the dogs are outside the house when they should be inside."

Sunday, August 10, 1969

About 1 A.M. the LaBiancas dropped Susan off at her apartment on Greenwood Place, in the Los Feliz district of Los Angeles. Leno and Rosemary lived in the same neighborhood, at 3301 Waverly Drive, not far from Griffith Park.

The LaBiancas did not immediately return home but first drove to the corner of Hillhurst and Franklin.

John Fokianos, who had a newsstand on that corner, recognized the green Thunderbird-plus-boat as it pulled into the Standard station across the street, and while it was making a U-turn that would bring it alongside his stand, he reached for a copy of the Los Angeles *Herald Examiner*, Sunday edition, and a racing form. Leno was a regular customer.

To Fokianos, the LaBiancas seemed tired from their long trip. Business was slow, and they chatted for a few minutes, "about Tate, the event of the day. That was the big news." Fokianos would recall that Mrs. LaBianca seemed very shaken by the deaths. He had some extra news fillers for the Sunday Los Angeles *Times*, which featured the murders, and he gave them one without charge.

He watched as they drove away. He did not notice the exact time, except that it was sometime between 1 and 2 A.M., probably closer to the latter, as not long after they left the bars closed and there was a flurry of business.

As far as is known, John Fokianos was the last person—excluding their killer(s)—to see Rosemary and Leno LaBianca alive.

At noon on Sunday the hall outside the autopsy room on the first floor of the Hall of Justice was packed with reporters and TV cameramen, all awaiting the coroner's announcement.

They would have a long wait. Although the autopsies had begun at 9:50 A.M., and a number of deputy coroners had been pressed into service, it would be 3 P.M. before the last autopsy was completed.

Dr. R. C. Henry conducted the Folger and Sebring autopsies, Dr. Gaston Herrera those of Frykowski and Parent. Dr. Noguchi supervised and directed all four; in addition, he personally conducted the other autopsy, which began at 11:20 A.M.

Sharon Marie Polanski, 10050 Cielo Drive, female Caucasian, 26 years, 5-3, 135 pounds, blond hair, hazel eyes. Victim's occupation, actress . . .

Autopsy reports are abrupt documents. Cold, factual, they can indicate how the victims died, and give clues as to their last hours, but nowhere in them do their subjects emerge, even briefly, as people. Each report is, in its own way, the sum total of a life, yet there are very few glimpses as to how that life was lived. No likes, dislikes, loves, hates, fears, aspirations, or other human emotions; just a final, clinical summing up: "The body is normally developed . . . The pancreas is grossly unremarkable . . . The heart weighs 340 grams and is symmetrical . . ."

Yet the victims had lived, each had a past.

Much of Sharon Tate's story sounded like a studio press release. It seemed she had always wanted to be an actress. At age six months she had been Miss Tiny Tot of Dallas, at sixteen years Miss Richland, Washington, then Miss Autorama. When her father, a career army officer, was assigned to San Pedro, she would hitchhike into nearby Los Angeles, haunting the studios.

In addition to her ambition, she had at least one other thing in her favor: she was a very beautiful girl. She acquired an agent who succeeded in getting her a few commercials, then, in 1963, an audition for the TV series "Petticoat Junction." Producer Martin Ransohoff saw the pretty twenty-year-old on the set and, according to studio flackery, told her, "Sweetie, I'm going to make you a star."

The star was a long time ascending. Singing, dancing, and acting lessons were interspersed with bit parts, usually wearing a black wig, in "The Beverly Hillbillies," "Petticoat Junction," and two Ransohoff films, *The Americanization of Emily* and *The Sandpiper*. While the latter film, co-starring Elizabeth Taylor and Richard Burton, was being filmed in Big Sur, Sharon fell in love with the magnificently scenic coastline. Whenever she wanted to escape the Hollywood hassle, she fled there. Scrubbed of makeup, she would check into rustic Deetjen's Big Sur Inn, often alone, sometimes with girl friends, and walk the trails, sun at the beach, and blend in with the regulars at Nepenthe. Many did not know, until after her death, that she was an actress.

According to close friends, though Sharon Tate looked the part of the starlet, she didn't live up to at least one portion of that image. She was not promiscuous. Her relationships were few, and rarely casual, at least on her part. She seemed attracted to dominant men. While in Hollywood, she had a long affair with a French actor. Given to insane rages, he once beat her so badly she had to be taken to the UCLA Medical Center for treatment.* Shortly after this, in 1963, Jay Sebring spotted Sharon at a studio preview, prevailed upon a friend for an introduction, and, after a brief but much publicized courtship, they became lovers, a relationship which lasted until she met Roman Polanski.

It was 1965 before Ransohoff decided his protégé was

*LAPD learned of him from Sharon's parents. They also learned, from one of Sebring's ex-girl friends, that he had had an argument with the hair stylist a few nights before the murder, in one of the Hollywood discothèques. After checking the man's alibi, they cleared him of any possible involvement in the murders. The argument itself was minor: he had interrupted Sebring while he was trying to pick up a girl.

ready for her first featured role, in *Eye of the Devil,* which starred Deborah Kerr and David Niven. Listed seventh in the credits, Sharon Tate played a country girl with bewitching powers. She had less than a dozen lines; her primary role was to look beautiful, which she did. This was to be true of almost all her movies.

In the film, Niven became the victim of a hooded cult which practiced ritual sacrifice.

Though set in France, the film was made in London, and it was here, in the summer of 1966, that she met Roman Polanski.

Polanski was at this time thirty-three, and already acclaimed as one of Europe's leading directors. He had been born in Paris, his father a Russian Jew, his mother Polish of Russian stock. When Roman was three, the family moved to Cracow. They were still there in 1940 when the Germans arrived and sealed off the ghetto. With his father's help, Roman managed to escape and lived with family friends until the war ended. Both his parents, however, were sent to concentration camps, his mother dying in Auschwitz.

Following the war, he spent five years at the Polish National Film Academy at Lodz. As his senior thesis, he wrote and directed *Two Men and a Wardrobe,* a much acclaimed surrealistic short. He made several other short films, among them *Mammals,* in which a Polish friend, Voytek Frykowski, played a thief. After an extended trip to Paris, Polanski returned to Poland to make *Knife in the Water,* his first feature-length effort. It won the Critics Award at the Venice Film Festival, was nominated for an Academy Award, and established Polanski, then only twenty-seven, as one of Europe's most promising filmmakers.

In 1965, Polanski made his first film in English, *Repulsion,* starring Catherine Deneuve. *Cul de Sac* followed, which won the Best Film Award in the Berlin Film Festival, the Critics Award in Venice, a Diploma of Merit in Edinburgh, and the Giove Capitaliano Award in Rome. In the news stories following the Tate murders, reporters were quick to note that in *Repulsion* Miss Deneuve went mad and murdered two men, while in *Cul de Sac* the inhabitants of an isolated castle each meet a bizarre fate until only one man is left alive. They also noted Polanski's "penchant for violence," without adding that most often in Polanski's films the violence was less explicit than implied.

Roman Polanski's personal life was no less controversial than his films. After his marriage to Polish film star Barbara Lass ended in divorce in 1962, Polanski became known as the playboy director. A friend would later recall him leafing through his address book, saying, "Who shall I gratify tonight?" Another friend observed that Polanski's immense talent was matched only by his ego. Non-friends, who were numerous, had stronger things to say. One, referring to the fact that Polanski was just over five feet tall, called him "the original five-foot Pole you wouldn't want to touch anyone with." Whether one was captivated by his gaminlike charm or repelled by his arrogance, he appeared to touch off strong emotions in nearly everyone whom he met.

It was not so with Sharon Tate, at least not at first. When Ransohoff introduced Roman and Sharon at a large party, neither was particularly impressed. The introduction was not accidental. On learning that Polanski was considering doing a film spoof of horror movies, Ransohoff had offered to produce it. He wanted Sharon for the female lead. Polanski gave her a screen test and decided she would be acceptable for the part. Polanski wrote, directed, and starred in the film, which eventually appeared as *The Fearless Vampire Killers,* but Ransohoff did the cutting, much to the displeasure of the Polish director, who disavowed the final print. Though the film was more camp than art, Polanski revealed another phase of his multi-faceted talent in his comic portrayal of the bumbling young assistant of a scholarly vampire hunter. Sharon, again, looked pretty and had less than a dozen lines. A victim of the vampire early in the picture, in the last scene she bites her lover, Polanski, creating still another monster.

Before the filming was over, and after what was for Polanski a very long courtship, Sharon and Roman became off-screen lovers too. When Sebring flew to London, Sharon told him the news. If he took it hard, he was careful not to show it, very quickly settling into the role of family friend. There were indications, asides made to a few associates, that Sebring hoped that Sharon would eventually tire of Roman, or vice versa, the presumption being that when this happened he intended to be around. Those who claimed that Sebring was still in love with Sharon were guessing—though Sebring knew hundreds of people, he apparently had few really close friends, and kept his inner feelings very much to himself—but it was a safe guess that although the nature of that love had changed, some deep attachment remained. After the breakup, Sebring was involved with many women, but, as revealed in the LAPD interview sheets, for the most part the relationships were more sexual than emotional, the majority "one night stands."

Paramount asked Polanski to do the film version of Ira Levin's novel *Rosemary's Baby*. The film, in which Mia Farrow played a young girl who had a child by Satan, was completed late in 1967. On January 20, 1968, to the surprise of many friends to whom Polanski had vowed never again to marry, he and Sharon were wed in a mod ceremony in London.

Rosemary's Baby premiered that June. That same month the Polanskis rented actress Patty Duke's home at 1600 Summit Ridge Drive in Los Angeles. It was while they were living there that Mrs. Chapman began working for them. In early 1969 they heard that 10050 Cielo Drive might be vacant. Though they never met in person, Sharon talked to Terry Melcher on the phone several times, making arrangements to take over his unexpired lease. The Polanskis signed a rental agreement on February 12, 1969, at $1,200 a month, and moved in three days later.

Though *Rosemary's Baby* was a smash success, Sharon's own career had never quite taken off. She had appeared semi-nude in the March 1967 issue of *Playboy* (Polanski himself took the photos on the set of *The Fearless Vampire Killers*), the accompanying article beginning, "This is the year that Sharon Tate happens . . ." But the prediction wasn't fulfilled, not that year. Though a number of reviewers commented on her striking looks, neither this nor two other films in which she played—*Don't Make Waves*, with Tony Curtis, and *The Wrecking Crew,* with Dean Martin—brought her much closer to stardom. Her biggest role came in the 1967 film *Valley of the Dolls,* in which she played the actress Jennifer who, on learning that she has breast cancer, takes an overdose of sleeping pills. Not long before her death, Jennifer remarks, "I have no talent. All I have is a body."

There were reviewers who felt that adequately summed up Sharon Tate's performance. To be fairer, to date she hadn't been given a single role which gave her a chance to bring out whatever acting ability she may have had.

She was not a star, not yet. Her career seemed to hesitate on the edge of a breakthrough, but it could easily have remained stationary, or gone the other way.

But for the first time in her life, Sharon's ambition had slipped to second place. Her marriage and her pregnancy had become her whole life. According to those closest to her, she seemed oblivious to all else.

There were rumors of trouble in her marriage. Several of her female friends told LAPD that she had waited to tell Roman of her pregnancy until after it was too late to abort. If she was concerned that even after marriage Polanski remained the playboy, she hid it. Sharon herself often told a story then current in the movie colony, of how Roman was driving through Beverly Hills when, spotting a pretty girl walking ahead of him, he yelled, "Miss, you have a bea-u-ti-ful arse." Only when the girl turned did he recognize his wife. Yet it was obvious that she hoped the baby would bring the marriage closer together.

Hollywood is a bitchy town. In interviewing acquaintances of the victims, LAPD would encounter an incredible amount of venom. Interestingly enough, in the dozens of interview sheets, no one who actually knew Sharon Tate said anything bad about her. Very sweet, somewhat naïve—these were the words most often used.

That Sunday a Los Angeles *Times* reporter who had known Sharon described her as "an astonishingly beautiful woman with a statuesque figure and a face of great delicacy."

But then he didn't see her as Coroner Noguchi did.

Cause of death: Multiple stab wounds of the chest and

back, penetrating the heart, lungs, and liver, causing massive hemorrhage. Victim was stabbed sixteen times, five of which wounds were in and of themselves fatal.

Jay Sebring, 9860 Easton Drive, Benedict Canyon, Los Angeles, male Caucasian, 35 years, 5-6, 120 pounds, black hair, brown eyes. Victim was a hair stylist and had a corporation known as Sebring International . . .

Born Thomas John Kummer, in Detroit, Michigan, he had changed his name to Jay Sebring shortly after arriving in Hollywood, following a four-year stint as a Navy barber, borrowing the last name from the famous Florida sports-car race because he liked the image it projected.

In his personal life, as in his work, appearances were all-important. He drove an expensive sports car, frequented the "in" clubs, even had his Levi jackets custom-made. He employed a full-time butler, gave lavish parties, and lived in a "jinxed" mansion, 9860 Easton Drive, Benedict Canyon. Once the love nest of actress Jean Harlow and producer Paul Bern, it was here, in Harlow's bedroom, that Bern had committed suicide, two months after their marriage. According to acquaintances, Sebring had bought the house because of its "far out" reputation.

It was widely reported that a motion-picture studio had flown Sebring to London just to cut George Peppard's hair, at a cost of $25,000. While the report was probably as factual as another also current, that he had a black belt in karate (he had taken a few lessons from Bruce Lee), there was no question that he was the leading men's hair stylist in the United States, and that more than any other single individual, he was responsible for the revolution in male hair care. In addition to Peppard, his customers included Frank Sinatra, Paul Newman, Steve McQueen, Peter Lawford, and numerous other motion-picture stars, many of whom had promised to invest in his new corporation, Sebring International. While keeping his original salon at 725 North Fairfax in Los Angeles, he planned to open a series of franchised shops and to market a line of men's toiletries bearing his name. The first shop had been opened in San Francisco in May 1969, Abigail Folger and Colonel and Mrs. Paul Tate being among those at the grand opening.

On April 9, 1968, Sebring had signed an application for a $500,000 executive protection policy with the Occidental Life Insurance Company of California. A background investigation, conducted by the Retail Credit Company, estimated his net worth at $100,000, of which $80,000 was the appraised worth of his residence. Sebring, Inc., the original business, had assets of $150,000, with liabilities of $115,000.

The investigators also looked into Sebring's personal life. He had married once, in October 1960, he and his wife, Cami, a model, separating in August 1963, their divorce becoming final in March 1965, the couple having had no children. The report also stated that Sebring had never "used drugs as a habit." LAPD knew otherwise.

They also knew something else the credit company investigators had never discovered. There was a darker side to Jay Sebring's nature that surfaced during numerous interviews conducted by the police. As noted in the official report: "He was considered a ladies' man and took numerous women to his residence in the Hollywood hills. He would tie the women up with a small sash cord and, if they agreed, would whip them, after which they would have sexual relations."

Rumors of this had long circulated around Hollywood. Now picked up by the press, they became the basis for numerous theories, chief among them that some sort of sadomasochistic orgy had been in progress on the night of August 9, 1969, at 10050 Cielo Drive.

LAPD never seriously considered Sebring's odd sexual habits a possible cause of the murders. None of the girls interviewed—and the number was large, Sebring frequently dating five or six different girls a week—claimed that Sebring had actually hurt them, though he often asked them to pretend pain. Nor, as far as could be determined, was Sebring involved in group sex: he was too afraid his private quirks would subject him to ridicule. The mundane truth appeared to be that behind the carefully cultivated public image there was a lonely, troubled man so insecure in his role that even in his sex life he had to revert to fantasy.

Cause of death: Exsanguination—victim literally bled to death. Victim had been stabbed seven times and shot once, at least three of the stab wounds, as well as the gunshot wound, being in and of itself fatal.

Abigail Anne Folger, female Caucasian, 25 years, 5–5, 120 pounds, brown hair, hazel eyes, residence since the first of April, 10050 Cielo Drive. Prior to that she lived at 2774 Woodstock Road. Occupation, heiress to the Folger coffee fortune . . .

Abigail "Gibby" Folger's coming-out party had been held at the St. Francis Hotel in San Francisco on December 21, 1961. The Italianate ball was one of the highlights of the social season, the debutante wearing a bright yellow Dior she had purchased in Paris the previous summer.

After that she had attended Radcliffe, graduating with honors; worked for a time as publicity director for the University of California Art Museum in Berkeley; quit that to work in a New York bookstore; then became involved in social work in the ghettos. It was while in New York, in early 1968, that Polish novelist Jerzy Kosinski introduced her to Voytek Frykowski. They left New York together that August, driving to Los Angeles, where they rented a house at 2774 Woodstock Road, off Mulholland in the Hollywood hills. Through Frykowski, she met the Polanskis, Sebring, and others in their circle. She was one of the investors in Sebring International.

Shortly after arriving in Southern California, she registered as a volunteer social worker for the Los Angeles County Welfare Department, and would get up at dawn each day for assignments that took her into Watts, Pacoima, and other ghetto areas. She continued this work until the day before she and Frykowski moved into 10050 Cielo Drive.

Something changed after that. Probably it was a combination of things. She became depressed over how little such work actually accomplished, how big the problems stayed. "A lot of social workers go home at night, take a bath, and wash off their day," she told an old San Francisco friend. "I can't. The suffering gets under your skin." In May, black city councilman Thomas Bradley ran against incumbent Samuel Yorty for mayor of Los Angeles. Bradley's defeat, after a campaign heavy with racial smears, left her disillusioned and bitter. She did not resume her social work. She was also disturbed about the way her affair with Frykowski was going, and with their use of drugs, which had passed the point of experimentation.

She talked about all these things with her psychiatrist, Dr. Marvin Flicker. She saw him five days a week, Monday through Friday, at 4:30 P.M.

She had kept her appointment that Friday.

Flicker told the police that he thought Abigail was almost ready to leave Frykowski, that she was attempting to build up enough nerve to go it alone.

The police were unable to determine exactly when Folger and Frykowski began to use drugs heavily, on a regular basis. It was learned that on their cross-country trip they had stopped in Irving, Texas, staying several days with a big dope dealer well known to local and Dallas police. Dealers were among their regular guests both at the Woodstock house and after they moved to Cielo Drive. William Tennant told police that whenever he visited the latter residence, Abigail "always seemed to be in a stupor from narcotics." When her mother last talked to her, about ten that Friday night, she said Gibby had sounded lucid but "a little high." Mrs. Folger, who was not unaware of her daughter's problems, had contributed large amounts of both money and time to the Haight-Ashbury Free Medical Clinic, to help in their pioneer work in treating drug abuse.

The coroners discovered 2.4 mg. of methylenedioxyamphetamine—MDA—in Abigail Folger's system. That this was a larger amount than was found in Voytek Frykowski's body—0.6 mg.—did not necessarily indicate that she had taken a larger quantity of the drug, but could mean she had taken it at a later time.

Effects of the drug vary, depending on the individual

and the dosage, but one thing was clear. That night she was fully aware of what was happening.

Victim had been stabbed twenty-eight times.

Wojiciech "Voytek" Frykowski, male Caucasian, 32 years, 5–10, 165 pounds, blond hair, blue eyes. Frykowski had been living with Abigail Folger in a common-law relationship . . .

"Voytek," Roman Polanski would later tell reporters, "was a man of little talent but immense charm." The two had been friends in Poland, Frykowski's father reputedly having helped finance one of Polanski's early films. Even in Poland, Frykowski had been known as a playboy. According to fellow émigrés, he had once taken on, and rendered inoperative, two members of the secret police, which may have had something to do with his exit from Poland in 1967. He had married twice, and had one son, who had remained behind when he moved to Paris. Both there and, later, in New York, Polanski had given him money and encouragement, hopeful—but knowing Voytek well, not too optimistic—that one of his grand plans would come through. None ever quite did. He told people that he was a writer, but no one could recall having read anything he had written.

Friends of Abigail Folger told the police that Frykowski had introduced her to drugs so as to keep her under his control. Friends of Voytek Frykowski said the opposite—that Folger had provided the drugs so as not to lose him.

According to the police report: "He had no means of support and lived off Folger's fortune . . . He used cocaine, mescaline, LSD, marijuana, hashish in large amounts . . . He was an extrovert and gave invitations to almost everyone he met to come visit him at his residence. Narcotic parties were the order of the day."

He had fought hard for his life. Victim was shot twice, struck over the head thirteen times with a blunt object, and stabbed fifty-one times.

Steven Earl Parent, male Caucasian, 18 years, 6–0, 175 pounds, red hair, brown eyes . . .

He had graduated from Arroyo High School in June; dated several girls but no one in particular; had a full-time job as delivery boy for a plumbing company, plus a part-time job, evenings, as salesman for a stereo shop, holding down the two jobs so he could save money to attend junior college that September.

Victim had one defensive slash wound, and had been shot four times.

During the flouroscopy examination that preceded the Sebring autopsy, Dr. Noguchi discovered a bullet lodged between Sebring's back and his shirt. Three more bullets were found during the autopsies; one in Frykowski's body, two in Parent's. These—plus the slug and fragments found in Parent's automobile—were turned over to Sergeant William Lee, Firearms and Explosives Unit, SID, for study. Lee concluded that all the bullets had probably been fired from the same gun, and that they were .22 caliber.

While the autopsies were in progress, Sergeants Paul Whiteley and Charles Guenther, two homicide detectives from the Los Angeles Sheriff's Office, approached Sergeant Jess Buckles, one of the Los Angeles Police Department detectives assigned to the Tate homicides, and told him something very curious.

On July 31 they had gone to 964 Old Topanga Road in Malibu, to investigate a report of a possible homicide. They had found the body of Gary Hinman, a thirty-four-year-old music teacher. He had been stabbed to death.

The curious thing: as in the Tate homicides, a message had been left at the scene. On the wall in the living room, not far from Hinman's body, were the words POLITICAL PIGGY, printed in the victim's own blood.

Whiteley also told Buckles that they had arrested a suspect in connection with the murder, one Robert "Bobby" Beausoleil, a young hippie musician. He had been driving a car that belonged to Hinman, there was blood on his shirt and trousers, and a knife had been found hidden in the tire well of the vehicle. The arrest had occurred on August 6; therefore he had been in custody at the time of the

Tate homicides. However, it was possible that he hadn't been the only one involved in the Hinman murder. Beausoleil had been living at Spahn's Ranch, an old movie ranch near the Los Angeles suburb of Chatsworth, with a bunch of other hippies. It was an odd group, their leader, a guy named Charlie, apparently having convinced them that he was Jesus Christ.

Buckles, Whiteley would later recall, lost interest when he mentioned hippies. "Naw," he replied, "we know what's behind these murders. They're part of a big dope transaction."

Whiteley again emphasized the odd similarities. Like mode of death. In both cases a message had been left. Both printed. Both in a victim's blood. And in both the letters PIG appeared. Any one of these things would be highly unusual. But *all*—the odds against its being a coincidence must be astronomical.

Sergeant Buckles, LAPD, told Sergeants Whiteley and Guenther, LASO, "If you don't hear from us in a week or so, that means we're on to something else."

A little more than twenty-four hours after the discovery of the Tate victims, the Los Angeles Police Department was given a lead by the Los Angeles Sheriff's Office, which, if followed, could possibly have broken the case.

Buckles never did call, nor did he think the information important enough to walk across the autopsy room and mention the conversation to his superior, Lieutenant Robert Helder, who was in charge of the Tate investigation.

At Lieutenant Helder's suggestion, Dr. Noguchi withheld specifics when he met with the press. He did not mention the number of wounds, nor did he say anything about two of the victims' having ingested drugs. He did, again, deny the already much repeated reports that there had been sexual molestation and/or mutilation. Neither was true, he stressed.

Asked about Sharon's child, he said that Mrs. Polanski was in the eighth month of her pregnancy; that the child was a perfectly formed boy; and that had he been removed by post-mortem cesarean within the first twenty minutes after the mother's death, his life probably could have been saved. "But by the time the bodies were discovered, it was too late."

Lieutenant Helder also talked to the press that day. Yes, Garretson was still in custody. No, he could not comment on the evidence against him, except to say that the police were now investigating his acquaintances.

Pressed further, Helder admitted, "There's no solid information that will limit us to a single suspect. It could've been one man. It could've been two. It could've been three.

"But," he added, "I don't feel that we have a maniac running around."

Lieutenant A. H. Burdick began the polygraph examination of William Garretson at 4:25 that afternoon, at Parker Center.

Burdick did not immediately hook up Garretson. In accordance with routine, the initial portion of the examination was conversational, the examiner attempting to put the suspect at ease while eliciting as much background information as possible.

Though obviously frightened, Garretson loosened up a little as he talked. He told Burdick that he was nineteen, from Ohio, and had been hired by Rudi Altobelli in March, just before Altobelli left for Europe. His job was simple: to look after the guest house and Altobelli's three dogs. In return, he had been given a place to stay, thirty-five dollars a week, and the promise of an airline ticket back to Ohio when Altobelli returned.

He had little to do with the people who lived in the main house, Garretson claimed. Several of his replies seemed to bear this out. He still referred to Frykowski, for example, as "the younger Polanski," while he appeared unfamiliar with Sebring, either by name or description, though he had seen the black Porsche in the driveway on several occasions.

Asked to relate his activities prior to the murders, Garretson said that on Thursday night an acquaintance had dropped by, accompanied by his girl. They had brought along a six-pack of beer and some pot. Garretson was sure it was Thursday night, as the man was married "and he brought her up there several other times, you know, on Thursday, when his wife lets him go out."

Q. "Did they use your pad?"

A. "Yes, they did, and I drank some beer while they made out . . ."

Garretson recalled that he drank four beers, smoked two joints, took one dexedrine, and was sick all day Friday.

About 8:30 or 9 P.M. Friday, Garretson said, he went down to the Sunset Strip, to buy a pack of cigarettes and a TV dinner. He guessed the time of his return at about ten, but couldn't be sure, not having a watch. As he passed the main house, he noticed the lights were on, but he didn't see anyone. Nor did he observe anything out of the ordinary.

Then "about a quarter of twelve or something like that, Steve [Parent] came up and, you know, he brought his radio with him. He had a radio, clock radio; and I didn't expect him or anything, and he asked me how I'd been and everything . . ." Parent plugged in the radio, to demonstrate how it worked, but Garretson wasn't interested.

Then "I gave him a beer . . . and he drank it and then he called somebody—somebody on Santa Monica and Doheny—and he said that he would be going there, and so then he left, and, you know, that's when—that's the last time I saw him."

When found in Parent's car, the clock radio had stopped at 12:15 A.M., the approximate time of the murder. Although it could have been a remarkable coincidence, the logical presumption was that Parent had set it while demonstrating it to Garretson, then unplugged it just before he left. This would coincide with Garretson's estimate of the time.

According to Garretson, after Parent left, he wrote some letters and played the stereo, not going to sleep until just before dawn. Though he claimed to have heard nothing unusual during the night, he admitted that he had been "scared."

Why? Burdick asked. Well, Garretson replied, not long after Steve left, he noticed that the handle of the door was turned down, as if someone had tried to open it. And when he tried to use the phone, to learn the time, he found it was dead.

Like the other officers, Burdick found it difficult to believe that Garretson, though admittedly awake all night, heard nothing, while neighbors even farther away heard shots or screams. Garretson insisted, however, that he had neither heard nor seen anything. He was less sure on another point—whether he had gone out into the back yard when he let Altobelli's dogs out. To Burdick he appeared evasive about this. From the yard, however, he couldn't see the main house, though he might have heard something.

As far as LAPD was concerned, the moment of truth was now arriving. Burdick began setting up the polygraph, at the same time reading Garretson the list of questions he intended to ask.

This, too, was standard operating procedure, and more than a little psychological. Knowing a certain question was going to be asked, but not when, built tension, accentuating the response. He then began the test.

Q. "Is your true last name Garretson?"

A. "Yes."

No significant response.

Q. "Concerning Steve, did you cause his death?"

A. "No."

Facing forward, Garretson couldn't see Burdick's face. Burdick kept his voice matter-of-fact as he moved on to the next question, in no way indicating that the steel pens had jerked across the graph.

Q. "You understood the questions?"

A. "Yes."

Q. "Do you feel responsible for Steve's death?"

A. "That he even knew me, yes."

Q. "Huh?"

A. "That he even knew me. I mean he wouldn't have come up that night, and nothing would have happened in other words to him."

Burdick relieved the pressure cup on Garretson's arm, told him to relax, talked to him informally for a while.

Then again the pressure, and the questions, only slightly changed this time.

Q. "Is your true last name Garretson?"

A. "Yes."

Q. "Did you shoot Steve?"

A. "No."

No significant response.

More test questions, followed by "Do you know who caused Mrs. Polanski's death?"

A. "No."

Q. "Did you cause Mrs. Polanski's death?"

A. "No."

Still no significant response.

Burdick now accepted Garretson's explanation, that he felt responsibility for Parent's death, but had no part in causing it or the other murders. The examination went on for another half hour or so, during which Burdick closed off several avenues of investigation. Garretson was not gay; he had never had sex with any of the victims; he had never sold drugs.

There was no indication that Garretson was lying, but he remained nervous throughout. Burdick asked him why. Garretson explained that when he was being taken to his cell, a policeman had pointed at him, saying, "There's the guy that killed all those people."

Q. "I would imagine it would shake you up. But that doesn't mean you're lying?"

A. "No, I'm just confused."

Q. "Why are you confused?"

A. "For one thing, how come I wasn't murdered?"

Q. "I don't know."

Although legally inadmissable as evidence, the police believe in the polygraph.* Though uninformed of it at the time, Garretson had passed. "At the conclusion of the examination," Captain Don Martin, commander, SID, wrote in his official report, "it was the examiner's opinion that

*In 1972 a Los Angeles Superior Court judge broke with precedent and permitted the results of a polygraph test to be received into evidence in a marijuana case.

Mr. Garretson was truthful and not criminally involved in the Polanski homicides."

Unofficially, though Burdick believed Garretson "clean" on participation, he felt he was a little "muddy" on knowledge. It was possible that he had heard something, then, fearful, hidden until dawn. This was just conjecture, however.

For all intents and purposes, with the polygraph William Eston Garretson ceased to be a "good suspect." Yet that bothersome question remained: Every single human being at 10050 Cielo Drive had been slaughtered save one; why?

Because there was no immediate answer, and certainly in part because, having been the only warm body on the premises, he had seemed such a likely suspect, Garretson was held for another day.

That same Sunday, Jerrold D. Friedman, a UCLA student, contacted the police and informed them that the call Steven Parent made at approximately 11:45 on Friday night had been to him. Parent was going to build a stereo set for Friedman, and he wanted to talk over the details. Friedman had tried to beg off, saying it was late, but finally gave in and told Parent he could drop by for a few minutes. Parent had asked him the time and, when he told him, said he would be there about 12:30.* According to Friedman, "he never got there."

That Sunday, LAPD not only lost their best suspect to date, another promising lead fizzled out. Sharon Tate's red Ferrari, which the police had thought might have been used as a getaway car, was located in a Beverly Hills garage where Sharon had taken it the previous week for repairs.

That evening Roman Polanski returned from London. Reporters who saw him at the airport described him as "terribly crushed" and "beaten by the tragedy." Though he refused to talk with the press, a spokesman for him denied there was any truth to the rumors of a marital rift. Polan-

*It was possible when Parent asked the time he also set the radio clock.

ski had remained in London, he said, because he hadn't finished his work there. Sharon had returned home early, by boat, because of airline restrictions against travel during the last two months of pregnancy.

Polanski was taken to an apartment inside the Paramount lot, where he remained in seclusion under a doctor's care. The police talked to him briefly that night, but he was, at that time, unable to suggest anyone with a motive for the murders.

Frank Struthers also returned to Los Angeles that Sunday night. About 8:30 P.M. the Saffies dropped him off at the end of the long driveway leading to the LaBianca residence. Lugging his suitcase and camping equipment up the driveway, the fifteen-year-old noticed that the speedboat was still on the trailer behind Leno's Thunderbird. That seemed odd; his stepfather didn't like to leave the boat out overnight. Stowing his equipment in the garage, he went to the back door of the residence.

Only then did he notice that all the window shades had been pulled down. He couldn't recall ever seeing them that way before, and it frightened him just a little bit. The light was on in the kitchen, and he knocked on the door. There was no response. He called out. Again no answer.

Really upset now, he walked to the closest pay phone, which was at a hamburger stand at Hyperion and Rowena. He dialed the number of the house, then, getting no response, tried to reach his sister at the restaurant where she worked. Susan wasn't working that night, but the manager offered to try her apartment. Frank gave him the number of the pay phone.

Shortly after nine she called. She hadn't seen or heard from their mother and stepfather since they had dropped her off at her apartment the previous night. Telling Frank to remain where he was, she called her boy friend, Joe Dorgan, and told him Frank thought something was wrong at the house. About 9:30, Joe and Susan picked up Frank at the hamburger stand, the three driving directly to 3301 Waverly Drive.

Rosemary often left a set of house keys in her own car.

They found them and opened the back door.* Dorgan suggested that Susan remain in the kitchen while he and Frank checked out the rest of the house. They proceeded through the dining room. When they got to the living room, they saw Leno.

He was sprawled on his back between the couch and a chair. There was a throw pillow over his head, some kind of cord around his neck, and the tops of his pajamas were torn open so his stomach was bare. Something was protruding from his stomach.

He was so still they knew he was dead.

Afraid Susan would follow and see what they had, they returned to the kitchen. Joe picked up the kitchen phone to call the police, then, worried that he might be disturbing evidence, put it back down, telling Susan, "Everything's O.K.; let's get out of here." But Susan knew everything wasn't O.K. On the refrigerator door someone had written something in what looked like red paint.

Hurrying back down the driveway, they stopped at a duplex across the street, and Dorgan rang the bell of 3308 Waverly Drive. The peephole opened. Dorgan said there had been a stabbing and he wanted to call the police. The person inside refused to open the door, saying, "We'll call the police for you."

LAPD's switchboard logged the call at 10:26 P.M., the caller complaining about some juveniles making a disturbance.

Unsure whether the person had really made the call, Dorgan had already pushed the bell of the other apartment, 3306. Dr. and Mrs. Merry J. Brigham let the three young people in. However, they were so upset Mrs. Brigham had to complete the call. At 10:35, Unit 6A39, a black-and-white manned by officers W. C. Rodriquez and J. C. Toney, was dispatched to the address, arriving very quickly, five to seven minutes later.

While Susan and Frank remained with the doctor and his wife, Dorgan accompanied the two Hollywood Division officers to the LaBianca residence. Toney covered

*Since no one tried the door before using the key, it is unknown whether it was locked.

the back door while Rodriquez went around the house. The front door was closed but not locked. After one look inside, he ran back to the car and called for a backup unit, a supervisor, and an ambulance.

Rodriquez had been on the force only fourteen months; he had never discovered a body before.

Within a few minutes, Ambulance Unit G-1 arrived, and Leno LaBianca was pronounced DOA—dead on arrival. In addition to the pillow Frank and Joe had seen, there was a bloody pillowcase over his head. The cord around his neck was attached to a massive lamp, the cord knotted so tightly it appeared he had been throttled with it. His hands were tied behind his back with a leather thong. The object protruding from his stomach was an ivory-handled, bi-tined carving fork. In addition to a number of stab wounds in the abdomen, someone had carved the letters WAR in the naked flesh.

The backup unit, 6L40, manned by Sergeant Edward L. Cline, arrived just after the ambulance. A veteran of sixteen years, Cline took charge, obtaining a pink DOA slip from the two attendants before they left.

The pair were already on their way down the driveway when Rodriquez called them back. Cline had found another body, in the master bedroom.

Rosemary LaBianca was lying face down on the bedroom floor, parallel to the bed and dresser, in a large pool of blood. She was wearing a short pink nightgown and, over it, an expensive dress, blue with white horizontal stripes, which Susan would later identify as one of her mother's favorites. Both nightgown and dress were bunched up over her head, so her back, buttocks, and legs were bare. Cline didn't even try to count the stab wounds, there were so many. Her hands were not tied but, like Leno, she had a pillowcase over her head and a lamp cord was wrapped around her neck. The cord was attached to one of a pair of bedroom lamps, both of which had overturned. The tautness of the cord, plus a second pool of blood about two feet from the body, indicated that perhaps she had tried to crawl, pulling the lamps over while doing so.

A second pink DOA slip was filled out, for Mrs. Rosemary LaBianca. Joe Dorgan had to tell Susan and Frank.

There was writing, in what appeared to be blood, in three places in the residence. High up on the north wall in the living room, above several paintings, were printed the words DEATH TO PIGS. On the south wall, to the left of the front door, even higher up, was the single word RISE. There were two words on the refrigerator door in the kitchen, the first of which was misspelled. They read HEALTER SKELTER.

Monday, August 11, 1969

At 12:15 A.M. the case was assigned to Robbery-Homicide. Sergeant Danny Galindo, who had spent the previous night on guard duty at the Tate residence, was the first detective to arrive, at about 1 A.M. He was joined shortly after by Inspector K. J. McCauley and several other detectives, while an additional unit, ordered by Cline, sealed off the grounds. As with the Tate homicides, however, the reporters, who had already begun to arrive, apparently had little difficulty obtaining inside information.

Galindo made a detailed search of the one-story residence. Except for the overturned lamps, there were no signs of a struggle. Nor was there any evidence that robbery had been the motive. Among the items that Galindo would log into the County Public Administrator's Report were: a man's gold ring, the main stone a one-carat diamond, the other stones also diamonds, only slightly smaller; two woman's rings, both expensive, both in plain view on a dresser in the bedroom; necklaces; bracelets; camera equipment; hand guns, shotguns, and rifles; a coin collection; a bag of uncirculated nickels, found in the trunk of Leno's Thunderbird, worth considerably more than their $400 face value; Leno LaBianca's wallet, with credit cards and cash, in the glove compartment of his car; several watches, one a high-priced stopwatch of the type used to clock race horses; plus numerous other easily fenced items.

Several days later Frank Struthers returned to the residence with the police. The only missing items, as far as he could determine, were Rosemary's wallet and her wristwatch.

Galindo was unable to find any indications of forced entry. However, testing the back door, he found it could be jimmied very easily. He was able to open it with only a strip of celluloid.

The detectives made a number of other discoveries. The ivory-handled carving fork found protruding from Leno's stomach belonged to a set found in a kitchen drawer. There were some watermelon rinds in the sink. There were also blood splatters, both there and in the rear bathroom. And a piece of blood-soaked paper was found on the floor in the dining room, its frayed end suggesting that possibly it had been the instrument used to print the words.

In many ways the activities at 3301 Waverly Drive the rest of that night were a replay of those that had occurred at 10050 Cielo Drive less than forty-eight hours earlier. Even to, in some cases, the same cast, with Sergeant Joe Granado arriving about 3 A.M. to take blood samples.

The sample from the kitchen sink wasn't sufficient to determine if it was animal or human, but all the other samples tested positive on the Ouchterlony test, indicating they were human blood. The blood in the rear bathroom, as well as all the blood in the vicinity of Rosemary LaBianca's body, was type A—Rosemary LaBianca's type. All the other samples, including that taken from the rumpled paper and the various writings, were type B—Leno LaBianca's type.

This time Granado didn't take *any* subtypes.

The fingerprint men from SID, Sergeants Harold Dolan and J. Claborn, lifted a total of twenty-five latents, all but six of which would later be identified as belonging to Leno, Rosemary, or Frank. It was apparent to Dolan, from examining those areas where fingerprints should have been but weren't, that an effort had been made to eradicate prints. For example, there was not even a smudge on the ivory handle of the carving fork, on the chrome handle of the refrigerator door, or on the enamel finish of the door itself—all surfaces that readily lent themselves to receiving latent fingerprints. The refrigerator door on close examination showed wipe marks.

After the police photographer had finished, a deputy coroner supervised the removal of the bodies. The pillowcases were left in place over the heads of the victims; the lamp cords were cut near the bases, so the knots remained intact for study. A representative of the Animal Regulation Department removed the three dogs, which, when the first officers arrived, had been found inside the house.

Left behind were the puzzle pieces. But this time at least a partial pattern was discernible, in the similarities:

Los Angeles, California; consecutive nights; multiple murders; victims affluent Caucasians; multiple stab wounds; incredible savagery; absence of a conventional motive; no evidence of ransacking or robbery; ropes around the neck of two Tate victims, cords around the necks of both LaBiancas. And the bloody printing.

Yet within twenty-four hours the police would decide there was no connection between the two sets of murders.

SECOND RITUAL
KILLINGS HERE

Los Feliz Couple Slain;
Link to 5-Way Murder Seen

The headlines screamed from the front pages that Monday morning; TV programs were interrupted for updates; to the millions of Angelenos who commuted to work via the freeways their car radios seemed to broadcast little else.*

It was then the fear began.

*Some of the details were garbled. It was reported, for example, that the pillowcases were white hoods; that the phrase DEATH TO PIGS had been printed in blood on the refrigerator door, when it actually appeared on the wall in the living room. But enough information had leaked out for the detectives again to have trouble finding polygraph keys.

When the news of the Tate homicides broke, even those acquainted with the victims were less fearful than shocked, for simultaneously came the announcement that a suspect had been arrested and charged with the murders. Garretson, however, had been in custody when these new murders took place. And with his release that Monday—still looking as puzzled and frightened as when the police "captured" him—the panic began. And spread.

If Garretson wasn't guilty, then it meant that whoever was was still at large. If it could happen in places as widely separated as Los Feliz and Bel Air, to people as disparate as movie colony celebrities and a grocery market owner and his wife, it meant it could happen anywhere, to anyone.

Sometimes fear can be measured. Among the barometers: In two days one Beverly Hills sporting goods store sold 200 firearms; prior to the murders, they averaged three or four a day. Some of the private security forces doubled, then tripled, their personnel. Guard dogs, once priced at $200, now sold for $1,500; those who supplied them soon ran out. Locksmiths quoted two-week delays on orders. Accidental shootings, suspicious persons reports—all suddenly increased.

The news that there had been twenty-eight murders in Los Angeles that weekend (the average being one a day) did nothing to decrease the apprehension.

It was reported that Frank Sinatra was in hiding; that Mia Farrow wouldn't attend her friend Sharon's funeral because, a relative explained, "Mia is afraid she will be next"; that Tony Bennett had moved from his bungalow on the grounds of the Beverly Hills Hotel to an inside suite "for greater security"; that Steve McQueen now kept a weapon under the front seat of his sports car; that Jerry Lewis had installed an alarm system in his home complete with closed circuit TV. Connie Stevens later admitted she had turned her Beverly Hills home into a fortress. "Mainly because of the Sharon Tate murders. That scared the daylights out of everyone."

Friendships ended, romances broke up, people were abruptly dropped from guest lists, parties canceled—for with the fear came suspicion. The killer or killers could be almost anyone.

A cloud of fright hung over southern California more dense than its smog. It would not dissipate for months. As late as the following March, William Kloman would write in *Esquire:* "In the great houses of Bel Air, terror sends people flying to their telephones when a branch falls from a tree outside."

POLITICAL PIGGY—Hinman.
PIG—Tate.
DEATH TO PIGS—LaBianca.

In each case, written in the blood of one of the victims.

Sergeant Buckles still didn't think it important enough to check further.

Deputy Medical Examiner David Katsuyama conducted the LaBianca autopsies. Before starting, he removed the pillowcases from the heads of the victims. Only then was it discovered that in addition to the carving fork embedded in his abdomen, a knife had been stuck in Leno LaBianca's throat.

Since none of the personnel at the scene had observed the knife, this became one of the LaBianca polygraph keys. There were two others. For some reason, though the phrase DEATH TO PIGS had leaked to the press, neither RISE nor HEALTER SKELTER had.

Leno A. LaBianca, 3301 Waverly Drive, male Caucasian, 44 years, 6–0, 220 pounds, brown eyes, brown hair . . .

Born in Los Angeles, son of the founder of the State Wholesale Grocery Company, Leno had gone into the family business after attending the University of Southern California, eventually becoming president of Gateway Markets, a Southern California chain.

As far as the police were able to determine, Leno had no enemies. Yet they soon discovered that he too had a secret side. Friends and relatives described him as quiet and conservative; they were amazed to learn, after his death, that he owned nine thoroughbred race horses, the most prominent being Kildare Lady, and that he was a chronic gambler, frequenting the tracks nearly every racing day, often betting $500 at a time. Nor did they know that he was, at the time of his death, some $230,000 in debt.

In the weeks ahead the LaBianca detectives would do a remarkable job of tracking their way through the tangled maze of Leno LaBianca's complex financial affairs. The possibility that Leno might have been the victim of loan sharks, however, fell apart when it was learned that Rosemary LaBianca was quite wealthy herself, having more than sufficient assets to pay off Leno's debts.

One of Leno's former partners, also Italian, who knew of his gambling habits, told the police he thought the murders might have been committed by the Mafia. He admitted he had no evidence to support this; however, the detectives did learn that for a short time Leno had been on the board of directors of a Hollywood bank which LAPD and LASO intelligence units believed was backed by "hoodlum money." They had been unable to prove this, though several other board members were indicted and convicted of a kiting scheme. The possibility of a Mafia link became one of a number of leads that would have to be checked out.

Leno did not have a criminal record; Rosemary had one traffic citation which dated back to 1957.

Leno left $100,000 in insurance, which, since it was to be divided equally among Susan, Frank, and the three children from his previous marriage, appeared to rule that out as a motive.

Leno LaBianca died in the same house in which he had been born, he and Rosemary moving into the family home, which Leno had purchased from his mother, in November 1968.

Cause of death: Multiple stab wounds. Victim had twelve stab wounds, plus fourteen puncture wounds made by a double-tined fork, for a total of twenty-six separate wounds, any one of six of which could in and of itself have been fatal.

Rosemary LaBianca, 3301 Waverly Drive, female Caucasian, 38 years, 5–5, 125 pounds, brown hair, brown eyes . . .

It was probable that even Rosemary did not know a great deal about her early years. It was believed that she had been born in Mexico, of American parents, then orphaned or abandoned in Arizona. She remained in an orphanage there until the age of twelve, when she was adopted by a family named Harmon, who took her to California. She had met her first husband while working as a carhop at the Brown Derby Drive-In in Los Feliz in the late 1940s, while still in her teens. They were divorced in 1958, and it was shortly after this, while working as a waitress at the Los Feliz Inn, that she met and married Leno LaBianca.

Her former husband was polygraphed, and cleared of any involvement in the crime. Former employers, ex-boy friends, current business associates were interviewed; none could recall anyone who disliked her.

According to Ruth Sivick, her partner in Boutique Carriage, Rosemary had a good head for business; not only was the shop successful, Rosemary also invested in stocks and commodities, and did well. How well was not known until her estate was probated, and it was learned she had left $2,600,000. Abigail Folger, the heiress in the Cielo slayings, had left less than one-fifth that.

Mrs. Sivick had last seen Rosemary on Friday, when they went buying for the store. Rosemary had called on Saturday morning, telling her they planned to drive to Lake Isabella, and wondering if she could drop by that afternoon and feed the dogs. The LaBiancas had three dogs. All had barked loudly when she approached the house at about 6 P.M. After feeding them—taking the dog food out of the refrigerator—Mrs. Sivick checked the doors—all were locked—and left.

Mrs. Sivick's testimony established that whoever wiped the refrigerator handle of prints had done so sometime after she had been there.

Rosemary LaBianca—carhop to millionairess to murder victim.

Cause of death: Multiple stab wounds. Victim had been stabbed a total of forty-one times, any one of six of which could in and of itself have been fatal.

All but one of Leno LaBianca's wounds were to the front of his body; thirty-six of the forty-one inflicted on Rosemary LaBianca were to her back and buttocks. Leno had no defensive wounds, indicating that his hands had probably been bound before he was stabbed. Rosemary had a defensive slash wound on her left jaw. This wound, plus the knife in Leno's throat, indicated that the placing of the pillowcases over the heads of the victims was a belated act, possibly even occurring after they had died.

The pillowcases were identified as the LaBiancas' own, having been removed from the two pillows on their bed.

The knife found in Leno's throat was also theirs; though it was from a different set than the fork, it matched others found in a kitchen drawer. The dimensions of its blade were: length, 4 7/8 inches; thickness, just under 1/16 inch; width at widest point, 13/16 inch; width at narrowest point, 3/8 inch.

The LaBianca detectives later noted in their report: "The knife recovered from his throat appeared to be the weapon used in both homicides."

It was a presumption, and nothing more, since for some reason Dr. Katsuyama, unlike his superior Dr. Noguchi, who handled the Tate autopsies, did not measure the dimensions of the wounds. Nor did the detectives assigned to the LaBianca case ask for these statistics.

The ramifications of this one presumption were immense. A single weapon indicated that there was probably a single killer. That the weapon used belonged in the residence meant that the killer had probably arrived unarmed, his decision to kill the pair occurring sometime after he entered the premises. This in turn suggested: (1) that the killer had arrived to commit a burglary or some other crime, then had been surprised when the LaBiancas returned home; or (2) that the victims knew the killer, trusting him enough to let him in at two in the morning or thereafter.

One little presumption, but it would cause many, many problems later.

As would the estimated time of death.

Asked by the detectives to determine the time, Katsuyama came up with 3 P.M. Sunday. When other evidence appeared to contradict this, the detectives went back to Katsuyama and asked him to recalculate. He now decided Leno LaBianca had died sometime between 12:30 A.M. and 8:30 P.M. on Sunday, and that Rosemary had died an hour earlier. However, Katsuyama cautioned, the time could be affected by room temperature and other variables.

All this was so indecisive that the detectives simply ignored it. They knew, from Frank Struthers, that Leno was a creature of habit. Every night he bought the paper, then read it before going to bed, always starting with the sports section. That section had been open on the coffee table, with Leno's reading glasses beside it. From this and other evidence (Leno was wearing pajamas, the bed hadn't yet been slept in, and so forth) they concluded that the murders had probably taken place within an hour or so after the LaBiancas had left Fokianos' newsstand, or sometime between 2 and 3 A.M. on Sunday.

As early as Monday, police were minimizing the similarities between the two crimes. Inspector K. J. McCauley told reporters: "I don't see any connection between this murder and the others. They're too widely removed. I just don't see any connection." Sergeant Bryce Houchin observed: "There is a similarity, but whether it's the same suspect or a copycat we just don't know."

There were several reasons for discounting the similarities. One was the absence of any apparent link between the victims; another the distance between the crimes. Still another, and more important in formulating a motive, drugs were found at 10050 Cielo Drive, while there were none at 3301 Waverly Drive.

There was one more reason, perhaps the most influential. Even before Garretson was released, the Tate detectives had not one but several very promising new suspects.

August 12-15, 1969

From William Tennant, Roman Polanski's business manager, LAPD learned that in mid-March the Polanskis had given a catered party at Cielo with over a hundred guests. As at any large Hollywood gathering, there were crashers, among them +Herb Wilson, +Larry Madigan, and +Jeffery Pickett, nicknamed "Pic."* The trio, all in their late twenties, were reputedly dope dealers. During the party Wilson apparently stepped on Tennant's foot. An argument ensued, Madigan and Pickett taking Wilson's side. Irritated, Roman Polanski had the three men evicted.

It was a minor incident, in and of itself hardly cause for five savage murders, but Tennant had heard something else: "Pic" had once threatened to kill Frykowski. This information had come to him through a friend of Voytek's, Witold Kaczanowski, an artist professionally known as Witold K.

Not unmindful of the similarity between "Pic" and the bloody-lettered PIG on the front door of the Tate residence, detectives interviewed Witold K. From him they learned that after the Polanskis had left for Europe, Wilson, Pickett, Madigan, and a fourth man, +Gerold Jones, were frequent visitors to the Cielo residence, Wilson and Madigan, according to Witold, supplying Voytek and Gibby with most of their drugs, including the MDA they had taken before they died. As for Jeffrey Pickett, when Gibby and Voytek took over Cielo, he moved into their Woodstock residence. Witold was staying there also. Once, during an argument, Pickett tried to strangle the artist.

*Everything in this book is based on fact. In a few instances the names of persons only tangentially involved have been changed for legal reasons, the cross symbol (+) indicating the substitution of a pseudonym for the true name. The persons were and are real, however, and the incidents depicted are entirely factual.

When Voytek learned of this, he told Pickett to get out. Enraged, Pic swore, "I'll kill them all and Voytek will be the first."

Numerous others also felt one or more of the men might be involved, and passed on their suspicions to the police. John and Michelle Phillips, formerly of the Mamas and Papas group and friends of four of the five Tate victims, said Wilson once drew a gun on Voytek. Various Strip habitués claimed Wilson often bragged that he was a hired killer; that Jones was an expert with knives, always carrying one for throwing; and that Madigan was Sebring's "candy man," or cocaine source.

More than ever convinced that the Tate homicides were the result of a drug burn or freakout, LAPD began looking for Wilson, Madigan, Pickett, and Jones.

For ten years Sharon Tate had sought stardom. Now she attained it, in just three days. On Tuesday, August 12, her name moved from the headlines onto theater marquees. *Valley of the Dolls* was rereleased nationally, opening in more than a dozen theaters in the Los Angeles area alone. It was quickly followed by *The Fearless Vampire Killers* and other films in which the actress had appeared, the only difference being that now she was given star billing.

That same day the police told reporters that they had officially ruled out any connection between the Tate and LaBianca homicides. According to the Los Angeles *Times*, "Several officers indicated they were inclined to believe the second slayings were the work of a copycat."

From the start, the two investigations had proceeded separately, with different detectives assigned to each. They would continue this way, each team pursuing its own leads.

They had one thing in common, though that similarity widened the distance between them. Both were operating on a basic assumption: in nearly 90 percent of all homicides the victim knows his killer. In both investigations the chief focus was now on acquaintances of the victims.

In checking out the Mafia rumor, the LaBianca detectives interviewed each of Leno's known business associates. All doubted the murders were Mafia originated. One man told the detectives that if the Mafia had been responsible, he "probably would have heard about it." It was a thorough investigation, the detectives even checking to see if the San Diego company where Leno had purchased his speedboat during their 1968 vacation was Mafia financed; it wasn't, though numerous other businesses in the Mission Bay area were allegedly backed by "Jewish Mafia money."

They even questioned Leno's mother, who told them, "He was a good boy. He never did belong to the association."

The elimination of a possible Mafia link, however, did not leave the LaBianca detectives without a suspect. In questioning neighbors of the pair, they learned that the house to the east, 3267 Waverly Drive, was vacant, and had been for several months. Prior to that it had been a hippie hangout. The hippies didn't interest them, but another former tenant, †Fred Gardner, did, very much.

From his rap sheet and from interviews they learned that Gardner, a young attorney, "has had mental problems in the past and claims he blacks out for periods of time and is not responsible for his actions . . ." During an argument with his father, he "grabbed a knife from the kitchen table and chased his father, stating that he would kill him . . ." In September 1968, after being married only two weeks, "for no apparent reason [he] administered a vicious beating to his wife, then grabbed a knife from the kitchen drawer and attempted to kill her. She warded off the blows and managed to escape and call the police." Booked for attempted murder, he was examined by a court-appointed psychiatrist, who found he had "uncontrolled aggressions of maniacal proportions." Despite this, the charge had been reduced to simple assault. He was released on probation, and returned to the practice of law.

Since then Gardner had been arrested a number of times, on drunk or drug charges. Following his last arrest, for forging a prescription, he was released on $900 bail, and promptly skipped. A warrant for his arrest had been issued on August 1, nine days before the LaBianca murders. He was believed to be in New York.

When the officers questioned Gardner's ex-wife, she told them she could recall seven separate occasions when Gardner visited the LaBiancas, each time returning with either money or whiskey. When she'd asked him about this, he'd allegedly replied, "It's O.K. I know them and they had better give it to me or else."

Had Gardner, with his penchant for kitchen knives, again tried to put the bite on the LaBiancas, this time the couple saying no? The officers contacted an FBI agent in New York to see if he could determine Gardner's present whereabouts.

Beloved Wife of Roman
Sharon Tate Polanski
1943 1969
Paul Richard Polanski
Their Baby

Wednesday was a day of funerals. More than 150 persons attended Sharon Tate's last rites at Holy Cross Cemetery. Among those present were Kirk Douglas, Warren Beatty, Steve McQueen, James Coburn, Lee Marvin, Yul Brynner, Peter Sellers, John and Michelle Phillips. Roman Polanski, wearing dark glasses and accompanied by his doctor, broke down several times during the ceremony, as did Sharon's parents and her two young sisters, Patricia and Deborah.

Many of the same people, including Polanski, later attended the services for Jay Sebring, at Wee Kirk o' the Heather, Forest Lawn. Additional celebrities included Paul Newman, Henry and Peter Fonda, Alex Cord, and George Hamilton, all former Sebring clients.

There were fewer people, and fewer flashbulbs, as, across the city, six of his high-school classmates carried Steven Parent's body from the small El Monte church where his services had taken place.

Abigail Folger was buried near where she had grown up in Northern California on the San Francisco Peninsula, following a requiem mass in Our Lady of the Wayside Church, which had been built by her grandparents.

Voytek Frykowski's body remained in Los Angeles until relatives in Poland could arrange for it to be returned there for burial.

While the Tate victims were being interred, the police were attempting to re-create their lives, in particular their last day.

Friday, August 8.

About 8 A.M. Mrs. Chapman arrived at Cielo. She did what dishes there were, then commenced her regular household chores.

About 8:30 Frank Guerrero arrived, to paint the room at the north end of the residence. This was to be the nursery. Before starting, Guerrero removed the screens from the windows.

At 11 A.M. Roman Polanski called from London. Mrs. Chapman overheard Sharon's side of the conversation. Sharon was worried that Roman wouldn't be home in time for his birthday, August 18. He apparently assured her that he would be back on August 12 as planned, as Sharon later told Mrs. Chapman this. Sharon informed Roman that she had enrolled him in a course for expectant fathers.

Sharon received several other calls, one of them having to do with a neighbor's kitten that had strayed onto the property; Sharon had been feeding it with an eyedropper. When Terry Melcher had moved out, he'd left behind a number of cats, Sharon promising to look after them. They had since multiplied, and Sharon was caring for all twenty-six, plus two dogs, hers and Abigail's.

Most of the day Sharon wore only bikini panties and a bra. This, according to Mrs. Chapman, was her usual at-home attire in hot weather.

Shortly before noon Mrs. Chapman, noticing that there were paw prints and dog splatters on the front door, washed down the whole exterior with vinegar and water. A small detail, which later would become extremely important.

Steven Parent had lunch at his home in El Monte. Before returning to work at the plumbing supply company, he asked his mother if she would lay out clean clothes so he could make a quick change before going to his second job, at the stereo shop, later that afternoon.

About 12:30 two of Sharon's friends, Joanna Pettet (Mrs. Alex Cord)* and Barbara Lewis, arrived at Cielo for lunch. Mrs. Chapman served them. It was all small talk, the women would later recall, mostly about the expected baby.

About 1 P.M. Sandy Tennant called Sharon. As previously noted, Sharon told her she wasn't planning a party that evening, but did invite her to drop by, an invitation Sandy declined.

(If one believed all the subsequent talk, half of Hollywood was invited to 10050 Cielo Drive for a party that night, and, at the last minute, changed their minds. According to Winifred Chapman, Sandy Tennant, Debbie Tate, and others close to Sharon, there was no party that night, nor was one ever planned. But LAPD probably spent a hundred man-hours attempting to locate people who allegedly attended the non-event.)

Having finished the first coat of paint, Guerrero left about 1:30. He didn't replace the screens, since he intended to return Monday to give the room a final coat. The police later concluded the killer(s) either didn't notice they were off or feared entering a freshly painted room.

About 2 P.M. Abigail purchased a bicycle from a shop on Santa Monica Boulevard, arranging for it to be delivered later that afternoon. About the same time David Martinez, one of Altobelli's two gardeners, arrived at 10050 Cielo and began work. Voytek and Abigail arrived not long after this, joining Sharon and her guests for a late lunch.

About 3 P.M. the second gardener, Tom Vargas, arrived. As he came in the gate, Abigail was driving out in her

*This would be actress Joanna Pettet's second close brush with violent death. She had also been a friend of Janice Wylie, who, together with her roommate Emily Hoffert, had been murdered in New York City in the summer of 1963, in what became known as the "career girls murder case."

Camaro. Five minutes later Voytek also left, driving the Firebird.

Joanna Pettet and Barbara Lewis departed about 3:30.

At about that same time Sebring's butler, Amos Russell, served Jay and his current female companion coffee in bed.* About 3:45 Jay called Sharon, apparently telling her he would be over earlier than expected. He later called his secretary, to pick up his messages, and John Madden, to discuss his visit to the San Francisco salon the next day. He didn't mention to either his plans for that evening, but he did tell Madden he had spent the day hard at work on a crest for the new franchise shops.

Just after Sebring called Sharon, Mrs. Chapman told her she had finished her work and was leaving for the day. Since it was so hot in the city, Sharon asked her if she would like to stay over. Mrs. Chapman declined. It was undoubtedly the most important decision she ever made.

David Martinez was just leaving, and he gave Mrs. Chapman a ride to the bus stop. Vargas remained behind, completing his work. While gardening near the house, he noticed Sharon asleep on the bed in her room. When a deliveryman from the Air Dispatch Company arrived with the two blue steamer trunks, Vargas, not wishing to disturb Mrs. Polanski, signed for them. The time, 4:30 P.M., was noted on the receipt. The trunks contained Sharon's clothing, which Roman had shipped from London.

Abigail kept her 4:30 appointment with Dr. Flicker.

Before Vargas left, about 4:45, he went back to the guest house and asked Garretson if he would do some watering over the weekend, as the weather was extremely hot and dry.

Across the city, in El Monte, Steven Parent hurried home, changed clothes, waved to his mother, and was off to his second job.

Between 5:30 and 6 P.M. Mrs. Terry Kay was backing out of her driveway at 9845 Easton Drive when she observed Jay Sebring driving down the road in his Porsche, seemingly in a hurry. Perhaps because her car was block-

*LAPD eventually located the girl and determined that she had not accompanied Sebring to the Tate residence that night.

ing his progress, he did not wave in his usual genial manner.

Sometime between 6 and 6:30 P.M. Sharon's thirteen-year-old sister Debbie called her, asking if she could drop by that evening with some friends. Sharon, who tired easily because of her advanced pregnancy, suggested they make it another time.

Between 7:30 and 8 P.M. Dennis Hurst arrived at the Cielo address to deliver the bicycle Abigail had purchased in his father's shop earlier that day. Sebring (whom Hurst later identified from photographs) answered the door. Hurst saw no one else and observed nothing suspicious.

Between 9:45 and 10 P.M. John Del Gaudio, manager of the El Coyote Restaurant on Beverly Boulevard, noted Jay Sebring's name on the waiting list for dinner: party of four. Del Gaudio didn't actually see Sebring or the others, and it is probable that he was off on the time, as waitress Kathy Palmer, who served the four, recalled they waited in the bar fifteen to twenty minutes before a table was available, then, after finishing dinner, left about 9:45 or 10. Shown photographs, she was unable to positively identify Sebring, Tate, Frykowski, or Folger.

If Abigail was along, they must have left the restaurant before ten, as it was about this time that Mrs. Folger called the Cielo number and talked to her, confirming that she planned to take the 10 A.M. United flight to San Francisco the next morning. Mrs. Folger told the police that "Abigail did not express any alarm or anxiety as to her personal safety or the situation at the Polanski house."

A number of people reported seeing Sharon and/or Jay at the Candy Store, the Factory, the Daisy, or various other clubs that night. None of the reports checked out. Several persons claimed to have talked by phone with one or another of the victims between 10 P.M. and midnight. When questioned, they suddenly changed their stories, or told them in such a way that the police concluded they were either confused or lying.

About 11 P.M. Steve Parent stopped at Dales Market in El Monte and asked his friend John LeFebure if he wanted to go for a ride. Parent had been dating John's younger sister Jean. John suggested they make it another night.

About forty-five minutes later Steve Parent arrived at the Cielo address, hoping to sell William Garretson a clock radio. Parent left the guest house about 12:15 A.M. He got as far as his Rambler.

The police also interviewed a number of other girls rumored to have been with Sebring on the evening of August 8.

"Ex-girl friend of Sebring, was supposed to have been with him on 8-8-69—not so—last slept with him 7-5-69. Cooperative, knew he used 'C'—she does not . . . "

". . . dated him steady for three months . . . knew nothing of his way-out bedroom activities . . ."

". . . was to go to a party at Cielo that night, but went to a movie instead . . ."

It was no small assignment, considering the number of girls the stylist had dated, yet none of the detectives was heard to complain. It wasn't every day they got the chance to talk to starlets, models, a *Playboy* centerfold, even a dancer in the Lido de Paris show at the Stardust Hotel in Las Vegas.

There was another barometer to the fear: the difficulty the police had in locating people. To have suddenly moved a few days after a crime would, in ordinary circumstances, be considered suspicious. But not in this case. From a not untypical report: "Asked why she had moved right after the murders, she replied that she wasn't sure why, that like everyone else in Hollywood she was just afraid . . ."

August 16-30, 1969

Though the police told the press there had been "no new developments," there were some that went unreported. After testing them for blood, Sergeant Joe Granado gave the three pieces of gun grip to Sergeant William Lee of the Firearms and Explosives Unit of SID. Lee didn't even have to consult his manuals; one look and he knew the grip was from a Hi Standard gun. He called Ed Lomax, product manager for the firm that owns Hi Standard, and arranged to meet him at the Police Academy. Lomax also made a quick ID. "Only one gun has a grip like that," he told Lee, "the Hi Standard .22 caliber Longhorn revolver." Popularly known as the "Buntline Special"—patterned after a pair of revolvers Western author Ned Buntline had made for Marshal Wyatt Earp—the gun had the following specifications: capacity 9 shots, barrel 9 1/2 inches, over-all length 15 inches, walnut grips, blue finish, weight 35 ounces, suggested retail price $69.95. It was, Lomax said, "rather a unique revolver"; introduced in April 1967, only 2,700 had been manufactured with this type grip.

Lee obtained from Lomax a list of stores where the gun had been sold, plus a photograph of the model, and LAPD began preparing a flyer which they planned to send to every police department in the United States and Canada.

A few days after the Lee-Lomax meeting, SID criminalist DeWayne Wolfer went to 10050 Cielo to conduct sound tests to see whether he could verify, or disprove, Garretson's claim that he had heard neither screams nor gunshots.

Using a general level sound meter and a .22 caliber revolver, and duplicating as closely as possible the conditions that existed on the night of the murders, Wolfer and an assistant proved (1) that if Garretson was inside the guest house as he claimed, he couldn't possibly have heard the shots that killed Steven Parent; and (2) that with the stereo on, with the volume at either 4 or 5, he couldn't have heard either screams or gunshots coming from in front of or inside the main residence.* The tests supported Garretson's story that he did not hear any shots that night.

Yet despite Wolfer's scientific findings, there were those at LAPD who still felt that Garretson must have heard something. It was almost as if he had been such a good suspect they were reluctant to admit him blameless. In a summary report on the case made up at the end of August, the Tate detectives observed: "In the opinion of the investigating officers and by scientific research by SID, it is highly unlikely that Garretson was not aware of the screams, gunshots and other turmoil that would result from a multiple homicide such as took place in his near proximity. These findings, however, did not absolutely preclude the fact that Garretson did not hear or see any of the events connected with the homicides."

The evening of Saturday, August 16, Roman Polanski was interviewed for several hours by LAPD. The following day he returned to 10050 Cielo Drive for the first time since the murders. He was accompanied by a writer and a photographer for *Life* and Peter Hurkos, the well-known psychic, who had been hired by friends of Jay Sebring to make a "reading" at the scene.

As Polanski identified himself and drove through the gate, the premises still being secured by LAPD, he commented bitterly to Thomas Thompson, the *Life* writer and a long-time acquaintance, "This must be the world-famous orgy house." Thompson asked him how long Gibby and Voytek had been staying there. "Too long, I guess," he answered.

The blue bedsheet that had earlier covered Abigail Folger was still on the lawn. The bloody lettering on the door had faded, but the three letters were still decipherable. The havoc inside seemed to take him aback for a minute,

*When Officer Whisenhunt searched the guest house following Garretson's arrest, he noticed the volume control on the set was between 4 and 5.

as did the dark stains in the entryway, and once inside the living room, the even larger ones in front of the couch. Polanski climbed the ladder to the loft, found the videotape LAPD had returned, and slipped it into his pocket, according to one of the officers who was present. On climbing back down, he walked from room to room, here and there touching things as if he could conjure up the past. The pillows were still bunched up in the center of the bed, as they had been that morning. They were always that way when he was gone, he told Thompson, adding simply, "She hugged them instead of me." He lingered a long time at the armoire where, in anticipation, Sharon had kept the baby things.

The *Life* photographer took a number of Polaroid shots first, to check lighting, placement, angles. Usually these are thrown away after the regular pictures are taken, but Hurkos asked if he might have several of them, to aid in his "impressions," and they were given to him, a gesture the photographer, and *Life*, would very soon regret.

As Polanski looked at the objects once familiar, now turned grotesque, he kept asking, "Why?" He posed outside the front door, looking as lost and confused as if he had stepped onto one of his own sets to discover everything immutably and grossly changed.

Hurkos later told the press: "Three men killed Sharon Tate and the other four—and I know who they are. I have identified the killers to the police and told them that these men must be stopped soon. Otherwise they will kill again." The killers, he added, were friends of Sharon Tate, turned into "frenzied homicidal maniacs" by massive doses of LSD. The killings, he was quoted as saying, erupted during a black magic ritual known as "goona goona," its suddenness catching the victims unawares.

If Hurkos did identify the three men to LAPD, no one bothered to make a report on it. All publicity to the contrary notwithstanding, those in law enforcement have a standard procedure for handling such "information": listen politely, then forget it. Being inadmissible as evidence, it is valueless.

Also skeptical of Hurkos' explanation was Roman Polanski. He would return to the house several times over the next few days, as if looking for the answer no one else had been able to give him.

There was an interesting juxtaposition of stories on the B, or lead local news, page of the Los Angeles *Times* that Sunday.

The big story, Tate, commandeered the top spot, with its headline, "ANATOMY OF A MASS/MURDER IN HOLLYWOOD."

Below it was a smaller story, its one-column head reading, "LABIANCA COUPLE,/VICTIMS OF SLAYER,/GIVEN FINAL RITES."

To the left of the Tate story, and just above an artist's drawing of the Tate premises, was a much briefer, seemingly unrelated item, chosen, one suspected, because it was small enough to fit the space. Its headline read, "POLICE RAID RANCH,/ARREST 26 SUSPECTS/IN AUTO THEFT RING."

It began: "Twenty-six persons living in an abandoned Western movie set on an isolated Chatsworth ranch were arrested in a daybreak raid by sheriff's deputies Saturday as suspects in a major auto theft ring."

According to deputies, the group had been stealing Volkswagens, then converting them into dune buggies. The story, which did not contain the names of any of those arrested but did mention that a sizable arsenal of weapons had been seized, concluded: "The ranch is owned by George Spahn, a blind, 80-year-old semi-invalid. It is located in the Simi Hills at 12000 Santa Susana Pass Road. Deputies said Spahn, who lives alone in a house on the ranch, apparently knew there were people living on the set but was unaware of their activity. They said he couldn't get around and he was afraid of them."

It was a minor story, and didn't even rate a follow-up when, a few days later, all the suspects were released, it being discovered they had been arrested on a misdated warrant.

Following a report that Wilson, Madigan, Pickett, and Jones were in Canada, LAPD sent the Royal Canadian Mounted Police a "want" on the four men; RCMP broadcast it; alert reporters picked it up; and within hours the news media in the United States were heralding "a break in the Tate case."

Although LAPD denied that the four men were suspects, saying they were only wanted for questioning, the impression remained that arrests were imminent. There were phone calls, among them one from Madigan, another from Jones.

Jones was in Jamaica, and said he would fly back voluntarily if the police wished to talk to him. They admitted they did. Madigan showed up at Parker Center with his attorney. He cooperated fully, agreeing to answer any questions except those which might tend to involve him in the use or sale of narcotics. He admitted having visited Frykowski at the Cielo residence twice during the week before the murders, so it was possible his prints were there. On the night of the murders, Madigan said, he had attended a party given by an airline stewardess who lived in the apartment below his. He had left about 2 or 3 A.M. This was later verified by LAPD, who also checked his prints against the unmatched latents found at the Cielo address, without success.

Madigan was given a polygraph, and passed, as did Jones, when he arrived from Jamaica. Jones said that he and Wilson had been in Jamaica from July 12 to August 17, at which time he had flown to Los Angeles and Wilson had flown to Toronto. Asked why they had gone to Jamaica, he said they were "making a movie about marijuana." Jones' alibi would have to be checked out, but after his polygraph, and a negative print check, he ceased to be a good suspect.

This left Herb Wilson and Jeffrey Pickett, nicknamed Pic. By this time LAPD knew where both men were.

The publicity had been bad. There was no disputing that. As Steven Roberts, Los Angeles bureau chief for the New York *Times*, later put it, "All the stories had a common thread—that somehow the victims had brought the murders on themselves . . . The attitude was summed up in the epigram: 'Live freaky, die freaky.' "

Given Roman Polanski's affinity for the macabre; rumors of Sebring's sexual peculiarities; the presence of both Miss Tate and her former lover at the death scene while her husband was away; the "anything goes" image of the Hollywood jet set; drugs; and the sudden clamp on police leaks, almost any kind of plot could be fashioned, and was. Sharon Tate was called everything from "the queen of the Hollywood orgy scene" to "a dabbler in satanic arts." Polanski himself was not spared. In the same newspaper a reader could find one columnist saying the director was so grief-stricken he could not speak, while a second had him nightclubbing with a bevy of airline stewardesses. If he wasn't personally responsible for the murders, more than one paper implied, he must know who committed them.

From a national news weekly:

"Sharon's body was found nude, not clad in bikini pants and a bra as had first been reported ... Sebring was wearing only the torn remnants of a pair of boxer shorts ... Frykowski's trousers were down to his ankles ... Both Sebring and Tate had X's carved on their bodies ... One of Miss Tate's breasts had been cut off, apparently as the result of indiscriminate slashing ... Sebring had been sexually mutilated ..." The rest was equally accurate: "No fingerprints were found anywhere ... no drug traces were found in any of the five bodies ..." And so on.

Though it read like something from the old *Confidential,* the article had appeared in *Time,* its writer apparently having some tall explaining to do when his editors became aware of his imaginative embellishments.

Angered by "a multitude of slanders," Roman Polanski called a press conference on August 19, where he castigated newsmen who "for a selfish reason" wrote "horrible things about my wife." There had been no marital rift, he reiterated; no dope; no orgies. His wife had been "beautiful" and "a good person," and "the last few years I spent with her were the only time of true happiness in my life ..."

Some of the reporters were less than sympathetic to Polanski's complaints about publicity, having just learned that he had permitted *Life* to take exclusive photos of the murder scene.

Not quite "exclusive." Before the magazine reached the

stands, several of the Polaroid prints appeared in the Hollywood *Citizen News*.

Life had been scooped, by its own photographs.

There were some things Polanski did not tell the press, or even his closest friends. One was that he had agreed to be polygraphed by the Los Angeles Police Department.

Polanski's polygraph examination was conducted by Lieutenant Earl Deemer at Parker Center.

Q. "Mind if I call you Roman? My name is Earl."

A. "Sure . . . I will lie one or two times during it, and I will tell you after, O.K.?"

Q. "Well—all right . . ."

Deemer asked Roman how he first met his wife.

Polanski sighed, then slowly began talking. "I first met Sharon four years ago at some kind of party Marty Ransohoff—a terrible Hollywood producer—had. The guy who makes 'Beverly Hillbillies' and all kinds of shit. But he seduced me with his talk about art, and I contracted with him to do this film, a spoof on the vampires, you know.

"And I met Sharon at the party. She was doing another film for him in London at the time. Staying in London alone. Ransohoff said, 'Wait until you see our leading lady, Sharon Tate!'

"I thought she was quite pretty. But I wasn't at that time very impressed. But then I saw her again. I took her out. We talked a lot, you know. At that time I was really swinging. All I was interested in was to fuck a girl and move on. I had a very bad marriage, you know. Years before. Not bad, it was beautiful, but my wife dumped me, so I was really feeling great, because I was a success with women and I just like fucking around. I was a swinger, uh?

"So I met her a couple of more times. I knew she was with Jay. Then [Ransohoff] wanted me to use her in the film. And I made tests with her.

"Once before I wanted to take her out, and she was being difficult, wanting to go out, not wanting to go out, so I said, 'Fuck you,' and I hung up. Probably that was the beginning of everything, you know."

Q. "You sweet-talked her."

A. "Right. She got intrigued by me. And I really played it cool, and it took me long dating before— And then I started seeing that she liked me.

"I remember I spent a night—I lost a key—and I spent a night in her house in the same bed, you know. And I knew there was no question of making love with her. That's the type of girl she was.

"I mean, that rarely happens to me!

"And then we went on location—it was about two or three months later. When we were on location shooting the film, I asked her, 'Would you like to make love with me?' and she said, very sweetly, 'Yes.' And then for the first time I was somewhat touched by her, you know. And we started sleeping regularly together. And she was so sweet and so lovely that I didn't believe it, you know. I'd had bad experiences and I didn't believe that people like that existed, and I was waiting a long time for her to show the color, right?

"But she was *beautiful*, without this phoniness. She was fantastic. She loved me. I was living in a different house. I didn't want her to come to my house. And she would say, 'I don't want to smother you. I only want to be with you,' etc. And I said, 'You know how I am; I screw around.' And she said, 'I don't want to change you.' She was ready to do everything, just to be with me. She was a *fucking angel*. She was a unique character, who I'll never meet again in my life."

Deemer asked about his first meeting with Sebring. It had occurred in a London restaurant, Polanski said, describing how nervous he had been, and how Jay had broken the ice by saying, "I dig you, man. I dig you." More important, "he seemed happy to see Sharon happy." Roman had remained slightly uncomfortable through their next several meetings. "But when I came to Los Angeles, started living here, he came to our parties, etc. And I started liking Jay very very much. He was a very sweet person. Oh, I know of his hangups. He liked to whip-tie girls. Sharon told me about it. He tied her once to the bed. And she told me about it. And was making fun of him . . . To her it was funny, but sad . . .

"And he was more and more often a guest of ours. He would just hang around, hang around, and sometimes Sharon would resent his staying too long, because he was always the last to leave, you know.

"I'm sure in the beginning of our relationship there was still his love for Sharon, but I think that largely it disappeared. I'm quite sure."

Q. "So there was no indication that Sharon went back to Sebring at any time?"

A. "*Not a chance!* I'm the bad one. I always screw around. That was Sharon's big hangup, you know. But Sharon was absolutely not interested in Jay."

Q. "Was she interested in any other men?"

A. "No! There was not a chance of any other man getting close to Sharon."

Q. "O.K., I know you have to get on your way. We might as well start. I'll tell you how this works, Roman." Deemer explained the mechanics of the polygraph, adding, "It's important for you to remain quiet. I know you talk a lot with your hands. You're emotional. You're an actor type person, so it's going to be a little difficult for you . . . But when the pressure is on, I want you to remain quiet. When it's off, you can talk and even wave your arms. Within reason."

After instructing Polanski to confine his answers to "yes" and "no" and to save any explanations for later, Deemer began the interrogation.

Q. "Do you have a valid California driver's license?"

A. "Yes."

Q. "Have you eaten lunch today?"

A. "No."

Q. "Do you know who took the life of Voytek and the others?"

A. "No."

Q. "Do you smoke cigarettes?"

A. "Yes." There was a long pause, then Polanski began laughing.

Q. "You know what you are going to do, with that screwing around? I'm going to have to start over again!"

A. "Sorry."

Q. "Look at the increase in your blood pressure when

you start to lie about your cigarettes. Boom, boom, boom, just like a staircase. O.K., let's start over again . . .

"Are you now in Los Angeles?"

A. "Yes."

Q. "Did you have anything to do with taking the life of Voytek and the others?"

A. "No."

Q. "Have you eaten lunch today?"

A. "No."

Q. "Do you feel any responsibility for the death of Voytek and the others?"

A. "Yes. I feel responsible that I wasn't there, that is all."

Q. "From running this thing through your mind, repeatedly, as I know you must have, who have you come up with as the target? I don't think it ever crossed your mind that Sharon might be the target, that anyone had that kind of mad on for her. Is there anyone else who was up there that you can think of who would be a target for this type of activity?"

A. "I've thought everything. I thought the target could be myself."

Q. "Why?"

A. "I mean, it could be some kind of jealousy or plot or something. It couldn't be Sharon directly. If Sharon were the target, it would mean that I was the target. It could be Jay was the target. It could be Voytek. It could also be sheer folly, someone just decided to commit a crime."

Q. "What would Sebring be doing, for instance, that would make him a target?"

A. "Some money thing, maybe. I've also heard a lot about this drug thing, drug deliveries. It's difficult for me to believe . . ." Polanski had always believed Sebring to be "a rather prosperous man," yet he'd recently heard he had large debts. "The indication to me is that he must have been in serious financial trouble, despite the appearances he gave."

Q. "That's a hell of a way to collect debts. It's no ordinary bill collector that goes up there and kills five people."

A. "No, no. What I'm talking about is for this reason

he might have got into some dangerous areas to make money, you understand? In desperation, he may have got mixed up with illegal people, you know?"

Q. "Eliminating Sharon and the kid, of the three remaining you think that Sebring would be the logical target, huh?"

A. "The whole crime seems so illogical.

"If I'm looking for a motive, I'd look for something which doesn't fit your habitual standard, with which you use to work as police—something much more far out . . ."

Deemer asked Polanski if he had received any hate mail after *Rosemary's Baby*. He admitted he had, surmising, "It could be some type of witchcraft, you know. A maniac or something. This execution, this tragedy, indicates to me it must be some kind of nut, you know.

"I wouldn't be surprised if I were the target. In spite of all this drug thing, the narcotics. I think the police like to jump too hastily on this type of lead, you know. Because it is their usual kind of lead. The only connection I know of Voytek with any kind of narcotic was he smoked pot. So did Jay. Plus cocaine. I knew he was sniffing. In the beginning I thought it was just an occasional kick. When I discussed it with Sharon, she said, 'Are you kidding? He's been doing it for two years, regularly.' "

Q. "Did Sharon mess with narcotics to any extent, other than pot?"

A. "No. She did take LSD before we met. Many times. And when we met we discussed it . . . I took it three times. When it was legal," he added, laughing. Then, serious again, Polanski recalled the only time they had taken it together. It was toward the end of 1965. It was his third trip, and Sharon's fifteenth or sixteenth. It had begun pleasantly enough, with them talking all night. But then "in the morning she started flipping out and screaming and I was scared to death. And after that she said, 'I told you I couldn't take it and this is the end.' And it was the end, for me and for her.

"But I can tell you this, without question. She took no drugs at all, except for pot, and not too much. And during her pregnancy there was no question, she was so in love with her pregnancy she would do nothing. I'd pour a glass of wine and she wouldn't touch it."

Once more Deemer took him through the questioning, then ended the examination, satisfied that Roman Polanski had no involvement in, or any hidden knowledge of, the murder of his wife and the others.

Before leaving, Roman told him, "I'm devoted now to this thing." He intended to question even his friends. "But I'm going to do it slowly, so they don't get suspicious. No one knows I'm here. I don't want them to know that I'm trying in any way to help the police, you know? I'm hoping in this way they'll have more sincerity."

A. "You have to go on living."

Polanski thanked him, lighted a cigarette, and left.

Q. "Hey, I thought you didn't smoke cigarettes!"

But Polanski had already gone.

On August 20, three days after Peter Hurkos accompanied Roman Polanski to the Cielo residence, a picture of Hurkos appeared in the *Citizen News*. It was captioned:

"FAMED PSYCHIC—Peter Hurkos, famed for his consultation in murder cases (including the current Sharon Tate massacre), opens Friday night at the Huntington Hartford, appearing through Aug. 30."

Madigan and Jones had been eliminated as suspects. Wilson and Pickett remained.

Because of his familiarity with the case, it was decided to send Lieutenant Deemer east to interview the two.

Jeffrey "Pic" Pickett had been contacted through a relative, and a meeting was set up in a Washington, D.C., hotel room. The son of a prominent State Department official, Pickett appeared to Deemer to be "under the influence of some narcotic, probably an excitant drug." He also had a bandaged hand. When Deemer expressed curiosity about it, Pickett vaguely replied that he had cut it on a kitchen knife. Though he agreed to a polygraph, Deemer found that Pickett couldn't remain still or follow instructions, so he interviewed him informally. He claimed that on the day of the murders he had been working in an auto company in Sheffield, Massachusetts. Asked if he owned any weapons, he admitted he had a Buck knife, purchased, he said, in Marlboro, Massachusetts, on a friend's credit card.

Later Pickett gave Deemer the knife. It was similar to the one found at Cielo. He also turned over a roll of videotape which he claimed showed Abigail Folger and Voytek Frykowski using drugs at a party at the Tate residence. Pickett didn't say how he came into possession of the film or what use he had intended to make of it.

Accompanied by Sergeant McGann, Deemer went to Massachusetts. A check of the time cards at the auto company in Sheffield revealed that Pickett's last workday was August 1, eight days before the homicides. Moreover, though two stores in Marlboro sold Buck knives, neither had ever stocked this particular model.

Pickett's status as a suspect rose appreciably, until the detectives interviewed the friend he had mentioned. Going through his credit card receipts, he produced the one for the Buck knife. It had been purchased in Sudbury, Massachusetts, on August 21, long after the murders. The friend and his wife also recalled something Pickett had apparently forgotten. He had gone to the beach with them the weekend of August 8-10. Pickett was subsequently polygraphed, twice. Both times it was decided he was telling the truth and was not involved. Eliminate Pickett.

Flying to Toronto, Deemer interviewed Herb Wilson. Although initially reluctant to submit to a polygraph, Wilson consented when Deemer agreed not to ask any questions that might make him liable to Canadian prosecution on narcotics charges. He passed. Eliminate Wilson.

The fingerprints of both Pickett and Wilson were checked against the unmatched Tate latents, with no match.

Although the first Tate investigative report—covering the period August 9-31—concluded that Wilson, Madigan, Pickett, and Jones "have been eliminated at the time of this report," in early September Deemer and McGann flew to Ocho Rios, Jamaica, to check out the alibis of Wilson and Jones. The pair claimed they had been there from July 8 until August 17, "making a movie about marijuana."

Interviews with realtors, servants, and airline ticket agencies supported half their story: they had been in Jamaica at the time of the murders. And it was quite possible they did have something to do with marijuana. Their only regular visitor, excluding female friends, was a pilot who, a few weeks before, had without explanation quit his well-paying job with a leading airline to make unscheduled solo runs between Jamaica and the United States.

As for their moviemaking, however, the detectives evinced some skepticism, the maid having told them the only camera she ever saw in the house was a small Kodak.

The videotape Pickett gave Deemer was viewed in the SID lab. It was decidedly different from the one previously found in the loft.

Apparently filmed during the period the Polanskis were away, it showed Abigail Folger, Voytek Frykowski, Witold K, and an unidentified young lady having dinner in front of the fireplace of the Tate residence. The video machine was simply turned on and left to run, those present after a time seeming to forget it.

Abigail wore her hair tied back in a rather severe chignon effect. She looked both older and more tired than in her other photos; Voytek looked dissipated. Though what appeared to be marijuana was smoked, Voytek seemed more drunk than high. At first Abigail treated him with the exasperated affection one would accord a spoiled child.

But then the mood gradually changed. In an obvious attempt to exclude Abigail, Voytek began speaking Polish. Abigail, in turn, was playing the grand dame, responding to his crude jests with witty repartee. Voytek began calling her "Lady Folger," then, as he became drunker, "Lady F." Abigail talked about him in the third person, as if he wasn't present, commenting upon, with some disgust, his habit of coming down off his drug trips by getting drunk.

To those viewing the tape it must have seemed nothing more than an overly long, exceedingly boring chronicle of a domestic argument. Except for two incidents, which, considering what would happen to two of those present, in this very house, gave it an eeriness as chilling as anything in *Rosemary's Baby*.

As she was serving the dinner, Abigail recalled a time when Voytek, stoned on drugs, looked into the fireplace and saw a strange shape. He had rushed for a camera, hoping to capture the image, a blazing pig's head.

The second incident was, in its own way, even more disturbing. The microphone had been left on the table, next to the roast. As the meat was being carved, it picked up, amazingly loud, over and over and over again, the sound of the knife grating on the bone.

Hurkos was not the only "expert" to volunteer a solution to the Tate homicides. On August 27, Truman Capote appeared on Johnny Carson's "Tonight Show" to discuss the crime.

One person, acting alone, had committed the murders, the author of *In Cold Blood* said authoritatively. He then proceeded to tell how, and why.

The killer, a man, had been in the house earlier. Something had happened "to trigger a kind of instant paranoia." The man then left the premises, went home to get a knife and a gun, and returned to systematically assassinate everyone in the place. According to Capote's deductions, Steven Parent was the last to die.

From the knowledge accumulated in over a hundred interviews with convicted murderers, Capote revealed that the killer was "a very young, enraged paranoid." While committing the murders, he probably experienced a sexual release, then, exhausted, went home and slept for two days.

Although Capote had taken up the single-suspect theory, the Tate detectives had by now abandoned it. Their sole reason for adopting it in the first place—Garretson—was no longer a factor. Because of the number of victims, the location of their bodies, and the use of two or more weapons, they were now convinced that "at least two suspects" were involved.

Killers. Plural. But as to their identity, they had not the slightest idea.

At the end of August there was a summing up, for both the Tate and the LaBianca detectives.

The "First Homicide Investigation Progress Report—

Tate" ran to thirty-three pages. Nowhere in it was there any mention of the LaBianca murders.

The "First Homicide Investigation Progress Report—LaBianca" was seventeen pages long. Despite the many similarities between the two crimes, it contained not one reference to the Tate homicides.

They remained two totally separate investigations.

Although Lieutenant Bob Helder had over a dozen detectives working full time on the Tate case, Sergeants Michael McGann, Robert Calkins, and Jess Buckles were the principal investigators. All were long-time veterans on the force, having worked their way up to the status of detective the hard way, from the ranks. They could remember when there was no Police Academy, and seniority was more important than education and merit examinations. They were experienced, and inclined to be set in their ways.

The LaBianca team, under Lieutenant Paul LePage, consisted, at various times, of from six to ten detectives, with Sergeants Frank Patchett, Manuel Gutierrez, Michael Nielsen, Philip Sartuchi, and Gary Broda the principal investigators. The LaBianca detectives were generally younger, better educated, and far less experienced. Graduates of the Police Academy for the most part, they were more inclined to the use of modern investigative techniques. For example, they obtained the fingerprints of almost everyone they interviewed; gave more polygraph examinations; made more *modus operandi* (MO) and fingerprint runs through the California State Bureau of Criminal Investigation and Identification (CII); and dug deeper into the backgrounds of the victims, even checking the outgoing calls Leno LaBianca had made from a motel while on vacation seven years ago.

They were also more inclined to consider "far out" theories. For example, while the Tate report didn't attempt to explain that bloody word on the front door, the LaBianca report speculated as to the meaning of the writings found inside the residence on Waverly Drive. It even suggested a connection so remote it couldn't even be called a wild guess. The report noted: "Investigation revealed that the singing group the Beatles' most recent album, No. SWBO

101, has songs titled 'Helter Skelter' and 'Piggies' and 'Blackbird.' The words in the song 'Blackbird' frequently say 'Arise, arise,' which might be the meaning of 'Rise' near the front door."

The idea was just sort of tossed in, by whom no one would later remember, and just as promptly forgotten.

The two sets of detectives had one thing in common, however. Though to date the LaBianca team had interviewed some 150 persons, the Tate investigators more than twice that, neither was much closer to "solving" the case than when the bodies were first discovered.

The Tate report listed five suspects—Garretson, Wilson, Madigan, Pickett, and Jones—all of whom had by this time been eliminated.

The LaBianca report listed fifteen—but included Frank and Susan Struthers, Joe Dorgan, and numerous others who were never serious suspects. Of the fifteen, only Gardner remained a good possible, and, though lacking a palm print for positive elimination (one had been found on a bank deposit slip on Leno's desk), his fingerprints had already been checked against those found in the residence with no match.

The progress reports were strictly intradepartmental; the press would never see them.

But already a few reporters were beginning to suspect that the real reason for the official silence was that there was nothing to report.

September 1969

About noon on Monday, September 1, 1969, ten-year-old Steven Weiss was fixing the sprinkler on the hill behind his home when he found a gun.

Steven and his parents lived at 3627 Longview Valley

Road in Sherman Oaks. Running parallel to Longview, atop the hill, was Beverly Glen.

The gun was lying next to the sprinkler, under a bush, about seventy-five feet—or halfway—up the steep hill. Steven had watched "Dragnet" on TV; he knew how guns should be handled. Picking it up very carefully by the tip of the barrel, so as not to eradicate prints, Steven took the gun back to his house and showed it to his father, Bernard Weiss. The senior Weiss took one look and called LAPD.

Officer Michael Watson, on patrol in the area, responded to the radio call. More than a year later Steven would be asked to describe the incident from the witness stand:

Q. "Did you show him [Watson] the gun?"
A. "Yes."
Q. "Did he touch the gun?"
A. "Yes."
Q. "How did he touch it?"
A. "With both hands, all over the gun."

So much for "Dragnet."

Officer Watson took the cartridges out of the cylinder; there were nine—seven empty shell casings and two live rounds. The gun itself was a .22 caliber Hi Standard Longhorn revolver. It had dirt on it, and rust. The trigger guard was broken, the barrel loose and slightly bent, as if it had been used to hammer something. The gun was also missing the right-hand grip.

Officer Watson took the revolver and shells back to Valley Services Division of LAPD, located in Van Nuys, and after booking them as "Found Evidence" turned them over to the Property Section, where they were tagged, placed in manila envelopes, and filed away.

Between September 3 and 5, LAPD sent out the first batch of confidential "flyers" on the wanted Tate gun. In addition to a photograph of a Hi Standard .22 caliber Longhorn revolver, and a list of Hi Standard outlets supplied by Lomax, Deputy Chief Robert Houghton sent a covering letter which asked police to interview anyone who had purchased such a gun, and to "visually check the weapon to see if the original grips are intact." To avoid leaks to the media, he suggested the following cover story:

such a gun had been recovered with other stolen property and the police wished to determine its ownership.

LAPD sent out approximately three hundred of the flyers, to various law-enforcement agencies in California, other parts of the United States, and Canada.

Someone neglected to mail one to the Valley Services Division of the Los Angeles Police Department in Van Nuys.

On September 10—one month after the Tate murders—a large advertisement appeared in newspapers in the Los Angeles area:

REWARD

$25,000

Roman Polanski and friends of the Polanski family offer to pay a $25,000 reward to the person or persons who furnish information leading to the arrest and conviction of the murderer or murderers of Sharon Tate, her unborn child, and the other four victims.

Information should be sent to
Post Office Box 60048,
Terminal Annex,
Los Angeles, California 90069.

Persons wishing to remain anonymous should provide sufficient means for later identification, one method of which is to tear this newspaper page in half, transmit one half with the information submitted, and save the remaining half for matching-up later. In the event more than one person is entitled to the reward, the reward will be divided equally between them.

In announcing the reward, Peter Sellers, who had put up a portion of the money, together with Warren Beatty, Yul Brynner, and others, said: "Someone must have knowledge or suspicions they are withholding, or may be afraid to reveal. Someone must have seen the blood-soaked clothing, the knife, the gun, the getaway car. Someone must be able to help."

Although unannounced in the press, others had already begun their own unofficial inquiries. Sharon's father, Colonel Paul Tate, had retired from the Army in August. Growing a beard and letting his hair grow long, the former intelligence officer began frequenting the Sunset Strip, hippie pads, and places where drugs were sold, looking for some lead to the killer(s) of his daughter and the others.

The police were fearful Colonel Tate's private investigation might become a private war, since there were reports he did not go on his forays unarmed.

Nor were the police happy about the reward. Besides the implication that LAPD wasn't capable of solving the case on its own, such an announcement usually yields only crackpot calls, and of these they already had a surplus.

Most had come in following the release of Garretson, the callers blaming the murders on everyone from the Black Power movement to the Polish Secret Police, their sources imagination, hearsay, even Sharon herself—returned during a seance. One wife called the police to accuse her husband: "He was evasive as to his whereabouts that night."

Hustlers, hairdressers, actors, actresses, psychics, psychotics—all got into the act. The calls revealed not so much the underside of Hollywood as the underside of human nature. The victims were accused of sexual aberrations as peculiar as the minds of the persons who called them in. Complicating LAPD's task were the large number of people—often not anonymous, and in some cases very well known—who seemed anxious to implicate their "friends"—if not directly connecting them with the murders, at least involving them with the drug scene.

There were proponents of every possible theory. The Mafia did it. The Mafia couldn't have done it because the killings were so unprofessional. The killings were *intentionally* unprofessional so the Mafia wouldn't be suspected.

One of the most persistent callers was Steve Brandt, a former gossip columnist. Because he had been a friend of four of the five Tate victims—he had been a witness at

Sharon's and Roman's marriage—the police took him seriously, at first, Brandt supplying considerable information on Wilson, Pickett, and their associates. But as the calls became more and more frequent, the names more and more prominent, it became obvious that Brandt was obsessed with the murders. Sure there was a death list and that he was next, Brandt twice attempted suicide. The first time, in Los Angeles, a friend arrived in time. The second time, in New York, he left a Rolling Stones concert to return to his hotel. When actress Ultra Violet called to make sure he was all right, he told her he had taken sleeping pills. She immediately called the desk man at the hotel, but by the time he reached the room Brandt was dead.

For such a well-publicized crime there were surprisingly few "confessions." It was as if the murders were so horrible that even the chronic confessors didn't want to become involved. A recently convicted felon, anxious to "make a deal," did claim another man had bragged of involvement in the killings, but, after investigation, the story proved bogus.

One after another, leads were checked out, then eliminated, leaving the police no closer to a solution than when the murders were discovered.

Though almost forgotten for a time, by mid-September the pair of prescription glasses found near the trunks in the living room of the Tate residence had, simply by the process of attrition, become one of the most important remaining clues.

Early that month the detectives showed the glasses to various optical company representatives. What they learned was in part discouraging. The frames were a popular model, the "Manhattan" style, readily available, while the prescription lenses were also a stock item, meaning they didn't have to be ground to order. But, on the plus side, they also learned several things about the person who had worn them.

Their owner was probably a man. He had a small, almost volley-ball-shaped head. His eyes were far apart. His left ear was approximately 1/4 to 1/2 inch higher than his right ear. And he was extremely myopic—if he didn't have an extra pair, he would probably have to replace the glasses soon.

A partial description of one of the Tate killers? Possibly. It was also possible that the glasses belonged to someone totally unconnected with the crime, or that they had been left behind as a false clue.

It was at least something to go on. Another flyer, with the exact specifications of the prescription, was sent to all members of the American Optometric Association, the California Optometric Association, the Los Angeles County Optometric Association, and the Ophthalmologists of Southern California, in hopes that it would yield more than had the flyer on the gun.

Of the 131 Hi Standard Longhorn revolvers sold in California, law-enforcement agencies had been able to locate and eliminate 105, a surprisingly large percentage, since many of the owners had moved to other jurisdictions. The search continued, but to date it hadn't yielded a single good suspect. A second gun letter was sent to thirteen different gunshops in the United States which, in recent months, had ordered replacement grips for the Longhorn model. Though the replies to this one wouldn't come back until much later, it too drew a blank.

Nor were the LaBianca detectives having any better luck. To date they had given eleven polygraphs; all had been negative. As a result of an MO run through the CII computer, the fingerprints of 140 suspects were checked; a palm print found on a bank deposit slip was checked against 2,150 suspects; and a fingerprint found on the liquor cabinet was checked against a total of 41,034 suspects. All uniformly negative.

At the end of September neither the Tate nor the LaBianca detectives bothered to write up a progress report.

October 1969

October 10. Two months had passed since the Tate homicides. "What is going on behind the scenes in the Los Angeles Police investigation (if there is such a thing) of the bizarre murder of Sharon Tate and four others?" the Hollywood *Citizen News* asked in a front-page editorial.

Officially, LAPD remained silent, as they had since their last news conference on the case, on September 3, when Deputy Chief Houghton, while admitting that they still didn't know who had committed the murders, said the detectives had made "tremendous progress."

"Exactly what progress?" reporters asked. The pressure was building; the fear remained, if possible even increased, owing to the suggestion, less than subtly hinted at by a popular TV commentator, that perhaps the police were covering for a person or persons "prominent in the entertainment industry."

Meanwhile the leaks continued. The media reported that narcotics had been found in several places at the Tate residence; that some of the victims had been on drugs at the time they died. By October it was also widely reported that the gun sought was a .22 (though it was identified as a pistol, rather than a revolver), and there was even one TV report—which the police quickly broke silence to deny—that pieces of the gun's grip had been found at the crime scene. The TV station stuck by its information, despite the official denial.

A .22, with a broken grip. Several times Bernard Weiss got to wondering about that gun his son Steven had found. Could it be the Tate murder weapon?

But that was ridiculous. After all, the police themselves had the gun, and, had it been the weapon, would surely have returned by now to ask more questions and search the hillside. Since turning the weapon over to them on

September 1, Weiss had heard nothing. When there was no follow-up, Steven had taken it on himself to make a search of the area. He'd found nothing. Still, Beverly Glen wasn't all that far from Cielo Drive, just a couple of miles.

But Bernard Weiss had better things to do than play detective. That was LAPD's responsibility.

On October 17, Lieutenant Helder and Deputy Chief Houghton told reporters that they had evidence which, if it could be traced, might lead to "the killers"—plural—of Sharon Tate and the four others. They refused to be more specific.

The press conference had been called in an attempt to relieve some of the pressure on LAPD. No solid information was released, but a number of current rumors were denied.

Less than a week later, on October 23, LAPD very hastily called another press conference, to announce that they had a clue to the identity of "the killer"—singular—of the five Tate victims: a pair of prescription eyeglasses that had been found at the scene.

The announcement was made only because several papers had that same day already printed the "wanted" flyer on the glasses.

Approximately 18,000 eye doctors had received the flyer from their various member associations; in addition, it had been printed verbatim in the *Optometric Weekly* and the *Eye, Ear, Nose, and Throat Monthly*, which had a combined national circulation of over 29,000. What was surprising was not that the story had leaked, but that it had taken so long for it to do so.

Starved for solid news, the press heralded "a major breakthrough in the case," overlooking the obvious fact that the police had had the glasses in their possession since the day the Tate victims were discovered.

Lieutenant Helder refused comment when a reporter, obviously with excellent connections inside the department, asked if it was true that to date the glasses flyer had yielded only seven suspects, all of whom had already been eliminated.

It was indicative of the desperation of the Tate detectives that the second, and last, Tate progress report, prepared the day before the press conference, stated: "At this time Garretson has not been positively eliminated."

The Tate report, covering the period September 1–October 22, 1969, ran to twenty-six pages, most of which were devoted to closing out the cases against Wilson, Pickett, et al.

The LaBianca report, closed out on October 15, was a little shorter, twenty-two pages, but far more interesting.

In one section of the report the detectives mentioned their use of the CII computer: "A MO run on all crimes where the victims were tied is presently being run. Future runs will be made concentrating on the peculiarities of the robberies, used gloves, wore glasses or disabled the phone."

Robberies. Plural. *Wore glasses, disabled the phone.* The phone at the LaBianca residence was not disabled, nor was there evidence that a LaBianca assailant wore glasses. These references were to Tate.

The conclusion is inescapable: The LaBianca detectives had decided—on their own, and without consulting the Tate detectives—to see if they could solve the Tate, as well as the LaBianca, case.

The second LaBianca report was interesting for still another reason.

It listed eleven suspects, the last of whom was one MANSON, CHARLES.

Part 2

THE KILLERS

"You couldn't meet a nicer group of people."
Leslie Van Houten, describing
the Manson Family
to Sergeant Michael McGann

"At twelve o'clock a meeting round the table
For a seance in the dark
With voices out of nowhere
Put on especially by the children for a lark."
The Beatles,
"Cry Baby Cry,"
"White Album"

"You have to have a real love in your heart to do this for people."
Susan Atkins, telling
Virginia Graham why she
stabbed Sharon Tate

October 15-31, 1969

The physical distance between Parker Center, headquarters of the Los Angeles Police Department, and the Hall of Justice, which houses the Los Angeles County Sheriff's Office, is four blocks. That distance can be traversed in the time it takes to dial a telephone.

But it isn't always that easy. Though LAPD and LASO cooperate on investigations that involve both jurisdictions, there exists between them a certain amount of jealousy.

One of the LaBianca detectives would later admit that he and his fellow officers *should* have checked with LASO homicide detectives in mid-August to see if they had any similar murders. But it wasn't until October 15, after most of their other leads had evaporated, that they did so.

When they did, they learned of the Hinman murder. And, unlike Sergeant Buckles of the Tate team, they found the similarities striking enough to merit further investigation.

There had been some recent developments in the Hinman case, Sergeants Whiteley and Guenther told them. Less than a week before, Inyo County officers had raided isolated Barker Ranch, located in an extremely rugged, almost inaccessible area south of Death Valley National Monument. The raid, based on charges ranging from grand theft to arson, had netted twenty-four members of a hippie cult known as the "Manson Family." Many of these same people—including their leader, Charles Manson, a thirty-four-year-old ex-con with a long and checkered criminal history—had also been arrested in an earlier raid conducted by LASO, which had occurred on August 16, at Spahn's Movie Ranch in Chatsworth.

During the Barker raid, which took place over a three-day period, two young girls had appeared out of the bushes near a road some miles from the ranch, asking the officers for protection. They claimed they had been attempting to flee the "Family" and were afraid for their lives. One was named Stephanie Schram, the other Kitty Lutesinger.

Whiteley and Guenther had been looking for Kitty Lutesinger ever since learning that she was a girl friend of Bobby Beausoleil, the suspect in the Hinman murder. Informed of her arrest, they drove 225 miles to Independence, the Inyo County seat, to question her.

Kitty, a freckled, frightened seventeen-year-old, was five months pregnant with Beausoleil's child. Though she had lived with the Family, she apparently was not trusted by them. When Beausoleil disappeared from Spahn Ranch in early August, no one would tell her where he had gone. Only after several weeks did she learn that he had been arrested, and, much later, that he had been charged with the murder of Gary Hinman.

Questioned about the murder, Kitty said she had heard that Manson had sent Beausoleil and a girl named Susan Atkins to Hinman's home to get money from him. A fight had ensued, and Hinman had been killed. Kitty couldn't recall who told her this, just that it was the talk at the ranch. She did recall, however, another conversation in which Susan Atkins told her and several other girls that she had been in a fight with a man who had pulled her hair, and that she had stabbed him three or four times in the legs.

Susan Atkins had been arrested in the Barker raid and booked under the name "Sadie Mae Glutz." She was still in custody. On October 13, the day after they talked to Kitty, Sergeants Whiteley and Guenther questioned her.

She told them that she and Bobby Beausoleil were sent to Gary Hinman's house to get some money he had supposedly inherited. When he wouldn't give it to them, Beausoleil pulled out a knife and slashed Hinman's face. For two days and two nights the pair had taken turns sleeping, so Hinman wouldn't escape. Then, on their last evening at the residence, while she was in the kitchen, she had heard Gary say, "Don't, Bobby!" Hinman then staggered into the kitchen bleeding from a chest wound.

Even after this, Hinman didn't die. After wiping the

house of prints (not effectively, since both a palm print and a fingerprint belonging to Beausoleil were found), they were going out the front door when they heard Hinman moaning. Beausoleil went back in, and she heard Gary cry out, "Oh, no, Bobby, please don't!" She also heard "a sound like gurgling as when people are dying."

Beausoleil then hot-wired Hinman's 1965 Volkswagen bus and they drove back to Spahn Ranch.

Whiteley and Guenther asked Susan if she would repeat her statement on tape. She declined. She was transported to the San Dimas sheriff's station, where she was booked for suspicion of murder.

Susan Atkins' statement—unlike that of Kitty Lutesinger—did not implicate Manson in the Hinman murder. Nor, contrary to what Kitty had said, did Susan admit to having stabbed anyone. Whiteley and Guenther strongly suspected she was telling only what she thought they already knew.

Nor were the two LaBianca detectives very impressed. Hinman had been close to the Manson family; several of its members—including Beausoleil, Atkins, even Manson himself—had lived with him at various times in the past. In short, there was a link. But there was no evidence that Manson or any of his followers knew the LaBiancas or the people at 10050 Cielo Drive.

Still, it was a lead, and they proceeded to check it out. Kitty had been released into the custody of her parents, who had a local address, and they interviewed her there. From LASO, Inyo County officials, Manson's parole officer, and others, they began assembling names, descriptions, and fingerprints of persons known to belong to or associate with the Family. Kitty had mentioned that while the Family was still living at Spahn, Manson had tried to enlist a motorcycle gang, the Straight Satans, as his personal bodyguard. With the exception of one biker named Danny, the group had laughed at Manson. Danny had stuck around for several months.

On learning that the motorcycle gang hung out in Venice, California, the LaBianca detectives asked Venice PD if they could locate a Straight Satan named Danny.

Something in Kitty Lutesinger's statement puzzled Whiteley and Guenther. At first they thought it was just a discrepancy. But then they got to wondering. According to Kitty, Susan Atkins had admitted stabbing a man three or four times in the legs.

Gary Hinman hadn't been stabbed in the legs.

But Voytek Frykowski had.

Although rebuffed once before, on October 20 the sheriff's deputies again contacted the Tate detectives at LAPD, telling them what they had learned.

It is possible to measure the Tate detectives' interest with some exactness. Not until October 31, eleven days later, did they interview Kitty Lutesinger.

November 1-12, 1969

November was a month for confessions. Which, initially, no one believed.

After being booked for the Hinman murder, Susan Denise Atkins, aka* Sadie Mae Glutz, was moved to Sybil Brand Institute, the women's house of detention in Los Angeles. On November 1, after completing orientation, she was assigned to Dormitory 8000, and given a bunk opposite one Ronnie Howard. Miss Howard, a buxom former call girl who over her thirty-some years had been known by more than a dozen and a half aliases, was at present awaiting trial on a charge of forging a prescription.

On the same day Susan moved into Dormitory 8000, one Virginia Graham did also. Miss Graham, herself an ex-call girl with a sizable number of aka's, had been picked up for violating her parole. Although they hadn't seen each other for five years, Ronnie and Virginia had

*Police shorthand for "also known as"; "t/n" means "true name."

not only been friends and business associates in the past, going out on "calls" together, but Ronnie had married Virginia's ex-husband.

As their work assignments, Susan Atkins and Virginia Graham were given jobs as "runners," carrying messages for the prison authorities. In the slow periods when there wasn't much work, they would sit on stools in "control," the message center, and talk.

At night, after lights-out, Ronnie Howard and Susan talked also.

Susan loved to talk. And Ronnie and Virginia proved rapt listeners.

On November 2, 1969, one Steve Zabriske appeared at the Portland, Oregon, Police Department and told Detective Sergeant Ritchard that a "Charlie" and a "Clem" had committed both the Tate and LaBianca murders.

He had heard this, the nineteen-year-old Zabriske said, from Ed Bailey and Vern Plumlee, two hippie types from California whom he had met in Portland. Zabriske also told Ritchard that Charlie and Clem were at present in custody in Los Angeles on another charge, grand theft auto.

Bailey had told him something else, Zabriske said: that he had personally seen Charlie shoot a man in the head with a .45 caliber automatic. This had occurred in Death Valley.

Sergeant Ritchard asked Zabriske if he could prove any of this. Zabriske admitted he couldn't. However, his brother-in-law, Michael Lloyd Carter, had also been present during the conversations, and would back him up if Sergeant Ritchard wanted to talk to him.

Sergeant Ritchard didn't. Since Zabriske "did not have last names nor did he have anything concrete to establish that he was telling the truth," Sergeant Ritchard, according to the official report, "did not place any credence on this interview and did not notify the Los Angeles Police Department . . ."

The girls in Dormitory 8000 called Sadie Mae Glutz—as Susan Atkins insisted on being known—"Crazy Sadie."

It wasn't just that ridiculous name. She was much too happy, considering where she was. She would laugh and sing at inappropriate times. Without warning, she would stop whatever she happened to be doing and start go-go dancing. She did her exercises sans underpants. She bragged that she had done everything sexual that could be done, and on more than one occasion propositioned other inmates.

Virginia Graham thought she was sort of a "little girl lost," putting on a big act so no one would know how frightened she really was.

One day while they were sitting in the message center, Virginia asked her, "What are you in for?"

"First degree murder," Susan matter-of-factly replied.

Virginia couldn't believe it; Susan looked so young.

In this particular conversation, which apparently took place on November 3, Susan said little about the murder itself, only that she felt a co-defendant, a boy who was being held in the County Jail, had squealed on her. In questioning Susan, Whiteley and Guenther hadn't told her that it was Kitty Lutesinger who had implicated her, and she presumed the snitch was Bobby Beausoleil.

The next day Susan told Virginia that the man she was accused of killing was named Gary Hinman. She said that she, Bobby, and another girl were involved. The other girl hadn't been charged with the murder, she said, though she had been in Sybil Brand not too long ago on another charge; right now she was out on bail and had gone to Wisconsin to get her baby.*

Virginia asked her, "Well, did you do it?"

Susan looked at her and smiled and said, "Sure." Just like that.

Only the police had it wrong, she said. They had her holding the man while the boy stabbed him, which was silly, because she couldn't hold a big man like that. It was the other way round; the boy held him and she had stabbed him, four or five times.

What stunned Virginia, she would later say, was that

*She was referring to Mary Brunner, first member of the Family, who had had a child by Manson. At this time the police were unaware of her involvement in the Hinman homicide.

Susan described it "just like it was a perfectly natural thing to do every day of the week."

Susan's conversations were not limited to murder. Subjects ranged from psychic phenomena to her experiences as a topless dancer in San Francisco. It was while there, she told Virginia, that she met "a man, this Charlie." He was the strongest man alive. He had been in prison but had never been broken. Susan said she followed his orders without question—they all did, all the kids who lived with him. He was their father, their leader, their love.

It was Charlie, she said, who had given her the name Sadie Mae Glutz.

Virginia remarked that she didn't consider that much of a favor.

Charlie was going to lead them to the desert, Susan said. There was a hole in Death Valley, only Charlie knew where it was, but deep down inside, in the center of the earth, there was a whole civilization. And Charlie was going to take the "family," the chosen few, and they were going to go to this bottomless pit and live there.

Charlie, Susan confided to Virginia, was Jesus Christ.

Susan, Virginia decided, was nuts.

On the night of Wednesday, November 5, a young man who might have been able to provide a solution to the Tate-LaBianca homicides ceased to exist.

At 7:35 P.M. officers from Venice PD, responding to a telephone call, arrived at 28 Clubhouse Avenue, a house near the beach rented by a Mark Ross. They found a youth—approximate age twenty-two, nickname "Zero," true name unknown—lying on a mattress on the floor in the bedroom. Deceased was still warm to the touch. There was blood on the pillow and what appeared to be an entrance wound in the right temple. Next to the body was a leather gun case and an eight-shot .22 caliber Iver & Johnson revolver. According to the other persons present—a man and three girls—Zero had killed himself while playing Russian roulette.

The stories of the witnesses—who identified themselves as Bruce Davis, Linda Baldwin, Sue Bartell, and Catherine

Gillies, and who said they had been staying at the house while Ross was away—tallied perfectly. Linda Baldwin stated that she had been lying on the right side of the mattress, Zero on the left side, when Zero noticed the leather case in a stand next to the bed and remarked, "Oh, here's a gun." He removed the gun from the case, Miss Baldwin said, commenting, "There's only one bullet in it." Holding the gun in his right hand, he had then spun the cylinder, placed the muzzle against his right temple, and pulled the trigger.

The others, in various parts of the house, had heard what sounded like a firecracker popping, they said. When they entered the bedroom, Miss Baldwin told them, "Zero shot himself, just like in the movies." Bruce Davis admitted he picked up the gun. They had then called the police.

The officers were unaware that all those present were members of the Manson Family, who had been living at the Venice residence since their release following the Barker Ranch raid. Since when questioned separately all told essentially the same story, the police accepted the Russian roulette explanation and listed the cause of death as suicide.

They had several very good reasons to suspect that explanation, although apparently no one did.

When officer Jerrome Boen later dusted the gun for latents, he found no prints. Nor were there prints on the leather gun case.

And when they examined the revolver, they found that Zero had really been bucking the odds. The gun contained seven live rounds and one spent shell. It had been fully loaded, with no empty chambers.

A number of Family members, including Manson himself, were still in jail in Independence. On November 6, LaBianca detectives Patchett and Sartuchi, accompanied by Lieutenant Burdick of SID, went there to interview them.

Patchett asked Manson if he knew anything about either the Tate or LaBianca homicides. Manson replied, "No," and that was that.

Patchett was so unimpressed with Manson that he didn't

even bother to write up a report on the interview. Of the nine Family members the detectives talked to, only one rated a memorandum. About 1:30 that afternoon Lieutenant Burdick interviewed a girl who had been booked under the name Leslie Sankston. "During this conversation," Burdick noted, "I inquired of Miss Sankston if she was aware that Sadie [Susan Atkins] was reportedly involved in the Gary Hinman homicide. She replied that she was. I inquired if she was aware of the Tate and LaBianca homicides. She indicated that she was aware of the Tate homicide but seemed unfamiliar with the LaBianca homicide. I asked her if she had any knowledge of persons in her group who might possibly be involved in either the Tate or LaBianca homicides. She indicated that there were some 'things' that caused her to believe someone from her group might be involved in the Tate homicide. I asked her to elaborate on the 'things' [but] she declined to indicate what she meant and stated that she wanted to think about it overnight, and that she was perplexed and didn't know what to do. She did indicate she might tell me the following day."

However, when Burdick again questioned her the next morning, "she stated she had decided she did not want to say anymore about the subject and the conversation was terminated."

Though the interviews yielded nothing, the LaBianca detectives did pick up one possible lead. Before leaving Independence, Patchett asked to see Manson's personal effects. Going through the clothing Manson had been wearing when arrested, Patchett noted that he used leather thongs both as laces in his moccasins and in the stitching of his trousers. Patchett took a sample thong from each back to Los Angeles for comparison with the thong used to tie Leno LaBianca's hands.

A leather thong is a leather thong, SID in effect told him; though the thongs were similar, there was no way to tell whether they had come from the same piece of leather.

LAPD and LASO have no monopoly on jealousy. To a certain extent it exists between almost all law-enforcement agencies, and even within some.

The Homicide Division of the Los Angeles Police Department is a single room, 318, on the third floor of Parker Center. Although it is a large room, rectangular in shape, there are no partitions, only two long tables, all the detectives working at either one or the other. The distance between the Tate and LaBianca detectives was only a few feet.

But there are psychological as well as physical distances and, as noted, while the Tate detectives were largely the "old guard," the LaBianca detectives were for the most part the "young upstarts." Also, there was apparently some residual bitterness stemming from the fact that several of the latter, rather than the former, had been assigned to L.A.'s last big publicity case, Sirhan Sirhan's assassination of Senator Robert F. Kennedy. In short, there was a certain amount of jealousy involved. And a certain lack of communication.

As a result, none of the LaBianca detectives walked those few feet to tell the Tate detectives that they were following a lead which might connect the two homicides. No one informed Lieutenant Helder, who was in charge of the Tate investigation, that they had gone to Independence and interviewed one Charles Manson, who was believed involved in a strikingly similar murder, or that while there one of his followers, a girl who went by the name of Leslie Sankston, had admitted that someone in their group might be involved in the *Tate* homicides.

The LaBianca detectives continued to go it on their own.

Had Leslie Sankston—true name Leslie Van Houten—yielded to that impulse to talk, she could have told the detectives a great deal about the Tate murders, but even more about the LaBianca slayings.

But by this time Susan Atkins was already doing enough talking for both of them.

On Thursday, November 6, at about 4:45 P.M., Susan had walked over to Virginia Graham's bed and sat down. They had finished work for the day, and Susan/Sadie was in a talkative mood. She began rapping about the LSD trips she had taken, karma, good and bad vibrations, and the Hinman murder. Virginia cautioned her that she shouldn't be talking so much; she knew a man who had been convicted just on what he told a cellmate.

Susan replied, "Oh, I know. I haven't talked about it to anyone else. You know, I can look at you and there's something about you, I know I can tell things to you." Also, she wasn't worried about the police. They weren't all that good. "You know, there's a case right now, they are so far off the track they don't even know what's happening."

Virginia asked, "What are you talking about?"

"That one on Benedict Canyon."

"Benedict Canyon? You don't mean Sharon Tate?"

"Yeah." With this Susan seemed to get very excited. The words came out in a rush. "You know who did it, don't you?"

"No."

"Well, you're looking at her."

Virginia gasped, "You've got to be kidding!"

Susan just smiled and said, "Huh-uh."*

Later Virginia Graham would be unable to remember exactly how long they had talked—she would estimate it as being between thirty-five minutes and an hour, maybe longer. She would also admit confusion as to whether some details were discussed that afternoon or in subsequent conversations, and the order in which some topics came up.

But the content she remembered. That, she would later say, she would never forget as long as she lived.

She asked the big question first: Why, Sadie, why? Because, Susan replied, we "wanted to do a crime that would shock the world, that the world would have to stand up and take notice." But why the Tate house? Susan's answer was chilling in its simplicity: "It is isolated." The place

*The Atkins-Graham-Howard conversations have been taken from LAPD's taped interviews with Virginia Graham and Ronnie Howard; my interviews with both; their trial testimony; and my interview with Susan Atkins. There are, of course, minor variations in wording. Major discrepancies will be noted.

had been picked at random. They had known the owner, Terry Melcher,* Doris Day's son, from about a year back, but they didn't know who would be there, and it didn't matter; one person or ten, they had gone there prepared to do everybody in.

"In other words," Virginia asked, "you didn't know Jay Sebring or any of the other people?"

"No," Susan replied.

"Do you mind me asking questions? I mean, I'm curious." Susan didn't mind. She told Virginia that she had kind brown eyes, and if you look through a person's eyes you can see the soul.

Virginia told Susan she wanted to know exactly how it had come down. "I'm dying of curiosity," she added.

Susan obliged. Before leaving the ranch, Charlie had given them instructions. They had worn dark clothing. They also brought along a change of clothes in the car. They drove up to the gate, then drove back down to the bottom of the hill, parked the car, and walked back up.

Virginia interrupted, "Then it wasn't just you?"

"Oh, no," Susan told her. "There were four of us." In addition to herself, there were two other girls and a man.

When they reached the gate, Susan continued, "he" cut the telephone wires. Virginia again interrupted to ask whether he wasn't worried he'd cut the electrical wires, extinguishing the lights and alerting the people that something was wrong. Susan replied, "Oh, no, he knew just what to do." Virginia got the impression, less from her words than from the way she said them, that the man had been there before.

Susan didn't mention how they got past the gate. She said they had killed the boy first. When Virginia asked why, Susan replied that he had seen them. "And he had to shoot him. He was shot four times."

At this point Virginia became somewhat confused.

*Virginia Graham had seen the owner of the house, Rudi Altobelli, interviewed on TV, and although she couldn't remember his name, she knew it wasn't Terry Melcher. This was one reason why, initially, she was inclined to disbelieve Susan Atkins' story. Susan, however, insisted Melcher was the owner, apparently believing he was.

Later she would state, "I think she told me—I'm not positive—I think she said that this Charles shot him." Earlier Virginia had got the impression that although Charlie had instructed them what to do, he hadn't come along. But now it appeared he had.

What Virginia didn't know was that there were two men named Charles in the Family: Charles Manson and Charles "Tex" Watson. The complications this simple misunderstanding would later cause would be immense.

On entering the house—Susan didn't say how they got in—they saw a man on the couch in the living room, and a girl, whom Susan identified as "Ann Folger," sitting in a chair reading a book. She didn't look up.

Virginia asked her how she knew their names. "We didn't," Susan replied, "not until the next day."

At some point the group apparently split up, Susan going on to the bedroom, while the others stayed in the living room.

"Sharon was sitting up in bed. Jay was sitting on the edge of the bed talking to Sharon."

"Oh, really?" Virginia asked. "What did she have on?"

"She had on a bikini bra and panties."

"You're kidding. And she was pregnant?"

"Yeah. And they looked up, and were they surprised!"

"Wow! Wasn't there some kind of a big hassle?"

"No, they were too surprised and they knew we meant business."

Susan skipped on. It was as if she was "tripping out," jumping abruptly from one subject to another. Suddenly they were in the living room and Sharon and Jay were strung up with nooses around their necks so if they tried to move they would choke. Virginia asked why they'd put a hood over Sebring's head. "We didn't put any hood over his head," Susan corrected her. "That's what the papers said, Sadie." "Well, there wasn't any hood," Susan reiterated, getting quite insistent about it.

Then the other man [Frykowski] broke and ran for the door. "He was full of blood," Susan said, and she stabbed him three or four times. "He was bleeding and he ran to the front part," out the door and onto the lawn, "and would you believe that he was there hollering 'Help, help, somebody please help me,' and nobody came?"

Bluntly, without elaboration, "Then we finished him off."

Virginia wasn't asking any questions now. What had begun as a little girl's fairy tale had become a horror-filled nightmare.

There was no mention of what had happened to Abigail Folger or Jay Sebring, only that "Sharon was the last to die." On saying this, Susan laughed.

Susan said that she had held Sharon's arms behind her, and that Sharon looked at her and was crying and begging, "Please don't kill me. Please don't kill me. I don't want to die. I want to live. I want to have my baby. I want to have my baby."

Susan said she looked Sharon straight in the eye and said, "Look, bitch, I don't care about you. I don't care if you're going to have a baby. You had better be ready. You're going to die, and I don't feel anything about it."

Then Susan said, "In a few minutes I killed her and she was dead."

After killing Sharon, Susan noticed there was blood on her hand. She tasted it. "Wow, what a trip!" she told Virginia. "I thought 'To taste death, and yet give life.' " Had she ever tasted blood? she asked Virginia. "It's warm and sticky and nice."

Virginia managed to ask a question. Hadn't it bothered her to kill Sharon Tate, with her pregnant?

Susan looked at Virginia quizzically and said, "Well, I thought you understood. I loved her, and in order for me to kill her I was killing part of myself when I killed her."

Virginia replied, "Oh, yeah, I do understand."

She had wanted to cut out the baby, Susan said, but there hadn't been time. They wanted to take out the eyes of the people, and squash them against the walls, and cut off their fingers. "We were going to mutilate them, but we didn't have a chance to."

Virginia asked her how she felt after the murders. Susan replied, "I felt so elated; tired, but at peace with myself. I knew this was just the beginning of helter skelter. Now the world would listen."

Virginia didn't understand what she meant by "helter skelter," and Susan tried to explain it to her. However, she talked so quickly and with such obvious excitement that Virginia had trouble following. As Virginia understood it, there was this group, these chosen people, that Charlie had brought together, and they were elected, this new society, to go out, all over the country and all over the world, to pick out people at random and execute them, to release them from this earth. "You have to have a real love in your heart to do this for people," Susan explained.

Four or five times while Susan was talking, Virginia had to caution her to keep her voice down, that someone might hear. Susan smiled and said she wasn't worried about that. She was very good at playing crazy.

After they'd left the Tate residence, Susan continued, she discovered that she had lost her knife. She thought maybe the dog had got it. "You know how dogs are sometimes." They had thought about going back to look for it but had decided against it. She had also left her hand print on a desk. "It dawned on me afterwards," Susan said, "but my spirit was so strong that obviously it didn't even show up, or they would have had me by now."

As Virginia understood it, after leaving the Tate residence, they had apparently changed clothes in the car. Then they had driven some distance, stopping at a place where there was a fountain or water outside, to wash their hands. Susan said a man came outside and wanted to know what they were doing. He started to holler at them. "And," Susan said, "guess who he was?"

"I don't know," Virginia replied.

"It was the sheriff of Beverly Hills!"

Virginia said she didn't think Beverly Hills had a sheriff.

"Well," Susan said petulantly, "the sheriff or mayor or something."

The man had started to reach into the car to grab the keys, and "Charlie turned on the key. Boy, we made it. We laughed all the way," Susan said, adding, "If he had only known!"

For a moment Susan remained silent. Then, with her

little girl's smile, she asked, "You know the other two the next night?"

Virginia flashed on the grocery store owner and his wife, the LaBiancas. "Yeah," she said, "was that you?"

Susan winked and said, "What do you think?

"But that's part of the plan," she continued. "And there's more—"

But Virginia had heard enough for one day. She excused herself to go take a shower.

Virginia would later recall thinking, She's got to be kidding! She's making all this up. This is just too wild, too fantastic!

But then she remembered what Susan was in for—first degree murder.

Virginia decided not to say anything to anyone. It was just too incredible. She also decided, if possible, to avoid Susan.

The following day, however, Virginia walked over to Ronnie Howard's bed to tell her something. Susan, who was lying on her own bed, interrupted: "Virginia, Virginia, remember that beautiful cat I was telling you about? I want you to dig on his name. Now listen, his name is Manson—*Man's Son!*" She repeated it several times to make sure Virginia understood. She said it in a tone of childlike wonder.

She just couldn't keep it to herself any longer. It was just too much. The first time she and Ronnie Howard were alone together, Virginia Graham told her what Susan Atkins had said. "Hey, what do you do?" she asked Ronnie. "If this is true—My God, this is terrible. I wish she hadn't told me."

Ronnie thought Sadie was "making it all up. She could have gotten it out of the papers."

The only way to know for sure, they decided, would be for Virginia to question her further, to see if she could learn something that only one of the killers would know.

Virginia had an idea how she could do this without arousing Susan's suspicions. Though she hadn't mentioned it to Susan Atkins, Virginia Graham had more than a passing interest in the Tate homicides. She had known Jay Sebring. A girl friend, who was working as a manicurist for Sebring, had introduced them at the Luau some years ago, shortly after Sebring opened his shop on Fairfax. It was a casual thing—he was neither client nor friend, just someone you'd nod and say "Hi" to at a party or in a restaurant. It was an odd coincidence, Susan copping out to her. But there was another coincidence even odder. Virginia had been to 10050 Cielo Drive. Back in 1962 she and her then husband and another girl had been looking for a quiet place, away from things, and had learned 10050 Cielo Drive was up for lease. There had been no one there to show them around, so they had just looked in the windows of the main house. She could remember little about it, only that it looked like a red barn, but the next day at lunch she told Susan about having been there and asked if the interior was still decorated in gold and white. It was just a guess. Susan replied, "Huh-uh," but didn't elaborate. Virginia then told her about knowing Sebring, but Susan didn't appear very interested. This time Susan wasn't as talkative, but Virginia persisted, picking up miscellaneous bits and pieces of information.

They'd met Terry Melcher through Dennis Wilson, one of the Beach Boys rock group. They—Charlie, Susan, and the others—had lived with Dennis for a time. Virginia got the idea they were hostile toward Melcher, that he was too interested in money. Virginia also learned that the Tate murders had taken place between midnight and one in the morning; that "Charlie is love, pure love"; and that when you stab someone "it feels good when the knife goes in."

She also learned that besides the Hinman, Tate, and La-Bianca murders, "there's more—and more before ... There's also three people out in the desert ..."

Bits and pieces. Susan had said nothing that would establish whether she was or wasn't telling the truth.

That afternoon Susan walked over and sat down on Virginia's bed. Virginia had been leafing through a movie magazine. Susan saw it and began talking. The story she related, Virginia would say much later, was even more bizarre than what Susan had already told her. It was so incredible that Virginia didn't even mention it to Ronnie Howard. No one would believe it, she decided. For Susan Atkins, in one spurt of non-stop talking, gave her a "death list" of persons who would be murdered next. All were celebrities. She then, according to Virginia, described in gruesome detail exactly how Elizabeth Taylor, Richard Burton, Tom Jones, Steve McQueen, and Frank Sinatra would die.

On Monday, November 10, Susan Atkins had a visitor at Sybil Brand, Sue Bartell, who told her about the death of Zero. After Sue left, Susan told Ronnie Howard. Whether she embellished it or not is unknown. According to Susan, one of the girls had been holding Zero's hand when he died. When the gun went off, "he climaxed all over himself."

Susan didn't seem disturbed to hear of Zero's death. On the contrary, it excited her. "Imagine how beautiful to be there when it happened!" she told Ronnie.

On Wednesday, November 12, Susan Atkins was taken to court for a preliminary hearing on the Hinman murder. While there, she heard Sergeant Whiteley testify that it was Kitty Lutesinger—not Bobby Beausoleil—who had implicated her. On being returned to jail, Susan told Virginia that the prosecution had a surprise witness; but she wasn't worried about her testimony: "Her life's not worth anything."

That same day Virginia Graham received some bad news. She was being transferred to Corona Women's Prison, to serve out the rest of her sentence. She was to leave that afternoon. While she was packing, Ronnie came up to her and asked, "What do you think?"

"I don't know," Virginia replied. "Ronnie, if you want to take it from here—"

"I've been talking to that girl every night," Ronnie said. "Boy, she's really weird. She could have, you know."

Virginia had forgotten to ask Susan about the word "pig," which the papers had said was printed in blood on the door of the Tate residence. She suggested that Ronnie question her about this, and anything else she could think of that might indicate whether she was telling the truth.

In the meantime, they decided not to mention it to anyone else.

That same day the LaBianca detectives received a call from Venice PD. Were they still interested in talking to one of the Straight Satans? If so, they were questioning one, a guy named Al Springer, on another charge.

The LaBianca detectives had Springer brought over to Parker Center, where they interviewed him on tape. What he told them was so unexpected they had trouble believing it. For Springer said that on August 11 or 12—two or three days after the Tate homicides—Charlie Manson had bragged to him about killing people, adding, "We knocked off five of them just the other night."

November 12-16, 1969

LaBianca detectives Nielsen, Gutierrez, and Patchett interviewed Springer on tape, in one of the interrogation cubicles of LAPD Homicide. Springer was twenty-six, five feet nine, weighed 130 pounds, and, except for his dusty, ragged "colors," as bikers' jackets are known, was surprisingly neat for a member of an "outlaw" motorcycle band.

Springer, it turned out, prided himself on his cleanliness. Which was one of the reasons he personally hadn't wanted to have anything to do with Manson and his girls, he said. But Danny DeCarlo, the club treasurer of the Straight Satans, had got mixed up with them and had missed meetings, so around August 11 or 12, he, Springer, had gone to Spahn Ranch to persuade Danny to come back. " . . . and there were flies all over the place and they were just like animals up there, I couldn't believe it, you know. You see, I'm really clean, really. Some of the guys get pretty nasty, but I myself, I like to keep things clean.

"Well, in comes this Charlie . . . He wanted Danny up there because Danny had his colors on his back, and all these drunkards, they come up there and start harrassing the girls and messing with the guys and Danny walks out with his Straight Satan colors on, and nobody messes with Charlie, see.

"So I tried to get Danny to come back, and Charlie is standing there, and Charlie says, he says, 'Now wait a minute, maybe I can give you a better thing than you've got already.' I said, 'What's that?' He says, 'Move up here, you can have all the girls you want, all the girls,' he says, 'are all yours, at your disposal, anything.' And he's a brainwashing type guy. So I said, 'Well, how do you survive, how do you support these twenty, thirty fucking broads, man?' And he says, 'I got them all hoofing for me.' He said, 'I go out at night and I do my thing.' 'Well,' I said, 'what's your thing, man; run your trip down.' He figured me being a motorcycle rider and all, I'd accept anything including murder.

"So he starts getting in my ear and says how he goes up and he lives with the rich people, and he calls the police 'pigs' and what not, he knocks on the door, they'll open the door, and he'll just drive in with his cutlass and start cutting them up, see."

Q. "This is what he told you?"

A. "This is what he told me verbally, right to my face."

Q. "You're kidding, is that what you really heard?"

A. "Yeah. I said, 'When's the last time you did it?' He says, 'Well, we knocked off five of them,' he says, 'just the other night.' "

Q. "So he told you that—Charlie stated that he knocked over five people?"

A. "Right. Charlie and Tex."

Springer couldn't recall the exact word Manson used: it wasn't "people"; it might have been "pigs" or "rich pigs."

The LaBianca detectives were so startled they had Springer run through it a second time, and a third.

A. "I think you've got your man right here, I really do."

Q. "I'm pretty sure we have, but in this day and age of feeding people their rights, if we're going to make a decent case on him, we can't do it with his statement."

Exactly when had Manson told him this? Well, it was the first time he went to Spahn, and that was either August 11 or 12—he couldn't remember which. But he sure remembered the scene. "I've never seen anything like it in my life. I've never been to a nudist colony or I've never seen real idiots on the loose . . ." Everywhere he looked there were naked girls. Maybe a dozen and a half were of age, eighteen or over, but about an equal number weren't. The young ones were hiding in the bushes. Charlie had told him he could have his pick. He'd also offered to buy him a dune buggy and a new motorcycle if he would stay.

It was true turnabout. Charlie Manson, aka Jesus Christ, trying to tempt a Straight Satan.

That Springer resisted the temptation may have been due in part to his knowledge that other members of his gang had been there on previous occasions: "Everybody got sick of catching the clap . . . the ranch was just out of hand . . ."

During Springer's first visit, Manson had demonstrated his prowess with knives, in particular a long sword. Springer had seen Charlie throw it maybe fifty feet, sticking it, say, eight times out of ten. This was the sword, Springer said, that Charlie used when he "put the chop" to people.

"Did you ever get a corpse with his ear cut off?" Springer abruptly asked. Apparently one of the detectives nodded, as Springer said, "Yeah, there's your man." Charlie had told him about cutting some guy's ear off. If Danny would come in, he could tell them about it. The only problem was, "Danny's scared of these creeps, they've tried to kill him already."

Springer had also mentioned a Tex and a Clem. The detectives asked him to describe them.

Clem was a certified idiot, Springer said: he was an escapee from Camarillo, a state mental hospital. Whatever Charlie said, Clem would parrot it. As far as he could tell, "Charlie and Tex are the ones that had the brains out there." Unlike Clem, Tex didn't say much; he "kept his mouth shut, real tight. He was real clean-cut. His hair was a little long, but he was—just like a college student." Tex seemed to spend most of his time working on dune buggies.

Charlie had a thing about dune buggies. He wanted to fix them with a switch on the dash that would turn the taillights off. Then, when the CHP (California Highway Patrol) pulled them over to cite them, there would be two guys armed with shotguns in the back, and as the CHP's came up alongside, "Pow, blow them up."

Q. "Why did he say he wanted to do that?"

A. "Ah, he wants to build up a thing where he can be leader of the world. He's crazy."

Q. "Does he have a name for his group?"

A. "The Family."

Back to that sword, could Springer describe it? Yeah, it was a cutlass, a real pirate's sword. Up until a few months ago, Springer said, it had belonged to the ex-president of the Straight Satans, but then it had disappeared, and he guessed one of the members had given it to Charlie.

He had heard, from Danny, that the sword had been used when they had killed a guy "called Henland, I believe it was." This was the guy who had his ear cut off.

What did he know about the "Henland" killing? they asked. According to Danny, a guy named "Bausley" and one or two other guys had killed him, Springer said. Danny had told him that "almost beyond a reasonable doubt he could prove that Bousley or Bausley or whatever killed this guy and evidently Charlie was in on it or something. Well, anyway, somebody cut his ear." Clem had also told him, Springer, "how they had cut some fucking idiot's ear off and wrote on the wall and put the Panther's hand or paw up there to blame the Panthers. Everything they did, they blamed on the niggers, see. They hate niggers because they had killed a nigger prior to that."

Five. Plus "Henland" (Hinman). Plus "a nigger." Total thus far: seven. The detectives were keeping track.

Had he seen any other weapons while at Spahn? Yeah, Charlie had shown him a whole gunrack full, the first time he went up there. There were shotguns, deer rifles, .45 caliber hand guns, "and I heard talk of and was told by

Danny that they had a .22 Buntline long barrel, a nine-round. This came from Danny, and he knows guns. And this is what was supposed to have killed that, ah, Black Panther."

Charlie had told him about it. As Al remembered it, Tex had burned this black guy in a deal for a whole bunch of grass. When Charlie refused to give back the guy's money, the black had threatened to get all his Panther brothers up to Spahn Ranch and wipe out the place. "So Charlie pulls out a gun, somebody else was going to do it, but Charlie pulls out a gun and he points it at the guy, and he goes click, click, click, click and the gun didn't go off, four or five times, and the guy stood up and he said, 'Ha, you coming here with an empty gun on me,' and Charlie says click, bam, in the heart area somewhere, and he told me this personally right to my face and that was what the Buntline was used on, the long-barrel job."

After the murder, which had occurred somewhere in Hollywood, the Panther's buddies "took the carcass off supposedly to some park, Griffith Park or one of them . . . This is all hearsay, but it is hearsay right from Charlie."

A. "Now, did anybody have their refrigerator wrote on?"

There was a sudden silence, then one of the LaBianca detectives asked, "Why does this come up?"

A. " 'Cause he told me something about writing something on the refrigerator."

Q. "Who said he wrote it on the refrigerator?"

A. "Charlie did. Charlie said they wrote something on the fucking refrigerator in blood."

Q. "What did he say he wrote?"

A. "Something about pigs or niggers or something like that."

If Springer was telling the truth, and *if* Manson wasn't just bragging to impress him, then it meant that Manson was probably also involved in the LaBianca murders. Bringing the total thus far to nine.

But the LaBianca detectives had good reason to doubt this statement, for, contrary to the press reports, DEATH TO

PIGS hadn't been printed in blood on the refrigerator door; the phrase had actually been printed on the living-room wall, as had the word RISE. What had been printed on the refrigerator door was HEALTER SKELTER.

While Springer was being questioned, one of the LaBianca detectives left the room. When he returned a few minutes later, another man was with him.

Q. "Here's another partner, Mike McGann, Al. Let me shove this table down here. He just came in, so you might want to bring him up on what we've talked about."

McGann was one of the Tate detectives. The LaBianca detectives had finally decided to walk those few feet, and share what they had learned. By this time the temptation to say "Hey, look what *we* found" must have been irresistible.

They had Springer run through it again. McGann listened, unimpressed. Springer then began talking about still another murder, that of a cowboy named "Shorty," whom he had met when he first visited the ranch. How and what had he heard about Shorty's death? one of the detectives asked. "I heard about that from Danny." Danny heard, from the girls, that Shorty "got to know too much and hear too much and got worried too much" and "so they just cut his arms and his legs and his head off . . ." Danny had felt very badly about this, because he had liked Shorty.

Ten. *If.*

Q. (*to McGann*) "Anything you want to get in on this?"

Q. "Yeah, I want to ask about why they killed this colored—the Panther supposedly. When did this take place, do you know?"

Springer wasn't sure, but he thought it was about a week before he went up to the ranch. Danny could probably tell them about that.

Q. "Did you connect up the five people that Charlie said that he killed in early August with any particular crime?"

A. "Right, the Tate crime."

Q. "You put that together?"

A. "Right."

They began zeroing in. Anybody else present when Charlie supposedly confessed those five murders to you? No. Was Tate ever specifically mentioned? No. Did you see anyone at the ranch who wore glasses? No. Ever see Manson with a gun? No, only a knife: "he's a knife freak." Were the cutlass and the other knives you saw sharpened on both sides? He thought so but wasn't sure; Danny had mentioned Charlie sending them out someplace to be sharpened. Ever see any rope up there? Yeah, they used all kinds of rope. Do you know there's a $25,000 reward on the Tate murders? Yeah, and "I sure could use it."

Springer had been to Spahn Ranch three times, his second visit occurring the day after his first. He'd lost his hat riding out and had gone back to look for it, but then his bike had broken down and he'd had to stay overnight to repair it. Again Charlie, Tex, and Clem had worked on him to join them. His third and last visit had taken place on the night of Friday, August 15. The detectives were able to establish the date because it was the night before the sheriff's raid on Spahn Ranch. Also, the Straight Satans held their club meetings on Friday, and they had discussed getting Danny away from Charlie. "A lot of the guys in the club were going to go up there and beat his ass, teach him a lesson not to brainwash our members . . ." Eight or nine of them did go to Spahn that night, "but it didn't happen that way."

Charlie had conned some of them. The girls had lured others into the bushes. And when they started breaking up things, Charlie told them that he had guns trained on them from the rooftops. Springer had one of his brothers check the gunrack that Charlie had shown him on his first visit. A couple of rifles were missing. After a time they'd left, in a cloud of exhaust fumes and threats, leaving one of their more sober members, Robert Reinhard, to bring Danny back the following day. But the next morning "the police were all over the place," arresting not only Charlie and the others but also DeCarlo and Reinhard.

All had been released a few days later and, according to Danny, Shorty had been killed not long after this.

Fearing he would be next, Danny had taken his truck and split to Venice. Late one night Clem and Bruce Davis, another of Charlie's boys, had snuck up on the truck. They had succeeded in prying open the door when Danny heard them and grabbed his .45. Danny felt sure, Springer said, that they had come "to off him." And he was scared now, not only for himself but because his little boy was living with him. Springer thought Danny was frightened enough to talk to them. Talking to the Venice detectives would be no problem, since "he's known them most of his life," but getting him to come down to Parker Center was something else. Springer, however, promised he'd try to get Danny to come in voluntarily, if possible the next day.

Springer didn't have a phone. The detectives asked if there was somewhere they could call "without putting any heat on you? Is there some gal you see quite a bit of?"

A. "Just my wife and kids."

The clean, neat, monogamous Springer didn't conform to their stereotype of a biker. As one of the detectives remarked, "You're going to give the motorcycle gang a whole new image in the world."

Although Al Springer appeared to be telling the truth, the detectives were not greatly impressed with his story. He was an outsider, not a member of the Family, yet the very first time he goes to Spahn Ranch, Manson confesses to him that he's committed at least nine murders. It just didn't make sense. It appeared far more likely that Springer was just regurgitating what Danny DeCarlo, who had been close to Manson, had told him. It was also possible that Manson, to impress the cyclists, had bragged about committing murders in which he wasn't even involved.

McGann, of the Tate team, was so unimpressed that later he wouldn't even be able to recall having heard of Springer, much less talking to him.

Although the interview had been taped, the LaBianca detectives had only one portion transcribed, and that not the section on their case, but the part, less than a page in length, with Manson's alleged confession, "We knocked off five of them just the other night." The LaBianca detectives then filed the tape and that single page in their "tubs," as police case files are known. With other developments in the case, they apparently forgot them.

Yet the Springer interview of November 12, 1969, was in a sense an important turning point. Three months after the Tate-LaBianca homicides, LAPD was finally seriously considering the possibility that the two crimes were not, as had long been believed, unrelated. And the focus of at least the LaBianca investigation was now on a single group of suspects, Charlie Manson and his Family. It appears almost certain that had the LaBianca detectives continued to pursue the Lutesinger-Springer-DeCarlo lead they would eventually—even if uninformed of Susan Atkins' confessions—have found the killers of Steven Parent, Abigail Folger, Voytek Frykowski, Jay Sebring, Sharon Tate, and Rosemary and Leno LaBianca.

In the meantime, two people—one at Sybil Brand, the other at Corona—were each, independent of the other, trying to tell someone what they knew about the killings. And having no luck.

There is some confusion as to exactly when Susan Atkins first discussed the Tate-LaBianca murders with Ronnie Howard. Whatever the date, there was a similarity in the way it came about, Susan first admitting her participation in the murder of Hinman, then, in her little-girl manner, attempting to surprise Ronnie with other, more startling revelations.

According to Ronnie, one evening Susan came over, sat down on her bed, and started rapping about her experiences. Susan said that she had "dropped acid" (taken LSD) many times, in fact she had done everything there was to do; there was nothing left; she'd reached a stage where nothing shocked her any more.

Ronnie replied that there wasn't much that would shock her, either. Since age seventeen, when she'd been sent to a federal penitentiary for two years for extortion, Ronnie had seen quite a lot.

"I bet I could tell you something that would really blow your mind," Susan said.

"I don't think so," Ronnie responded.

"You remember the Tate deal?"

"Yes."

"I was there. We did it."

"Really, anyone can say that."

"No, I'll tell you." And tell her Susan Atkins did.

Susan would flash from one thought to another with such rapidity that Ronnie was often left confused. Too, Ronnie's recollection of details—especially names, dates, places—was not as good as Virginia's. Later she would be unsure, for example, exactly how many persons were involved: at one time she thought Susan said five—herself, two other girls, Charlie, and a guy who stayed in the car; another time it was four, with no mention of the man in the car. She knew a girl named Katie was involved in a murder, but which murder—Hinman, Tate, or LaBianca—Ronnie wasn't sure. But she also recalled details Susan either hadn't told Virginia or Virginia had forgotten. Charlie had a gun; the girls all had knives. Charlie had cut the telephone wires, shot the boy in the car, then awakened the man on the couch (Frykowski), who looked up to see a gun pointing in his face.

Sharon Tate's plea and Susan's brutal response were nearly identical in both Ronnie's and Virginia's accounts. However, the description of how Sharon died differed somewhat. As Ronnie understood it, two other people held Sharon while, to quote Susan, "I proceeded to stab her."

"It felt so good the first time I stabbed her, and when she screamed at me it did something to me, sent a rush through me, and I stabbed her again."

Ronnie asked where. Susan replied in the chest, not the stomach.

"How many times?"

"I don't remember. I just kept stabbing her until she stopped screaming."

Ronnie knew a little bit about the subject, having once stabbed her ex-husband. "Did it feel sort of like a pillow?"

"Yeah," Susan replied, pleased that Ronnie understood. "It was just like going into nothing, going into air." But the killing itself was something else. "It's like a sexual release," Susan told her. "Especially when you see the blood spurting out. It's better than a climax."

Remembering Virginia's question, Ronnie asked Susan about the word "pig." Susan said that she printed the word on the door, after first dipping a towel in Sharon Tate's blood.

At one point in the conversation Susan asked, "Don't you remember that guy that was found with the fork in his stomach? We wrote 'arise' and 'death to pigs' and 'helter skelter' in blood."

"Was that you and your same friends?" Ronnie asked.

"No, just three this time."

"All girls?"

"No, two girls and Charlie. Linda wasn't in on this one."

Susan rapped on about a variety of subjects: Manson (he was both Jesus Christ and the Devil); helter skelter (Ronnie admittedly didn't understand it but thought it meant "you have to be killed to live"); sex ("the whole world is like one big intercourse—everything is in and out—smoking, eating, stabbing"); how she would play crazy to fool the psychiatrists ("All you have to do is act normal," Ronnie advised her); children (Charlie had helped deliver her baby, whom she had named Zezozose Zadfrack Glutz; within a couple of months after his birth she had begun fellating him); bikers (with the motorcycle gangs on their side, they "would really throw some fear into the world"); and murder. Susan loved to talk about murder. "More you do it, the better you like it." Just the mention of it seemed to excite her. Laughingly, she told Ronnie about some man whose head "we cut off," either out in the desert or in one of the canyons.

She also told Ronnie, "There are eleven murders that they will never solve." And there were going to be more, many more. Although Charlie was in jail "in Indio," most of the Family was still free.

As Susan talked, Ronnie Howard realized that there were still some things that could shock her. One was that this little girl, who was twenty-one but often seemed much younger, probably *had* committed all these murders. Another was Susan's assertion that this was only the beginning, that more murders would follow.

Ronnie Howard would later state: "I'd never informed on anyone in the past, but this one thing I could not go along with. I kept thinking that if I didn't say anything these people would probably be set free. They were going to pick other houses, just at random. I just couldn't see all those innocent people being killed. It could have been my house next time or yours or anyone's."

Ronnie decided she "just had to tell the police."

It would seem that if one were in jail, talking to a policemen would be relatively easy. Ronnie Howard discovered otherwise.

The dates, again, are vague, but, according to Ronnie, she told +Sergeant Broom,* one of the female deputies at Sybil Brand, that she knew who had committed the Tate and LaBianca murders; that the person who told her had been involved and was now in custody; but that the other killers were on the loose and unless they were apprehended soon there would be more murders. Ronnie wanted permission to call LAPD.

Sergeant Broom said she would pass the request to her superior, +Lieutenant Johns.

After waiting three days and hearing nothing, Ronnie asked Sergeant Broom about the request. Lieutenant Johns didn't think there was anything to the story, the sergeant told her. By this time the lieutenant had probably forgotten all about it, Sergeant Broom said, adding, "Why don't you do the same thing, Ronnie?"

By now, according to Ronnie, she was literally begging. People were going to die unless she warned the police in time. Could you call *for* me? Ronnie asked. *Please!*

It was against the rules for a guard to make a call for an inmate, Sergeant Broom informed her.

On Thursday, November 13, biker Danny DeCarlo came down to Parker Center, where he was interviewed

*Since neither the deputy nor her lieutenant was available for interviews, therefore making it impossible to present their version of these incidents, pseudonyms have been used for both.

by the LaBianca detectives. It was not a long interview, and it was not taped. Although DeCarlo had a great deal of information about the activities of Manson and his group, having lived with them for more than five months, at no time had Charlie admitted to him that he was involved in either the Tate or the LaBianca murders.

This made the officers even more skeptical about Springer's tale, and it was probably at this point that they decided to write him off as a reliable source. When Springer came back the following week, he was given some photos to identify but was asked few questions.

Arrangements were made to interview DeCarlo on tape, and at length, on Monday, November 17. He was to come in about 8:30 in the morning.

Ronnie Howard kept after Sergeant Broom, who finally mentioned the subject to Lieutenant Johns a second time. The lieutenant suggested that she ask Ronnie for some details.

Sergeant Broom did, and Ronnie—still without identifying the people involved—told her a little of what she had learned. The killers knew Terry Melcher. They had shot the boy, Steven Parent, first, four times, because he saw them. Sharon Tate had been the last to die. The word "pig" had been written in her blood. They were going to cut out Sharon's baby, but didn't. Again she stressed that more killings were planned.

Sergeant Broom apparently misunderstood Ronnie, for she told Lieutenant Johns that they *had* cut out the baby. And Lieutenant Johns knew this wasn't true.

Your informant is lying, Sergeant Broom informed Ronnie, and told her why.

Ronnie, now almost hysterical, told Sergeant Broom that she had misunderstood what she'd said. Could she talk to Lieutenant Johns herself?

But Sergeant Broom decided that she had already bothered the lieutenant enough. As far as she was concerned, she informed Ronnie, the matter was closed.

There was an irony here, although Ronnie Howard was unaware of it, and wouldn't have appreciated it had she known: Sergeant Broom dated one of the Tate detectives.

But apparently they had other, more important things to talk about.

Virginia Graham was having her own troubles with bureaucracy. Although, unlike Ronnie Howard, she was not yet completely convinced that Susan Atkins was telling the truth, the possibility that there might be more murders worried her too. On November 14, two days after her transfer to Corona, she decided she had to tell someone what she had heard. There was one person at the prison she knew and trusted, Dr. Vera Dreiser, a staff psychologist.

In order for an inmate to talk to a staff member at Corona, it is necessary to fill out a "blue slip," or request form. Virginia made one out, writing on it, "Dr. Dreiser, it is very important that I speak with you."

The form was returned with a notation stating that Miss Graham should fill out another blue slip, to see Dr. Owens, administrator of the unit to which she was assigned. But Virginia didn't want to speak to Dr. Owens. Again she requested a personal interview with Dr. Dreiser.

The request was granted. But not until December. And by then the whole world knew what Virginia Graham had wanted to tell Dr. Dreiser.

November 17, 1969

Danny DeCarlo was due at LAPD Homicide at 8:30 that Monday morning. He didn't show. The detectives called his home first, getting no answer, then his mother's number. No, she hadn't seen Danny, and she was a little worried. Danny was supposed to leave his son with her, so she could baby-sit while he went down to LAPD, but he hadn't even called.

It was possible DeCarlo had skipped. He had been very

frightened when the detectives talked to him the previous Thursday.

There was another possibility, one that they didn't want to think about.

That same day Ronnie Howard had a court appearance in Santa Monica, on the forgery charge. When inmates of Sybil Brand are due in court, they are first transported to the men's jail on Bouchet Street, where a bus picks them up and delivers them to the assigned departments. Before the arrival of the bus, there are usually a few minutes during which each girl is permitted to make one call from a pay phone.

Ronnie saw her chance and got in line. However, time began running out and there were still two girls ahead of her. She paid each fifty cents to let her call first.

Ronnie called the Beverly Hills Police Department and asked to speak to a homicide detective. When one came on the line, she gave him her name and booking number, and told him she knew who had committed the Tate and LaBianca murders. The officer said those cases were being handled by the Hollywood Division of LAPD, and suggested she call there.

Ronnie then called Hollywood PD, giving a second homicide officer the same information. He wanted to send someone over immediately, but she told him she would be in court the rest of the day.

She hung up, however, before the officer could ask which court she would be in.

All day in court Ronnie Howard had the feeling that she was being watched. She was sure that two men, sitting in the back of the courtroom, were homicide detectives, and expected at any minute they would arrange to speak to her. But they never did. When court adjourned, she was taken by bus back to Sybil Brand, Dormitory 8000, and Susan Atkins.

Shortly before 5 P.M., Danny DeCarlo arrived at LAPD Homicide. He had been on his way downtown earlier when he noticed he was low on gas and had pulled into a service station. On leaving, he had made an illegal turn, had been spotted by a black-and-white, and, after the officers checked and found he had some outstanding traffic tickets, had been hauled in. It had taken all day to secure his release.

Unlike Al Springer, Danny DeCarlo looked, talked, and acted like a biker. He was short, five feet four, weighed 130 pounds, had a handlebar mustache, tattoos on both arms, and burn scars on one arm and both legs from motorcycle pile-ups. Wary, frequently glancing back over his shoulder as if expecting to find someone there, he spoke in a colorful jargon that the interviewing officers—Nielsen, Gutierrez, and McGann—unconsciously adopted. Now twenty-five, he had been born in Toronto, then given U.S. citizenship after serving four years in the Coast Guard, his job: weapons expert. Currently he was in business with his father, selling firearms. When it came to the guns at Spahn Ranch, the detectives couldn't have found a better source. When he wasn't getting drunk and chasing girls—which he admitted occupied most of his time—he looked after the weapons. He not only cleaned and repaired them, he slept in the gunroom where they were kept. When a weapon was taken out, Danny knew about it.

He also knew a great deal about Spahn's Movie Ranch, which was located in Chatsworth, not more than twenty miles from downtown Beverly Hills, yet, seemingly, a world away. Once William S. Hart, Tom Mix, Johnny Mack Brown, and Wallace Beery had made movies here; it was said that Howard Hughes had come to Spahn, to oversee personally the filming of portions of *The Outlaw;* and the rolling hills behind the main buildings provided settings for *Duel in the Sun*. Now, except for an occasional Marlboro commercial or a "Bonanza" episode, the main business was renting horses to weekend riders. The movie sets—Longhorn Saloon, Rock City Cafe, Undertaking Parlor, Jail—which fronted on Santa Susana Pass Road, were old now, run down, as was George Spahn, the eighty-one-year-old, near blind owner of the ranch. For years Ruby Pearl, a onetime circus bareback rider turned horse wrangler, had run the riding stable part of the business for George: getting hay, hiring and firing cowboys, making sure they looked after the horses and stable and kept their hands off the too young girls who came for riding lessons. Almost sightless, George depended on Ruby, but at the end of the day she went home to a husband and another life.

Over the years George had sired ten children, each of whom he had named after a favorite horse. He could recall in detail the namesakes but was less clear about the kids. All lived elsewhere, and only a few visited him with any regularity. When the Manson Family arrived, in August 1968, George was living alone in a filthy trailer, feeling old, lonely, and neglected.

This was long before Danny DeCarlo became involved with the Family, but he had often heard the tale from those who were there.

Manson, who originally asked Spahn's permission to stay for a few days, but neglected to mention that there were twenty-five to thirty people with him, assigned Squeaky to look after George.

Squeaky—t/n Lynette Fromme—had been with Manson more than a year at that time, having been one of the first girls to join him. She was thin, red-headed, covered with freckles. Though nineteen, she looked much younger. DeCarlo told the detectives, "She had George in the palm of her hand. She cleaned for him, cooked for him, balanced his checkbook, made love with him."

Q. (*unbelievingly*) "She did?! That old son of a gun!"

A. "Yeah . . . Charlie's trip was to get George so he had so much faith in Squeaky that come time for George to go off into the happy hunting ground he'd turn the ranch over to Squeaky. That was their thing. Charlie'd always tell her what to tell George . . . and she'd report back to Charlie anything anyone else told him."

Squeaky maintained that she was George's eyes. According to DeCarlo, they saw only what Charlie Manson wanted them to see.

Possibly because he suspected, possibly because his own children on their occasional visits strongly resisted the idea, George never did get around to willing the property to Squeaky. Which, the detectives surmised, was probably why he was still alive out at Spahn Ranch.

George Spahn had frustrated one of Charlie's plans. Danny DeCarlo had played along with, then failed to come through on another—Manson's scheme to get the motorcycle gangs to join him in "terrorizing society," as DeCarlo put it. Danny had met Manson in March 1969, just after separating from his wife. He had gone to Spahn to repair some bikes, and had stayed; "I had a ball," he later admitted. Manson's girls had been taught that having babies and caring for men were their sole purpose in life. DeCarlo liked being cared for, and the girls, at least at first, appeared very affectionate toward "Donkey Dan,"* a nickname they had bestowed upon him because of certain physical endowments.

There were problems. Charlie was against drinking; Danny liked nothing better than to swill beer and lie in the sun—later he testified that while at Spahn he was smashed "probably 90 percent of the time." And, with the exception of a couple of "special sweeties," DeCarlo eventually tired of most of the girls: "They would always try preaching to me. It was always the same shit Charlie preached to them."

With the August 15 visit of the Straight Satans, Manson must have realized that he would never succeed in getting the bikers to join him. After that, Danny was ignored, left out of Family conferences, while the girls denied him their favors. Though he went to Barker Ranch with the group, he stayed only three days. He split, DeCarlo said, because he had begun to believe all the "murder talk" he had heard, and because he had strong suspicions that unless he left he might be next. "After that," he said, "I started watching my back."

When the LaBianca detectives had talked to DeCarlo the previous Thursday, he'd promised to try to locate Manson's sword. He turned it over to Sergeant Gutierrez, who booked it as the personal property of "Manson, Charles M.," probable crime "187 PC"—murder.

*Manson told DeCarlo that because he, Manson, was less amply endowed, he needed DeCarlo to keep the girls from running away. This sounds like a Manson con, though DeCarlo maintains it was true.

The sword had accumulated a history. A few weeks after Danny moved to Spahn, the president of the Straight Satans, George Knoll, aka "86 George," had visited him. Manson had admired George's sword and had conned him out of it by promising to pay a twenty-dollar traffic ticket George owed. According to Danny, the sword became one of Charlie's favorite weapons; he had a metal scabbard built for it, next to the steering wheel of his personal dune buggy. When the Straight Satans came to get Danny the night of August 15, they spotted the sword and reclaimed it. On learning that it was "dirty," i.e., had been used in a crime, they had broken it in half. It was in two pieces when DeCarlo handed it over to Gutierrez.

Over-all length, 20 inches; blade length, 15 inches. The width of its razor-sharp blade, the tip of which had been honed on both sides, was 1 inch.

This was the sword, according to DeCarlo, that Manson had used to slice Gary Hinman's ear.

From DeCarlo the detectives now learned that, in addition to Bobby Beausoleil and Susan Atkins, three others had been involved in the murder of Hinman: Manson, Mary Brunner, and Bruce Davis. DeCarlo's primary source was Beausoleil, who, on returning to Spahn after the murder, had bragged to DeCarlo about what he had done. Or, as Danny put it, "He came back with a big head the next day, you know, just like he got him a cherry."

The story, as DeCarlo claimed Beausoleil had related it to him, went as follows. Mary Brunner, Susan Atkins, and Bobby Beausoleil had dropped in on Hinman, "bullshitting about old times and everything like that." Bobby then asked Gary for all his money, saying they needed it. When Gary said he didn't have any money, Bobby pulled out a gun—a 9mm. Polish Radom automatic—and started pistol-whipping him. In the scuffle the gun went off, the bullet hitting no one but ricocheting through the kitchen. (LASO found a 9 mm. slug lodged under the kitchen sink.)

Beausoleil then called Manson at Spahn Ranch and told him, "You'd better get up here, Charlie. Gary ain't cooperating."* A short time later Manson and Bruce Davis arrived at the Hinman residence. Puzzled and hurt, Gary pleaded with Charlie, asking him to take the others and leave; he didn't want any trouble; he couldn't understand why they were doing this to him; they had always been friends. According to DeCarlo, "Charlie didn't say anything. He just hit him with the sword. Whack. Cut part of his ear off or all of it. [Hinman's left ear had been split in half.]

"So Gary went down, and was really going through some changes about losing his ear . . ." Manson gave him a choice: sign over everything he had, or die. Manson and Davis then left.

Though Beausoleil did obtain the "pink slips" (California automobile ownership papers) on two of Hinman's vehicles, Gary continued to insist he had no money. When more pistol-whipping failed to convince him, Bobby again called Manson at Spahn, telling him, "We ain't going to get nothing out of him. He ain't going to give up nothing. And we can't just leave. He's got his ear hacked off and he'll go to the police." Manson replied, "Well, you know what to do." And Beausoleil did it.

"Bobby said he went up to Gary again. Took the knife and stuck him with it. He said he had to do it three or four times . . . [Hinman] was really bleeding, and he was gasping for air, and Bobby said he knelt down next to him and said, 'Gary, you know what? You got no reason to be on earth any more. You're a pig and society don't need you, so this is the best way for you to go, and you should thank me for putting you out of your misery.' Then [Hinman] made noises in his throat, his last gasping breath, and wow, away he went."

Q. "So Bobby told him he was a 'pig'?"

A. "Right. You see, the fight against society was the number one element in this—"

Q. (*skeptically*) "Yeah. We'll get into his philosophy and all that bullshit later . . ."

They never did.

*Since the Hinman residence in Malibu and Spahn's Movie Ranch in Chatsworth were in the same dialing area, this was not a toll call; therefore the telephone company kept no record of it.

DeCarlo went on. Before leaving the house, they wrote on the wall " 'white piggy' or 'whitey' or 'kill the piggies,' something along that line." Beausoleil also dipped his hand in Hinman's blood and, using his palm, made a paw print on the wall; the plan was "to push the blame onto the Black Panthers," who used the paw print as their symbol. Then they hot-wired Hinman's Volkswagen microbus and his Fiat station wagon and drove both back to Spahn Ranch, where Beausoleil bragged about his exploits to DeCarlo.

Later, apparently fearful that the palm print might be identifiable, Beausoleil returned to the Hinman residence and attempted, unsuccessfully, to wipe it off the wall. This was several days after Hinman's death, and Beausoleil later told DeCarlo that he "could hear the maggots eating away on Gary."*

As killers, they had been decidedly amateurish. Not only was the palm print identifiable, so was a latent fingerprint Beausoleil had left in the kitchen. They kept Hinman's Volkswagen and his Fiat at the ranch for several days, where a number of people saw them.† Hinman had played bagpipes, a decidedly uncommon musical instrument. Beausoleil and the girls took his set back to Spahn Ranch, where for a time they remained on a shelf in the kitchen; DeCarlo for one had tried to play them. And Beausoleil did not discard the knife but continued to carry

*Beausoleil, Brunner, and Atkins went to Hinman's residence on Friday, July 25, 1969. Manson slashed Hinman's ear sometime late that night. Hinman was not killed, however, until Sunday, July 27, and it was not until the following Thursday, July 31, that his body was discovered by LASO, following a report from a friend who had been trying to reach Hinman for several days.

†Ironically, on July 28, two LASO deputies—Olmstead and Grap—visited Spahn Ranch on another matter. While there they saw the Fiat, ran a spot check on the license, and learned that it belonged to Gary Hinman. Grap knew Hinman; he also knew he was a friend of the people at Spahn Ranch, and therefore didn't feel there was anything suspicious about the station wagon's being there. At this time, although Hinman was dead, his body had not yet been discovered.

After the discovery of the body on July 31, LASO put out a "want" on Hinman's vehicles. Grap didn't learn of it, or Hinman's death, until much later. If he had known, of course, he could have directed the investigation to Spahn Ranch and the Manson Family months before Kitty Lutesinger implicated Atkins and the others.

it with him; it was in the tire well when he was arrested on August 6, driving Hinman's Fiat.

DeCarlo drew a picture of the knife Beausoleil claimed he had used to stab Hinman. It was a pencil-thin, miniature bowie, with an eagle on the handle and a Mexican inscription. It tallied perfectly with the knife recovered from the Fiat. DeCarlo also sketched the 9 mm. Radom, which as yet hadn't been recovered.

The detectives asked him what other hand guns he had seen at Spahn.

A. "Well, there was a .22 Buntline. When they did that Black Panther, I didn't want to touch it. I didn't want to clean it. I didn't want to be nowhere around it."

DeCarlo claimed he didn't know whose gun it was, but he said, "Charlie always used to carry it in a holster on the front of him. It was more or less always with him."

Sometime "around July, maybe June," the gun "just popped up." When was the last time he saw it? "I know I didn't see it for at least a week before the raid."

The Spahn Ranch raid had taken place on August 16. A week earlier would be August 9, the date of the Tate homicides.

Q. "Did you ever ask Charlie, 'Where's your gun?' "

A. "He said, 'I just gave it away.' He liked it, so I figured it was maybe just stashed."

The detectives had DeCarlo draw the Buntline. It was nearly identical with the photo of the Hi Standard Longhorn model sent out in the LAPD flyer. Later DeCarlo was shown the flyer and asked, "Does this look like the gun you mentioned?"

A. "It sure does."

Q. "What's the difference between that gun and the gun that you saw?"

A. "No difference at all. Only the rear sight blade was different. It didn't have any."

The detectives had DeCarlo run down what he knew about the murder of the Black Panther. Springer had first mentioned the killing to them when they interviewed him. In the interim they had done some checking and had come up with a slight problem: no such murder had ever been reported.

According to DeCarlo, after Tex burned the guy for $2,500 on a grass deal, the Panther had called Charlie at Spahn Ranch, threatening that if he didn't make good he and his brothers were going to wipe out the whole ranch. That same night Charlie and a guy named T. J. went to the Panther's place, in North Hollywood. Charlie had a plan.

He put the .22 Buntline in his belt in back. On a signal T. J. was to yank out the gun, step out from behind Charlie, and plug the Panther. Nail him right there. Only T. J. had chickened out, and Manson had to do the shooting himself. Friends of the black, who were present when the shooting occurred, had later dumped the body in Griffith Park, Danny said.

Danny had seen the $2,500 and had been present the next morning when Manson criticized T. J. for backing down. DeCarlo described T. J. as "a really nice guy; his front was trying to be one of Charlie's boys, but he didn't have it inside." T. J. had gone along with Manson on everything up to this, but he told him, "I don't want to have nothing to do with snuffing people." A day or two later he "fled in the wind."

Q. "Who else got murdered up there? What about Shorty? Do you know anything about that?"

There was a long pause, then: "That was my ace in the hole."

Q. "How so?"

A. "I was going to save that for the last."

Q. "Well, might as well clear the thing up now. Has Charlie got something he can smear on you that—"

A. "No, no way at all. Nothing."

One thing did worry DeCarlo, however. In 1966 he had been convicted of a felony, smuggling marijuana across the Mexican border, a federal charge; he was currently appealing the sentence. He was also under indictment on two other charges: along with Al Springer and several other Straight Satans, he had been charged with selling a stolen motorcycle engine, which was a local charge, and giving false information while purchasing a firearm (using an alias and not disclosing that he had a prior felony conviction), which was federal. Manson was still on parole from a federal pen. "So what if they send me to the same place? I don't want to feel a shank in my back and find that little son of a bitch behind me."

Q. "Let me explain something to you, Danny, so you know where you stand. We're dealing with a guy here who we are pretty sure is responsible for about thirteen murders. Some of which you don't know about."

The figure thirteen was just a guess, but DeCarlo surprised them by saying, "I know about—I'm pretty sure he did Tate."

Q. "O.K., we've talked about the Panther, we've talked about Gary Hinman, we're going to talk about Shorty, and you think he did Tate, that's eight. Now, we've got five more. All right? Now, our opinion of Charlie is that he's got a little mental problem.

"But we're in no way going to jeopardize you or anyone else if, for no other reason, we don't want another murder. We're in business to stop murders. And in this business there's no sense in solving thirteen murders if somebody else is going to get killed. That just makes fourteen."

A. "I'm a nasty motorcycle rider."

Q. "I don't care what you are personally."

A. "The police's general opinion of me is nothing."

Q. "That's not my opinion."

A. "I'm not an outstanding citizen—"

Q. "As I told you the other day, Danny, you level with us, all the way, right down the line, no bullshitting—I'm not going to bullshit you, you're not going to bullshit me—we level with each other and I'll go out for you a hundred percent. And I mean it. So that you don't have to go to the joint."

Q. (*another detective*) "We've dealt with motorcycle riders before, and with all kinds of people. We've gone out on a limb to help them because they've helped us. We'll do our very best to make sure that nobody gets killed, whether he's a motorcycle rider or the best citizen in the world...

"Now tell us what you know about Shorty."

Early that same evening, November 17, 1969, two LAPD homicide officers, Sergeants Mossman and Brown, appeared at Sybil Brand Institute and asked to see one Ronnie Howard.

The interview was brief. They heard enough, however, to realize they were on to something big. Enough, too, to decide it wasn't the best idea to leave Ronnie Howard in the same dormitory with Susan Atkins. Before leaving Sybil Brand, they arranged to have Ronnie moved to an isolation unit. Then they drove back to Parker Center, anxious to tell the other detectives that they had "cracked the case."

Nielsen, Gutierrez, and McGann were still questioning DeCarlo about the murder of Shorty. They already knew something about it, even before talking to Springer and DeCarlo, since Sergeants Whiteley and Guenther had begun their own investigation into the "possible homicide" after talking to Kitty Lutesinger.

They knew "Shorty" was Donald Jerome Shea, a thirty-six-year-old male Causcasian who had worked at Spahn Ranch on and off for some fifteen years as a horse wrangler. Like most of the other cowboys who drifted in and out of Spahn's Movie Ranch, Shorty was just awaiting the day when some producer discovered he had all the potentials of a new John Wayne or Clint Eastwood. Whenever the prospect of any acting job materialized, Shorty would quit work and go in search of that ever elusive stardom. Which explained why, when in late August he disappeared from Spahn, no one thought too much about it. At first.

Kitty had also told LASO that Manson, Clem, Bruce, and possibly Tex had been involved in the killing, and that some of the girls in the Family had helped obliterate all traces of the crime. One thing they didn't know, and now asked Danny, was, "Why did they do it?"

A. "Because Shorty was going to old man Spahn and snitching. And Charlie didn't like snitches."

Q. "Just about the petty bullshit at the ranch?"

A. "That's right. Shorty was telling old man Spahn that he should put him in charge and he would clean everybody up." He would, in short order, run off Manson and his Family. Shorty, however, made a fatal mistake: he forgot that little Squeaky was not only George's eyes, she was also Charlie's ears.

There were other reasons, which Danny enumerated. Shorty had married a black topless dancer; Charlie "had a thing" about interracial marriages, and blacks. ("Charlie had two enemies," DeCarlo said, "the police and the niggers, in that order.") Charlie also suspected that Shorty had helped set up the August 16 raid on Spahn—Shorty had been "offed" about ten days later.* And there was the possibility, though this was strictly conjecture on DeCarlo's part, that Shorty had overheard something about some of the other murders.

Bruce Davis had told him about Shorty's murder, DeCarlo said. Several of the girls had also mentioned it, as had both Clem and Manson. Danny was unclear as to some of the details—how they had managed to catch Shorty off guard, and where—but as for the mode of death, he was more than graphic. "Like they were going to do Caesar," they went to the gunroom and picked up a sword and four German bayonets, the latter purchased from an Army surplus store for a buck each and honed to razor sharpness, then, getting Shorty off by himself, they "stuck him like carving up a Christmas turkey . . . Bruce said they cut him up in nine pieces. They cut his head off. Then they cut his arms off too, so there was no way they could possibly identify him. They were laughing about that."

After killing him, they covered the body with leaves (DeCarlo guessed, but was not sure, that this had occurred in one of the canyons behind the ranch buildings); some of the girls had helped dispose of Shorty's bloody clothing, his automobile, and other possessions; then "Clem came back the next day or that night and buried him good."

Q. (*unidentified voice*) "Can we break this up for about fifteen minutes, maybe send Danny up to get some coffee? There's been an accident and they want to talk to you guys."

Q. "Sure."

*The exact date of Shea's death still remains unknown. It is believed to have occurred on either the night of Monday, August 25, or Tuesday, August 26, 1969.

Q. "I'm going to send Danny up to the eighth floor. I want him back down here in fifteen minutes."

A. "I'll wait right here." Danny was not anxious to be seen wandering the halls of LAPD.

Q. "It won't take more than fifteen minutes. We'll close the door so nobody will know you're in here."

There had been no accident. Mossman and Brown had returned from Sybil Brand. As they related what they had heard, the fifteen minutes stretched to nearly forty-five. Although the Atkins-Howard conversations left many unanswered questions, the detectives were now convinced that the Tate and LaBianca cases had been "solved."* Susan Atkins had told Ronnie Howard details—the unpublished words written at the LaBianca residence, the lost knife at Tate—which only one of the killers could know. Lieutenants Helder (Tate) and LePage (LaBianca) were notified.

When the detectives returned to the interrogation room, they were in a lighthearted mood.

Q. "Now, when we left Shorty, he was in nine pieces and his head and arms were off . . ."

DeCarlo was not told what they had learned. But he must have sensed a change in the questioning. The matter of Shorty was quickly wrapped up. Tate was now the topic. Exactly why did Danny think Manson was involved?

Well, there were two incidents. Or maybe it was the same incident, Danny was not sure. Anyway, "they went out on one caper and they came back with seventy-five bucks. Tex was in on that. And he fucked up his foot, fucking somebody out of it. I don't know whether he put his lights out or not, but he got seventy-five bucks."

There were no calendars at Spahn Ranch, DeCarlo had told them earlier; no one paid much attention to what day it was. The one date everyone at the ranch remembered, however, was August 16, the day of the raid. It was before this.

Q. "How much before?"

A. "Oh, two weeks."

*As will become all too apparent, in this instance "solved" was a misstatement if ever there was one.

If DeCarlo's estimate was correct, this would also be before Tate. What was the other incident?

A. "They went out one night, everybody went but Bruce."

Q. "Who went?"

A. "Charlie, Tex, and Clem. Them three. O.K., the next morning—"

One of the detectives interrupted. Had he actually seen them leave? No, only the next morning— Another interruption: Did any of the girls go that night?

A. "No, I think— No, I am almost positive it was just them three that went."

Q. "Well, do you remember, were the rest of the girls there that night?"

A. "See, the girls were scattered all over the place, and there is no possible way that I could have kept track of who was there and who wasn't there . . ."

So it was possible the girls could have gone without DeCarlo's knowing about it. Now, what about the date?

This one Danny remembered, more or less, because he was rebuilding the engine on his bike and had to go into town to get a bearing. It was "around the ninth, tenth, or eleventh" of August. "And they split that night and they came back the next morning."

Clem was standing in front of the kitchen, DeCarlo said. Danny walked up to him and asked, "What'd you do last night?" Clem, according to Danny, smiled "that real stupid smile of his." Danny glanced back over his shoulder and saw that Charlie was standing behind him. He got the impression that Clem had been about to answer but that Charlie had signaled him to be quiet. Clem said something like "Don't worry about it, we did all right." At this point Charlie walked off. Before starting after him, Clem put his hand on Danny's arm and said, "We got five piggies." There was a great big grin on his face.

Clem told DeCarlo, "We got five piggies." Manson told Springer, "We knocked off five of them just the other night." Atkins confessed to Howard that she stabbed Sharon Tate and Voytek Frykowski. Beausoleil confessed to DeCarlo that he had stabbed Hinman. Atkins told

Howard that *she* had done the stabbing. Suddenly the detectives had a surfeit of confessors. So many that they were thoroughly confused as to who was involved in which homicides.

Skipping Hinman, which, after all, was the sheriff's case, and concentrating on Tate, they had two versions:

(1) DeCarlo felt that Charlie, Clem and Tex—without the help of any of the girls—had killed Sharon Tate and the others.

(2) Ronnie Howard understood Susan Atkins to say that she, two other girls (the names "Linda" and "Katie" had been mentioned, but whether they were involved in this particular homicide was unclear), plus "Charles," plus possibly one other man, had gone to 10050 Cielo Drive.

As for the LaBianca murders, all they knew was that there were "two girls and Charlie," that "Linda wasn't in on this one," and that Susan Atkins was somehow involved in that collective "we."

The detectives decided to try another approach—through the other girls at the ranch. But first they wanted to wrap up a few loose ends. What clothing had the three men been wearing? Dark clothing, DeCarlo replied. Charlie had on a black sweater, Levi's, moccasins; Tex was dressed similarly, he thought, though he may have been wearing boots, he wasn't sure; Clem wore Levi's and moccasins, too, plus an olive-drab field jacket. Had he noticed any blood on their clothes when he saw them the next morning? No, but then he hadn't been looking for any. Did he have any idea which vehicle they took? Sure, Johnny Swartz' '59 Ford; it was the only car working at that time. Any idea where it was now? It had been hauled off during the August 16 raid and, so far as Danny knew, was probably still in the impound garage in Canoga Park. Swartz was one of the ranch hands at Spahn, not a Family member, but he let them borrow his car. Any idea what Tex's true name was? "Charles" was his first name, Danny said; he'd seen the last name once, on a pink slip, but couldn't recall it. Was it "Charles Montgomery"? the detectives asked, using a name Kitty Lutesinger had supplied. No, that didn't sound familiar. What about Clem—does the name "Tufts" ring any bell? No, he'd never heard

Clem called that, but, "That boy that was found shot up in Topanga Canyon, the sixteen-year-old kid. Wasn't his name Tufts?" One of the detectives replied, "I don't know. That's the sheriff's case. We got so many murders now."

O.K., now about the girls. "How well did you know the broads out there?"

A. "Pretty well, man." [Laughter]

The detectives began going through the names the girls had used when arrested in the Spahn and Barker raids. And they immediately encountered problems. Not only had they used aliases when booked, they also used them at the ranch. And not a single alias but several, seemingly changing names like clothes, whenever the mood hit them. As a further complication, they even traded aliases.

As if these weren't problems enough, Danny provided another. He was extremely reluctant to admit that any of the girls might be capable of murder.

The guys were something else. Bobby, Tex, Bruce, Clem, any would kill, DeCarlo felt, if Charlie told him to. (All, it later turned out, had.)

Ella Jo Bailey was eliminated; she'd left Spahn Ranch before the murders. Mary Brunner and Sandra Good were out also; they'd been in jail both nights.

What about Ruth Ann Smack, aka Ruth Ann Huebelhurst? (These were booking names. Her true name was Ruth Ann Moorehouse, and she was known in the Family as "Ouisch." Danny knew this, but for personal reasons didn't bother to enlighten the detectives.)

Q. "What do you know about her?"

A. "She used to be one of my favorite sweeties."

Q. "Do you think she would have the guts to get into a cold-blooded murder?"

Danny hesitated a long time before answering. "You know, that little girl there is so sweet. What really made me sick to my stomach is when she came up one night, when I was up there in the desert, and she said, 'I can hardly wait to get my first pig.'

"Little seventeen-year-old! I looked on her like she was my daughter, just the sweetest little thing you would ever want to meet in your life. She was so beautiful and so sweet. And Charlie fucked her thinking around so much it turned your guts."

The date when she told DeCarlo this was determined to be about September 1. If she hadn't killed by then, she couldn't have been in on LaBianca or Tate. Eliminate Ruth Ann.

Ever know a Katie? Yeah, but he didn't know what her real name was. "I never knew anybody by their real name," DeCarlo said. Katie was an older broad, not a runaway. She was from down around Venice. His description of her was vague, except that she had so much hair on her body that none of the guys wanted to make it with her.

What about a Linda? She was a short broad, Danny said. But she didn't stay long, maybe only a month or so, and he didn't know much about her. She'd left by the time they raided Spahn Ranch.

When Sadie went out on "creepy-crawly" missions, did she carry any weapons? one of the detectives asked.

A. "She carried a little knife . . . They had a bunch of little hunting knives, Buck hunting knives."

Q. "Buck knives?"

A. "Buck knives, right . . ."

They now began firing specific questions at DeCarlo. Ever see any credit cards with an Italian name on them? Anybody ever talk about somebody who owned a boat? Ever hear anyone use the name "LaBianca"? Danny gave "No" answers to all.

What about glasses, anybody at Spahn wear them? "None of 'em wore glasses because Charlie wouldn't let 'em wear glasses." Mary Brunner had had several pairs; Charlie had broken them.

DeCarlo was shown some two-strand nylon rope. Ever see any rope like this up at Spahn? No, but he had seen some three-strand. Charlie had bought about 200 feet of it at the Jack Frost surplus store in Santa Monica, in June or July.

Was he sure about that? Sure he was sure; he'd been along when Charlie bought it. Later he'd coiled it so it wouldn't develop snags. It was the same as they used in the Coast Guard, on PT boats; he'd handled it hundreds of times.

Although DeCarlo was unaware of it, the Tate-Sebring rope was also three-strand.

Probably by prearrangement, the detectives began to lean on DeCarlo, adopting a tougher tone.

Q. "Did you ever caper with any of the guys?"

A. "Fuck no. No way at all. Ask any of the girls."

Q. "Did you have anything to do with Shorty's death?"

DeCarlo denied it, vehemently. Shorty had been his friend; besides, "I've got no balls for putting anybody's lights out." But there was just enough hesitation in his reply to indicate he was hiding something. Pressed, DeCarlo told them about Shorty's guns. Shorty had a matched pair of Colt .45s. He was always hocking, then reclaiming the pistols. In late August or early September—after Shorty had disappeared but supposedly before DeCarlo knew what had happened to him—Bruce Davis had given him Shorty's pawn tickets on the guns, in repayment for some money he owed DeCarlo. Danny had reclaimed the pistols. Later, learning that Shorty had been killed, he'd sold the guns to a Culver City shop for seventy-five dollars.

Q. "That puts you in a pretty shitty spot, you're aware of that?"

Danny was. And he got in even deeper when one of the detectives asked him if he knew anything about lime. When arrested, Mary Brunner was carrying a shopping list made up by Manson. "Lime" was one of the items listed. Any idea why Charlie would want some lime?

Danny recalled that Charlie had once asked him what to use "to decompose a body." He had told him lime worked best, because he had once used it to get rid of a cat that had died under a house.

Q. "Why did you tell him that?"

A. "No particular reason, he was just asking me."

Q. "What did he ask you?"

A. "Oh, the best way to ah, ah, you know, to get rid of a body real quick."

Q. "Did you ever think to say, 'Now what in the fuck makes you ask a question like that, Charlie?' "

A. "No, because he was nuts."

Q. "When did that conversation take place?"

A. "Right around, ah, right around the time Shorty disappeared."

It looked bad, and the detectives left it at that. Although privately they were inclined to accept DeCarlo's tale, suspecting, however, that although he probably had not taken part in the murder, he still knew more than he was telling, it gave them some additional leverage to try and get what they wanted.

They wanted two things.

Q. "Anybody left up at Spahn Ranch that knows you?"

A. "Not that I know of. I don't know who's up there. And I don't want to go up there to find out. I don't want nothing to do with the place."

Q. "I want to look around there. But I need a guide."

Danny didn't volunteer.

They made the other request straight out.

Q. "Would you be willing to testify?"

A. "*No, sir!*"

There were two charges pending against him, they reminded him. On the stolen motorcycle engine, "Maybe we can get it busted down to a lesser charge. Maybe we can go so far as to get it knocked off. As far as the federal thing is concerned, I don't know how much weight we can push on that. But here again we can try."

A. "If you try for me, that's fine. That's all I can ask of you."

If it came down to being a witness or going to jail—

DeCarlo hesitated. "Then when *he* gets out of jail—"

Q. "He isn't going to get out of jail on no first degree murder beef when you've got over five victims involved. If Manson was the guy that was in on the Tate murder. We don't know that for a fact yet. We've got a great deal of information that way."

A. "There's also a reward involved in that."

Q. "Yes, there is. Quite a bit of a reward. Twenty-five

grand. Not to say that one guy is going to get it, but even split that's a hell of a piece of cash."

A. "I could send my boy through military school with that."

Q. "Now, what do you think, would you be willing to testify against this group of people?"

A. "He's going to be sitting there looking at me, Manson is, isn't he?"

Q. "If you go to trial and testify, he is. Now, how scared of Manson are you?"

A. "I'm scared shitless. I'm petrified of him. He wouldn't hesitate for a second. If it takes him ten years, he'd find that little boy of mine and carve him to pieces."

Q. "You give that motherfucker more credit than he deserves. If you think Manson is some kind of a god that is going to break out of jail and come back and murder everybody that testified against him—"

But it was obvious DeCarlo didn't put that past Manson.

Even if he remained in jail, there were the others.

A. "What about Clem? Have you got him locked up?"

Q. "Yeah. Clem is sitting in the cooler up in Independence, with Charlie."

A. "What about Tex and Bruce?"

Q. "They're both out. Bruce Davis, the last I heard, sometime earlier this month, was in Venice."

A. "Bruce is down in Venice, huh? I'll have to watch myself . . . One of my club brothers said he spotted a couple of the girls down in Venice, too."

The detectives didn't tell DeCarlo that when Davis was last seen, on November 5, it was in connection with another death, the "suicide" of Zero. By this time LAPD had learned that Zero—aka Christopher Jesus, t/n John Philip Haught—had been arrested in the Barker raid. Earlier, in going through some photographs, DeCarlo had identified "Scotty" and "Zero" as two young boys from Ohio, who had been with the Family for a short time but "didn't fit in." One of the detectives had remarked, "Zero's no longer with us."

A. "What do you mean he's 'no longer with us'?"

Q. "He's among the dead."

A. *"Oh, shit, is he?"*

Q. "Yeah, he got a little too high one day and he was playing Russian roulette. He parked a bullet in his head."

While the detectives had apparently bought the story of Zero's death, as related by Bruce Davis and the others, Danny didn't, not for a minute.

No, Danny didn't want to testify.

The detectives left it at that. There was still time for him to change his mind. And, after all, they now had Ronnie Howard. They let Danny go, after making arrangements for him to call in the next day.

One of the detectives commented, after Danny had left but while the tape was still on, "I kind of feel like we've done a day's work."

The DeCarlo interview had lasted over seven hours. It was now past midnight on Tuesday, November 18, 1969. I was already asleep, unaware that in a few hours, as a result of a meeting between the DA and his staff that morning, I would be handed the job of prosecuting the Tate-LaBianca killers.

Part 3

THE INVESTIGATION—PHASE TWO

"No sense makes sense."
Charles Manson

November 18, 1969

By now the reader knows a great deal more about the Tate-LaBianca murders than I did on the day I was assigned that case. In fact, since large portions of the foregoing story have not been made public before this, the reader is an insider in a sense highly unusual in a murder case. And, in a way, I'm a newcomer, an intruder. The sudden switch from an unseen background narrator to a very personal account is bound to be a surprise. The best way to soften it, I suspect, would be to introduce myself; then, when we've got that out of the way, we'll resume the narrative together. This digression, though unfortunately necessary, will be as brief as possible.

A conventional biographical sketch would probably have read more or less as follows: Vincent T. Bugliosi, age thirty-five, Deputy District Attorney, Los Angeles, California. Born Hibbing, Minnesota. Graduate Hollywood High School. Attended the University of Miami on a tennis scholarship, B.A. and B.B.A. degrees. Deciding on the practice of law, attended UCLA, LL.B. degree, president graduating class 1964. Joined the Los Angeles County District Attorney's Office same year. Has tried a number of highly publicized murder cases—Floyd-Milton, Perveler-Cromwell, etc.—obtaining convictions in all. Has tried 104 felony jury trials, losing only one. In addition to his duties as deputy DA, Bugliosi is a professor of criminal law at Beverly School of Law, Los Angeles. Served as technical consultant and edited the scripts of two pilot films for Jack Webb's TV series "The D.A." Series star Robert Conrad patterned his part after the young prosecutor. Married. Two children.

That's probably about how it would read, yet it tells nothing about how I feel toward my profession, which is even more important.

"The primary duty of a lawyer engaged in public prosecution is not to convict, but to see that justice is done . . ."

Those words are from the old Canon of Ethics of the American Bar Association. I'd thought of them often during the five years I'd been a deputy DA. In a very real sense they had become my personal credo. If, in a given case, a conviction is justice, so be it. But if it is not, I want no part of it.

For far too many years the stereotyped image of the prosecutor has been either that of a right-wing, law-and-order type intent on winning convictions at any cost, or a stumbling, bumbling Hamilton Burger, forever trying innocent people, who, fortunately, are saved at the last possible minute by the foxy maneuverings of a Perry Mason.

I've never felt the defense attorney has a monopoly on concern for innocence, fairness, and justice. After joining the DA's office, I tried close to a thousand cases. In a great many I sought and obtained convictions, because I believed the evidence warranted them. In a great many others, in which I felt the evidence was insufficient, I stood up in court and asked for a dismissal of the charges, or requested a reduction in either the charges or the sentence.

The latter cases rarely make headlines. Only infrequently does the public learn of them. Thus the stereotype remains. Far more important, however, is the realization that fairness and justice have prevailed.

Just as I never felt the slightest compunction to conform to this stereotype, so did I rebel against another. Traditionally, the role of the prosecutor has been twofold: to handle the legal aspects of the case; and to present in court the evidence gathered by law-enforcement agencies. I never accepted these limitations. In past cases I always joined in the investigation—going out and interviewing witnesses myself, tracking down and developing new leads, often finding evidence otherwise overlooked. In some cases, this led to the release of a suspect. In others, to a conviction that otherwise might not have been obtained.

For a lawyer to do less than his utmost is, I strongly feel, a betrayal of his client. Though in criminal trials one tends to focus on the defense attorney and his client the accused, the prosecutor is also a lawyer, and he too has a client: the People. And the People are equally entitled to their day in court, to a fair and impartial trial, and to justice.

The Tate-LaBianca case was the farthest thing from my mind on the afternoon of November 18, 1969. I'd just completed a long trial and was on my way back to my office in the Hall of Justice when Aaron Stovitz, head of the Trials Division of the District Attorney's Office, one of the top trial lawyers in an office of 450 deputy district attorneys, grabbed me by the arm and, without a word of explanation, hurried me down the hall into the office of J. Miller Leavy, director of Central Operations.

Leavy was talking to two LAPD lieutenants I'd worked with on previous cases, Bob Helder and Paul LePage. Listening for a minute, I heard the word "Tate." Turning to Aaron, I asked, "Are *we* going to handle it?"

He nodded affirmatively.

My only comment was a low whistle.

Helder and LePage gave us a sketchy résumé of what Ronnie Howard had said. As a follow-up to Mossman and Brown's visit the previous night, two other officers had gone to Sybil Brand that morning and talked to Ronnie for a couple of hours. They had obtained considerably more detail, but there were still huge gaps in the story.

To say that the Tate and LaBianca cases had been "solved" at this point would be a gross overstatement. Obviously, in any murder case finding the killer is extremely important. But it's only a first step. Neither the finding, the arresting, nor the indicting of a defendant has evidentiary value and none are proof of guilt. Once the killer is identified, there remains the difficult (and sometimes insurmountable) problem of connecting him with the crime by strong, admissible evidence, then proving his guilt beyond a reasonable doubt, be it before a judge or a jury.

And as yet we hadn't even made the first step, much less the second. In talking to Ronnie Howard, Susan Atkins had implicated herself and "Charles," presumably meaning Charles Manson. But Susan had also said that others were involved, and we lacked their actual identities. This was on Tate. On LaBianca there was virtually no information.

One of the first things I wanted to do, after reviewing the Howard and DeCarlo statements, was to go to Spahn Ranch. Arrangements were made for me to go out the next morning with several of the detectives. I asked Aaron if he wanted to come along, but he couldn't make it.*

When I returned home late that afternoon and told my wife, Gail, that Aaron and I had been assigned the Tate case, she shared my excitement. But with reservations. She had been hoping that we could take a vacation. It had been months since I'd taken a full day off. Even when I was at home in the evenings, I was either reading transcripts, researching law, or preparing arguments. Although every day I made sure I spent some time with our two children, Vince, Jr., three, and Wendy, five, when I was on a big case I totally immersed myself in it. I promised Gail I'd try to take a few days off, but I honestly had to admit that it might be a while before I could do so.

At that time we were, fortunately, unaware that I would be living with the Tate-LaBianca cases for almost two years, averaging one hundred hours per week, rarely, if ever, getting to bed before 2 A.M. seven days per week. And that the few moments Gail, the kids, and I had together would be devoid of privacy, our home transformed into a fortress, a bodyguard not only living with us but accompanying me everywhere I went, following a threat by Charles Manson that he would "kill Bugliosi."

* Although Aaron was my superior in the office, we had been assigned the case as co-prosecutors, each of us having an equal say in its handling. Though neither of us could have foreseen that months later Aaron would be yanked off the case, leaving me to go it alone, I did realize from the start that owing to his other duties as head of the Trials Division his participation would be limited.

November 19-21, 1969

We'd picked a hell of a day for a search. The wind was incredible. By the time we reached Chatsworth, it was almost buffeting us off the road.

It wasn't a long drive, well under an hour. From the Hall of Justice in downtown Los Angeles it's about thirty miles to Chatsworth. Going north on Topanga Canyon Boulevard past Devonshire for about two miles, we made a sharp left onto Santa Susana Pass Road. Once heavily traveled but in recent years bypassed for a faster freeway, the two-lane road winds upward a mile or two. Then, suddenly, around a bend and to the left, there it was, Spahn's Movie Ranch.

Its ramshackle Main Street was less than twenty yards from the highway, in plain view. Wrecked automobile and truck bodies littered the area. There wasn't a sign of life.

There was an unreality to the place, accentuated by the roaring wind and the appearance of total desertion, but even more so by the knowledge, if the Atkins-Howard story was true, of what had begun and ended here. A run-down movie set, off in the middle of nowhere, from which dark-clad assassins would venture out at night, to terrorize and kill, then return before dawn to vanish into the surroundings. It might have been the plot of a horror film, except that Sharon Tate and at least eight other real human beings were now dead.

We pulled off onto the dirt road, stopping in front of the Long Branch Saloon. In addition to myself, there were Lieutenant Helder and Sergeant Calkins of the Tate team; Sergeant Lee of SID; Sergeants Guenther, Whiteley, and William Gleason from LASO; and our guide, Danny DeCarlo. Danny had finally agreed to accompany us, but only on one condition: that we handcuff him. That way, if any members of the Family were still around, they wouldn't think he was voluntarily "flapping to the fuzz."

Though the sheriff's deputies had been to the ranch before, we needed DeCarlo for a specific purpose: to point out the areas where Manson and the Family target-practiced. The object of our search: any .22 caliber bullets and/or shell casings.

But first I wanted to obtain George Spahn's permission to search the ranch. Guenther pointed out his shack, which was to the right and apart from the Western set. We knocked and a voice, that of a young girl, said, "Come right on in."

It was as if every fly in the area had taken shelter there during the storm. Eighty-one-year-old George Spahn was sitting in a decaying armchair, wearing a Stetson and dark glasses. In his lap was a Chihuahua, at his feet a cocker spaniel. A hippie girl of about eighteen was fixing his lunch, while a transistor radio, tuned to a cowboy station, blared "Young Love" by Sonny James.

It seemed as staged as the setting itself: according to DeCarlo, Manson called his girls "young loves."

Because of Spahn's near blindness, Calkins handed him his badge to feel. Once we had identified ourselves, Spahn seemed to relax. Asked for permission to search, he magnanimously replied, "It's my ranch and you're welcome to search it any time you want to, day or night, and as often as you like." I explained his legal rights. Under the law, no search warrant was required, only his permission. If he did give permission, however, it might be necessary at some later date for him to testify to this in court. Spahn still agreed.

There was no mention of Manson and his Family. But Spahn must have known that they were in some way the reason for our being there. Although on other occasions I would interview George at length, our conversation at this time was brief and confined to the search.

Once we went back outside, people began appearing from almost every building. There must have been ten to fifteen, most of them young, most in hippie-type clothes, although a few appeared to be ranch hands. How many, if any, were actual members of the Family we didn't know.

While looking around, I heard some odd sounds coming from a doghouse. Leaning down and looking in, I saw two dogs and, crouched in the corner, a toothless, white-haired old woman of about eighty. I later checked with one of the ranch hands to see if she needed help, but he said she was happy where she was.

It was a very strange place.

About a hundred yards behind the main cluster of buildings there was a drop down to a creek, then, beyond it, the hills rose up and became a part of the Santa Susana mountain range. Rocky, brush covered, the area looked far more rugged than it actually was. I wondered how many times as a boy I'd seen this scene in B-grade cowboy films. According to Lutesinger and DeCarlo, it was here, in the canyons and gullies behind the ranch, and across the road, in Devil's Canyon, that the Family hid out from the police. Here, too, somewhere in this area, if the various accounts were correct, were the remains of Donald "Shorty" Shea.

Charlie's favorite firing spot, DeCarlo said, was in the creek bed, well out of sight from the road. As targets he used fence posts and a trash can. Under the direction of Sergeant Lee, we began searching. Though no shell casings had been found at 10050 Cielo Drive—the Buntline being a revolver, which doesn't automatically eject its shell casings—we wanted to collect both in case the gun or additional evidence was found.

While we were searching the creek bed, I kept thinking about George Spahn, alone and almost defenseless in his blindness. I asked, "Anybody bring a tape recorder?" Calkins had; it was in the back of his car. "Let's go back and get Spahn's consent on tape," I said. "Between now and the time we go to trial, I don't want some s.o.b. putting a knife to Spahn's throat, forcing him to say he didn't give us permission." We went back and taped Spahn's consent. It was for his protection as well as our own; knowing the tape existed could be discouragement.

DeCarlo indicated another area, about a quarter of a mile up one of the canyons, where Charlie and the men sometimes target-practiced. We found a number of bullets and shell casings there. Because of the wind and dust, the search was less thorough than I'd hoped for; however, Sergeant Lee promised to return at a later date and see what he could find.

Altogether, that day we found approximately sixty-eight .22 caliber bullets (approximate because some were fragments rather than whole slugs) and twenty-two shell casings of the same caliber. Lee put them in envelopes, noting where and when found, and took them back to the police lab with him.

While looking around the corral area, I spotted some white nylon rope, but it was two-strand, not three.

Guenther and Whiteley had made their own find, in Danny DeCarlo. That afternoon they interviewed him on the Hinman murder and Beausoleil's confession. The only problem was that the Beausoleil trial had been going on for a week now, and both the prosecution and defense had rested.

Against the objections of Beausoleil's attorney, a continuance was obtained until the following Monday, at which time the prosecution hoped to reopen its case to introduce the confession.

It was agreed that if DeCarlo testified in the Beausoleil trial, LASO would drop the motorcycle engine theft charge against him.

On my return to the Hall of Justice there was a meeting in the office of the then Assistant District Attorney, Joseph Busch. Present in addition to Busch, Stovitz, and myself from the DA's Office were Lieutenant Paul LePage (LaBianca) and Sergeant Mike McGann (Tate) representing LAPD.

The police wanted to wrap up the case, Lieutenant LePage informed us. The public pressure on LAPD to solve these murders was unbelievable. Every time Chief Edward M. Davis encountered a reporter, he was asked, "What, if anything, is happening on Tate?"

LAPD wanted to offer Susan Atkins immunity, in exchange for telling what she knew about the murders.

I was in total disagreement. "If what she told Ronnie Howard is true, Atkins personally stabbed to death Sharon

Tate, Gary Hinman, and who knows how many others! *We don't give that gal anything!*"

Chief Davis wanted to rush the case to the grand jury, LePage said. But before that he wanted to break the news that we had caught the killers in a big press conference.

"We don't even *have* a case to take to the grand jury," I told LePage. "We're not even sure who the killers are, or if they're free or in custody. All we have is a good lead, but we're getting there. Let's see if, on our own, we can get enough evidence to nail all of them. If we can't, then, as a last resort—a very, very last resort—we can turn to Atkins."

I could sympathize with LAPD; the media were blasting the department almost daily. On the other hand, it would be nothing compared to the public response if we let Susan Atkins walk off scot-free. I couldn't forget Susan describing how it felt to taste Sharon Tate's blood: "Wow, what a trip!"

LePage was firm; LAPD wanted to make a deal. I conferred with Busch and Stovitz; they were far less adamant than I. Against my very strong objections, Busch told LePage that the DA's Office would be willing to settle for a second degree murder plea for Atkins.

Susan Atkins would be offered a deal. The precise terms, or whether she would even accept them, remained unknown.

At eight that night, the citizens of Los Angeles still thinking that the Tate-LaBianca killers were completely unknown, two cars sped out of Los Angeles, their destination the last home of the Manson Family: Death Valley.

It seemed more than ironic that, following the murders, Manson had chosen as his refuge a place so aptly named.

Sergeants Nielsen, Sartuchi, and Granado were in one car, Sergeants McGann, Gene Kamadoi, and I were in the other. We broke a few speed limits along the way, arriving in Independence, California, at 1:30 A.M.

Independence, seat of Inyo County, is not a large town. The county itself, though second largest in the state, has less than 16,000 residents, just over one per square mile.

If one were looking for a hideaway, he could find few better.

We checked into the Winnedumah Hotel for what amounted to little more than a long nap. When I got up at 5:30, the temperature had dropped below zero. I slipped my clothes on over my pajamas and was still cold.

Before leaving Los Angeles, I had telephoned Frank Fowles, Inyo County DA, and we had arranged to meet at a nearby café at 6 A.M. Fowles, his deputy Buck Gibbens, and their investigator Jack Gardiner were already there. The three men were, I would soon learn, very conscientious; the help they would give us in the months ahead would be considerable. At the moment they were also very excited. Unexpectedly, they were in the middle of one of the most publicized murder cases in modern history, the Tate case. Then, with puzzled looks, they'd glance across the table at the big-city prosecutor, pajamas sticking out of his cuffs.

Fowles told me that although they had seized some of Manson's belongings during the October raid on Barker Ranch, a number of things remained there, including an old school bus, which was littered with clothing and other items. I suggested that before leaving Independence we obtain a search warrant for the ranch that specifically mentioned the bus.

This caught Fowles by surprise. I explained that if we did find evidence, and wished to use it in a trial, we didn't want it suppressed just because someone suddenly appeared with a pink slip saying, "I'm the real owner of the bus. I only loaned it to Charlie, and you didn't get my permission."

Fowles understood that. It was only, he explained cryptically, that they didn't do things quite that way in Inyo County. We returned to his office and, after waiting for the typist to come to work, I dictated the warrant.

It was necessary to state exactly what we were looking for. Among the items I enumerated were: a .22 caliber revolver; knives and other weapons; rope; wire cutters; wallet, driver's license, and credit cards belonging to Rosemary LaBianca; motor plates to any vehicle; any male and/or female clothing, including footwear.

It was also necessary that I cite the crime—187 PC, murder—and the suspected perpetrators—"tentatively believed to be CHARLES MANSON, CLEM TUFTS, CHARLES MONTGOMERY, SADIE GLUTZ, and one or more additional females." The information was based on the testimony of two "untested informants," whom I did not name but who were Ronnie Howard and Danny DeCarlo.

When typed, the warrant ran to sixteen pages. It was an impressive document, the evidence cited therein more than sufficient to obtain a search warrant. Only I was aware how weak our case actually was.

With McGann and me tagging along, Fowles took the warrant to the office of Judge John P. McMurray. The white-haired jurist was, I guessed, in his seventies; he told us he was near retirement.

A search warrant! Judge McMurray looked at it with amusement. This was the first one he had seen in eighteen years, he told us. In Inyo, he explained, men are men. If you knock on a door and the people inside don't want to let you in, you assume they are hiding something, and bust the door in. A search warrant indeed! But he read and signed it.*

The trip to Barker Ranch would take three hours, leaving us little more than an hour to search before the sun set. En route Fowles told me some of the things he had learned about the Manson Family.† The first few members—in effect, a scouting party—had appeared in the area in the fall of 1968. Since you have to be somewhat different to want to live on the edge of Death Valley, residents of the area had developed a tolerance for people who elsewhere would have been considered odd types. The hippies were no

*In 1971, California Governor Ronald Reagan arranged to have Judge McMurray taken out of retirement to try the Angela Davis case. The defense challenged him for cause.

†Exact dates, details, quotes from the investigating officers, etc. I would obtain the following day when going over reports of the various law-enforcement agencies.

When booked, almost all the Family members used aliases. In a number of cases their true names were not known until much later. To avoid confusing the reader as much as I was confused at the time, true names and most-used aliases have been inserted in brackets.

stranger than others who passed through—prospectors, desert rats, chasers after legendary lost mines. There were only a few minor brushes with the authorities—the girls were advised to desist from panhandling in Shoshone, and one made the mistake of giving a marijuana cigarette to a fifteen-year-old girl, who just happened to be the sheriff's niece—until September 9, 1969, when National Park Rangers discovered that someone had attempted to burn a Michigan loader, a piece of earth-moving equipment that was parked in the race-track area of Death Valley National Monument. It appeared a senseless act of vandalism. Automobile tracks leading away from the area were determined to belong to a Toyota. Several persons recalled seeing the hippies driving a red Toyota and a dune buggy. On September 21, Park Ranger Dick Powell spotted a 1969 red Toyota in the Hail and Hall area. The four females and one male who were riding in it were questioned but not detained. Powell later ran a license check, learning that the plates on the Toyota belonged to another vehicle. On September 24, Powell returned to look for the group, but they had gone. On September 29, Powell, accompanied by California Highway Patrolman James Pursell, decided to check out Barker Ranch. They found two young girls there, but no vehicles. As they had found standard in their contacts with this group, the girls gave vague, uncommunicative answers to their questions. As the officers were leaving the area, they encountered a truck driven by Paul Crockett, forty-six, a local miner. With him was Brooks Poston, eighteen, who had previously been a member of the hippie band but was now working for Crockett. On hearing that there were two girls at the ranch, Crockett and Poston appeared apprehensive and, when questioned, finally admitted that they feared for their lives.

Powell and Pursell decided to accompany them back to Barker. The two girls had vanished, but the officers presumed they were still nearby, probably watching them. They began questioning Crockett and Poston.

The officers had come looking for arson suspects, and a possible stolen vehicle. They found something totally unexpected. From Pursell's report: "The interview resulted in some of the most unbelievable and fantastic information we had ever heard: tales of drug use, sex orgies, the actual attempt to re-create the days of Rommel and the Desert Corps by tearing over the countryside by night in numerous dune buggies, the stringing of field phones around the area for rapid communication, the opinion of the leader that he is Jesus Christ and seemed to be trying to form a cult of some sort . . ."

The surprises weren't over. Before leaving Barker, Powell and Pursell decided to check out some draws back of the ranch. To quote Powell: "In doing so we stumbled into a group of seven females, all nude or partially so, hiding behind various clumps of sagebrush." They saw one male, but he ran away when they approached. They questioned the girls but received no useful information. In searching the area, the officers found the red Toyota and a dune buggy, carefully camouflaged with tarps.

The officers had a problem. Because of the Panamint mountain range, they couldn't use their police radio. They decided to leave and return later with more men. Before departing, they removed several parts from the engine of the Toyota, rendering it inoperative; the dune buggy had no engine, so they weren't concerned with it.

They would later learn that "as soon as we left, the suspects pulled a complete Volkswagen engine from under a pile of brush, put it in the disabled dune buggy, and drove off within two hours."

A check on the two vehicles revealed "wants" on both. The Toyota had been rented from a Hertz agency in Encino, a town near Los Angeles, on a credit card stolen in a residential burglary. The dune buggy had been stolen off a used-car lot only three days before Powell and Pursell saw it.

On the night of October 9, officers from the California Highway Patrol, the Inyo County Sheriff's Office, and National Park rangers assembled near Barker for a massive raid on the ranch, to commence the following morning.

At about 4 A.M., as several of the officers were proceeding down one of the draws some distance from the ranch, they spotted two males asleep on the ground. Between them was a sawed-off shotgun. The two, Clem Tufts [t/n Steve Grogan] and Randy Morglea [t/n Hugh Rocky

Todd], were placed under arrest. Though the officers were unaware of it, the pair had been stalking human game: Stephanie Schram and Kitty Lutesinger, two seventeen-year-old girls who had fled the ranch the previous day.

Another male, Robert Ivan Lane [aka Soupspoon], was apprehended on a hill overlooking the ranch. Lane had been acting as lookout but had fallen asleep. There was still another lookout post, this one a very well disguised dugout, its tin roof hidden by brush and dirt, on a hill south of the ranch. The officers had almost passed it when they saw a female emerge from the brush, squat, and urinate, then disappear back into the bushes. While two officers covered the entrance with their rifles, one climbed above the dugout and dropped a large rock on the tin roof. The occupants rushed out. Apprehended were: Louella Maxwell Alexandria [t/n Leslie Van Houten, aka Leslie Sankston]; Marnie Kay Reeves [t/n Patricia Krenwinkel]; and Manon Minette [t/n Catherine Share, aka Gypsy].

Those inside the ranch house were caught unawares, and offered no resistance. They were: Donna Kay Powell [t/n Susan Denise Atkins, aka Sadie Mae Glutz]; Elizabeth Elaine Williamson [t/n Lynette Fromme, aka Squeaky]; and Linda Baldwin [t/n Madaline Cottage, aka Little Patty.]

Other members of the raiding party surrounded nearby Myers Ranch, where the group had also been staying, arresting: Sandra Collins Pugh [this was her married name; her maiden name was Sandra Good, aka Sandy]; Rachel Susan Morse [t/n Ruth Ann Moorehouse, aka Ouisch]; Mary Ann Schwarm [t/n Diane Von Ahn]; and Cydette Perell [t/n Nancy Pitman, aka Brenda McCann.]

A total of ten females and three males were arrested during this first sweep of the Barker Ranch area. They ranged in age from sixteen to twenty-six, with the average nineteen or twenty. Two babies were also found: Zezozose Zadfrack Glutz, age one year, whose mother was Susan Atkins; and Sunstone Hawk, age one month, whose mother was Sandra Good. Both were badly sunburned. Mrs. Powell, wife of ranger Dick Powell, who had been brought along as matron, took care of them.

A search of the area revealed a number of hidden vehicles, mostly dune buggies, mostly stolen; a mailbag with a .22 Ruger single-shot pistol inside, also stolen; a number of knives; and caches of food, gasoline, and other supplies. Also found were more sleeping bags than people, indicating that there might be others still in the area.

The officers decided to take the prisoners into Independence and book them, then make a surprise raid at a later date, in case the others returned.

The strategy paid off. The second raid occurred on October 12, two days after the first. CHP officer Pursell and two Park rangers arrived in the area before their support and were hiding in the brush, waiting for the others, when they saw four males walk from one of the washes to the ranch house and enter. Pursell spotted sheriff's deputy Don Ward of the backup unit approaching in the distance. It was already after 6 P.M., the dusk rapidly becoming dark. Not wanting to risk a gunfight at night, Pursell decided to act. While Powell covered the front of the building, Pursell drew his gun and, to quote from his report, "I quickly moved to the back door, flung it open, and making as much use of the wall on the left of the doorway as possible, I ordered all occupants to remain still and place their hands on their heads."

The group, most of whom had been sitting around the kitchen table, were ordered outside, lined up, and searched. There were three females: Dianne Bluestein [t/n Dianne Lake, aka Snake]; Beth Tracy [t/n Collie Sinclair]; and Sherry Andrews [t/n Claudia Leigh Smith]. Plus four males: Bruce McGregor Davis [aka Bruce McMillan]; Christopher Jesus [t/n John Philip Haught, aka Zero, who in less than a month would be shot to death while allegedly playing Russian roulette]; Kenneth Richard Brown [aka Scott Bell Davis, Zero's partner from Ohio]; and one Lawrence Bailey [aka Larry Jones.]

There was no sign of the group's leader, Charles Manson. Pursell decided to recheck the house. It was completely dark now. However, a homemade candle was burning in a glass mug on the table, and, taking that, he began searching the rooms. On entering the bathroom, "I was forced to move the candle around quite a bit, as it made a very poor light. I lowered the candle toward the hand basin, and small cupboard below, and saw long hair hanging out of the top of the cupboard, which was partially open." It seemed impossible that a person could get into such a small space, but, without Pursell's having to say anything, "a figure began to emerge from the tiny cupboard. After I recovered from the initial shock, I advised the subject to continue out and not make any false moves. As he emerged, he made a comment, more or less in a humorous vein, about being glad to get out of that cramped space.

"The subject was dressed entirely in buckskins, much differently than all the others we had found . . . I asked the subject who he was. He immediately replied, 'Charlie Manson.' He was taken to the back door and turned over to the officers outside."

On re-entering the house, Pursell found still another male, who was just emerging from the bedroom. He was David Lee Hamic [aka Bill Vance, an ex-con with more aliases than Manson.] Pursell noted the time: 6:40 P.M.

None of the suspects were armed, although several sheath knives were found on the kitchen table.

The prisoners were handcuffed and, hands on heads, walked single file toward Sourdough Springs, where the officers had left two pickups. En route they encountered two more females driving a car loaded with groceries. Also placed under arrest were: Patti Sue Jardin [t/n Catherine Gillies], and Sue Bartell [aka Country Sue] All the suspects were loaded in the back of one pickup, the second following immediately behind to provide illumination. As they neared the Lotus Mine area, about three miles from Barker, Manson told the officers that he had left his pack there, near the side of the road. Pursell: "He asked us to stop and pick it up, which we agreed to do; however, we could not locate it by his directions, and we refused to let him loose to search himself as he requested."

On the way to Independence, Manson told Pursell and Ward that the blacks were going to take over the country and that he and his group only wanted to find a quiet, peaceful place away from the conflict. But the establishment, as represented by the police, wouldn't let them alone. He also told them that they, being both cops and white, were in deep trouble and should escape to the desert or somewhere while they still had the chance.

Also during the ride, again according to Pursell, "two things happened which indicated to me the leadership exerted over the group by subject Manson. At least twice Charlie made statements that would cause the others to say 'amen' two or three times in unison. Also, a few times when the others would become involved in whispered, giggly conversations, Charlie would simply look at them and immediately they would fall silent.

"The amazing part of the stare," Pursell noted, "was how obvious the results were without a word being spoken."

On arriving in Independence, the suspects were charged with grand theft auto, arson, and various other offenses. The leader of the Family was fingerprinted, photographed, and booked as "MANSON, CHARLES M., aka JESUS CHRIST, GOD."

According to Frank Fowles, although all but three of the eleven vehicles recovered were stolen, there was insufficient evidence to link most of the group with the thefts, and after a few days more than half of those arrested were released. Though most had left the area, two of the girls, Squeaky and Sandy, had rented a motel room and were staying in Independence, so they could run errands for Manson and the others still in custody.

I asked Fowles if he knew why the group had come to the area in the first place. He told me that one of the girls, Cathy Gillies, was the granddaughter of the woman who owned Myers Ranch. The Family had apparently camped there first, then moved to nearby Barker. After the raid a sheriff's deputy interviewed Mrs. Arlene Barker, who was living at Indian Ranch in the Panamint Valley. She told him that about a year ago Manson had visited her, asking permission to camp at Barker Ranch. Like George Spahn, Mrs. Barker presumed there were only a few people and that they intended to stay only a few days. On this visit Manson gave her a gold record which had been presented to the Beach Boys, commemorating one million dollars in sales of their LP "The Beach Boys Today." Manson told her that he was the composer or arranger for the group. Manson had contacted her again, two or three weeks before the October raid, wanting to buy Barker Ranch. She told him she wanted cash; Manson said he'd see her again when he had it.

Apparently Manson felt that if he actually owned the property he would have fewer problems with local law-enforcement agencies.

I was unaware until much later that Manson supposedly had an alternate plan, to get control of Myers Ranch, which called for murdering Cathy's grandmother, and that the plan had been frustrated by something very simple and commonplace: while en route to her home, the three killers he'd chosen had a flat tire.

I asked Fowles about the evidence recovered in the raids and subsequent searches. Were any of the knives Buck brand? Yes, several. Any rope? No. What about wire cutters? Yes, there was a big red pair; they'd found them in the back of what they later learned was Manson's personal, or command, dune buggy. Aside from the Ruger .22 and Clem's shotgun, any other firearms? Not one, Fowles said. In none of the searches did the officers turn up the machine guns, shotguns, rifles, pistols, and large stores of ammunition Crockett, Poston, and others said the Family had.

Throughout the trials that followed, we would remain very aware that those members of the Family still at large probably had access to a sizable cache of arms and ammunition.

Barker Ranch was located in Golar Wash, one of seven dry washes in the Panamint range, approximately twenty-two miles southeast of Ballarat. He had been all over the country, Fowles told me; those dry washes comprised the roughest terrain he had ever seen; we'd have to walk much of it, he said, otherwise our heads would bounce through the roof of the four-wheel-drive jeep Fowles had chosen for the trip.

"Ah, come on, Frank," I said, "it can't be that rough."

It was. The washes were extremely narrow and rock-strewn. Going up them, we'd frequently gain one foot, then with an angry screech of rubber, slide back two. You could smell the tires burning. Finally, Fowles and I got out of the vehicle and walked in front of it, removing boulders as McGann drove forward, foot after foot. It took us two hours to travel five miles.

I asked Fowles to have photographs taken of the washes. I wanted to show the jury how isolated and remote an area the killers had chosen for their hiding place. Circumstantial evidence, a tiny speck, but of such specks, one after another, are strong cases made.

No one would have chosen to live at either Barker or Myers Ranch, which were about a quarter of a mile apart, except for one thing: there was water. There was even a swimming pool at Barker, though, like the stone ranch house and outlying shacks, it was in disrepair. The house was small—living room, bedroom, kitchen, bathroom. I also wanted photos of the cabinet under the sink where Manson hid. It measured 3 by 1½ by 1½ feet. I could see why Pursell was so surprised.

When I saw the large school bus, I couldn't believe Manson had brought it up one of the washes. He hadn't, Fowles told me; he'd driven it in over the road on the Las Vegas side. Even that had been an ordeal, and the condition of the bus showed it. It was a battered green and white. On the side was an American flag decal with the slogan AMERICA—LOVE IT OR LEAVE IT. While Sartuchi and the others searched the house, I went to work on the abandoned bus.

The placement of the warrant took some thought. It had to be left in sight. However, if it was, anyone could come along and remove it. I didn't want a defense attorney contending we hadn't fulfilled the requirements of the search. I put it on one of the racks just under the roof of the bus. You *could* see it, if you looked up.

At least a foot of clothing was piled on the floor. I later learned that wherever the Family stayed, they kept a community clothing pile. When an item was needed, they'd root through the pile until they found it. I got down on my hands and knees and began rooting too. I was looking for two things in particular: clothing with bloodstains, and boots. A bloody boot-heel print had been found on the front porch of the Tate residence. There was a small mark, a little indentation, in the heel that I was hoping we could match up. Although I found several boots, none had such a mark. And when Joe Granado applied the benzidine test to the clothing, the results were uniformly negative. I had all the clothing taken back to L.A. anyway, hoping SID might come up with something in the lab.

There were eight to ten magazines in the bus, half of which were *National Geographics*. Looking through them, I noticed something curious: all dated from 1939 to 1945 and all had articles on Hitler. One also had photographs of Rommel and his Desert Corps.

But that was about all we found. Our search appeared to have yielded little, if anything, of evidentiary value. However, I was anxious to go through the items picked up in the raids.

On the way back to Independence we stopped in Lone Pine. While I was nursing a beer with the officers, Sartuchi remarked that he and Patchett had interviewed Manson in Independence some weeks earlier, questioning him about the Tate as well as the LaBianca murders. The following day when I called Lieutenant Helder, I mentioned this, thinking he probably had a report on the interview. Helder was amazed; he had no idea anyone from LAPD had ever talked to Manson. This was my first indication that the Tate and LaBianca detectives hadn't exactly been working hand in glove.

Helder did have some news. It wasn't good. Sergeant Lee had run a ballistics comparison on the .22 caliber bullets we'd found at Spahn: all were negative to those recovered at 10050 Cielo Drive.

I wasn't about to give up that easily. I still wanted a much more thorough search of Spahn Ranch.

We stayed at the Winnedumah again that night. Up early the next morning, I walked to the courthouse. I'd forgotten what fresh air smelled like. That trees, grass, have scents. In L.A. there are no smells, just smog. A couple of blocks from the courthouse I saw two young girls, one carrying a baby. It was a wild guess but I asked, "Are you Sandy and Squeaky?" They admitted they were. I identified myself and said that I would like to talk to them in the District Attorney's office at 1 P.M. They said they would come if I would buy them some candy. I said I would.

In the DA's office, Fowles opened his files and gave me everything he had on the Manson Family. Sartuchi set to work photocopying.

In going through the documents, I spotted a reference to Crockett and Poston: "Inyo County Deputy Sheriff Don Ward talked to the two miners in Shoshone and has their entire conversation recorded." I wanted to interview the pair, but it would save time if I heard the tape first, so I asked McGann to contact Ward and get it for me.

There was also an October 2, 1969, California Highway Patrol report in which it was stated: "Deputy Dennis Cox has F.I.R. card on suspect Charles Montgomery, 23 years of age (dob 12-2-45)." Field Interrogation Reports are three-by-five cards that are made whenever a person is stopped and questioned. I wanted to see that card. We still knew very little about Tex, who hadn't been arrested in either the Spahn or Barker raids.

After going through the large stack of documents, I started on the evidence seized in the October 10-12 raid. I had Granado test the knives for blood: negative. The wire cutters were large and heavy. It would have been difficult to shinny up a telephone pole with them; still, maybe they were the only pair available. I gave them to the officers so SID could make comparison cuts on the Tate telephone wires. Boots, but no discernible heel mark; I put them aside for SID. I checked the labels on all the clothing, noting that a number of the women's garments, though now filthy, came from expensive shops. I had them taken to L.A. for analysis. I also wanted Winifred Chapman and Susan Struthers to look at them, to see if any of the items might have been the property of Sharon Tate, Abigail Folger, or Rosemary LaBianca.

Squeaky and Sandy kept the appointment. I'd done a little checking before talking to them. Though the information was sketchy, I knew that both had been born in Southern California, and had come from fairly well-to-do families. Squeaky's parents lived in Santa Monica; her father was an aeronautical engineer. Sandy's parents had divorced and remarried; her father was a San Diego stockbroker. According to DeCarlo, when Sandy joined the Family, sometime early in 1968, she had some $6,000 in stocks, which she sold, giving the money to Manson. She and her baby were now on welfare. Both girls had started college, then dropped out, Squeaky attending El Camino Junior College in Torrance, Sandy the University of Oregon and San Francisco State. Squeaky had been one of the earliest members of the Family, I later learned, casting her lot with Manson just months after he got out of prison in 1967.

They were the first Family members I had talked to, other than DeCarlo, who was a fringe member at best, and I was immediately struck by their expressions. They seemed to radiate inner contentment. I'd seen others like this—true believers, religious fanatics—yet I was both shocked and impressed. Nothing seemed to faze them. They smiled almost continuously, no matter what was said. For them all the questions had been answered. There was no need to search any more, because they had found the truth. And their truth was "Charlie is love."

Tell me about this love, I asked them. Do you mean this in the male-female sense? Yes, that too, they answered, but that was only a part. More all-encompassing? Yes, but "Love is love; you can't define it."

Did Charlie teach you this? I asked, genuinely curious. Charlie did not need to teach them, they said. Charlie only turned them around so they could look at themselves and see the love within. Did they believe that Charlie was Jesus Christ? They only smiled enigmatically, as if sharing a secret no one else could possibly understand.

Although Squeaky was twenty-one and Sandy twenty-five, there was a little-girl quality to them, as if they hadn't aged but had been retarded at a certain stage in their childhood. Little girls, playing little-girl games. Including murder? I wondered.

Is your love for Charlie, say, different from your love for George Spahn? I asked Squeaky. No, love is love, Squeaky said; it's all the same. But she'd hesitated just a moment before answering, giving the impression that though these were the words she was supposed to say, there was heresy in them, in denying that Charlie was special. Perhaps to overcome this, she told me about her relationship with George Spahn. She was in love with George, Squeaky said; if he asked her to marry him, she would. George was, she went on, a beautiful person inside. He was also, she added, in an obvious attempt to shock me, very good in bed. She was quite graphic.

"I'm not that interested in your sex life, Squeaky," I told her. "But I am very, very interested in what you know about the Tate, LaBianca, Hinman, and other murders."

Neither expression changed in the slightest. The smiles remained. They knew nothing about any crimes. All they knew about was love.

I talked to them for a long time, asking specific questions now, but still getting pat answers. On asking where they were on a certain date, for example, they'd reply, "There is no such thing as time." The answers were both non-responsive and a guard. I wanted to get past that guard, to learn what they really felt. I couldn't.

I sensed something else. Each was, in her own way, a pretty girl. But there was a sameness about them that was much stronger than their individuality. I'd notice it again later that afternoon, in talking to other female members of the Family. Same expressions, same patterned responses, same tone of voice, same lack of distinct personality. The realization came with a shock; they reminded me less of human beings than Barbie dolls.

Looking at Sandy's almost beatific smile, I remembered something that Frank Fowles had told me, and a chill ran up and down my spine.

While she was still in jail in Independence, Sandy had been overheard talking to one of the other girls in the Family. Sandy had told her, "I've finally reached the point where I can kill my parents."

Leslie, Ouisch, Snake, Brenda, Gypsy—Frank Fowles arranged to have them brought over from the jail, where they were still being held on charges stemming from the

Barker raid. Like Squeaky and Sandy, they accepted my "bribe," candy and gum, and told me nothing of importance. Their answers were as if rehearsed; often they gave identical responses.

If we were to get any of them to talk, I knew, we would have to separate them. There was a cohesion, a kind of cement, that held them together. A part of it was undoubtedly their strange—and to me still puzzling—relationship with Charles Manson. Part was their shared experiences, the world known as the Family. But I couldn't help wondering if another of the ingredients wasn't fear: fear of what the others would say if they talked, fear of what the others would do.

The only way we could find out would be to keep them apart, and owing to the smallness of the jail, it couldn't be done in Independence.

Besides Manson, there was only one male Family member still in custody: Clem Tufts, t/n Steve Grogan. Jack Gardiner, Fowles' investigator, gave me the eighteen-year-old Grogan's rap sheet:

3-23-66, Possession dangerous drugs, 6 mos. probation; 4-27-66, Shoplifting, Cont'd on probation; 6-23-66, Disturbing the peace, Con't on probation; 9-27-66, Probation dismissed; 6-5-67, Possession marijuana, Counseled & released; 8-12-67, Shoplifting, Bail forfeiture; 1-22-68, Loitering, Closed after investigation; 4-5-69, Grand theft money & Prowling, Released insuff. evidence; 5-20-69, Grand theft auto, Released insuff. evidence; 6-11-69, Child molesting & Indecent exposure . . .

Grogan had been observed exposing himself to several children, ages four to five years. "The kids wanted me to," he explained to arresting officers, who had caught him in the act. "I violated the law, the thing fell out of my pants and the parents got excited," he later told a court-appointed psychiatrist. After interviewing Grogan, the psychiatrist ruled *against* committing him to Camarillo State Hospital, because "the minor is much too aggressive to remain in a setting which does not provide containment facilities."

The court decided otherwise, sending him to Camarillo

for a ninety-day observation period. He remained a grand total of two days, then walked away, aided, I would later learn, by one of the girls from the Family.

His escape had occurred on July 19, 1969. He was back at Spahn in time for the Hinman, Tate, and LaBianca murders. He was arrested in the August 16 Spahn raid, but was released two days later, in time to behead Shorty Shea.

Currently, as a result of the Barker raid, he was charged with grand theft auto and possession of an illegal weapon, i.e., the sawed-off shotgun. I asked Fowles the present status of the case.

He said that, at the instigation of Grogan's attorney, he had been examined by two psychiatrists, who had decided that he was "presently insane."

I told Fowles I hoped he would request a jury trial and fight the insanity plea. If I brought Clem to trial in Los Angeles, charged with participating in the Tate murders, I didn't want the defense introducing evidence that a court in Inyo County had already found him insane. Frank agreed to go along with this.

At the moment our case against Grogan was so thin as to be nonexistent. There was no proof that Donald "Shorty" Shea was even dead; to date, no body had been found. As for the Tate murders, all we had was DeCarlo's statement that Clem had told him, "We got five piggies."

There was no way we could use that statement in court if there was a joint trial. In 1965 the California Supreme Court ruled, in the case of *People* vs. *Aranda*, that the prosecution cannot introduce into evidence a statement made by one defendant which implicates a co-defendant.

Since *Aranda* would have a bearing on all the trials involving the Manson Family members, a simplified explanation is in order. For example, if there were a joint trial, with more than one defendant, we couldn't use Susan Atkins' statement to Ronnie Howard, "We did it," the plural being inadmissible because it implicated co-defendants. We could, however, use her statement, "I stabbed Sharon Tate." It is possible to "sanitize" some statements so they don't violate *Aranda*. Susan Atkin's admission to Whiteley and Guenther, "I went to Gary's house with Bobby

Beausoleil" could be edited to "I went to Gary's house," although a good defense attorney can fight, and—depending on the prosecutor and judge—sometimes win the exclusion of even that. But when it came to the pronoun "we," there was no way we could get around it.

Therefore, Manson's statement to Springer, "We knocked off five of them just the other night," was useless. As was Clem's remark to DeCarlo, "We got five piggies."

Manson and Grogan could have made such confessions on nationwide TV and, if there was a joint trial, we could never use their remarks against them.

So we had virtually nothing on Clem.

In going through Grogan's file, I noticed that one of his brothers had made application for the California Highway Patrol; I made note of this, thinking maybe his brother could influence Clem to cooperate with us. DeCarlo had described Grogan in two words: "He's nuts." In his police photograph—big, wide grin, chipped front tooth, moronic stare—he did look idiotic. I asked Fowles for copies of the recent psychiatric reports.

Asked, "Why do you hate your father?" Grogan replied, "I'm my father and I don't hate myself." He denied the use of drugs. "I have my own bennies, adrenalin. It's called fear." He claimed that "love is everything," but, according to one psychiatrist, "he also revealed that he could not accept the philosophy of interracial brotherhood. Quotes supposedly from the Bible with sexual correlation were given in defense of his attitude."

Other quotes from Clem: "I'm dying a little every day. My ego is dying and knows he's dying and struggles hard. When you're free of ego you're free of everything ... Whatever you say is right for yourself ... Whoever you think I am, that's who I am."

The philosophy of Clem? Or Charles Manson? I'd heard the same thoughts, in several instances even identical words, from the girls.

If the psychiatrists had examined one of Manson's followers and, on the basis of such responses, found him insane, what of his leader?

I saw Charles Manson for the first time that day. He was walking from the jail to the courtroom for arraignment on the Michigan loader arson charge, and was accompanied by five sheriff's deputies.

I hadn't realized how small he was. He was just five feet two. He was thin, of slight build, a shade hunchbacked, wore his brown hair very long, almost to his shoulders, and had a good start on a beard, grown—I'd noticed in comparing the LASO and Inyo mug shots—after his arrest in the Spahn Ranch raid. He wore fringed buckskins, which were not inexpensive. Though handcuffed, his walk was casual, not stiff, as though he was completely at ease.

I could not believe that this little guy had done all the things it was said he had. He looked anything but a heavyweight. Yet I knew that to underrate him would be the biggest mistake I could make. For if the Atkins and DeCarlo stories were true, he was not only capable of committing murder himself, he also possessed the incredible power to command others to kill for him.

Manson's girls had talked a great deal about the Indian concept of karma. It was like a boomerang, they said. Whatever you threw out would, eventually, come back to you. I wondered if Manson himself really believed this and if he sensed that, nearly three and a half months after these hideous murders, his own karma was finally returning. He must. You don't assign five sheriff's deputies to an arson suspect. If he didn't know now, he would soon enough, when the jail grapevine repeated some of the questions we'd been asking.

Before leaving Independence, I gave Frank Fowles both my home and office numbers. If there were any developments, I wanted to be notified, whatever the hour. Manson had pleaded not guilty to the arson charge, and his bail had been set at $25,000. If anyone attempted to meet it, I wanted to know immediately, so we could move fast on the murder charges. It might mean revealing our case before we were ready to do so, but the alternative was worse. Aware that he was suspected of murder, once free Manson would probably split. And with Manson at large it would be extremely difficult to get anyone to talk.

November 22-23, 1969

That weekend I went through LAPD's files on the Tate-LaBianca murders; the Inyo County files; LASO's reports on the Spahn Ranch raid and other contacts with the Family; and numerous rap sheets. LAPD had conducted over 450 interviews on Tate alone; although they had netted less than had a ten-cent phone call from an ex-hooker, I had to familiarize myself with what had and hadn't been done. I was especially interested in seeing if I could find any link between the Tate-LaBianca victims and the Manson clan. Also, I was looking for some clue as to the motive behind the slayings.

Occasionally writers refer to "motiveless crimes." I've never encountered such an animal, and I'm convinced that none such exists. It may be unconventional; it may be apparent only to the killer or killers; it may even be largely unconscious—but every crime is committed for a reason. The problem, especially in this case, was finding it.

After listening to the seven-hour taped interview with Daniel DeCarlo, I began studying the criminal record of one Manson, Charles M.

I wanted to get to know the man I would be up against.

Charles Manson was born "no name Maddox" on November 12, 1934, in Cincinnati, Ohio, the illegitimate son of a sixteen-year-old girl named Kathleen Maddox.*

Though Manson himself would later state that his mother was a teen-age prostitute, other relatives say she was simply "loose." One remarked, "She ran around a lot,

*As with almost everything else written about Manson's early years, even his date of birth is usually given erroneously, although for an understandable reason. Unable to remember her child's birthday, the mother changed it to November 11, which was Armistice Day and an easier date to remember.

drank, got in trouble." Whatever the case, she lived with a succession of men. One, a much older man named William Manson, whom she married, was around just long enough to provide a surname for the youth.

The identity of Charles Manson's father was something of a mystery. In 1936 Kathleen filed a bastardy suit in Boyd County, Kentucky, against one "Colonel Scott,"* a resident of Ashland, Kentucky. On April 19, 1937, the court awarded her a judgment of $25, plus $5 a month for the support of "Charles Milles Manson." Though it was an "agreed judgment," Colonel Scott apparently didn't honor it, for as late as 1940 Kathleen was attempting to file an attachment on his wages. Most accounts state that Colonel Scott died in 1954; though this has never been officially verified, Manson himself apparently believed it. He also stated on numerous occasions that he never met his father.

According to her own relatives, Kathleen would leave the child with obliging neighbors for an hour, then disappear for days or weeks. Usually his grandmother or maternal aunt would have to claim him. Most of his early years were spent with one or the other, in West Virginia, Kentucky, or Ohio.

In 1939 Kathleen and her brother Luther robbed a Charleston, West Virginia, service station, knocking out the attendant with Coke bottles. They were sentenced to five years in the state penitentiary for armed robbery. While his mother was in prison, Manson lived with his aunt and uncle in McMechen, West Virginia. Manson would later tell his counselor at the National Training School for Boys that his uncle and aunt had "some marital difficulty until they became interested in religion and became very extreme."

A very strict aunt, who thought all pleasures sinful but who gave him love. A promiscuous mother, who let him do anything he wanted, just so long as he didn't bother her. The youth was caught in a tug-of-war between the two.

Paroled in 1942, Kathleen reclaimed Charles, then

*His first name remains unknown. Even in official records he is referred to as "Colonel Scott."

eight. The next several years were a blur of run-down hotel rooms and newly introduced "uncles," most of whom, like his mother, drank heavily. In 1947 she tried to have him put in a foster home, but, none being available, the court sent him to the Gibault School for Boys, a caretaking institution in Terre Haute, Indiana. He was twelve years old.

According to school records, he made a "poor institutional adjustment" and "his attitude toward schooling was at best only fair." Though "during the short lapses when Charles was pleasant and feeling happy he presented a likable boy," he had "a tendency toward moodiness and a persecution complex . . ." He remained at Gibault ten months, then ran away, returning to his mother.

She didn't want him, and he ran away again. Burglarizing a grocery store, he stole enough money to rent a room. He then broke into several other stores, stealing, among other things, a bicycle. Caught during a burglary, he was placed in the juvenile center in Indianapolis. He escaped the next day. When he was apprehended, the court—erroneously informed that he was Catholic—made arrangements through a local priest to have him accepted at Father Flanagan's Boys Town.

He didn't make its distinguished alumni list. Four days after his arrival, he and another boy, Blackie Nielson, stole a car and fled to the home of Blackie's uncle in Peoria, Illinois. En route they committed two armed robberies—one a grocery store, the other a gambling casino. Among criminals, as in the law itself, a distinction is made between non-violent and violent crimes. Manson had "graduated," committing his first armed robbery at age thirteen.

The uncle was glad to see them. Both boys were small enough to slip through skylights. A week after their arrival in Peoria, the pair broke into a grocery store and stole $1,500. For their efforts, the uncle gave them $150. Two weeks later they tried a repeat, but this time they were caught. Both talked, implicating the uncle. Still only thirteen, Charles Manson was sent to the Indiana School for Boys at Plainfield.

He remained there three years, running away a total of

eighteen times. According to his teachers, "He professed no trust in anyone" and "did good work only for those from whom he figured he could obtain something."

In February 1951, Charles Manson and two other sixteen-year-olds escaped and headed for California. For transportation they stole cars. For support they burglarized gas stations—Manson would later estimate they hit fifteen or twenty—before, just outside Beaver, Utah, a roadblock set up for a robbery suspect netted them instead.

In taking a stolen vehicle across a state line, the youths had broken a federal law, the Dyer Act. This was the beginning of a pattern for Charles Manson of committing federal crimes, which carry far stiffer sentences than local or state offenses.

On March 9, 1951, Manson was ordered confined to the National Training School for Boys, in Washington, D.C., until reaching his majority.

Detailed records were kept on Charles Manson during the time he was there.* On arrival, he was given a battery of aptitude and intelligence tests. Manson's IQ was 109. Though he had completed four years of school, he remained illiterate. Intelligence, mechanical aptitude, manual dexterity: all average. Subject liked best: music. Observed his first case worker, with considerable understatement, "Charles is a sixteen-year-old boy who has had an unfavorable family life, if it can be called family life at all." He was, the case worker concluded, aggressively antisocial.

One month after his arrival: "This boy tries to give the impression that he is trying hard to adjust although he actually is not putting forth any effort in this respect ... I feel in time he will try to be a wheel in the cottage."

After three months: "Manson has become somewhat of an 'institution politician.' He does just enough work to get by on ... Restless and moody most of the time, the boy would rather spend his class time entertaining his friends." The report concluded: "It appears that this boy is a very

*I would not obtain the results of these until much later; however, portions are quoted here.

emotionally upset youth who is definitely in need of some psychiatric orientation."

Manson was anxious to be transferred to Natural Bridge Honor Camp, a minimum security institution. Because of his run-away record, school officials felt the opposite—i.e., transfer to a reformatory-type institution—was in order, but they decided to withhold decision until after the boy had been examined by a psychiatrist.

On June 29, 1951, Charles Manson was examined by a Dr. Block. The psychiatrist noted "the marked degree of rejection, instability, and psychic trauma" in Manson's background. His sense of inferiority in relation to his mother was so pronounced, Block said, that he constantly felt it necessary "to suppress any thoughts about her." Because of his diminutive stature, his illegitimacy, and the lack of parental love, "he is constantly striving for status with the other boys." To attain this, Manson had "developed certain facile techniques for dealing with people. These for the most part consist of a good sense of humor" and an "ability to ingratiate himself . . . This could add up to a fairly 'slick' institutionalized youth, but one is left with the feeling that behind all this lies an extremely sensitive boy who has not yet given up in terms of securing some kind of love and affection from the world."

Though the doctor observed that Manson was "quite unable to accept any kind of authoritative direction," he found that he "accepted with alacrity the offer of psychiatric interviews."

If he found this suspicious, the doctor did not indicate it in his report. For the next three months he gave Manson individual psychotherapy. It may be presumed that Charles Manson also worked on the doctor, for in his October 1 report Dr. Block was convinced that what Manson most required were experiences which would build up his self-confidence. In short, he needed to be trusted. The doctor recommended the transfer.

It would appear that Charles Manson had conned his first psychiatrist. Though the school authorities considered him at best a "calculated risk," they accepted the doctor's recommendation, and on October 24, 1951, he was transferred to Natural Bridge Camp.

That November he turned seventeen. Shortly after his birthday he was visited by his aunt, who told the authorities that she would supply a home and employment for him if he was released. He was due for a parole hearing in February 1952, and, with her offer, his chances looked good. Instead, less than a month before the hearing, he took a razor blade and held it against another boy's throat while he sodomized him.

As a result of the offense, he lost ninety-seven days good-time and, on January 18, 1952, he was transferred to the Federal Reformatory at Petersburg, Virginia. He was considered "dangerous," one official observing, "He shouldn't be trusted across the street." By August he had committed eight serious disciplinary offenses, three involving homosexual acts. His progress report, if it could be called that, stated, "Manson definitely has homosexual and assaultive tendencies." He was classified "safe only under supervision." For the protection of himself as well as others, the authorities decided to transfer him to a more secure institution, the Federal Reformatory at Chillicothe, Ohio. He was sent there on September 22, 1952.

From the Chillicothe files: "Associates with trouble makers ... seems to be the unpredictable type of inmate who will require supervision both at work and in quarters ... In spite of his age, he is criminally sophisticated ... regarded as grossly unsuited for retention in an open reformatory type institution such as Chillicothe ..." This from a report written less than a month after his transfer there.

Then, suddenly, Manson changed. For the rest of the year there were no serious disciplinary offenses. Except for minor infractions of the rules, and a consistently "poor attitude toward authority," his good conduct continued into 1953. A progress report that October noted: "Manson has shown a marked improvement in his general attitude and cooperation with officers and is also showing an active interest in the educational program ... He is especially proud of the fact that he raised his [educational level from lower fourth to upper seventh grade] and that he can now read most material and use simple arithmetic."

Because of his educational advancement and his good

work habits in the transportation unit, where he repaired and maintained vehicles belonging to the institution, on January 1, 1954, he was given a Meritorious Service Award. Far more important to Charles Manson, on May 8, 1954, he was granted parole. He was nineteen.

One of the conditions of his parole was that he live with his aunt and uncle in McMechen. He did, for a time, then, when his mother moved to nearby Wheeling, he joined her. They seemed drawn together, yet unable to stand each other for any length of time.

Since fourteen, Charles Manson's only sexual contacts had been homosexual. Shortly after his release he met a seventeen-year-old McMechen girl, Rosalie Jean Willis, a waitress in the local hospital. They were married in January 1955. For support Manson worked as a busboy, service-station helper, parking-lot attendant. He also boosted cars. He would later admit to stealing six. He appeared to have learned nothing; he took at least two across state lines. One, stolen in Wheeling, West Virginia, he abandoned in Fort Lauderdale, Florida. The second, a 1951 Mercury, he drove from Bridgeport, Ohio, to Los Angeles in July 1955, accompanied by his now pregnant wife. Manson had finally made it to the Golden State. He was arrested less than three months later, and admitted both Dyer Act violations. Taken to federal court, he pleaded guilty to the theft of the Mercury, and asked for psychiatric help, stating, "I was released from Chillicothe in 1954 and, having been confined for nine years, I was badly in need of psychiatric treatment. I was mentally confused and stole a car as a means of mental release from the confused state of mind that I was in."

The judge requested a psychiatric report. Manson was examined on October 26, 1955, by Dr. Edwin McNiel. He gave the psychiatrist a much abbreviated version of his past, stating that he was first sent to an institution "for being mean to my mother." Of his wife, Manson said, "She is the best wife a guy could want. I didn't realize how good she was until I got in here. I beat her at times. She writes to me all the time. She is going to have a baby."

He also told McNiel that "he spent so much time in institutions that he never really learned much of what 'real life on the outside was all about.' He said that now he has a wife and is about to become a father it has become important to him to try to be on the outside and be with his wife. He said she is the only one he has ever cared about in his life."

Dr. McNiel observed: "It is evident that he has an unstable personality and that his environmental influences throughout most of his life have not been good . . . In my opinion this boy is a poor risk for probation; on the other hand, he has spent nine years in institutions with apparently little benefit except to take him out of circulation. With the incentive of a wife and probable fatherhood, it is possible that he might be able to straighten himself out. I would, therefore, respectfully recommend to the court that probation be considered in this case under careful supervision." Accepting the suggestion, on November 7, 1955, the court gave Manson five years probation.

There remained the Florida charge. Though his chances of getting probation on it were excellent, before the hearing he skipped. A warrant was issued for his arrest. He was picked up in Indianapolis on March 14, 1956, and returned to Los Angeles. His probation was revoked, and he was sentenced to three years imprisonment at Terminal Island, San Pedro, California. By the time Charles Manson, Jr., was born, his father was back in jail.

"This inmate will no doubt be in serious difficulty soon," wrote the orientation officer. "He is young, small, baby-faced, and unable to control himself . . ."

Given another battery of tests, Manson received average marks in all the categories except "word meaning," where he had a high score. His IQ was now 121. With some perception, when it came to his work assignment Manson requested "a small detail where he is not with too many men. He states he has a tendency to cut up and misbehave if he is around a gang . . ."

Rosalie moved in with his mother, now living in Los Angeles, and during his first year at Terminal Island she visited him every week, his mother somewhat less frequently. "Manson's work habits and attitudes range from good to poor," noted his March 1957 progress report. "However, as the time of his parole hearing approaches, his work performance report has jumped from good to excellent, showing that he is capable of a good adjustment if he wants to."

His parole hearing was set for April 22. In March his wife's visits ceased. Manson's mother told him Rosalie was living with another man. In early April he was transferred to the Coast Guard unit, under minimal custody. On April 10 he was found in the Coast Guard parking lot, dressed in civilian clothes, wiring the ignition of a car. Subsequently indicted for attempted escape, he pleaded guilty, and an extra five years probation was tacked onto the end of his current sentence. On April 22 the parole request was denied.

Rosalie filed for divorce not long after this, the divorce becoming final in 1958. She retained custody of Charles, Jr., remarried, and had no further contact with Manson or his mother.

April 1958, annual review: His work performance was "sporadic," his behavior continued to be "erratic and moody." Almost without exception, he would let down anyone who went to bat for him, the report noted. "For example, he was selected to attend the current Dale Carnegie Course, being passed over a number of other applicants because it was felt that this course might be beneficial in his case and he urgently desired enrollment. After attending a few sessions and apparently making excellent progress, he quit in a mood of petulance and has since engaged in no educational activity."

Manson was called "an almost classic text book case of the correctional institutional inmate . . . His is a very difficult case and it is impossible to predict his future adjustment with any degree of accuracy."

He was released September 30, 1958, on five years parole.

By November, Manson had found a new occupation: pimping. His teacher was +Frank Peters, a Malibu bartender and known procurer, with whom he was living.

Unknown to Manson, he was under surveillance by the FBI, and had been since his release from prison. The federal agents, who were looking for a fugitive who had once lived with Peters, told Manson's parole officer that his "first string" consisted of a sixteen-year-old girl named Judy, whom he had personally "turned out"; as additional support, he was getting money from "Fat Flo," an unattractive Pasadena girl who had wealthy parents.

His parole officer called him in for a talk. Manson denied he was pimping; said he was no longer living with Peters; promised never to see Judy again; but stated that he wished to continue his relationship with Flo, "for money and sex." After all, he said, he had "been in a long time." After the interview the parole officer wrote: "This certainly is a very shaky probationer and it seems just a matter of time before he gets in further trouble."

On May 1, 1959, Manson was arrested attempting to cash a forged U.S. Treasury check for $37.50 in Ralph's, a Los Angeles supermarket. According to the arresting officers, Manson told them he had stolen the check from a mailbox. Two more federal offenses.

LAPD turned Manson over to Secret Service agents for questioning. What then happened was somewhat embarrassing. "Unfortunately for them," read a report of the incident, "the check itself has disappeared; they feel certain subject took it off table and swallowed it when they momentarily turned their backs." The charges remained, however.

In mid-June an attractive nineteen-year-old girl named Leona called on Manson's parole officer and told him she was pregnant by Charlie. The parole officer was skeptical and wanted to see a medical report. He also began checking her background.

With the aid of an attorney, Manson obtained a deal: if he would plead guilty to forging the check, the mail theft charge would be dropped. The judge ordered a psychiatric examination, and Dr. McNiel examined Manson a second time.

When Manson appeared in court on September 28, 1959, Dr. McNiel, the U.S. Attorney's Office, and the probation department *all* recommended against probation. Leona also appeared and made a tearful plea in Manson's behalf. They were deeply in love, she told the judge, and would marry if Charlie were freed. Though it was proved that Leona had lied about being pregnant, and that she had an arrest record as a prostitute under the name Candy Stevens, the judge, evidently moved by Leona's plea and Manson's promise to make good, gave the defendant a ten-year sentence, then suspended it and placed him on probation.

Manson returned to pimping and breaking federal laws.

By December he had been arrested by LAPD twice: for grand theft auto and the use of stolen credit cards. Both charges were dismissed for lack of evidence. That month he also took Leona-aka-Candy and a girl named Elizabeth from Needles, California, to Lordsburg, New Mexico, for purposes of prostitution, violating the Mann Act, still another federal beef.

Held briefly, questioned, then released, he was given the impression that he had "beat the rap." He must have suspected that the investigation was continuing, however. Possibly to prevent Leona from testifying against him, he did marry her, though he didn't inform his probation officer of this. He remained free throughout January 1960, while the FBI prepared its case.

Late in February, Manson's probation officer was visited by an irate parent, +Ralph Samuels, from Detroit. Samuels' daughter +Jo Anne, nineteen, had come to California in response to an ad for an airline stewardess school, only to learn, after paying her tuition, that the school was a fraud. She had $700 in savings, however, and together with another disillusioned student, +Beth Beldon, had rented an apartment in Hollywood. About November 1959, Jo Anne had the misfortune to meet Charles Manson, who introduced himself, complete with printed card, as "President, 3-Star-Enterprises, Nite Club, Radio and TV Productions." Manson conned her into investing her savings in his nonexistent company; drugged and raped her roommate; and got Jo Anne pregnant. It was an ectopic pregnancy, the fetus growing in one of the Fallopian tubes, and she nearly died.

The probation officer could offer little more than a sympathetic ear, however, for Charles Manson had disappeared. A bench warrant was issued, and on April 28 a federal grand jury indicted him on the Mann Act violation. He was arrested June 1 in Laredo, Texas, after police picked up one of his girls on a prostitution charge, and brought back to Los Angeles, where, on June 23, 1960, the court ruled he had violated his probation and ordered him returned to prison to serve out his ten-year sentence. The judge observed: "If there ever was a man who demonstrated himself completely unfit for probation, he is it." This was the same judge who had granted him probation the previous September.

The Mann Act charge was later dropped. For a full year Manson remained in the Los Angeles County Jail, while appealing the revocation. The appeal was denied, and in July 1961 he was sent to the United States Penitentiary at McNeil Island, Washington. He was twenty-six.

According to staff evaluation, Manson had become something of an actor: "He hides his loneliness, resentment, and hostility behind a façade of superficial ingratiation . . . An energetic, young-appearing person whose verbalization flows quite easily, he gestures profusely and can dramatize situations to hold the listener's attention." Then a statement which, in one form or another, was to reappear often in his prison records, and, much later, in post-prison interviews: "He has commented that institutions have become his way of life and that he receives security in institutions which is not available to him in the outside world."

Manson gave as his claimed religion "Scientologist," stating that he "has never settled upon a religious formula for his beliefs and is presently seeking an answer to his question in the new mental health cult known as Scientology."

Scientology, an outgrowth of science-fiction writer L. Ron Hubbard's Dianetics, was just coming into vogue at this time. Manson's teacher, i.e., "auditor," was another convict, Lanier Rayner. Manson would later claim that while in prison he achieved Scientology's highest level, "theta clear."*

Although Manson remained interested in Scientology much longer than he did in any other subject except music, it appears that, like the Dale Carnegie course, he stuck with it only as long as his enthusiasm lasted, then dropped it, extracting and retaining a number of terms and phrases ("auditing," "cease to exist," "coming to Now") and some concepts (karma, reincarnation, etc.) which, perhaps fittingly, Scientology had borrowed in the first place.

He was still interested in Scientology when his annual progress report was written that September. Furthermore, according to the report, that interest "has led him to make a semi-professional evaluation of his personality which strangely enough is quite consistent with the evaluations made by previous social studies. He appears to have developed a certain amount of insight into his problems through his study of this discipline. Manson is making progress for the first time in his life."

The report also noted that Manson "is active in softball, basketball and croquet" and "is a member of the Drama Club and the Self Improvement Group." He had become "somewhat of a fanatic at practicing the guitar."†

He held one fairly responsible job eleven months, the longest he held any prison assignment, before being caught with contraband in his cell and reassigned to janitorial work.

The annual report that September took a close, hard look at the twenty-eight-year-old convict:

"Charles Manson has a tremendous drive to call attention to himself. Generally he is unable to succeed in positive acts, therefore he often resorts to negative behavior to satisfy this drive. In his effort to 'find' himself, Manson peruses different religious philosophies, e.g., Scientology and Buddhism; however, he never remains long enough

*In one of his pamphlets, Hubbard defined a "clear" as "one who has straightened up this lifetime." It is rather hard to see how this might apply to Charles Manson.

†He in fact requested a transfer to Leavenworth, considered a much tougher institution, because "he claimed he would be allowed to practice his guitar more often." The request was denied.

with any given teachings to reap meaningful benefits. Even these attempts and his cries for help represent a desire for attention, with only superficial meaning. Manson has had more than the usual amount of staff attention, yet there is little indication of change in his demeanor. In view of his deep-seated personality problems ... continuation of institutional treatment is recommended."

On October 1, 1963, prison officials were informed, "according to court papers received in this institution, that Manson was married to a Leona Manson in 1959 in the State of California, and that the marriage was terminated by divorce on April 10, 1963, in Denver, Colorado, on grounds of mental cruelty and conviction of a felony. One child, Charles Luther Manson, is alleged to have been of this union."

This is the only reference, in any of Manson's records, to his second marriage and second child.

Manson's annual review of September 1964 revealed a clear conduct record, but little else encouraging. "His past pattern of employment instability continues ... seems to have an intense need to call attention to himself ... remains emotionally insecure and tends to involve himself in various fanatical interests."

Those "fanatical interests" weren't identified in the prison reports, but at least several are known. In addition to Scientology and his guitar, there was now a third. In January 1964 "I Want to Hold Your Hand" became the No. 1 song on U.S. record charts. With the New York arrival of the "four Liverpool lads" the following month, the United States experienced, later than Great Britain but with no less intensity, the phenomenon known as Beatlemania. According to former inmates at McNeil, Manson's interest in the Beatles was almost an obsession. It didn't necessarily follow that he was a fan. There was more than a little jealousy in his reaction. He told numerous people that, given the chance, he could be much bigger than the Beatles. One person he told this to was Alvin Karpis, lone survivor of the Ma Barker gang. Manson had struck up a friendship with the aging gangster after learning he could play the steel guitar. Karpis taught Manson how. Again an observable pattern. Manson managed to get something from almost everyone with whom he associated.

May 1966: "Manson continues to maintain a clear conduct record . . . Recently he has been spending most of his free time writing songs, accumulating about 80 or 90 of them during the past year, which he ultimately hopes to sell following release . . . He also plays the guitar and drums, and is hopeful that he can secure employment as a guitar player or as a drummer or singer . . .

"He shall need a great deal of help in the transition from institution to the free world."

In June 1966, Charles Manson was returned to Terminal Island for release purposes.

August 1966: "Manson is about to complete his ten-year term. He has a pattern of criminal behavior and confinement that dates to his teen years. This pattern is one of instability whether in free society or a structured institutional community. Little can be expected in the way of change in his attitude, behavior, or mode of conduct . . ." This last report noted that Manson had no further interest in academic or vocational training; that he was no longer an advocate of Scientology; that "he has come to worship his guitar and music"; and, finally, "He has no plans for release as he says he has nowhere to go."

The morning Charles Manson was to be freed, he begged the authorities to let him remain in prison. Prison had become his home, he told them. He didn't think he could adjust to the world outside.

His request was denied. He was released at 8:15 A.M. on March 21, 1967, and given transportation to Los Angeles. That same day he requested and received permission to go to San Francisco. It was there, in the Haight-Ashbury section, that spring, that the Family was born.

Charles Manson was thirty-two years old. Over seventeen of those years—more than half his life—had been spent in institutions. In those seventeen years, Manson had only been examined by a psychiatrist three times, and then very superficially.

I was surprised, in studying Manson's record, to find no sustained history of violence—armed robbery age thirteen, homosexual rape age seventeen, wife beating age twenty, that was it. I was more than surprised, I was amazed at the number of federal offenses. Probably ninety-nine out of one hundred criminals never see the inside of a federal court. Yet here was Manson, described as "criminally sophisticated," violating the Dyer Act, the Mann Act, stealing from the mails, forging a government check, and so on. Had Manson been convicted of comparable offenses in state courts, he probably would have served *less than five years* instead of over seventeen.

Why? I could only guess. Perhaps, as he said before his reluctant release from Terminal Island, prison was the only home he had. It was also possible that, consciously or unconsciously, he sought out those offenses that carried the most severe punishments. A third speculation—and I wasn't overlooking the possibility that it could be a combination of all three—was a need, amounting almost to a compulsion, to challenge the strongest authority.

I was a long way from understanding Charles Manson. Though I could see patterns in his conduct, which might be clues to his future actions, a great deal was missing.

Burglar, car thief, forger, pimp—was this the portrait of a mass murderer?

I had far more questions than answers. And, as yet, not even a clue as to the motive.

November 24-26, 1969

Although Lieutenants Helder and LePage remained in charge of the Tate and LaBianca cases, the assignments were more jurisdictional than operational, since each was in charge of numerous other homicide investigations. Nineteen detectives had originally been assigned to the two cases. That number had now been cut to six. Moreover, for some odd reason, though there were only two victims in the LaBianca slayings, four detectives remained assigned to that case: Sergeants Philip Sartuchi, Mike Nielsen, Manuel "Chick" Gutierrez, and Frank Patchett. But on Tate, where there were five victims, there were only two detectives: Sergeants Robert Calkins and Mike McGann.

I called Calkins and McGann in for a conference and gave them a list of things I needed done. A few samples:

Interview Terry Melcher.

Check the fingerprints of every known Family member against the twenty-five unmatched latents found at 10050 Cielo Drive.

Put out a "want" on Charles "Tex" Montgomery, using the description on Inyo Deputy Sheriff Cox's August 21, 1969, F.I.R. card (M/C/6 feet/145 pounds/slim build/ruddy complexion/born December 2, 1945). If the case breaks before we arrest him, I told them, we may never find him.

Show photos of every Family member to Chapman; Garretson; the Tate gardeners; and the families, friends, and business associates of the victims. If there's a link, I want to know about it.

Check everyone in the Family to see who wears glasses, and determine if the pair found at the Tate murder scene belongs to a Family member.

"How do we do that?" Calkins asked. "They're not about to admit it."

"I presume you talk to their acquaintances, parents, relatives, to any of the Family members like Kitty Lutesinger and Stephanie Schram who are willing to cooperate," I told him. "If you can check out the glasses with eye doctors all over the United States and Canada, you can certainly check out some thirty-five people."

This was our initial estimate of the size of the Family. We'd later learn that at various times it numbered a hundred or more. The hard-core members—i.e., those who remained for any length of time and who were privy to what was going on—numbered between twenty-five and thirty.

Something occurred to me. "You *did* check out Garretson, didn't you, to see if those glasses were his?"

They weren't sure. They'd have to get back to me on that.

I later learned that although Garretson had been the first—and, for a time, the *only*—suspect in the murders, no one had thought to ascertain if those glasses, the single most important clue found at the murder scene, belonged to him. They hadn't even asked him if he wore glasses. It turned out he sometimes did. I learned this in talking to his attorney, Barry Tarlow. Eventually I was able to get LAPD to contact the police in Lancaster, Ohio, Garretson's home town, where he had returned after his release, and they obtained the specifics of Garretson's prescription from his local optometrist. Not even close.

From the evidence I'd seen, I didn't believe Garretson was involved in the murders, but I didn't want a defense attorney popping up in court pointing a finger, or rather a pair of eyeglasses, at an alternate suspect.

I was also curious about whom those glasses belonged to.

After Calkins and McGann left, I got in touch with the LaBianca detectives and gave them similar instructions regarding the photos and the Waverly Drive latents.

Five of the Manson girls were still in jail in Independence. LAPD decided to bring them to Los Angeles for individual interrogation. They would be confined at Sybil Brand but a "keep away" would be placed on each. This meant they could have no contact with each other or with anyone else LAPD designated—for example, Susan Atkins.

It was a good move on LAPD's part. There was a chance that, questioned separately, one or more might decide to talk.

That evening TV commentator George Putnam startled his listeners with the announcement that on Wednesday he would reveal who had committed the Tate murders. Our office called LAPD, who had their public relations spokesman, Lieutenant Hagen, contact Putnam and other representatives of the media asking them to hold off, because publicity now would hurt our investigation. All the newspapers, wire services, and radio and TV stations agreed to sit on the story, but only for one week, until Monday, December 1. The news was too big, and each was afraid someone else would try for a scoop.

There had been a leak. It wouldn't be the last.

On Tuesday, the twenty-fifth, Frank Fowles, the Inyo County DA, called, and we traded some information.

Fowles told me that Sandra Good had been overheard talking again. She had told another Family member that Charlie was going to "go alibi." If he was brought to trial for the Tate-LaBianca murders, they would produce evidence showing he wasn't even in Los Angeles at the time the murders occurred.

I told Fowles of a rumor I'd heard. According to McGann, a police informant in Las Vegas had told him that Charles "Tex" Montgomery and Bruce Davis had been seen there the previous day, driving a green panel Volkswagen. They had allegedly told someone that they were attempting to raise enough money to bail out Manson; failing in that, they intended to kill someone.

Fowles had heard similar rumblings among the Manson girls. He took them seriously enough to send his own family out of Inyo County over the Thanksgiving weekend. He remained behind, however, ready to forestall any bail attempt.

After hanging up, I called Patchett and Gutierrez of the LaBianca team and told them I wanted a detailed report on Manson's activities the week of the murders. Unlike the Tate detectives, they didn't ask how to do it. They went out and did it, eventually giving me evidence which, together with other information we obtained, would blow any alibi defense to smithereens.

That afternoon McGann and Patchett re-interviewed Ronnie Howard, this time on tape. She provided several details she'd recalled since LAPD last talked to her, but nothing that was of help in the current investigation. We still didn't know who all the killers were.

Wednesday, November 26. "Hung jury on Beausoleil," one of the deputy DAs yelled in the door of my office. "Eight to four for conviction."

The case had been so weak our office hadn't sought the death penalty. Also, the jury hadn't believed Danny DeCarlo. Brought in at the last minute, without adequate preparation, he had not been a convincing witness.

Later that day LASO asked my office if I would take over the prosecution of Beausoleil in his new trial, and I was assigned this case in addition to the two cases I was already handling.

That same morning Virginia Graham decided she had to tell someone what she knew. A few days earlier her husband had visited her at Corona. Whispering through the wire screen in the visitor's room, she told him she had heard something about the Benedict Canyon murders, and didn't know what to do.

He advised her: "Mind your own business."

But, she would later state: "I can see a lot of things I don't say anything about, but this is sick. This is so bad that I don't know who could mind their own business with this."*

Having failed to get an appointment with Dr. Dreiser, Virginia instead went to her counselor. The authorities at Corona called LAPD. At 3:15 that afternoon Sergeant Nielsen arrived at the prison and began taping her story.

Unlike Ronnie, who was unsure whether four or five people were involved in the Tate homicides, Virginia recalled Sadie's saying there were three girls and one man. Like Ronnie, however, she presumed the man, "Charles," was Manson.

The individual questioning of the five girls took place that afternoon and evening at Sybil Brand.

Sergeant Manuel "Chick" Gutierrez interviewed Dianne Bluestein, aka Snake, t/n Dianne Lake, given age twenty-one, true age sixteen. The interview was taped. Listening to the tapes later, I couldn't believe what I was hearing.

Q. "My name is Sergeant Gutierrez and I'm with the

*Virginia Graham would later state that she was unaware that Ronnie Howard had already talked to the police. However, a group of girls were transferred from Sybil Brand to Corona shortly before this, and it's possible they carried along some jail scuttlebutt.

Los Angeles Police Department and I work homicide. . . . I've talked to several of the girls. The girls have been real nice and we've had some long, long chats. We know a lot of things that went on over at Spahn. We know a lot that happened other places. We know who is involved, and who is not involved. We also know things that maybe you don't know, that we're not going to tell you until the right time comes up, but we've got to talk to everybody who was involved, and I think you know what I'm talking about. I'm talking about Charlie and the Family and everybody. I don't know how tight you are with the Family. You're probably real tight with them, but somebody's going to go down the tubes, and somebody's going to get the pill in the gas chamber for a whole bunch of murders which you are a part of, or so some other people have indicated."

There was no evidence whatsoever that Dianne was involved in any of the murders, but "Chick" wasn't deterred by this.

"Now, I'm here for one specific reason, and that's to listen to you, see what you've got to say, so I can go to the District Attorney and tell him, 'Look, this is what Dianne told me, and she's willing to turn state's evidence in return for her full release.' We're not interested in nailing you. We're interested in the big guy, and you know who we're talking about, right, honey?"

A. [No audible answer]

Q. "Now, somebody's going to go to that gas chamber, you know that. This is just too big. This is the biggest murder of the century. You know that and I know it. So, in order to protect yourself from getting even indicted or spending the rest of your life in jail, then you're going to have to come up with some answers . . . We know of about fourteen murders right now, and you know which ones I'm talking about."

A. [Unintelligible]

Gutierrez accused her of involvement in all fourteen. He then said: "I'm prepared to give you complete immunity, which means that if you are straight with me, right down the line, I'll be straight with you, and I'll guarantee you that you will walk out of that jail a free woman ready to start over again and never go back up there to Independence to do any time. I wouldn't say that unless I meant it, right?"

Actually, Sergeant Gutierrez did not have the authority to guarantee this. The granting of immunity is a complicated procedure, involving the approval not only of the Police Department but also of the District Attorney's Office, with the final decision being made by the Court. Gutierrez offered it to her as casually as if it were a stick of gum.

Commenting on her silence, Sergeant Gutierrez said, "Now, what's that going to prove, huh? Right now the only thing you're proving to me, honey, is that, heck, you're out there sticking your nose out for a guy by the name of Charlie. Now, what's Charlie? He got you guys in all this problem. You could have been out right now doing your thing, but here you're holding silent for what? For Charlie? Charlie ain't never going to get out of that jail. You know that, right? Didn't we start out on good terms? Huh?"

A. "Yes."

Q. "O.K. And I'm not about to beat you over the head with a hammer or hose and all that. All I want to do is talk to you friendly . . ."

Gutierrez interviewed Dianne for nearly two hours, obtaining from the sixteen-year-old little more than the admission that she liked candy bars.

Later Dianne Lake would become one of the prosecution's most important witnesses. But credit for this goes to the Inyo County authorities, in particular Gibbens and Gardiner, who, instead of threats, tried patient, sympathetic understanding. It made all the difference.

Having got nothing from Dianne, Gutierrez next interviewed Rachel Morse, aka Ouisch, t/n Ruth Ann Moorehouse, age eighteen, Ruth Ann was the girl Danny DeCarlo identified as his "favorite sweetie," the same girl who at Barker Ranch had told him she couldn't wait to get her first pig.

Unlike Dianne, Ruth Ann answered Gutierrez' questions, though most of her replies were lies. She claimed she'd never heard of Shorty, Gary Hinman, or anyone named Katie. The reason she knew so little, she explained, was that she had been with the Family only a short time, a month or so before the Spahn Ranch raid (all five girls said this, obviously by prearrangement).

Q. "I want to know everything you know, because you're going to testify before that grand jury."

A. "I don't know anything."

Q. "Then you're going to hang with the rest of them. You're going to go to the joint. If you don't start cooperating, you're going to go to the joint, and let me tell you what it is down there. They may drop that pill on you. They may drop that cyanide pill on you."

A. (*nearly screaming*) "I haven't done anything! I don't know anything about it!"

Then, later:

Q. "How old are you?"

A. "Eighteen."

Q. "That's old enough to go to the gas chamber."

There was also no evidence linking her to any of the homicides, but Gutierrez told her, "Fourteen murders, and you're involved in each one!" He also promised her complete immunity ("You're either going to go up for murder or you are going to go free"), and added, "Also, there is a $25,000 reward."

Manon Minette, aka Gypsy, t/n Catherine Share, who at twenty-seven was the oldest female member of the Family, gave the detectives nothing of value. Nor did Brenda McCann, t/n Nancy Pitman, age eighteen.

It was otherwise, however, with twenty-year-old Leslie Sankston.

Leslie, whose true name, Van Houten, was not known to us at this time, was interviewed by Mike McGann. McGann tried using her parents, conscience, the hideousness of the murders, the implication that others had talked and involved her—none worked. What did work was Leslie's little-girl cuteness, her I-know-something-you-don't game playing. Repeatedly she trapped herself.

Q. "What did you hear about the Tate murders up there?"

A. "I'm deaf. I didn't hear nothing." [Laughs]

Q. "Five people were killed up there, on the hill. And I know three for sure that went up there. I think I know the fourth. And I don't know the fifth. But I suspect you do. Why are you holding back? You know what happened."

A. "I have a pretty good idea."

Q. "I want to know who was involved. How it went down. The little details."

A. "I told Mr. Patchett [in Independence] I'll tell him if I changed my mind. I haven't changed my mind yet."

Q. "You're going to have to talk about it someday."

A. "Not today . . . How did you ever trace it back to Spahn?"

Q. "Who did you see leave the night of the eighth of August?"

A. [Laughs] "Oh, I went to bed early that night. Really, I don't want to talk about it."

Q. "Who went?"

A. "That's what I don't want to talk about."

All these were little admissions, if not of participation, at least of knowledge.

Though she didn't want to talk about the murders, she didn't mind talking about the Family. "You couldn't meet a nicer group of people," she told McGann. "Of all the guys at the ranch, I liked Clem the best; he's fun to be with." Clem, with the idiot grin, who liked to expose himself to little children. Sadie was "really kind of a nice person. But she tends to be on the rough side . . ." As Sharon Tate, Gary Hinman, and others had discovered. Bruce Davis was all talk, Leslie continued, always going on about how he was going to dynamite someone, but she was sure it was "only talk." She commented on some of the others, but not Charlie. In common with the four other girls who had been brought down from Independence, she avoided the subject of Manson.

Q. "The Family is no more, Leslie." Charlie was in jail; Clem was in jail; Zero had killed himself playing Russian roulette—

A. "*Zero!*"

Obviously shocked, she dropped her little-girl role and

pressed McGann for details. He told her that Bruce Davis had been present.

A. "Was Bruce playing it too?"

Q. "No."

A. (*sarcastically*) "Zero was playing Russian roulette all by himself!"

Q. "Kind of odd, isn't it?"

A. "Yeah, it's odd!"

Sensing an advantage, McGann moved in. He told her that he knew five people had gone to the Tate residence, three girls and two men, and that one of the men was Charles Manson.

A. "I don't think Charlie was in on any of them."

Leslie said she had heard only four people went to Tate. "I would say that three of them were girls. I would say that there were probably more girls involved than men." Then, later, "I heard one girl who didn't murder someone while they was, they were up there."

Q. "Who is that?"

A. "A girl by the name of Linda."

Susan Atkins had told Ronnie Howard, in regard to the killings the second night, "Linda wasn't in on this one," presumably meaning she had been along the first night, but until now we had been unsure of this.

Questioned, Leslie said she didn't know Linda's last name; that she was at Spahn only a short time and hadn't been arrested with them; and that she was a small girl, maybe five feet two, thin, with light-brown hair.

McGann asked her *who* had told her that Linda had been along on Tate. Leslie replied, petulantly, "I don't remember. I don't remember who told me little details!" Why was she so upset? McGann asked. "Because so many of my friends are getting knocked off, for reasons I don't even know about."

McGann showed her the mug shots taken after the Barker raid. Though she had been present, she claimed she couldn't recognize most of the people. When handed one of a girl booked as "Marnie Reeves," Leslie said, "That's Katie."

Q. "Katie is Marnie Reeves?"

Leslie equivocated. She wasn't sure. She really didn't

know any of these people all that well. Though she had lived with the Family at both Spahn and Barker, she associated mostly with the motorcycle riders. She thought they were neat.

McGann brought the questioning back to the murders. Leslie began playing games again, and in the process making admissions. She implied that she knew of eleven murders—Hinman 1, Tate 5, LaBianca 2, Shea 1, for a total of 9—but she declined to identify the other two. It was as if she were keeping score in a baseball game.

There was a break in the questioning. It's standard police procedure to leave a suspect alone for a while, to think about his or her answers, to provide a transition between "soft" and "hard" interrogation. It also gives the officers an opportunity to visit the can.

When McGann returned, he decided to shock Leslie some more.

Q. "Sadie has already told fifteen people in the jailhouse that she was there, that she took part in it."

A. "That's incredible." Then, after a thoughtful pause, "Didn't she mention anyone else?"

Q. "No. Except for Charlie. And Katie."

A. "She mentioned Charlie and Katie?"

Q. "That's right."

A. "That's pretty nauseating."

Q. "She said Katie was there, and I know it was Marnie Reeves, and you know it was Marnie Reeves."

At this point, McGann later told me, Leslie nodded her head affirmatively.

Q. "Sadie also said, 'I went out the next night and killed two more people, out in the hills.' "

A. *"Sadie said that!"*

Leslie was astonished. With good reason. Though we were as yet unaware of it, Leslie knew Susan Atkins had never entered the LaBianca residence. She knew that because she was one of the persons who had.

After this, Leslie refused to answer any further questions. McGann asked her why.

A. "Because if Zero was suddenly found playing Russian roulette I could be found playing Russian roulette."

Q. "We'll give you twenty-four-hour protection from now on."

A. (*laughing sarcastically*) "Oh, that would really be nice! I'd rather stay in jail."

From Leslie we learned that three girls had gone to the Tate residence: Sadie, Katie, and Linda. We also learned that Linda was "one girl who didn't murder someone," the clear implication being that the two other girls had. Beyond Leslie's limited description of Linda, however, we knew nothing about her.

We also knew that Katie was "Marnie Reeves." According to her Inyo arrest sheet, she was five feet six, weighed 120 pounds, had brown hair and blue eyes. Her photograph revealed a not very attractive girl, with very long hair and a somewhat mannish face. She looked older than twenty-two, the age she gave. In comparing the Barker and Spahn photos, it was discovered that she had been arrested in the earlier raid also, at that time giving the name "Mary Ann Scott." It was possible that "Katie," "Marnie Reeves," and "Mary Ann Scott" were all three aliases. She had been released a few days after her arrest at Barker, and her current whereabouts were unknown.

In return, Leslie had learned a few things from McGann: that Tex, Katie, and Linda were still free; and, more important, that Susan Atkins, aka Sadie Mae Glutz, was the snitch.

Even with a "keep away" on the girls, it wouldn't be long before this information got back to Manson.

November 27-30, 1969

We could have used a private line between Independence and L.A.; Fowles and I were averaging easily a dozen calls a day. Thus far, no attempt to meet Manson's bail, or any sign of Tex or Bruce. However, there were reporters all over Independence, and KNXT was sending in a camera crew tomorrow to film Golar Wash. I had Lieutenant Hagen call the TV station. They told him they didn't plan to use the film until Monday, the first, the agreed date, but wouldn't promise an extension to Wednesday, which I wanted.

Although nothing had seen print, the leaks continued. Chief Davis was enraged; he wanted to break the news himself. Someone was talking, and he wanted to know who. Determined to catch the culprit, he suggested that everyone working on the case, at LAPD and in the DA's Office, take a polygraph.

Even his own office ignored the suggestion, and I resisted the impulse to suggest that we concentrate on catching the killers instead.

On Saturday, Sergeant Patchett interviewed Gregg Jakobson. A talent scout, who was married to the daughter of old-time comedian Lou Costello, Jakobson had first met Charles Manson about May 1968, at the Sunset Boulevard home of Dennis Wilson, one of the Beach Boys rock group.

It was Jakobson who had introduced Manson to Terry Melcher, Doris Day's son, while Melcher was still living at 10050 Cielo Drive. In addition to producing his mother's TV show, Melcher was involved in a number of other enterprises, including a record company, and Jakobson had attempted to persuade him to record Manson. After listening to him play and sing, Melcher had said no.

Though Melcher had been unimpressed by Manson, Jakobson had been fascinated with the "whole Charlie Manson package," songs, philosophy, life style. Over a period of about a year and a half, he'd had many talks with Manson. Charlie loved to rap about his views on life, Gregg said, but Patchett wasn't particularly interested in this, and moved on to other subjects.

Did he know a Charles "Tex" Montgomery? Patchett asked. Yes, very well, Jakobson replied; only his real name wasn't Montgomery—it was Watson.

Sunday, November 30. At LAPD from 8:30 A.M. to midnight.

Charles Denton Watson had been arrested in Van Nuys, California, on April 23, 1969, for being on drugs. Though he had been released the next day, he had been fingerprinted at the time of his arrest.

10:30 A.M. Latent Prints Section called Lieutenant Helder. The print of Watson's right ring finger matched a latent found on the front door of the Tate residence.

Helder and I jumped up and down like little kids. This was the first physical evidence connecting the suspects to the crime scene.

Helder sent out fifteen detectives to see if they could locate Watson at any of his old addresses, but they had no luck. They did learn, however, that Watson was from a small town in Texas, McKinney.

Checking an atlas, we found that McKinney was in Collin County. Patchett called the sheriff of Collin, informing him that a former local resident, Charles Denton Watson, was wanted for 187 PC, murder, in California.

The sheriff's name was Tom Montgomery. A coincidence, Watson's using as alias the last name of the local sheriff? It was more than that: Sheriff Montgomery was Watson's second cousin.

"Charles is living here now," Sheriff Montgomery said. "He has an apartment in Denton. I'll bring him in."

The sheriff, we later learned, called Watson's uncle, Maurice Montgomery, saying, "Can you bring Charles over to the jail? We've got some trouble."

Maurice picked up his nephew and drove him to McKinney in his pickup truck. "He didn't say much on the way," the uncle later said. "I didn't know what it was all about, but I guess he knew all the time."

Watson supposedly refused comment and was lodged in the local jail.

Texans are straight shooters, LAPD told me. They'll hold him until we get around to sending an arrest warrant.

Not wanting to take any chances, I suggested we send someone to McKinney with the warrant, and it was decided that Sartuchi and Nielsen would leave at eleven the next morning.

Manson, Atkins, and Watson were now in custody, but two other suspects were still at large. From one of the ranch hands at Spahn, LAPD heard that Linda's last name was Kasabian, and that she was supposedly in a convent in New Mexico.* Marnie Reeves was rumored to be on a farm outside Mobile, Alabama.

That same day Patchett interviewed Terry Melcher regarding his contacts with Manson. He confirmed what Jakobson had already said: he had gone to Spahn Ranch twice, to hear Manson and the girls perform, and was "not enthused"; he had also seen Manson twice before this, while visiting Dennis Wilson. Melcher, however, added one important detail Jakobson hadn't mentioned.

On one of the latter occasions, late at night, Wilson had given him a ride back to his house on Cielo Drive. Manson had come along, sitting in the back seat of the car, singing and playing his guitar. They'd driven up to the gate and let him out, Melcher said, Wilson and Manson then driving off.

We now knew that Charles Manson had been to 10050 Cielo Drive on at least one occasion prior to the murders, although there was no evidence that he had ever been inside the gate.

At 5:30 that Sunday afternoon, while still at LAPD, I talked to Richard Caballero. A former deputy DA now in private practice, Caballero was representing Susan Atkins on the Hinman charge. Earlier Caballero had contacted Aaron Stovitz, wanting to know what the DA's Office had on his client. Aaron laid it out for him: while at Sybil Brand, Susan Atkins had confessed to two other inmates that she was involved not only in the Hinman but also the Tate and LaBianca murders. Aaron gave Caballero copies of the taped statements Ronnie Howard and Virginia Graham had given LAPD.

Under the law of discovery, the prosecution must make available to a defense attorney any and all evidence

*This was probably garbled, "convent" having been mistaken for "commune."

against his client. This is a one-way street. While the defense therefore knows in advance exactly what evidence the prosecution has, the defense isn't required to tell the prosecution anything. Although discovery usually occurs after a formal request to the Court, Aaron wanted to impress Caballero with the strength of our case, hoping his client would decide to cooperate.

Caballero came to Parker Center to see me and the detectives, wanting to know what kind of deal we could offer. In accordance with the earlier discussion between our office and LAPD, we said that if Susan would cooperate with us, we would probably let her plead guilty to second degree murder—i.e., we would not seek the death sentence, but we would ask for life imprisonment.

Caballero went to Sybil Brand and talked to his client. He would later testify: "I told her what the problems were, what the evidence was against her as it was related to me. That included the Hinman case (to which she had already confessed to LASO) and the Tate-LaBianca case. As a result of all this, I indicated to her that there is no question in my mind but they were going to seek the death penalty and that they would probably get it. I told her, 'They have enough evidence to convict you. You will be convicted.' "

About 9:30, Caballero returned to LAPD. Susan was undecided. She might be willing to testify before the grand jury, but he was sure she would never testify against the others at the trial. She was still under Manson's domination. Any minute she could bolt back to him. He said he'd let me know what she finally decided.

It was left hanging there. Though we had the Howard-Graham statements implicating Atkins, and physical evidence linking Watson to the Tate murder scene, our whole case against Manson and the others rested on the decision of Sadie Mae Glutz.

December 1, 1969

7 A.M. Aaron reached me at home. Sheriff Montgomery had just called. If he didn't have a warrant in two hours, he was going to release Watson.

I rushed down to the office and made out a complaint. McGann and I took it to Judge Antonio Chavez, who signed the warrant, LAPD teletyping it to Sheriff Montgomery with just minutes to spare.

I also made out two other complaints: one against Linda Kasabian, the other against Patricia Krenwinkel. The latter, LAPD had learned from LASO, was the real name of Marnie Reeves, aka Katie. Following the Spahn raid, her father, Joseph Krenwinkel, an Inglewood, California, insurance agent, had arranged for her release. On learning this, Sergeant Nielsen had called Krenwinkel, asking where he could reach his daughter. He had told him she was staying with relatives in Mobile, Alabama, and had given him the address. LAPD had then contacted Mobile Police Chief James Robinson, and he had men out looking for her now. Judge Chavez signed these warrants also.

Buck Compton, the Chief Deputy District Attorney, called to inform me that Chief Davis had scheduled a press conference for two that afternoon. Aaron and I were to be in his office at 1:30. "Buck, this is way too premature!" I told him. "We don't even have enough on Manson for an indictment, much less a conviction. As for Krenwinkel and Kasabian, if the story breaks before they're picked up, we may never catch them. Can't we persuade Davis to hold off?" Buck promised to try.

At least part of my worry was unnecessary. Patricia Krenwinkel was arrested in Mobile a few minutes before we arrived in Compton's office. Mobile police had gone to the home of her aunt, Mrs. Garnett Reeves, but Patricia wasn't there. However, Sergeant William McKellar and his partner were driving down the road that runs in front of the residence when they saw a sports car with a boy and a girl inside. As the two cars passed, McKellar "noticed the female passenger pulled her hat down lower over her face." Convinced this was "an effort to avoid identification," the officers pulled a quick U and sirened the car to a halt. Though the girl fitted the teletype description, she said her name was Montgomery (the same alias Watson had used). On being taken to the aunt's home, however, she admitted her true identity. The young man, a local acquaintance, was questioned and released. Patricia Krenwinkel was read her rights and placed under arrest at 3:20 P.M., Mobile time.

1:30 P.M. Buck, Aaron, and I met with Chief Davis. I told Davis that I'd scraped together barely enough evidence against Krenwinkel and Kasabian to get warrants, but it was all inadmissible hearsay: Leslie Sankston's statement to McGann; Susan Atkins' statements to Virginia Graham and Ronnie Howard. We can't get a grand jury indictment on this, I told him, adding, "If Susan Atkins doesn't cooperate, we've had it."

There were over two hundred reporters and cameramen waiting in the police auditorium, Davis said, representing not only all the networks and wire services but newspapers from all over the world. There was no way he could call it off now.

Shortly before the press conference Lieutenant Helder called both Roman Polanski and Colonel Paul Tate, telling them the news. For Colonel Tate, the news meant the end of his months-long private investigation; despite his diligence, he had not come up with anything that was of use to us. But at least now the wondering and suspicion were over.

2 P.M. Facing fifteen microphones and dozens of bright lights, Chief Edward M. Davis announced that after 8,750 hours of police work LAPD had "solved" the Tate case. Warrants had been issued for the arrests of three persons:

Charles D. Watson, twenty-four, who was now in custody in McKinney, Texas; Patricia Krenwinkel, twenty-one, who was in custody in Mobile, Alabama; and Linda Kasabian, age and present whereabouts unknown. It was anticipated that an additional four or five persons would be named in indictments which would be sought from the Los Angeles County grand jury. (Neither Charles Manson nor Susan Atkins was mentioned by name in the press conference.)

These persons, Davis continued, were also involved in the murder deaths of Rosemary and Leno LaBianca.

This came as a big surprise to most of the newsmen, since LAPD had maintained almost from the start that there was no connection between the two homicides. Though a few reporters had suspected the crimes were linked, they had been unable to sell their theories to LAPD.

Davis went on to say: "The Los Angeles Police Department wishes to express their appreciation for the magnificent cooperation rendered by other law enforcement agencies during the development of information regarding both of the above cases, in particular, the Los Angeles Sheriff's office."

Davis did not mention that it had taken LAPD over two months to follow up the lead LASO had supplied them the day after the Tate murders.

Questioned by reporters, Davis credited "tenacious investigation carried on by robbery-homicide detectives" with forcing the break in the case. He stated that the investigators "developed a suspicion which caused them to do a vigorous amount of work in this Spahn Ranch area and the people connected with Spahn Ranch which led us to where we are today."

There was also no mention of that ten-cent telephone call.

The reporters ran for the phones.

Caballero called Aaron. He wanted to interview Susan Atkins on tape, but he didn't want to do it at Sybil Brand, where there was a chance one of the other Manson girls would hear of it. Also, he felt Susan would be inclined to talk more freely in other surroundings. He suggested having her brought to his own office.

Though unusual, the request wasn't unprecedented. Aaron made up a removal order, which was signed by Judge William Keene, and that evening Susan Atkins, escorted by two sheriff's deputies, was taken to Caballero's office, where Caballero and his associate, Paul Caruso, interviewed her on tape.

The tape was for two purposes, Caballero told Aaron. He wanted it for the psychiatrists in case he decided on an insanity plea. And if we went ahead on the deal, he would let us listen to it before we took the case to the grand jury.

December 2, 1969

LAPD called a few minutes after I arrived at the office. All five suspects were now in custody, Linda Kasabian just having voluntarily surrendered to Concord, New Hampshire, police. According to her mother, Linda had admitted to being present at the Tate residence but claimed she had not participated in the murders. It looked as if she wasn't going to fight extradition.

A somewhat different decision had been reached in Texas.

McKinney was less than thirty miles north of Dallas, and only a few miles from Farmersville, where Charles Watson had grown up and gone to school. Audie Murphy had been a Farmersville boy. Now they had another local celebrity.

The news had already broken by the time Sartuchi and Nielsen reached McKinney. Stories in the Texas papers described Watson as having been an A student in high school, a football, basketball, and track star, who still held the state record for the low hurdles. Most local residents expressed shocked disbelief. "Charles was the boy next door," one said. "It was drugs that did it," an uncle told reporters. "He started taking them at college and that was where the trouble started." The principal of Farmersville High was quoted as saying, "It almost makes you afraid to send your kids off to college any more."

On the instruction of Watson's attorney, Bill Boyd, the Los Angeles detectives were not allowed to speak to his client. Sheriff Montgomery wouldn't even permit them to fingerprint him. Sartuchi and Nielsen did see Watson, however—accidentally. While they were talking to the sheriff, Watson passed them on the stairs, on his way to the visitor's room. According to their report, he was well dressed, clean-shaven, with short, not long, hair. He appeared in good health and looked like "a clean-cut college boy."

While in McKinney, the detectives established that Watson had gone to California in 1967 and that he hadn't moved back until November 1969—long after the murders.

Sartuchi and Nielsen returned to Los Angeles convinced we'd have little cooperation from the local authorities. It wasn't only a matter of relatives; somehow the whole affair had become involved in state politics!

"Little cooperation" would be a gross exaggeration.

Reporters were busy tracing the wanderings of the nomadic Family and interviewing those members not in custody. I asked Gail to save the papers, knowing the interviews might be useful at a later date. Though still uncharged with the murders, Charles Manson had now taken center stage. Sandy: "The first time I heard him sing it was like an angel . . ." Squeaky: "He gave off a lot of magic. But he was sort of a changeling. He seemed to change every time I saw him. He seemed ageless . . ."

There were also interviews with acquaintances and relatives of the suspects. Joseph Krenwinkel recalled how in September 1967 his daughter Patricia left her Manhattan Beach apartment, her job, and her car, not even picking up a paycheck due her, to join Manson. "I am convinced he was some kind of hypnotist."

Krenwinkel was not the only one to make that suggestion. Attorney Caballero talked to reporters outside the Santa Monica courtroom where his client had just entered a not guilty plea to the Hinman murder. Susan Atkins was under the "hypnotic spell" of Manson, Caballero said, and had "nothing to do with the murders" despite her presence at the Hinman and Tate residences.

Caballero also told the press his client was going to go before the grand jury and tell the complete story. This was the first confirmation we had that Susan Atkins had agreed to cooperate.

That same day LAPD interviewed Barbara Hoyt, whose parents had persuaded her to contact the police. Barbara had lived with the Family off and on since April 1969, and had been with them at Spahn, Myers, and Barker ranches.

The pretty seventeen-year-old's story came out in bits and pieces, over several interviews. Among her disclosures:

One evening while at Spahn, about a week after the August 16 raid, she had heard screams that seemed to come from down the creek. They lasted a long time, five to ten minutes, and she was sure they were Shorty's. After that night she never saw Shorty again.

The next day she heard Manson tell Danny DeCarlo that Shorty had committed suicide, "with a little help from us." Manson had also asked DeCarlo if lime would dispose of a body.

While at Myers Ranch, in early September 1969, Barbara had overheard Manson tell someone—she wasn't sure whom—that it had been real hard killing Shorty, once he had been "brought to Now." They'd hit him over the head with a pipe, Manson said, then everyone stabbed him, and finally Clem had chopped his head off. After that they'd cut him up in nine pieces.

While still at Myers, Barbara had also overheard Sadie tell Ouisch about the murders of Abigail Folger and Sharon Tate. Sometime later Ouisch told Barbara that she knew of ten other people the group had murdered.

Not long after this, Barbara and another girl—Sherry Ann Cooper, aka Simi Valley Sherri—fled the Family's Death Valley hideout. Manson caught up with them in

Ballarat, but, because other people were present, had let them go, even giving them twenty dollars for their bus fare to Los Angeles.*

Although very frightened, Barbara agreed to cooperate with us.

That cooperation would nearly cost her life.

About this same time another of Manson's girls agreed to help the police. She was the last person from whom I expected cooperation—Mary Brunner, the first member of the Manson Family.

Following his release from prison in March 1967, Charles Manson had gone to San Francisco. A prison acquaintance found him a room across the bay in Berkeley. In no hurry to find a job, subsisting mostly by panhandling, Manson would wander Telegraph Avenue or sit on the steps of the Sather Gate entrance to the University of California, playing his guitar. Then one day along came this librarian. As Charlie related the story to Danny DeCarlo, "She was out walking her dog. High-button blouse. Nose stuck up in the air, walking her little poodle. And Charlie's fresh out of the joint and along he comes talking his bullshit."

Mary Brunner, then twenty-three, had a B.A. degree in history from the University of Wisconsin and was working as an assistant librarian at the University of California. She was singularly unattractive, and Manson apparently was one of the first persons who thought her worth cultivating. It was possible he recalled the days when he lived off Fat Flo.

"So one thing led to another," DeCarlo resumed. "He moved in with her. Then he comes across this other girl. 'No, there will be no other girls moving in with me!' Mary says. She flatly refused to consider the idea. After the girl had moved in, two more came along. And Mary says, "I'll accept one other girl but never three!' Four, five, all the

*We later received information indicating that Manson may have sent three of his followers to Los Angeles with instructions to either bring back the girls or kill them, but we were never able to prove this. This was the same trip when a flat tire prevented the murder of Cathy Gillies' grandmother, the owner of Myers Ranch.

way up to eighteen. This was in Frisco. Mary was the first."

The Family had been born.

By this time Manson had discovered the Haight. According to a tale Manson himself often told his followers, one day a young boy handed him a flower. "It blew my mind," he'd recall. Questioning the youth, he learned that in San Francisco there was free food, music, dope, and love, just for the taking. The boy took him to Haight-Ashbury, Manson later told Steve Alexander, a writer for the underground paper *Tuesday's Child:* "And we slept in the park and we lived on the streets and my hair got a little longer and I started playing music and people liked my music and people smiled at me and put their arms around me and hugged me—I didn't know how to act. It just took me away. It grabbed me up, man, that there were people that are real."

They were also young, naïve, eager to believe, and, perhaps even more important, belong. There were followers aplenty for any self-styled guru. It didn't take Manson long to sense this. In the underground milieu into which he'd stumbled, even the fact that he was an ex-convict conferred a certain status. Rapping a line of metaphysical con that borrowed as much from pimping as joint jargon and Scientology, Manson began attracting followers, almost all girls at first, then a few young boys.

"There are a lot of Charlies running around, believe me," observed Roger Smith, Manson's parole officer during his San Francisco period.

But with one big difference: somewhere along the line—I wasn't yet sure *how* or *where* or *when*—Manson developed a control over his followers so all-encompassing that he could ask them to violate the ultimate taboo—say "Kill" and they would do it.

Many automatically assumed the answer was drugs. But Dr. David Smith, who got to know the group through his work in the Haight-Ashbury Free Medical Clinic, felt "sex, not drugs, was the common denominator" in the Manson Family. "A new girl in Charlie's Family would bring with her a certain middle-class morality. The first thing Charlie did was to see that all this was worn down.

That way he was able to eliminate the controls that normally govern our lives."

Sex, drugs—they were certainly part of the answer, and I'd soon learn a great deal more about how Manson used both—but they were only part. There was something more, a lot more.

Manson himself de-emphasized the importance of drugs, at least as far as he was concerned. During this period he took his first LSD trip. He later said that it "enlightened my awareness" but added "being in jail for so long had already left my awareness pretty well open." Aware Charlie was.

Manson claimed he foresaw the decline of the Haight even before it came into full flower. Saw police harassment, bad trips, heavy vibes, people ripping off one another and OD'ing in the streets. During the famous Summer of Love, with free rock concerts and Owsley's acid and a hundred more young people arriving every day, he got an old school bus, loaded up his followers, and split, "looking for a place to get away from the Man."

Mary Brunner eventually left her job and joined Manson's wandering caravan. She had a child by him, Michael Manson, the whole Family participating in the delivery, Manson himself biting through the umbilical cord.

Interviewed in Eau Claire, Wisconsin, where she had gone following her release from jail, Mary Brunner agreed to cooperate with the police in return for immunity in the Hinman murder. She supplied numerous details regarding that crime. She also said that in the latter part of September 1969, Tex Watson had told her about the murder of Shorty. They had buried his body near the railroad tracks at Spahn, Tex said, and Gypsy abandoned his car in Canoga Park near a residence the Family had previously occupied on Gresham Street. On the basis of this information, LASO began a search for both the body and the vehicle.

Obviously, Mary Brunner would be an important witness in both the Hinman and Shea cases. Though she had been in jail when the Tate and LaBianca murders occurred, for a time I even considered using her as a witness in that case, since she could testify to the beginnings of the

Family. But I remained very leery of her. According to others I interviewed, her devotion to Manson was fanatical. I just couldn't visualize her testifying against the father of her child.

The Tate case had been big news abroad since the murders occurred, eclipsing even the incident at Chappaquiddick. The arrests commanded just as much attention.

Because of the time difference, it was nearly midnight of December 1 before reports of the "hippie kill cult" reached London. As in the United States, the sensational dispatches dominated the headlines of the papers the next day, led off radio and TV broadcasts.

At eleven that morning a maid in the Talgarth Hotel, on Talgarth Road in London, tried to open the door of a room occupied by an American youth named Joel Pugh. It was locked from the inside. Shortly after 6 P.M. the hotel manager unlocked the door with a passkey. "It only opened about one foot," he stated. "There seemed to be a weight behind it." Kneeling down and reaching in, "I felt what seemed like an arm." He hastily called the police. A constable from Hammersmith station arrived minutes later and pushed the door open. Behind it was the body of Joel Pugh. He was lying on his back, unclothed except for a sheet over the lower half of his body. His throat had been slit, twice. There was a bruise on his forehead, slash marks on both wrists, and two bloody razor blades, one less than two feet from the body. There were no notes, although there were some "writings" in reverse on the mirror, along with some "comic-book type drawings."

According to the manager, Pugh had checked into the room on October 27 with a young lady who had left after three weeks. A "hippie in appearance," Pugh was quiet, went out rarely, seemed to have no friends.

There being "no wound not incapable of being self-inflicted," the coroner's inquest concluded that Pugh "took his own life while the balance of his mind was disturbed."

Although the circumstances of the death, including the wounds themselves, were equally if not more consistent with murder, it was considered a routine suicide. No one thought the drawings or writings important enough to take down (the manager later recalled only the words "Jack and Jill"). No attempt was made to determine the time of death. Nor, though Pugh's room was on the ground floor and could be entered and left through the window, did anyone feel it necessary to check for latent prints.

At the time no one connected the death with the big American news that day. If it hadn't been for a brief reference in a letter over a month later, we probably would have remained unaware that Joel Dean Pugh, age twenty-nine, former Manson Family member and husband of Family member Sandra Good, had joined the lengthening list of mysterious deaths connected with the case.

When she and Squeaky moved out of their motel room in Independence, Sandy left some papers behind. Among them was a letter from an unidentified former Family member which contained the line: "I would not want what happened to Joel to happen to me."

December 3, 1969

About eight that night Richard Caballero brought the Susan Atkins tape to LAPD. He requested that no copy be made; however, I was allowed to take notes. In addition to myself, both Lieutenants Helder and LePage and four or five detectives were present while the tape was being played. We said little as, with all the casualness of a child reciting what she did that day in school, Susan Atkins matter-of-factly described the slaughter of seven people.

The voice was that of a young girl. But except for occasional giggles—"And Sharon went through quite a few changes [laughs], quite a few changes"—it was flat, emotionless, dead. It was as if all the human feelings had been erased. *What kind of creature is this?* I wondered.

I'd soon know. Caballero had agreed that before we took the case to the grand jury, I could personally interview Susan Atkins.

The tape lasted about two hours. Although the monumental job of proving their guilt remained, when the tape had ended—Caballero saying to Susan, "O.K., now we're going to get you something to eat, including some ice cream"—we at least knew, for the first time, exactly who had been involved in the Tate and LaBianca murders.

Though Manson had sent the killers to 10050 Cielo Drive, he had not gone along himself. Those who did go were Charles "Tex" Watson, Susan Atkins, Patricia Krenwinkel, and Linda Kasabian. One man, three girls, who would mercilessly shoot and stab five people to death.

Manson, however, did enter the Waverly Drive residence the next night, to tie up Rosemary and Leno LaBianca. He then sent in Watson, Krenwinkel, and Leslie Van Houten, aka Sankston, with instructions to "kill them."

Susan Atkins herself hadn't been inside the LaBianca residence. She had remained in the car with Clem and Linda. But she had heard—from Manson, Krenwinkel, and Van Houten—what had occurred inside.

Though the tape cleared up some mysteries, many remained. And there were discrepancies. For example, although Susan admitted stabbing the big man (Frykowski) five or six times, "in self-defense," she said nothing about stabbing Sharon Tate. In contrast to what she had told Virginia Graham and Ronnie Howard, Susan now claimed that she had held Sharon while Tex stabbed her.

Returning to my office, I did what I do after every interview—converted my notes into a tentative interrogation. I had a lot of questions I wanted to ask Sadie Mae Glutz.

Linda Kasabian waived extradition proceedings and was flown back to Los Angeles that same day. She was booked into Sybil Brand at 11:15 P.M. Aaron was there, as was Linda's attorney, Gary Fleischman. Though Fleischman permitted her to ID some photographs of various Family members which Aaron had, he would not let Aaron question her. Aaron did ask her how she felt, and she replied, "Tired, but relieved." Aaron got the impression that Linda herself was anxious to tell what she knew but that Fleischman was holding out for a deal.

December 4, 1969

CONFIDENTIAL MEMORANDUM

TO: EVELLE J. YOUNGER
District Attorney

FROM: AARON H. STOVITZ
Head, Trials Division

SUBJECT: SUSAN ATKINS

A meeting was held today in Mr. Younger's office, commencing at 10:20 A.M. and concluding at 11 A.M. Present at the meeting were Mr. Younger, Paul Caruso, Richard Caballero, Aaron Stovitz and Vincent Bugliosi.

Discussion was had as to whether or not immunity should be given to Susan Atkins in exchange for her testimony at the Grand Jury hearing and subsequent trial. It was decided that she would *not* be given immunity.

Mr. Caballero made it known that at this moment his client may not testify at the trial due to her fear of the physical presence of Charles Manson and the other participants in the Sharon Tate murders.

Discussion was held concerning the value of Susan Atkins' testimony. Agreement was reached upon the following points:

1. That Susan Atkins' information has been vital to law enforcement.

2. In view of her past cooperation and in the event that she testifies truthfully at the Grand Jury, the prosecution will not seek the death penalty against her in any of the three cases that are now known to

the police; namely, the Hinman murder, the Sharon Tate murders, and the LaBianca murders.

3. The extent to which the District Attorney's Office will assist Defense Counsel in an attempt to seek less than a first degree murder, life sentence, will depend upon the extent to which Susan Atkins continues to cooperate.

4. That in the event that Susan Atkins does not testify at the trial or that the prosecution does not use her as a witness at the trial, the prosecution will not use her testimony, given at the Grand Jury, against her.

Caballero had made an excellent deal, as far as his client was concerned. If she testified truthfully before the grand jury, we could not seek the death penalty against her in the Hinman, Tate, and LaBianca cases; nor could we use her grand jury testimony against her or any of her co-defendants when they were brought to trial. As Caballero later put it, "She gave up nothing and got everything in return."

For our part, I felt we got very much the short end. Susan Atkins would tell her story at the grand jury. We'd get an indictment. And that would be all we would have, a scrap of paper. For Caballero was convinced she would never testify at the trial. He was worried that even now she might suddenly change her mind.

We had no choice but to rush the case to the grand jury, which was meeting the following day.

Our case was getting a little stronger. The previous day Sergeant Sam McLarty of the Mobile Police Department had taken Patricia Krenwinkel's prints. On receiving the exemplar from Mobile, Sergeant Frank Marz of LAPD "made" one print. The print of the little finger on Krenwinkel's left hand matched a latent print officer Boen had lifted from the frame on the left French door *inside* Sharon Tate's bedroom. This was the blood-splattered door that led outside to the pool.

We now had a second piece of physical evidence linking still another of the suspects to the crime scene.

But we didn't have either suspect. Like Watson, Krenwinkel intended to fight extradition. She would be held fourteen days without bond. If extradition papers were not there before the fifteenth day, she would be released.

Caballero drove me to his office in Beverly Hills. By the time we arrived, about 5:30 P.M., Susan Atkins was already there, having been taken out of Sybil Brand on the basis of another court order, requested by Aaron. Caballero had suggested that Susan would be much more apt to speak freely with me in the relaxed atmosphere of his office than at Sybil Brand, and Miller Leavy, Aaron, and I had agreed.

Although she had opened up to both Virginia Graham and Ronnie Howard, my interview with Susan Atkins on the Tate-LaBianca murders was the first she had had with any law-enforcement officer. It would also be the last.

Twenty-one years old, five feet five, 120 pounds, long brown hair, brown eyes, a not unattractive face, but with a distant, far-off look, similar to the expressions of Sandy and Squeaky but even more pronounced.

Although this was the first time I had seen Susan Atkins, I already knew quite a bit about her. Born in San Gabriel, California, she had grown up in San Jose. Her mother had died of cancer while Susan was still in her teens, and, after numerous quarrels with her father, she'd dropped out of high school and drifted to San Francisco. Hustler, topless dancer, kept woman, gun moll—she'd been all these things even before meeting Charles Manson. I had a certain amount of pity for her. I tried my best to understand her. But I couldn't summon up very much compassion, not after having seen the photographs of what had been done to the Tate victims.

After Caballero introduced us, I informed her of her constitutional rights and obtained permission to interview her.

A male and female deputy sheriff sat just outside the open door of Caballero's office, watching Susan's every move. Caballero remained for most of the interview, leaving only to take a few phone calls. I had Susan tell me the whole story, from the time she first met Manson in

Haight-Ashbury in 1967 to the present. Periodically I'd halt her narrative to ask questions.

"Were you, Tex, or any of the others under the influence of LSD or any other drug on the night of the Tate murders?"

"No."

"What about the next night, the night the LaBiancas were killed?"

"No. Neither night."

There was something mysterious about her. She would talk rapidly for a few minutes, then pause, head slightly cocked to the side, as if sensing voices no one else could.

"You know," she confided, "Charlie is looking at us right now and he can hear everything we are saying."

"Charlie is up in Independence, Sadie."

She smiled, secure in the knowledge that she was right and I, an outsider, an unbeliever, was wrong.

Looking at her, I thought to myself, This is the star witness for the prosecution? I'm going to build my case upon the testimony of this very, very strange girl?

She was crazy. I had no doubt about it. Probably not legally insane, but crazy nonetheless.

As on the tape, she admitted stabbing Frykowski but denied stabbing Sharon Tate. I'd conducted hundreds of interviews; you get a sort of visceral reaction when someone is lying. I felt that she *had* stabbed Sharon but didn't want to admit it to me.

I had to interview over a dozen witnesses that same night: Winifred Chapman, the first police officers to arrive at Cielo and Waverly, Granado and the fingerprint men, Lomax from Hi Standard, Coroner Noguchi and Deputy Medical Examiner Katsuyama, DeCarlo, Melcher, Jakobson. Each presented special problems. Winifred Chapman was petulent, querulous: she wouldn't testify to seeing any bodies, or any blood, or . . . Coroner Noguchi was a rambler: he had to be carefully prepared so he would stick to the subject. Danny DeCarlo hadn't been believable in the Beausoleil trial: I had to make sure the grand jury believed him. It was necessary not only to extract from very disparate witnesses, many of them experts in their individual fields, exactly what was relevant, but to bring these pieces together into a solid, convincing case.

Seven murder victims, multiple defendants: a case like this was not only probably unprecedented, it required weeks of preparation. Because of Chief Davis' rush to break the news, we'd had only days.

It was 2 A.M. before I finished. I still had to convert my notes to interrogation. It was 3:30 before I finished. I was up at 6 A.M. In three hours we had to take the Tate and LaBianca cases before the Los Angeles County grand jury.

December 5, 1969

"Sorry. No comment." Although grand jury proceedings are by law secret—neither the DA's Office, the witnesses, nor the jurors being allowed to discuss the evidence—this didn't keep the reporters from trying. There must have been a hundred newsmen in the narrow hallway outside the grand jury chambers; some were atop tables, so it looked as if they were stacked to the ceiling.

In Los Angeles the grand jury consists of twenty-three persons, picked by lot from a list of names submitted by each Superior Court judge. Of that number twenty-one were present, two-thirds of whom would have to concur to return an indictment. The proceedings themselves are usually brief. The prosecution presents just enough of its case to get an indictment and no more. Though in this instance the testimony would extend over two days, the "star witness for the prosecution" would tell her story in less than one.

Attorney Richard Caballero was the first witness, testifying that he had informed his client of her rights. Caballero then left the chambers. Not only are witnesses not allowed to have their attorneys present, each witness testifies outside the hearing of the other witnesses.

THE SERGEANT AT ARMS "Susan Atkins."

The jurors, seven men and fourteen women, looked at her with obvious curiosity.

Aaron informed Susan of her rights, among which was her right not to incriminate herself. She waived them. I then took over the questioning, establishing that she knew Charles Manson and taking her back to the day they first met. It was over two years ago. She was living in a house on Lyon Street in the Haight-Ashbury district of San Francisco, with a number of other young people, most of whom were into drugs.

A. ". . . and I was sitting in the living room and a man walked in and he had a guitar with him and all of a sudden he was surrounded by a group of girls." The man sat down and began to play, "and the song that caught my attention most was 'The Shadow of Your Smile,' and he sounded like an angel."

Q. "You are referring to Charles Manson?"

A. "Yes. And when he was through singing, I wanted to get some attention from him, and I asked him if I could play his guitar . . . and he handed me the guitar and I thought, 'I can't play this,' and then he looked at me and said, 'You can play that if you want to.'

"Now he had never heard me say 'I can't play this,' I only thought it. So when he told me I could play it, it blew my mind, because he was inside my head, and I knew at that time that he was something that I had been looking for . . . and I went down and kissed his feet."

A day or two later Manson returned to the house and asked her to go for a walk. "And we walked a couple blocks to another house and he told me he wanted to make love with me.

"Well, I acknowledged the fact that I wanted to make love with him, and he told me to take off my clothes, so I uninhibitedly took off my clothes, and there happened to be a full-length mirror in the room, and he told me to go over and look at myself in the mirror.

"I didn't want to do it, so he took me by my hand and stood me in front of the mirror, and I turned away and he said, 'Go ahead and look at yourself. There is nothing wrong with you. You are perfect. You have always been perfect.' "

Q. "What happened next?"

A. "He asked me if I had ever made love with my father. I looked at him and kind of giggled and I said, 'No.' And he said, 'Have you ever thought about making love with your father?' I said, 'Yes.' And he told me, 'All right, when you are making love . . . picture in your mind that I am your father.' And I did, I did so, and it was a very beautiful experience."

Susan said that before she met Manson she felt she was "lacking something." But then "I gave myself to him, and in return for that he gave me back to myself. He gave me the faith in myself to be able to know that I am a woman."

A week or so later, she, Manson, Mary Brunner, Ella Jo Bailey, Lynette Fromme, and Patricia Krenwinkel, together with three or four boys whose names she couldn't remember, left San Francisco in an old school bus from which they had removed most of the seats, furnishing it with brightly colored rugs and pillows. For the next year and a half they roamed—north to Mendocino, Oregon, Washington; south to Big Sur, Los Angeles, Mexico, Nevada, Arizona, New Mexico; and, eventually, back to L.A., living first in various residences in Topanga Canyon, Malibu, Venice, and then, finally, Spahn Ranch. En route others joined them, a few staying permanently, most only temporarily. According to Susan, they went through changes, and learned to love. The girls made love with each of the boys, and with each other. But Charlie was complete love. Although he did not have sex with her often—only six times in the more than two years they were together—"he would give himself completely."

Q. "Were you very much in love with him, Susan?"

A. "I was in love with the reflection and the reflection I speak of is Charlie Manson's."

Q. "Was there any limit to what you would do for him?"

A. "No."

I was laying the foundation for the very heart of my case against Manson, that Susan and the others would do anything for him, up to and including murder at his command.

Q. "What was it about Charlie that caused you girls to be in love with him and to do what he wanted you to do?"

A. "Charlie is the only man I have ever met . . . on the face of this earth . . . that is a complete man. He will not take back-talk from a woman. He will not let a woman talk him into doing anything. He is a man."

Charlie had given her the name Sadie Mae Glutz because "in order for me to be completely free in my mind I had to be able to completely forget the past. The easiest way to do this, to change identity, is by doing so with a name."

According to Susan, Charlie himself went under a variety of names, calling himself the Devil, Satan, Soul.

Q. "Did Mr. Manson ever call himself Jesus?"

A. "He personally never called himself Jesus."

Q. "Did you ever call him Jesus?" From my questioning the night before, I anticipated that Susan would be evasive about this, and she was.

A. "He represented a Jesus Christ-like person to me."

Q. "Do you think Charlie is an evil person?"

A. "In your standards of evil, looking at him through your eyes, I would say yes. Looking at him through my eyes, he is as good as he is evil, he is as evil as he is good. You could not judge the man."

Although Susan didn't state that she believed Manson was Christ, the implication was there. Though I was at this time far from understanding it myself, it was important that I give the jury some explanation, however partial, for Manson's control over his followers. Incredible as all this was to the predominantly upper-middle-class, upper-middle-aged grand jurors, it was nothing compared to what they would hear when she described those two nights of murder.

I worked up to them gradually, having her describe Spahn Ranch and the life there, and asking her how they survived. People gave them things, Susan said. Also, they panhandled. And "the supermarkets all over Los Angeles throw away perfectly good food every day, fresh vegetables and sometimes cartons of eggs, packages of cheese that are stamped to a certain date, but the food is still good, and us girls used to go out and do 'garbage runs.' "

DeCarlo had told me of one such garbage run, when, to the astonishment of supermarket employees, the girls had driven up in Dennis Wilson's Rolls-Royce.

They also stole—credit cards, other things.

Q. "Did Charlie ask you to steal?"

A. "No, I took it upon myself. I was—we'd get programmed to do things."

Q. "Programmed by Charlie?"

A. "By Charlie, but it's hard for me to explain it so that you can see the way—the way I see. The words that would come from Charlie's mouth would not come from inside him, [they] would come from what I call the Infinite."

And sometimes, at night, they "creepy-crawled."

Q. "Explain to these members of the jury what you mean by that."

A. "Moving in silence so that nobody sees us or hears us . . . Wearing very dark clothing . . ."

Q. "Entering residences at night?"

A. "Yes."

They would pick a house at random, anywhere in Los Angeles, slip in while the occupants were asleep, creep and crawl around the rooms silently, maybe move things so when the people awakened they wouldn't be in the same places they had been when they went to bed. Everyone carried a knife. Susan said she did it "because everybody else in the Family was doing it" and she wanted that experience.

These creepy-crawling expeditions were, I felt sure the jury would surmise, dress rehearsals for murder.

Q. "Did you call your group by any name, Susan?"

A. "Among ourselves we called ourselves the Family." It was, Susan said, "a family like no other family."

I thought I heard a juror mutter, "Thank God!"

Q. "Susan, were you living at Spahn Ranch on the date of August the eighth, 1969?"

A. "Yes."

Q. "Susan, on that date did Charlie Manson instruct you and some other members of the Family to do anything?"

A. "I never recall getting any actual instructions from

Charlie other than getting a change of clothing and a knife and was told to do exactly what Tex told me to do."

Q. "Did Charlie indicate to you the type of clothing you should take?"

A. "He told me . . . wear dark clothes."

Susan ID'd photos of Watson, Krenwinkel, and Kasabian, as well as a photo of the old Ford in which the four of them left the ranch. Charlie waved to them as they drove off. Susan didn't notice the time, but it was night. There was a pair of wire cutters in the back seat, also a rope. She, Katie, and Linda each had a knife; Tex had a gun and, she believed, a knife too. Not until they were en route did Tex tell them, to quote Susan, that they "were going to a house up on the hill that used to belong to Terry Melcher, and the only reason why we were going to that house was because Tex knew the outline of the house."

Q. "Did Tex tell you why you four were going to Terry Melcher's former residence?"

Matter-of-factly, with no emotion whatsoever, Susan replied, "To get all of their money and to kill whoever was there."

Q. "It didn't make any difference who was there, you were told to kill them; is that correct?"

A. "Yes."

They got lost on the way. However, Tex finally recognized the turnoff and they drove to the top of the hill. Tex got out, climbed the telephone pole, and, using the wire cutters, severed the wires. (LAPD still hadn't got back to me regarding the test cuts made by the pair found at Barker.) When Tex returned to the car, they drove back down the hill, parked at the bottom, then, bringing along their extra clothing, walked back up. They didn't enter the grounds through the gate "because we thought there might be an alarm system or electricity." To the right of the gate was a steep, brushy incline. The fence wasn't as high here. Susan threw over her clothing bundle, then went over herself, her knife in her teeth. The others followed.

They were stowing their clothing in the bushes when Susan saw the headlights of a car. It was coming up the driveway in the direction of the gate. "Tex told us girls to lie down and be still and not make a sound. He went out of sight . . . I heard him say 'Halt.' " Susan also heard another voice, male, say "Please don't hurt me, I won't say anything." "And I heard a gunshot and I heard another gunshot and another one and another one." Four shots, then Tex returned and told them to come on. When they got to the car, Tex reached inside and turned off the lights; then they pushed the car away from the gate, back up the driveway.

I showed Susan a photo of the Rambler. "It looked similar to it, yes." I then showed her the police photograph of Steven Parent inside the vehicle.

A. "That is the thing I saw in the car."

There were audible gasps from the jurors.

Q. "When you say 'thing,' you are referring to a human being?"

A. "Yes, human being."

The jurors had looked at the heart of Susan Atkins and seen ice.

They went on down the driveway, past the garage, to the house. Using a scale diagram I'd had prepared, Susan indicated their approach to the dining-room window. "Tex opened the window, crawled inside, and the next thing I knew he was at the front door."

Q. "Did all of you girls enter at that time?"

A. "Only two of us entered, one stayed outside."

Q. "Who stayed outside?"

A. "Linda Kasabian."

Susan and Katie joined Tex. There was a man lying on the couch (Susan ID'd a photo of Voytek Frykowski). "The man stretched his arms and woke up. I guess he thought some of his friends were coming from somewhere. He said, 'What time is it?' . . . Tex jumped in front of him and held a gun in his face and said, 'Be quiet. Don't move or you're dead.' Frykowski said something like 'Who are you and what are you doing here?' "

Q. "What did Tex say to that, if anything?"

A. "He said, 'I am the Devil and I'm here to do the Devil's business . . .' "

Tex then told Susan to check for other people. In the

first bedroom she saw a woman reading a book. (Susan ID'd a photo of Abigail Folger.) "She looked at me and smiled and I looked at her and smiled." She went on. A man and a woman were in the next bedroom. The man, who was sitting on the edge of the bed, had his back to Susan. The woman, who was pregnant, was lying on the bed. (Susan ID'd photos of Jay Sebring and Sharon Tate.) The pair were talking and neither saw her. Returning to the living room, she reported to Tex that there were three more people.

Tex gave her the rope and told her to tie up the man on the couch. After she'd done this, Tex ordered her to get the others. Susan walked into Abigail Folger's bedroom, "put a knife in front of her, and said, 'Get up and go into the living room. Don't ask any questions. Just do what I say.' " Katie, also armed with a knife, took charge of Folger while Susan got the other two.

None offered any resistance. All had the same expression on their faces, "Shock."

On entering the living room, Sebring asked Tex, "What are you doing here?" Tex told him to shut up, then ordered the three to lie on their stomachs on the floor in front of the fireplace. "Can't you see she's pregnant?" Sebring said. "Let her sit down."

When Sebring "didn't follow Tex's orders ... Tex shot him."

Q. "Did you see Tex shoot Jay Sebring?"

A. "Yes."

Q. "With the gun that he had taken from Spahn Ranch?"

A. "Yes."

Q. "What happened next?"

A. "Jay Sebring fell over in front of the fireplace and Sharon and Abigail screamed."

Tex ordered them to be quiet. When he asked if they had any money, Abigail said she had some in her purse in the bedroom. Susan went with her to get it. Abigail handed her seventy-two dollars and asked if she wanted her credit cards. Susan said she didn't. On their return to the living room, Tex told Susan to get a towel and retie Frykowski's hands; she did, she said, but couldn't get the knot very tight. Tex then took the rope and tied it first around Sebring's neck, then the necks of Abigail and Sharon. He threw the end of the rope over the beam in the ceiling and pulled on it, "which made Sharon and Abigail stand up so they wouldn't be choked to death . . ." Then, "I forget who said it, but one of the victims said, 'What are you going to do with us?' and Tex said, 'You are all going to die.' And at that time they began to plead for their lives."

Q. "What is the next thing that happened?"

A. "Then Tex ordered me to go over and kill Frykowski."

As she raised her knife, Frykowski, who had managed to free his hands, jumped up and "knocked me down, and I grabbed him as best I could, and then it was a fight for my life as well as him fighting for his life.

"Somehow he got ahold of my hair and pulled it very hard and I was screaming for Tex to help me, or somebody to help me, and Frykowski, he was also screaming.

"Somehow he got behind me, and I had the knife in my right hand and I was—I was—I don't know where I was at but I was just swinging with the knife, and I remember hitting something four, five times repeatedly behind me. I didn't see what it was I was stabbing."

Q. "But did it appear to be a human being?"

A. "I never stabbed a human being before, but I just know it was going into something."

Q. "Could it have been Frykowski?"

A. "It could have been Frykowski, it could have been a chair, I don't know what it was."

Susan had changed her story. In my interview with her, and on the tape, she had admitted to stabbing Frykowski "three or four times in the leg." Also, if the story she told Virginia Graham was true, she knew exactly how it felt to stab someone, i.e., Gary Hinman.

Frykowski ran for the front door, "yelling for his life, for somebody to come help him." Tex got to him and hit him over the head several times with "I believe a gun butt." Tex later told her that he had broken the gun hitting Frykowski and that it wouldn't work any more.* Apparently Tex had a knife ready, as he began stabbing Frykowski "as best he could because Frykowski was still fighting." Meanwhile, "Abigail Folger had gotten loose from the rope and was in a fight with Katie, Patricia Krenwinkel . . ."

THE FOREMAN "We have a grand juror who would like to be excused for just a couple of minutes."

A recess was taken. There was more than one pale face in the jury box.

We resumed where Susan had left off. Someone was moaning, she said. Tex ran over to Sebring, "and bent down and viciously stabbed him in the back many times . . .

"Sharon Tate, I remember seeing her struggling with the rope." Tex ordered Susan to take care of her. Susan locked her arm around Sharon's neck, forcing her back onto the couch. She was begging for her life. "I looked at her and said, 'Woman, I have no mercy for you.' And I knew that I was talking to myself, not to her . . ."

Q. "Did Sharon say anything about the baby at that point?"

A. "She said, 'Please let me go. All I want to do is have my baby.'

"There was a lot of confusion going on . . . Tex went over to help Katie . . . I saw Tex stab Abigail Folger and just before he stabbed—maybe an instant before he stabbed her—she looked at him and let her arms go and looked at all of us and said, 'I give up. Take me.' "

I asked Susan how many times Tex had stabbed Abigail. "Only once," Susan replied. "She grabbed her middle section of her body and fell to the floor."

Tex then ran outside. Susan released her grip on Sharon but continued to guard her. When Tex returned, he told Susan, "Kill her." But, according to the story Susan was now telling, "I couldn't." Instead, "in order to make a diversion so that Tex couldn't see that I couldn't kill her, I grabbed her hand and held her arms, and then I saw Tex

*Although Frykowski had been shot twice, Susan couldn't recall the shooting, leaving in doubt exactly when this occurred.

stab her in the heart area around the chest." Sharon then fell from the couch to the floor. (Susan only mentioned Tex stabbing Sharon Tate once. According to the autopsy report, she had been stabbed sixteen times. According to Ronnie Howard, Susan told her, "I just kept stabbing her until she stopped screaming.")

The next thing she remembered, Susan now testified, was that she, Tex, and Katie were outside, and "I saw Abigail Folger on the front lawn, bent over falling onto the grass . . . I didn't see her go outside . . . and I saw Tex go over and stab her three or four—I don't know how many times . . ." (Abigail Folger had twenty-eight stab wounds.) "While he was doing that, Katie and I were looking for Linda, because she wasn't around . . . and then Tex walked over to Frykowski and kicked him in the head." Frykowski was on the front lawn, away from the door. When Tex kicked him, "the body didn't move very much. I believe it was dead at that time." (Which was not surprising, since Voytek Frykowski had been shot twice, struck over the head thirteen times with a blunt object, and stabbed fifty-one times.)

Then "Tex told me to go back into the house and write something on the door in one of the victims' blood . . . He said, 'Write something that will shock the world.' . . . I had previously been involved in something similar to this [Hinman], where I saw 'political piggy' written on the wall, so that stuck very heavily in my mind . . ." Re-entering the house, she picked up the same towel she had used to tie Frykowski's hands, and walked over to Sharon Tate. Then she heard sounds.

Q. "What kind of sounds were they?"

A. "Gurgling sounds like blood flowing into the body out of the heart."

Q. "What did you do then?"

A. "I picked up the towel and turned my head and touched her chest, and at the same time I saw she was pregnant and I knew that there was a living being inside of that body and I wanted to but I didn't have the courage to go ahead and take it . . . And I got the towel with Sharon Tate's blood, walked over to the door, and with the towel I wrote PIG on the door."

Susan then threw the towel back into the living room; she didn't look to see where it landed. (It fell on Sebring's face, hence the "hood" referred to in the press.)

Sadie, Tex, and Katie then picked up the bundles of spare clothing they'd hidden in the bushes. They left by the gate, Tex pushing the button, and hurried down the hill. "When we got to the car, Linda Kasabian started the car, and Tex ran up to her and said, 'What do you think you're doing? Get over on the passenger side. Don't do anything until I tell you to do it.' Then we drove off."

They changed clothing in the car, all except Linda, who, not having been in the house, had no blood on her. As they were driving away, Susan realized she had lost her knife, but Tex was against going back.

They drove somewhere along "Benedict Canyon, Mulholland Drive, I don't know [which street] . . . until we came to what looked like an embankment going down like a cliff with a mountain on one side and a cliff on the other." They pulled off and stopped, and "Linda threw all the bloody clothes over the side of the hill . . ." The weapons, the knives and gun, were tossed out at "three or four different places, I don't remember how many."

Susan then described, as she had to Virginia Graham and Ronnie Howard, how after they'd pulled off onto a side street and used a garden hose to wash off the blood, a man and a woman rushed out of the house and threatened to report them to the police. "And Tex looked at him and said, "Gee, I'm sorry. I didn't think you were home. We were just walking around and wanted a drink of water. We didn't mean to wake you up or disturb you.' And the man looked down the street and said, 'Is that your car?' And Tex said, 'No, I told you we were just walking.' The man said, 'I know that is your car. You better get in and get going.' "

They got in the car, and the man, apparently having decided to detain them, reached in to get the keys. Tex quickly started the car, however, and drove off fast.

After stopping at a service station on Sunset Boulevard, where they took turns going to the bathroom to check for "any other blood spots," they drove back to Spahn Ranch, arriving there, Susan guessed, about 2 A.M.

When they pulled up in front of the boardwalk of the old movie set, Charles Manson was waiting for them. He walked over to the car, leaned inside, and asked, "What are you doing home so early?"

According to Susan, Tex told Manson "basically just what we had done. That it all happened perfectly. There was a lot of—it happened very fast—a lot of panic, and he described it, 'Boy, it sure was helter skelter.' "

While at the service station, Susan had noticed blood on the door handles and steering wheel. She now went into the ranch kitchen and got a rag and a sponge and wiped it off.

Q. "How was Charles Manson acting when you arrived back at Spahn Ranch?"

A. "Charles Manson changes from second to second. He can be anybody he wants to be. He can put on any face he wants to put on at any given moment."

Patricia "was very silent." Tex was "nervous like he had just been through a traumatic experience."

Q. "How did you feel about what you had just done?"

A. "I almost passed out. I felt as though I had killed myself. I felt dead. I feel dead now."

After she'd finished cleaning the car, Susan and the others had gone to bed. She thought she had made love to someone, maybe Clem, but then again maybe she had imagined it.

The noon recess was called.

Throughout her testimony Susan had referred to the victims by name. After the recess I established that she hadn't known their names that night, nor had she ever seen any of them before. ". . . when I first saw them, my reaction was, 'Wow, they sure are beautiful people.' "

Susan first learned their identities the day after the murders, while watching the news on TV in the trailer next to George Spahn's house. Tex, Katie, and Clem were also there, and maybe Linda, though Susan wasn't sure.

Q. "As you were watching the television news coverage, did anyone say anything?"

Someone—Susan thought the words came from her

own mouth, but she wasn't positive—said either, "The Soul sure did pick a lulu," or "The Soul sure did a good job." She did remember saying that what had happened had "served its purpose." Which was? I asked.

A. "To instill fear into the establishment."

I asked Susan if any other members of the Family knew they had committed the Tate murders.

A. "The Family was so much together that nothing ever had to be said. We all just knew what each other would do or had done."

We came now to the second night, the evening of August 9 and the early-morning hours of August 10.

That evening Manson again told Susan to get an extra set of clothing. "I looked at him and I knew what he wanted me to do, and I gave a sort of sigh and went and did what he asked me to do."

Q. "Did he say what you were going to go out and do that night?" I asked.

A. "He said we were going to go out and do the same thing we did the last night . . . only two different houses . . ."

It was the same car and the same cast—Susan, Katie, Linda, and Tex—with three additions: Charlie, Clem, and Leslie. Susan didn't notice any knives, only a gun, which Charlie had.

They stopped in front of a house, "somewhere in Pasadena, I believe," Charlie got out, and the others drove around the block, then came back and picked him up. "He said he saw pictures of children through the window and he didn't want to do that house." In the future, however, Manson explained, they might have to kill the children also.

They stopped in front of another house, but saw some people nearby so remained in the car and after a few minutes drove off. At some point Susan fell asleep, she said. When she awakened, they were in a familiar neighborhood, near a house where, about a year before, she, Charlie, and about fifteen others had gone to an LSD party. The house had been occupied by a "Harold." She couldn't recall his last name.

Charlie got out, only he didn't walk up the driveway of

this particular house but the one next door. Susan went back to sleep. She woke up when Charlie returned. "He said, 'Tex, Katie, Leslie, go into the house. I have the people tied up. They are very calm.'

"He said something to the effect that last night Tex let the people know they were going to be killed, which caused panic, and Charlie said that he reassured the people with smiles in a very quiet manner that they were not to be harmed . . . And so Tex, Leslie, and Katie got out of the car."

Susan ID'd photographs of Tex, Leslie, and Katie. Also of the LaBianca residence, the long driveway, and the house next door.

I asked Susan what else Charlie told the trio. She replied that she "thought," but it may be "my imagination that tells me this," that "Charlie instructed them to go in and kill them." She did recall him saying that they were "to paint a picture more gruesome than anybody had ever seen." He'd also told them that after they were done they were to hitchhike back to the ranch.

When Charlie returned to the car, he had a woman's wallet with him. Then they drove around "in a predominantly colored area."

Q. "What happened next?"

Susan said they stopped at a gas station. Then "Charlie gave Linda Kasabian the woman's wallet and told her to put it in the bathroom in the gas station and leave it there, hoping that somebody would find it and use the credit cards and thus be identified with the murder . . ."

I wondered about that wallet. To date, none of Rosemary LaBianca's credit cards had been used.

After leaving the station, Susan said, she went back to sleep. "It was like I was drugged" though "I was not on drugs at the time." When she woke up, they were back at the ranch.

(At this time we were unaware that Susan Atkins had made some significant omissions in her grand jury testimony—including three other attempts at murder that night. Had we known of them, we probably would have asked for an indictment of Clem. As it was, however, all we had against him was Susan's statement that he had been in the car. And we still had a slim hope that his brother, whom we'd contacted at the Highway Patrol Academy, might persuade him to cooperate with us.)

Susan had not entered the LaBianca residence. However, the next morning Katie told her what had happened inside.

A. "She told me that when they got in the house they took the woman in the bedroom and put her on the bed and left Tex in the living room with the man . . . And then Katie said the woman heard her husband being killed and started to scream, 'What are you doing to my husband?' And Katie said that she then proceeded to stab the woman . . ."

Q. "Did she say what Leslie was doing while—"

A. "Leslie was helping Katie hold the woman down because the woman was fighting all the way up until she died . . ." Later Katie told Susan that the last words the woman spoke—"What are you doing to my husband?"—would be the thought she would carry with her into infinity.

Afterwards, Katie told Susan, they wrote " 'Death to all pigs' on the refrigerator door or on the front door, and I think she said they wrote 'helter skelter' and 'arise.' "

Then Katie walked into the living room from the kitchen with a fork in her hand, and "she looked at the man's stomach and she had the fork in her hand and she put the fork in the man's stomach and watched it wobble back and forth. She said she was fascinated by it."

Susan also said that it was "Katie, I believe," who carved the word "war" on the man's stomach.

The three then took a shower and, since they were hungry, they went to the kitchen and fixed themselves something to eat.

According to Susan, Katie also told her that they presumed the couple had children and that they would probably find the bodies when they came over for Sunday dinner later that day.

After leaving the residence, "they dumped the old clothing in a garbage can a few blocks, maybe a mile, away from the house." Then they hitchhiked back to Spahn Ranch, arriving about dawn.

I had only a few more questions for Susan Atkins.

Q. "Susan, did Charlie oftentimes use the word 'pig' or 'pigs'?"

A. "Yes."

Q. "How about 'helter skelter'?"

A. "Yes."

Q. "Did he use the word 'pigs' and 'helter skelter' very, very frequently?"

A. "Well, Charlie talks a lot . . . In some of the songs he wrote, 'helter skelter' was in them and he'd talk about helter skelter. We all talked about helter skelter."

Q. "You say 'we'; are you speaking of the Family?"

A. "Yes."

Q. "What did the word 'pig' or 'pigs' mean to you and your Family?"

A. " 'Pig' was a word used to describe the establishment. But you must understand that all words had no meanings to us and that 'helter skelter' was explained to me."

Q. "By whom?"

A. "Charlie. I don't even like to say Charlie—I'd like to say the words came from his mouth—that helter skelter was to be the last war on the face of the earth. It would be all the wars that have ever been fought built one on top of the other, something that no man could conceive of in his imagination. You can't conceive of what it would be like to see every man judge himself and then take it out on every other man all over the face of the earth."

After a few more questions, I brought Susan Atkins' testimony to an end. As she nonchalantly stepped down from the witness stand, the jurors stared at her in disbelief. Not once had she shown a trace of remorse, sorrow, or guilt.

There were only four more witnesses that day. After Susan Atkins was taken from the room, Wilfred Parent was brought in to identify his son in a high-school prom picture. After identifying photos of the other Tate victims, Winifred Chapman testified that she had washed the front door of the Tate residence shortly before noon on Friday, August 8. This was important, since it meant that in order to leave a print Charles "Tex" Watson had to have been on the premises sometime after Mrs. Chapman left at four that afternoon.

Aaron questioned Terry Melcher. He described meeting Manson; told of how Manson had been along when Dennis Wilson drove him home to 10050 Cielo Drive one night; and described, very briefly, his two visits to Spahn Ranch, the first to audition Manson, the second to introduce him to Michael Deasy, who had a mobile recording unit and who he felt might be more interested in recording Manson than he was.*

According to various Family members, Melcher had made numerous promises to Manson, and hadn't come through on them. Melcher denied this: the first time he went to Spahn, he had given Manson fifty dollars, all the money he had in his pocket, because "I felt sorry for these people"; but it was for food, not an advance on a recording contract; and he'd made no promises. As for Manson's talent, he "wasn't impressed enough to allot the time necessary" to prepare and record him.

I wanted to interview Melcher in depth—I had a feeling that he was withholding something—but, like most of the other grand jury witnesses, he was here for a very limited purpose, and any real digging would have to wait.

Los Angeles Coroner Thomas Noguchi testified to the autopsy findings on the five Tate victims. When he had concluded, the session was adjourned until Monday.

That the proceedings were secret encouraged speculation, which, in some cases, appeared not as conjecture but fact. The headline on the Los Angeles *Herald Examiner* that afternoon read:

TATE KILLERS WILD ON
LSD, GRAND JURORS TOLD

It wasn't true; Susan Atkins had stated the very opposite, that the killers were not on drugs either night. But

*Manson gave Deasy some LSD. He had such a frightening "trip" that he wanted nothing more to do with Manson or his Family.

the myth was born, and it persisted, perhaps because it was the easiest explanation for what had happened.

Though, as I'd soon learn, drugs were one of several methods Manson used to obtain control over his followers, they had no part in these crimes, for a very simple reason: on these two nights of savage slaughter, Charles Manson wanted his assassins in complete control of their faculties.

The reality, and its implications, were far more frightening than the myth.

December 6-8, 1969

On Saturday, Joe Granado went to the impound garage in Canoga Park to examine John Swartz' 1959 Ford, which had been held there since the August 16 Spahn raid. This was the car Susan Atkins said the killers had used on both nights.

Granado got a positive benzidine reaction on a spot in the upper right-hand corner of the glove compartment, indicating blood, but there wasn't enough to determine whether it was animal or human.

When I finally got Joe's written report, I noticed the blood wasn't mentioned. Asked about this, Joe said the amount was so small he hadn't bothered to note it. I had Joe prepare a new report, this time including reference to the blood. Our case thus far was basically circumstantial, and in such a case each speck of evidence counts.

"I just had a talk with Gary Fleischman, Vince," Aaron said. "He wants a deal for his client Linda Kasabian. Complete immunity in exchange for her testimony at the trial. I told him maybe we could go along with her pleading to voluntary manslaughter, but we couldn't give her—"

"Christ, Aaron," I interrupted. "It's bad enough that we had to give Susan Atkins something! Look at it this way—Krenwinkel's in Alabama, Watson's in Texas; for all we know, we may not be able to extradite them before the others go on trial; and Van Houten wasn't along on the night of the Tate murders. If we give deals to Atkins and Kasabian, who are we going to prosecute for the five Tate killings? Just Charlie? The people of this city won't tolerate that. They're shocked and outraged by these crimes. Drive through Bel Air sometime; the fear is still so real you can feel it."

According to Fleischman, Linda was anxious to testify. He had urged her to fight extradition; she'd gone against his advice and come back to California because she wanted to tell the whole story.

"O.K., what can she testify to? According to Susan, Linda never entered either the Tate or LaBianca residences. As far as we know, she wasn't an eyewitness to any of the murders, with the possible exception of Steven Parent. More important, as long as we have Susan, Linda's testimony would be valueless to us, since Susan and Linda are both accomplices. As you well know, the law is clear on this: the testimony of one accomplice can't be used to corroborate the testimony of another accomplice. What we really need, more than anything else, is corroboration."

This was one of our biggest problems. In a sense it didn't matter who ended up as our star witness; without corroboration our case would be lost as a matter of law. We not only had to find corroboration against *each* of the defendants, that corroborating evidence had to be completely independent of the accomplice's testimony.

Aaron had seen Linda briefly, when she was booked into Sybil Brand. I'd never seen her. For all I knew, she was probably just as freaky as Sadie Mae Glutz.

"Now if Susan bolts back to Charlie," I told Aaron, "and we're left without a major witness for the trial—as well we might be—then we can talk about a deal for Linda. In fact, if that happens, Linda may be our only hope."

When the grand jury reconvened on Monday, we moved quickly through the remaining testimony. Sergeant Michael McGann described what he had found at 10050

Cielo Drive on the morning of August 9, 1969. Sergeant Frank Escalante testified to having rolled Charles Watson's prints on April 23, 1969, when he was arrested on a drug charge; Jerrome Boen of SID described how he lifted the latent from the front door of the Tate residence; and Harold Dolan, also of SID, testified to having compared it to the Watson exemplar, finding eighteen points of identity, eight more than LAPD requires for a positive identification. Sergeant William Lee testified regarding the pieces of gun grip and the .22 caliber bullets. Edward Lomax of Hi Standard matched the grips with his firm's .22 caliber Longhorn revolver, and gave statistics indicating that the gun itself, because of its low production figures, was "rather unique." Gregg Jakobson told of touting Manson to Melcher. Granado testified regarding the rope, the blood on the gun grips, and his discovery of the Buck knife.

It was for the most part highly technical testimony, and the appearance of Daniel DeCarlo provided a respite, as well as more than a little local color.

Aaron asked Danny: "Did you have any particular reason for staying at the ranch?"

A. "Lots of pretty girls up there."

How did he get along with particular girls—for example, Katie?

A. "We talked, that is about it, but I never did nothing. You know, I never snatched her up or anything."

Q. "And is your motorcycle club the kind that goes into a town and scares everybody?"

A. "No, that only happens in the movies."

DeCarlo's appearance, however, was intended for more than comic relief. He testified that Manson, Watson, and others, including himself, target-practiced with a .22 caliber Buntline revolver at Spahn. He said that he had last seen the gun "maybe a week, week and a half" before the sixteenth of August, and never after that. The drawing of the revolver which he had made for LAPD before he knew it was the Tate murder weapon was introduced into evidence. DeCarlo also recalled how he and Charlie had bought the three-strand nylon rope (which, being an ex-Coast Guardsman, he called "line") at the Jack Frost store in Santa Monica in June 1969, and, shown the rope found at Cielo, said it was "identical."

After Susan Atkins, the outlaw motorcyclist looked almost like a model citizen.

Deputy Medical Examiner David Katsuyama followed DeCarlo. Katsuyama had conducted the LaBianca autopsies. I'd have many, many problems with this witness. The grand jury provided only a sample. Aaron was to show Katsuyama a photo of Leno LaBianca's hands, which were bound with a leather thong. DeCarlo was then to retake the stand and describe how Charlie always wore leather thongs around his neck. Sergeant Patchett was to follow and introduce the thongs he had found in Independence among Manson's personal effects. He was also prepared to testify that they were "similar."

Aaron showed Katsuyama the photo, asking what material had been used to tie Leno LaBianca's hands. "Electrical cord," he replied. I managed to suppress a groan: the electrical cord had been around the necks of the LaBianca victims. Would he look at the photo a little more closely? It still looked like electrical cord to him. I finally had to show Katsuyama his own autopsy notes, where he'd written: "The hands are tied together with a rather thin leather thong."

Roxie Lucarelli, an officer with LAPD and a lifelong friend of Leno's, identified photos of the LaBiancas, both Susan and Frank Struthers being still too shaken by the deaths to testify. Sergeant Danny Galindo told what he had found at 3301 Waverly Drive the night of August 10-11, 1969, and stated that a search of the residence revealed no trace of Rosemary LaBianca's wallet.

Of the five girls brought down from Independence, Catherine Share, aka Gypsy, refused to testify, and we had not called Leslie Van Houten, since we were not aware that she was one of the LaBianca killers. The three remaining—Dianne Lake, aka Snake; Nancy Pitman, aka Brenda; and Ruth Ann Moorehouse, aka Ouisch—all denied any knowledge of the murders.

I'd anticipated this. However, I had another reason for calling them. If they appeared as defense witnesses when we went to trial, any discrepancy between what they told the grand jury and the trial jury would give me a prior inconsistent statement with which to impeach their testimony.

At 4:17 P.M. the Los Angeles County grand jury began their deliberations. Exactly twenty minutes later they returned the following indictments: Leslie Van Houten, two counts of murder and one count of conspiracy to commit murder; Charles Manson, Charles Watson, Patricia Krenwinkel, Susan Atkins, and Linda Kasabian, seven counts of murder and one count of conspiracy to commit murder.

We'd got the indictments. And that was about all we had.

December 9-12, 1969

Neither Aaron nor I logged the calls we received, but it would be a safe guess that we were getting upward of a hundred a day, to most of which our only response was "no comment." The press was frantic. Although the indictments had been made public, the grand jury transcript itself had been "sealed"; it would remain secret until a week to ten days after the last defendant was arraigned. It was rumored that one magazine offered $10,000 just to look at a copy.

An officer, Thomas Drynan, called from Oregon. He had arrested Susan Atkins in 1966, as part of a holdup gang. At the time she had been carrying a .25 caliber pistol and had told Drynan that if he hadn't drawn first she would have shot and killed him. At this stage of the investigation such information had no relevance. There was always a chance, however, that it might be useful later, and I made a note of his name and telephone number.

My cubicle in the Hall of Justice measured 20 feet by 10 feet, the furnishings consisting of a battered desk, a rickety cot brought in for cat naps at lunch hour, a filing cabinet, a couple of chairs, and a large table, usually piled high with transcripts and exhibits. A reporter once described the decor as 1930 Chicago. At that I was lucky, since the other deputy DAs had to share their offices. When I had a witness to interview, I'd have to drive everyone else out—not always diplomatically. That left the phone, which, since none of us had secretaries, we had to answer ourselves.

Each day brought new developments. Thus far, although sheriff's deputies had dug up a sizable portion of Spahn Ranch, no trace of the remains of Donald "Shorty" Shea had been found. However, acting on the information supplied by Mary Brunner, LASO searched the neighborhood adjacent to 20910 Gresham Street, Canoga Park, and found, just around the corner from the former Family residence, Shea's 1962 Mercury. It was dirt-covered and rain-streaked, apparently having been abandoned some months before. Inside the vehicle was a footlocker containing Shea's personal effects; dusting it, LASO found a set of palm prints, which were later matched to Family member Bruce Davis. Shea's cowboy boots were also in the car. They were caked with dried blood.

Independence, California, 4 P.M., December 9. Charles Milles Manson, aka Jesus Christ, age thirty-five, address transient, occupation musician, was charged with the Tate-LaBianca murders. Sartuchi and Gutierrez were bringing him to Los Angeles.

We scheduled Manson's arraignment on a different date than that of the other defendants, fearing that if Atkins and Manson met in the courtroom he'd persuade her to repudiate her testimony.

A reporter located Susan Atkins' father in San Jose. He said he didn't believe this claim that Susan was under the "hypnotic spell" of Manson. "I think she is just trying to talk her way out of it. She's sick and she needs help." According to the reporter, Mr. Atkins blamed Susan's involvement on her use of drugs and the leniency of the courts. He said he'd tried for three years to get the courts to keep his rebellious daughter off the streets; had they done so, he implied, this might not have happened.

For Susan, I realized, the Family was her only family. I understood now why Caballero felt it was only a matter of time before she returned to the fold.

On December 10, Susan Atkins, Linda Kasabian, and Leslie Van Houten were brought before Judge William Keene. All three requested and were granted continuances before entering pleas.

This was the first time I had seen Kasabian. She was short, about five feet one, with long, dark-blond hair and green eyes, and was quite obviously pregnant. She looked older than twenty. In contrast to Susan and Leslie, who smiled and giggled through most of the proceedings, Linda seemed on the edge of tears.

Following the grand jury hearing, Judge Keene had called Aaron and me into chambers. At that time he'd told us that since the DA's Office was not discussing the case with the press, he saw no need to issue a "publicity order" (or, as it is most often called, a "gag order") covering the case. However, owing to the incredible amount of pre-trial publicity—a New York *Times* reporter told me that already it far exceeded that given the first Sam Sheppard trial—Judge Keene, without consulting our office, now went ahead and issued a detailed publicity order. Later amended several times, it would run to a dozen pages. In essence, it forbade anyone connected with the case—prosecutors, defense attorneys, police officers, witnesses, and so forth—to discuss the evidence with any representative of the media.

Though unknown to me at the time, the order was already too late to prevent an inside account of the murders from making headlines around the world. The previous evening, attorney Richard Caballero, acting on the basis of an agreement with Susan Atkins, had arranged the sale of the publication rights to her story.

Call from LAPD. Charles Koenig, an attendant at the Standard service station at 12881 Ensenada Boulevard in Sylmar, was cleaning the women's rest room when he noticed the toilet was running. Lifting the lid off the tank, he found, on top of the mechanism, damp but above the waterline, a woman's wallet. He'd checked the driver's license and credit cards, saw the name "Rosemary LaBianca," and immediately called LAPD.

SID was checking the wallet for prints but, because of both the material and the dampness, they doubted they'd find any.

Just the discovery of the wallet was enough for me, for it provided another piece of independent evidence supporting Susan Atkins' story. Apparently the wallet had been there, undiscovered, since Linda Kasabian placed it there the night of the LaBianca murders, exactly four months ago.

At 11 A.M. on December 11 buckskin-clad Charles Manson was brought before Judge William Keene. The courtroom was so packed with reporters and spectators you couldn't have squeezed another person in with a shoehorn. Since Manson lacked funds to hire an attorney, Keene appointed Paul Fitzgerald of the Public Defender's Office to represent him. I'd come up against Paul before on several jury trials and knew he had a good reputation in his office. Manson was arraigned, and a postponement granted until December 22 for the entering of his plea.

In Independence, Sandra Good had told me that once, in the desert, Charlie had picked up a dead bird, breathed on it, and the bird had flown away. Sure, Sandy, sure, I replied. Since then I'd heard a great deal about Manson's alleged "powers"; Susan Atkins, for example, felt he could see and hear everything she did or said.

Midway through the arraignment I looked at my watch. It had stopped. Odd. It was the first time I could remember that happening. Then I noticed that Manson was staring at me, a slight grin on his face.

It was, I told myself, simply a coincidence.

Following the arraignment, Paul Fitzgerald told Ron Einstoss, veteran crime reporter for the Los Angeles *Times:* "There's no case against Manson and these defendants. All the prosecution has are two fingerprints and Vince Bugliosi."

Fitzgerald was right about our case being weak. But I

didn't intend that it should remain that way. Nearly three weeks ago I'd given the Tate detectives, Calkins and McGann, an initial list of things to do, among which were to interview Terry Melcher; check the prints of every known Family member against the unmatched Tate latents; show photographs of Family members to friends and relatives of the victims; determine if the glasses belonged to anyone in the Family.

I called in Calkins and McGann and asked for a progress report. I learned that only one of the things on the list had been done. Melcher had been interviewed. By the LaBianca detectives.

To date LAPD hadn't even begun looking for the Tate weapons and clothing, though Susan Atkins' statements gave us some good clues as to the general area where they should be. Arrangements were made through our office for Susan to be taken from Sybil Brand the following Sunday, to see if she could point out the spots where Linda Kasabian had thrown the various items.

Fitzgerald was not the only one who felt we had no case. The consensus in the DA's Office and the Los Angeles legal community—which I picked up from many sources, usually with some such remark as "Too bad you had to get involved in such a bummer"—was that the case against Manson and most of the other defendants would be thrown out on an 1118 motion.

Under section 1118.1 of the California Penal Code, if at the end of the People's case the court feels the prosecution has failed to put on enough evidence to sustain a conviction on appeal, the judge is empowered to acquit the defendants. They aren't even required to put on a defense to the charges.

Some felt it wouldn't even get that far. *Newsweek* quoted an unnamed Los Angeles County deputy district attorney as saying that our case against Manson was so anemic that it would be thrown out even before we went to trial.

Such talk, in addition to the national exposure that would be accorded any defense attorney connected with the case, was, I suspected, the reason Manson was having so many visitors at the Los Angeles County Jail.

As one deputy sheriff put it, "It's like a bar association convention over here." (Between December 11, 1969, and January 21, 1970, Manson had 237 separate visits, 139 of which were by one or more attorneys.) Among the first lawyers to call on him were Ira Reiner, Daye Shinn, and Ronald Hughes, none of whom I knew at that time, though I'd know all three much better before the trial ended.

Rumors multiplied like bacteria. One was that, prior to the imposition of the gag order, Caballero had sold Atkins' story to a European press syndicate, with the stipulation that the story was not to be released in the United States until after the grand jury transcript was made public. If true, I seriously doubted if American papers would respect such an agreement. There were bound to be leaks.

December 14, 1969

I didn't have to look for a newsstand that sold foreign papers. When I got up that Sunday morning, I needed only to walk out the front door, reach down, and pick up the Los Angeles *Times*.

SUSAN ATKINS' STORY OF
2 NIGHTS OF MURDER

The story covered nearly three pages. Though obviously edited and rewritten, with some additional material on her childhood, it was essentially the same story Susan Atkins had related on the tape made in Caballero's office.

Not until the trial itself would the story-behind-the-story come out. The following is reconstructed from the courtroom testimony. I can make no claim as to its accuracy, only that this is what the various participants testified under oath.

Before the imposition of the gag order, Lawrence Schiller, a self-described Hollywood "journalist and communicator," approached Richard Caballero and his law associate, Paul Caruso, asking if they would be interested in selling Susan Atkins' first-person account of the murders. After consulting with Susan, an agreement was reached and a "ghost"—Los Angeles *Times* reporter Jerry Cohen, on leave of absence from the paper—was hired to write the account.* Using as his main source the December 1 tape, Cohen completed the story in just two days, while locked in a room in Schiller's home. To make sure he maintained "exclusivity," Schiller saw that Cohen had neither carbon paper nor access to a phone, and he destroyed all but the finished draft.

According to their subsequent courtroom testimony, Caballero and Caruso understood that initially the story was to appear in Europe only, with a publication date of Sunday, December 14.

According to Schiller, on December 12 he made three Xerox copies of the manuscript: one was given to Caballero; one to a German editor who had bought the rights for his magazine and who translated it as he flew back to Germany; and the third flown by special courier to the London *News of the World*, which had paid $40,000 for exclusive English rights. Schiller put the original in his own safe.

The following day, Saturday, December 13, Schiller learned (1) that the Los Angeles *Times* also had a Xerox copy of the manuscript, and (2) that the *Times* intended to run it in full the following day. Screaming copyright infringement, Schiller tried, unsuccessfully, to stop publication.

Exactly how the Los Angeles *Times* obtained the story remains unknown. During the trial Caballero more than

*Schiller, though listed as co-author, not only didn't write the story, he never even met Susan Atkins.

According to evidence introduced during the trial, the terms of the agreement were: 25 percent to Schiller; of the remaining 75 percent, 60 percent to Susan Atkins, 40 percent to her attorneys.

hinted that he suspected Schiller, while Schiller attempted to put the blame on Caballero.

Whatever the ethics of the whole matter, the Atkins story created immense problems which would plague both the defense and the prosecution throughout the trial. The story was not only reprinted in newspapers all over the world; even before the trial started it appeared as a paperback book, titled *The Killing of Sharon Tate.** It was felt by some that the Atkins revelations would make it impossible for the defendants to obtain a fair trial. Although neither Aaron nor I nor, eventually, the trial judge, shared this view, we were all too aware, from the moment the story broke, that finding twelve jurors who hadn't read or heard of the account, and then keeping any mention of it out of the courtroom itself, would be a difficult task.

Few of the Angelenos who read Susan Atkins' story in the *Times* that Sunday were aware that she was at the same time riding around Los Angeles and its environs in a nondescript, though heavily guarded, automobile. We were hoping she would point out the places where the clothing and weapons had been discarded following the Tate murders.

On returning to Sybil Brand that night, Susan wrote a letter to a former cellmate, Kitt Fletcher, in which she told of her excursion: "My attorney is great. He has had me out to his office twice and today he got me out for 7 hours. We went riding in a car up to the Tate mansion and through the canyons. The LAPD wanted me to see if I could recall where certain things happened. It was such a beautiful day my memory vanished."

As in most jails, the mail at Sybil Brand was censored, both letters received and letters sent being read by the authorities. Those which contained what appeared to be incriminating statements were photocopied and given to our office. Under existing case law, this could be done without violating a prisoner's constitutional rights.

Susan/Sadie was in a letter-writing mood. Several of her letters contained damaging admissions which, unlike

*Published by New American Library, which is owned by the Times Mirror Company, which also owns the Los Angeles *Times*.

her grand jury testimony, could be used against her in the trial, if we chose to do so. To Jo Stevenson, a friend in Michigan, she'd written on the thirteenth: "You rember the Sharon Tate murder and LaBianca murder? Well because of my big mouth to a cell-mate they just indicted me and 5 other people . . ."*

Even more incriminating, and revealing, was a "kite" Susan sent Ronnie Howard. In jail parlance, a kite is any illegal communication. The letter, which Susan smuggled to Ronnie via the underground at Sybil Brand, read as follows:

"I can see your side of this clearly. Nor am I mad at you. I am hurt in a way only I understand. I blame no one but myself for even saying anything to anybody about it . . . Yes, I wanted the world to know M. It sure looks like they do now. There was a so called motive behind all this. It was to instill fear into the pigs and to bring on judgment day which is here now for all.

"In the word kill, the only thing that dies is the ego. All ego must die anyway, it is written. Yes, it could have been your house, it could have been my fathers house also. In killing someone phisally you are only releasing the soul. Life has no boundris and death is only an illusion. If you can believe in the second coming of Crist, M is he who has come to save . . . Maybe this will help you to understand . . . I did not admit to being in the 2nd house because I was not in the 2nd house.

"I went before the grand jury because my attorney said your testimony was enough to convict me and all the others. He also said it was my only chance to save myself. Then I was out to save myself. I have gone through some changes since then . . . I know now it has all been perfect. Those people died not out of hate or anything ugly. I am not going to defend our beliefs. I am just telling you the way it is . . . As I write to you I feel more at ease inside. When I first heard you were the informer I wanted to slit your throat. Then I snapped that I was the real informer and it was my throat I wanted to cut. Well that's all over with now as I let the past die away from my mind. You

*Spelling and punctuation errors in the Atkins letters are as in the originals.

know it will all turn out ok in the end anyway, M or no M, Sadie or no Sadie, love will still run forever. I am giving up me to become that love a little more every day . . ."

Quoting a lyric from one of Manson's songs, Susan ended the letter: "Cease to exist, just come and say you love me. As I say I love you or I should say I love Me (my love) in you.

"I hope now you understand a little more. If not, ask."

Ronnie, who was now living in deathly fear of Susan, turned the letter over to her attorney, Wesley Russell, who passed it on to our office. It would prove far more damaging to Susan Atkins than the confession which appeared in the Los Angeles *Times*.

December 15-25, 1969

When on a case, I made it a habit periodically to scour LAPD's "tubs," or files, often finding something useful to my case whose evidentiary value wasn't apparent to the police.

In going through the LaBianca tubs, I made two discoveries. The first was the Al Springer interview. Only one page had been transcribed, the one on which Springer related how Manson had told him, "We knocked off five of them just the other night."

As desperate as we were for evidence, none of the detectives had mentioned the Springer statement to me, nor, when I questioned Lieutenants Helder and LePage, were they aware they had a confession by Manson in their files. I took the tape and had it transcribed, adding "Interview Al Springer" to my own already lengthy list of Things to Do. Though, because of *Aranda*, Manson's confession couldn't be used against him at the trial, it was quite possible he had made other admissions that could.

The second find was a photocopy of a letter mailed to Manson while he was in jail in Independence. The content was innocuous; however, it was signed "Harold." Susan Atkins had told the grand jury that a guy named "Harold" had been living at the house next door to the LaBianca residence when she, Charlie, and a number of others had gone there for an LSD party a year or so earlier. I had a feeling this might be the same person, and made another note for the LaBianca detectives: "Find Harold." This shouldn't be too difficult, as he had given an address in Sherman Oaks and two telephone numbers.

Why? The biggest and most puzzling question of all remained: what was Manson's motive? On learning that Manson often told his followers that he was a Scorpio, and thinking that possibly his belief in astrology might be a factor, I obtained back copies of the Los Angeles *Times* and checked Carroll Righter's "Astrological Forecast" for his sign.

> August 8: Do whatever you think will help you to extend your sphere of influence. Take care of that private task wisely and well. Get the information at the right source. Then use it cleverly.
>
> August 9: If you go about it tactfully, you can get a reluctant associate to understand what you have in mind. Cooperate with this individual when some problem arises.
>
> August 10: There are fine opportunities all around you. Don't hesitate to seize the best one. Extend your sphere of influence . . .

You could, I realized, read just about any meaning you wanted into such forecasts. Including plans for murder?

It was indicative of our desperation that I went to such unlikely lengths in trying to ascertain why Manson had ordered these murders.

I didn't even know whether Manson read newspapers.

Since the story first broke, LAPD had been receiving inquiries from various police departments regarding unsolved murders in their jurisdictions which they believed could have been committed by one or more members of the Manson Family. I went through these reports, eliminating a great many, setting others aside as "possibles."* Though my principal concern was the Tate-LaBianca homicides, I wanted to see if there was a discernible pattern which might help explain the killings at Cielo and Waverly Drives. Thus far, if there was one, I couldn't find it.

In her printed "confession" Susan Atkins had described how, after changing clothes in the car, the Tate killers drove "along a steep embankment," with a mountain on one side, a ravine on the other. "We stopped and Linda got out of the car and threw all the clothes, all drippy with blood . . . over the side."

With the *Times* story on the seat beside them, a TV camera crew from Channel 7, KACB-TV, attempted to re-create the scene. Driving from the gate at 10050 Cielo Drive, they proceeded down Benedict Canyon, all but the driver changing clothes on the way. It took them six minutes and twenty seconds—during which they later admitted they felt more than a little foolish—to complete their change of apparel. At the first spot where they could pull off the road—a wide shoulder opposite 2901 Benedict Canyon Road—they stopped and got out.

Mountain on one side, ravine on the other. Newscaster Al Wiman looked down the steep embankment and, pointing to some dark objects about fifty feet down, said, laughing, "Looks like clothing down there." King Baggot, the cameraman, and Eddie Baker, the sound man, looked too and had to agree.

It was just too easy—if the clothing was in plain view from the road, surely LAPD would have found it by now. Still, they decided to check it out. They were about to descend the slope when the car radio buzzed: they were needed on another story.

While on the other assignment they couldn't get those dark objects out of mind. About 3 P.M. they returned to the spot. Baker went down first, followed by Baggot. They found three sets of clothing: one pair of black trousers, two pairs of blue denim pants, two black T-shirts,

*These will be discussed in a later chapter.

one dark velour turtleneck, and one white T-shirt which was spotted with some substance that looked like dried blood. Some of the clothing was partly covered by dirt slides; all of it, however, was in an area about twelve feet square, as if thrown there in one bundle.

They yelled the news up to Wiman, who called LAPD. By the time McGann and three other detectives arrived, shortly before five, it was beginning to get dark, so the TV crew set up artificial lighting. While the detectives placed the clothing in plastic bags, Baggot filmed the incident.

On learning of the find, I asked the Tate detectives to conduct a thorough search of the area, to see if they could locate any of the weapons. I had to make the request not once but many, many times. In the interim, a week after the initial discovery, Baggot and Baker returned to the scene and conducted their own search, finding a knife. It was an old, badly rusted kitchen knife, which, because of its dimensions and dull edge, was eliminated as one of the murder weapons, but it was in plain view less than a hundred feet from where the clothing had been found.

That a TV crew had found the clothing was an embarrassment to LAPD. Faces at Parker Center, however, would be far redder before the end of the following day.

On Tuesday, December 16, Susan Atkins appeared before Judge Keene and pleaded not guilty to all eight counts of the indictment. Keene set a trial date of February 9, 1970. Since this was the same date set for the retrial of Bobby Beausoleil, I was taken off the Beausoleil-Hinman case, and it was assigned to Deputy DA Burton Katz. I wasn't unhappy about this; I had more than enough to do on Tate-LaBianca.

That Tuesday was, for Bernard Weiss, a most trying day.

Weiss hadn't read Susan Atkins' story when it appeared in the Los Angeles *Times,* but a colleague at work had, and he mentioned to Weiss that a .22 caliber revolver had definitely been used in the Tate murders. Odd coincidence, wasn't it, his boy finding a similar type gun?

Weiss thought it might be something more than that.

After all, his son had found the revolver on September 1, a little over two weeks after the Tate murders; they lived not far from the Tate residence; and the road right above the hill where Steven had found the gun was Beverly Glen. That morning Weiss called the Valley Services Division of LAPD in Van Nuys and told them he thought they might have the missing Tate gun. Van Nuys referred him to LAPD Homicide at Parker Center.

Weiss called there about noon, and repeated his story. He observed that the gun his son had found had a broken trigger guard and part of the wooden grip was missing. "Well, it sounds enough like the gun," the detective told him. "We'll check it out."

Weiss anticipated that the detective would call him back; he didn't. That evening on arriving home, Weiss read the Atkins story. It convinced him. About 6 P.M. he again called LAPD Homicide. The officer he'd talked to at noon was out, so he had to repeat the story a third time. This officer told him, "We don't keep guns that long. We throw them in the ocean after a while." Weiss said, "I can't believe you'd throw away what could be the single most important piece of evidence in the Tate case." "Listen, mister," the officer replied, "we can't check out every citizen report on every gun we find. Thousands of guns are found every year." The discussion became an argument, and they hung up on each other.

Weiss then called one of his neighbors, Clete Roberts, a newscaster for Channel 2, and told Roberts the story. Roberts in turn called someone at LAPD.

Although it remains unclear which of the five calls triggered a response, at least one did. At 10 P.M.—three and a half months after Weiss gave the gun to officer Watson—Sergeants Calkins and McGann drove over to Van Nuys and picked up the .22 caliber Hi Standard Longhorn revolver.

POLICE FIND GUN BELIEVED USED
IN SLAYING OF 3 TATE VICTIMS

News of the find "leaked" to the Los Angeles *Times* four days later. It was a somewhat selective leak. There were no details as to when or where the gun was found, or by whom, the implication being that it had been discovered by LAPD sometime after the clothing, and in the same general area.

The cylinder contained two live rounds and seven empty shell casings. This tallied perfectly with the original autopsy reports, which stated that Sebring and Frykowski had each been shot once, and Parent five times. There was only one problem: I'd already discovered the autopsy reports were in error.

After Susan Atkins testified that Tex Watson shot Parent four (not five) times, I'd asked Coroner Noguchi to re-examine the Parent autopsy photos. When he did, he found that two of the wounds had been made by the same bullet. This reduced the number of times Parent was shot to four; it also left one bullet unaccounted for.

This time I had Noguchi re-examine *all* the autopsy photos. In doing so, he found that Frykowski had been shot not once but twice, the coroners performing the autopsy having overlooked a gunshot wound in the left leg. So the count was again consistent, even if the reports were not.

Bill Lee of SID compared the three pieces of gun grip with the butt of the revolver: a perfect fit. Joe Granado tested some brown spots on the barrel: blood, human, same type and subtype as Jay Sebring's. After test-firing the gun, Lee placed the test bullets and the Tate bullets under a comparison microscope. Three of the four bullets recovered after the Tate murders were either too fragmented or battered for the stria to be matched up. With the fourth, the Sebring bullet, he made a positive ID. There was no doubt whatsoever, he told me, that it had been fired from the .22 Longhorn.

One very important step remained: linking the gun to Charles Manson. I asked the Tate detectives to show it to DeCarlo, to determine if it was the same gun with which Manson and the other men used to target-practice at Spahn. I also requested as complete a history of the gun as they could manage, from the day it was manufactured by Hi Standard to the day it was found by Steven Weiss.

It was decided that there was insufficient evidence to convict either Gypsy or Brenda, and the two hard-core Manson Family members were released from custody. Although Brenda returned to her parents for a short time, both soon rejoined Squeaky, Sandy, and the other Family members at Spahn, lonely George having weakened and let them move back to the ranch.

Manson's frequent court appearances gave me opportunities to study him. Though he'd had little formal schooling, he was fairly articulate, and definitely bright. He picked up little nuances, seemed to consider all the hidden sides of a question before answering. His moods were mercurial, his facial expressions chameleonlike. Underneath, however, there was a strange intensity. You felt it even when he was joking, which, despite the seriousness of the charges, was often. He frequently played to the always packed courtroom, not only to the Family faithful but to the press and spectators as well. Spotting a pretty girl, he'd often smile or wink. Usually they appeared more flattered than offended.

Though their responses surprised me, they shouldn't have. I'd already heard that Manson was receiving a large volume of mail, including many "love letters," the majority of which were from young girls who wanted to join the Family.

On December 17, Manson appeared before Judge Keene and asked to have the Public Defender dismissed. He wanted to represent himself, he said.

Judge Keene told Manson that he was not convinced that he was competent to represent himself, or, in legal jargon, to proceed "in pro per" (in propria persona).

MANSON "Your Honor, there is no way I can give up my voice in this matter. If I can't speak, then our whole thing is done. If I can't speak in my own defense and converse freely in this courtroom, then it ties my hands behind my back, and if I have no voice, then there is no sense in having a defense."

Keene agreed to reconsider Manson's motion on the twenty-second.

Manson's insistence that only he could speak for himself, as well as his obvious enjoyment at being in the spotlight, led me to one conclusion: when the time came, he probably wouldn't be able to resist taking the stand.

I began keeping a notebook of questions I intended to ask him on cross-examination. Before long there was a second notebook, and a third.

On the nineteenth Leslie Van Houten also asked to have her present attorney, Donald Barnett, dismissed. Keene granted the motion and appointed Marvin Part to be Miss Van Houten's attorney of record.

Only later would we learn what was happening behind the scenes. Manson had set up his own communications network. Whenever he heard that an attorney for one of the girls had initiated a move on behalf of his client which could conceivably run counter to Manson's own defense, within days that attorney would be removed from the case. Barnett had wanted a psychiatrist to examine Leslie. Learning of this, Manson vetoed the idea, and when the psychiatrist appeared at Sybil Brand, Leslie refused to see him. Her request for Barnett's dismissal came immediately after.

Manson's goal: to run the entire defense himself. In court as well as out, Charlie intended to retain complete control of the Family.

Manson wanted to represent himself, he told the court, because "lawyers play with people, and I am a person and I don't want to be played with in this matter." Most lawyers were only interested in one thing, publicity, Manson said. He'd seen quite a few of them lately and felt he knew what he was talking about. Any attorney previously associated with the DA's Office was not acceptable to him, he added. He had learned that two other defendants had court-appointed attorneys who were once deputy DAs (Caballero and Part).

Judge Keene explained that many lawyers engaged in the practice of criminal law first gained experience in the office of the District Attorney, the City Attorney, or the

U.S. Attorney. Knowing how the prosecution worked was often a benefit to their clients.

MANSON "It sounds good from there, but not from here."

"Your Honor," Manson continued, "I am in a difficult position. The news media has already executed and buried me . . . If anyone is hypnotized, the people are hypnotized by the lies being told to them . . . There is no attorney in the world who can represent me as a person. I have to do it myself."

Judge Keene had a suggestion. He would arrange for an experienced attorney to confer with him. Unlike other attorneys to whom Manson had talked, this attorney would have no interest in representing him. His function would be solely to discuss with him the legal issues, and the possible dangers, of defending himself. Manson accepted the offer and, after court, Keene arranged for Joseph Ball, a former president of the State Bar Association and former senior counsel to the Warren Commission, to meet with Manson.

Manson talked to Ball and found him "a very nice gentleman," he told Judge Keene on the twenty-fourth. "Mr. Ball probably understands maybe everything there is to know about law, but he doesn't understand the generation gap; he doesn't understand free love society; he doesn't understand people who are trying to get out from underneath all of this . . ."

Ball, in turn, found Manson "an able, intelligent young man, quiet-spoken and mild-mannered . . ." Although he had attempted to persuade him, without success, that he could benefit from the services of a skilled lawyer, Ball was obviously impressed with Manson. "We went over different problems of law, and I found he had a ready understanding . . . Remarkable understanding. As a matter of fact, he has a very fine brain. I complimented him on the fact. I think I told you that he had a high IQ. Must have, to be able to converse as he did." Manson "is not resentful against society," Ball said. "And he feels that if he goes to trial and he is able to permit jurors and the Court to hear him and see him, they will realize he is not the kind of man who would perpetrate horrible crimes."

After Ball had finished, Judge Keene questioned Manson for more than an hour about his knowledge of courtroom procedure, and the possible penalties for the crimes with which he was charged, throughout almost begging him to reconsider his decision to defend himself.

MANSON "For all my life, as long as I can remember, I've taken your advice. Your faces have changed, but it's the same court, the same structure ... All my life I've been put in little slots, Your Honor. And I went along with it ... I have no alternative but to fight you back any way I know because you and the District Attorney and all the attorneys I have ever met are all on the same side. The police are on the same side and the newspapers are on the same side and it's all pointed against me, personally ... No. I haven't changed my mind."

THE COURT "Mr. Manson, I am imploring you not to take this step; I am imploring you to either name your own attorney, or, if you are unable to do so, to permit the Court to name one for you."

Manson's mind was made up, however, and Judge Keene finally concluded: "It is, in this Court's opinion, a sad and tragic mistake that you are making by taking this course of action, but I can't talk you out of it. ... Mr. Manson, you are your own lawyer."

It was Christmas Eve. I worked until 2 A.M., then took the next day off.

December 26-31, 1969

A call from LAPD. A cook at the Brentwood Country Club says that the chief steward there, Rudolf Weber, was the man in front of whose house the Tate killers stopped to hose off about 1 A.M. on August 9.

Bringing along a police photographer to take photos of the area, Calkins and I went to see Weber at his home at 9870 Portola Drive, a side street just off Benedict Canyon Drive, less than two miles from the Tate residence. As I listened to Weber's story, I knew he was going to be a good witness. He had an excellent memory, told exactly what he remembered, didn't try to fill in what he did not. He was unable to make a positive identification from the large batch of photos I showed him, but his general description fitted: all four were young (Watson, Atkins, Krenwinkel, and Kasabian were all in their early twenties), the man was tall (Watson was six feet one), and one of the girls was short (Kasabian was five feet one). His description of the car—which had never appeared in the press—was accurate down to the faded paint around the license plates. How was it he could recall such a detail about the car but not their faces? Very simple: when he followed the four down to the car, he turned the flashlight on the license plate; when he saw them on the street, near the hose, they were in the dark.

Weber had a surprise—a big one. Following the incident, thinking perhaps the four people had committed a burglary in the area, he had written down the license number of the vehicle. He had since thrown the piece of paper away—my heart sank—but he still remembered the number. It was GYY 435.

How in the world could he remember that? I asked him. In his job as steward he had to remember numbers, he replied.

Anticipating that this point might be brought up by the defense, I asked Weber if he had read the Atkins story. He said he hadn't.

On returning to my office, I checked the impound report on John Swartz' car: "1959 Ford 4 Dr., Lic. # GYY 435."

When I interviewed Swartz, the former Spahn ranch hand told me that Manson and his girls often borrowed the car; in fact, he had taken the back seat out so they could fit the big boxes in when they went on their "garbage runs." With the exception of one particular night, they always asked his permission before taking the car.

What night was that? Well, he wasn't exactly sure of the date, but it was a week, two weeks before the raid. What happened that particular night? Well, he'd already gone to bed in his trailer when he heard his car start up. He got up and looked out the window just in time to see the taillights pulling away. Any idea what time that was? Well, he usually went to bed around ten or thereabouts, so it was after that. When he woke up the next morning, Swartz said, the car was back. He'd asked Charlie why they'd taken the car without asking, and Charlie had told him that he hadn't wanted to wake him up.

Any other nights during this same period when Manson borrowed the car? I inquired. Yeah, one other night Charlie, the girls, and some other guys—he was unable to remember which girls and guys—said they were going downtown to play some music.

Swartz was unable to date this particular night except that it was around the same time they took the car without permission. Before or after? He couldn't remember. Consecutive nights? Couldn't remember that either.

I asked Swartz if he had ever belonged to the Family. "*Never,*" he very emphatically replied. One time, after the raid, and after Shorty had dropped from sight, he and Manson had an argument, Swartz said. Charlie had told him, "I could kill you any time. I could come into your sleeping quarters any time." After that Swartz quit his job at Spahn, where he had been working off and on since 1963, and got a job at another ranch.

What did he know about Shorty's disappearance? Well, a week or two after the raid Shorty just wasn't around any more. He'd asked Charlie if he knew where he was, and Charlie had told him, "He's gone to San Francisco about a job. I told him about a job there." He didn't exactly feel confident with that explanation, he said, not after having noticed that Bill Vance and Danny DeCarlo each had one of Shorty's .45 caliber pistols.

Shorty would never willingly part with those matched pistols, Swartz said, no matter how hard up he was.

Under the Constitution of the United States, extradition is mandatory, not discretionary.* When a state has a valid and duly executed indictment—as we did in the case of Charles "Tex" Watson—there is no legitimate reason why the accused shouldn't be extradited forthwith.

Certain powers in Collin County, Texas, felt otherwise. Bill Boyd, Watson's attorney, told the press he'd fight to keep his client in Texas if it meant going all the way to the United States Supreme Court.

Bill Boyd's father, Roland Boyd, was a powerful southern politician of the Sam Rayburn school. He was also the campaign manager of a candidate who was running for attorney general of Texas. It was his candidate, Judge David Brown, who heard the Watson extradition request, and granted delay after delay after delay to young Boyd's client.

Bill Boyd was himself an aspiring politician. Tom Ryan, the local DA, told a Los Angeles *Times* reporter: "I've heard it said that Bill wants to be President of the United States. And after that he wants to be God."

Time magazine reported: "As swarms of reporters begged for jailhouse interviews with his client, Boyd began dropping ten-gallon hints that Watson's family might go along 'if the offer is substantial.' One photographer offered $1,800. 'We need lots and lots of money,' retorted Boyd. How much? 'About $50,000,' said the lawyer. Though the press balked, Boyd still has not lowered his client's price—and he is quite sure that eventually he will get it."

Meanwhile, Tex apparently wasn't suffering unduly. We heard, from various sources, that his one-man cell was comfortably furnished, that he had his own record player and records. His vegetarian meals were cooked by his mother. He also wore his own clothing, which she laundered. And he was not completely lacking company, his cell adjoining that occupied by the female prisoners.

*Subdivision 2 of Article IV reads: "A person charged in any state with treason, felony, or any other crime, who shall flee from justice, and be found in another state, shall on demand of the executive authority of the state from which he fled, be delivered up, to be removed by the state having jurisdiction of the crime."

Though the extradition of Watson was proving difficult, there were indications that Katie Krenwinkel might decide to return voluntarily, on Manson's orders. Squeaky, acting as Charlie's liaison, had sent Krenwinkel a barrage of letters and telegrams, photocopies of which we received from the Mobile, Alabama, authorities: "Together we stand . . . If you go extra is good . . ."

I also presumed that the togetherness referred to in each of the messages meant that Manson intended to conduct a joint, or umbrella, defense.

Since the Family had contacted Krenwinkel but, as far as we could determine, not Watson, I carried my conjecture a step further, guessing that when the case went to trial Manson and the girls would try to put the hat on Watson.

Presuming they would try to prove that Tex, not Charlie, was the mastermind behind the Tate-LaBianca murders, I began collecting every bit of evidence I could find on the Manson-Watson relationship, and the role each played in the Family.

When interrogated in Los Angeles, sixteen-year-old Dianne Lake had been threatened with the gas chamber. And had said nothing. Inyo County Deputy DA Buck Gibbens and investigator Jack Gardiner tried kindness, something Dianne had known little of during her life.

Dianne's parents had "turned hippy" while she was still a child. By age thirteen she was a member of the Hog Farm commune, and had been introduced to group sex and LSD. When she joined Manson, just before her fourteenth birthday, it was with her parents' approval.

Apparently not finding Dianne submissive enough, Manson had, on various occasions: punched her in the mouth; kicked her across a room; hit her over the head with a chair leg; and whipped her with an electrical cord. Despite such treatment, she stayed. Which implies something tragic about the alternatives available to her.

After her return to Independence, Gibbens and Gardiner had a number of lengthy conversations with Dianne. They convinced her that other people did care about her. Gardiner's wife and children visited her regularly.

Hesitantly at first, Dianne began telling the officers what she knew. And, contrary to what she had told the grand jury, she knew a great deal. Tex, for example, had admitted to her that he'd stabbed Sharon Tate. He did it, he told her, because Charlie had ordered the killings.

On December 30, Sartuchi and Nielsen interviewed Dianne in Independence. She told them that one morning, maybe a week or two weeks before the August 16 raid, Leslie had come into the back house at Spahn with a purse, a rope, and a bag of coins. She hid them under a blanket. When, a short time later, a man arrived and knocked on the door, Leslie hid herself. She told Dianne the man had given her a ride from Griffith Park and she didn't want him to see her.

The two LaBianca detectives exchanged looks. Griffith park was not far from Waverly Drive.

After the man left, Leslie came out from under the blanket and Dianne helped her count the money. There was about eight dollars in change, in a plastic sack.

Because of Leno LaBianca's coin collection, the detectives were very interested in that bag of change.

Q. "O.K., you say you helped Leslie count the money or coins. Did you see any coins in there from another country?"

A. "Canada."

Leslie then built a fire and burned the purse (Dianne recalled it as being brown leather), some credit cards (one was an oil company card), and the rope (it was about 4 feet long and 1 to 1½ inches in diameter). Then she took off her own clothing and burned it too. Had Dianne noticed any blood spots on the clothing? No.

Later, in late August or early September, while they were at Willow Springs, about ten miles from Barker Ranch, Leslie told Dianne that she had stabbed someone who was already dead. Was it a woman or a man? Leslie hadn't said.

Leslie also told Dianne that the murder had occurred someplace near Griffith Park, near Los Feliz; that someone had written something in blood on the refrigerator door; and that she, Leslie, then wiped everything so there would be no prints, even wiping things they hadn't touched. When they left, they took some food with them. What kind of food? A carton of chocolate milk.

Had Leslie said anything about the Tate murders? Leslie had told her she wasn't in on that.

Sartuchi attempted to get more details. The only other thing Dianne could recall was that there had been a big boat outside the house. But she couldn't remember whether Leslie had told her about the boat or whether she had read it in the paper. She did, however, remember Leslie describing it.

Prior to this, the only evidence we had linking Leslie Van Houten with the LaBianca murders was the testimony of Susan Atkins. Since Susan was an accomplice, this would not stand up in court without independent corroboration.

Dianne Lake supplied it.

There was a question, however, as to whether Dianne would be able to testify at the trial. She was obviously emotionally disturbed. She had occasional LSD flashbacks. She feared Manson, and she loved him. At times she thought he was inside her head. Shortly after the first of the year the Inyo County court arranged for her to be sent to Patton State Hospital, in part for treatment for her emotional problems, in part because the court didn't know what else to do with her.

Additions to my list of Things to Do: Check to see if any LaBianca credit cards are still missing. When doctors permit, interview Dianne; find out if anyone else present during back-house incident or Willow Springs conversation. Check with Katsuyama to see if any of the LaBianca stab wounds were post-mortem, i.e., inflicted after death. Ask Susan Struthers if her mother had a brown leather purse and if it is missing. Ask Susan and/or Frank Struthers if either Rosemary or Leno liked chocolate milk.

Tiny details, but they could be important.

The "Harold" whose letter I'd found in the Tate tubs *was* the same "Harold" Susan Atkins had mentioned in her grand jury testimony. His full name was Harold True, and he was a student. When LAPD found him, I was busy with another interview, so Aaron volunteered to talk to him.

From True, who remained friendly to Manson, visiting him several times at the County Jail, Aaron learned that he had met Charlie in March of 1968, while the Family was living in Topanga Canyon. The next day Charlie and about ten others (including Sadie, Katie, Squeaky, and Brenda, but not Tex or Leslie) had shown up at 3267 Waverly Drive, the house True shared with three other youths, and stayed overnight. Manson had visited him maybe four or five times there, before True and the others moved out in September 1968. While they were still living at Waverly, True said, neighbors had frequently complained about their noisy parties.

Aaron hadn't asked True if the LaBiancas had been among the neighbors who complained, and I made a note to check this. When I did, I learned that True couldn't recall having ever seen the LaBiancas; as best he could remember, 3301 Waverly Drive was vacant all the time they were living there.

Going back to the LaBianca investigative reports, I saw that Leno and Rosemary hadn't moved into 3301 Waverly Drive until November 1968, which was after True and the others moved out.

I'd been looking for a possible incident involving the LaBiancas and the Family. I didn't find it. We were left with two facts, however: Manson had been to the house next door to the LaBianca residence on five or six occasions, and he had been as far as the gate to the Tate residence at least once.

Coincidence? Anticipating that this was probably what the Manson defense would argue, I jotted down some ideas for my rebuttal.

Charles Manson was not without a sense of humor. While in the County Jail he had somehow managed to obtain an application for a Union Oil Company credit card. He filled it in, giving his correct name and the jail address. He listed "Spahn's Movie Ranch" as his previous residence, and gave George Spahn as a reference. As for his occupation, he put "Evangelist"; type of business, "Religious"; length of employment, "20 years." He also wrote, in the blank for wife's first name, "None," and gave as his number of dependents "16."

The card was smuggled out of jail and mailed from Pasadena. Someone at Union Oil—obviously not a computer—recognized the name, and Charles Manson didn't get the two credit cards he'd requested.

Another characteristic I'd noticed while observing Manson in court was his cockiness. One possible reason for this was his new notoriety. At the beginning of December 1969 few had ever heard of Charles Manson. By the end of that month the killer had already upstaged his famous victims. An enthusiastic Family member was heard to brag, "Charlie made the cover of *Life!*"

But it was something more. You got the feeling that, despite his verbal utterances, Manson was convinced that he was going to beat the rap.

He wasn't the only one to feel this. Leslie Van Houten wrote her parents that even if convicted she'd be out in seven years (in California a person given life imprisonment is eligible for parole in seven years), while Bobby Beausoleil wrote several of his girl friends that he expected to be acquitted in his new trial, after which he was going to start his own Family.

The problem, at year's end, was that there was a very good chance that at least Manson would be right.

"What if Manson demands an immediate trial?"

Aaron and I discussed this at length. A defendant has a constitutional right to a speedy trial and a statutory right to go to trial within sixty days after the return of the indictment. If Manson insisted on this, we were in deep trouble.

We needed more time, for two reasons. We still desperately lacked evidence to corroborate the testimony of Susan Atkins, presuming—and it was a very big presumption—that she agreed to testify. And two of the defendants, Watson and Krenwinkel, were still out of state. They just happened to be the only two defendants against whom there was scientific evidence of guilt, i.e., the fingerprints at the Tate residence. If there was to be a joint trial, which we wanted, we needed at least one of the two sitting behind that defense table.

I suggested we bluff. Every time we were in court, we should indicate that we wanted to go to trial as quickly as possible. Our hope was that Manson would think this was bad, and start stalling himself.

It was a gamble. There was a very real possibility that Charlie might call our bluff, saying, with his strange little grin, "O.K., let's go to trial right now."

Part 4

THE SEARCH FOR THE MOTIVE

The Bible, the Beatles, and Helter Skelter

"If I'm looking for a motive, I'd look for something which doesn't fit your habitual standard, with which you use to work as police—something much more far out."

Roman Polanski to
Lieutenant Earl Deemer

January 1970

Confidential Memo. From: Deputy DA Vincent Bugliosi. To: District Attorney Evelle Younger. Subject: Status of Tate & LaBianca cases.

The memo ran to thirteen pages, but the heart of it consisted of a single paragraph:

"Without Susan Atkins' testimony on the Tate case, the evidence against two out of the five defendants [Manson and Kasabian] is rather anemic. Without her testimony on the LaBianca case, the evidence against five out of the six defendants [everyone except Van Houten] is non-existent."

That was it. Without Sadie, we still didn't have a case.

On January 2, I called a meeting of the Tate and LaBianca detectives, giving them a list of forty-two things that had to be done.

Many were repeat requests: Go to the areas where the clothing and the gun were found and search for knives. Has Granado been able to "make" the boots we picked up in November with the bloody boot-heel print on the Tate walkway? SID must have something by now on the wire cutters, also the clothing the TV crew found. Where is the tape Inyo County Deputy Sheriff Ward made with the two miners, Crockett and Poston? Where are the reports on the Tate, LaBianca, and Spahn Ranch toll calls? Telephone company destroys its records after six months; hurry on this.

Many of the requests were elementary follow-up steps that I felt the detectives should have already done on their own, without our prompting: Get Atkins printing exemplar and compare it with PIG on the front door at Tate. Get same on defendants Van Houten, Krenwinkel, and Watson and compare with printing at the LaBianca residence. Submit a complete report on the stolen credit cards involved in this case (we were hoping to find a sales slip on the rope or the Buck knives). DeCarlo said he was along when Manson purchased the three-strand nylon rope at the Jack Frost store in Santa Monica in June 1969: ask Frost employees if they sold such a rope; also show them the "Family album" to see if they can recall Manson and/or DeCarlo. Also show photos of Manson, Atkins, Kasabian, and the others to employees of the Standard station in Sylmar where Rosemary LaBianca's wallet was found.

After giving the detectives the list, I asked, "I presume that, above and beyond what I've given you, you guys are also conducting your own independent investigations?" The long silence that followed was in itself the answer. Then Calkins complained, "How are we supposed to know to do these things? We're policemen, not lawyers."

"Wait a minute," I said. "These forty-two things have nothing to do with the law. Each and every one pertains to securing evidence and strengthening our case against these people."

"But that isn't our job," Calkins continued to protest.

His remark was so astonishing I came close to losing my temper. "*Investigating a case, gathering evidence, connecting defendants with the corpus delicti of the crime—that isn't a police job?* Come on, Bob. You're the detectives. Aaron and I are the lawyers. Each of us has his own job to do. And if either of us falls down on the job, Manson is going to walk. Think about that."

I could understand if the detectives had other duties, but they were assigned full time to the case.

Unlike Calkins, Mike McGann rarely complained, but he rarely came through either. To a man, the LaBianca detectives were far more conscientious. In the weeks ahead I began giving them assignments that related specifically to the Tate, as well as the LaBianca, murders, knowing they'd do their best. I did this only after checking with Lieutenant Helder, who candidly agreed that Calkins and McGann simply weren't getting the job done.

If it was any consolation to the police—and I'm sure it wasn't—my own list was much longer than theirs. It ranged from such simple items as a reminder to get the Beatles' album that contained the song "Helter Skelter" to more than fifty names of potential witnesses I needed to interview. It also included such detailed specifics as: Obtain exact measurements of all LaBianca wounds—original officers failed to ask Deputy Medical Examiner Katsuyama for this—in order to determine dimensions of knives used.

The measurements of the LaBianca wounds were extremely important. If the wound patterns were consistent with those made by the LaBianca kitchen knives, then the logical inference was that the defendants had entered the residence unarmed, then killed the LaBiancas with their own knives. If Manson had intended to kill these people, the defense would surely ask, would he have sent in unarmed people to do the job?

Of even greater importance was another item which appeared on all the assignment lists: Get incidents—and witnesses who can testify to same—where Manson ordered or instructed *anyone* to do *anything*.

Put yourself in the jury box. Would you believe the prosecutor if he told you that a little runt out at Spahn Ranch sent some half dozen people, the majority of them young girls, out to murder for him, their victims not persons they knew and had a grudge against but complete strangers, including a pregnant woman, and that without argument they did it?

To convince a jury of this, I would have first to convince them of Manson's domination over the Family, and particularly over his co-defendants. A domination so total, so complete, that they would do anything he told them to do. Including murder.

Each time I interviewed anyone connected with the Family, I would ask for an example of Manson's control. Often the witness would be unable to recall specific examples, and I'd have to dig to bring them out: Why did Manson beat Dianne Lake; was it because she failed to do something he told her to do? Who assigned the chores at the ranch? Who put out the guards and lookouts? Can you recall a single instance where Tex ever talked back to Charlie?

Getting this evidence was especially difficult because Manson rarely gave direct orders. Usually he'd suggest, rather than command, though his suggestions had the force of commands.

Domination. Unless we could prove this, beyond all reasonable doubt, we'd never obtain a conviction against Manson.

As the defense attorneys requested discovery, I'd take them to my office and let them go through our files on the case. Since Manson was now acting as his own attorney, the files were also made available to him, the only difference being that they were carted over to the County Jail and he examined them there. Eventually, by a court order, secretaries in our office photostated everything in our files, with a copy for each defense counsel.

Only two things were held back. I argued to the court, "We would vehemently resist furnishing Mr. Manson with addresses, and particularly telephone numbers, of prospective witnesses, Your Honor." I also strongly opposed providing the defense with copies of the death photos. We had heard that a German magazine had a standing offer of $100,000 for them. I did not want the families of the victims to open a magazine and see the terrible butchery inflicted on their loved ones.

With only these two exceptions—the court ruling in our favor on both—the prosecution, by law, gave the defense anything they wanted and, discovery being a one-way street, they in turn gave us *nothing.* We couldn't even get a list of the witnesses they intended to call. I was still reading newspaper and magazine articles to pick up leads.

Even this wasn't as simple as it sounds. Many former associates of the Family were in fear of their lives. Several, including Dennis Wilson of the Beach Boys, had received death threats. Since few sources wished to be quoted by name, pseudonyms were often used in the articles. In several instances, I tracked down someone only to find a person I'd already interviewed. And, in more than a few cases, I found fiction posing as fact.

One article claimed that Manson and various other Family members had been present at a party Roman and

Sharon gave at 10050 Cielo in early 1969. Once located, the writer told me his source was Alan Warnecke, a close friend of Terry Melcher's. When I talked to Warnecke, he denied saying any such thing. Eventually I assembled a list of persons who had attended the party, and as many as could be located were interviewed. None had seen Manson or the others at 10050 Cielo Drive, either on the night in question or any other time.

Peter Maas, author of *The Valachi Papers,* wrote an article entitled "The Sharon Tate Murders," which appeared in the *Ladies' Home Journal.* In it was the following paragraph:

"'How are you going to get the establishment? You can't sing to them. I tried that. I tried to save them, but they wouldn't listen. Now we got to destroy them.' —Charlie Manson to a friend in the summer of 1969."

This was powerful evidence, if true, and I was anxious to learn the source of Maas' quotation.

After easily a dozen calls, I located Maas in New York City. Asked the source of several other statements, he quickly supplied them. But when it came to the key quote mentioned above, which the *Journal* had seen fit to highlight with italics on the first page of the article, Maas said he couldn't remember who had told him that.

Cross off another seemingly promising lead.

On August 9, 1968—exactly a year before the Tate murders—Gregg Jakobson had arranged a recording session for Manson at a studio in Van Nuys. I went there to listen to the tapes, which were now in the possession of Herb Weiser, a Hollywood attorney representing the studio.

My own admittedly unprofessional appraisal was that Manson was no worse than many performers in current vogue.* However, Charlie's musical ability was not my

*A folk-song expert later listened to the tapes and found the songs "extremely derivative." From his notes: "Somewhere along the line Manson has picked up a pretty good guitar beat. Nothing original about the music. But the lyrics are something else. They contain an amazing amount of hostility ('You'll get yours yet,' etc.). This is rare in folk songs, except in the old murder ballads, but even there it is always past tense. In Manson's lyrics these are things that are *going to happen.* Very spooky. Overall judgment: a moderately talented amateur."

major concern. Both Atkins and DeCarlo had said that the words "helter skelter" appeared in at least one of Manson's own songs. I'd asked both, "Are you sure he wasn't just playing the Beatles' song "Helter Skelter"? No, each had replied; this was Charlie's own composition. If anywhere in his lyrics I could find "helter skelter," "pig," "death to pigs," or "rise," it would be strong circumstantial evidence.

No luck.

It looked, for a time, as if we'd have better luck with the Watson extradition. On January 5, following a hearing in Austin, Texas Secretary of State Martin Dies, Jr., ordered Watson returned to California. Boyd returned to McKinney and filed a writ of habeas corpus, asking that Dies' order be vacated. The writ was filed with Judge Brown. On January 16, Brown granted a thirty-day continuance on Boyd's request. Tex remained in Texas.

In Los Angeles, Linda Kasabian was arraigned on the sixth and pleaded "not guilty." That same day attorney Marvin Part requested that a court-appointed psychiatrist examine his client, Leslie Van Houten. Judge Keene appointed Dr. Blake Skrdla, who was to make a confidential report to Part. Earlier Part had requested and received permission to interview Leslie on tape. Though the prosecution would neither hear the tape nor see the report, it was a fairly safe assumption that Part, like his predecessor Barnett, was considering an insanity plea.

We didn't have to wait very long for Manson's reaction.

On the nineteenth Leslie requested that Part be relieved as her attorney and Ira Reiner appointed instead.

Owing to the possibly sensitive nature of the testimony, Judge George M. Dell decided to hear the matter in chambers, outside the presence of the public and press.*

Part opposed the substitution, arguing that Leslie Van Houten was mentally incapable of making a rational decision. "This girl will do anything that Charles Manson or any member of this so-called Manson Family says . . . This

*The transcripts of in-chambers proceedings were sealed until after the conclusion of the trial. Though there were occasional leaks, in most instances those proceedings are reported here for the first time.

girl has no will of her own left . . . Because of this hold that Charles Manson and the Family has over her, she doesn't care whether she is tried together and gets the gas chamber, she just wants to be with the Family."

The appointment of Reiner, Part claimed, would constitute a conflict of interest, one that would definitely hurt Miss Van Houten.

Part told the court how the switch had come about. A week or so ago Squeaky had visited Leslie. Although Part was also present, Squeaky had told her, "*We* think you ought to have another lawyer," and had shown her Reiner's card. Leslie had replied, "I'll do anything that Charlie wants me to do." A few days later Leslie (1) refused to be examined by the psychiatrist, and (2) informed Part that he was no longer her attorney and that Reiner was.

Part wanted Judge Dell to listen to the tape he had made with Leslie. He was sure that, having heard it, the Court would realize that Leslie Van Houten was incapable of acting in her own best interests.

It was now obvious that Part felt a joint trial and an "umbrella" defense would hurt his client. The other defendants were charged with seven murders, Leslie with only two. And the evidence against her was slight. "To the best of my knowledge," Part said, referring to the Dianne Lake statement which he had received through discovery, "all she did was perhaps stab somebody who was already dead."

Judge Dell then questioned Ira Reiner, who admitted that he had talked to Manson "roughly a dozen times." He also admitted that Manson was one of several people who had suggested he represent Leslie. He had never actually represented Manson, however, and he had only gone to see Miss Van Houten after receiving a written request from her.

Judge Dell questioned Leslie outside the presence of the two attorneys. She remained firm in her resolve: she wanted Reiner.

Part, literally, begged Judge Dell to listen to the tape he had made with Leslie. Part said, "That girl is insane in a way that is almost science fiction."

Judge Dell said he would rather not hear the tape. He was concerned with one issue only: whether Miss Van Houten's mental state was such that she could intelligently make a substitution of counsel. To determine this, he appointed three psychiatrists to listen to the tape and examine Leslie, their confidential report, on that single issue, to be made directly to him.

Manson himself appeared before Judge Dell on the seventeenth.

MANSON "I have a motion here—it's a strange motion—probably never been a motion like this ever before—"

THE COURT "Try me."

After examining it, the judge had to agree: "It certainly is an interesting document."

"Charles Manson, also known as Jesus Christ, Prisoner," assisted by six other pro pers, who called themselves "The Family of Infinite Soul, Inc.," had filed a habeas corpus motion on behalf of Manson-Christ, charging that the sheriff was depriving him of his spiritual, mental, and physical liberty, in an unconstitutional manner not in harmony with man's or God's law, and asking that he be released forthwith.

Judge Dell denied the motion.

MANSON "Your Honor, behind the big words and all the confusion and the robes you hide the truth."

THE COURT "Not intentionally."

MANSON "Like sometimes I wonder if you know what is going on."

THE COURT "Sometimes I do too, Mr. Manson. I admit there is some self-doubt . . . Yet we in the black robes do our thing, too."

Manson requested a number of items—a tape recorder, unlimited telephone privileges, and so on—which he claimed both the Sheriff's Office and the DA's Office were denying him. Dell corrected him.

THE COURT "The prosecutor is willing to go further than the sheriff has, as a matter of fact."

MANSON "Well, I was going to ask him if he would call the whole thing off. It would save a lot of trouble."

THE COURT "Disappoint all these people? Never, Mr. Manson."

When Manson again appeared before Judge Dell, on the twenty-eighth, he was still complaining about the limitations of his pro per privileges. For example, he wanted to interview Robert Beausoleil, Linda Kasabian, and Sadie Mae Glutz, but their attorneys had denied permission. Judge Dell informed him they had that right.

MANSON "I got a message from Sadie. She told me that the District Attorney had made her say what she had said."

Manson was playing to the press, certain that they would pick up the charge, and they did. It was the next best thing to calling Susan on the phone and telling her how to recant.

Aaron played out our bluff, stating that the People were prepared to go to trial.

Manson, to our relief, wanted more time.

Judge Dell assigned the case to Judge William Keene, and granted a continuance to February 9, at which time the trial date would be set.

Our relief was real. Not only was our case still weak, Aaron and I couldn't even agree on the motive.

The prosecution does not have the legal burden of proving motive. But motive is extremely important evidence. A jury wants to know why. Just as showing that a defendant has a motive for committing a crime is circumstantial evidence of guilt, so is the absence of motive circumstantial evidence of innocence.

In this case, even more than in most others, proving motive was important, since these murders appeared completely senseless. It was doubly important in Manson's case, since he was not present when the murders took place. If we could prove to the jury that Manson, and Manson alone, had a motive for these murders, then this would be very powerful circumstantial evidence that he also ordered them.

Aaron and I had been friends for a long time. We had developed a mutual respect that allowed us to say exactly what we felt, and quite often our discussions were heated. This one was no exception. Aaron thought that we should argue that the motive was robbery. I told him quite frankly that I felt his theory was ridiculous. What had they stolen? Seventy-some dollars from Abigail Folger, Rosemary LaBianca's wallet (which they ditched, money intact), possibly a sack of coins, and a carton of chocolate milk. That was it. As far as we knew, nothing else had been taken from either residence. There was, the police reports reiterated, no evidence of ransacking or theft. Items worth thousands of dollars, though in plain view, were left behind.

As an alternative motive, Aaron suggested that maybe Manson was trying to get enough money to bail out Mary Brunner, the mother of his child, who had been arrested on the afternoon of August 8 for using a stolen credit card. Again I played the Devil's advocate. Seven murders, five one night, two the next; 169 separate stab wounds; words written in the victims' own blood; a knife stuck in the throat of one victim, a fork in his stomach, the word WAR carved on his stomach—all this to raise $625 bail?

It wasn't that we lacked a motive. Though Aaron and LAPD disagreed with me, I felt we had one. It was just that it was almost unbelievably bizarre.

When I interviewed Susan Atkins on December 4, she told me, "The whole thing was done to instill fear in the establishment and cause paranoia. Also to show the black man how to take over the white man." This, she said, would be the start of "Helter Skelter," which, when I questioned her before the grand jury the next day, she defined as "the last war on the face of the earth. It would be all the wars that have ever been fought built one on top of the other . . ."

"There was a so called motive behind all this," Susan wrote Ronnie Howard. "It was to instill fear into the pigs and to bring on judgment day which is here now for all."

Judgment Day, Armageddon, Helter Skelter—to Manson they were one and the same, a racial holocaust which would see the black man emerge triumphant. "The karma is turning, it's blackie's turn to be on top." Danny DeCarlo said Manson preached this incessantly. Even a near stranger such as biker Al Springer, who visited Spahn Ranch only a few times, told me he thought "helter skelter" must be Charlie's "pet words," he used them so often.

That Manson foresaw a war between the blacks and the whites was not fantastic. Many people believe that such a war may someday occur. What *was* fantastic was that he was convinced he could personally start that war himself—that by making it look as if blacks had murdered the seven Caucasian victims he could turn the white community against the black community.

We knew there was at least one secondary motive for the Tate murders. As Susan Atkins put it in the Caballero tape, "The reason Charlie picked that house was to instill fear into Terry Melcher because Terry had given us his word on a few things and never came through with them." But this was obviously not the primary motive, since, according to Gregg Jakobson, Manson knew that Melcher was no longer living at 10050 Cielo Drive.

All the evidence we'd assembled thus far, I felt, pointed to one primary motive: Helter Skelter. It was far out, but then so were the murders themselves. It was admittedly bizarre, but from the first moment I was assigned to the case, I'd felt that for murders as bizarre as these the motive itself would have to be almost equally strange, not something you'd find within the pages of a textbook on police science.

The jury would never buy Helter Skelter, Aaron said, suggesting that we offer something they would understand. I told him it wouldn't take me two seconds to dump the whole Helter Skelter theory if he could find another motive in the evidence.

Aaron, however, was right. The jury would never accept Helter Skelter, as is. We were missing far too many bits and pieces, and one all-important link.

Presuming that Manson actually believed that he could start a race war with these acts, what would he, Charlie Manson, personally gain by it?

To this I had no answer. And without it the motive made no sense.

"Always think of the Now . . . No time to look back . . . No time to say how." This rhyme was repeated in almost every letter Sandy, Squeaky, Gypsy, or Brenda sent to the defendants. Its meaning was obvious: Don't tell them anything.

Through a barrage of letters, telegrams, and attempted visits, the Manson girls tried to get Beausoleil, Atkins, and Kasabian to dump their present attorneys, repudiate any incriminating statements they may have made, and engage in a united defense.

Though Beausoleil agreed that "the whole thing balances on whether the Family stays together in their heads & doesn't break up & start testifying against itself," he decided, "I'm going to keep my present lawyer."

Bobby Beausoleil had always been somewhat independent. Less handsome than "pretty" (the girls had nicknamed him "Cupid"), Beausoleil had had bit parts in several movies, written music, formed a rock group, and had his own harem, all before meeting Manson. Leslie, Gypsy, and Kitty had all lived with Bobby before joining Charlie.

Beausoleil requested that Squeaky and the others not visit him so often. They were taking up all his visiting time, when the person he really wanted to see was Kitty, who was expecting his child in less than a month.

Beausoleil wasn't the only one being pressured. Without Susan Atkins, the prosecution had no case against Manson, and Manson knew it. Family members called Richard Caballero at all hours of the day and night. When cajoling didn't work, they tried threats. Less because of their pressure than that of his own client, Caballero finally gave in and let some of the Manson girls—though not Manson himself—visit Susan.

It was, at best, a holding action. At any moment Susan could insist on seeing Charlie, and Caballero would be unable to prevent it. After Susan's story had appeared in the Los Angeles *Times*, little signs had appeared on the walls at Sybil Brand reading, "SADIE GLUTZ IS A SNITCH." This greatly upset Susan. And each time something like this happened, the scales seemed to tip a little more in Manson's favor.

Manson was also aware that if Susan Atkins refused to testify at the trial, our only hope lay with Linda Kasabian. After a time Linda's attorney, Gary Fleischman, refused to see Gypsy, so persistent had her visits become. If Linda didn't testify, Gypsy told him on numerous occasions, everyone would get off. Fleischman did take her along one time when he went to see his client. Gypsy told Linda—in the presence of several persons—that she should lie and say that on the nights of the Tate-LaBianca murders she had never left Spahn Ranch but remained with her at the waterfall. Gypsy promised to back up her story.

Given a choice between Susan and Linda as the star witness for the prosecution, I much preferred Linda: she hadn't killed anyone. But in the rush to get the case to the grand jury, we'd made the deal with Susan and, like it or not, we were stuck with it. Unless Susan bolted.

Yet this posed its own problems. If Susan didn't testify, we'd need Linda, but without Susan's testimony we had no evidence against Linda, so what could we offer her? Fleischman wanted immunity for his client, yet from Linda's standpoint it would be better to be tried and acquitted than get immunity, testify against Manson and the others, and risk retribution by the Family.

We were very worried at this point. Exactly how worried is evidenced by a telephone call I made. After Manson had been indicted for the Tate-LaBianca murders, the Inyo County authorities had dropped the arson charges against him, though they had a strong case. I called Frank Fowles and asked him to refile the charges, which he did, on February 6. We were that afraid that Manson would be set free.

February 1970

That an accused mass murderer could emerge a counterculture hero seemed unconceivable. But to some Charles Manson had become a cause.

Just before she went underground, Bernardine Dohrn told a Students for a Democratic Society convention: "Offing those rich pigs with their own forks and knives, and then eating a meal in the same room, far out! The Weathermen dig Charles Manson."

The underground paper *Tuesday's Child*, which called itself the Voice of the Yippies, blasted its competitor the Los Angeles *Free Press* for giving too much publicity to Manson—then spread his picture across the entire front page with a banner naming him MAN OF THE YEAR.

The cover of the next issue had Manson on a cross.

Manson posters and sweat shirts appeared in psychedelic shops, along with FREE MANSON buttons.

Gypsy and other spokesmen for the Family took to the late-night radio talk shows to play Charlie's songs and denounce the prosecution for "framing an innocent man."

Stretching his pro per privileges to their utmost limits, Manson himself granted a number of interviews to the underground press. He was also interviewed, by phone from the County Jail, by several radio stations. And his visitor's list now included, among the "material witnesses," some familiar names.

"I fell in love with Charlie Manson the first time I saw his cherub face and sparkling eyes on TV," exclaimed Jerry Rubin. On a speaking tour during a recess in the Chicago Seven trial, Rubin visited Manson in jail, giving rise to the possibility that Manson might be considering the use of disruptive tactics during his own trial. According to Rubin, Charlie rapped for three hours, telling him, among other things, "Rubin, I am not of your world.

I've spent all my life in prison. When I was a child I was an orphan and too ugly to be adopted. Now I am too beautiful to be set free."

"His words and courage inspired us," Rubin later wrote. "Manson's soul is easy to touch because it lays quite bare on the surface."*

Yet Charles Manson—revolutionary martyr—was a difficult image to maintain. Rubin admitted being angered by Manson's "incredible male chauvinism." A reporter for the *Free Press* was startled to find Manson both anti-Jewish and anti-black. And when one interviewer tried to suggest that Manson was as much a political prisoner as Huey Newton, Charlie, obviously perplexed, asked, "Who's he?"

As yet the pro-Mansonites appeared to be a small, though vocal minority. If the press and TV reports were correct, a majority of young people whom the media had lumped together under the label "hippies" disavowed Manson. Many stated that the things he espoused—such as violence—were directly contrary to their beliefs. And more than a few were bitter about the guilt by association. It was almost impossible to hitchhike any more, one youth told a New York *Times* reporter. "If you're young, have a beard, or even long hair, motorists look at you as if you're a 'kill crazy cultist,' and jam the gas."

The irony was that Manson never considered himself a hippie, equating their pacifism with weakness. If the Family members had to have a label, he told his followers, he much preferred calling them "slippies," a term which, in the context of their creepy-crawly missions, was not inappropriate.

What was most frightening was that the Family itself was growing. The group at Spahn had increased significantly. Each time Manson made a courtroom appearance, I spotted new faces among the known Family members.

It could be presumed that many of the new "converts" were sensation seekers, drawn like moths to the glare of publicity.

***We Are Everywhere*, by Jerry Rubin (New York: Harper & Row, 1971).

What we didn't know, however, was how far they would go to gain attention or acceptance.

Leslie Van Houten was legally sane, Judge Dell ruled on February 6, basing his decision on the confidential reports of the three psychiatrists, and granting her motion for a substitution of attorneys.

In court the same day, Manson unexpectedly called our bluff: "Let's have an early trial setting. Let's go tomorrow or Monday. That's a good day for a trial." Keene set a trial date of March 30, the date already assigned Susan Atkins. That gave us a little more time, but not nearly enough.

On February 16, Keene heard Manson's motion for a change of venue. "You know, there has been more publicity on this, even more than the guy who killed the President of the United States," Manson said. "You know, it is getting so far out of proportion that to me it is a joke, but actually the joke might cost me my life."

Though the other defense attorneys would later submit similar motions, arguing that it would be impossible for their clients to obtain fair trials in Los Angeles because of the extensive pre-trial publicity, Manson didn't argue this too strongly. The motion was really "trivial," he said, because "it doesn't seem it could be done anywheres."

Though Keene disagreed with Manson's contention that he couldn't obtain a fair trial, he did observe, in denying the motion, that "a change of venue, even if warranted, would be ineffectual."

This was also the view of the prosecution. It was doubtful if there was any place in California, or the rest of the United States, where the publicity had not reached.

Each time the defense made a motion—and there would be hundreds before the end of the trial—the prosecution had to be prepared to answer. Though Aaron and I shared the verbal arguments, I prepared the written briefs, many of which required considerable legal research. All this was in addition to the heavy investigative responsibilities I had taken on.

Yet the latter job had its special satisfactions. At the start of February there were still huge holes in our case, big areas where we had almost no information whatsoever. For example, I still had very little insight into what made Charles Manson tick.

By the end of the month I had that, and a great deal more. For by then I understood, for the first time, Manson's motive—the reason why he'd ordered these murders.

I rarely interview a witness just once. Often the fourth or fifth interview will bring out something previously forgotten or deemed insignificant, which, in proper context, may prove vital to my case.

When I had questioned Gregg Jakobson before the grand jury, my primary concern had been to establish the link between Manson and Melcher.

Reinterviewing the talent scout, I was surprised to discover that since meeting Manson at Dennis Wilson's home in the early summer of 1968, Jakobson had had over a hundred long talks with Charlie, mostly about Manson's philosophy. An intelligent young man, who flirted off and on with the hippie life style, Gregg had never joined the Family, though he'd often visited Manson at Spahn Ranch. Besides seeing in Manson certain commercial possibilities, Jakobson had found him "intellectually stimulating." He was so impressed that he often touted him to others, such as Rudi Altobelli, the owner of 10050 Cielo Drive, who had been both Terry Melcher's and Sharon Tate's landlord.

I was surprised at the wide variety of people Manson knew. Charlie was a chameleon, Gregg said; he often professed that "he had a thousand faces and that he used them all—he told me that he had a mask for everyone."

Including the jury? I wondered, realizing that if Manson put on the mask of the peace-loving hippie at the trial, I'd be able to use Gregg's remark to unmask him.

I asked Gregg why Manson felt it necessary to don masks.

A. "So he could deal with everyone on their own level, from the ranch hand at Spahn, to the girls on the Sunset Strip, to me."

I was curious as to whether Manson had a "real" face. Gregg thought he had. Underneath it all he had very firm beliefs. "It was rare to find a man who believed in his convictions as strongly as Charlie did—who couldn't be swayed."

What were the sources of Manson's beliefs? I asked.

Charlie rarely, if ever, gave anyone else credit for his philosophy, Gregg replied. But it was obvious that Charlie was not above borrowing.

Had Manson ever mentioned Scientology or The Process?

The Process, also known as the Church of the Final Judgment, was a very strange cult. Led by one Robert DeGrimston, t/n Robert Moore—who, like Manson, was an ex-Scientologist—its members worshiped both Satan and Christ. I'd only begun to look into the group, acting on the basis of a newspaper story which indicated Manson might have been influenced by them.

However, Jakobson said Manson had never mentioned either Scientology or The Process. Gregg himself had never heard of the latter group.

Did Charlie ever quote anyone? I asked Gregg.

Yes, he replied, "The Beatles and the Bible." Manson would quote, verbatim, whole lyrics from the Beatles' songs, finding in them a multitude of hidden meanings. As for the Bible, he most often quoted Revelation 9. But in both cases he usually used the quotations as support for his own views.

Though I was very interested in this odd coupling, and would later question Gregg in depth about it, I wanted to know more about Manson's personal beliefs and attitudes.

Q: "What did Manson say, if anything, about right and wrong?"

A: "He believed you could do no wrong, no bad. Everything was good. Whatever you do is what you are supposed to do; you are following your own karma."

The philosophical mosaic began taking shape. The man I was seeking to convict had no moral boundaries. It was not that he was immoral, but totally amoral. And such a person is always dangerous.

Q: "Did he say it was wrong to kill a human being?"

A: "He said it was not."

Q: "What was Manson's philosophy re death?"

A: "There was no death, to Charlie's way of thinking. Death was only a change. The soul or spirit can't die ... That's what we used to argue all the time, the objective and the subjective and the marriage of the two. He believed it was all in the head, all subjective. He said that death was a fear that was born in man's head and can be taken out of man's head, and then it would no longer exist ...

"Death to Charlie," Gregg added, "was no more important than eating an ice cream cone."

Yet once, in the desert, Jakobson had run over a tarantula, and Manson had angrily berated him for it. He had denounced others for killing rattlesnakes, picking flowers, even stepping on a blade of grass. To Manson it was not wrong to kill a human being, but it was wrong to kill an animal or plant. Yet he also said that nothing was wrong, everything that happened was right.

That Manson's philosophy was riddled with such contradictions apparently bothered his followers little if at all. Manson said that each person should be independent, but the whole Family was dependent on him. He said that he couldn't tell anyone else what to do, that they should "do what your love tells you," but he also told them, "I am your love," and his wants became theirs.

I asked Gregg about Manson's attitude toward women. I was especially interested in this because of the female defendants.

Women had only two purposes in life, Charlie would say: to serve men and to give birth to children. But he didn't permit the girls in the Family to raise their own children. If they did, Charlie claimed, they would give them their own hangups. Charlie believed that if he could eliminate the bonds created by parents, schools, churches, society, he could develop "a strong white race." Like Nietzsche, whom Manson claimed to have read, Charlie "believed in a master race."

"According to Charlie," Gregg continued, "women were only as good as their men. They were only a reflection of their men, all the way back to daddy. A woman was an accumulation of all the men she had been close to."

Then why were there so many women in the Family? I asked; there were at least five girls to every man.

It was only through the women, Gregg said, that Charlie could attract the men. Men represented power, strength. But he needed the women to lure the men into the Family.

As with others I interviewed, I asked Gregg for examples of Manson's domination. Gregg gave me one of the best I'd yet found: he said he had had dinner with the Family on three occasions; each time Manson sat alone on the top of a large rock, the other members of the Family sitting on the ground in a circle around him.

Q. "Did Tex Watson ever get up on the rock?"

A. "No, of course not."

Q. "Did anyone else in the Family get up there?"

A. "Only Charlie."

I needed many, many more examples like this, so that when I offered all of them at the trial, the jury would be led to the irresistible conclusion that Manson had such a hold over his followers, and specifically his co-defendants, that never in a million years would they have committed these murders without his guidance, directions, and orders.

I asked Gregg about Charlie's ambitions. "Charlie wanted to be a successful recording artist," Gregg said. "Not so much as a means to making money as to get his word out to the public. He needed people to live with him, to make love, to liberate the white race."

What was Manson's attitude toward blacks?

Gregg replied that Charlie "believed there were different levels when it came to race, and the white man occupied a higher level than the black." This was why Charlie was so strongly opposed to black-white sex; "you would be interfering with the path of evolution, you would be mixing up nervous systems, less evolved with more evolved."

According to Jakobson, "Charlie believed that the black man's sole purpose on earth was to serve the white man. He was to serve the white man's needs." But blackie had been on the bottom too long, Charlie said. It was now his turn to take over the reins of power. This was what Helter Skelter, the black-white revolution, was all about.

Gregg and I would talk about this on more than a half

dozen separate occasions. What before had been only fragments, bits and pieces, now began slipping into place.

The picture that eventually emerged, however, was so incredibly bizarre as to be almost beyond belief.

There is a special feeling you develop over years of interviewing people. When someone is lying or not telling everything he knows, you can often sense it.

On reinterviewing Terry Melcher, I became convinced that he was withholding something. There wasn't time for pussyfooting. I told Terry I wanted to talk to him again, only this time he should have his attorney, Chet Lappen, present. When we met in Lappen's office on the seventeenth, I put it to him bluntly: "You're not leveling with me, Terry. You're keeping something back. Whatever it is, eventually it will come out. It would be far better if you told me about it now rather than have the defense surprise us with it on cross-examination."

Terry wavered for a few minutes, then decided to tell me.

The day after news of Manson's involvement in the Tate murders broke, Terry had received a telephone call from London. The caller was Rudi Altobelli, the owner of 10050 Cielo Drive. Rudi had told him, in confidence, that one day in March 1969, while he was taking a shower in the guest house, Manson had knocked on the door. Manson claimed to be looking for Terry, who had moved out some months before, but Altobelli, who was a successful business manager for a number of theatrical stars, suspected that Manson had actually come looking for him, as Manson had worked the conversation around to his own music and songs. In a rather subtle fashion, Altobelli had made it clear that he wasn't interested, and Manson had left.

The guest house! "Terry," I said, "why didn't you tell me this before?"

"I wasn't sure it was relevant."

"Christ, Terry, this places Manson inside the gate of the Tate residence. As you well know, to reach the guest house he'd have to first pass the main house. This means Manson was familiar with the layout of the house and grounds. I don't know what could be any *more* relevant. Where's Altobelli now?"

"Cape Town, South Africa," Melcher reluctantly replied. Checking his address book, he gave me the number of the hotel where he was staying.

I called Cape Town. Mr. Altobelli had just checked out of the hotel, leaving no forwarding address. However, Terry told me that Rudi was planning to return to Los Angeles for a few days sometime soon.

"The minute he hits L.A. I want to know it," I told him. As a safeguard I put out a few feelers of my own, asking others who knew Altobelli to contact me if they saw or heard from him.

The same day I talked to Melcher, half our extradition problems were solved: Patricia "Katie" Krenwinkel waived further proceedings and asked to be returned to California immediately. When she made her first courtroom appearance on the twenty-fourth, she requested Paul Fitzgerald of the Public Defender's Office as her attorney. Fitzgerald told the judge that, barring a possible conflict of interest, his office would be willing to represent her.

Actually there were two possible conflicts of interest: the Public Defender's Office was already representing Beausoleil on the Hinman murder, and Fitzgerald had earlier represented Manson, albeit briefly, before he went in pro per.

A month later Paul Fitzgerald resigned from the Public Defender's Office, after that office decided there was indeed a conflict of interest involved. Whether Fitzgerald's motive was purely idealistic, or he hoped to make a name for himself in private practice by winning an acquittal for his client, or both, the fact remained that he gave up a $25,000 a year salary and a promising career as a public defender to represent Patricia Krenwinkel with virtually no pay.

Terry Melcher didn't call. But another of my contacts did, reporting that Rudi Altobelli had returned to Los Angeles the previous day. I called Altobelli's attorney, Barry

Hirsch, and arranged a meeting. Before leaving the office, I prepared a subpoena and stuck it in my pocket.

Rather than ask Altobelli whether the guest house incident really occurred, and risk a possible denial, I simply laid it out: "Rudi, the reason I'm here is because I want to ask you about the time Manson came to the guest house. Terry told me about it." *Fait accompli.*

Yes, Manson had been there, Rudi said. But did this mean he would have to testify?

Rudi Altobelli was a bright, urbane, and, as I'd later discover, at times quite witty man. The roster of entertainment figures he'd represented included such stars as Katharine Hepburn, Henry Fonda (who for a time had rented the guest house at 10050 Cielo Drive), Samantha Eggar, Buffy Sainte-Marie, Christopher Jones, and Sally Kellerman, to name only a few. However, in common with almost all the other witnesses in this case, he was scared.

On his return from Europe following the murders, he'd found that 10050 Cielo Drive had been sealed by the police. Needing a place to stay, and unsure whether he might have been one of the intended victims—and still might be—he picked the safest place he could think of. He moved in with Terry Melcher and Candice Bergen, who were occupying a beach house in Malibu owned by Terry's mother, Doris Day. Though Terry and Rudi had spent many hours discussing the murders, and possible suspects, Manson's name was never mentioned, Rudi said. When the news broke that Manson had been accused of the murders, a possible motive being his grudge against Melcher, Altobelli decided that he had probably chosen the least safe place in Southern California. He still shivered when recalling it.

He had another reason for fear. In a sense, he too had rejected Manson.

"Tell me about it, Rudi," I suggested. "Then we'll discuss whether you have to testify or not. But first, how do you know it was Manson?"

Because he'd met Manson once before, Altobelli said, during the summer of 1968, at Dennis Wilson's house. Manson was living there at the time, and Rudi had dropped in while Dennis was playing a tape of Manson's music. He'd listened politely, commented that it was "nice," the minimal courtesy possible, then left.

At various times Dennis and Gregg had tried to interest him in Manson and his philosophy. Having worked hard for what money he had, Altobelli said, he was not sympathetic to Manson's sponging, and had told them exactly that.

The incident had occurred about eight or nine on the evening of Sunday, March 23, 1969—Rudi remembered the date because he and Sharon had flown to Rome together the next day, Rudi on business, Sharon to rejoin her husband and to make a movie there. Rudi was alone in the guest house, taking a shower, when Christopher started barking. Grabbing a robe, he went to the door and saw Manson on the porch. While it was possible that Manson had knocked and the shower had muffled the sound, Rudi was irritated that he had opened the outside door and walked onto the porch uninvited.

Manson started to introduce himself but Rudi, somewhat brusquely, without opening the screen door that separated the porch from the living room, said, "I know who you are, Charlie, what do you want?"

Manson said he was looking for Terry Melcher. Altobelli said Terry had moved to Malibu. When Manson asked for his address, Altobelli said he didn't know it. Which was not true.

Prolonging the conversation, Manson asked him what business he was in. Though Altobelli felt sure Manson already knew the answer, he replied, "The entertainment business." He added, "I'd like to talk to you longer, Charlie, but I'm leaving the country tomorrow and have to pack."

Manson said he would like to talk to him when he returned. Rudi told him that he wouldn't be back for over a year. Another untruth, but he had no desire to talk further with Manson.

Before Manson left, Rudi asked him why he had come back to the guest house. Manson replied that the people at the main house had sent him back. Altobelli said that he didn't like to have his tenants disturbed, and he would appreciate it if he wouldn't do so in the future. With that Manson left.

Though one question was uppermost in my mind, before asking it I had Altobelli describe Manson, the lighting on the porch, exactly where each was standing. Since he had met Manson on a prior occasion, there was no question that this was a positive identification, but I wanted to be absolutely sure.

Then I asked it, and held my breath until he answered. "Rudi, who was up front that night?"

"Sharon, Gibby, Voytek, and Jay."

Four of the five Tate victims! This meant that Manson could have seen any or all of them. Prior to my talking to Rudi, we had assumed that Manson had never seen the people he had ordered killed.

"Rudi, all those people are dead. Was there anyone else up front who could testify to this?"

Rudi thought a moment. He had been up at the main house earlier in the evening, actually returning to the guest house only a few minutes before Manson arrived. "I'm not sure," he said, "but I'm almost positive Hatami was there."

Shahrokh Hatami, a native of Iran, was Sharon's personal photographer, and a good friend of both Polanskis. Hatami had been at the house that afternoon, Rudi knew, photographing Sharon while she was packing for her trip.

"I don't want to testify, Mr. Bugliosi," Rudi suddenly said.

"I can understand that. If there is any way I can avoid it, I won't call you to the stand. But realistically, considering the importance of what you've told me, the odds are that I will have to call you." We discussed the subject at some length before I gave him the subpoena.

I then asked him, "Tell me about Sharon."

In the short time he had known her, Rudi said, he had grown very fond of her. She was a beautiful person. Of course she was physically beautiful, but by this he meant something else. She had a kind of warmth, a niceness, which you sensed immediately on meeting her, but which, thus far in her career, no director had ever managed to bring out on the screen. They'd had many long talks. She'd called 10050 Cielo Drive her "love house."

Rudi then told me something he said he had never told anyone else. I knew there was no way I could use it in the trial: it was hearsay, and though there are many exceptions to the hearsay rule, this couldn't come in under any of them.

On the flight to Rome, Sharon had asked him: "Did that creepy-looking guy come back there yesterday?"

So Sharon had seen Manson, the creepy-looking little guy who four and a half months later would mastermind her murder!

Something must have happened to have caused such a strong reaction. A confrontation of some sort. Could it be that Voytek, who had an unpredictable temper, had got into an argument with Manson? Or that Manson had said something offensive to Sharon, and Jay had come to her defense?

I called LAPD and told them to find Shahrokh Hatami.

Lieutenant Helder contacted a friend of Colonel Tate's, who in turn located Hatami. I interviewed him in my office. Very emotionally, the Iranian photographer told me how much he had loved Sharon. "Not romantic, but"—he apologized for his broken English—"one human being loving qualities other human being has."

I told him I doubted if it could be better expressed.

Yes, he'd once sent someone to the back house. One time. He didn't know the date, but it was the day before Sharon left for Europe. It was in the afternoon. He'd looked out the window and noticed a man walking into the yard, hesitant, as if he didn't know where he was going, yet cocky, as if he thought he owned the place. His manner irritated Hatami, and he went out on the porch and asked him what he wanted.

I asked Hatami to describe the man. He said he was short, like Roman Polanski (Polanski was five feet five, Manson five feet two), late twenties, thin, with long hair. What color hair? Dark brown. He didn't have a beard but looked as if he needed a shave. How could he tell that?

He'd walked off the porch onto the stone walk to confront him; they were at most three or four feet apart.

With the exception of the age—Manson was thirty-four, but could easily have been mistaken for younger—the description fitted.

The man said he was looking for someone, mentioning a name Hatami did not recognize.

Could it have been Melcher? I asked. Possible, Hatami said, but he really couldn't remember. It had meant nothing to him at the time.

"This is the Polanski residence," Hatami told him. "This is not the place. Maybe the people you want is back there," pointing. "Take the back alley."

By "back alley" Hatami meant the dirt pathway in front of the residence which led to the guest house. But, as I'd later argue to the jury, to an American "back alley" meant a place where there were garbage cans, refuse. Manson must have felt he was being treated like an alley cat.

I asked Hatami, "What tone of voice did you use?" He illustrated, speaking loudly and angrily. Roman was away, Hatami said, and he felt protective of Sharon. "I wasn't happy that he was coming on the property, and looking at people he doesn't know."

How did the man react? He appeared upset, Hatami said; he turned and walked away without saying "excuse me" or anything.

Just before this, however, Sharon came to the door and said, "Who is it, Hatami?" Hatami told her that a man was looking for someone.

Showing Hatami a diagram of the house and grounds, I had him point to the spots where each was standing. Sharon was on the porch, the man on the walk not more than six to eight feet away, with no obstruction between them. There could be no question that Charles Manson saw Sharon Tate, and she him. Sharon had undoubtedly looked right into the eyes of the man who would order her death. We now had, for the first time, evidence that prior to the murders Manson had seen one of his victims.

Hatami had remained on the walk, Sharon on the porch, while the man went down the path toward the guest house. According to Hatami, he came back up the path in "a minute or two, no more," and left the premises without saying anything.

It was not as abrasive an incident as I was looking for, but, together with Melcher's rejection and Altobelli's subtle putdown, Hatami's "take the back alley" was more than sufficient cause for Manson to have strong feelings against 10050 Cielo Drive. Too, not only were these people obviously establishment, they were establishment in the very fields—entertainment, recording, motion pictures—in which Manson had tried to make it and failed.

There was one discrepancy: the time. Hatami was positive the incident had occurred during the afternoon. Altobelli, however, was equally insistent that it was between eight and nine in the evening when Manson appeared on the guest house porch. While it was possible one or the other was confused, the most logical explanation was that Manson had gone to the guest house that afternoon, found no one there (Altobelli was out most of the afternoon, making arrangements for his trip), then returned that evening. This was supported by Hatami's statement that Manson had come back up the path after "a minute or two, no more," which hardly left time for his conversation with Altobelli.

I had Hatami look at photographs of a dozen or so men. He picked out one, saying it looked like the man, though he couldn't be absolutely sure. It was a photograph of Charles Manson.

In interviewing Hatami, I hadn't mentioned Manson's name. Not until the interview was almost over did Hatami realize that the man he had spoken to that day might have been the man accused of plotting Sharon's murder.

Melcher to Altobelli to Hatami. If I hadn't suspected that Melcher was withholding something, it was possible that we might never have placed Manson inside the gate of 10050 Cielo Drive.

A similar chain, which had begun with my discovery of a short notation in the Inyo County files, led me to the missing piece in the motive for both the Tate and LaBianca murders.

Finally, nearly three months after first requesting it, I obtained the tape Inyo County Deputy Sheriff Don Ward had made with the two miners, Paul Crockett and Brooks Poston.

Ward had interviewed the pair on October 3, 1969, at Independence. This was a week before the Barker raid, and nearly a month and a half before LAPD learned of the Manson Family's possible involvement in the Tate-LaBianca murders. Ward's interview had nothing to do with those murders, only the activities of the "hippie types" who were now living in Golar Wash.

Crockett, a weather-worn miner in his mid-forties, had been prospecting in the Death Valley area in the spring of 1969 when he came across Manson's advance party at Barker Ranch. At this time it consisted of only two persons, a young runaway named Juanita Wildebush and Brooks Poston, a slender, rather docile eighteen-year-old who had been with the Family since June 1968. Nights, Crockett would visit the pair, and the talk would invariably turn to one subject, Charlie. "And I couldn't believe what they were saying," Crockett observed. "I mean, it was so utterly ridiculous." It became obvious to Crockett that these people believed this Charlie to be the second coming of Christ. It was just as obvious that they feared him. And so Crockett, who was no stranger to mysticism, did something perhaps a little odd but at least psychologically effective. He told them that, just like Charlie, he too had powers. And "I planted them with the idea that I had the power to keep Charlie from coming back up there."

Other Family members—including Paul Watkins, Tex Watson, Brenda McCann, and Bruce Davis—would occasionally show up at Barker with messages and supplies, and it didn't take long for the word to get back to Manson.

Initially he scoffed at the idea. But each time he tried to go to Barker something happened: the truck broke down, Spahn Ranch was raided, and so on. Meanwhile Juanita eloped with Bob Berry, Crockett's partner, and Crockett succeeded in "unconverting" several of Manson's most important male followers: Poston; Paul Watkins, who often acted as Manson's second in command; and, somewhat later, Juan Flynn, a tall, strapping Panamanian cowboy who had worked at Spahn.

When Crockett first met young Poston, he was "a zombie." The phrase was Poston's own. He said that he had wanted to leave the Family many times, but "Manson had a vise grip on my mind, and I couldn't break the grip. I didn't know how to leave . . ."

Crockett discovered that Manson had "programmed all his people to the extent that they're just like him. He has put all kinds of things in their heads. I didn't believe it could be done, but he has done it and I seen it working." Crockett began "deprogramming" Poston. He put him to work in his various mining ventures, built up his body, got him to thinking of other things than Manson.

When Manson finally reached Barker, in September 1969, Crockett, meeting him for the first time, found him "a very clever man—he borders on genius." Then Manson told him "some of the weirdest stories. I thought it was all make-believe, to start with." Before long, Crockett was not only convinced that Manson was insane, he was sure "he would think no more of killing one of us than he would of stepping on a flower; in fact, he'd rather do that than step on a flower."

Deciding that his own life expectancy was directly proportionate to his usefulness to Manson, Crockett made himself very useful, volunteering his truck to haul in supplies, and so forth. He and the former Mansonites now living with him in a small cabin near Barker also began taking precautions.

Among the weird tales Manson had told Crockett: That the black man "was getting ready to blow the whole thing open . . . Charlie has set up the whole thing, it's kind of like a storybook . . . He says Helter Skelter is coming down."

"Helter Skelter is what he calls the Negro revolt," Poston explained. "He says the Negroes are going to revolt and kill all the white men except the ones that are hiding in the desert . . ." Long before this Manson had told Poston, "When Helter Skelter comes down, the cities are going to be mass hysteria and the cops—the piggies, he calls them—won't know what to do, and the beast will fall and the black man will take over . . . that the battle of Armageddon will be at hand."

Poston told Deputy Ward, "One of Charlie's basic creeds is that all that girls are for is to fuck. And that's all they're for. And there is no crime, there is no sin, everything is all right, that it's all just a game, like the game of a little kid, only it's a grown-up game, and that God's getting ready to pull down the curtain on this game and start it over again with his chosen people . . ."

His chosen people were the Family, Charlie said. He would lead them to the desert, where they would multiply until they numbered 144,000. He got this, Poston said, "from reading things into the Bible, from Revelations."*

Also in Revelation, as well as in Hopi Indian legends, there was mention of a "bottomless pit," Poston said. The entrance to this pit, according to Charlie, was "a cave that he says is underneath Death Valley that leads down to a sea of gold that the Indians know about." Charlie claimed that "every tuned-in tribe of people that's ever lived have escaped the destruction of their race by going underground, literally, and they're all living in a golden city where there's a river that runs through it of milk and honey, and a tree that bears twelve kinds of fruit, a different fruit each month, or something like that, and you don't need to bring candles nor any flashlights down there. He says it will be all lit up because . . . the walls will glow and it won't be cold and it won't be too hot. There will be warm springs and fresh water, and people are already down there waiting for him."

Both Atkins and Jakobson had already told me about Charlie's "bottomless pit." The Family loved to hear Charlie sermonize about this hidden "land of milk and honey." They not only believed, they were so convinced that such a place existed that they spent days searching for the hole in the ground which would lead them to the underground paradise.

There was also a kind of desperation in the search, because it was here, underground in the bottomless pit, that they intended to hide and wait out Helter Skelter.

*Manson apparently got the 144,000 figure from Revelation 7, which mentions the twelve tribes of Israel, each numbering 12,000.

It was obvious to both Crockett and Poston that Manson believed Helter Skelter was imminent. And there were the preparations. Manson had arrived at Barker Ranch in September 1969 with about eight others, all heavily armed. More Family members arrived the following week, driving stolen dune buggies and other vehicles. They began setting up lookout posts and fortifications, hiding caches of guns, gasoline, and supplies.

(It did not occur to Crockett and Poston—since neither was aware of the Family's involvement in the Tate-LaBianca murders—that Manson might be fearful of something other than blacks.)

Manson hadn't given up on Poston, but Crockett's "deprogramming" had been very effective. Manson was even more upset about Paul Watkins' leaving him, since Watkins, a good-looking youth with a way with women, had been Manson's chief procurer of young girls.

Crockett, Poston, and Watkins had begun sleeping with their shotguns within reach. On at least three occasions Charlie, Clem, and/or the girls tried to creepy-crawl the cabin. Each time the trio had been lucky and had heard something, aborting the plan. Then one night Juan Flynn arrived "to shoot some bull," and admitted Manson had suggested he kill Crockett. Crockett persuaded Juan—who was far too independent to ever join the Family—that he should leave the area.

Crockett, accustomed to living as free and unencumbered as a mountain goat, was a mite stubborn. He felt he had as much right to be in Death Valley as Manson did. But he was also a realist. With Flynn gone and Watkins in town getting supplies, he and Poston were vastly outnumbered. Figuring "my usefulness to Charlie had already vanished and that he would, if he considered it necessary, liquidate me immediately, if not sooner," Crockett had Poston fill the canteens and pack some grub. Under cover of night they fled the area on foot, walking over twenty rugged miles to Warmsprings, then catching a ride to Independence, where they told Deputy Sheriff Ward about Charles Manson and his Family.

After hearing the tape, I arranged through Frank Fowles for Crockett and Poston to come to Los Angeles.

Though it was Crockett who had broken Manson's hold over Poston, the latter was by far the most articulate. Incidents, dates, places—snap, snap, snap. Crockett, by contrast, was evasive. "I can feel their vibrations. I can't talk freely to you because they might know what I am saying."

Crockett doubted if we could ever convict Manson, because "he does nothing himself. His people do it all for him. He doesn't do anything anybody could pin on him." He added that "all the women have been programmed to do exactly as he says, and they all have knives. He's got those girls so programmed that they don't even exist. They are a copy of him."

Though I was interested in Crockett's contacts with Manson and the Family, I was hopeful that he could give me something more important.

Crockett had helped Poston, Watkins, and Flynn break away from Manson. To do this he must have gained some insight into how Manson had gained control over them in the first place. Others had also said that Manson "programmed" his followers. Did he understand how he accomplished this?

Crockett said he did, but when he tried to articulate it, he became bogged down in a morass of words and definitions, finally saying, "I can't explain it. It's all part of the occult."

I decided I wouldn't be able to use Crockett as a witness.

It was otherwise with Brooks Poston. The tall, gangly youth, with the air of the hayseed about him, was a fund of information about Manson and the Family.

A highly impressionable seventeen-year-old, Brooks Poston had met Manson at Dennis Wilson's house, and from that moment until he finally broke with Manson more than a year later to follow Crockett, "I believed Charlie was JC."

Q. "JC?"

A. "Yeah, that's how Charlie always used to refer to Jesus Christ."

Q. "Did Manson ever tell you that he was JC, or Jesus Christ?"

It wasn't so much stated as implied, Brooks said. Charlie claimed that he had lived before, nearly two thousand years ago, and that he had once died on the cross. (Manson had also told Gregg Jakobson that he had already died once, and that "death is beautiful.")

Charlie had a favorite story which he was fond of telling the Family, complete with dramatic gestures and moans of pain. Brooks had heard it often. According to Charlie, while he was living in Haight-Ashbury, he had taken a "magic mushroom" (psilocybin) trip. He was lying on a bed, but it became a cross, and he could feel the nails in his feet and hands and the sword in his side, and when he looked down at the foot of the cross he saw Mary Magdalene (Mary Brunner), and she was crying, and he said, "I'm all right, Mary." He had been fighting it, but now he gave up, surrendered himself to death, and when he did, he could suddenly see through the eyes of everyone at the same time, and at that moment he became the whole world.

With such clues, his followers had little trouble guessing his true identity.

I was curious about something. Up until his arrest in Mendocino County on July 28, 1967,* Charlie had always used his real name, Charles Milles Manson. On that occasion, however, and thereafter, he called himself Charles *Willis* Manson. Had Manson ever said anything about his name? I asked. Crockett and Poston both told me that they had heard Manson say, very slowly, that his name was "Charles' Will Is Man's Son," meaning that his will was that of the Son of Man.

Although Susan Atkins had emphasized Charlie's surname in talking to Virginia Graham, I hadn't really thought, until now, how powerful that name was. Man Son. It was tailor-made for the Infinite Being role he was now seeking to portray.

*Manson was charged with interfering with the questioning of a suspected runaway juvenile, Ruth Ann Moorehouse. He was given thirty days, suspended, and placed on three years probation. Asked his occupation when booked, he said he was a minister.

But Charlie carried all this yet a step further, Poston said. Manson claimed that the members of the Family were the original Christians, reincarnated, and that the Romans had returned as the establishment.

It was now time, Manson told his closest followers, for the Romans to have their turn on the cross.

Exactly how did Manson "program" someone? I asked Brooks.

He had various techniques, Poston said. With a girl, it would usually start with sex. Charlie might convince a plain girl that she was beautiful. Or, if she had a father fixation, have her imagine that he was her father. (He'd used both techniques with Susan Atkins.) Or, if he felt she was looking for a leader, he might imply that he was Christ. Manson had a talent for sensing, and capitalizing on, a person's hangups and/or desires. When a man first joined the group, Charlie would usually take him on an LSD trip, ostensibly "to open his mind." Then, while he was in a highly suggestible state, he would talk about love, how you had to surrender yourself to it, how only by ceasing to exist as an individual ego could you become one with all things.

As with Jakobson, I queried Poston as to the sources of Manson's philosophy. Scientology, the Bible, and the Beatles. These three were the only ones he knew.

A peculiar triumvirate. Yet by now I was beginning to suspect the existence of at least a fourth influence. The old magazines I'd found at Barker, Gregg's mention that Charlie claimed to have read Nietzsche and that he believed in a master race, plus the emergence of a startling number of disturbing parallels between Manson and the leader of the Third Reich, led me to ask Poston: "Did Manson ever say anything about Hitler?"

Poston's reply was short and incredibly chilling.

A. "He said that Hitler was a tuned-in guy who had leveled the karma of the Jews."

I spent most of two days interviewing Crockett and Poston, obtaining much new information, some of it very incriminating. For example, Manson had once suggested

Poston take a knife, go into Shoshone, and kill the sheriff. In the first real test of his newly found independence, Poston had refused to even consider the idea.

Before Crockett and Poston returned to Shoshone, I told them I wanted to talk to Juan Flynn and Paul Watkins. They weren't sure if Juan would talk to me—that big Panamanian cowboy was an independent cuss—but they thought Paul might. Since he was no longer procuring girls for Charlie, he had some free time on his hands.

Watkins agreed to the interview, and I arranged for Watkins, Poston, and Crockett to stay in a motel in downtown L.A.

"Paul, I need a new love."

Paul Watkins was describing for me how Manson would send him out to recruit young girls. Watkins admitted that he liked his special role in the Family. The only problem was, after he'd located a likely candidate, Charlie would insist on sleeping with her first.

Why didn't Manson pick up the girls himself? I asked.

"He was too old for most of the girls," the nineteen-year-old Watkins replied. "He frightened them. Also, I had a good line." It was also obvious that Watkins was better-looking than Charlie.

I asked Paul where he found the girls. He might go down to the Sunset Strip, where the teenyboppers hung out. Or drive the highways watching for girls who were hitchhiking. Once Charlie, through the connivance of an older woman who posed as Watkins' mother, even had him arrange a phony registration at a Los Angeles high school so he could be closer to the action.

Watkins also described the orgies that took place at the Gresham Street house and at Spahn. For a while there was one about every week. They would always start with drugs—grass, Peyote, LSD, whatever was available—Manson rationing them out, deciding how much each person needed. "Everything was done at Charlie's direction," Paul said. Charlie might dance around, everyone else following, like a train. As he'd take off his clothes, all the rest would take off their clothes. Then, when everyone was naked, they'd lie on the floor, "and they'd play the game of taking twelve deep breaths and releasing them and close eyes and then rub against each other" until "eventually all were touching." Charlie would direct the orgy, arranging bodies, combinations, positions. "He'd set it all up in a beautiful way like he was creating a masterpiece in sculpture," Watkins said, "but instead of clay he was using warm bodies." Paul said that the usual objective during the orgies was for all the Family members to achieve a simultaneous orgasm, but they were never successful.

Manson often staged these events to impress outsiders. If there were guests who he felt could be of some use to him, he'd say to the Family, "Let's get together and show these people how to make love." Whatever the reaction, the impression was a lasting one. "It was like the Devil buying your soul," Watkins said.

Manson also used these occasions to "eradicate hang-ups." If a person indicated reluctance to engage in a certain act, Manson would force that person to commit it. Male-female, female-female, male-male, intercourse, cunnilingus, fellatio, sodomy—there could be no inhibitions of any kind. One thirteen-year-old girl's initiation into the Family consisted of her being sodomized by Manson while the others watched. Manson also "went down on" a young boy to show the others he had rid himself of all inhibitions.

Charlie used sex, Paul said. For example, when it became obvious that DeCarlo was making no effort to persuade his motorcycle gang to join the Family, Manson told the girls to withhold their favors from Danny.

The fact that Manson directed even the sex lives of his followers was powerful evidence of his domination. I asked Watkins for other examples specifically involving co-defendants. He recalled that once at Spahn Ranch, Charlie told Sadie: "I'd like half a coconut, even if you have to go to Rio de Janeiro to get it." Sadie got right up and was on her way out the door when Charlie said, "Never mind."

It was a test. It was also, by inference, evidence that Susan Atkins would do anything Charles Manson asked her to do.

As with the others, I questioned Watkins about Manson's programming techniques. He told me something very interesting, which apparently the other Family members didn't know. He said that when Manson passed out the LSD, he always took a smaller dose than the others. Though Manson never told him why he did so, Paul presumed that during the "trip" Manson wanted to retain control over his own mental faculties. It is said that LSD is a mind-altering drug which tends to make the person ingesting it a little more vulnerable and susceptible to the influence of third parties. Manson used LSD "trips," Paul said, to instill his philosophies, exploit weaknesses and fears, and extract promises and agreements from his followers.

As Manson's second in command, Watkins had enjoyed Charlie's confidence more than most of the others. I asked him if Manson had ever mentioned Scientology or The Process. Watkins had never heard of The Process, but Manson had told him that while he was in prison he had studied Scientology, becoming a "theta," which Manson defined as being "clear." Watkins said that in the summer of 1968 he and Charlie had dropped into a Church of Scientology in downtown Los Angeles, and Manson asked the receptionist, "What do you do after 'clear'?" When she was unable to tell him anything he hadn't already done, Manson walked out.

One aspect of Manson's philosophy especially puzzled me: his strange attitude toward fear. He not only preached that fear was beautiful, he often told the Family that they should live in a constant state of fear. What did he mean by that? I asked Paul.

To Charlie fear was the same thing as awareness, Watkins said. The more fear you have, the more awareness, hence the more love. When you're really afraid, you come to "Now." And when you are at Now, you are totally conscious.

Manson claimed that children were more aware than adults, because they were naturally afraid. But animals were even more aware than people, he said, because they always lived at Now. The coyote was the most aware creature there was, Manson maintained, because he was completely paranoid. Being frightened of everything, he missed nothing.

Charlie was always "selling fear," Watkins continued. He *wanted* people to be afraid, and the more afraid the better. Using this same logic, "Charlie said that death was beautiful, because people feared death."

I would learn, from talking to other Family members, that Manson would seek out each individual's greatest fear—not so the person could confront and eliminate it, but so he could re-emphasize it. It was like a magic button, which he could push at will to control that person.

"Whatever you do," Watkins advised me, as had both Crockett and Poston, "don't ever let Charlie know you are afraid of him." One day at Spahn, without warning or provocation, Manson had jumped on Watkins and started strangling him. At first Paul resisted, but then, gasping for breath, he suddenly gave up, stopped resisting. "It was really weird," Watkins said. "The instant I stopped fearing him, his hands flew off my throat and he jumped back as if he'd been attacked by an unseen force."

"Then it's like the barking dog," I commented. "If you show fear, it will attack; if you don't it won't?"

"Exactly. *Fear turns Charlie on.*"

Paul Watkins was inherently more independent than Brooks Poston, much less the follower type. Yet he too had remained with the Family for a long period. Other than the girls, was there some reason why he stayed?

"I thought Charlie was Christ," he told me, not blinking an eye.

Both Watkins and Poston had severed the umbilical linking them to Manson. But both admitted to me that they still weren't completely free of him, that even now they would sometimes lapse back into a state where they could feel Manson's vibrations.

It was Paul Watkins who finally supplied the missing link in Manson's motive for the murders. Yet, if I hadn't talked to Jakobson and Poston, I might have missed its importance, for it was from all three, Gregg, Brooks, and Paul, that I obtained the keys to understanding (1) Charles Manson's unique interpretation of the Book of Revelation, and (2) his decidedly curious and complex attitude toward the English musical group the Beatles.

Several persons had told me Manson was fond of quoting from the Bible, particularly the ninth chapter of Revelation. Once Charlie had handed Jakobson a Bible, already open to the chapter, and, while he read it, supplied his own interpretation of the verses. With only one exception, which will be noted, what Gregg told me tallied with what I later heard from Poston and Watkins.

The "four angels" were the Beatles, whom Manson considered "leaders, spokesmen, prophets," according to Gregg. The line "And he opened the bottomless pit . . . And there came out of the smoke locusts upon the earth; and unto them was given power . . ." was still another reference to the English group, Gregg said. Locusts—Beatles—one and the same. "Their faces were as the faces of men," yet "they had hair as the hair of women." An obvious reference to the long-haired musicians. Out of the mouths of the four angels "issued fire and brimstone." Gregg: "This referred to the spoken words, the lyrics of the Beatles' songs, the power that came out of their mouths."

Their "breastplates of fire," Poston added, were their electric guitars. Their shapes "like unto horses prepared unto battle" were the dune buggies. The "horsemen who numbered two hundred thousand thousand," and who would roam the earth spreading destruction, were the motorcyclists.

"And it was commanded them that they should not hurt the grass of the earth, neither any green thing, neither any tree; but only those men which have not the seal of God in their foreheads." I wondered about that seal on the forehead. How did Manson interpret that? I asked Jakobson.

"It was all subjective," Gregg replied. "He said there would be a mark on people." Charlie had never told him exactly what the mark would be, only that he, Charlie, "would be able to tell, he would know," and that "the mark would designate whether they were with him or against him." With Charlie, it was either one or the other, Gregg said; "there was no middle road."

One verse spoke of worshipping demons and idols of gold and silver and bronze. Manson said that referred to the material worship of the establishment: of automobiles, houses, money.

Q. "Directing your attention to Verse 15, which reads: 'And the four angels were loosed, which were prepared for an hour, and a day, and a month, and a year, for to slay the third part of men.' Did he say what that meant?"

A. "He said that those were the people who would die in Helter Skelter . . . one third of mankind . . . the white race."

I now knew I was on the right track.

Only on one point did Jakobson's recollection of Manson's interpretation differ from that of the others. The first verse of Revelation 9 refers to a fifth angel; the chapter ends, however, referring to only four. Originally there were five Beatles, Gregg explained, one of whom, Stuart Sutcliffe, had died in Germany in 1962.

Poston and Watkins—who, unlike Jakobson, were members of the Family—interpreted this much differently. Verse I reads: "And the fifth angel sounded, and I saw a star fall from heaven unto the earth: and to him was given the key of the bottomless pit."

To members of the Family the identity of that fifth angel, the ruler of the bottomless pit, was never in doubt. It was Charlie.

Verse II reads: "And they had a king over them, which is the angel of the bottomless pit, whose name in the Hebrew tongue is Abaddon, but in the Greek tongue hath his name Apollyon."

The king also had a Latin name, which, though it appears in the Catholic Douay Version, was inadvertently omitted by the translators of the King James version. It was Exterminans.

Exterminans, t/n Charles Manson.

As far as Jakobson, Watkins, and Poston knew, Manson placed no special meaning on the last verse of Revelation 9. But I found myself thinking of it often in the months ahead:

"Neither repented they of their murders, nor of their sorceries, nor of their fornication, nor of their thefts."

"The important thing to remember about Revelation 9," Gregg told me, "is that Charlie believed this was happening *now*, not in the future. It's going to begin now and it's time to choose sides ... either that or flee with him to the desert."

According to Jakobson, Manson believed "the Beatles were spokesmen. They were speaking to Charlie, through their songs, letting him know from across the ocean that this is what was going to go down. He believed this firmly ... He considered their songs prophecy, especially the songs in the so-called White Album ... He told me that many, many times."

Watkins and Poston also said that Manson and the Family were convinced that the Beatles were speaking to Charlie through their music. For example, in the song "I Will" are the lines: "And when at last I find you/ Your song will fill the air/ Sing it loud so I can hear you/ Make it easy to be near you ..." Charlie interpreted this to mean the Beatles wanted him to make an album, Poston and Watkins said. Charlie told them that the Beatles were looking for JC and he was the JC they were looking for. He also told them that the Beatles knew that Christ had returned to earth again and that he was living somewhere in Los Angeles.

"How in the world did he come up with that?" I asked them.

In the White Album is a song called "Honey Pie," a lyric of which reads: "Oh honey pie my position is tragic/ Come and show me the magic/ Of your Hollywood song." A later lyric goes: "Oh Honey pie you are driving me frantic/ Sail across the Atlantic/ To be where you belong."

Charlie, of course, wanted *them* to sail across the Atlantic, to join him in Death Valley. While residing in the Gresham Street house (in January and February of 1969, just after the White Album was released), Manson and the girls sent several telegrams, wrote a number of letters, and made at least three telephone calls to England, attempting to reach the Beatles. No luck.

The line "I'm in love but I'm lazy" from "Honey Pie" meant to Charlie that the Beatles loved JC but were too lazy to go looking for him; too, they'd just gone all the way to India, following a man who they'd finally decided was a false prophet, the Maharishi. They were also calling for JC/Charlie in the first eight lines of the song "Don't Pass Me By," in "Yer Blues," and, in the earlier Magical Mystery Tour album, in "Blue Jay Way."

Much of this I would never use at the trial; it was simply too absurd.

The Beatles' White Album, Manson told Watkins, Poston, and others, "set up things for the revolution." *His* album, which was to follow, would, in Charlie's words, "blow the cork off the bottle. That would start it."

Much of the time at the Gresham Street house, according to Poston, Watkins, and others, was spent composing songs for Charlie's album. Each was to be a message song, directed to a particular group of people, such as the bikers, outlining the part they'd play in Helter Skelter. Charlie worked hard on these songs; they had to be very subtle, he said, like the Beatles' own songs, their true meaning hidden beneath the awareness of all but the tuned-in people.

Manson was counting on Terry Melcher to produce this album. According to numerous Family members (both Melcher and Jakobson denied this), Terry had promised to come and listen to the songs one evening. The girls cleaned the house, baked cookies, rolled joints. Melcher didn't show. Manson, according to Poston and Watkins, never forgave Terry for this. Melcher's word was no good, he said angrily on a number of occasions.

Though the Beatles had made many records, it was the double-disk White Album, which Capitol issued in December 1968, that Manson considered most important. Even the fact that the cover was white—with no other design except the embossed name of the group—held significance for him.

It was, and remains, a startling album, containing some of the Beatles' finest music, and some of their strangest. Its thirty songs range from tender love ballads to pop parodies to cacophonies of noise made by taking loops of very diverse tapes and splicing them together. To Charles

Manson, however, it was prophecy. At least this is what he convinced his followers.

That Charlie had renamed Susan Atkins "Sadie Mae Glutz" long before the White Album appeared containing the song "Sexy Sadie" was additional proof to the Family that Manson and the Beatles were mentally attuned.

Almost every song in the album had a hidden meaning, which Manson interpreted for his followers. To Charlie "Rocky Raccoon" meant "coon" or the black man. While to everyone except Manson and the Family it was obvious that the lyrics of "Happiness Is a Warm Gun" had sexual connotations, Charlie interpreted the song to mean that the Beatles were telling blackie to get guns and fight whitey.

According to Poston and Watkins, the Family played five songs in the White Album more than all the others. They were: "Blackbird," "Piggies," "Revolution I," "Revolution 9," and "Helter Skelter."

"Blackbird singing in the dead of night/ Take these broken wings and learn to fly/ All your life/ You were only waiting for this moment to arise," went the lyrics of "Blackbird." According to Jakobson, "Charlie believed that the moment was now and that the black man was going to arise, overthrow the white man, and take his turn." According to Watkins, in this song Charlie "figured the Beatles were programming the black people to get it up, get it on, start doing it."

On first hearing the song, I'd thought that the LaBianca killers had made a mistake, writing "rise" instead of "arise." However, Jakobson told me that Charlie said the black man was going to "rise" up against the white man. " 'Rise' was one of Charlie's big words," Gregg said, providing me with the origin of still another of the key words.

Both the Tate and LaBianca murders had occurred in "the dead of night." However, if the parallel had special significance to Manson, he never admitted it to anyone I interviewed, nor, if he knew it, did he admit the dictionary meaning of the phrase "helter skelter." The song "Helter Skelter" begins: "When I get to the bottom I go back to the top of the slide/ Where I stop and I turn and I go for a ride . . ." According to Poston, Manson said this was a reference to the Family emerging from the bottomless pit.

There was a simpler explanation. In England, home of the Beatles, "helter skelter" is another name for a slide in an amusement park.

If you listen closely, you can hear grunts and oinks in the background of the song "Piggies."* By "piggies," Gregg and the others told me, Manson meant anyone who belonged to the establishment.

Like Manson himself, the song was openly critical of the piggies, noting that what they really needed was a damned good whacking.

"By that he meant the black man was going to give the piggies, the establishment, a damned good whacking," Jakobson explained. Charlie really loved that line, both Watkins and Poston said; he was always quoting it.

I couldn't listen to the final stanza without visualizing what had happened at 3301 Waverly Drive. It describes piggy couples dining out, in all their starched finery, eating bacon with their forks and knives.

Rosemary LaBianca: forty-one knife wounds. Leno LaBianca: twelve knife wounds, punctured with a fork seven times, a *knife* in his throat, a *fork* in his stomach, and, on the wall, in his own blood, DEATH TO PIGS.

"There's a chord at the end of the song 'Piggies,' " Watkins said. "It goes down and it's a really weird chord. After the sound of piggies snorting. And in the 'Revolution 9' song, there's that same chord, and after it they have a little pause and snort, snort, snort. But in the pause, there is machine-gun fire.

"And it's the same thing with the 'Helter Skelter' song," Paul continued. "They had this really weird chord. And in the 'Revolution 9' song there's the same chord again, with machine guns firing and people dying and screaming and stuff."

*Unlike ex-Beatles John Lennon and Paul McCartney, George Harrison refused the authors permission to quote from the lyrics of any of his songs, including "Piggies."

The White Album contains two songs with the word "revolution" in their titles.

The printed lyrics of "Revolution 1," as given on the jacket insert, read: "You say you want a revolution/ Well you know/ We all want to change the world . . ./ But when you talk about destruction/ Don't you know that you can count me out."

When you listen to the record itself, however, immediately after "out" you hear the word "in."

Manson took this to mean the Beatles, once undecided, now favored the revolution.

Manson made much of these "hidden lyrics," which can be found in a number of the Beatles' songs but are especially prevalent in the White Album. They were, he told his followers, direct communications to him, Charlie/JC.

Later on the lyrics go: "You say you got a real solution/ Well you know/ We'd all love to see the plan."

The meaning of this was obvious to Manson: Sing out, Charlie, and tell us how we can escape the holocaust.

Of all the Beatles' songs, "Revolution 9" is easily the weirdest. Reviewers couldn't decide whether it was an exciting new direction for rock or an elaborate put-on. One critic said it reminded him of "a bad acid trip."

There are no lyrics as such, nor is it music in any conventional sense; rather, it is a montage of noises—whispers, shouts, snatches of dialogue from the BBC, bits of classical music, mortars exploding, babies crying, church hymns, car horns, and football yells—which, together with the oft reiterated refrain "Number 9, Number 9, Number 9," build to a climax of machine-gun fire and screams, to be followed by the soft and obviously symbolic lullaby "Good Night."

Of all the songs in the White Album, Jakobson said, Charlie "spoke mostly of 'Revolution 9.' " He said "it was the Beatles' way of telling people what was going to happen; it was their way of making prophecy; it directly paralleled the Bible's Revelation 9."

It was also the battle of Armageddon, the coming black-white revolution portrayed in sound, Manson claimed, and after having listened to it myself, I could easily believe that if ever there were such a conflict, this was probably very much what it would sound like.

According to Poston: "When Charlie was listening to it, he heard in the background noise, in and around the machine-gun fire and the oinking of pigs, a man's voice saying 'Rise.'" Listening to the recording again, I also heard it, twice repeated: the first time almost a whisper, the second a long-drawn-out scream.* This was potent evidence. Through both Jakobson and Poston, I'd now linked Manson, irrevocably, with the word "rise" printed in blood at the LaBianca residence.

In "Revolution I" the Beatles had finally decided to commit themselves to the revolution. In "Revolution 9" they were telling the black man that *now* was the time to rise and start it all. According to Charlie.

Manson found many other messages in this song (including the words "Block that Nixon"), but as far as his philosophy of Helter Skelter was concerned, these were the most important.

Charles Manson was already talking about an imminent black-white war when Gregg Jakobson first met him, in the spring of 1968. There was an underground expression current at the time, "the shit is coming down," variously interpreted as meaning the day of judgment was at hand or all hell was breaking loose, and Charlie often used it in reference to the coming racial conflict. But he wasn't rabid about it, Gregg said; it was just one of many subjects they discussed.

"When I first met Charlie [in June 1968], he really didn't have any of this Helter Skelter stuff going," Paul Watkins told me. "He talked a little bit about the 'shit coming down,' but just barely . . . He said when the shit comes down the black man will be on one side and the white will be on the other, and that's all he said about it."

Then, that December, Capitol issued the Beatles' White Album, one of the songs of which was "Helter Skelter."

*"It is first heard two minutes and thirty-four seconds into the song, just after the crowd sounds that follow "lots of stab wounds as it were" and "informed him on the third night" and just before "Number 9, Number 9."

The final stanza went: "Look out helter skelter helter skelter helter skelter/ Look out [background scream] helter skelter/ She's coming down fast/ Yes she is/ Yes she is."

Manson apparently first heard the White Album in Los Angeles, while on a trip there from Barker Ranch, where most of the Family remained. When Manson returned to Death Valley on December 31, 1968, he told the group, according to Poston, "Are you hep to what the Beatles are saying? Helter Skelter is coming down. The Beatles are telling it like it is."

It was the same expression, except that in place of the word for defecation Manson now substituted "Helter Skelter."

Another link had been made, this time to the bloody words on the refrigerator door at the LaBianca residence.

Though this was the first time Manson used the phrase, it was not to be the last.

Watkins: "And he started rapping about this Beatle album and Helter Skelter and all these meanings that I didn't get out of it . . . and he builds this picture up and he called it Helter Skelter, and what it meant was the Negroes were going to come down and rip the cities all apart."

After this, Watkins said, "We started listening to the Beatles' album constantly . . ."

Death Valley is very cold in the winter, so Manson found a two-story house at 20910 Gresham Street in Canoga Park, in the San Fernando Valley, not too far from Spahn Ranch. In January 1969, Watkins said, "we all moved into the Gresham Street house to get ready for Helter Skelter. So we could watch it coming down and see all of the things going on in the city. He [Charlie] called the Gresham Street house 'The Yellow Submarine' from the Beatles' movie. It was like a submarine in that when you were in it you weren't allowed to go out. You could only peek out of the windows. We started designing dune buggies and motorcycles and we were going to buy twenty-five Harley sportsters . . . and we mapped escape routes to the desert . . . supply caches . . . we had all these different things going.

"I watched him building this big picture up," Paul noted. "He would do it very slowly, very carefully. I swallowed it hook, line, and sinker.

"Before Helter Skelter came along," Watkins said with a sigh of wistful nostalgia, "all Charlie cared about was orgies."

Before Jakobson and I had ever discussed the Beatles, I asked him: "Did Charlie ever talk to you about a black-white revolution?"

A. "Yeah, that was Helter Skelter, and he believed it was going to happen in the near future, almost immediately."

Q. "What did he say about this black-white revolution? How would it come about and what would it accomplish?"

A. "It would begin with the black man going into white people's homes and ripping off the white people, physically destroying them, until there was open revolution in the streets, until they finally won and took over. Then black man would assume white man's karma. He would then be the establishment."

Watkins: "He used to explain how it would be so simple to start out. A couple of black people—some of the spades from Watts—would come up into the Bel Air and Beverly Hills district ... up in the rich piggy district ... and just really wipe some people out, just cutting bodies up and smearing blood and writing things on the wall in blood ... all kinds of super-atrocious crimes that would really make the white man mad ..."

Poston said very much the same thing before I ever talked to Watkins, but with the addition of one very important detail: "He [Manson] said a group of real blacks would come out of the ghettos and do an atrocious crime in the richer sections of Los Angeles and other cities. They would do an atrocious murder with stabbing, killing, cutting bodies to pieces, smearing blood on the walls, writing 'pigs' on the walls ... in the victims' own blood."

This was tremendously powerful evidence—linking Manson not only with the Tate murders, where PIG had been printed in Sharon Tate's blood on the front door of the residence, but also with the LaBianca murders, where

DEATH TO PIGS had been printed in Leno LaBianca's blood on the living-room wall—and I questioned Poston in depth as to Manson's exact words, where the conversation had occurred, when, and who else was present. I then questioned everyone Poston mentioned who was willing to cooperate.

Ordinarily, I try to avoid repetitious testimony in a trial, knowing it can antagonize the jury. However, Manson's Helter Skelter motive was so bizarre that I knew if it was expounded by only one witness no juror would ever believe it.

The conversation had occurred in February 1969, at the Gresham Street house, Poston said.

We now had evidence that six months before the Tate-LaBianca murders Charles Manson was telling the Family exactly how the murders would occur, complete even to writing "pigs" in the victims' own blood.

We now had also linked Manson with every one of the bloody words found at both the Tate and LaBianca residences.

But this would only be the beginning, Manson told Watkins. These murders would cause mass paranoia among the whites: "Out of their fear they would go into the ghetto and just start shooting black people like crazy." But all they would kill would be "the ones that were with whitey in the first place."

The "true black race"—whom Manson identified at various times as the Black Muslims and the Black Panthers—"wouldn't even be affected by it." They would be in hiding, waiting, he said.

After the slaughter, the Black Muslims would "come out and appeal to the whites, saying, 'Look what you have done to my people.' And this would split whitey down the middle," Watkins said, "between the hippie-liberals and all the uptight conservatives . . ." And it would be like the War between the States, brother against brother, white killing white. Then, after the whites had mostly killed off each other, "the Black Muslims would come out of hiding and wipe them *all* out."

All except Charlie and the Family, who would have taken refuge in the bottomless pit in Death Valley.

The karma would then have turned. "Blackie would be on top." And he would begin to "clean up the mess, just like he always has done . . . He will clean up the mess that the white man made, and build the world back up a little bit, build the cities back up. But then he wouldn't know what to do with it. He couldn't handle it."

According to Manson, Watkins said, the black man had a problem. He could only do what the white man had taught him to do. He wouldn't be able to run the world without whitey showing him how.

Watkins: "Blackie then would come to Charlie and say, you know, 'I did my thing. I killed them all and, you know, I am tired of killing now. It is all over.'

"And then Charlie would scratch blackie's fuzzy head and kick him in the butt and tell him to go pick cotton and go be a good nigger, and we would live happily ever after . . ." The Family, now grown to 144,000, as predicted in the Bible—a pure, white master race—would emerge from the bottomless pit. And "It would be our world then. There would be no one else, except for us and the black servants."

And, according to the gospel of Charlie—as he related it to his disciple Paul Watkins—he, Charles Willis Manson, the fifth angel, JC, would then rule that world.

Paul Watkins, Brooks Poston, and Gregg Jakobson had not only defined Manson's motive, Helter Skelter, Watkins had supplied that missing link. In his sick, twisted, disordered mind, Charles Manson believed that *he* would be the ultimate beneficiary of the black-white war and the murders which triggered it.

One day at the Gresham Street house, while they were on an acid trip, Manson had reiterated to Watkins and the others that blackie had no smarts, "that the only thing blackie knows is what whitey has told him or shown him" and "so someone is going to have to show him how to do it."

I asked Watkins: "How to do what?"

A. "How to bring down Helter Skelter. How to do all these things."

Watkins: "Charlie said the only reason it hadn't come down already was because whitey was feeding his young daughters to the black man in Haight-Ashbury, and he said that if his music came out, and all of the beautiful people—'love' he called it—left Haight-Ashbury, blackie would turn to Bel Air to get his rocks off."

Blackie had been temporarily "pacified" by the young white girls, Manson claimed. But when he took away the pacifier—when his album came out and all the young loves followed Pied Piper Charlie to the desert—blackie would need another means of getting his frustrations out and he would then turn to the establishment.

But Terry Melcher didn't come through. The album wasn't made. Sometime in late February of 1969 Manson sent Brooks and Juanita to Barker Ranch. The rest of the Family moved back to Spahn and began preparing for Helter Skelter. "Now there was an actual physical effort to get things together, so they could move to the desert," Gregg said. Jakobson, who visited the ranch during this period, was startled at the change in Manson. Previously he had preached oneness of the Family, complete in itself, self-sufficient; now he was cultivating outsiders, the motorcycle gangs. Before this he had been anti-materialistic; now he was accumulating vehicles, guns, money. "It struck me that all this contradicted what Charlie had done and talked to me about before," Gregg said, explaining that this was the beginning of his disenchantment and eventual break with Manson.

The newly materialistic Manson came up with some wild moneymaking schemes. For example, someone suggested that the girls in the Family could earn $300 to $500 a week apiece working as topless dancers. Manson liked the idea—with ten broads pulling in $3,000 a week and upward he could buy jeeps, dune buggies, even machine guns—and he sent Bobby Beausoleil and Bill Vance to the Girard Agency on the Sunset Strip to negotiate the deal.

There was only one problem. With all his powers, Manson was unable to transform molehills into mountains.

HELTER SKELTER

A CHILLING 64-PAGE
PHOTOGRAPHIC
RECORD OF THE VICTIMS,
THE KILLERS, THE EVIDENCE.

LOS ANGELES AND VICINITY
Freeways
Other streets and roads
0
5
10
Miles
SANTA SUSANA MTS
SAN FERNANDO
Spahn Ranch
SIMI HILLS
CHATSWORTH
CANOGA PARK
BURBANK
GLENDALE
Gun found
Clothing found
Griffith Park
La Bianca residence
To Pasadena
HOLLYWOOD
SANTA MONICA MTS
Benedict Canyon
Tate residence
BEVERLY HILLS
Topanga Canyon
Hinman residence
MALIBU
SANTA MONICA
LOS ANGELES
VENICE
INGLEWOOD
PACIFIC OCEAN
EL SEGUNDO
LYNWOOD
TORRANCE
REDONDO BEACH
CALIFORNIA
Area of main map
SAN PEDRO
LONG BEACH
H. Faye

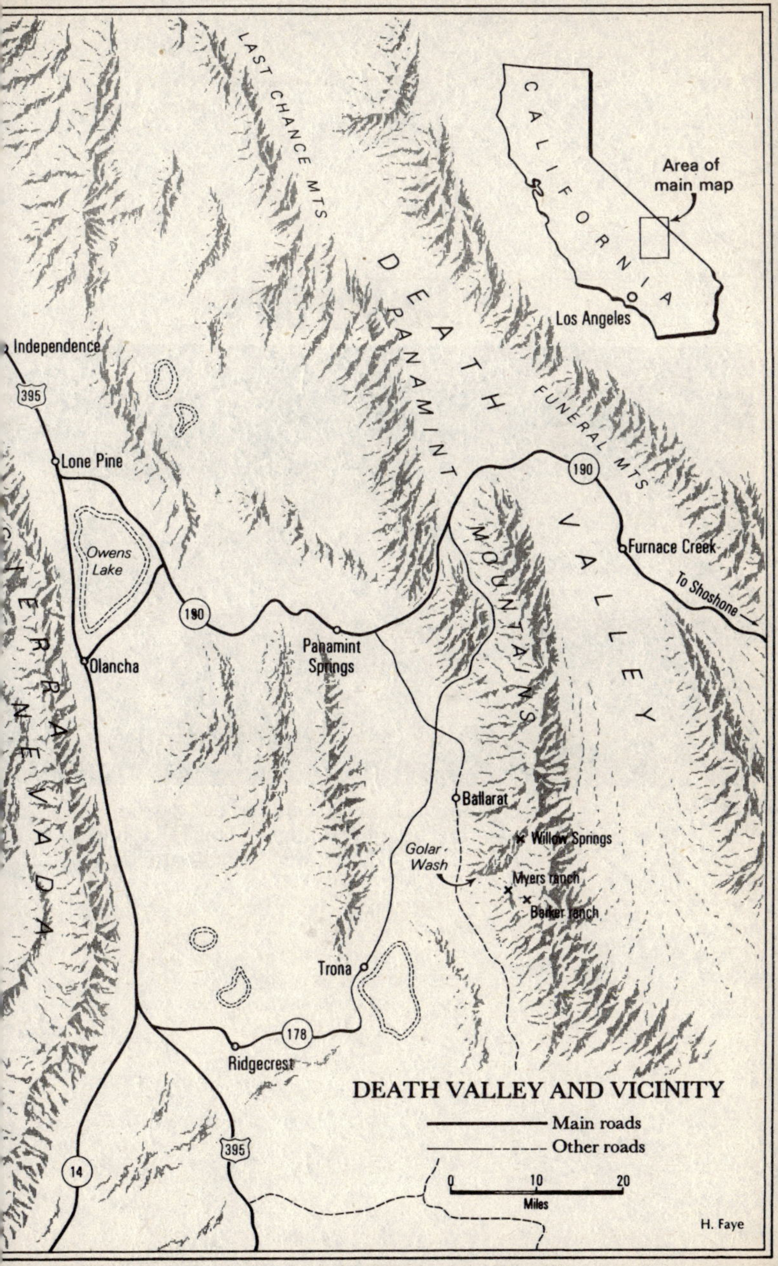

LAST CHANCE MTS
CALIFORNIA
Area of main map
Los Angeles
DEATH
PANAMINT
FUNERAL MTS
Independence
395
Lone Pine
Owens Lake
190
Furnace Creek
To Shoshone
VALLEY
MOUNTAINS
Panamint Springs
Olancha
SIERRA NEVADA
Ballarat
Willow Springs
Golar Wash
Myers ranch
Barker ranch
Trona
178
Ridgecrest
14
DEATH VALLEY AND VICINITY
Main roads
Other roads
0
10
20
Miles
H. Faye

The Murders

10050 Cielo Drive, a secluded cul-de-sac
high above the City of the Angels. Until that night,
Sharon Tate called it her "love house."

First the telephone
wires were cut.

Fearing the gate was electrified,
the killers avoided it.

Instead, they scaled
the embankment to the right
of the gate.

Later, on fleeing the premises,
one of the killers left a
bloody fingerprint on the button
of the gate-control
mechanism. Still later, an LAPD
officer pushed the button,
creating a superimposure which
eradicated the print.

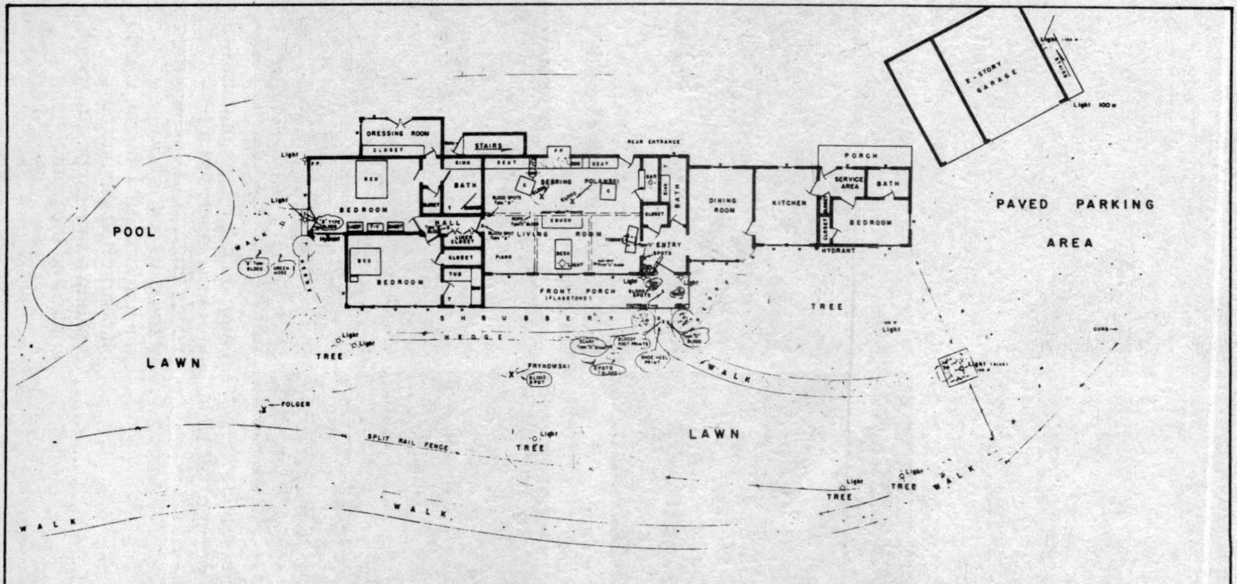

Scale diagram of the Tate residence, showing the location of four of the five bodies. Parent's Rambler was to the right, farther up the paved parking area that led to the gate. The guest house was located to the left, a considerable distance beyond the pool.

Steven Earl Parent,
18, at his high-school prom.
A hi-fi enthusiast,
he was working at two jobs
to save enough
money for college that fall.

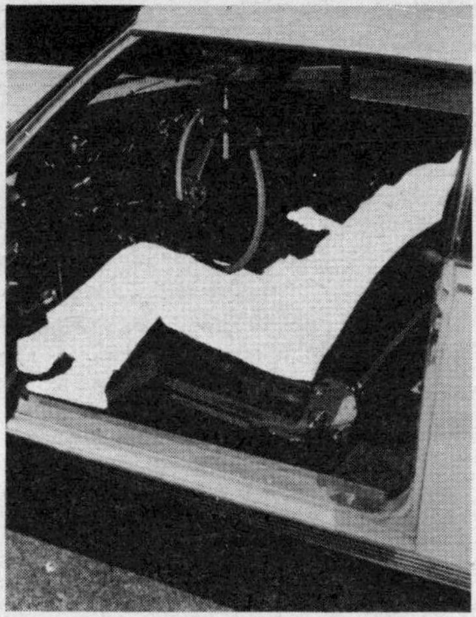

Steven Earl Parent—murder victim.
In the wrong place
at the wrong time, Parent was
driving toward the gate
when the killers arrived. He was
the first to die.

After discovering Parent's body,
the first officers proceeded up the driveway to the residence.
They found the house and grounds frighteningly quiet.

Coffee heiress Abigail Folger, 25, and her Polish lover Voytek Frykowski, 32. They had begun moving out of the Cielo Drive residence, but Sharon asked them to stay until her husband, movie director Roman Polanski, returned the following week.

Abigail Folger—murder victim. Her body was also on the lawn, a short distance beyond Frykowski's. She had been stabbed so often her white gown appeared red.

Voytek Frykowski—murder victim. Found sprawled on the lawn near the front door, Frykowski had fought hard for his life. He had been shot twice, hit over the head thirteen times with a blunt object, and stabbed fifty-one times.

The walkway leading to the front door of the Tate residence. The pools of blood were mute evidence of the furious struggle that occurred here. Only on getting closer did the officers see the bizarre message the killers had left. Printed on the door, in Sharon Tate's own blood, were the letters PIG.

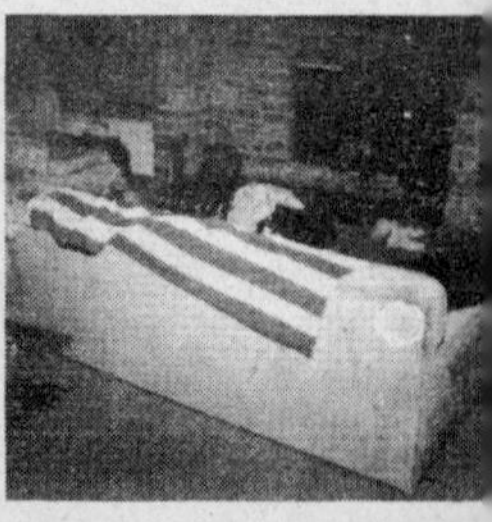

Internationally known men's hair stylist
Jay Sebring, 35, had once been engaged to Sharon Tate.
According to some, he was still in love with her.

An American flag was draped over the back of the couch in the living room. On the other side, in front of the fireplace, was a scene so incredible it horrified even the most case-hardened detectives.

Beautiful honey-blond actress
Sharon Tate, 26. Though featured in *Valley of the Dolls*,
only in death would she receive star billing.

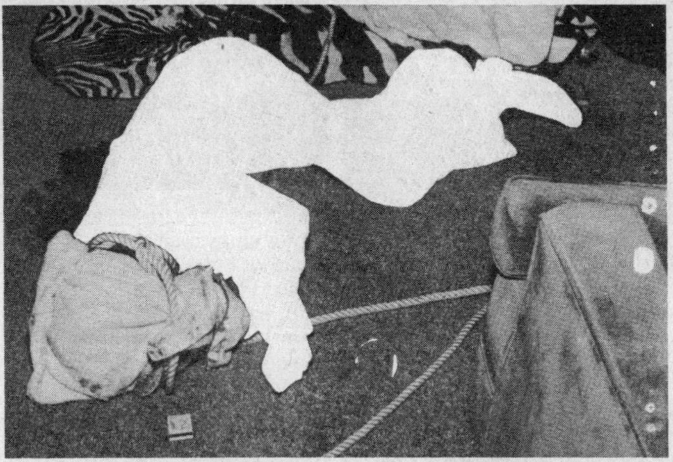

Jay Sebring—murder victim. A bloody towel covered his face. A rope, looped around his neck, led to still another body.

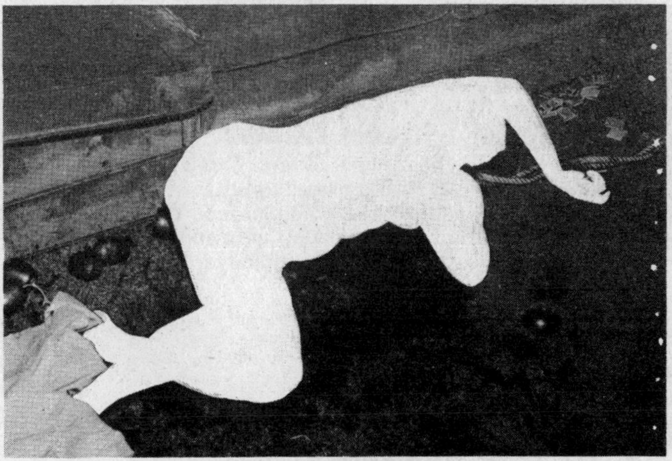

Sharon Tate Polanski—
murder victim. Eight months pregnant, she pleaded for the life of her child. "Look, bitch, I have no mercy for you," one of her killers replied.

The loft over the living room. Before she was stabbed to death, Sharon Tate was hanged from one of the rafters. The rope, left behind by the killers, became an important clue.

Other clues included: a pair of eyeglasses; three pieces of broken gun grip; and this Buck knife, found sticking up from the cushion of a chair in the living room.

The Folger-Frykowski bedroom. Abigail Folger was reading when the killers came down the hall. Apparently thinking they were friends of the Polanskis, she looked up and smiled.

Sharon Tate's bedroom, as it appeared the morning after the murders. The bassinet, atop the armoire, would never be used.

Chased by one of the killers, Abigail Folger had attempted to escape via the door leading from Sharon's bedroom to the pool outside, but they caught her on the lawn.

The guest house at the far end of the estate. Hearing the barking of a dog and a voice saying, "Shhh, be quiet," the police surrounded it, arresting the only person still alive on the premises, nineteen-year-old caretaker William Garretson. Though charged with the five murders, he was released after passing a polygraph test.

Aerial view of the LaBianca residence—
3301 Waverly Drive, in the Los Feliz section of Los Angeles.
The house formerly occupied by Harold True, 3267, is to
the right. The killers parked where the vehicle appears, walked
up the curved driveway toward 3267,
then cut across to the LaBianca home.

Above and right. Again, as with the five murders the previous night, the police found a number of bizarre clues: DEATH TO PIGS and RISE on the living-room walls, and the misspelled HEALTER SKELTER on the refrigerator door, all printed in the blood of one of the victims.

Leno LaBianca was sitting on the couch, reading the Sunday paper, when the deadly nightmare began.

The bedroom. Hearing the screams of her husband, Rosemary LaBianca began to struggle. Her assailants kept stabbing her even after she was dead.

Owner of a chain of grocery stores, Leno LaBianca, 44, seemed to have nothing in common with the Tate victims, and, despite the many similarities, the police quickly concluded the two crimes were unrelated.

Rosemary LaBianca, 38. A few days before her death she confided to a friend that someone had been inside their home while she and Leno were away.

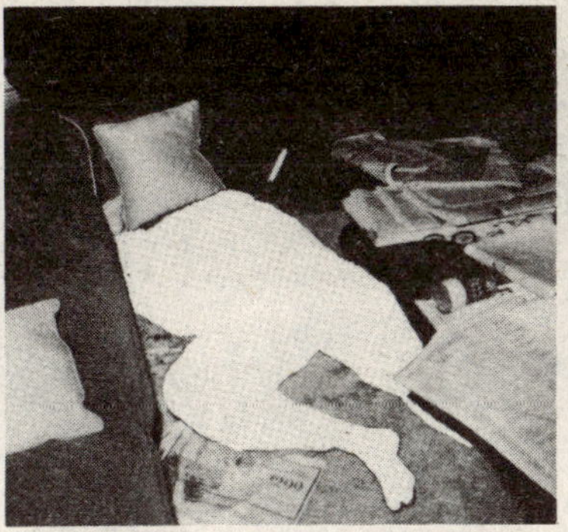

Leno LaBianca—murder victim. In addition to the multiple stab wounds, a knife and fork were found protruding from his body, and the word WAR had been carved on his stomach.

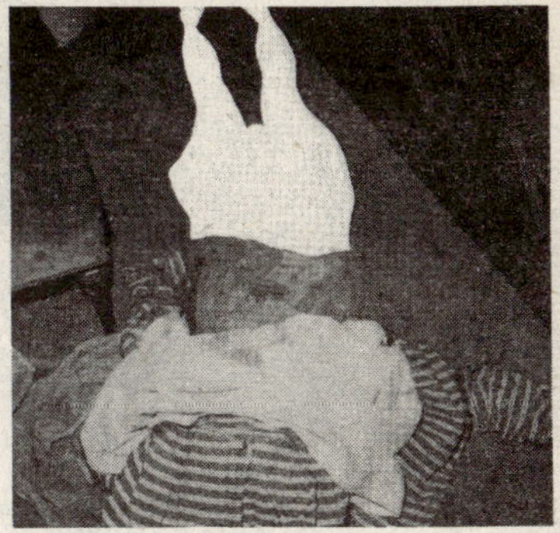

Rosemary LaBianca—murder victim. Wielding knives very similar to those used the previous night, the killers stabbed her forty-one times.

Less than twenty-four hours after the discovery of the word PIG printed on the front door of the Tate residence, one of the homicide detectives assigned to the case was told of a strikingly similar murder which had occurred in Malibu only three weeks earlier, in which the words POLITICAL PIGGY had been printed in the blood of the victim, musician Gary Hinman. Even after the bloody words DEATH TO PIGS were found at the LaBianca residence, he didn't feel the lead worth investigating.

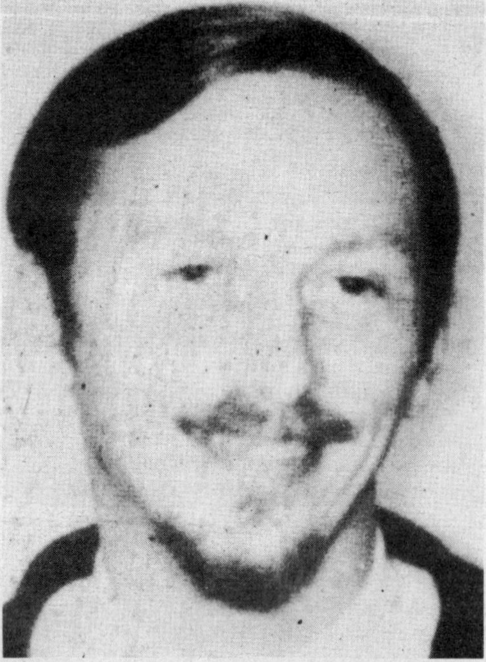

Music teacher Gary Hinman—murder victim. He made the mistake of befriending his killers.

John Philip Haught, aka Christopher Jesus, aka Zero. Murder victim or suicide? The others present claimed he had been playing Russian roulette. Only the gun was fully loaded and clean of prints.

Aspiring actor and Spahn Ranch cowboy Donald "Shorty" Shea—murder victim. Like Sharon Tate, he was hoping for stardom and found death instead. His body has never been found.

Attorney Ronald Hughes—murder victim. His attempt to defend one of the Tate-LaBianca killers cost him his life. As revealed here for the first time, the slaying of Hughes was "the first of the retaliation murders."

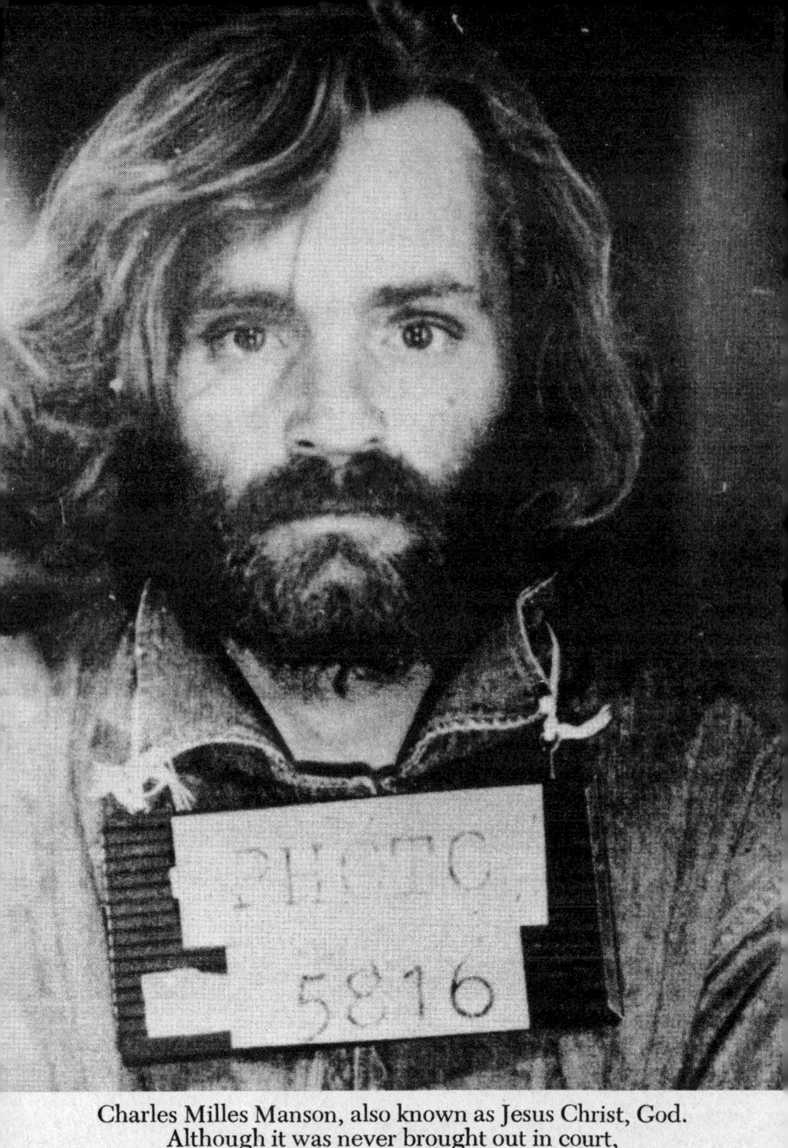

Charles Milles Manson, also known as Jesus Christ, God.
Although it was never brought out in court,
Manson bragged of committing thirty-five murders.

The Manson

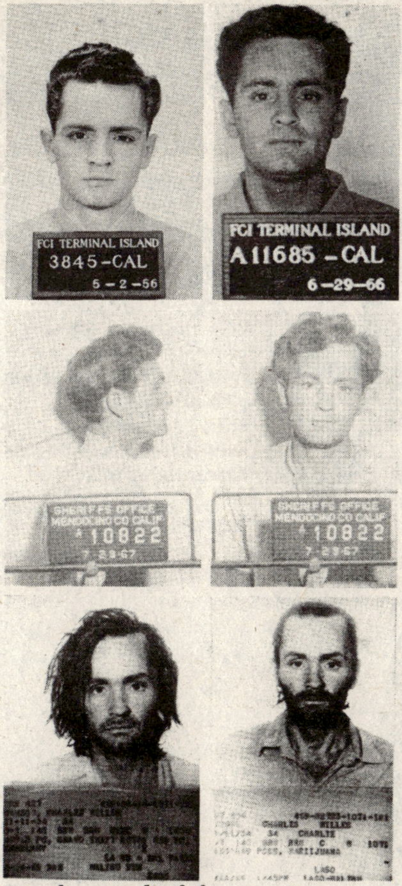

Burglar, car thief, forger, pimp.
By the age of thirty-two, Manson had spent seventeen years—more than half his life—in prison.
What happened to transform a small-time hood into one of the most notorious mass murderers of our time?

Family Album

Charles Manson at the time of the Spahn Ranch raid, August 16, 1969. A week after the Tate murders, all but one of the killers were under arrest, on suspicion of car theft. All were released within forty-eight hours, when it was discovered the warrant was misdated.

Following the October 10-12, 1969, raid on isolated Barker Ranch in Death Valley, Manson was booked for grand theft auto and arson. Standing only five feet two, he hardly looked like a man who could, and did, command others to kill for him.

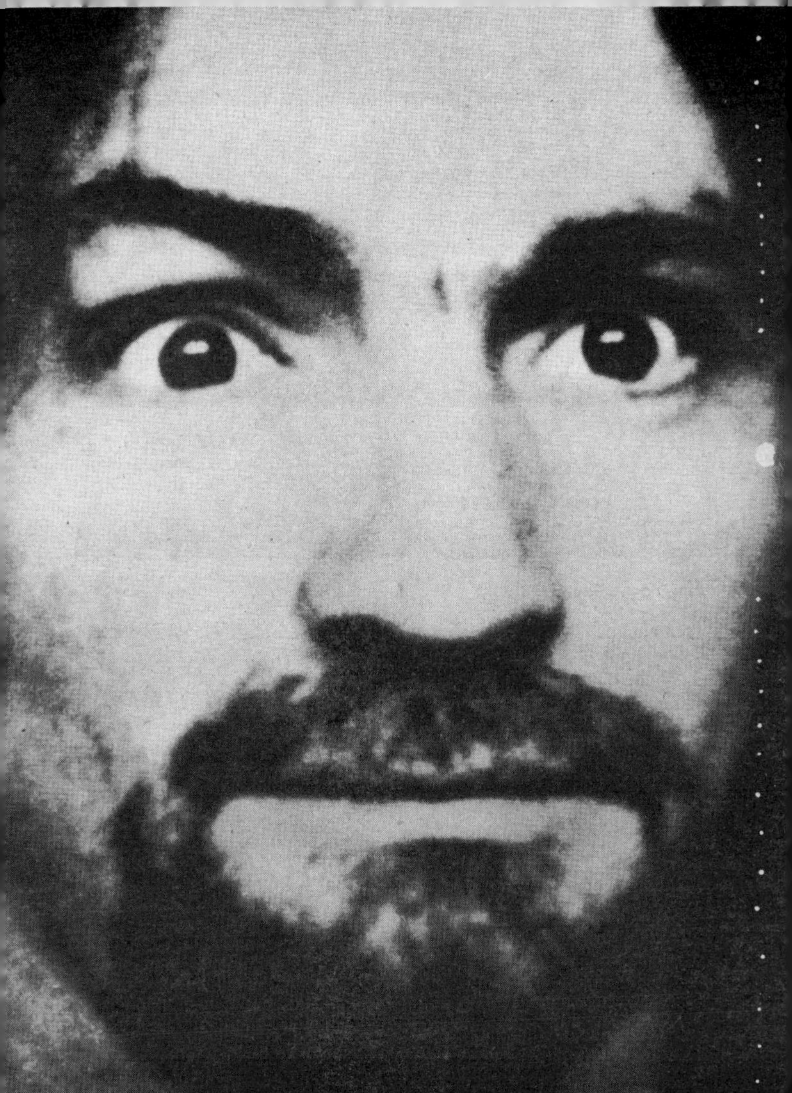

The most widely publicized photograph of Charles Manson. When it appeared on newsstands all over the world, Family members were heard to exclaim proudly, "Charlie made the cover of *Life!*"
PHOTO COURTESY OF ROBERT HENDRICKSON AND LAURENCE MERRICK

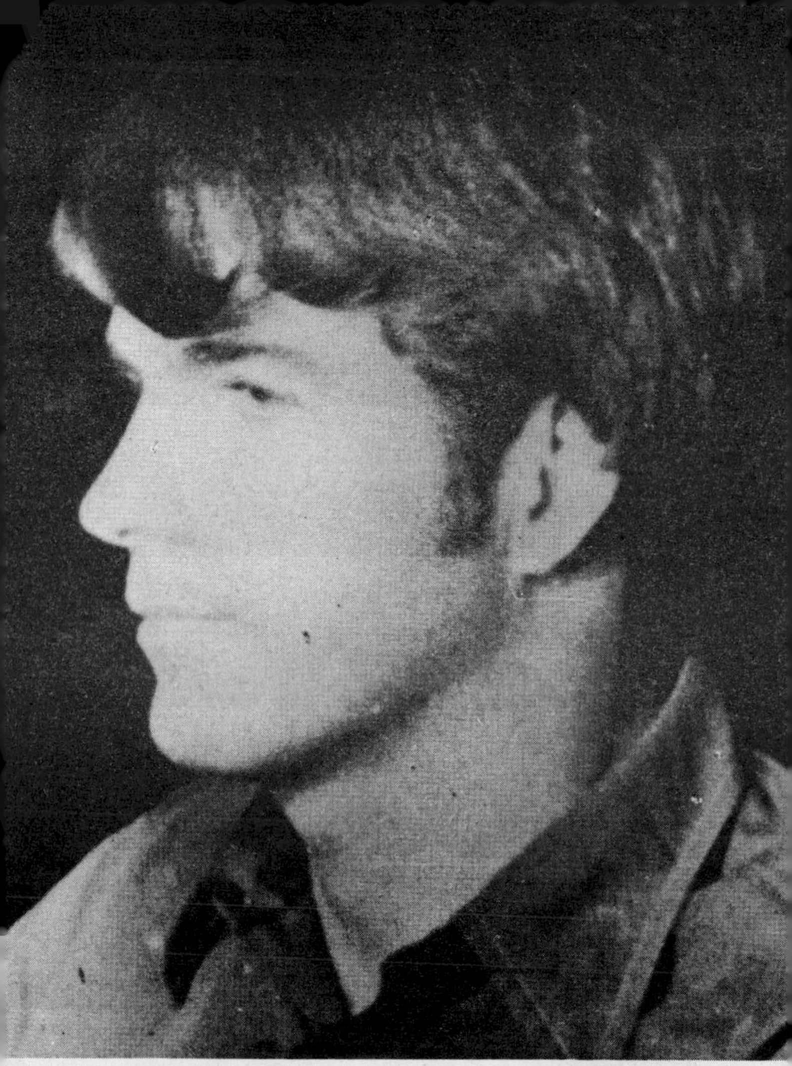

Charles Watson,
aka Tex, age 23—murderer.

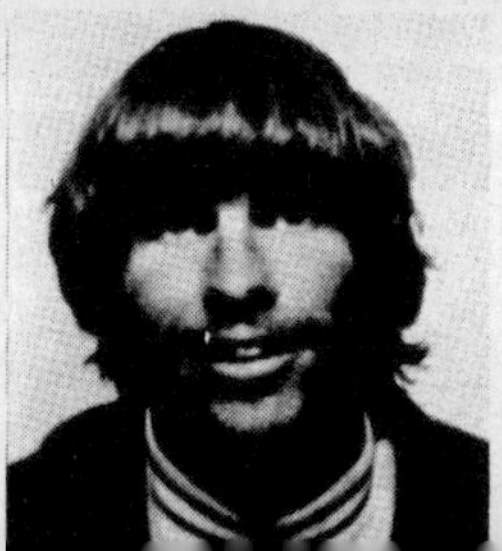

Susan Denise Atkins,
aka Sadie Mae Glutz, 21—murderer.

LARGE PHOTO COURTESY OF ROBERT HENDRICKSON AND LAURENCE MERRICK

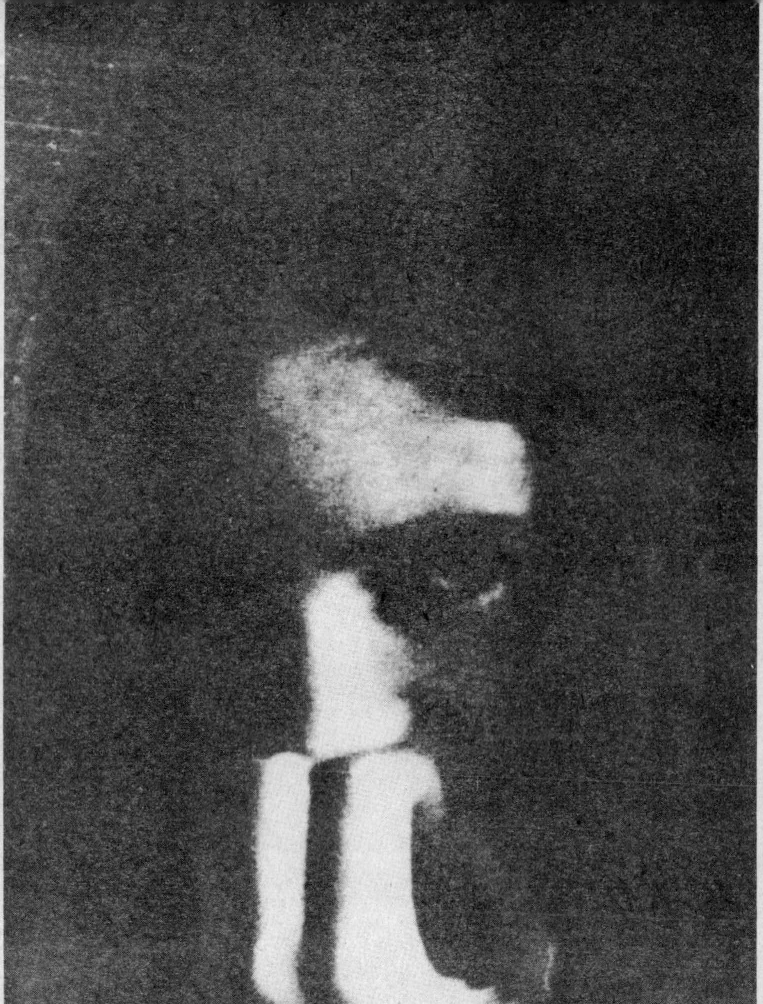

Leslie Van Houton, aka LuLu,
age 20—murderer.
LARGE PHOTO COURTESY OF ROBERT HENDRICKSON
AND LAURENCE MERRICK

Patricia Krenwinkel,
aka Katie, age 21—murderer.
LARGE PHOTO COURTESY OF ROBERT HENDRICKSON AND LAURENCE MERRICK

Lynette Fromme, aka Squeaky, age 20. Acting head of the Family in Manson's absence, she was arrested in connection with the attempted murder of prosecution witness Barbara Hoyt and given a ninety-day sentence.

PHOTO COURTESY OF ROBERT HENDRICKSON AND LAURENCE MERRICK

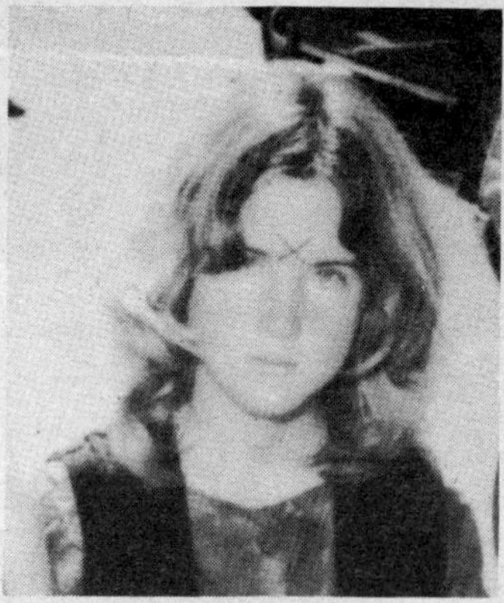

Sandra Good, aka Sandy, age 25. The daughter of a San Diego stockbroker and a former student at San Francisco State College, she bragged that the Manson Family had killed defense attorney Ronald Hughes.

Ruth Ann Moorehouse, aka Ouisch, age 17. Arrested in connection with the attempted murder of a prosecution witness, she was released on her own recognizance, then failed to appear for sentencing.

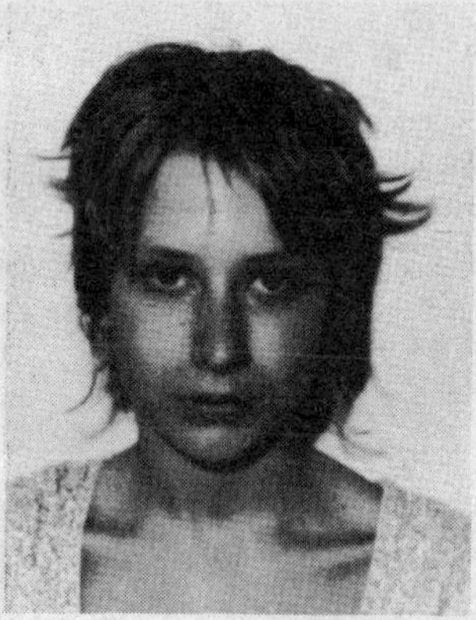

Catherine Gillies, aka Capistrano, age 18. Her grandmother owned Myers Ranch. Manson's plan to hasten her inheritance was frustrated by a flat tire.

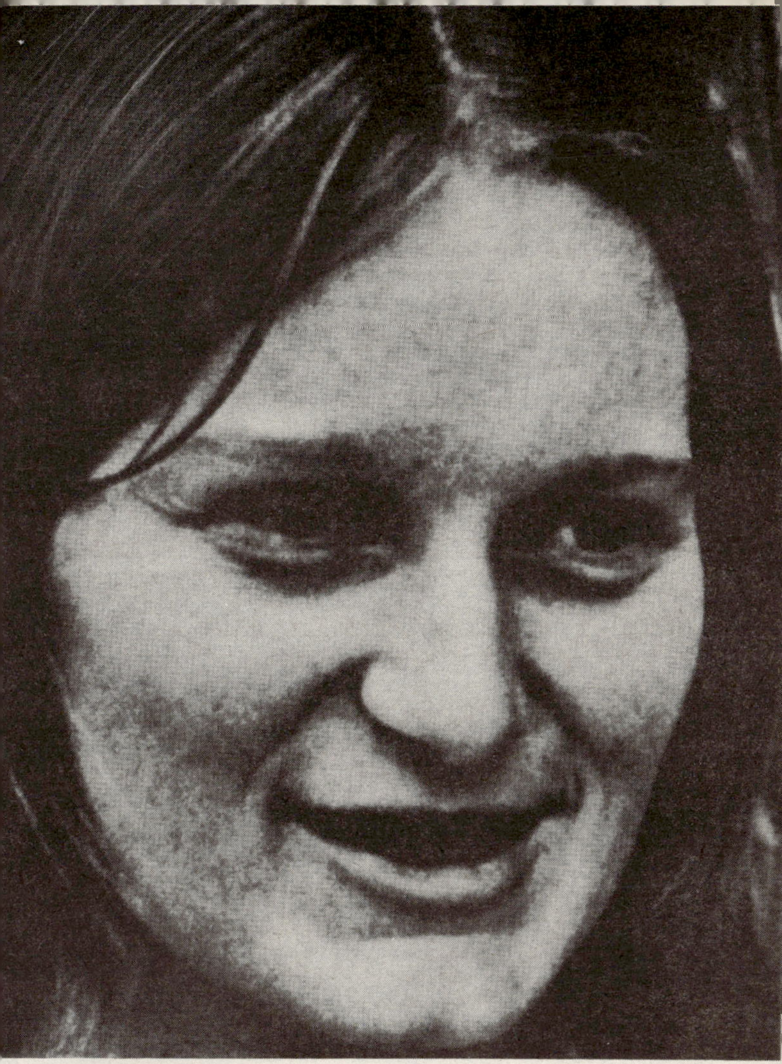

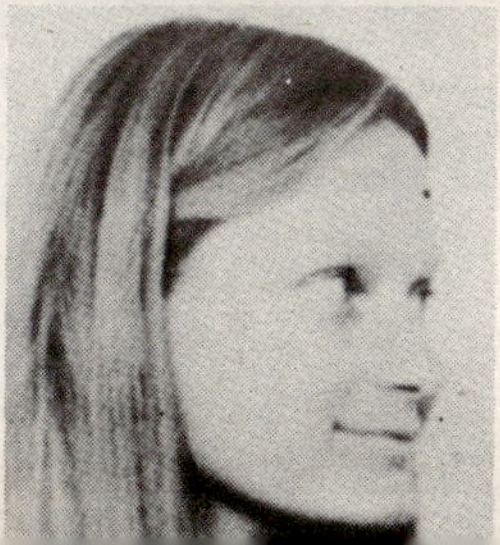

Mary Theresa Brunner,
age 25—murderer.

LARGE PHOTO COURTESY OF ROBERT HENDRICKSON AND LAURENCE MERRICK

Steve Grogan,
aka Clem, age 17—murderer.
LARGE PHOTO COURTESY OF ROBERT HENDRICKSON AND LAURENCE MERRICK

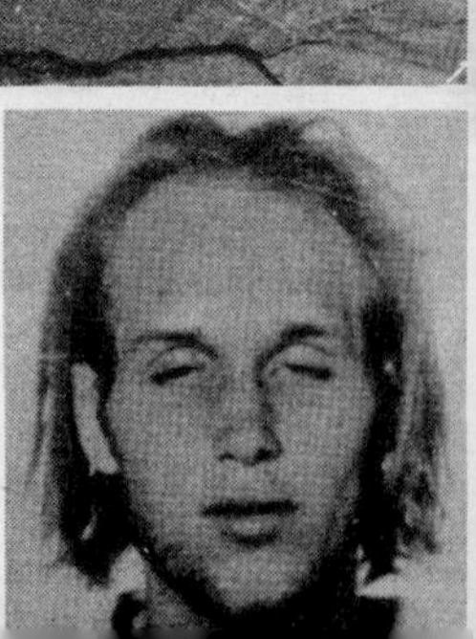

Bruce McGregor Davis,
age 26—murderer.

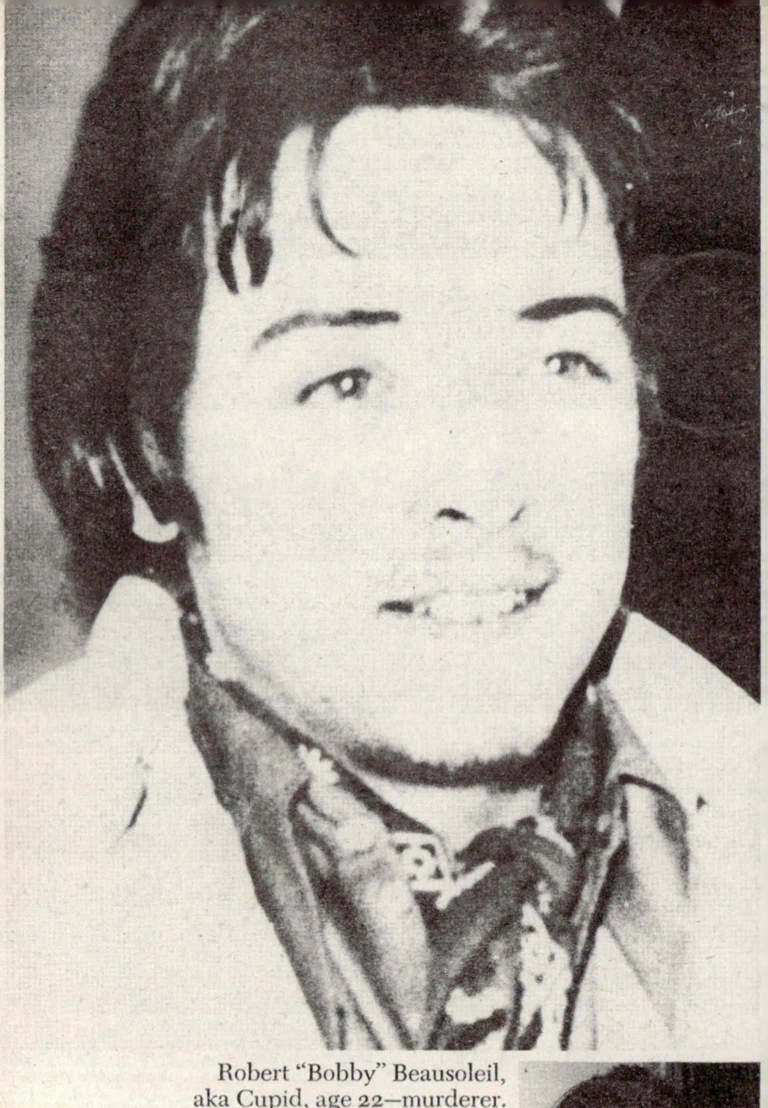

Robert "Bobby" Beausoleil,
aka Cupid, age 22—murderer.
LARGE PHOTO COURTESY OF ROBERT HENDRICKSON AND LAURENCE MERRICK

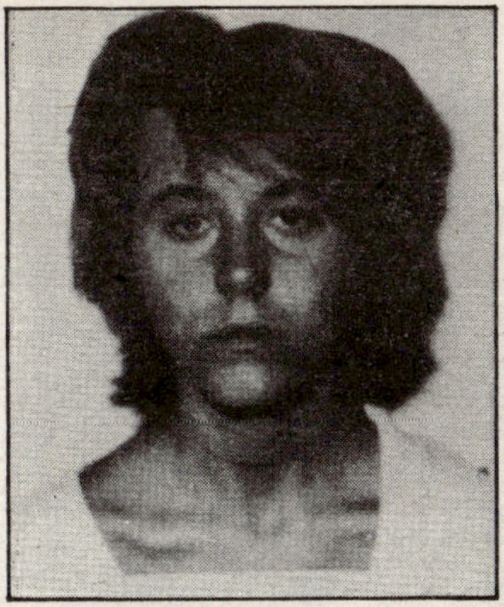

Nancy Pitman, aka Brenda McCann, age 18.
She pleaded guilty to being an accessory in the 1972 murder of Lauren Willett, who, together with her murdered husband, James, may have known too much about the slaying of Hughes. Manson once designated Pitman his chief assassin.

Catherine Share, aka Gypsy, age 27. Convicted with five others of armed robbery in a bizarre plot to hijack a 747 and obtain the release of Manson and the other Family members.
PHOTO COURTESY OF ROBERT HENDRICKSON AND LAURENCE MERRICK

A few of the Manson Family children. Manson placed great emphasis on children because, he said, they had no egos and had not yet been contaminated by their parents and society.

At present, some of the children have been adopted. Most, however, are wards of the courts and live in foster homes. The court records on the children have been sealed.

PHOTOS COURTESY OF ROBERT HENDRICKSON AND LAURENCE MERRICK

From Spahn's Movie

Right: Aerial photo of Spahn's Movie Ranch. Above shows the main buildings. From this ramshackle movie set, a world of make-believe, the killers went out on their all-too-real nightly missions of murder.

Eighty-one and near blind, ranch owner George Spahn depended on the Manson girls to be his eyes, unaware they were also serving as ears for Charlie. Spahn is shown here with Family member Gypsy.

PHOTO COURTESY OF ROBERT HENDRICKSON AND LAURENCE MERRICK

Ranch to Death Valley

During the August 16, 1969, raid on Spahn Ranch, sheriff's deputies arrested twenty-six persons. Only Manson hid, under one of the buildings. *From far left to right:* Straight Satan motorcycle gang member Danny DeCarlo; Charles Manson; Straight Satan Robert Reinhard; and ranch hand Juan Flynn.

Manson Family members and ranch hands alike were pulled in during the massive raid, which netted a huge cache of arms, including a submachine gun. However, a dozen Buck knives, purchased shortly before the Tate murders, had mysteriously disappeared.

To reach isolated Barker Ranch, where the Family hid following the Shea murder, it was necessary to go up this incredibly rugged dry wash. Only a four-wheel-drive vehicle could make it, and then only if someone walked ahead and moved the boulders out of the way.

PHOTO COURTESY OF TOM ROSS

The submachine gun in its violin case and
Manson's command dune buggy.
In a special scabbard next to the steering wheel is the
sword which Manson used to slice musician
Gary Hinman. It was also taken along on the night
of the LaBianca murders.

Barker Ranch. Manson gave its absentee owner one of
the Beach Boys' gold records in return for letting the Family stay
there. Though in disrepair, the ranch was an oasis
compared to most of Death Valley, even having a swimming pool.
The Family's school bus, in the background,
was brought in from the less rugged Las Vegas side.

Lookouts were posted in dugouts surrounding Barker Ranch, but the pre-dawn raid caught the Family off guard. Among those arrested and taken to Independence to be booked were Gypsy *(far left)* and Katie, Brenda, Squeaky, and Sadie *(far right)*. Standing alongside the jeep is Little Patty. The police were still unaware the nomadic band was guilty of anything more serious than auto theft.

Entering the bathroom, officer James Pursell noticed hair sticking out of a cabinet under the sink. Inside he found Charles Manson. The cabinet measured only 3 by 11/2 by 11/2 feet.
PHOTO COURTESY OF TOM ROSS

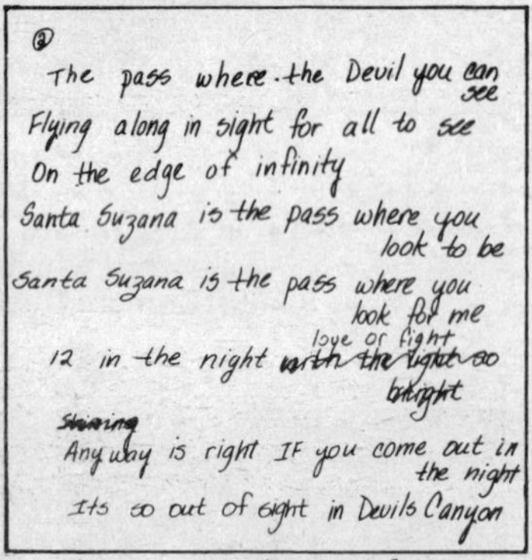

②
The pass where the Devil you can see
Flying along in sight for all to see
On the edge of infinity
Santa Suzana is the pass where you look to be
Santa Suzana is the pass where you look for me
12 in the night ~~with the light so bright~~ love or fight
~~Shining~~ Any way is right IF you come out in the night
Its so out of sight in Devils Canyon

Among the items seized in the Barker raid was a knapsack containing dozens of movie magazines and the lyrics of a number of Manson's songs. A frustrated musician who failed to make the big time, Manson numbered among his targets those who had. Devil's Canyon is located across from Spahn Ranch, near Santa Susana Pass. Perhaps coincidentally, perhaps not, the Tate murders occurred just after "12 in the night."

The Physical Evidence

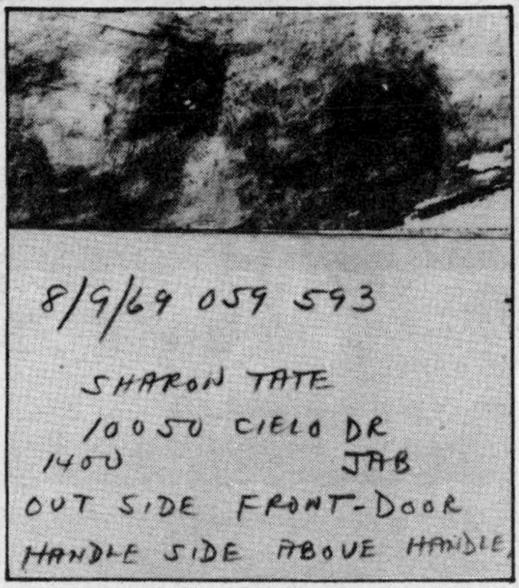

LAPD fingerprint expert Jerrome Boen pointing to the latent print recovered from the front door of the Tate residence. To the right is the lift card he prepared.

Although only twelve points are marked here, a comparison between the latent *(left)* and the print of the right ring finger on a fingerprint exemplar belonging to Charles "Tex" Watson *(right)* revealed eighteen points of similarity. LAPD requires only ten points for a positive identification.

The location and lift card of the latent fingerprint found on the inside of the French doors that led from Sharon Tate's bedroom outside.

The latent *(left)* and the print of the left little finger on a fingerprint exemplar belonging to Patricia Krenwinkel revealed seventeen points of similarity, seven more than required for a positive identification.

Following the clues in Susan Atkins' published confession, on December 15, 1969, a TV crew discovered the bloody clothing the killers had worn and discarded on the night of the Tate murders—over four months earlier. Officers from LAPD are shown placing the evidence in plastic bags for inspection in the SID lab.

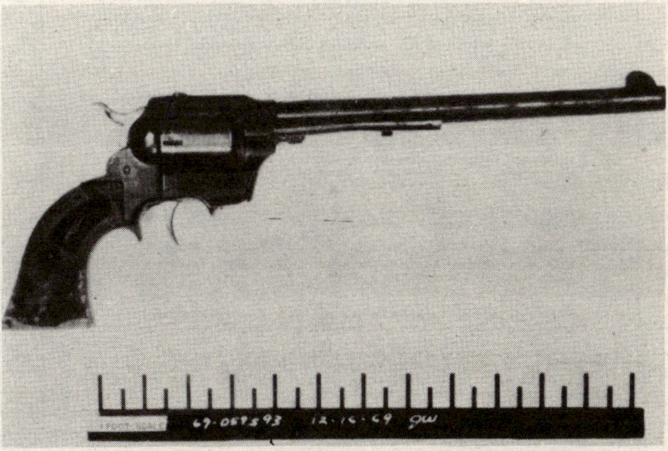

The nine-shot, .22 caliber Hi Standard Longhorn revolver used by Charles "Tex" Watson to shoot Parent, Sebring, and Frykowski. It was found by ten-year-old Steven Weiss on a hillside behind his home on September 1, 1969. Though the Valley Services Division of LAPD, located in Van Nuys, picked up the gun that same day, it was filed away under "Found Evidence."

CITY OF LOS ANGELES

CALIFORNIA

OFFICE OF THE
CHIEF OF POLICE
THOMAS REDDIN

DEPARTMENT OF
POLICE
150 N LOS ANGELES ST
LOS ANGELES CALIF 90012
PHONE 624 5211

IN REPLYING PLEASE GIVE
OUR REF NO 1.6

SAM YORTY
MAYOR

The following information and request for assistance is confidential. It is imperative for a successful conclusion of this case that the contents of this letter not be released to the news media or the general public.

During the early morning hours of August 9, 1969, a series of murders occurred in the City of Los Angeles. Pieces of a broken revolver grip were found at the scene. These have been identified as those originally used on the right side of a Hi Standard 22 long rifle "Long Horn" revolver, catalog number 9399. Revolver further described as follows: 9½" barrel, 9 shot capacity, 15" overall length, walnut grips, blue finish, weight 35 oz., price $75. Photo enclosed.

This particular revolver has only been manufactured since February, 1967. Through the cooperation of the Hi Standard Manufacturing Company of Hamden, Connecticut, we were furnished the serial numbers of all revolvers sold to California Hi Standard distributors. These serial numbers were checked through the CII and the enclosed listed weapon(s) were sold in your jurisdiction.

It is requested that you ascertain if this purchaser still has the revolver in his possession and visually check the weapon to see if the original grips are intact.

As a cover story, we suggest the following. "Your Department has some recovered property that is obviously stolen. One of the articles recovered was a revolver of the above description with the serial numbers partially obliterated. Your Department checked with the CII and ascertained that the purchaser in your jurisdiction has such a weapon. You are checking with him to obtain a lead on the obviously stolen property you have recovered."

In the event the purchaser has moved, please attempt to determine his present address.

In the event the purchaser has sold his revolver, please determine to whom he sold the weapon, their physical description and present address.

In the event the purchaser has loaned his revolver to someone, please determine to whom he loaned the weapon, their physical description and present address and the date of loan.

It is requested that you phone collect Robbery-Homicide Division, Area Code 213, MAdison 4-5211, Extension 2531, the results of your investigation. Direct your information to Lt. R. Helder and Sgts. J. Buckles and M. McGann.

R. A. Houghton

ROBERT A. HOUGHTON, Deputy Chief
Commander, Detective Bureau

Enclosures (2)

Between September 3 and 5, 1969, LAPD sent this letter, together with a photograph of the Hi Standard model, to police departments all over the United States and Canada. They neglected to send one to their own division in Van Nuys, and it was not until December 16, after persistent calls from Steven Weiss' father, that the police discovered they already had the Tate murder gun.

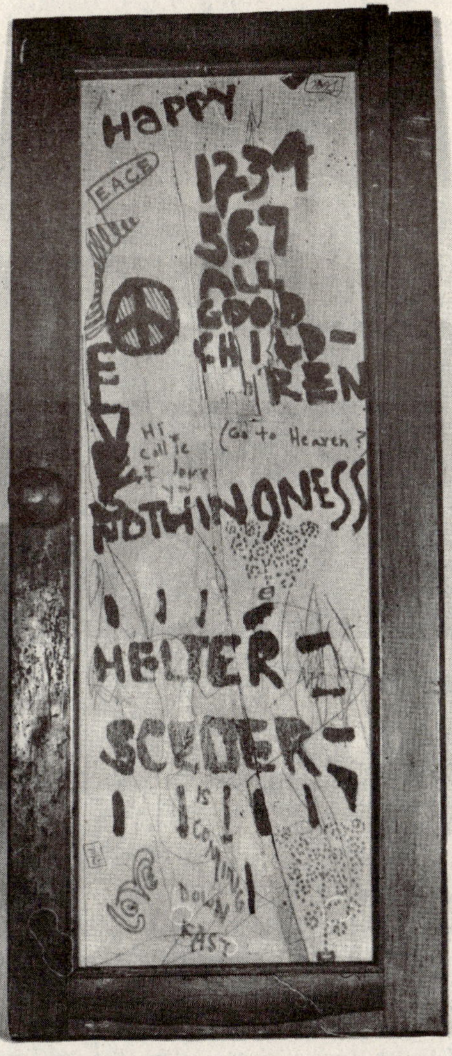

The "HELTER SKELTER" door found at Spahn Ranch. Although the words HEALTER SKELTER had been found printed at the LaBianca residence, its importance was missed.

THE PEOPLE VS. CHARLES MANSON

Prosecutor Vincent Bugliosi, chosen from a staff of 450 lawyers and assigned to the Tate-LaBianca case in November 1969, he personally gathered much of the evidence which led to the convictions and death penalty verdicts against Charles Manson, Susan Atkins, Patricia Krenwinkel, and Leslie Van Houten, after one of the longest and most sensational trials in American history.

PHOTO COURTESY OF CURT GUNTHER

Ronnie Howard. Also known by some twenty other aliases, the former call girl listened in disbelief as her cellmate Susan Atkins bragged of her participation in the Tate, LaBianca, and Hinman murders. Although Atkins first confessed to another inmate, Virginia Graham, it was Howard who first contacted the police.
PHOTO COURTESY OF ROBERT HENDRICKSON AND LAURENCE MERRICK

Linda Kasabian, star witness for the prosecution. Ordered by Manson to slit the throat of an actor, the little hippie girl told him, "I'm not you, Charlie. I can't kill anybody."
PHOTO COURTESY OF ROBERT HENDRICKSON AND LAURENCE MERRICK

Witness Juan Flynn, being interviewed by prosecutor Vincent Bugliosi during a recess in the Tate-LaBianca murder trial. Though marked for death by the Family, the colorful Panamanian cowboy lived to testify that Manson told him, "Don't you know I'm the one who's doing all of these killings?"

  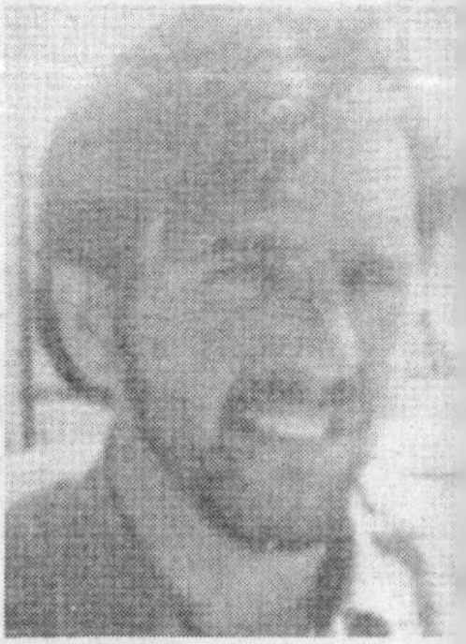

Left: Kitty Lutesinger. Girl friend of killer Bobby Beausoleil, she told sheriff's investigators about Susan Atkins' involvement in the Hinman murder and inadvertently linked her to the Tate homicides. *Center:* Biker Al Springer. When he said Manson was responsible for the Tate-LaBianca murders, the detectives were skeptical. He vanished before he could share in the $25,000 reward. *Right:* Straight Satan Danny DeCarlo. He liked booze and broads but not murder. The motorcycle rider linked the rope, the sword, and the knives to Manson—but suddenly hedged when it came to the gun.

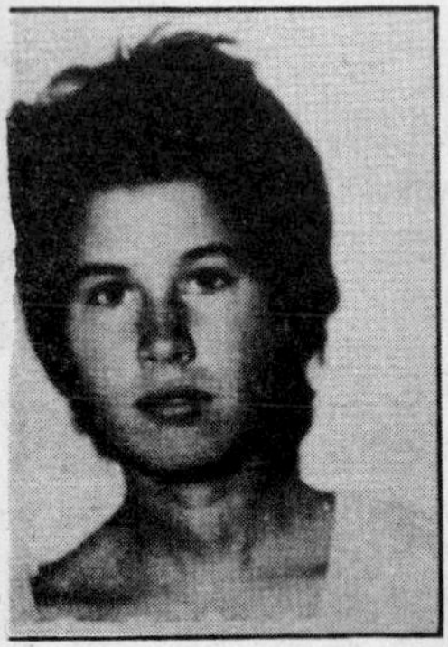  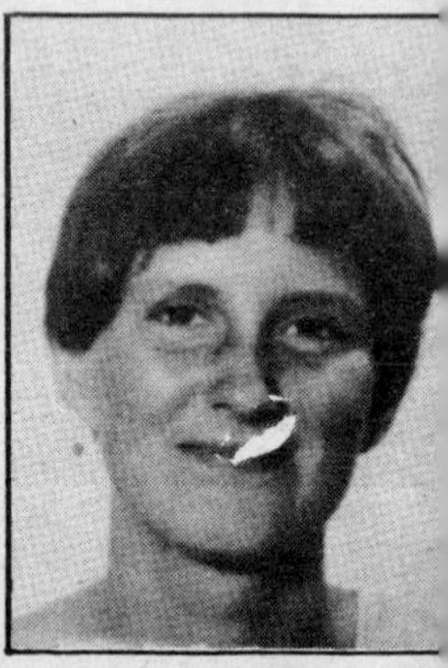

Left: Dianne Lake, aka Snake. With the Family since the age of thirteen, she began a new life after the trial. *Center:* Barbara Hoyt. Her cooperation almost cost her her life. The Family's attempt to eliminate her, by giving her an LSD-laden hamburger, backfired, changing her to a helpful witness. *Right:* Stephanie Schram. Manson found her in Big Sur and planned to use her as his alibi for the two nights of murder.

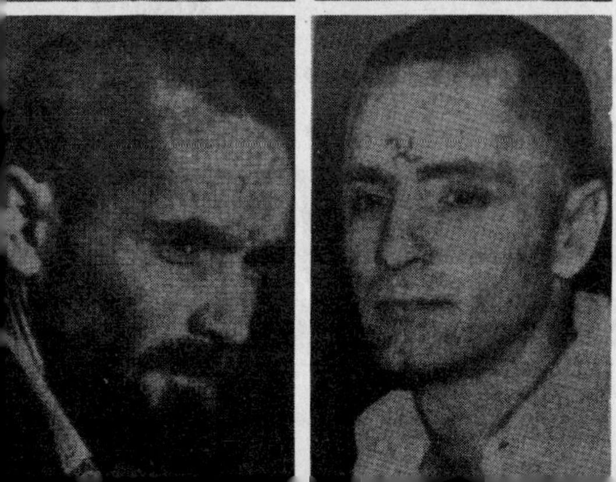

The Faces of Charles Manson. According to his disciple Squeaky: "He was a changeling. He seemed to change every time I saw him."

The Story on Page One

Calley May Learn Fate Today

TUESDAY FINAL

RACING ENTRIES

Los Angeles Times

VOL. XC   SIX PARTS—PART ONE   TUESDAY MORNING, MARCH 30, 1971   92 PAGES   DAILY 10c

Jurors Tell Feelings

MANSON, 3 GIRLS SENTENCED TO DIE

TUESDAY PREVIEW EDITION

EXTRA

Los Angeles Times

LATE SPORTS

VOL. XC   FIVE PARTS—PART ONE   ★★★   TUESDAY MORNING, JANUARY 26, 1971   72 PAGES   DAILY 10c

MANSON VERDICT

ALL GUILTY!

NEWS SUMMARY

First-Degree Conviction on

Dodgers Get Richie Allen

Story in Sports

JURORS OUT IN SALAZAR INQUEST

Story in Cols. 6-7

LOS ANGELES EVENING AND SUNDAY

HERALD EXAMINER

United Press International • Associated Press • Dow Jones

MONDAY, OCTOBER 5, 1970 PRICE TEN CENTS

8 STAR

LATEST SPORTS

TODAY'S COMPLETE NEW YORK AND AMERICAN STOCKS

MANSON LEAPS AT JUDGE, HURLS THREAT

'I'm Going

Polanski On Recovery Road (*Story in Col. 1*)

Valley Times

San Fernando Valley's Own Daily Newspaper

FINAL ★★★

SIX INDICTED IN TATE CASE

TUESDAY PREVIEW EDITION

COMPLETE STOCKS

Los Angeles Times

LATE SPORTS

VOL. LXXXIX FIVE PARTS—PART ONE ★★★ TUESDAY MORNING, AUGUST 4, 1970 74 PAGES DAILY 10c

MANSON GUILTY, NIXON DECLARES

Rams Game Saturday

Defense Says Mistrial Will Be Asked

House OKs 18 Vote I[illegible] A[illegible] Elections

Story in Cols. 7

Nixon Appeals To Senate for SST

Story in Cols. 1-3

HERALD EXAMINER
United Press International • Associated Press • Dow Jones
SUNSET RACE RESULTS COMPLETE STOCKS
VOL. C NO. 360 TUESDAY MAR[illegible] PRICE TEN CENTS

MANSON DEATH THREAT

Warns of Terror If Doomed to Die

Cult Head: 'Not Going To Take It'

Double School

Blue Chips Skid, Stocks Off 12

Story in Cols 7-8

WAR ON POVERTY: LBJ LOOKS BACK

Story Page A-6

LOS ANGELES EVENING AND SUNDAY
HERALD EXAMINER
United Press International • Associated Press • Dow Jones
8 STAR LATEST SPORTS TODAY'S COMPLETE NEW YORK AND AMERICAN STOCKS
WEDNESDAY OCTOBER

CATCH MANSON PAL IN SPECTACULAR ESCAPE

Prisoner

Willy Brandt

Tate Slaying Trial Begins

Story in Cols. 1-3

For 'Conscientious Objectors' A Victory

Story in Cols. 6-7

LOS ANGELES EVENING AND SUNDAY
HERALD EXAMINER
United Press International • Associated Press • Dow Jones
8 STAR TODAY'S NEWS TODAY!
VOL. C NO. 81 MONDAY, JUNE 15, 1970 PRICE 10 CENTS

WORLD SPACE RECORD

Russ Cosmonauts Near Third Week

Soyuz 9 May Orbit

Reds Beat

LOS ANGELES

FREE PRESS

25¢

KRLA's Pop Chronicles

Free Party to say good-by to Temple

How to start an anti-war military paper

141 Places to go this week—see page 32

Volume 7, #5 Issue 289 | $6.00 PER YEAR | Copyright 1970 The Los Angeles Free Press, Inc. | Phone: YES-1970 | January 30 – February 4

EXCLUSIVE ! EXCLUSIVE !

MANSON INTERVIEW !

First interview with Charles Manson in jail

Los Angeles Herald-Examiner, Sunday, Dec. 7, 1969

Main Characters in Tate Murder Drama

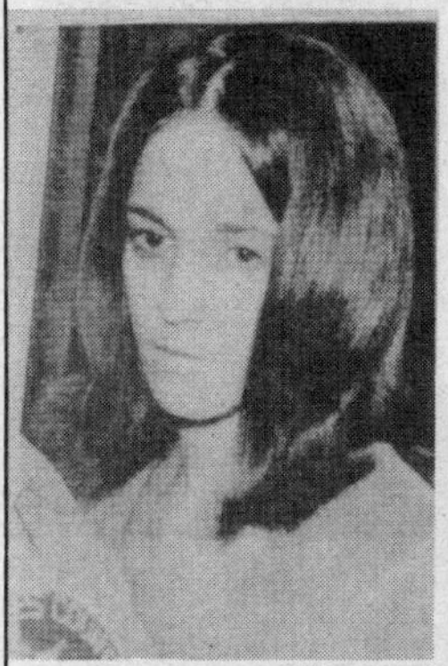

—Herald-Examiner Photo

Miss Susan Atkins . . . she gave valuable testimony to the County Grand Jury.

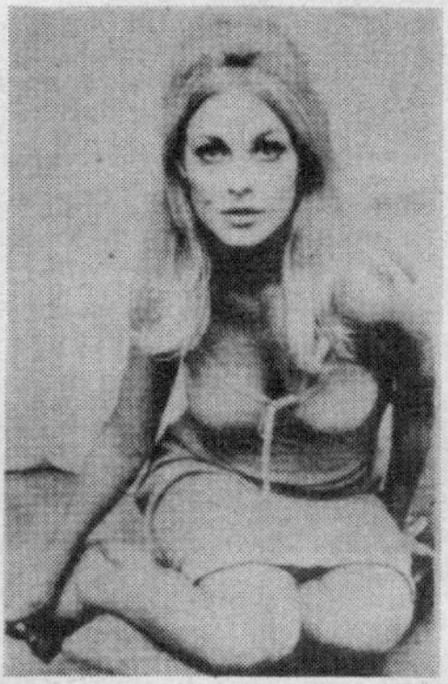

—AP Wirephoto

Miss Sharon Tate . . . TV and movie actress was one of five slain last August.

—AP Wirephoto

Charles Manson . . . is alleged leader of hippie group.

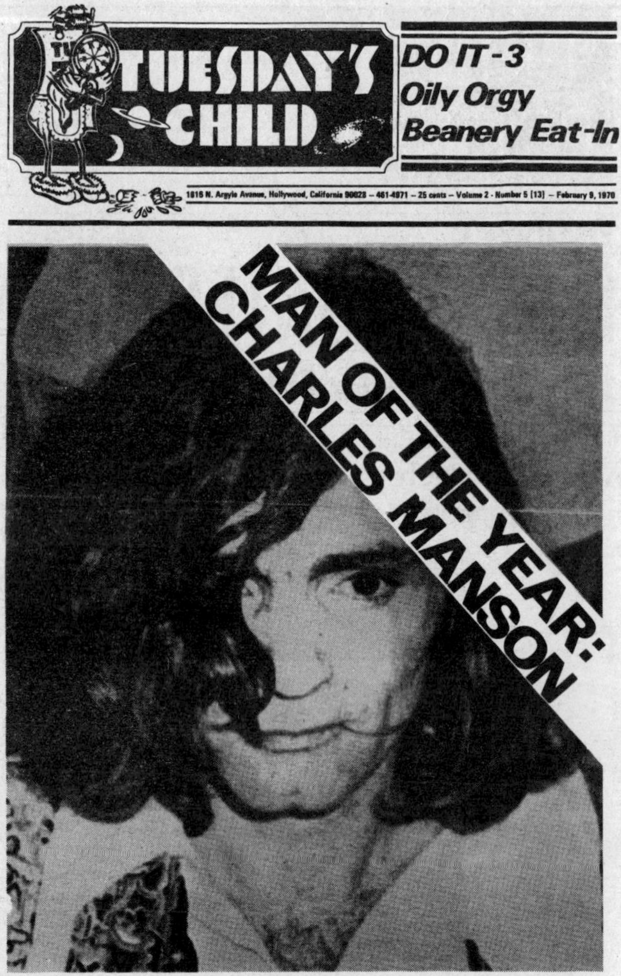

TUESDAY'S CHILD

DO IT-3
Oily Orgy
Beanery Eat-In

1816 N. Argyle Avenue, Hollywood, California 90028 – 461-4971 – 25 cents – Volume 2 · Number 5 [13] – February 9, 1970

MAN OF THE YEAR:
CHARLES MANSON

Monster or Revolutionary Martyr?
The underground press was divided as to whether

Manson was a sick symbol
of our times or Christ returned. His cult still survives.

NATIONAL CREDIT CARD APPLICATION

UNION

Union Oil Company of California

PS	For Credit Department use		
	Cards 1 2 3 __	Code	T P
	Approved by		

Please print

Name–(full first name–second initial–last name) Charles M. Manson ✓	Age 35	No. of dependents 16	Wife's first name none
Street address 441 N. Bauchet	How long at address — Years 10 Mos.		Own ☐ Buying ☐ Rent ☒
City, state and zip code Los Angeles, Calif		Social Security no. 560-84-8462	
Previous address (street–city–state) Spahn's Movie Ranch Chatsworth, Calif.		How long at address 1 Years — Mos.	
Employer's name (if self-employed–name of business) Evangalist	Type of business Religious	Length of employment 20 Years — Mos.	
Business address (street–city–state)	Position	Monthly salary ☐ 300-399 ☐ 400-499 ☐ 500-699 ☒ 700 & over	
Previous employer (if above employment is less than 2 years)	Position	Length of employment Years Mos.	
Wife's employer	Position	Monthly salary ☐ 200-299 ☐ 300-399 ☐ 400 & over	Length of employ. Yrs. Mos.

Credit is established with: (include name of oil company credit cards and account number)		
Name/address George Spahn Chatsworth	☐ 30 Day ☐ Budget	Bank used Republic National
Name/address A Joint Venture 13150 Chandler Van Nuys, Calif	☐ 30 Day ☐ Budget	Branch No Hollywood
Name/address	☐ 30 Day ☐ Budget	Account no. ☒ Checking ☐ Savings
Name/address	☐ 30 Day ☐ Budget	
Number of cards desired 2	Mail statements to ☒ Residence ☐ Business	Applicant agrees to terms and conditions of use printed on credit card.
Date / /	Residence phone no. 680-9600	Signature Charles M Manson

PLEASE ALLOW APPROXIMATELY 3 WEEKS FOR CREDIT INVESTIGATION AND ISSUANCE

A rare example of Manson's sense of humor.
He applied for a credit card while on trial for mass murder.

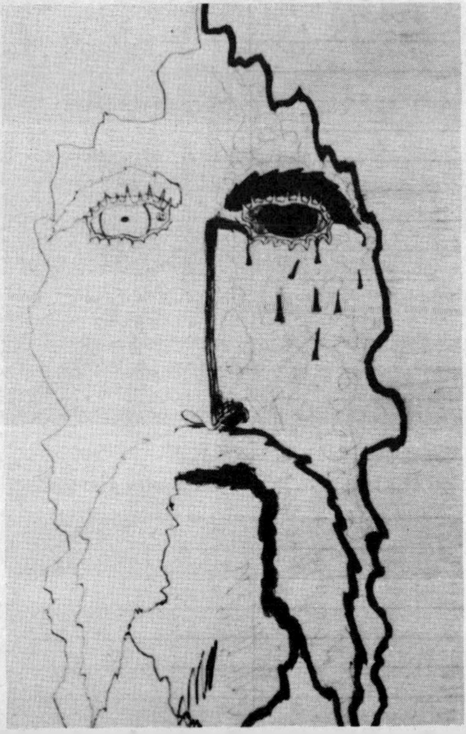

Another side of Manson is revealed in one of his doodlings, made during the trial.

"The Bug." Prosecutor Bugliosi, as depicted by Susan Atkins and Leslie Van Houten during the trial. The three female defendants sketched, giggled, or looked bored as witness after witness testified to their savage slaughter.

Prosecutor Bugliosi talks to reporters congratulating him outside the courtroom moments after the jury returned verdicts of guilty against all the defendants on every count of the indictment with which they were charged.
ASSOCIATED PRESS

Manson's attorney Irving Kanarek. The press focused on his bombast and missed his effectiveness. He fought as if he personally were on trial.
PHOTO COURTESY OF ROBERT HENDRICKSON AND LAURENCE MERRICK

Charles "Tex" Watson fought extradition for months, then was tried separately. Though the judge referred to him as "poor Tex," Bugliosi obtained a conviction and death penalty verdict against Watson also.
PHOTO COURTESY OF ROBERT HENDRICKSON AND LAURENCE MERRICK

"We're waiting for our father to be set free." During the trials, Manson Family members conducted a vigil outside the Hall of Justice, at the corner of Temple and Broadway. *Left to right:* Sandy, Ouisch, Cathy, and Mary.
PHOTO COURTESY OF ROBERT HENDRICKSON AND LAURENCE MERRICK

"I have X'd myself from your world."
When Manson carved an X
on his forehead, his followers did
likewise. Later, again
following Manson's lead, they changed
the X's into swastikas.
Left to right: Squeaky, Sandy,
Ouisch, Cathy.
PHOTO COURTESY OF ROBERT HENDRICKSON
AND LAURENCE MERRICK

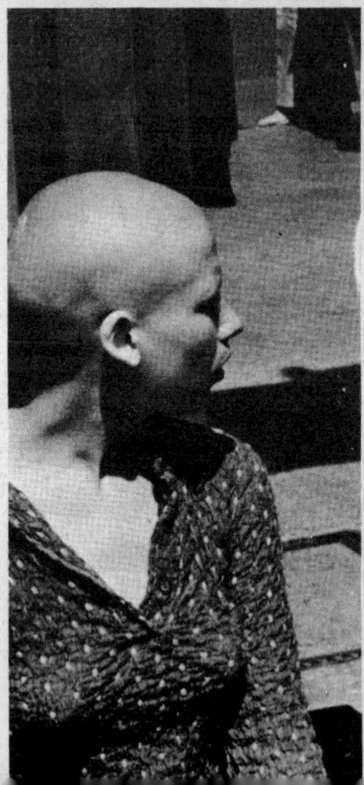

Following the guilty verdicts,
Manson, Atkins, Krenwinkel, and
Van Houten shaved their heads,
as did the girls on the corner, who told
reporters: "You'd better
watch your children because Judgment
Day is coming!"
Left to right, facing camera: Crystal,
Mary, Kitty.
With backs to camera, left to right:
Sandy and Squeaky.
PHOTO COURTESY OF ROBERT HENDRICKSON
AND LAURENCE MERRICK

Charles Manson on his way to Death Row, San Quentin Prison. With the abolition of the death sentence, Manson's own sentence was commuted to life imprisonment.

PHOTO COURTESY OF ROBERT HENDRICKSON AND LAURENCE MERRICK

With the exception of Sadie and a few others, Charlie's girls simply did not have impressive busts. For some reason Manson seemed to attract mostly flat-chested girls.

While at the Gresham Street house, Manson had told Watkins that the atrocious murders would occur that summer. It was almost summer now and the blacks were showing no signs of rising up to fulfill their karma. One day in late May or early June of 1969, Manson took Watkins aside, down near the old trailer at Spahn, and confided: "The only thing blackie knows is what whitey has told him." He then added, "*I'm* going to have to show him how to do it."

According to Watkins: "I got some weird pictures from that." A few days later Watkins took off for Barker, fearful that if he stuck around he would see those weird pictures materialize into nihilistic reality.

It was September of 1969 before Manson himself returned to Barker Ranch, to find that Watkins and Poston had defected. Though Manson told Watkins about "cutting Shorty into nine pieces," he made no mention whatsoever of the Tate-LaBianca murders. In discussing Helter Skelter with Watkins, however, Manson said, without explanation, "I had to show blackie how to do it."

LAPD had interviewed Gregg Jakobson in late November of 1969. When he attempted to tell them about Manson's far-out philosophy, one of the detectives replied, "Ah, Charlie's a madman; we're not interested in all that." The following month two detectives went to Shoshone and talked to Crockett and Poston; LAPD also contacted Watkins. All three were asked what they knew about the Tate-LaBianca murders. And all three said they didn't know anything, which, in their minds, was true, none having previously made the connection between Manson and these murders. After the interview with Poston and Crockett, one of the detectives remarked, "Looks like we made a trip for nothing."

Initially, I found it difficult to believe that none of the four even suspected that Manson might be behind the Tate-LaBianca murders. There were, I discovered, several probable reasons for this. When Manson had told Jakobson how Helter Skelter would start, he had said nothing about writing words in blood. He had told this to both Watkins and Poston, even telling Poston about the word "pigs," but there were no newspapers at Barker Ranch, and its location was such that there was no radio reception. Though they had heard about the murders on their infrequent supply trips into Independence and Shoshone, both stated they hadn't picked up many details.

The main reason, however, was simply a fluke. Though the press did report that there was bloody writing at the LaBianca residence, LAPD had succeeded in keeping one fact secret: that two of the words were HEALTER SKELTER.

Had this been publicized, undoubtedly Jakobson, Watkins, Poston, and numerous others would have connected the LaBianca murders—and probably the Tate murders also, because of their proximity in time—with Manson's insane plan. And it seems a safe assumption that at least one would have communicated his suspicions to the police.

It was one of those odd happenstances, for which no one was at fault, the repercussions of which no one could foresee, but it appears possible that had this happened, the killers might have been apprehended days, rather than months, after the murders, and Donald "Shorty" Shea, and possibly others, might still be alive.

Though I was now convinced we had the motive, other leads failed to pan out.

None of the employees of the Standard station in Sylmar or the Jack Frost store in Santa Monica could identify anyone in our "Family album." As for the LaBianca credit cards, all appeared to be accounted for, while Susan Struthers was unable to determine if a brown purse was missing from her mother's personal effects. The problem was that Rosemary had several brown purses.

By the time LAPD requested the Spahn Ranch phone records, most of the billings for May and July 1969 had been "lost or destroyed." All the numbers for the other months—April to October 1969—were identified and, though we obtained some minor background information on the activities of the Family, we were unable to find any link between the killers and the victims. Nor did any appear in the phone records of the Tate and LaBianca residences.

Exposure to rain and sunlight over a prolonged period of time breaks down human blood components. Many of the spots on the clothing the TV crew had found gave a positive benzidine reaction, indicating blood, but Granado was unable to determine whether it was animal or human. However, Granado did find human blood, type B, on the white T-shirt (Parent, Folger, and Frykowski were type B), and human blood, "possible type O," on the dark velour turtleneck (Tate and Sebring were type O). He did not test for subtypes.

He also removed some human hair from the clothing, which he determined had belonged to a woman, and which did not match that of the two female victims.

I called Captain Carpenter at Sybil Brand and requested a sample of Susan Atkins' hair. On February 17, Deputy Sheriff Helen Tabbe took Susan to the jail beauty shop for a wash and set. Afterwards she removed the hair from Susan's brush and comb. Later a sample of Patricia Krenwinkel's hair was similarly obtained. Granado eliminated the Krenwinkel sample but, although he wasn't able to state positively that they were the same, he found the Atkins sample "very, very similar" to that taken from the clothing, concluding it was "very likely" the hair belonged to Susan Atkins.*

Some white animal hairs were also found on the clothing. Winifred Chapman said they looked like the hair from Sharon's dog. Since the dog had died shortly after Sharon's death, no comparison could be made. I intended to introduce the hair into evidence anyway, and let Mrs. Chapman state what she had told me.

On February 11, Kitty Lutesinger had given birth to Bobby Beausoleil's child. Even before this, she was an unwilling witness, and the little information I got from her came hard. Later she would return to the Family, leave it, go back. Unsure of what she might say on the stand, I eventually decided against calling her as a witness.

*The points of similarity included color, diameter, length, as well as the medullary characteristics.

I made the same decision in relation to biker Al Springer, though for different reasons. Most of his testimony would be repetitive of DeCarlo's. Also, his most damning testimony—Manson's statement, "We got five of them the other night"—was inadmissible because of *Aranda*. I did interview Springer, several times, and one remark Manson made to him, re the murders, gave me a glimpse into Manson's possible defense strategy. In discussing the many criminal activities of the Family, Manson had told Springer: "No matter what happens, the girls will take the rap for it."

I interviewed Danny numerous times, one session lasting nine hours, obtaining considerable information that hadn't come out in previous interviews. Each time I picked up a few more examples of Manson's domination: Manson would tell the Family when it was time to eat; he wouldn't permit anyone to be served until he was seated; during dinner he would lecture on his philosophy.

I asked Danny if anyone ever interrupted Manson while he was talking. He recalled that one time "a couple of broads" started talking.

Q. "What happened?"

A. "He threw a bowl of rice at them."

Although DeCarlo was extremely reluctant to testify, Sergeant Gutierrez and I eventually persuaded him that it was in his own best interests to do so.

I had less success with Dennis Wilson, singer and drummer for the Beach Boys. Though Wilson initially claimed to know nothing of importance, he finally agreed to "level" with me, but he refused to testify.

It was obvious that Wilson was scared, and not without good reason. On December 4, 1969, three days after LAPD announced they had broken the case, Wilson had received an anonymous death threat. It was, I learned, not the only such threat, and the others were not anonymous.

Though denying any knowledge of the Family's criminal activities, Wilson did supply some interesting background information. In the late spring of 1968, Wilson had twice picked up the same pair of female hitchhikers while driving through Malibu. The second time he took the girls home with him. For Dennis, home was 14400 Sunset Boulevard, a palatial residence formerly owned by humorist Will Rogers. The girls—Ella Jo Bailey and Patricia Krenwinkel—stayed a couple of hours, Dennis said, mostly talking about this guy named Charlie.

Wilson had a recording session that night and didn't get home until 3 A.M. When he pulled into the driveway, a strange man stepped out of his back door. Wilson, frightened, asked, "Are you going to hurt me?" The man said, "Do I look like I'm going to hurt you, brother?" He then dropped to his knees and kissed Wilson's feet—obviously one of Charlie's favorite routines. When Manson ushered Wilson into his own home, he discovered he had about a dozen uninvited house guests, nearly all of them girls.

They stayed for several months, during which time the group more than doubled in number. (It was during Manson's "Sunset Boulevard period" that Charles "Tex" Watson, Brooks Poston, and Paul Watkins became associated with the Family.) The experience, Dennis later estimated, cost him about $100,000. Besides Manson's constantly hitting him for money, Clem demolished Wilson's uninsured $21,000 Mercedes-Benz by plowing it into a mountain on the approach to Spahn Ranch; the Family appropriated Wilson's wardrobe, and just about everything else in sight; and several times Wilson found it necessary to take the whole Family to his Beverly Hills doctor for penicillin shots. "It was probably the largest gonorrhea bill in history," Dennis admitted. Wilson even gave Manson nine or ten of the Beach Boys' gold records and paid to have Sadie's teeth fixed.

The newly divorced Wilson obviously found something attractive about Manson's life style. "Except for the expense," Dennis told me, "I got along very well with Charlie and the girls." He and Charlie would sing and talk, Dennis said, while the girls cleaned house, cooked, and catered to their needs. Wilson said he liked the "spontaneity" of Charlie's music, but added that "Charlie never had a musical bone in his body." Despite this, Dennis tried hard to "sell" Manson to others. He rented a recording studio in Santa Monica and had Manson recorded. (Though I was very interested in hearing the tapes, Wilson claimed that he had destroyed them, because "the vibrations connected with them don't belong on this earth.") Wilson also introduced Manson to a number of people in or on the fringes of the entertainment industry, including Melcher, Jakobson, and Altobelli. At one party, Charlie gave Dean Martin's daughter, Deana, a ring and asked her to join the Family. Deana told me she kept the ring, which she later gave to her husband, but declined Manson's invitation. As did the other Beach Boys, none of whom shared Dennis' fondness for the "scruffy little guru," as one described him.

Wilson denied having any conflicts with Manson during this period. However, in August 1968, three weeks before his lease was to expire, Dennis moved in with Gregg, leaving to his manager the task of evicting Charlie and the girls.

From Sunset Boulevard the Family moved to Spahn Ranch. Although Wilson apparently avoided the group for a time, he did see Manson occasionally. Dennis told me that he didn't have any trouble with Charlie until August 1969—Dennis could not recall the exact date, but he did know it was after the Tate murders—when Manson visited him, demanding $1,500 so he could go to the desert. When Wilson refused, Charlie told him, "Don't be surprised if you never see your kid again." Dennis had a seven-year-old son, and obviously this was one reason for his reluctance to testify.

Manson also threatened Wilson himself, but Dennis did not learn of this until an interview I conducted with both Wilson and Jakobson. According to Jakobson, not long after Dennis refused Manson's request, Charlie handed Gregg a .44 caliber bullet and told him, "Tell Dennis there are more where this came from." Knowing how the other threat had upset Dennis, Gregg hadn't mentioned it to him.

This incident had occurred in late August or early September of 1969. Jakobson was startled by the change in Manson. "The electricity was almost pouring out of him. His hair was on end. His eyes were wild. The only thing I can compare it to . . . is that he was just like an animal in a cage."

It was possible there was still another threat, but this is

strictly conjecture. In going through the Spahn Ranch phone bills, I found that on September 22, 1969, someone called Dennis Wilson's private number from the pay phone at Spahn and that the following day Wilson had the phone disconnected.

Looking back on his involvement with the Family, Dennis told me: "I'm the luckiest guy in the world, because I got off only losing my money."

From rock star to motorcycle rider to ex-call girl, the witnesses in this case all had one thing in common: they were afraid for their lives. They needed only to pick up a newspaper or turn on TV to see that many of the Family members were still roaming the streets; that Steve Grogan, aka Clem, was out on bail, while the Inyo County grand theft charges against Bruce Davis had been dismissed for lack of evidence. Neither Grogan, Davis, nor any of the others suspected of beheading Shorty Shea had been charged with that murder, there being as yet no physical proof that Shea was dead.

Perhaps in her cell at Sybil Brand, Susan Atkins recalled the lyrics of the Beatles' song "Sexy Sadie":

> "Sexy Sadie what have you done
> You made a fool of everyone . . .
> Sexy Sadie you broke the rules
> You laid it out for all to see . . .
> Sexy Sadie you'll get yours yet
> However big you think you are . . ."

Or perhaps it was simply that the numerous messages Manson was sending, by other Family members, were getting to her.

Susan called in Caballero and told him that under no circumstances would she testify at the trial. And she demanded to see Charlie.

Caballero told Aaron and me that it looked as if we'd lost our star witness.

We contacted Gary Fleischman, Linda Kasabian's attorney, and told him we were ready to talk.

From the start Fleischman, dedicated to the welfare of his client, had wanted nothing less than complete immunity for Linda Kasabian. Not until after I had talked to Linda myself did I learn that she had been willing to talk to us immunity or not, and that only Fleischman had kept her from doing so. I also learned that she had decided to return to California voluntarily, against the advice of Fleischman, who had wanted her to fight extradition.

After a number of discussions, our office agreed to petition the Superior Court for immunity, *after* she had testified. In return it was agreed: (1) that Linda Kasabian would give us a full and complete statement of her involvement in the Tate-LaBianca Murders; (2) that Linda Kasabian would testify truthfully at all trial proceedings against all defendants; and (3) that in the event Linda Kasabian did not testify truthfully, or that she refused to testify, for whatever reason, she would be prosecuted fully, but that any statement that she gave the prosecution would not be used against her.

The agreement was signed by Younger, Leavy, Busch, Stovitz, and myself on February 26, 1970.

Two days later I interviewed Linda Kasabian. It was the first time she had discussed the Tate-LaBianca murders with anyone connected with law enforcement.

As noted, given a choice between Susan and Linda, I'd preferred Linda, sight unseen: she hadn't killed anyone and therefore would be far more acceptable to a jury than the bloodthirsty Susan. Now, talking to her in Captain Carpenter's office at Sybil Brand, I was especially pleased that things had turned out as they had.

Small, with long light-brown hair, Linda bore a distinct resemblance to the actress Mia Farrow. As I got to know her, I found Linda a quiet girl, docile, easily led, yet she communicated an inner sureness, almost a fatalism, that made her seem much older than her twenty years. The product of a broken home, she herself had had two unsuccessful marriages, the last of which, to a young hippie, Robert Kasabian, had broken up just before she went to Spahn Ranch. She had one child, a girl named Tanya, age two, and was now eight months pregnant with another, conceived, she thought, the last time she and her husband were together. She had remained with the Family less than a month and a half—"I was like a little blind girl in the forest, and I took the first path that came to me." Only now, talking about what had happened, did she feel she was emerging from the darkness, she said.

On her own since sixteen, Linda had wandered from the east coast to the west, "looking for God." In her quest she had lived in communes and crash pads, taken drugs, had sex with almost anyone who showed an interest. She described all this with a candor that at times shocked me, yet which, I knew, would be a plus on the witness stand.

From the first interview I believed her story, and I felt that a jury would also. There were no pauses in her answers, no evasions, no attempts to make herself appear something she was not. She was brutally frank. When a witness takes the stand and tells the truth, even though it is injurious to his own image, you know he can't be impeached. I knew that if Linda testified truthfully about those two nights of murder, it would be immaterial whether she had been promiscuous, taken dope, stolen. The question was, could the defense attack her credibility regarding the events of those two nights? And I knew the answer from our very first interview: they wouldn't be able to do so, because she was so obviously telling the truth.

I talked to her from 1 to 4:30 P.M. on the twenty-eighth. It was the first of many long interviews, a half dozen of them lasting six to nine hours, all of which took place at Sybil Brand, her attorney usually the only other person present. At the end of each interview I'd tell her that if, back in her cell, anything occurred to her which we hadn't discussed, to "jot it down." A number of these notes became letters to me, running to a dozen or more pages. All of which, together with my interview notes, became available to the defense under discovery.

The more times a witness tells his story, the more opportunities there are for discrepancies and contradictions, which the opposing side can then use for impeachment purposes. While some attorneys try to hold interviews and pre-trial statements to a minimum so as to avoid such problems, my attitude is the exact opposite. If a witness is lying, I want to know it before he ever takes the stand. In the more than fifty hours I spent interviewing Linda Kasabian, I found her, like any witness, unsure in some details, confused about others, but never once did I catch her even attempting to lie. Moreover, when she was unsure, she admitted it.

Though she added many details, Linda Kasabian's story of those two nights was basically the same as Susan Atkins'. There were only a few surprises. But they were big ones.

Prior to my talking to Linda, we had assumed that she had probably witnessed only one murder, the shooting of Steve Parent. We now learned that she had also seen Katie chasing Abigail Folger across the lawn with an upraised knife and Tex stabbing Voytek Frykowski to death.

She also told me that on the night the LaBiancas were killed, Manson had attempted to commit three other murders.

Part 5

"DON'T YOU KNOW WHO YOU'RE CRUCIFYING?"

"For there shall arise false Christs,
and false prophets, and shall shew
great signs and wonders; insomuch that,
if it were possible, they shall deceive
the very elect . . . Wherefore, if they
shall say unto you, Behold, he is in
the desert; go not forth . . ."

Matthew 24:24,26

"Just before we got busted in the desert,
there was twelve of us apostles and Charlie."

Family member
Ruth Ann Moorehouse

"I may have implied on several occasions
to several different people that I may
have been Jesus Christ, but I haven't
decided yet what I am or who I am."

Charles Manson

March 1970

On March 3, accompanied by attorney Gary Fleischman and some dozen LAPD and LASO officers, I took Linda Kasabian out of Sybil Brand. For Linda it was a trip back in time, to an almost unbelievable night nearly seven months ago.

Our first stop was 10050 Cielo Drive.

In late June of 1969, Bob Kasabian had called Linda at her mother's home in New Hampshire, suggesting a reconciliation. Kasabian was living in a trailer in Topanga Canyon with a friend, Charles Melton. Melton, who had recently inherited $20,000, and had already given away more than half, planned to drive to the tip of South America, buy a boat, and sail around the world. He'd invited Linda and Bob, as well as another couple, to come along.

Linda, together with her daughter, Tanya, flew to Los Angeles, but the reconciliation was unsuccessful.

On July 4, 1969, Catherine Share, aka Gypsy, visited Melton, whom she had met through Paul Watkins. Gypsy told Linda about "this beautiful man named Charlie," the Family, and how life at Spahn was all love, beauty, and peace. To Linda it was "as if the answer to an unspoken prayer."* That same day Linda and Tanya moved to Spahn. Though she didn't meet Manson that day, she did meet most of the other members of the Family, and they talked of little else. It was obvious to her that "they worshiped him."

That night Tex took her into a small room and told her "far-out things—nothing was wrong, all was right—things

*My interviews with Linda Kasabian were not taped. Exact quotations are from either my interview notes, her trial testimony, or her narrative letters to me.

I couldn't comprehend." Then "He made love to me, and a strange experience took place—it was like being possessed." When it was over, Linda's fingers were clenched so tightly they hurt. Gypsy later told her that what she had experienced was the death of the ego.

After making love, Linda and Tex talked, Linda mentioning Melton's inheritance. Tex told her that she should steal the money. According to Linda, she told him she couldn't do that—Melton was a friend, a brother. Tex told her that she could do no wrong and that everything should be shared. The next day Linda went back to the trailer and stole $5,000, which she gave to either Leslie or Tex. She had already turned over all her possessions to the Family, the girls having told her, "What's yours is ours and what's ours is yours."

Linda met Charles Manson for the first time that night. After all she had heard about him, she felt as if she were on trial. He asked why she had come to the ranch. She replied that her husband had rejected her. Manson reached out and felt her legs. "He seemed pleased with them," Linda recalled. Then he told her she could stay. Before making love to her, he told her that she had a father hang-up. Linda was startled by his perception, because she disliked her stepfather. She felt that Manson could see inside her.

Linda Kasabian became a part of the Family—went on garbage runs, had sex with the men, creepy-crawled a house, and listened as Manson lectured about the Beatles, Helter Skelter, and the bottomless pit. Charlie told her that the black man was together but the white man was not. However, he knew a way to unite the white man, he said. It was the only way. But he didn't tell her what it was.

Nor did she ask. From the first time they met, Manson had stressed, "Never ask why." When something he said or did puzzled her, she was reminded of this. Also of another of his favorite axioms, "No sense makes sense."

The whole Family, Linda said, was "paranoid of blackie." On weekends George Spahn did a brisk business renting horses. Occasionally among the riders there would be blacks. Manson maintained they were Panthers, spying on the Family. He always hid the young girls when they were around. At night everyone was required to wear dark clothing, so as to be less conspicuous, and eventually Manson posted armed guards, who roamed the ranch until dawn.

Gradually Linda became convinced that Charles Manson was Jesus Christ. He never told her this directly, but one day he asked her, "Don't you know who I am?"

She replied, "No, am I supposed to know something?"

He didn't answer, just smiled, and playfully twirled her around.

Yet she had doubts. The mothers were not allowed to care for their own children. They separated her and Tanya, Linda explained, because they wanted "to kill the ego that I put in her" and "at first I agreed to it, I thought that it was a good idea that she should become her own person." Also, several times she saw Manson strike Dianne Lake. Linda had been in many communes—from the American Psychedelic Circus in Boston to Sons of the Earth Mother near Taos—but she'd never seen anything like this, and, forgetting Charlie's commandment, she did ask Gypsy why. Gypsy told her that Dianne really wanted to be beaten, and Charlie was only obliging her.

Overriding all doubts was one fact: she had fallen in love with Charles Manson.

Linda had been at Spahn Ranch a little over a month when, on the afternoon of Friday, August 8, 1969, Manson told the Family: *"Now is the time for Helter Skelter."*

Had Linda stopped there, supplying that single piece of testimony and nothing else, she would have been a valuable witness. But Linda had a great deal more to tell.

That Friday evening, about an hour after dinner, seven or eight members of the Family were standing on the boardwalk in front of the saloon when Manson came out and, calling Tex, Sadie, Katie, and Linda aside, told each to get a change of clothing and a knife. He also told Linda to get her driver's license. Linda, I later learned, was the only Family member with a valid license, excepting Mary Brunner, who had been arrested that afternoon. This was, I concluded, probably one of the reasons why

Manson had picked Linda to accompany the others, each of whom, unlike her, had been with him a year or more.

Linda couldn't find her own knife (Sadie had it), but she obtained one from Larry Jones. The handle was broken and had been replaced with tape. Brenda found Linda's license and gave it to her just about the time Manson told Linda, "Go with Tex and do whatever Tex tells you to do."

According to Linda, in addition to Tex, Katie, and herself, Brenda McCann and Larry Jones were present when Manson gave this order.

Brenda remained hard core and refused to cooperate with law enforcement. Larry Jones, t/n Lawrence Bailey, was a scrawny little ranch hand who was always trying to ingratiate himself with the Family. However, Jones had what Manson considered negroid features and, according to Linda, Charlie was always putting him down, referring to him as "the drippings from a white man's dick." Since Jones had been present when Manson instructed the Tate killers, he could be a very important witness—providing independent corroboration of Linda Kasabian's testimony—and I asked LAPD to bring him in. They were unable to find him. I then gave the assignment to the DA's Bureau of Investigation, who located Jones, but he wouldn't give us the time of day.

Linda said that after Manson instructed her to go with Tex, the group piled into ranch hand Johnny Swartz' old Ford.

I asked Linda what each was wearing. She wasn't absolutely sure, but she thought Sadie had on a dark-blue T-shirt and dungarees, that Katie's attire was similar, and that Tex was wearing a black velour turtleneck and dark dungarees.

When shown the clothing the TV crew had found, Linda identified six of the seven items, failing to recall only the white T-shirt. The logical assumption was that she hadn't seen it because it had been worn under one of the other shirts.

What about footwear? I asked. The girls, she believed,

were all barefoot. She thought, but couldn't be sure, that Tex had on cowboy boots.

A number of bloody footprints had been found at the Tate murder scene. After eliminating those belonging to LAPD personnel, two remained unidentified: a boot-heel print and the print of a bare foot—thus supporting Linda's recollections. Again, as with Susan Atkins, I badly needed independent corroboration of Linda's testimony.

I then asked Linda the same question I'd asked Susan—had any of them been on drugs that night?—and received the same reply: no.

As Tex started to drive off, Manson said, "Hold it," or "Wait." He then leaned in the window on the passenger side and said, "Leave a sign. You girls know what to write. Something witchy."

Tex handed Linda three knives and a gun, telling her to wrap them in a rag and put them on the floor. If stopped by the police, Tex said, she was to throw them out.

Linda positively identified the .22 caliber Longhorn revolver. Only at this time, she said, the grip had been intact and the barrel unbent.

According to Linda, Tex did not tell them their destination, or what they were going to do; however, she presumed they were going on another creepy-crawly mission. Tex did say that he had been to the house and knew the layout.

As we drove up Cielo Drive in the sheriff's van, Linda showed me where Tex had turned, in front of the gate at 10050, then parked, next to the telephone pole. He had then taken a pair of large, red-handled wire cutters from the back seat and shinnied up the pole. From where she was sitting, Linda couldn't see Tex cutting the wires, but she saw and heard the wires fall.

When shown the wire cutters found at Barker Ranch, Linda said they "looked like" the pair used that night. Since the wire cutters had been found in Manson's personal dune buggy, her identification linked them not just to the Family but to Manson himself. I was especially pleased at this evidence, unaware that link would soon be severed, literally.

When Tex returned to the car, they drove to a spot near the bottom of the hill and parked. The four then took the weapons and extra clothing and stealthily walked back up to the gate. Tex also had some white rope, which was draped over his shoulder.

As Linda and I got out of the sheriff's van and approached the gate at 10050 Cielo Drive, two large dogs belonging to Rudi Altobelli began barking furiously at us. Linda suddenly began sobbing. "What are you crying about, Linda?" I asked.

Pointing to the dogs, she said, "Why couldn't they have been here that night?"

Linda pointed to the spot, to the right of the gate, where they had climbed the embankment and scaled the fence. As they were descending the other side, a pair of headlights suddenly appeared in the driveway. "Lay down and be quiet," Tex ordered. He then jumped up and ran to the automobile, which had stopped near the gate-control mechanism. Linda heard a man's voice saying, "Please don't hurt me! I won't say anything!" She then saw Tex put the gun in the open window on the driver's side and heard four shots. She also saw the man slump over in the seat.

(Something here puzzled me, and still does. In addition to the gunshot wounds, Steven Parent had a defensive stab wound that ran from the palm across the wrist of his left hand. It severed the tendons as well as the band of his wristwatch. Obviously, Parent had raised his left hand, the hand closest to the open window, in an effort to protect himself, the force of the blow being sufficient to hurl his watch into the back seat. It therefore appeared that Tex must have approached the car with a knife in one hand, a gun in the other, and that he first slashed at Parent, then shot him. Yet neither Susan nor Linda saw Tex with a knife at this point, nor did either recall the stabbing.)

Linda saw Tex reach in the car and turn off the lights and ignition. He then pushed the car some distance up the driveway, telling the others to follow him.

The shooting put her in a state of shock, Linda said.

"My mind went blank. I was aware of my body, walking toward the house."

As we went up the driveway, I asked Linda which lights had been on that night. She pointed to the bug light on the side of the garage, also the Christmas-tree lights along the fence. Little details, yet important if the defense contended Linda was fabricating her story from what she had read in the papers, since neither these, nor numerous other details I collected, had appeared in the press.

As we approached the residence, I noticed that Linda was shivering and her arms were covered with goose bumps. Though it wasn't cold that day, Linda was now nine months pregnant, and I slipped off my coat and put it over her shoulders. The shivering continued, however, all the time we were on the premises, and often, in pointing out something, she would begin crying. There was no question in my mind that the tears were real and that she was deeply affected by what had happened in this place. I couldn't help contrasting Linda with Susan.

When they reached the house, Linda said, Tex sent her around the back to look for an unlocked window or door. She reported that everything was locked, though she hadn't actually checked. (This explained why they ignored the open nursery window.) Tex then slit a screen on one of the front windows with a knife. Though the actual screen had since been replaced, Linda pointed to the correct window. She also said the slash was horizontal, as it had been. Tex then told her to go back and wait by the car in the driveway.

Linda did as she was told. Perhaps a minute or two later Katie came back and asked Linda for her knife (this was the knife with the taped handle) and told her, "Listen for sounds."

A few minutes later Linda heard "horrifying sounds" coming from the house. A man moaned, "No, no, no," then screamed very loudly. The scream, which seemed continuous, was punctuated with other voices, male and female, begging and pleading for their lives.

Wanting "to stop what was happening," Linda said, "I started running toward the house." As she reached the walk, "there was a man, a tall man, just coming out of the door, staggering, and he had blood all over his face, and he was standing by a post, and we looked into each other's eyes for a minute, I don't know however long, and I said, 'Oh, God, I'm so sorry.' And then he just fell into the bushes.

"And then Sadie came running out of the house, and I said, 'Sadie, *please* make it stop! People are coming!' Which wasn't true, but I wanted to make it stop. And she said, 'It's too late.' "

Complaining that she had lost her knife, Susan ran back into the house. Linda remained outside. (Susan had earlier told me, and the grand jury, that Linda had never entered the residence.) Turning, Linda saw a dark-haired woman in a white gown running across the lawn; Katie was pursuing her, an upraised knife in her hand. Somehow, the tall man managed to stagger from the bushes next to the porch onto the lawn, where he had again fallen. Linda saw Tex hit him over the head with something—it could have been a gun but she wasn't sure—then stab him repeatedly in the back as he lay on the ground.

(Shown a number of photographs, Linda identified the tall man as Voytek Frykowski, the dark-haired woman as Abigail Folger. Examining the autopsy report on Frykowski, I found that five of his fifty-one stab wounds were to the back.)

Linda turned and ran down the driveway. For what seemed like maybe five minutes, she hid in the bushes near the gate, then climbed the fence again and ran down Cielo to where they had parked the Ford.

Q. "Why didn't you run to one of the houses and call the police?" I asked Linda.

A. "My first thought was 'Get help!' Then my little girl entered my mind—she was back [at the ranch] with Charlie. I didn't know where I was or how to get out of there."

She got in the car and had started the engine when "all of a sudden they were there. They were covered with blood. They looked like zombies. Tex yelled at me to turn off the car and get over. He had a terrible look in his eyes." Linda slid over to the passenger side. "Then he started in on Sadie and yelled at her for losing her knife."

Tex had put the .22 revolver on the seat between them. Linda noticed that the grip was broken, and Tex told her it had smashed when he hit the man over the head. Sadie and Katie complained that their heads hurt because the people had pulled their hair while they were fighting with them. Sadie also said the big man had hit her over the head and that "the girl"—it was unclear whether she meant Sharon or Abigail—had cried for her mother. Katie also complained that her hand hurt, explaining that when she stabbed, she kept hitting bones, and since the knife didn't have a regular handle, it bruised her hand.

Q. "How did *you* feel, Linda?"

A. "In a state of shock."

Q. "What about the others, how did they act?"

A. "As if it was all a game."

Tex, Sadie, and Katie changed their clothing while the car was in motion, Linda holding the wheel for Tex. Linda herself didn't change, since there was no blood on her. Tex told them he wanted to find a place to hose the blood off, and he turned off Benedict Canyon onto a short street not too far from the Tate residence.

Linda's account of the hosing incident paralleled Susan Atkins' and Rudolf Weber's. Weber's house was located 1.8 miles from the Tate premises.

From there Tex turned onto Benedict Canyon again and drove along through a dark, hilly country area. He stopped the car on a dirt shoulder off the road, and Tex, Sadie, and Katie gave Linda their bloody clothing, which, on Tex's instructions, she rolled up in one bundle and threw down the slope. Since it was dark, she couldn't see where it landed.

After driving off, Tex told Linda to wipe the knives clean of fingerprints, then throw them out the window. She did, the first knife hitting a bush at the side of the road, the second, which she tossed out a few seconds later, striking the curb and bouncing back into the road. Looking back, she saw it lying there. Linda believed she threw the gun out a few minutes later but she wasn't sure; it was possible that Tex did it.

After driving for a time, they stopped at a gas station—Linda was unable to recall the street—where Katie and Sadie took turns going into the rest room to wash the rest of the blood off their bodies. Then they drove back to Spahn Ranch.

Linda did not have a watch but guessed it must have been about 2 A.M. Charles Manson was standing on the boardwalk in the same spot where he had been when they drove off.

Sadie said she saw some blood on the outside of the car, and Manson had the girls get rags and sponges and wash the car inside and out.

He then told them to go to the bunkhouse. Brenda and Clem were already there. Manson asked Tex how it had gone. Tex told him that there was a lot of panic, that it was real messy, and that there were bodies lying all over the place, but that everyone was dead.

Manson asked the four, "Do you have any remorse?" All shook their heads and said, "No."

Linda did feel remorse, she told me, but she didn't admit it to Charlie because "I was afraid for my life. I could see in his eyes he knew how I felt. And it was against his way."

Manson told them, "Go to bed and say nothing to the others."

Linda slept most of the day. It was almost sundown when Sadie told her to go into the trailer, that the TV news was coming on. Although Linda could not recall seeing Tex, she remembered Sadie, Katie, Barbara Hoyt, and Clem being there.

It was the big news. For the first time Linda heard the names of the victims. She also learned that one, Sharon Tate, had been pregnant. Only a few days earlier Linda had learned that she herself was pregnant.

"As we were watching the news," Linda said, "in my head I kept saying, 'Why would they do such a thing?' "

After Linda and I left the Tate residence, I asked her to show us the route they had taken. She found the dirt shoulder where they had pulled off to dispose of the clothing, but was unable to find the street where Tex had turned off Benedict Canyon, so I had the sheriff's deputy who was driving take us directly to Portola. Once on the street, Linda immediately identified 9870, pointing to the hose in front. Number 9870 was Rudolf Weber's house. She also pointed to the spot where they had parked the car. It was the same spot Weber had indicated. Neither his address, nor even the fact that he had been located, had appeared in the press.

We were back on Benedict looking for the area where Linda had thrown out the knives when one of the deputies said, "We've got company."

Looking out the window, we saw we were being followed by a Channel 2 TV unit. Its presence in the area may have been a coincidence, but I doubted it. More likely, someone at the jail or in the courts had alerted the press that we were taking Linda out. All this time only a few people knew that Linda Kasabian would be a witness for the prosecution. I'd hoped to keep this secret as long as possible. I'd also hoped to take Linda to the LaBianca residence and several other sites, but now that would have to wait. Telling Linda to turn her head away so she wouldn't be recognized, I asked the driver to hightail it back to Sybil Brand.

Once on the freeway, we tried to outrun the TV unit, but without success. They filmed us all the way. It was like a Mack Sennett comedy, only with the press in pursuit of the fuzz.

After Linda was back in jail, I asked Sergeant McGann to get some cadets from the Police Academy, or a troop of Boy Scouts, and conduct a search for the knives. From Linda's testimony, we knew that they had probably been thrown out of the car somewhere between the clothing site and the hill where young Steven Weiss had found the gun, an area of less than two miles. We also knew that since Linda had looked back and seen one of the knives lying in the road, there must have been some illumination nearby, which could be another clue.

The following day, March 4, Gypsy made another visit to Fleischman's office. She told him, in the presence of his law partner Ronald Goldman, "If Linda testifies, thirty people are going to do something about it."

I'd already checked out the security at Sybil Brand. Until her baby was born, Linda was being kept in an isolation cell off the infirmary. She had no contact with the other inmates; deputies brought her meals. After the baby was born, however, she would be reassigned to one of the open dormitories, where she might be threatened, even killed, by Sadie, Katie, or Leslie. I made a note to talk to Captain Carpenter to see if other arrangements could be made.

Attorney Richard Caballero had been able to postpone the inevitable, but he couldn't prevent it. The meeting between Susan Atkins and Charles Manson took place in the Los Angeles County Jail on March 5. Caballero, who was present, would later testify: "One of the first things they wanted to know was whether either one had gotten to see Linda Kasabian yet." Neither having done so, it was decided both should keep trying.

Manson asked Susan, "Are you afraid of the gas chamber?"

Susan grinned and replied that she wasn't.

With that, Caballero must have realized that he had lost her.

Susan and Charlie talked for an hour or so more, but Caballero hadn't the foggiest idea of what they said. "At some point in the conversation they began to talk in sort of a double talk or pig Latin," and "when they reached that point they lost me."

However, the looks they exchanged said it all. It was like a "joyous homecoming." Sadie Mae Glutz had returned to the irresistible Charles Manson.

She fired Caballero the next day.

On March 6, Manson appeared in court and argued a number of novel motions. One asked that the "Deputy District Attorneys in charge of the trial be incarcerated for a period of time under the same circumstances that I have been subject to . . ." Another requested that he "be free to travel to any place I should deem fit in preparing my defense . . ."

There were more, and Judge Keene declared himself

"appalled" at Manson's "outlandish" requests. Keene then said he had reviewed the entire file on the case, from his "nonsensical" motions to his numerous violations of the gag order. He had also discussed Manson's conduct with Judges Lucas and Dell, before whom Manson had also appeared, concluding that it had become "abundantly clear to me that you are incapable of acting as your own attorney."

Infuriated, Manson shouted, "It's not me that's on trial here as much as this court is on trial!" He also told the judge, "Go wash your hands. They're dirty."

THE COURT "Mr. Manson, your status, at this time, of acting as your own attorney is now vacated."

Against Manson's strong objections, Keene appointed Charles Hollopeter, a former president of the Los Angeles Criminal Courts Bar, as Manson's attorney of record.

"You can kill me," Manson said, "but you can't give me an attorney. I won't take one."

Keene told Manson that if he found an attorney of his own choosing, he would consider a motion to substitute him for Hollopeter. I knew Hollopeter by reputation. Since he'd never be Charlie's bootlicker, I guessed he'd last about a month; I was too generous.

Toward the end of the proceedings, Manson shouted, *"There is no God in this courtroom!"* As if on cue, a number of Family members jumped up and yelled at Keene, "You are a mockery of justice! You are a joke!" The judge found three of them—Gypsy, Sandy, and Mark Ross—in contempt, and sentenced each to five days in the County Jail.

When Sandy was searched prior to being booked, among the items found in her purse was a Buck knife.

After this, the sheriff's deputies, who are in charge of maintaining security in the Los Angeles criminal courts, began searching all spectators before they entered the courtroom.

On March 7, Linda Kasabian was taken to the hospital. Two days later she gave birth to a boy, whom she named Angel. On the thirteenth she was returned to the jail, without the child, Linda's mother having taken him back to New Hampshire.

In the interim I had talked to Captain Carpenter, and he had agreed to let Linda remain in her former cell just off the infirmary. I checked it out myself. It was a small room, its furnishings consisting of a bed, toilet bowl, wash-basin, and a small desk and chair. It was clean but bleak. Far more important, it was safe.

Every few days I called McGann. No, he hadn't got around to looking for the knives yet.

On March 11, Susan Atkins, after formally requesting that Richard Caballero be relieved as her attorney, asked for Daye Shinn in Caballero's place.

Inasmuch as Shinn, one of the first attorneys to call on Manson after he was brought down from Independence, had represented Manson on several matters and had visited him more than forty times, Judge Keene felt there might be a possible conflict of interest involved.

Shinn denied this. Keene then warned Susan of the possible dangers of being represented by an attorney who had been so closely involved with one of her co-defendants. Susan said she didn't care; she wanted Shinn. Keene granted the substitution.

I hadn't come up against Shinn before. He was about forty, Korean born; according to the press, his main practice, before allying himself with the Manson defense, had been obtaining Mexican domestics for Southern California families.

On leaving the courtroom, Shinn told waiting reporters that Susan Atkins "definitely will deny everything she told the grand jury."

On March 15 we took Linda Kasabian out again. Only this time we used not a conspicuous sheriff's van but unmarked police cars.

I wanted Linda to trace the route the killers had taken the night the LaBiancas were killed.

After dinner that night—Saturday, August 9, 1969—Linda and several other Family members were standing outside the kitchen at Spahn. Manson called Linda, Katie, and Leslie aside and told them to get a change of clothing and meet him in the bunkhouse.

This time he mentioned nothing to Linda about knives, but he did tell her again to get her driver's license.

"I just looked at him and, you know, just sort of pleaded with my eyes, please don't make me go, because," Linda said, "I just knew we were going out again, and I knew it would be the same thing, but I was afraid to say anything."

"Last night was too messy," Manson told the group when they assembled in the bunkhouse. "This time I'm going to show you how to do it."

Tex complained that the weapons they had used the previous night weren't effective enough!

Linda saw two swords in the bunkhouse, one of which was the Straight Satans' sword. She did not see anyone pick them up, but later she noticed the Satans' sword and two smaller knives under the front seat of the car. In questioning DeCarlo, I'd learned that one night about this time he'd noticed that the sword had been taken out.

Again the group piled into Swartz' Ford. This time Manson himself slipped into the driver's seat, with Linda next to him, Clem on the passenger side, Tex, Sadie, Katie, and Leslie crowded in back. All wore dark clothing, Linda said, except for Clem, who had on an olive-drab field jacket. As he often did, Manson wore a leather thong around his neck, the two ends extending down to his breastbone, where they were looped together. I asked Linda if anyone else was wearing such a thong; she said no.

Before they left, Manson asked Bruce Davis for some money. Just as DeCarlo took care of the Family guns, Davis acted as comptroller for the group, taking care of the stolen credit cards, fake ID, and so forth.

As they drove off, Manson told them that tonight they would divide into two groups: each would take a separate house. He said he'd drop off one group, then take the second group with him.

When they stopped to buy gas (using cash, not a credit card), Manson told Linda to take over the driving. Questioning Linda, I established that Manson—and Manson alone—gave all the instructions as to where they were to go and what they were to do. At no time, she said, did Tex Watson instruct anyone to do anything. Charlie was in complete command.

Following Manson's directions, Linda took the freeway to Pasadena. Once off it, he gave her so many directions she was unsure where they were. Eventually he told her to stop in front of a house, which Linda described as a modern, one-story, middle-class-type home. This was the place where, as described by Susan Atkins, Manson got out, had them drive around the block, then got back in, telling them that, having looked in the window and seen photographs of children, he didn't want to "do" that particular house, though, he added, in the future it might be necessary to kill children also. Linda's account was essentially the same as Susan's.

After riding around Pasadena for some time, Manson again took over the driving. Linda: "I remember we started driving up a hill with lots of houses, nice houses, rich houses, and trees. We got to the top of the hill and turned around and stopped in front of a certain house." Linda couldn't remember if it was one story or two, only that it was big. Manson, however, said the houses were too close together here, so they drove off.

Shortly after this, Manson spotted a church. Pulling into the parking lot next to it, he again got out. Linda believed, but wasn't absolutely sure, that he told them he was going to "get" the minister or priest.

However, he returned a few minutes later, saying the church door was locked.

Susan Atkins had neglected to mention the church in her account. I learned of it for the first time from Linda Kasabian.

Manson again told Linda to drive, but the route he gave her was so confusing that she soon became lost. Later, driving up Sunset from the ocean, there occurred another incident which Susan Atkins had neglected to mention.

Observing a white sports car ahead of them, Manson

told Linda, "At the next red light, pull up beside it. I'm going to kill the driver."

Linda pulled up next to the car, but just as Manson jumped out, the light changed to green and the sports car zoomed away.

Another potential victim, unaware to this day how close to death he had come.

Thus far, their wanderings appeared totally at random, Manson seemingly having no particular victims in mind. As I'd later argue to the jury, up to this time no one in the vast, sprawling metropolis of seven million people, whether in a home, a church, or even a car, was safe from Manson's insatiable lust for death, blood, and murder.

But after the sports-car incident, Manson's directions became very specific. He directed Linda to the Los Feliz section of Los Angeles, not far from Griffith Park, having her stop on the street in front of a home in a residential area.

Linda recognized the house. In June of 1968 she and her husband had been driving from Seattle to Taos when they stopped off in Los Angeles. A friend had taken them to the house—3267 Waverly Drive—for a peyote party. One of the men who were living there, she recalled, was named Harold. In another of the many coincidences which abounded in this case, Linda had also been to the Harold True residence, though at a time none of the Family members were there.

Linda asked, "Charlie, you're not going to do that house, are you?"

Manson replied, "No, the one next door."

Telling the others to stay in the car, Manson got out. Linda noticed him shove something into his belt, but she couldn't see what it was. She watched him walking up the driveway until it curved and he disappeared from sight.

I presumed, although I couldn't be sure of this, that Manson had a gun.

For Rosemary and Leno LaBianca, the horror that would end in their deaths had begun.

Linda guessed the time was about 2 A.M. Some ten minutes later, she said, Manson returned to the car.

I asked Linda if he was still wearing the leather thong around his neck. She said she hadn't noticed, though she did notice, later that night, that he no longer had it. I showed her the leather thong used to bind the wrists of Leno LaBianca, and she said it was "the same kind" Manson had been wearing.

Manson told Tex, Katie, and Leslie to get out of the car and bring their clothing bundles with them. Obviously they were to be the first team. Linda heard some, though not all, of the conversation. Manson told the trio that there were two people inside the house, that he had tied them up and told them that everything was going to be all right, and that they shouldn't be afraid. He also instructed Tex, Katie, and Leslie that they were not to cause fear and panic in the people as had happened the night before.

The LaBiancas had been creepy-crawled, pacified with Charles Manson's unctuous assurances, then set up to be slaughtered.

Linda heard only bits and pieces of the rest of the conversation. She did not hear Manson specifically order the three to kill the two persons. Nor did she see them carrying any weapons. She believed she heard Manson say, "Don't let them know you are going to kill them." And she definitely heard him instruct them that when they were done they were to hitchhike back to the ranch.

As the trio started toward the house, Manson got back in the car and handed Linda a woman's wallet, telling her to wipe off the prints and remove the change. In opening it, she noticed the driver's license, which had a photo of a woman with dark hair. She recalled the woman's first name was "Rosemary," while the last name "was either Mexican or Italian." She also remembered seeing a number of credit cards and a wrist watch.

When I asked Linda the color of the wallet, she said it was red. Actually it was brown. She also claimed to have removed all the change, but when the wallet was found there were still some coins in one of the inner compartments. Both were understandable errors, I felt, particularly overlooking the extra change compartment.

Manson again took over the driving. Linda was now on the passenger side, Susan and Clem in back. Manson told Linda that when they reached a predominantly colored area he wanted her to toss the wallet out onto a sidewalk, so a black person would find it, use the credit cards, and be arrested. This would make people think the Panthers had committed the murders, he explained.

Manson drove onto the freeway not far from where they had dropped off Tex, Katie, and Leslie. After driving for a long time, he pulled off the freeway and stopped at a nearby service station. Apparently having changed his plans, Manson now told Linda to put the wallet in the women's rest room. Linda did, only she hid it too well, lifting the top of the toilet tank and placing it over the bulb, where it would remain undiscovered for four months.

I asked Linda if she could remember anything distinctive about the station. She remembered there was a restaurant next door and that it seemed "to radiate the color orange."

There was a Denny's Restaurant next to the Standard station in Sylmar, with a large orange sign.

While Linda was in the rest room, Manson went to the restaurant, returning with four milk shakes.

Probably at the same time the LaBiancas were being murdered, the man who had ordered their deaths was sipping a milk shake.

Again Manson had Linda drive. After a long time, perhaps an hour, they reached the beach somewhere south of Venice. Linda recalled seeing some oil storage tanks. All four got out of the car, Sadie and Clem, at Charlie's instructions, dropping behind while he and Linda walked ahead in the sand.

Suddenly Manson was again all love. It was as if the events of the last forty-eight hours had never happened. Linda told Charlie that she was pregnant. Manson took Linda's hand and, as she described it, "it was sort of nice, you know, we were just talking, I gave him some peanuts, and he just sort of made me forget about everything, made me feel good."

Would the jury understand this? I thought so, once they

understood Manson's charismatic personality and Linda's love for him.

Just as they reached a side street, a police car pulled up and two officers got out. They asked the pair what they were doing.

Charlie replied, "We were just going for a walk." Then, as if they should recognize him, he asked, "Don't you know who I am?" or "Don't you remember my name?" They said, "No," then returned to the patrol car and drove off, without asking either for identification. It was, Linda said, "a friendly conversation," lasting only a minute.

Finding the two officers on duty in the area that night should be fairly easy, I thought, unaware how wrong I could be.

Clem and Sadie were already back in the car when they returned. Manson then told Linda to drive to Venice. En route he asked the three if they knew anyone there. None did. Manson then asked Linda, "What about the man you and Sandy met in Venice? Wasn't he a piggy?" Linda replied, "Yes, he's an actor." Manson told her to drive to his apartment.

I asked Linda about the actor.

One afternoon in early August, Linda said, she and Sandy had been hitchhiking near the pier when this man picked them up. He told them he was Israeli or Arab—Linda couldn't recall which—and that he had appeared in a movie about Kahlil Gibran. The two girls were hungry, and he drove them to his apartment and fixed them lunch. Afterward, Sandy napped and Linda and the man made love. Before the girls left, he gave them some food and spare clothing. Linda couldn't remember the man's name, only that it was foreign. However, she felt sure she could find the apartment house, as she had located it when Manson asked her to drive there that night.

When they pulled up in front, Manson asked Linda if the man would let her in. "I think so," she replied. What about Sadie and Clem? Linda said she guessed so. Manson then handed her a pocketknife and demonstrated how he wanted her to slit the actor's throat.

Linda said she couldn't do it. "I'm not you, Charlie," Linda told Manson. "I can't kill anybody."

Manson asked her to take him to the man's apartment. Linda led Charlie up the stairs, but deliberately pointed to the wrong door.

On returning to the car, Manson gave the trio explicit instructions. They were to go to the actor's apartment. Linda was to knock. When the man let her in, Sadie and Clem were to go in also. Once they were inside, Linda was to slit the man's throat and Clem was to shoot him. When finished, they were to hitchhike back to the ranch.

Linda saw Manson hand Clem a gun, but was unable to describe it. Nor did she know if Sadie also had a knife.

"If anything goes wrong," Manson told them, "just hang it up, don't do it." He then slid into the driver's seat and drove off.

Like the church and sports-car incidents, Susan Atkins had not mentioned the Venice incident to me, nor had she said anything about it when testifying before the grand jury. While I felt that she might have forgotten the two earlier incidents, I suspected the third was omitted intentionally, since it directly involved her as a willing partner in still another attempted murder. It was possible, however, that had I had more time to interview Susan, this too might have come out.

The actor's apartment was on the top, or fifth, floor, but Linda did not tell Clem or Sadie this. Instead, on reaching the fourth floor, she knocked on the first door she saw. Eventually a man sleepily asked, "Who is it?" She replied, "Linda." When the man opened the door a crack, Linda said, "Oh, excuse me, I have the wrong apartment."

The door was open only a second or two and Linda caught just a glimpse of the man. She had the impression, though she was unsure of this, that he was middle-aged.

The three then left the building, but not before Sadie, ever the animal, defecated on the landing.

It was obvious that Linda Kasabian had prevented still another Manson-ordered murder. As independent evidence corroborating her story, it was important that we locate not only the actor but the man who answered the door.

Perhaps he'd remember being awakened at 4 or 5 A.M. by a pretty young girl.

From the apartment house Clem, Sadie, and Linda walked to the beach, a short distance away. Clem wanted to ditch the gun. He disappeared from sight behind a sandpile, near a fence. Linda presumed that he had either buried the gun or tossed it over the fence.

Walking back to the Pacific Coast Highway, they hitched a ride to the entrance of Topanga Canyon. There was a hippie crash pad nearby, next door to the Malibu Feedbin, and Sadie said she knew a girl who was staying there. Linda recalled there was also an older man there, and a big dog. The three stayed about an hour, smoking some weed, then left.

They then hitched two rides, the last taking them all the way to the entrance of Santa Susana Pass Road, where Clem and Linda got out. Sadie, Linda learned the next day, remained in the car until it reached the waterfall area.

When Linda and Clem arrived at the ranch, Tex and Leslie were already there, asleep in one of the rooms. She didn't see Katie, though she learned the next day that, like Sadie, she had gone on to the camp by the waterfall. Linda went to bed in the saloon.

Two days later Linda Kasabian fled Spahn Ranch. The manner of her departure, however, would cause the prosecution a great deal of concern.

Rather than taking Linda directly to the LaBianca residence, I had the sheriff's deputy drive to the Los Feliz area, to see if Linda could find the house itself. She did, pointing out both the LaBianca and True houses, the place where they had parked, the driveway up which Manson had walked, and so on.

I also wanted to find the two houses in Pasadena where Manson had stopped earlier that night, but, though we spent hours looking for them, we were, at this time, unsuccessful. Linda did find the apartment house where the actor had lived, 1101 Ocean Front Walk, and pointed out both his apartment, 501, and the door on which she had knocked, 403. I asked Patchett and Gutierrez to locate and interview both the actor and the man who had been living in 403.

Linda also showed us the sandpile near the fence where she believed Clem had disposed of the gun, but though we got out shovels and dug up the area, we were unable to locate the weapon. It was possible that someone had already found it, or that Clem or one of the other Family members had reclaimed it later. We never did learn what type of gun it was.

Having been out since early in the morning, we stopped at a Chinese restaurant for lunch. That afternoon we returned to Pasadena and must have driven past forty churches before Linda found the one where Manson had stopped. I asked LAPD to photograph it and the adjoining parking lot as a trial exhibit.

Linda also identified the Standard station in Sylmar where she'd left the wallet, as well as Denny's Restaurant next door.

Despite all our security precautions, we were spotted. The next day the *Herald Examiner* reported: "In addition to winning immunity, Mrs. Kasabian was given a 'bonus' in the form of a Chinese dinner at Madam Wu's Garden Restaurant in Santa Monica. Restaurant employees confirmed Mrs. Kasabian, defense attorney Fleischman and Prosecutor Bugliosi ate there Sunday."

The paper neglected to mention that our party included a half dozen LAPD officers and two LASO deputies.

We took Linda out twice more, trying to find the two houses in Pasadena. On both occasions we were accompanied by South Pasadena PD officers who directed us to neighborhoods similar to those Linda had described. We finally found the large house atop the hill. Though I had it and the adjoining houses photographed—they were close together, as Manson had said—I decided against talking to the owners, sure they would sleep better not knowing how close to death they had come. We were never able to locate the first house—which both Susan and Linda had described—where Manson looked in the window and saw the photographs of the children.

We did grant Linda one special privilege, which might have been called a "bonus." On the three occasions we took her out of Sybil Brand, we let her call her mother in New Hampshire and talk to her two children. Her attorney paid for the calls. Though Angel was only a month old and much too young to understand, just speaking to them obviously meant a great deal to Linda.

Yet she never asked to do this. She never asked for anything. She told me not once but several times that although she was pleased to be getting immunity, because it meant that eventually she could be with her children, it didn't matter that much if she didn't get it. There was a sort of sad fatalism about her. She said she knew she had to tell the truth about what had happened, and that she had known she would be the one to tell the story ever since the murders occurred. Unlike the other defendants, she seemed burdened with guilt, though, again unlike them, she hadn't physically harmed anyone. She was a strange girl, marked by her time with Manson, yet not molded by him in the same way the others were. Because she was compliant, easily led, Manson apparently had had little trouble controlling her. Up to a point. But she had refused to cross that point. "I'm not you, Charlie. I can't kill anybody."

Once I asked her what she thought about Manson now. She was still in love with him, Linda said. "Some things he said were the truth," she observed thoughtfully. "Only now I realize he could take a truth and make a lie of it."

Shortly after the story broke that Linda Kasabian would testify for the prosecution, Al Wiman, the reporter with the Channel 7 crew which had found the clothing, showed up in my office. If Kasabian was cooperating with us, then she must have indicated where she threw the knives, Wiman surmised. He begged me to pinpoint the area; his station, he promised, would supply a search crew, metal detectors, everything.

"Look, Al," I told him, "you guys have already found the clothing. How is it going to look at the trial if you find the knives too? Tell you what. I'm trying to get someone out. If they won't go, then I'll tell you."

After Wiman left, I called McGann. *Two weeks* had passed since I'd asked him to look for the knives; he still hadn't done it. My patience at an end, I called Lieutenant Helder and told him about Wiman's offer. "Think how LAPD is going to look if it comes out during the trial that a ten-year-old boy found the gun and Channel 7 found both the clothing and the knives."

Bob had a crew out the next day. No luck. But at least during the trial we'd be prepared to prove that they had looked. Otherwise, the defense could contend that LAPD was so skeptical of Linda Kasabian's story that they hadn't even bothered to mount a search.

That they'd failed to find the knives was a disappointment, but not too much of a surprise. Over seven months had passed since the night Linda tossed the knives out of the car. According to her testimony, one had bounced back into the road, while the other had landed in the bushes nearby. The street, though in the country, was much traveled. It was quite possible they had been picked up by a motorist or passing cyclist.

I had no idea how often the police had interviewed Winifred Chapman, the Polanskis' maid. I'd talked to her a number of times myself before I realized there was one question so obvious we'd all overlooked it.

Mrs. Chapman had stated that she washed the front door of the Tate residence just after noon on Friday, August 8. This meant Charles Watson had to have left his print there sometime after this.

However, there was a *second* print found at the Tate residence, Patricia Krenwinkel's, located inside the door that led from Sharon Tate's bedroom to the pool.

I asked Mrs. Chapman: "Did you ever wash that door?" Yes. How often? A couple of times a week. She had to, she explained, because the guests usually used that door to get to the pool.

The big question: "Did you wash it the week of the murders, and, if so, when?"

A. "Tuesday was the last time. I washed it down, inside and out, with vinegar and water."

Under discovery, I was only required to make a note of the conversation and put it in our tubs. However, in fairness to both Fitzgerald and his client, I called Paul and told him, "If you're planning on having Krenwinkel testify that she went swimming at the Tate residence a couple of weeks before the murders and left her print at that time, better forget it. Mrs. Chapman is going to testify she washed that door on Tuesday, August 5."

Paul was grateful for the information. Had he based his defense on this premise, Mrs. Chapman's testimony could have been devastating.

There was, in such conversations, something assumed though unstated. Whatever his public posture, I was sure that Fitzgerald knew that his client was guilty, and he knew that I knew it. Though only on rare occasions does a defense attorney slip up and admit this in court, when it comes to in-chambers discussions and private conversations, it's often something else.

There were two items of evidence in our files which I did not point out to the defense. I was sure they had already seen them—both were among the items photocopied for them—but I was hoping they wouldn't realize their importance.

One was a traffic ticket, the other an arrest report. Separately each seemed unimportant. Together they made a bomb that would demolish Manson's alibi defense.

On first learning from Fowles that Manson might claim that he was not in the Los Angeles area at the time of the murders, I had asked LaBianca detectives Patchett and Gutierrez to see if they could obtain evidence proving his actual whereabouts on the subject dates. They did an excellent job. Together with information obtained from credit card transactions and interviews, they were able to piece together a timetable of Manson's activities during the week preceding the start of Helter Skelter.

On about August 1, 1969, Manson told several Family members that he was going to Big Sur to seek out new recruits.

He apparently left on the morning of Sunday, August 3, as sometime between seven and eight he purchased gas at a station in Canoga Park, using a stolen credit card. From Canoga Park, he headed north toward Big Sur. At about four the next morning, he picked up a young girl, Stephanie Schram, outside a service station some distance south of Big Sur, probably at Gorda. An attractive seventeen-year-old, Stephanie was hitchhiking from San Francisco to San Diego, where she was living with her married sister. Manson and Stephanie camped in a nearby canyon that night—probably Salmon or Limekiln Creek, both hippie hangouts—Manson telling her his views on life, love and death. Manson talked a lot about death, Stephanie would recall, and it frightened her. They took LSD and had sex. Manson was apparently unusually smitten with Stephanie. Usually he'd have sex with a new girl a few times, then move on to a new "young love." Not so with Stephanie. He later told Paul Watkins that Stephanie, who was of German extraction, was the result of two thousand years of perfect breeding.

On August 4, Manson, still using the stolen credit card, purchased gas at Lucia. Ripping off the place, which bore a large sign reading "Hippies Not Allowed," must have given him a special satisfaction, as he did it again the next day.

On the night of the fifth Manson and Stephanie drove north to a place whose name Stephanie couldn't recall but which Manson described as a "sensitivity camp." It was, he told her, a place where rich people went on weekends to play at being enlightened. He was obviously describing Esalen Institute.

Esalen was, at this time, just coming into vogue as a "growth center," its seminars including such diverse figures as yogis and psychiatrists, salvationists and satanists. Obviously Manson felt Esalen a prime place to espouse his philosophies. It is unknown whether he had been there on prior occasions, those involved in the Institute refusing to even acknowledge his visits there.*

*At 3:07 P.M., July 30, 1969, someone at the Tate residence called the Esalen Institute, Big Sur, California, telephone number 408-667-2335. It was a brief station-to-station call, total charge 95 cents. It is unknown who placed the call, or—since the number is that of the switchboard—who was called.

Since the call occurred just six days before Charles Manson's visit to Esalen, it arouses a certain amount of speculation. A few things are known, however: none of the Tate victims was at Big Sur during the period Manson was there; Abigail Folger had attended semi-

Manson took his guitar and left Stephanie in the van. After a time she fell asleep. When she awakened the next morning, Manson had already returned. He was in less than a good mood, as, later that day, he unexpectedly struck her. Still later, at Barker Ranch, Manson would tell Paul Watkins—to quote Watkins—that while at Big Sur he had gone "to Esalen and played his guitar for a bunch of people who were supposed to be the top people there, and they rejected his music. Some people pretended that they were asleep, and other people were saying, 'This is too heavy for me,' and 'I'm not ready for that,' and others were saying, 'Well, I don't understand it,' and some just got up and walked out."

Still another rejection by what Manson considered the establishment—this occurring just three days before the Tate murders.

With his single recruit, Manson left Big Sur on August 6, making gas purchases that same day at San Luis Obispo and Chatsworth, a few miles from Spahn Ranch. According to Stephanie, they had dinner at the ranch that night and she met the Family for the first time. She felt uncomfortable with them, and, learning that Manson shared his favors with the other girls, told him she would stay only if he would promise to remain with her, and her alone, for two weeks. Surprisingly, Manson agreed. They spent that night in the van, parked not far from the ranch, then drove to San Diego the next day to pick up Stephanie's clothes.

En route, about ten miles south of Oceanside on Interstate 5, they were stopped by California Highway Patrol officer Richard C. Willis. Though pulled over for a mechanical violation, Manson was cited only for having no valid driver's license in his possession. Manson gave his correct name and the ranch address, and signed the ticket

---

nars at Esalen in the past; and several of her San Francisco friends visited there periodically. It is possible that she was simply trying to locate someone, but this is just a guess.

Though both the call and Manson's visit to Esalen remain mysterious, I should perhaps note that, with a single exception—the Hatami-Tate-Manson confrontation on March 23, 1969—I was unable to find a prior link of any kind between any of the Tate-LaBianca victims and their killers.

himself. Officer Willis noted on the ticket that Manson was driving a "1952 cream-colored Ford bakery van, license number K70683." The date was Thursday, August 7, 1969; the time 6:15 P.M.

The ticket, which Patchett and Gutierrez found, proved Manson was in Southern California the day before the Tate murders.

While Stephanie was getting her clothes together, Manson talked to her sister, who was also a Beatles fan. She had the White Album, and Manson told her the Beatles had laid out "the whole scene" in it. He warned her that the blacks were getting ready to overthrow the whites and that only those who fled to the desert and hid in the bottomless pit would be safe. As for those who remained in the cities, Manson said, "People are going to be slaughtered, they'll be lying on their lawns dead."

Just a little over twenty-four hours later, his prediction would be fulfilled, in all its gory detail, at 10050 Cielo Drive. With a little help from his friends.

That night, according to Stephanie, she and Charlie parked somewhere in San Diego and slept next to the van, returning to Spahn Ranch the following day, arriving there about two in the afternoon.

Stephanie was a bit vague when it came to dates. She "thought" the day they returned to Spahn Ranch was Friday, August 8, but she wasn't sure. I anticipated that the defense would make the most of this, but I wasn't concerned, because that second piece of evidence conclusively placed Manson back at the ranch on Friday, August 8, 1969.

According to Linda Kasabian, on the afternoon of August 8 Manson gave Mary Brunner and Sandra Good a credit card and told them to purchase some items for him. At four that afternoon the two girls were apprehended while driving away from a Sears store in San Fernando, after store employees checked and found the credit card was stolen. The San Fernando PD arrest report stated that they were driving a "van 1952 Ford license K70683."

Because of the fine job of digging by the LaBianca detectives, we now had physical proof that Manson was back at Spahn Ranch on Friday, August 8, 1969.

Though both the traffic ticket and arrest report were in the discovery materials, so were hundreds of other documents. I was hoping that the defense would overlook their common denominator: that vehicle description with its telltale license number.

If Manson went with an alibi defense, and I proved that alibi was fabricated, this would be strong circumstantial evidence of his guilt.

There was, of course, other evidence placing Manson at Spahn Ranch that day. In addition to the testimony of Schram, DeCarlo, and others, Linda Kasabian said that when the Family got together that afternoon, Manson discussed his visit to Big Sur, saying that the people there were "really not together, they were just off on their little trips" and that "the people wouldn't go on his trip."

It was just after this that Manson told them: "Now is the time for Helter Skelter."

Bits and pieces, often largely circumstantial. Yet patiently dug out and assembled, they became the People's case. And with almost every interview it became a little stronger.

I spent many hours interviewing Stephanie Schram, who, together with Kitty Lutesinger, had fled Barker Ranch just hours before the October 1969 raid, shotgun-wielding Clem in close pursuit. I often wondered what would have happened to the two girls had the raid been timed just a day later or Clem been a little faster.

Unlike Kitty, Stephanie had severed all contact with the Family. Though we had kept her current address from the defense, Squeaky and Gypsy found her working at a dog-grooming school. "Charlie wants you to come back," they told her. Stephanie replied, "No thanks." Considering what she knew, her forthright refusal was a brave act.

From Stephanie I learned that while at Barker Manson had conducted a "murder school." He had given a Buck knife to each of the girls, and had demonstrated how they should "slit the throats of pigs," by yanking the head back by the hair and drawing the knife from ear to ear (using Stephanie as a very frightened model). He also said they should "stab them in either their ears or eyes and then wiggle the knife around to get as many vital organs as possible." The details became even gorier: Manson said that if the police pigs came to the desert, they should kill them, cut them in little pieces, boil the heads, then put the skulls and uniforms on posts, to frighten off others.*

Stephanie had told LAPD that Manson had spent the nights of Friday, August 8, and Saturday, August 9, with her. On questioning her, I learned that about an hour after dinner on August 8, Manson took her to the trailer at Spahn and told her to go to sleep, that he would join her soon. However, she didn't see him again until shortly before dawn the next morning, at which time he awakened her and took her with him to Devil's Canyon, the camp across the road from the ranch.

That night—August 9—Stephanie said, "when it got dark, he left and he came back either sometime during the night or early in the morning."

If Manson was planning on using Stephanie Schram as an alternative alibi, we were now more than ready for him.

On March 19, Hollopeter, Manson's court-appointed attorney, made two motions: that Charles Manson be given a psychiatric examination, and that his case be severed from that of the others.

Enraged, Manson tried to fire Hollopeter.

Asked whom he wished to represent him, Manson replied, "Myself." When Judge Keene denied the change, Manson picked up a copy of the Constitution and, saying it meant nothing to the Court, tossed it in a wastebasket.

Manson eventually requested that Ronald Hughes be substituted for Hollopeter. Like Reiner and Shinn, Hughes had been one of the first attorneys to call on Manson. He had remained on the periphery of the case ever since, his chief function being to run errands for Manson, as indi-

*Much later I discovered that LASO deputies George Palmer and William Gleason had obtained much of this same information from Stephanie Schram on December 3, 1969, but LASO had not informed LAPD of this.

cated by a document Manson had signed on February 17, designating him one of his legal runners.

Keene granted the substitution. Hollopeter, whom the press called "one of L.A. county's most successful defense attorneys," was out, after thirteen days; Hughes, who had never before tried a case, was in.

Something of an intellectual, Hughes was a huge, balding man with a long, scraggly beard. His various items of apparel rarely matched and usually evidenced numerous food stains. As one reporter remarked, "You could usually tell what Ron had for breakfast, for the past several weeks." Hughes, whom I would get to know well in the months ahead, and for whom I developed a growing respect, once admitted to me that he had bought his suits for a dollar apiece at MGM; they were from Walter Slezak's old wardrobe. The press was quick to dub him "Manson's hippie lawyer."

Hughes' first two acts were to withdraw the motions for the psychiatric examination and the severance. Granted. His third and fourth were requests that Manson be allowed to revert to pro per status and to deliver a speech to the Court. Denied.

Although Manson was displeased with Keene's last two rulings, he couldn't have been too unhappy with the defense team, which now consisted of four attorneys—Reiner (Van Houten), Shinn (Atkins), Fitzgerald (Krenwinkel), and Hughes (Manson)—each of whom had been associated with him since early in the case.

Unknown to us, there were still changes ahead. Among the casualties would be both Ira Reiner and Ronald Hughes, each of whom dared go against Manson's wishes. Reiner would lose considerable time and money for having linked himself with the Manson defense. His loss would be small, however, compared to that of Hughes, who, just eight months later, would pay with his life.

On March 21, Aaron and I were walking down the corridor in the Hall of Justice when we spotted Irving Kanarek emerging from the elevator.

Although little known elsewhere, Kanarek was something of a legend in the Los Angeles courts. The attorney's obstructionist tactics had caused a number of judges to openly censure him from the bench. Kanarek stories were so common, and usually incredible, as to seem fictional when they were actually fact. Prosecutor Burton Katz, for example, recalled that Kanarek once objected to a prosecution witness's stating his own name because, having first heard his name from his mother, it was "hearsay." Such frivolous objections were minor irritations compared with Kanarek's dilatory tactics. As samples:

In the case of *People* vs. *Goodman*, Kanarek had stretched a simple theft case, which should have taken a few hours or a day at most, to three months. The amount stolen: $100. The cost to the taxpayers: $130,212.

In the case of *People* vs. *Smith and Powell,* Kanarek spent twelve and a half months on pre-trial motions. After an additional two months trying to pick a jury, Kanarek's own client fired him in disgust. *A year and a half* after Irving Kanarek came onto the case, the jury still hadn't been selected, nor a single witness called.

In the case of *People* vs. *Bronson,* Superior Court Judge Raymond Roberts told Kanarek: "I am doing my best to see that Mr. Bronson gets a fair trial in spite of you. I have never seen such obviously stupid, ill-advised questions of a witness. Are you paid by the word or by the hour that you can consume the Court's time? You are the most obstructionist man I have ever met."

Outside the presence of the jury, Judge Roberts defined Kanarek's modus operandi as follows: "You take interminable lengths of time in cross-examining on the most minute, unimportant details; you ramble back and forth with no chronology of events, to just totally confuse everybody in the courtroom, to the utter frustration of the jury, the witnesses, and the judge."

After examining the transcript, the Appellate Court found the judge's remarks were not prejudicial but were substantiated by the trial record.

"All we need, Vince," Aaron remarked jocularly to me, "is to have Irving Kanarek on this case. We'd be in court ten years."

The next day Ronald Hughes told a reporter that "he may ask Van Nuys attorney I. A. Kanarek to enter the case as Manson's lawyer. He mentioned that he and Manson conferred with Kanarek at the County Jail Monday night."

Though no miracle was involved, the Black Panther whom Charles Manson had shot and killed in July 1969 had resurrected. Only he wasn't a Panther, just a "former dope dealer," and, contrary to what Manson and the Family had believed, after Manson shot him he hadn't died, though his friends had told Manson that he had. His name was Bernard Crowe, but he was best known by the descriptive nickname Lotsapoppa. Our long search for Crowe ended when an old acquaintance of mine, Ed Tolmas, who was Crowe's attorney, called me. He told me he had learned we were looking for his client and arranged for me to interview Crowe.

Crowe's story of the incident was essentially the same as that DeCarlo had told LAPD, although even Charlie didn't know the surprise ending.

After Manson and T. J. had left the Hollywood apartment where the shooting took place, Crowe, who had been playing dead, told his friends to call an ambulance. They did, then split. When questioned by the police at the hospital, Crowe said he didn't know who had shot him or why. He nearly didn't make it; he was on the critical list for eighteen days. The bullet was still lodged next to his spine.

I was interested in Crowe for two reasons. One, the incident proved that Charles Manson was quite capable of killing someone on his own. Though I knew I couldn't get this into evidence during the guilt phase of the trial, I was hopeful of introducing it during the penalty phase, when other crimes can be considered. Two, from the description it appeared that the gun Manson had shot Crowe with was the same .22 caliber Longhorn revolver which, just a little over a month later, Tex Watson would use in the Tate homicides. If we could remove the bullet from Crowe's body and match it up with the bullets test-fired from the .22 caliber revolver, we'd have placed the Tate murder weapon in Manson's own hand.

Sergeant Bill Lee of SID wasn't optimistic about the bullet. He told me that since it had been embedded in the body for over nine months, it was likely that acids had obliterated the stria to an extent where a positive identification would be difficult. Still, it might be possible. I then talked to several surgeons: they could take out the bullet, they told me, but the operation was risky.

I laid it out for Crowe. We'd like to have the bullet, and would arrange to have it removed at the Los Angeles County Hospital. But there were serious risks involved, and I didn't minimize them.

Crowe declined the operation. He was sort of proud of the bullet, he said. It made quite a conversation piece.

Eventually Manson would have learned, through discovery, of the resurrection of Bernard Crowe. Before this, however, Crowe was jailed on a marijuana charge. As he was being escorted down the hall, he passed Manson and his guard, who were on their way back from the attorney room. Charlie did a quick about-face, then told Crowe, according to the deputies who were present, "Sorry I had to do it, but you know how it is."

Crowe's response, if there was one, went unreported.

Toward the end of March the prosecution nearly lost one of its key witnesses.

Paul Watkins, once Manson's chief lieutenant, was pulled out of a flaming Volkswagen camper and rushed to Los Angeles County General Hospital with second-degree burns on 25 percent of his face, arms, and back. When sufficiently recovered to talk to the police, Watkins told them he had fallen asleep while reading by candlelight, and either that, or a marijuana cigarette he had been smoking, could have caused the fire.

These were only guesses, Watkins told them, as he was "unsure of the origin of the blaze."

Three days *before* the fire, Inyo County authorities had heard a rumor that Watkins was going to be killed by the Family.

As far back as November 1969, I'd asked LAPD to infiltrate the Family. I not only wanted to know what they were planning as far as defense strategy was concerned; I told the officers, "It would be tragic if there was another murder which we could have prevented."

I made this request at least ten times, LAPD finally contending that if they did plant an undercover agent in the Family, he would have to commit crimes, for example, smoke marijuana. For there to be a crime, I noted, there had to be criminal intent; if he was doing it as part of his job, to catch a criminal, it wouldn't be a crime. When they balked at this, I said he didn't even have to be a police officer. If they had paid informers in narcotics, bookmaking, even prostitution cases, surely they could manage to come up with one in one of the biggest murder cases of our time. No dice.

Finally I turned to the DA's Bureau of Investigation, and they found a young man willing to accept the assignment. I admired his determination, but he was clean-cut, with short hair, and looked as straight as they come. As desperate as we were for information, I couldn't send him into that den of killers; once they stopped laughing, they'd chop him to pieces. Eventually I had to abandon the idea. We remained in the dark as to what the Family was planning to do next.

April 1970

The words PIG, DEATH TO PIGS, RISE, and HEALTER SKELTER contain only thirteen different letters. Handwriting experts told me it would be extremely difficult—if not impossible—to match the bloody words found at the Tate and LaBianca residences with printing exemplars obtained from the defendants.

It wasn't only the small number of letters involved. The words were printed, not written; the letters were oversize; in both cases unusual writing implements had been used, a towel at the Tate residence, probably a rolled-up piece of paper at the LaBiancas; and all but the two words found on the refrigerator door at the latter residence had been printed high up on the walls, the person responsible having to stretch unnaturally high to make them.

As evidence, they appeared worthless.

However, thinking about the problem, I came up with an idea which, if successful, could convert them into very meaningful evidence. It was a gamble. But if it worked, it would be worth it.

We knew who had printed the words. Susan Atkins had testified before the grand jury that she had printed the word PIG on the front door of the Tate house, while Susan had told me, when I interviewed her, that Patricia Krenwinkel had admitted printing the words at the LaBiancas. Though Susan's grand jury testimony and her statements to me were inadmissible because of the deal we had made with her, she had confessed the printing at Tate to Ronnie Howard, so we had her on that. But we had nothing admissible on Krenwinkel.

The Fifth Amendment to the U.S. Constitution provides that no person "shall be compelled in any criminal case to be a witness against himself." The U.S. Supreme Court has ruled that this is limited to verbal utterances, and that a defendant cannot refuse to give physical evidence of himself, like appearing in a lineup, submitting to a breath-analysis test for drunken driving, giving fingerprint and handwriting exemplars, hair samples, and so on. After researching the law, I drew up very explicit instructions for Captain Carpenter at Sybil Brand, stating exactly how to request the printing exemplars of Susan Atkins, Patricia Krenwinkel, and Leslie Van Houten.

Each was to be informed: "(1) You have no constitutional right to refuse; (2) you have no constitutional right to have your attorney present; (3) your constitutional right to remain silent does not include the right to withhold printing exemplars; and (4) if you submit to this process, this can be used as evidence by the prosecution in your case."

Captain Carpenter assigned Senior Deputy H. L. Mauss to obtain the exemplars. According to my instructions, she informed Susan Atkins of the above, then told her: "The word PIG was printed in blood at the Tate residence. We want you to print the word PIG." Susan, without complaint, printed the exemplar as requested.

Leslie Van Houten and Patricia Krenwinkel were brought in individually and given similar instructions concerning their rights. However, each was told, *orally:* "The words HELTER SKELTER, DEATH TO PIGS, and RISE were printed in blood at the LaBianca residence. We want you to print those words."

In my memo to Captain Carpenter there was one additional instruction for the deputy: "Do not write any of this for them." I wanted to see if Krenwinkel misspelled "helter" as "healter" as she had on the refrigerator door.

Leslie Van Houten printed the exemplar.

Patricia Krenwinkel refused.

We'd won the gamble. We could now use her refusal in the trial as circumstantial evidence of her guilt.

As evidence, this was doubly important, since, before this, I'd had absolutely *no* independent evidence corroborating Linda Kasabian's testimony regarding Patricia Krenwinkel's involvement in the LaBianca murders. And without corroborating evidence, as a matter of law, Krenwinkel would have been entitled to an acquittal on those charges.

Though we'd won that gamble, Krenwinkel herself could just as easily have emerged the winner. Leslie could have refused to make an exemplar also, which would have diluted the force of Katie's refusal. Or Katie could have made the exemplar, the handwriting experts then failing to match her printing with that found at the LaBiancas.

We were less lucky when it came to putting the Tate-Sebring rope and the wire cutters in Manson's possession before the murders, evidence I was counting on to provide the necessary corroboration of Linda Kasabian's testimony as to Manson.

We knew from DeCarlo, who had been present, that Manson had purchased about 200 feet of the white, three-strand nylon rope at the Jack Frost surplus store in Santa Monica in June 1969. However, when Tate detectives finally interviewed Frost—three and a half months after my initial request—he was unable to find a purchase order for the rope. Nor could he definitely state that this was the same rope he had stocked.* An attempt to identify the manufacturer, then trace it back to Frost, also failed. Frost usually picked up his stock in odd lots from jobbers or through auctions, rather than directly from the manufacturer.

Just as these were blind alleys, so was one other—literally. According to DeCarlo, Manson had given part of the rope to George Spahn, for use on the ranch. Spahn's near blindness, however, eliminated him as a witness.

It was then I thought of Ruby Pearl.

For some reason, though the police had visited Spahn Ranch numerous times, none of the officers had interviewed Ruby, George's ranch manager. I found her a fund of valuable information. Examining the Tate-Sebring rope, she not only said it looked like the rope Manson had, she also supplied numerous examples of Manson's domination; recalled seeing the .22 Longhorn at the ranch many times; identified the leather thong found at the LaBiancas' as similar to the ones Manson often wore; and told me that, prior to the arrival of the Family at Spahn, she had never seen any Buck knives there, but that in the summer of 1969 "suddenly it seemed everyone had one."

While disappointed that we couldn't obtain documented proof of the rope sale, I was pleased with Ruby. Being an experienced horse wrangler—as well as a tough, gallant lady who showed not the slightest fear of the Family†—her testimony would carry weight. There was a fine streak of stubborn authority about her.

Another find was Randy Starr, whom I interviewed the same day as Ruby. A sometime movie stunt man who spe-

*Frost recalled stocking some three-strand, white nylon rope, but he believed it was ½ inch thick. The Tate-Sebring rope was ⅝ inch thick. While it was possible that Frost had been mistaken, or the rope had been mislabeled, the defense could argue that it simply wasn't the same rope.

†When Manson was brought to Los Angeles from Independence, Ruby Pearl visited him at the jail. "I only came here for one reason, Charlie," she told him. "I want to know where Shorty was buried."

Manson, unwilling to meet her gaze, looked down at the floor and remarked, "Ask the Black Panthers."

"Charlie, you know the Black Panthers have never been up to the ranch," she responded, turning her back on him and walking out.

cialized in fake hangings, Starr said the Tate-Sebring rope was "identical" to a rope he'd once used to help Manson pull a vehicle out of the creek bed. Starr told me, "Manson always kept the rope behind the seat in his dune buggy."

Even more important was Randy Starr's positive identification of the .22 Longhorn revolver, for Starr had once owned the gun and had given it to Manson.*

One question remained unanswered. Why, on the night of the Tate murders, did the killers bring along 43 feet 8 inches of rope? To tie up the victims? Manson accomplished this the next night with a single leather thong. I obtained a glimpse of a possible answer during one of my interviews with DeCarlo. According to Danny, in late July of 1969, Manson had told him that the establishment pigs "ought to have their throats cut and be hung up by their feet." This would really throw the fear into people, Manson said.

The logical inference, I felt, was that the killers brought along the rope intending to hang their victims. It was only a guess, but I suspected it was correct.

The wire cutters presented their own problems. Linda Kasabian said the pair found in Manson's dune buggy looked like the pair that had been in the car that night. Fine. Joe Granado of SID used them to test-cut a section of the Tate telephone wire and concluded that the two cuts were the same. Great. But then officer DeWayne Wolfer, considered LAPD's foremost expert on physical evidence, made some test cuts also, and he concluded that these wire cutters couldn't have been the ones used.

Not about to give up, I asked Wolfer if the tautness of the wire could have been a factor. Possibly, he said. I then asked Wolfer to accompany telephone company representatives to 10050 Cielo Drive and make another cut, only

*The gun, serial number 1902708, had been among a number of weapons taken from the Archery Headquarters in El Monte, California, during a burglary on the night of March 12, 1969. According to Starr, he obtained it in a trade with a man known only as "Ron." Manson was always borrowing the gun for target practice, and Randy finally gave it to him in trade for a truck that had belonged to Danny DeCarlo.

this time I wanted him to sever the wire while it was strung up and tight, the way it was the night of the murders. Wolfer eventually made the test, but his opinion remained unchanged: the actual cut made on the night of the murders and the test cut did not match.

While it was possible that the cutting edge of the wire cutters could have been damaged subseqeunt to the Tate murders, Wolfer's tests literally severed this important link between Manson and the Tate evidence.

When I'd accompanied LAPD to Spahn Ranch on November 19, 1969, we'd found a number of .22 caliber bullets and shell casings. Because of the terrific windstorm, and the necessity of following up other leads, our search had been cursory, however, and I'd asked Sergeant Lee to return and conduct a more thorough search. The much repeated request became even more important when, on December 16, 1969, LAPD obtained the .22 caliber Longhorn revolver. Yet it was not until April 15, 1970, that Lee returned to Spahn. Again concentrating on the gully area some two hundred feet behind George Spahn's residence, Lee found twenty-three more .22 caliber shell casings. Since twenty-two had been found during the first search, this brought the total to forty-five.*

It was not until after the latter search that Lee ran comparison tests on any of the Spahn shell casings. When he finally did, he concluded that fifteen of the forty-five had been fired from the Tate murder gun.†

Belatedly, but fortunately in time for the trial, we now had scientific evidence linking the gun to Spahn Ranch.

Only one thing would have made me happier: if Lee had returned and found the rest of the shell casings before the gun was discovered. As it was, the defense could contend that during the four and a half months between the

*None of the .22 caliber bullets recovered during the two searches matched up with the bullets found at the murder scene or those test-fired from the weapon.

†Lee determined this by comparing the rim marks on the Spahn shell casings with (1) the rim marks on the shell casings found in the cylinder of the weapon; (2) the rim marks of shell casings test-fired from the gun; and (3) the firing pin of the gun.

two searches the police and/or prosecution had "planted" this evidence.

For months one item of physical evidence had especially worried me: the pair of eyeglasses found near the trunks in the living room at the Tate murder scene. The natural conclusion was that if they didn't belong to any of the victims, they must belong to one of the killers. Yet neither Watson, Atkins, Krenwinkel, nor Kasabian wore glasses.

I anticipated that the defense would lean heavily on this, arguing that since they didn't belong to any of the defendants, at least one of the killers was still at large. From there it was only a short step to the conclusion that maybe the wrong people were on trial.

This posed an extremely serious problem for the prosecution. That problem, though not the mystery itself, vanished when I talked to Roseanne Walker.

Since Susan Atkins had confessed the murders to both Virginia Graham and Ronnie Howard, it occurred to me that she might have made incriminating statements to others, so I asked LAPD to locate any girls Atkins had been particularly close to at Sybil Brand.

One former inmate who agreed to talk to me, though she wasn't very happy about it, was Roseanne Walker. A pathetic, heavyset black girl who had been sent to Sybil Brand on five drug-related charges, Roseanne had been a sort of walking commissary, selling candy, cigarettes, and makeup to the other inmates. Not until the fifth or sixth time I interviewed her did Roseanne recall a conversation which, though it seemed unimportant to her, I found very significant.

Susan and Roseanne were listening to the radio one day, when the newscaster began talking about a pair of eyeglasses LAPD had found at the Tate murder scene. Amused, Susan remarked, "Wouldn't it be too much if they arrested the person the glasses belonged to, when the only thing he was guilty of was losing his glasses?"

Roseanne replied that maybe the glasses did belong to the killer.

Susan said, "That ain't the way it went down."

Susan's remark clearly indicated that the glasses did *not* belong to the killers.

Other problems remained. One of the biggest concerned Linda Kasabian's escape from Spahn Ranch.

Linda told me that she decided to flee after the night of the LaBianca murders; however, Manson sent her to the waterfall area later that day (August 11) and she was afraid to leave that night because of the armed guards he had posted.

Early the next morning (August 12) Manson sought her out. She was to put on a "straight" dress, then take a message to Mary Brunner and Sandra Good at Sybil Brand, as well as Bobby Beausoleil at the County Jail. The message: "Say nothing; everything's all right." After borrowing a car from Dave Hannum, a new ranch hand at Spahn, Linda went to Sybil Brand, but learned that Brunner and Good were in court; at the County Jail her identification was rejected and she wasn't allowed to see Beausoleil. When she returned to the ranch and told Manson she had been unsuccessful, he told her to try again the next day.

Linda saw her chance. That night she packed a shoulder bag with some clothing and Tanya's diapers and pins, and hid it in the parachute room. Early the next morning (August 13) she again borrowed Hannum's car. On going to get the bag, however, she found Manson and Stephanie Schram sleeping in the room. Deciding to forget the bag, she went to get Tanya, but discovered that the children had been moved to the waterfall area. There was no way she could go there to get Tanya, she said, without having to explain her actions. So she left the ranch without her.

Instead of going to Los Angeles as instructed, Linda began driving to Taos, New Mexico, where her husband was now living. Hannum's car broke down outside Albuquerque. When she tried to have it repaired, using a credit card Bruce Davis had earlier given her for gas, the gas station owner checked and learned the card was no longer valid. Linda then wrote a letter to Hannum, enclosing the keys, telling him where he could find the car, and apologizing. She then hitchhiked the rest of the way.

(Susan Atkins apparently intercepted the letter, as she gave Hannum the information and keys, but didn't show him the rest of the letter. Understandably unhappy, Hannum took a bus to Albuquerque to reclaim the vehicle.)

Linda found her husband living with another girl in a commune at Lorien, outside Taos. She told him about the Tate murders, the events of the second night, and leaving Tanya at Spahn. Bob Kasabian suggested they return to Spahn together and get Tanya, but Linda was afraid Manson would kill them all. Kasabian said he wanted to think about it for a few days. Unwilling to wait, Linda hitchhiked into Taos and went to see Joe Sage. Sage, who had a reputation for helping people, was a rather colorful character. When the fifty-one-year-old Zen monk wasn't busy running his Macrobiotic Church, he was campaigning for president of the United States on an anti-pollution ticket. Linda asked Sage for enough money to return to Los Angeles to get her little girl. Sage, however, began questioning Linda, and eventually she told him and a youth named Jeffrey Jacobs about the murders.

Not believing Linda's tale, Sage placed a call to Spahn Ranch, talking first to an unidentified girl, then to Manson himself. Sage asked Manson—whose reaction can only be imagined—if Linda's story was true. Manson told him Linda had flipped out; that her ego was not ready to die, and so she had run away.

Linda did not talk to Charlie, but she did talk to one of the other girls—she believed, but was not sure, it was Squeaky—who told her about the August 16 raid. The authorities had kept Tanya, she learned; she was now in a foster home. Linda also spoke to Patricia Krenwinkel, Katie saying something to the effect, "You just couldn't wait to open your big mouth, could you?"

Linda subsequently called the Malibu police station and learned the name of the social worker who was handling Tanya's case.* Sage gave Linda enough money for round-

*On calling the social worker, Linda learned that another girl, posing as Tanya's mother, had attempted to reclaim Tanya a short time before. Though I couldn't prove it, I suspected that Manson had sent one of his girls to get Tanya, as insurance that Linda wouldn't talk.

trip air fare, as well as the name of a Los Angeles attorney, Gary Fleischman, who he felt might be able to help her reclaim Tanya. When Linda saw Fleischman, she did not tell him about the murders, only that she had left the ranch to look for her husband. Eventually, after a court hearing, the mother and daughter were reunited and flew back to Taos. Bob was still involved with the other girl, however, and Linda took Tanya and hitchhiked first to Miami, Florida, where her father was living, then to her mother's home in Concord, New Hampshire. It was here, on December 2, 1969, when the news broke that she was being sought in connection with the Tate murders, that Linda turned herself in to the local police. Waiving extradition, she was returned to Los Angeles the next day.

I asked Linda, "Why, between the time you reclaimed Tanya and the date of your arrest in December, didn't you contact the police and tell them what you knew about the murders?"

She was afraid of Manson, Linda said, afraid that he might find and kill both her and Tanya. Also, she was pregnant, and didn't want to go through this ordeal until after the baby was born.

There were, of course, other reasons, the most important being her distrust of the police. In the drug-oriented world she inhabited, police were considered neither friends nor allies. I felt that this explanation, if properly argued, would satisfy the jury.

An even bigger question remained: "How could you leave your daughter in that den of killers?"

I was concerned not only with the jury's reaction to this, but also with the use to which the defense could put it. That Linda had left Tanya with Manson and the others at Spahn Ranch could be circumstantial evidence that she did not really believe them to be killers, clearly contradicting the main thrust of her testimony. Therefore both the question and her answer became extremely important.

Linda replied that she felt Tanya would be safe there, *just so long as she did not go to the police.* "Something within me told me that Tanya would be all right," Linda said, "that nothing would happen to her, and that now was the time to leave. I knew I would come back and get her. I was just confident that she would be all right."

Would the jury accept this? I didn't know. This was among my many concerns as the trial date drew ever closer.

When contacted by Lieutenant Helder and Sergeant Gutierrez, both Sage and Jacobs verified Linda's story. I was unable to use either as a witness, however, most of their testimony being inadmissible hearsay. Ranch hand David Hannum said he had begun work at Spahn on August 12, and that Linda had borrowed his car that same day, as well as the next. And a check of the jail records verified that Brunner and Good *had* been in court on August 12.

The various interviews yielded unexpected bonuses. Hannum said that once when he killed a rattlesnake, Manson had angrily castigated him, yelling, "How would you like it if I chopped your head off?" He then added, "I'd rather kill people than animals." At the same time I interviewed Linda's husband, Robert Kasabian, I also talked to Charles Melton, the hippie philanthropist from whom Linda had stolen the $5,000. Melton said that in April 1969 (before Linda ever met the Family) he had gone to Spahn Ranch to see Paul Watkins. While there, Melton had met Tex, who, admiring Melton's beard, commented, "Maybe Charlie will let me grow a beard someday."

It would be difficult to find a better example of Manson's domination of Watson.

These were pluses. There were minuses. And they were big ones.

To prove to the jury that Linda's account of these two nights of murder wasn't fabricated out of whole cloth, I desperately needed some third person to corroborate any part of her story. Rudolf Weber provided that corroboration for the first night. But for the second night I had no one. I gave LAPD this all-important priority assignment: Find the two officers who spoke to Manson and Linda on the beach, the man whose door Linda knocked on that night, the man and woman at the house next to the

Malibu Feedbin, or any of the drivers who gave them rides. I'd like to have had all these people, but if they could turn up even one, I'd be happy.

Linda had located the spot where the two police officers stopped and questioned them. It was near Manhattan Beach. But, Los Angeles being the megalopolis that it is, it turned out to be an area where there were overlapping jurisdictions, not one but three separate law-enforcement agencies patrolling it. And a check of all three failed to turn up anyone who could recall such an incident.

We had better luck when it came to locating the actor Linda had mentioned. LaBianca detectives Sartuchi and Nielsen found him still living in Apartment 501, 1101 Ocean Front Walk, Venice. Not Israeli but Lebanese, his name was Saladin Nader, age thirty-nine. Unemployed since starring in *Broken Wings*, the movie about the poet Kahlil Gibran, he remembered picking up the two hitchhiking girls in early August 1969. He described both Sandy and Linda accurately, including the fact that Sandy was noticeably pregnant; picked out photos of each; and related essentially the same story Linda had told me, neglecting to mention only that he and Linda had gone to bed.

After questioning Nader, the investigating officers, according to their report, "explained to subject the purpose of the interview, and he displayed amazement that such sweet and sociable young ladies would attempt to inflict any harm upon his body after he assisted them to the best of his ability."

Though their stories jibed, Nader was only partial support for Linda's testimony, as (fortunately for him, and thanks to Linda) he did not encounter the group that night.

One floor down was the apartment of the man on whose door Linda had knocked. Linda had pointed out the door, 403, for us, and I'd asked Gutierrez and Patchett to try to locate the man, hopeful he'd recall the incident. When I got their report, it was on the tenant of 404. Returning, they learned from the landlady that 403 had been vacant during August 1969. It was possible some transient may have been staying there, she said—it wouldn't have been the first time—but beyond that we drew a blank.

According to the rental manager of 3921 Topanga Canyon Boulevard—the house next to the Malibu Feedbin where Linda said she, Sadie, and Clem had stopped just before dawn—a group of hippies had moved into the unrented building about nine months ago. There had been, he said, as many as fifty different persons living there, but he didn't know any of them. Sartuchi and Nielsen, however, did manage to locate two young girls who had lived there from about February to October 1969. Both were friends of Susan Atkins, and both recalled meeting Linda Kasabian. One recalled that once Susan, another girl, and a male had visited them. She remembered the incident—though not the date, the time, or the other persons present—because she was "on acid" and the trio "appeared evil." Both girls admitted that during this period they were "stoned" so much of the time their recollections were hazy. As witnesses, they would be next to useless.

Nor was LAPD able to locate any of the drivers who had picked up the hitchhikers that night.

The LaBianca detectives handled all these investigations. Going over their reports, I was convinced they had done everything possible to run down the leads. But we were left with the fact that of the six to eight persons who could have corroborated Linda Kasabian's story of the events of that second night, we hadn't found even one. I anticipated that the defense would lean heavily on this.

Any defendant may file at least one affidavit of prejudice against a judge and have him removed from the case. It isn't even necessary to give a reason for such a challenge. On April 13, Manson filed such an affidavit against Judge William Keene. Judge Keene accepted Manson's challenge, and the case was reassigned to Judge Charles H. Older. Though more affidavits were expected—each defendant was allowed one—the defense attorneys, after a brief huddle, decided to accept Older.

I'd never tried a case before him. By reputation, the fifty-two-year-old jurist was a "no nonsense" judge. A World War II fighter pilot who had served with the Flying

Tigers, he had been appointed to the bench by Governor Ronald Reagan in 1967. This would be his biggest case to date.

The trial date was set for June 15. Because of the delay, we were again hopeful that Watson might be tried with the others, but that hope was quickly dashed when Watson's attorney requested, and received, still another postponement in the extradition proceedings.

The retrial of Beausoleil for the Hinman murder had begun in late March. Chief witness for the prosecution was Mary Brunner, first member of the Manson Family, who testified that she had witnessed Beausoleil stab Hinman to death. Brunner was given complete immunity in exchange for her testimony. Claiming that he had only been a reluctant witness, Beausoleil himself took the stand and fingered Manson as Hinman's murderer. The jury believed Brunner. In Beausoleil's first trial the case against him had been so weak that our office hadn't asked for the death penalty. This time prosecutor Burton Katz did, and got it.

Two things concerned me about the trial. One was that Mary Brunner did everything she could to absolve Manson—making me wonder just how far Sadie, Katie, and Leslie would be willing to go to save Charlie—and the other that Danny DeCarlo hedged on many of his previous statements to LAPD. I was worried that Danny might be getting ready to split, all too aware that he had little reason to stick around. Though the motorcycle engine theft charge had been dropped in return for his testimony in the Hinman case, we had made no deal with him on Tate-LaBianca. Moreover, although he had a good chance of sharing the $25,000 reward, it was not necessary that he testify to obtain it.

DeCarlo and Brunner did testify that same month before the grand jury, which brought additional indictments against Charles Manson, Susan Atkins, and Bruce Davis on the Hinman murder. But testifying before a grand jury in secret and having to face Manson himself in court were two different things.

Nor could I blame Danny for being apprehensive. As

soon as the grand jury indictments were made public, Davis, who had been living with the Family at Spahn, vanished.

May 1970

In early May, Crockett, Poston, and Watkins encountered Clem, Gypsy, and a youth named Kevin, one of the newer Family members, in Shoshone. Clem told Watkins: "Charlie says that when he gets out you all had better not be around the desert."

From a source at Spahn Ranch we learned that Family members there appeared to be "preparing for some activity."

The Manson girls were interviewed so often that they were on a first-name basis with many of the reporters. Inadvertently, several times they implied that Charlie would be out soon. Perhaps significantly, the girls said nothing about his being "acquitted" or "released."

It was obvious that something was being planned.

On May 11, Susan Atkins filed a declaration repudiating her grand jury testimony. Both Manson and Atkins used the declaration as basis for habeas corpus motions, which were subsequently denied.

Aaron and I conferred with District Attorney Younger. Sadie couldn't have it both ways. Either she had told the complete truth before the grand jury and, according to our agreement, we would not seek a first degree murder conviction against her, or, according to her recent declaration, she recanted her testimony, in which case the agreement was breached.

My personal opinion was that Susan Atkins had testified "substantially truthfully" before the grand jury, with these exceptions: her omission of the three other murder attempts the second night; her hedging on whether she had stabbed Voytek Frykowski (which she admitted to me when I interviewed her); and my instinctive, but strong, feeling (corroborated by her confessions to Virginia Graham and Ronnie Howard) that she had lied when she testified that she had not stabbed Sharon Tate. Under Atkins' agreement with our office, "substantially" wasn't good enough—she had to tell the complete truth.

With her declaration, however, the issue was closed. On the basis of her repudiation, Aaron and I asked Younger's permission to seek the death penalty against Susan Atkins as well as the other defendants. He granted it.

Sadie's about-face was not unexpected. Another change, however, caught almost everyone off guard. In court to petition for a new trial, Bobby Beausoleil produced an affidavit, signed by Mary Brunner, stating that her testimony in his trial "was not true," and that she had lied when she said Beausoleil stabbed Hinman to death.

Although obviously stunned, prosecutor Burt Katz argued that the other evidence in the trial was sufficient to convict Beausoleil.

Investigating further, Burt learned that a few days before she was due to testify, Mary Brunner had been visited by Squeaky and Brenda at her parents' home in Wisconsin. She was again visited by Squeaky, this time accompanied by Sandy, two days before she signed the affidavit. Burt charged that the girls, representing Manson, had coerced Mary Brunner into repudiating her testimony.

Called to the stand, Mary Brunner first denied this, then, after conferring with counsel, did another about-face, and repudiated her repudiation. Her testimony in the trial was true, she said. Still later she *again* reversed herself.

Eventually, Beausoleil's motion for a new trial was denied, and he was sent to San Quentin's Death Row to wait out his appeal. The District Attorney's Office was left with a perplexing legal dilemma, however. After her testimony in the Beausoleil trial, the Court had granted Mary Brunner complete immunity for her part in the Hinman murder.

Except for the possibility that she might be tried for

perjury, it looked as if Mary Brunner had managed to beat the rap.

Indicted on the Hinman murder, Manson appeared before Judge Dell to request that he be allowed to represent himself. When Dell denied the motion, Manson requested that Irving Kanarek and Daye Shinn be made his attorneys. Judge Dell ruled there would be "a clear conflict of interest" if Shinn represented both Manson and Susan Atkins. This left Kanarek.

Commenting, "I think we are well aware of Mr. Kanarek and his record," Manson told Judge Dell, "I do not wish to hire this man as my attorney, but you leave me no alternative. I understand what I am doing. Believe me, I understand what I am doing. *This is the worst man in town I could pick,* and you are pushing him on me." If Dell would permit him to represent himself, Manson said, then he would forget about having Kanarek.

"I am not going to be blackmailed," Dell told Manson.

MANSON "Then I will take it up to the bigger father."

Judge Dell said that Manson could, of course, appeal his decision. However, since Manson was already appealing the revocation of his pro per status in the Tate-La-Bianca proceedings, Dell was willing to postpone a final decision until that writ was either accepted or rejected.

Aaron and I discussed the possible Kanarek substitution with District Attorney Younger. In view of his record, with Kanarek on the case the prospect that the trial might last two or more years was very real. Younger asked us if there was any legal basis for removing an attorney from a case. We told him we knew of none; however, I'd research the law. Younger asked me to prepare an argument for the Court, and suggested that it stress Kanarek's incompetency. From what I had learned of Kanarek, I did not feel that he was incompetent. His obstructionism, I felt, was the major issue.

I had no trouble obtaining evidence of this. From judges, deputy DAs, even jurors, I heard examples of his dilatory, obstructionist tactics. One deputy DA, on learning that he had to oppose Kanarek a second time, quit the office; life was too short for that, he said.

Anticipating that Manson would ask to substitute Kanarek on Tate-LaBianca as well as Hinman, I began preparing my argument. At the same time I had another idea which just might make that argument unnecessary.

Maybe, with the right bait, I could persuade Manson to dump Kanarek himself.

On May 25, I was going through LAPD's tubs on the LaBianca case when I noticed, standing against the wall, a wooden door. On it was a multicolored mural; the lines from a nursery rhyme, "1, 2, 3, 4, 5, 6, 7—All Good Children Go to Heaven"; and, in large letters, the words "HELTER SKELTER IS COMING DOWN FAST."

Stunned, I asked Gutierrez, "Where in the hell did you get that?"

"Spahn Ranch."

"When?"

He checked the yellow property envelope affixed to the door.

"November 25, 1969."

"You mean for five months, while I've been desperately trying to link the killers with Helter Skelter, you've had this door, with those very words on it, the same bloody words that were found at the LaBianca residence?"

Gutierrez admitted they had. The door, it turned out, had been found on a cabinet in Juan Flynn's trailer. It had been considered so unimportant that to date no one had even bothered to book it into evidence.

Gutierrez did so the next day.

Again, as I had on numerous other occasions, I told the detectives that I wanted to interview Juan Flynn.

I had no idea how much Flynn actually knew. Along with Brooks Poston and Paul Watkins, the Panamanian cowboy had been interviewed by the authors of a quickie paperback that appeared even before the trial, but he obviously held back a great deal, since many of the incidents I'd learned about from Brooks and Paul were not included.

June 1-14, 1970

Two weeks before the start of the Tate-LaBianca trial, Manson requested, and obtained, the substitution of Irving Kanarek for Ronald Hughes.

I asked for a conference in chambers. Once there, I pointed out that the legal issues in this case were tremendously complex. Even with attorneys known to handle matters expeditiously, the trial could last four or more months. "But," I added, "it is my frank opinion that if Mr. Kanarek is permitted to represent Mr. Manson, the case could last several years." I noted, "It is common knowledge among the legal profession that Mr. Kanarek is a professional obstructionist. I believe the man is conscientious. I believe he is sincere." However, I continued, "there is no way for the Court to stop Mr. Kanarek. Even holding him in contempt will not stop this man, because he will gladly spend the night in jail."

Rather than have the trial become "a burlesque on justice," I had an alternative suggestion, I told the Court. It was one I had considered for a long time and, though I had discussed it with Aaron, I knew it would come as a surprise to everyone else.

"As a possible solution, the prosecution has no objection to permitting Mr. Manson to represent himself, as he has desired throughout, and let him have an attorney of his choice to assist him . . ."

Manson looked at me with a startled expression. This was probably the last thing he had expected to hear from the prosecution.

Although I was hoping that, given this opportunity, Manson would dump Kanarek, I was sincere in making the suggestion. From the start Manson had maintained that only he could speak for himself. He'd strongly implied that, failing in this, he'd make trouble. And there was no question in my mind that this was his reason for choosing Kanarek.

Too, even though lacking formal education, Manson was bright. Having dominated them in the past, he could cross-examine such prosecution witnesses as Linda Kasabian, Brooks Poston, and other ex-Family members with probably more effectiveness than many "straight" attorneys. And, to assist him in legal matters, he would have not only his own lawyer but three other experienced attorneys alongside him at the counsel table. Also, looking far ahead, I was concerned that the denial of Manson's request to defend himself might be an issue on appeal.

Aaron then quoted Manson's own statement, made in Judge Dell's court, that Kanarek was the worst man he could pick.

Kanarek objected so strongly to the proceedings that Judge Older remarked, "Now the things that Mr. Stovitz and Mr. Bugliosi said about you, Mr. Kanarek, while they might appear to be unfair, there certainly is, as a matter of common knowledge among the judges in this court, a good deal of truth in what they say. I am not impugning your personal motives, but you do have a reputation for taking an inordinately long time to do what someone else can do in a much shorter period . . ."

However, Older said, the only reason he was considering the matter was that he wanted to be absolutely sure Manson wanted Kanarek as his attorney. His remarks before Judge Dell had injected some doubt on that point.

In one respect, Manson replied, Kanarek would be the best attorney in town, "in a lot of respects, he would be the worst attorney that I could take." But, Manson continued, "I don't think there is any attorney that can represent me as well as I can myself. I am smart enough to realize that I am not an attorney, and I will sit behind these men and I won't make a scene. I am not here to make trouble . . .

"There is a lot involved here that does not meet the eye. A person is born, he goes to school, he learns what he is told in a book, and he lives his life by what he knows. The only thing he knows is what someone has told him. He is educated; he does what an educated person does.

"But go out of this realm, you go into a generation gap, a free-love society, you get into insane drugs or smoking marijuana." And in this other world the reality differs, Manson noted. Here experience alone is the teacher; here you discover "there is no way that you can know the taste of water unless you drink it or unless it has rained on you or unless you jump in the river."

THE COURT "All I want to do, Mr. Manson, is find out if you are happy with Mr. Kanarek or if you have second thoughts."

MANSON "I thought I explained that. I would not be happy with anyone but myself. No man can represent me."

I asked the Court's permission to question Manson. Though Kanarek objected, Charlie was agreeable. I asked him if he had consulted the other defense attorneys as to whether he should be represented by Kanarek. I had heard that two of them, Fitzgerald and Reiner, were very unhappy about Kanarek's entry into the case.

MANSON "I don't ask other men's opinions. I have my own."

BUGLIOSI "Do you feel Mr. Kanarek can give you a fair trial?"

MANSON "I do. I feel *you* can give me a fair trial. You showed me your fairness already."

BUGLIOSI "I will give you a fair trial, Charlie, but I am out to convict you."

MANSON "What's a fair trial?"

BUGLIOSI "That's when the truth comes out."

Declaring, "It would be a miscarriage of justice to permit you to represent yourself in a case having the complications this case has," Older again asked Manson, "Are you affirming Mr. Kanarek as your attorney?"

"I am forced into a situation," Manson replied. "My second alternative is to cause you as much trouble as possible."

A little over a week later we'd get our first sample of what he had in mind.

On being taken to Patton State Hospital in January, sixteen-year-old Dianne Lake had been labeled "schizophrenic" by a staff psychologist. Though I knew the defense would probably try to use this to discredit her testimony, I wasn't too worried, since psychologists are not doctors and are not qualified to make medical diagnoses. The staff psychiatrists, who were doctors, said her problems were emotional, not mental: behavioral disorders of adolescence plus possible drug dependence. They also felt she had made excellent progress and were now sure she would be able to testify at the trial.

With Sergeant Patchett, I visited Patton in early June. The little ragamuffin I'd first seen in the jail in Independence now looked like any teen-ager. She was getting straight A's in school, Dianne told me proudly; not until getting away from the Family, she said, had she realized how good life was. Now, looking back, she felt she had been in a "pit of death."

In interviewing Dianne, I learned a number of things which hadn't come out in her earlier interviews. While they were in the desert together, at Willow Springs, Patricia Krenwinkel had told her that she had dragged Abigail Folger from the bedroom into the living room of the Tate residence. And Leslie Van Houten, after admitting to her that she had stabbed someone, had commented that at first she had been reluctant to do so, but then she'd discovered the more you stabbed, the more fun it was.

Dianne also said that on numerous occasions, in June, July, and August of 1969, Manson had told the Family, "We have to be willing to kill pigs in order to help the black man start Helter Skelter."

And several times—she believed it was in July, about a month before the Tate-LaBianca murders—Manson had also told them, "*I'm* going to have to start the revolution."

The interview lasted several hours. One thing Dianne said struck me as very sad. Squeaky, Sandy, and the other girls in the Family could never love anyone else, not even their parents, she told me. "Why not?" I asked. "Because," she replied, "they've given all their love to Charlie."

I left Patton with the very strong feeling that Dianne Lake had now escaped that fate.

In court on June 9, Manson suddenly turned in his chair so his back was to the judge. "The Court has shown me no respect," Manson said, "so I am going to show the Court the same thing." When Manson refused to face the Court, Judge Older, after several warnings, had the bailiffs remove him from the courtroom. He was taken to the lockup adjoining the court, which was equipped with a speaker system so he could hear, though not participate in, the proceedings.

Although Older gave him several opportunities to return, on the understanding that he would agree to conduct himself properly, Manson rejected them.

We had not given up in our attempt to have Irving Kanarek taken off the case. On June 10, I filed a motion requesting an evidentiary hearing on the Kanarek-Hughes substitution. The thrust of my motion: Manson did not have the constitutional right to have Kanarek as his lawyer.

The right of counsel of one's choice, I argued, was not an unlimited, unqualified, absolute right. This right was given to defendants seeking a favorable verdict for themselves. It was obvious from Manson's statements that he wasn't picking Kanarek for this reason, but rather to subvert, thwart, and paralyze the due and proper administration of justice. "And we submit that he cannot use the right to counsel of his choice in such an ignoble fashion."

Kanarek responded that he would be glad to let the Court read the transcripts of his cases, to see if he used dilatory tactics. I thought I saw Judge Older wince at this, but I wasn't sure. Older's somber expression rarely changed. It was very difficult to guess what he was thinking.

In researching Kanarek's record, I had learned something which was not part of my hour-long argument. For all his filibustering, disconnected ramblings, senseless motions, and wild, irresponsible charges, Irving Kanarek frequently scored points. He noted, for example, that our office hadn't tried to challenge Ronald Hughes, who had never tried a case before, on the grounds that his representation might hurt Manson. And, in conclusion, Kanarek, very much to the point, asked that the prosecution's motion be struck "on the basis there is no basis for it in law."

I'd frankly admitted this in my argument, but had noted that this was "a situation so aggravated that it literally cries out to the Court to take a pioneer stand."

Judge Older disagreed. My motion for an evidentiary hearing was denied.

Although District Attorney Younger had Older's ruling appealed to the California Supreme Court, it was let stand. Though we had tried to save the taxpayers perhaps several million dollars and everyone involved a great deal of time and unnecessary effort, Irving Kanarek would remain on the Tate-LaBianca cases just as long as Charles Manson wanted him.

"If Your Honor does not respect Mr. Manson's rights, you need not respect mine," Susan Atkins said, rising and turning her back to the Court. Leslie Van Houten and Patricia Krenwinkel followed suit. When Older suggested that the defense attorneys confer with their clients, Fitzgerald admitted that would do little good, "because there is a minimum of client control in this case." After several warnings, Older had the girls removed to one of the vacant jury rooms upstairs, and a speaker was placed there also.

I had mixed feelings about all this. If the girls parroted Manson's actions during the trial, it would be additional evidence of his domination. However, their removal from the courtroom might also be considered reversible error on appeal, and the last thing we wanted was to have to try the whole case over again.

Under the current law, *Allen* vs. *Illinois*, defendants can be removed from a courtroom if they engage in disruptive conduct. Another case, however, *People* vs. *Zamora*, raised a subtler point. In that case, in which there were twenty-two defendants, the counsel tables were so situated that it was extremely difficult for the attorneys to communicate with their clients while court was in session. This led to a reversal by the Appellate Court, which ruled that the right of counsel implies the right of consultation between a defendant and his lawyer during the trial.

I mentioned this to Older, suggesting that some type of telephonic communication be set up. Older felt it unnecessary.

After the noon recess the girls professed a willingness to return. Speaking for all three, Patricia Krenwinkel told Older, "We should be able to be present at this play here."

To Krenwinkel it was just that—a play. Remaining standing, she turned her back to the bench. Atkins and Van Houten immediately mimicked her. Older again ordered all three removed.

Bringing all the defendants back into court the next day, Judge Older warned them that if they persisted in their conduct before a jury, they could badly jeopardize their cases. "So I would ask you to seriously reconsider what you are doing, because I think you are hurting yourselves." After again attempting to revert to pro per status, Manson said, "O.K., then you leave me nothing. You can kill me now."

Still standing, Manson bowed his head and stretched out his arms in a crucifixion pose. The girls quickly emulated him. When the deputies attempted to seat them, all resisted, Manson ending up scuffling with a deputy on the floor. Two deputies bodily carried him to the lockup, while the matrons took the girls out.

KANAREK "I would ask medical assistance for Mr. Manson, Your Honor."

THE COURT "I will ask the bailiff to check and see if he needs any. If he does, he will get it."

He didn't. Once in the lockup, out of sight of the press and spectators, Manson became an entirely different person. He donned another mask, that of the complaisant prisoner. Having spent more than half his life in reformatories and prisons, he knew the role all too well. Thoroughly "institutionalized," he played by the rules, rarely causing trouble in the jail itself.

After the noon recess we had several examples of Kanarek in action. Arguing a search-and-seizure motion, he said that Manson's arrest was illegal because "Mr. Caballero and Mr. Bugliosi conspired to have Miss Atkins make certain statements" and that "the District Attorney's Office suborned the perjury."

As ridiculous as this was, subornation of perjury is an extremely serious charge, and since Kanarek was making it in open court, in front of the press, I reacted accordingly.

BUGLIOSI "Your Honor, if Mr. Kanarek is going to have diarrhea of the mouth, I think he should make an offer of proof back in chambers. This man is totally irresponsible. I urgently request the Court we go back in chambers. God knows what this man is going to say next."

THE COURT "Confine yourself to the argument, Mr. Kanarek."

The argument, when Kanarek did eventually get around to making it, left even the other defense attorneys looking stunned. Kanarek stated that since "the warrant of arrest for the defendant Manson was based on illegally obtained and perjured testimony, therefore the seizure of the person of Mr. Manson was illegal. The person of Mr. Manson must, therefore, be suppressed from evidence."

While I was wondering how you could suppress a person, Kanarek provided an answer: he asked that "that piece of physical evidence which is Mr. Manson's physical body" not "be before the Court conceptually to be used in evidence." Presumably, by Kanarek's convoluted logic, witnesses shouldn't even be allowed to identify Manson.

Older denied the motion.

Another aspect of Irving Kanarek was exhibited that day: a suspicious distrust that at times bordered on paranoia. The prosecution had told the Court that we would not introduce Susan Atkins' grand jury testimony in the trial. One would think the introduction of this testimony—in which Susan stated that Charles Manson ordered the Tate-LaBianca murders—would have been the last thing Manson's attorney would want in evidence. But Kanarek, suddenly wary, charged that if we weren't using those statements, "they must be tainted in some way."

Older recessed court for the weekend. The preliminaries were over. The trial would begin the following Monday—June 15, 1970.

Part 6

THE TRIAL

"If the tale that is unfolding were not
so monstrous, aspects of it would break the heart."
Jean Stafford

June 15-July 23, 1970

Judge Charles Older's court, Department 104, was located on the eighth floor of the Hall of Justice. As the first panel of sixty prospective jurors was escorted into the crowded courtroom, their expressions changed from boredom to curiosity. Then, as eyes alighted on the defendants, mouths dropped open in abrupt shock.

One man gasped, loud enough for those around him to hear, *"My God, it's the Manson trial!"*

In chambers the chief topic was sequestration. Judge Older had decided that once jury selection was completed, the jurors would be locked up until the end of the trial—"to protect them from harassment and to prevent their being exposed to trial publicity." Arrangements had already been made for them to occupy part of a floor at the Ambassador Hotel. Although spouses could visit on weekends, at their own expense, bailiffs would take all necessary precautions to see that the jury remained isolated from both outsiders and any news about the case. No one was sure how long this would be—estimates of the trial's length ranged from three to six months and up—but obviously it would be severe hardship for those chosen.

STOVITZ "Your Honor has—and I don't say this in comedy—sentenced some felons for less than three months in custody."

THE COURT "No doubt about it."

FITZGERALD "Not at the Ambassador, though."

Although all the attorneys had some reservations about sequestration, only one strongly opposed it: Irving Kanarek. Since Kanarek had screamed the loudest about the taint of publicity adverse to his client, I concluded that Manson, not Kanarek, must have been behind the motion.

And I had my own opinion as to why Charlie didn't want the jury locked up.

Rumor had it that Judge Older himself had already received several threats. A secret memo he'd sent the sheriff, outlining courtroom security measures, ended with the following paragraph:

"The sheriff shall provide the trial judge with a driver-bodyguard, and security shall be provided at the trial judge's residence on a 24-hour basis, until such time as all trial and post-trial proceedings have been concluded."

Twelve names were drawn by lot. When the prospective jurors were seated in the jury box, Older explained that the sequestration could last "as much as six months." Asked if any felt this would constitute undue hardship, eight of the twelve raised their hands.*

Envisioning a mass exodus from the courtroom, Older was very strict when it came to excuses for cause. However, anyone who stated that he or she could not vote the death penalty under any circumstances was automatically excused, as was anyone who had read Susan Atkins' confession. This was usually approached obliquely, the prospective juror being asked something like "Have you read where any defendant has made any type of incriminating statement or confession?" to which several answered on the order of "Yes, that thing in the L.A. *Times*." Questioning on this and other issues dealing with pre-trial publicity was done individually and in chambers, to avoid contaminating the whole panel.

After Older finished the initial questioning, the attorneys began their individual voir dire (examination). I was disappointed in Fitzgerald, who led off. His questions were largely conversational, and quite often showed no sign of prior thought. For example: "Have you or any member of your family ever been the unfortunate victim of a homicide?" Fitzgerald asked this not once but twice, before one of his fellow lawyers nudged him and suggested that if the prospective juror was a homicide victim he wouldn't be of much use on a jury.

*Later, after obtaining revised estimates from the various attorneys, Judge Older changed this to "three or more months," after which the hardship excuses abruptly declined.

Reiner was much better. It was obvious that he was doing his best to separate his client, Leslie Van Houten, from the other defendants. It was also obvious that in doing so he was incurring Manson's wrath. Kanarek objected to Reiner's questions almost as often as did the prosecution.

Shinn asked the first prospective juror only eleven questions, seven of which Older ruled improper. His entire voir dire, including objections and arguments, took only thirteen pages of transcript.

Kanarek began by reading a number of questions obviously written by Manson. This apparently didn't satisfy Charlie, as he asked Older if he could ask the jurors "a few simple, tiny, childlike questions that are real to me in my reality." Refused permission, Manson instructed Kanarek: "You will not say another word in court."

Manson contended, Kanarek later told the Court, that he was already presumed guilty; therefore there was no need to question the jurors, since it didn't matter who was selected.

To my amazement, Kanarek, usually a very independent sort, actually followed Manson's instructions and declined to ask further questions.

Lawyers are not supposed to "educate" jurors during voir dire, but every lawyer worth his salt tries to predispose a jury to his side. For example, Reiner asked: "Have you read anything in the press, or heard anything on TV, to the effect that Charles Manson has a kind of 'hypnotic power' over the female defendants?" Obviously Reiner was less interested in the answer than in implanting this suggestion in the minds of the jurors. Similarly, walking the thin line between inquiry and instruction, I asked each juror: "Do you understand that the People only have the burden of proving a defendant guilty beyond a *reasonable* doubt; we do not have the burden of proving his guilt beyond *all* doubt—only a *reasonable* doubt?"

Initially, Older would not permit the attorneys to instruct the prospective jurors in the law. I had a number of heated discussions with him about this before he let us couch such questions in general terms. This was, I felt, an important victory. For example, I didn't want to go through the whole trial only to have some juror decide, "We can't convict Manson of the five Tate murders because he wasn't there. He was back at Spahn Ranch."

The heart of our case against Manson was the "vicarious liability" rule of conspiracy—each conspirator is criminally responsible for all the crimes committed by his co-conspirators if said crimes were committed to further the object of the conspiracy. This rule applies even if the conspirator was not present at the scene of the crime. For example: A, B and C decide to rob a bank. A plans the robbery, B and C carry it out. Under the law, A, though he never entered the bank, is as responsible as B and C, I pointed out to the jury.

From the prosecution's point of view, it was important that each juror understand such gut issues as reasonable doubt, conspiracy, motive, direct and circumstantial evidence, and the accomplice rule.

We hoped Judge Older would not declare Linda Kasabian an accomplice. But we were fairly sure he would,* in which case the defense would make much of the fact that no defendant can be convicted of any crime on the uncorroborated testimony of an accomplice. In researching the law, I found a California Supreme Court case, *People* vs *Wayne*, in which the Court said only "slight" evidence was needed to constitute corroboration. After I brought this to Older's attention, he permitted me to use the word "slight" in my questioning. This, too, I considered a significant victory.

Though Older had ascertained that each prospective juror could, if the evidence warranted it, vote a verdict of death, I went beyond this, asking each if he could conceive of circumstances wherein he would be willing to vote such a verdict against (1) a young person; (2) a female defendant; or (3) a particular defendant even though the evidence showed that he himself did not do any actual killing. Obviously I wanted to eliminate anyone who answered any of these questions negatively.

Manson and the girls caused no disruptions during jury selection. In chambers during the individual voir dire,

*He later did.

however, Manson would often stare at Judge Older for literally hours. I could only surmise that he had developed his incredible concentration while in prison. Older totally ignored him.

One day Manson tried it with me. I stared right back, holding his gaze until his hands started shaking. During the recess, I slid my chair over next to his and asked, "What are you trembling about, Charlie? Are you afraid of me?"

"Bugliosi," he said, "you think I'm bad and I'm not."

"I don't think you're all bad, Charlie. For instance, I understand you love animals."

"Then you know I wouldn't hurt anyone," he said.

"Hitler loved animals too, Charlie. He had a dog named Blondie, and from what I've read, Adolf was very kind to Blondie."

Usually a prosecutor and a defendant won't exchange two words during an entire trial. But Manson was no ordinary defendant. And he loved to rap. In this, the first of many strange, often highly revealing conversations we had, Manson asked me why I thought he was behind these murders. "Because both Linda and Sadie told me you were," I replied. "Now, Sadie doesn't like me, Charlie, and she thinks you're Jesus Christ. So why would she tell me this if it wasn't true?"

"Sadie's just a stupid little bitch," Manson said. "You know, I only made love to her two or three times. After she had her baby and lost her shape, I couldn't have cared less about her. That's why she told that story, to get attention. I would never personally harm anyone."

"Don't give me that crap, Charlie, because I won't buy it! What about Lotsapoppa? You put a bullet in his stomach."

"Well, yeah, I shot that guy," Manson admitted. "He was going to come up to Spahn Ranch and get all of us. That was kinda in self-defense."

Manson was enough of a jailhouse lawyer to know that I couldn't use anything he told me unless I'd first informed him of his constitutional rights. Yet this, and many subsequent admissions, surprised me. There was a strange sort of honesty about him. It was devious, it was never direct, but it was there. Whenever I pinned him down, he might evade, but not once in this, or the numerous other conversations we had, did he flatly deny that he had ordered the murders.

An innocent man protests his innocence. Instead, Manson played word games. If he took the stand and did this, I felt the jury would see through him.

Would Manson take the stand? The general consensus was that Manson's prodigious ego, plus the opportunity to use the witness stand as a forum to expound his philosophy before the world press, would impel him to testify. But—though I had already put in many hours preparing my cross-examination—no one but Manson really knew what he would do.

Toward the end of the recess, I told him, "I've enjoyed talking to you, Charlie, but it would be much more interesting if we did it with you on the stand. I have lots and lots of things I'm curious about."

"For instance?"

"For instance," I replied, "where in the world—Terminal Island, Haight-Ashbury, Spahn Ranch—did you get the crazy idea that other people don't like to live?"

He didn't answer. Then he began to smile. He'd been challenged. And knew it. Whether he'd decide to accept the challenge remained to be seen.

Though silent in court, Manson remained active behind the scenes.

On June 24, Patricia Krenwinkel interrupted Fitzgerald's voir dire to ask that he be relieved as her attorney. "I have talked with him about the way I wish this to be handled right now, and he doesn't do as I ask," she told the Court. "He is to be my voice, which he is not . . ." Older denied her request.

Later the defense attorneys had a meeting with their clients. Fitzgerald, who had given up his Public Defender's job to represent Krenwinkel, emerged with tears in his eyes. I felt very badly about this and, putting my arm around his shoulder, told him, "Paul, don't let it get you down. She'll probably keep you. And if she doesn't, so what? They're just a bunch of murderers."

"They're savages, ingrates," Fitzgerald said bitterly. "Their only allegiance is to Manson."

Fitzgerald didn't tell me what had occurred during the meeting, but it wasn't hard to guess. Directly, or through the girls, Manson had probably told the attorneys: Do it my way or you're off the case. Fitzgerald and Reiner told Los Angeles *Times* reporter John Kendall that all the attorneys had been instructed to "remain silent" and not question prospective jurors.

When, the following day, Reiner disobeyed this order and continued his voir dire, Leslie Van Houten tried to fire him, repeating almost verbatim the words Krenwinkel had used. Older denied her request also.

What Reiner was going through could be gleaned from some of his questions. For example, he asked one prospective juror: "Even if it appears that Leslie Van Houten desired to stand or fall with the other defendants, could you nevertheless acquit her if the evidence against her was insufficient?"

On July 14 both the prosecution and the defense agreed to accept the jury. The twelve were then sworn. The jury consisted of seven men and five women, ranging in age from twenty-five to seventy-three, in occupation from an electronics technician to a mortician.*

It was very much a mixed jury, neither side getting exactly what it wanted.

Almost automatically, the defense will challenge anyone connected with law enforcement. Yet Alva Dawson, the oldest member of the jury, had worked sixteen years as a deputy sheriff with LASO, while Walter Vitzelio had been a plant security guard for twenty years, and had a brother who was a deputy sheriff.

*The twelve jurors were: John Baer, an electrical tester; Alva Dawson, a retired deputy sheriff; Mrs. Shirley Evans, a school secretary; Mrs. Evelyn Hines, a dictaphone-teletype operator; William McBride II, a chemical company employee; Mrs. Thelma McKenzie, a clerical supervisor; Miss Marie Mesmer, former drama critic for the now defunct Los Angeles *Daily News;* Mrs. Jean Roseland, an executive secretary; Anlee Sisto, an electronics technician; Herman Tubick, a mortician; Walter Vitzelio, a retired plant guard; and William Zamora, a highway engineer.

On the other hand, Herman Tubick, the mortician, and Mrs. Jean Roseland, a secretary with TWA, each had two daughters in approximately the same age group as the three female defendants.

Studying the jurors' faces as they were sworn, I felt that most appeared pleased to have been selected. After all, they had been chosen to serve on one of the most famous trials of all time.

Older was quick to bring them back to earth. He instructed them that when they came to court the following morning they should bring their suitcases, clothing, and personal items, as from that point on they would be sequestered.

There remained the selection of the alternate jurors. Because of the anticipated length of the trial, Older decided to pick six, an unusually large number. Again we went through the whole voir dire.

Only this time it was without Ira Reiner. On July 17, Leslie Van Houten formally requested that Reiner be relieved as her attorney and Ronald Hughes appointed instead.

After questioning Hughes, Manson, and Van Houten on the possibility of a conflict of interest, Judge Older granted the substitution. Reiner was out, receiving not even so much as a thank-you for the eight months he had devoted to the case. Manson's former attorney, the "hippie lawyer" Ronald Hughes, with his Santa Claus beard and Walter Slezak suits, became Leslie Van Houten's attorney of record.

Ira Reiner had been fired for one reason, and one reason only. He had tried to represent his client to the best of his ability. And he had properly decided that his client was not Charles Manson but Leslie Van Houten.

There was a slight but perceptible smile on Manson's face. With good reason. He had succeeded in forming a united defense team. Although Fitzgerald remained its nominal head, it was obvious who was calling the shots.

On July 21 the six alternates were sworn, and they too were sequestered.* Jury selection had taken five weeks, during which 205 people had been examined and nearly 4,500 pages of transcript accumulated.

It had been a rough five weeks. Older and I had clashed on several occasions, Reiner and Older even oftener. And Older had threatened four of the attorneys with contempt, carrying through on one.

Three were for violations of the gag order: Aaron Stovitz was cited for an interview he had given the magazine *Rolling Stone;* Paul Fitzgerald and Ira Reiner for their quoted remarks in the Los Angeles *Times* story "TATE SUSPECTS TRY TO SILENCE LAWYERS." Though Older eventually dropped the contempt citations against all three, Irving Kanarek was less lucky. On July 8 he was seven minutes late to court. He had a valid reason—it was very difficult to find a parking space at the time court convened—but Older, who had previously threatened Kanarek with contempt when he was just three minutes late, was not sympathetic. He ruled Kanarek in contempt and fined him twenty-five dollars.

While we were busy selecting a jury, two of Manson's killers were set free.

Mary Brunner was reindicted and rearrested for the Hinman murder. Her attorneys filed a writ of habeas corpus. Ruling that she had fufilled the conditions of the immunity agreement, Judge Kathleen Parker granted the writ and Brunner was released.

Meanwhile, Clem, t/n Steve Grogan, pleaded guilty to a grand theft auto charge stemming from the Barker raid. Van Nuys Judge Sterry Fagan heard the case. He was aware of Grogan's lengthy rap sheet. Moreover, the probation department, usually very permissive, in this case recommended that Grogan be sentenced to a year in the County Jail. Aaron also informed the judge that Clem was

*The six alternate jurors were: Miss Frances Chasen, a retired civil service employee; Kenneth Daut, Jr., a state Division of Highways employee; Robert Douglass, an employee of the Army Corps of Engineers; John Ellis, a telephone installer; Mrs. Victoria Kampman, a housewife; and Larry Sheely, a telephone maintenance man.

exceedingly dangerous; and that he had not only been along on the night the LaBiancas were killed, but we also had evidence that he had beheaded Shorty Shea. Yet unbelievably enough, Judge Fagan gave Clem straight probation!

On learning that Clem had returned to the Family at Spahn Ranch, I contacted his probation officer, asking him to revoke Clem's probation. There was more than ample cause. Among the terms of his probation were that he maintain residence at the home of his parents; seek and maintain employment; not use or possess any narcotics; not associate with known narcotics users. Moreover, he had been seen on several occasions, even photographed, with a knife and a gun.

His probation officer refused to act. He later admitted to LAPD that he was afraid of Clem.

Though Bruce Davis had gone underground, most of the other hard-core Family members were very much in evidence. Some dozen of them, including Clem and Mary, haunted the entrances and corridors of the Hall of Justice each day, where they would cast cold, accusing stares at the prosecution witnesses as they arrived to testify.

The problem of their presence in the courtroom—a concern since Sandy had been found carrying a knife—was solved by Aaron. Prospective witnesses are excluded when other witnesses are testifying. Aaron simply subpoenaed all the known Family members as prosecution witnesses, an act which raised a tremendous furor from the defense but made everyone else breathe a little easier.

July 24-26, 1970

TATE MURDER TRIAL STARTS TODAY

HINT PROSECUTION WILL REVEAL "SURPRISE MOTIVE"

SHARON'S FATHER EXPECTED TO BE FIRST WITNESS

Many of the spectators had been waiting since 6 A.M., hoping to get a seat and a glimpse of Manson. When he was escorted into the courtroom, several gasped. On his forehead was a bloody X. Sometime the previous night he had taken a sharp object and carved the mark in his flesh.

An explanation was not long forthcoming. Outside court his followers passed out a typewritten statement bearing his name:

"I have X'd myself from your world ... You have created the monster. I am not of you, from you, nor do I condone your unjust attitude toward things, animals, and people that you do not try to understand ... I stand opposed to what you do and have done in the past ... You make fun of God and have murdered the world in the name of Jesus Christ ... My faith in me is stronger than all of your armies, governments, gas chambers, or anything you may want to do to me. I know what I have done. Your courtroom is man's game. Love is my judge ..."

THE COURT "People vs. Charles Manson, Susan Atkins, Patricia Krenwinkel, and Leslie Van Houten.

"All parties and counsel and jurors are present ...

"Do the People care to make an opening statement?"

BUGLIOSI "Yes, Your Honor."

I began the People's opening statement—which was a preview of the evidence the prosecution intended to introduce in the trial—by summarizing the charges, naming the defendants, and, after relating what had occurred at 10050 Cielo Drive in the early-morning hours of August 9, 1969, and at 3301 Waverly Drive the following night, identifying the victims.

"A question you ladies and gentlemen will probably ask yourselves at some point during this trial, and we expect the evidence to answer that question for you, is this:

"What kind of a diabolical mind would contemplate or conceive of these seven murders? What kind of mind would want to have seven human beings brutally murdered?

"We expect the evidence at this trial to answer that question and show that defendant Charles Manson owned that diabolical mind. Charles Manson, who the evidence will show at times had the infinite humility, as it were, to refer to himself as Jesus Christ.

"Evidence at this trial will show defendant Manson to be a vagrant wanderer, a frustrated singer-guitarist, a pseudo-philosopher, but, most of all, the evidence will conclusively prove that Charles Manson is a killer who cleverly masqueraded behind the common image of a hippie, that of being peace loving . . .

"The evidence will show Charles Manson to be a megalomaniac who coupled his insatiable thirst for power with an intense obsession for violent death."

The evidence would show, I continued, that Manson was the unquestioned leader and overlord of a nomadic band of vagabonds who called themselves the "Family." After briefly tracing the history and composition of the group, I observed: "We anticipate that Mr. Manson, in his defense, will claim that neither he nor anyone else was the leader of the Family and that he never ordered anyone in the Family to do anything, much less commit these murders for him."

KANAREK "Your Honor, he is now making an opening statement for us!"

THE COURT "Overruled. You may continue, Mr. Bugliosi."

BUGLIOSI "We therefore intend to offer evidence at this trial showing that Charles Manson was in fact the dictatorial leader of the Family; that everyone in the Family was slavishly obedient to him; that he always had the other members of the Family do his bidding for him; and that eventually they committed the seven Tate-LaBianca murders at his command.

"This evidence of Mr. Manson's total domination over the Family will be offered as circumstantial evidence that on the two nights in question it was he who ordered these seven murders."

The principal witness for the prosecution, I told the jury, would be Linda Kasabian. I then briefly stated what Linda would testify to, interrelating her story with the physical evidence we intended to introduce: the gun, the rope, the clothing the killers wore the night of the Tate murders, and so forth.

We came now to the question that everyone had been asking since these murders occurred: *Why?*

The prosecution does not have the burden of proving motive, I told the jury. We needn't introduce one single, solitary speck of evidence as to motive. However, when we have evidence of motive we introduce it, because if one has a motive for committing a murder, this is circumstantial evidence that it was he who committed the murder. "In this trial, we *will* offer evidence of Charles Manson's motives for ordering these seven murders."

If Manson and the defense were waiting to hear the word "robbery," they'd wait in vain. Instead, Manson's own beliefs came back at them.

"We believe there to be more than one motive," I told the jury. "Besides the motives of Manson's passion for violent death and his extreme anti-establishment state of mind, the evidence in this trial will show that there was a further motive for these murders, which is perhaps as bizarre, or perhaps even more bizarre, than the murders themselves.

"Briefly, the evidence will show Manson's fanatical obsession with Helter Skelter, a term he got from the English musical group the Beatles.

"Manson was an avid follower of the Beatles and believed that they were speaking to him across the ocean through the lyrics of their songs. In fact, Manson told his followers that he found complete support for his philosophy in the words of those songs . . .

"To Charles Manson, Helter Skelter, the title of one of their songs, meant the black man rising up and destroying the entire white race; that is, with the exception of Charles Manson and his chosen followers, who intended to escape from Helter Skelter by going to the desert and living in a bottomless pit, a place that Manson derived from Revelation 9, a chapter in the last book of the New Testament . . .

"Evidence from several witnesses will show that Charles Manson hated black people, but that he also hated the white establishment, whom he called 'pigs.'

"The word 'pig' was found printed in blood on the outside of the front door to the Tate residence.

"The words 'death to pigs,' 'helter skelter,' and 'rise' were found printed in blood inside the LaBianca residence.

"The evidence will show that one of Manson's principal motives for these seven savage murders was to ignite Helter Skelter; in other words, start the black-white revolution by making it look as though the black man had murdered these seven Caucasian victims. In his twisted mind, he thought this would cause the white community to turn against the black community, ultimately leading to a civil war between blacks and whites, a war which Manson told his followers would see bloodbaths in the streets of every American city, a war which Manson predicted and foresaw the black man as winning.

"Manson envisioned that black people, once they destroyed the entire white race, would be unable to handle the reins of power because of inexperience, and would therefore have to turn over the reins to those white people who had escaped from Helter Skelter; i.e., Charles Manson and his Family.

"In Manson's mind, his Family, and particularly he, would be the ultimate beneficiaries of a black-white civil war.

"We intend to offer the testimony of not just one witness but many witnesses on Manson's philosophy, because the evidence will show that it is so strange and so bizarre that if you heard it only from the lips of one person you probably would not believe it."

Thus far all the emphasis had been on Manson. Convicting Manson was the first priority. If we convicted the others and not Manson, it would be like a war crimes trial in which the flunkies were found guilty and Hitler went free. Therefore I stressed that it was Manson who had ordered these murders, though his co-defendants, obedient to his every command, actually committed them.

There was a danger in this, however. I was giving the attorneys for the three girls a ready-made defense. In the penalty phase of the trial, they could argue that since Atkins, Krenwinkel, and Van Houten were totally under Manson's domination, they were not nearly as culpable as he, and therefore should receive life imprisonment rather than the death penalty.

Anticipating long in advance that I'd have to prove the very opposite, I laid the groundwork in my opening statement:

"What about Charles Manson's followers, the other defendants in this case, Susan Atkins, Patricia Krenwinkel, and Leslie Van Houten?

"The evidence will show that they, along with Tex Watson, were the actual killers of the seven Tate-LaBianca victims.

"The evidence will also show that they were *very willing* participants in these mass murders, that by their overkill tactics—for instance, Rosemary LaBianca was stabbed forty-one times, Voytek Frykowski was stabbed fifty-one times, shot twice, and struck violently over the head thirteen times with the butt of a revolver—these defendants displayed that *even apart* from Charles Manson, murder ran through their own blood."

After mentioning Susan Atkins' confessions to Virginia Graham and Ronnie Howard; the fingerprint which placed Patricia Krenwinkel at the Tate murder scene; and the evidence which implicated Leslie Van Houten in the LaBianca murders, I observed: "The evidence will show that Charles Manson started his Family in the Haight-Ashbury district of San Francisco in March of 1967. The Family's demise, as it were, took place in October of 1969 at Barker Ranch, a desolate, secluded, rock-strewn hideout from civilization on the shadowy perimeters of Death Valley. Between these two dates, seven human beings and an eight-and-a-half-month baby boy fetus in the womb of Sharon Tate met their death at the hands of these members of the Family.

"The evidence at this trial will show that these seven incredible murders were perhaps the most bizarre, savage, nightmarish murders in the recorded annals of crime.

"Mr. Stovitz and I intend to prove not just beyond a reasonable doubt, which is our only burden, but beyond *all* doubt that these defendants committed these murders, and are guilty of these murders; and in our final arguments to you at the conclusion of the evidence, we intend to ask you to return verdicts of first degree murder against each of these defendants."

Noting that it would be a long trial, with many witnesses, I recalled the old Chinese proverb, "The palest ink is better than the best memory," urging the jury to take detailed notes to aid them in their deliberations.

I closed by telling the jury that we felt confident that they would give both the defendants and the People of the State of California the fair and impartial trial to which each was entitled.

Kanarek had interrupted my opening statement nine times with objections, all of which the Court had overruled. When I finished, he moved that the whole statement be stricken or, failing in that, a mistrial declared. Older denied both motions. Fitzgerald told the press my remarks were "scurrilous and slanderous," and called the Helter Skelter motive "a truly preposterous theory."

I had a strong feeling that by the time of his closing argument to the jury, Paul wouldn't even bother to argue this.

The defense reserving its opening statements until after the prosecution had completed its case, the People called their first witness, Colonel Paul Tate.

With military erectness, Sharon's father took the stand and was sworn. Though forty-six, he looked younger, and sported a well-trimmed beard. Before entering the courtroom, he had been thoroughly searched, it being rumored that he had vowed to kill Manson. Even though he glanced only briefly at the defendants, and exhibited no discernible reaction, the bailiffs watched him every minute he was in the courtroom.

Our direct examination was brief. Colonel Tate described his last meeting with Sharon, and identified photos of his daughter, Miss Folger, Frykowski, Sebring, and the house at 10050 Cielo Drive.

Wilfred Parent, who followed Colonel Tate to the stand, broke down and cried when shown a photograph of his son, Steven.

Winifred Chapman, the Tate maid, was next. I questioned her in detail about the washing of the two doors; then, wanting to establish a chronology for the jurors, I took her up to her departure from the residence on the afternoon of August 8, 1969, intending to recall her to the stand later so she could testify to her discoveries the next morning.

On cross-examination Fitzgerald brought out that she hadn't mentioned washing the door in Sharon's bedroom until months after the murders, and then she had told this not to LAPD but to me.

This was to be the start of a pattern. Having questioned each of the witnesses not once but a number of times, I had uncovered a great deal of information not previously related to the police. In many instances I had been the only one who had interviewed the witness. Though Fitzgerald initially planted the idea, Kanarek would nurture it until, in his mind at least, it budded into a full-bloomed conspiracy, with Bugliosi framing the whole case.

Kanarek had only one question for Mrs. Chapman, but it was a good one. Had she ever seen the defendant Charles Manson before her appearance in court? She replied that she had not.

Although he had recently married and was not anxious to leave his bride, William Garretson had flown back from his home in Lancaster, Ohio, where he had returned after being released by LAPD. The former caretaker came across as sincere, though rather shy. Although I intended to call both officers Whisenhunt and Wolfer, the former to testify to finding the setting on Garretson's stereo at between 4 and 5, the latter to describe the sound tests he had conducted, I did question Garretson in detail as to the events of that night, and I felt the jury believed him when he claimed he hadn't heard any gunshots or screams.

I asked Garretson: "How loud were you playing your stereo?"

A. "It was about medium . . . It wasn't very loud."

This, I felt, was the best evidence Garretson was telling the truth. Had he been lying about hearing nothing, then surely he would have lied and said the stereo was loud.

Most of Fitzgerald's questions concerned Garretson's arrest and alleged rough handling by the police. At one point later in the trial Fitzgerald would maintain that Garretson was involved in at least some of the Tate homicides. Since there wasn't even a hint of this in his cross-examination, I'd conclude that he was belatedly looking for a convenient scapegoat.

Kanarek again asked the same question. No, he'd never seen Manson before, Garretson replied.

When I'd interviewed Garretson prior to his taking the stand, he'd told me that he still had nightmares about what had happened. That weekend, before his return to Ohio, Rudi Altobelli, who was now living in the main house, arranged for Garretson to revisit 10050 Cielo Drive. He found the premises quiet and peaceful. After that, he told me, the nightmares stopped.

By the end of the day we had finished with three more witnesses: Frank Guerrero, who had been painting the nursery that Friday; Tom Vargas, the gardener, who testified to the arrivals and departures of the various guests that day and to his signing for the two steamer trunks; and Dennis Hurst, who identified Sebring from a photograph as the man who came to the front door when he delivered the bicycle about eight that night.

The stage was now set for the prosecution's main witness, whom I intended to call to the stand first thing Monday morning.

On hearing my opening statement, Manson must have realized that I had his number.

At the conclusion of court that afternoon sheriff's deputy Sergeant William Maupin was escorting Manson from the lockup to the ninth floor of the jail when—to quote from Maupin's report—"inmate Manson stated to undersigned that it would be worth $100,000 to be set free. Inmate Manson also commented on how much he would like to return to the desert and the life he had before his arrest. Inmate Manson commented additionally that money meant nothing to him, that several people had contacted him regarding large sums of money. Inmate Manson also stated that an officer would only receive a six month sentence if caught releasing an inmate without authority."

Maupin reported the bribe offer to his superior, Captain Alley, who in turn informed Judge Older. Though the incident was never made public, Older gave the attorneys Maupin's report the next day. Reading it, I wondered what Manson would try next.

Over the weekend, Susan Atkins, Patricia Krenwinkel, and Leslie Van Houten lit matches, heated bobby pins red-hot, then burned X marks on their foreheads, after which they ripped open the burnt flesh with needles, to create more prominent scars.

When the jurors were brought into court Monday morning, the X's were the first thing they saw—graphic evidence that when Manson led, the girls followed.

A day or so later Sandy, Squeaky, Gypsy, and most of the other Family members did the same thing. As new disciples joined the group, this became one of the Family rituals, complete to tasting the blood as it ran down their faces.

July 27-August 3, 1970

Eight sheriff's deputies escorted Linda Kasabian from Sybil Brand to the Hall of Justice, through an entrance that circumvented those patrolled by the Family. When they reached the ninth floor, however, Sandra Good suddenly appeared in the corridor and screamed, *"You'll kill us all; you'll kill us all!"* Linda, according to those who witnessed the encounter, seemed less shaken than sad.

I saw Linda just after she arrived. Though her attorney, Gary Fleischman, had purchased a new dress for her, it had been misplaced, and she was wearing the same maternity dress she'd worn when pregnant. The baggy tent made her look more hippie-like than the defendants. After I'd explained the problem to Judge Older, he heard other matters in chambers until the dress was located and brought over. Later a similar courtesy would be extended to the defense when Susan Atkins lost her bra.

BUGLIOSI "The People call Linda Kasabian."

The sad, resigned look she gave Manson and the girls contrasted sharply with their obviously hostile glares.

CLERK "Would you raise your right hand, please?"

KANAREK "Object, Your Honor, on the grounds this witness is not competent and she is insane!"

BUGLIOSI "Wait a minute! Your Honor, I move to strike that, and I ask the Court to find him in contempt for gross misconduct. This is unbelievable on his part!"

Unfortunately, it was all too believable—exactly the sort of thing we had feared since Kanarek came on the case. Ordering the jury to disregard Kanarek's remarks, Older called counsel to the bench. "There is no question about it," Older told Kanarek, "your conduct is outrageous . . ."

BUGLIOSI "I know the Court cannot prevent him from

speaking up, but God knows what he is going to say in the future. If I were to say something like this in open court, I would probably be thrown off the case by my office and disbarred . . ."

Defending Kanarek, Fitzgerald told the Court that the defense intended to call witnesses who would testify that Linda Kasabian had taken LSD at least three hundred times. The defense would contend, he said, that such drug use had rendered her mentally incapable of testifying.

Whatever their offer of proof, Older said, matters of law were to be discussed either at the bench or in chambers, *not* in front of the jury. As for Kanarek's outburst, Older warned him that if he did that once more, "I am going to take some action against you."

Linda was sworn. I asked her: "Linda, you realize that you are presently charged with seven counts of murder and one count of conspiracy to commit murder?"

A. "Yes."

Kanarek objected, moving for a mistrial. Denied. It was some ten minutes later before I was able to get in the second question.

Q. "Linda, are you aware of the agreement between the District Attorney's Office and your attorneys that if you testify to everything you know about the Tate-LaBianca murders, the District Attorney's Office will petition the Court to grant you immunity from prosecution and dismiss all charges against you?"

A. "Yes, I am aware."

Kanarek objected on four different grounds. Denied. By bringing this in first, we defused one of the defense's biggest cannons.

Q. "Besides the benefits which will accrue to you under the agreement, is there any other reason why you have decided to tell everything you know about these seven murders?"

Another torrent of objections from Kanarek before Linda was able to answer: "I strongly believe in the truth, and I feel the truth should be spoken."

Kanarek even objected to my asking Linda the number of children she had. Often he used a shotgun approach—"Leading and suggestive; no foundation; conclusion and hearsay"—in hope that at least some of the buckshot would hit. Many of his grounds were totally inapplicable. He would object to a "conclusion," for example, when no conclusion was called for, or yell "Hearsay" when I was simply asking her what she did next.

Since I'd anticipated this, it didn't bother me. However, it took over an hour to get Linda up to her first meeting with Manson, her description of life at Spahn Ranch, and, over Kanarek's very heated objections, her definition of what she meant by the term "Family."

A. "Well, we lived together as one family, as a family lives together, as a mother and father and children, but we were all just one, and Charlie was the head."

I was questioning Linda about the various orders Manson had given the girls when, unexpectedly, Judge Older began sustaining Kanarek's hearsay objections. I asked to approach the bench.

Lay people believe hearsay is inadmissible. Actually there are so many exceptions to the hearsay rule that many lawyers feel the law should read, "Hearsay is admissible except in these few instances."* I told Older: "I had anticipated many legal problems in this case, and I have done research on them—because I kind of play the Devil's advocate—but I never anticipated I'd have any trouble showing Manson's directions to members of the Family."

Older said he sustained the objections because he couldn't think of any exception to the hearsay rule that would permit the introduction of such statements.

This was crucial. If Older ruled such conversations inadmissible, there went the domination framework, and our case against Manson.

Shortly after this, court recessed for the day. Aaron, J. Miller Leavy, and I were up late that night, looking for citations of authority. Fortunately, we found two cases—*People* vs. *Fratiano* and *People* vs. *Stevens*—in which the Court ruled you can show the existence of a conspiracy by showing the relationship between the parties, including statements made to each other. Shown the cases the next

*For example, Susan Atkins' confessions to Virginia Graham and Ronnie Howard were hearsay, but admissible under the admission exception to the hearsay rule.

morning, Judge Older reversed himself and overruled Kanarek's objections.

Opposition now came from a totally unexpected direction: Aaron.

Linda had already testified that Manson ordered the girls to make love to male visitors to induce them to join the Family, when I asked her: "Linda, do you know what a sexual orgy is?"

Kanarek immediately objected, as did Hughes, who remarked, in a somewhat revealing choice of words: "We are not trying the sex lives of these people. We are trying the murder lives of these people."

Not only were the defense attorneys shouting objections, many of which Older sustained; Aaron leaned over to me and said, "Can't we skip this stuff? We're just wasting time. Let's get into the two nights of murder."

"Look, Aaron," I told him sotto voce, "I'm fighting the judge, I'm fighting Kanarek, I'm not going to fight you. I've got enough problems. This is important and I'm going to get it in."

As Linda finally testified, in between Kanarek's objections, *Manson* decided when an orgy would take place; *Manson* decided who would, and who would not, participate; and *Manson* then assigned the roles each would play. From start to finish he was the maestro, as it were, orchestrating the whole scene.

That Manson controlled even this most intimate and personal aspect of the lives of his followers was extremely powerful evidence of his domination.

Moreover, among the twenty-some persons involved in the particular orgy Linda testified to were Charles "Tex" Watson, Susan Atkins, Leslie Van Houten, and Patricia Krenwinkel.

The sexual acts were not detailed, nor did I question Linda about other such "group encounters." Once the point was made, I moved on to other testimony—Helter Skelter, the black-white war, Manson's belief that the Beatles were communicating with him through the lyrics of their songs, his announcement, late on the afternoon of August 8, 1969, that "Now is the time for Helter Skelter."

Describing her appearance on the stand, the Los Angeles *Times* noted that even in discussing the group's sex life, Linda Kasabian was surprisingly "serene, soft-spoken, even demure."

Her testimony was also at times very moving. Telling how Manson separated the mothers and their children, and relating her own feelings on being parted from Tanya, Linda said, "Sometimes, you know, when there wasn't anybody around, especially Charlie, I would give her my love and feed her."

Linda was describing Manson's directions to the group just before they left Spahn Ranch that first night when Charlie, seated at the counsel table, put his hand up to his neck and, with one finger extended, made a slitting motion across his throat. Although I was looking the other way and didn't see the gesture, others, including Linda, did.

Yet there was no pause in her reply. She went on to relate how Tex had stopped the car in front of the big gate; the cutting of the telephone wires; driving back down the hill and parking, then walking back up. As she described how they had climbed the fence to the right of the gate, you could feel the tension building in the courtroom. Then the sudden headlights.

A. "And a car pulled up in front of us and Tex leaped forward with a gun in his hand . . . And the man said, 'Please don't hurt me, I won't say anything!' And Tex shot him four times."

As she described the murder of Steven Parent, Linda began sobbing, as she had each time she had related the story to me. I could tell the jury was moved, both by the mounting horror and her reaction.

Sadie giggled. Leslie sketched. Katie looked bored.

By the end of the day I had brought Linda to the point where Katie was chasing the woman in the white gown (Folger) with a knife and Tex was stabbing the big man (Frykowski): "He just kept doing it and doing it and doing it."

Q. "When the man was screaming, do you know what he was screaming?"

A. "There were no words, it was beyond words, it was just screams."

Reporters keeping track of Kanarek's objections gave up on the third day, when the count passed two hundred. Older warned Kanarek that if he interrupted either the witness or the prosecution again, he would find him in contempt. Often a dozen transcript pages separated my question and Linda's answer.

BUGLIOSI "We are going to have to go back, Linda. There has been a blizzard of objections."

KANAREK "I object to that statement."

When Kanarek again interrupted Linda in mid-sentence, Older called us to the bench.

THE COURT "Mr. Kanarek, you have directly violated my order not to repeatedly interrupt. I find you in contempt of Court and I sentence you to one night in the County Jail starting immediately after this court adjourns this afternoon until 7 A.M. tomorrow morning."

Kanarek protested that "rather than my interrupting the witness, the witness interrupted me"!

By day's end Kanarek would have company. Among the items I wished to submit for identification purposes was a photograph which showed the Straight Satans' sword in a scabbard next to the steering wheel of Manson's own dune buggy. Since the photograph had been introduced in evidence in the Beausoleil trial, I didn't get it until it was brought over from the other court. "The District Attorney is withholding great quantities of evidence from us," Hughes charged.

BUGLIOSI "For the record, I just saw it for the first time a few minutes ago myself."

HUGHES "That is a lot of shit, Mr. Bugliosi."

THE COURT "I hold you in direct contempt of Court for that statement."

Though in complete agreement with Older's earlier citing of Kanarek, I disagreed with his finding against Hughes, feeling if he was in contempt of anyone, it was me, not the Court. Too, it was based on a simple misunderstanding, one which, when explained to him, Hughes quickly accepted. Older was less understanding.

Given a choice between paying a seventy-five-dollar fine or spending the night in jail, Hughes told the Court: "I am a pauper, Your Honor." With no sympathy whatsoever, Older ordered him remanded into custody.

Kanarek learned nothing from his night in jail. The next morning he was right back interrupting both my questions and Linda's replies. Admonishments from the bench accomplished nothing; he'd apologize, then immediately do the same thing again. All this concerned me much less than the fact that he occasionally succeeded in keeping out testimony. Usually when Older sustained an objection, I could work my way around it, introducing the testimony in a different way. For example, when Older foreclosed me from questioning Linda about the defendants watching the news of the Tate murders on TV the day after those murders occurred, because he couldn't see the relevance of this, I asked Linda if, on the night of the murders, she was aware of the identities of the victims.

A. "No."

Q. "When was the first time you learned the names of these five people?"

A. "The following day on the news."

Q. "On television?"

A. "Yes."

Q. "In Mr. Spahn's trailer?"

A. "Yes."

Q. "Did you see Tex, Sadie, and Katie during the day following these killings, other than when you were watching television with them?"

A. "Well, I saw Sadie and Katie in the trailer. I cannot remember seeing Tex on that day."

The relevance of this would become obvious when Barbara Hoyt took the stand and testified (1) that Sadie came in and told her to switch channels to the news; (2) that before this particular day Sadie and the others never watched the news; and (3) that immediately after the newscaster finished with Tate and moved on to the Vietnam war, the group got up and left.

In my questioning of Linda regarding the second night, there was one reiterated theme: Who told you to turn off the freeway? Charlie. Was anyone else in the car giving directions other than Mr. Manson? No. Did anyone question any of Mr. Manson's commands? No.

In her testimony regarding both nights, there were also literally a multitude of details which only someone who had been present on those nights of horrendous slaughter could have known.

Realizing very early how damaging this was, Manson had remarked, loud enough for both Linda and the jury to hear, "You've already told three lies."

Linda, looking directly at him, had replied, "Oh, no, Charlie, I've spoken the truth, and you know it."

By the time I had finished my direct examination of Linda Kasabian on the afternoon of July 30, I had the feeling the jury knew it too.

When I know the defense has something which might prove harmful to the prosecution's case, as a trial tactic I usually put on that evidence myself first. This not only converts a damaging left hook into a mere left jab, it also indicates to the jury that the prosecution isn't trying to hide anything. Therefore, I'd brought out, on direct, Linda's sexual permissiveness and her use of LSD and other drugs.* Prepared to destroy her credibility with these revelations, the defense found itself going over familiar ground. In doing so, they sometimes even strengthened our case.

It was Fitzgerald, Krenwinkel's defense attorney, not the prosecution, who brought out that during the period Linda was at Spahn, "I was not really together in myself . . . I was extremely impressionistic . . . I let others put ideas in me"; and—even more important—that she feared Manson.

Q. "What were you afraid of?" Fitzgerald asked.

A. "I was just afraid. He was a heavy dude."

Asked to explain what she meant by this, Linda replied, "He just had something, you know, that could hold you. He was a heavyweight. He was just heavy, period."

Fitzgerald also elicited from Linda that she loved Manson; that "I felt he was the Messiah come again."

*She had taken LSD about fifty times, she testified, the last time being in May 1969, three months prior to the murders.

Linda then added one statement which went a long way toward explaining not only why she but also many of the others had so readily accepted Manson. When she first saw him, she said, "I thought . . . 'This is what I have been looking for,' and this is what I saw in him."

Manson—a mirror which reflected the desires of others.

Q. "Was it also your impression that other people at the ranch loved Charlie?"

A. "Oh, yes. It seemed that the girls worshiped him, just would die to do anything for him."

Helter Skelter, Manson's attitude toward blacks, his domination of his co-defendants: in each of these areas Fitzgerald's queries brought out additional information which bolstered Linda's previous testimony.

Often his questions backfired, as when he asked Linda: "Do you remember who you slept with on August 8?"

A. "No."

Q. "On the tenth?"

A. "No, but eventually I slept with all the men."

Time and again Linda volunteered information which could have been considered damaging, yet, coming from her, somehow seemed only honest and sincere. She was so open that it caught Fitzgerald off guard.

Avoiding the word "orgy," he asked her, regarding the "love scene that took place in the back house . . . did you enjoy it?"

Linda frankly answered: "Yeah, I guess I did. I will have to say I did."

If possible, at the end of Fitzgerald's cross-examination Linda Kasabian looked even better than she had at the end of the direct.

It was Monday, August 3, 1970. I was on my way back to court from lunch, a few minutes before 2 P.M., when I was abruptly surrounded by newsmen. They were all talking at once, and it was a couple of seconds before I made out the words: "Vince, have you heard the news? *President Nixon just said that Manson's guilty!*"

August 3-19, 1970

Fitzgerald had a copy of the AP wire. In Denver for a conference of law-enforcement officials, the President, himself an attorney, was quoted as complaining that the press tended "to glorify and make heroes out of those engaged in criminal activities."

He continued: "I noted, for example, the coverage of the Charles Manson case . . . Front page every day in the papers. It usually got a couple of minutes in the evening news. Here is a man who was guilty, directly or indirectly, of eight murders. Yet here is a man who, as far as the coverage is concerned, appeared to be a glamorous figure."

Following Nixon's remarks, presidential press secretary Ron Ziegler said that the President had "failed to use the word 'alleged' in referring to the charges."*

We discussed the situation in chambers. Fortunately, the bailiffs had brought the jury back from lunch before the story broke. They remained sequestered in a room upstairs, and so, as yet, there was no chance of their having been exposed.

Kanarek moved for a mistrial. Denied. Ever suspicious that the sequestration was not effective, he asked that the

*On the way back to Washington on *Air Force One,* President Nixon issued a supplementary statement:

"I have been informed that my comment in Denver regarding the Tate murder trial in Los Angeles may continue to be misunderstood despite the unequivocal statement made at the time by my press secretary.

"The last thing I would do is prejudice the legal rights of any person, in any circumstances.

"To set the record straight, I do not now and did not intend to speculate as to whether the Tate defendants are guilty, in fact or not. All the facts in the case have not yet been presented. The defendants should be presumed to be innocent at this stage of the trial."

jurors be voir dired to see if any had heard the news. As Aaron put it, "It would be like waving a red flag. If they didn't know about it before, they certainly will after the voir dire."

Older denied the motion "without prejudice," so it could be renewed at a later time. He also said he would tell the bailiffs to inaugurate unusually stringent security measures. Later that afternoon the windows of the bus used to transport the jury to and from the hotel were coated with Bon Ami to prevent the jurors from seeing the inevitable headlines. There was a TV set in their joint recreation room at the Ambassador; ordinarily they could watch any program they wished, except the news, a bailiff changing the channels. Tonight it would remain dark. Newspapers would also be banned from the courtroom, Older specifically instructing the attorneys to make sure none were on the counsel table, where they might inadvertently be seen by the jury.

When we returned to court, there was a smug grin on Manson's face. It remained there all afternoon. It isn't every criminal who merits the attention of the President of the United States. Charlie had made the big time.

The jury was brought down, and Atkins' defense attorney, Daye Shinn, began his cross-examination of Linda.

Apparently intent on implying that I had coached Linda in her testimony, he asked: "Do you recall what Mr. Bugliosi said to you during your first meeting?"

A. "Well, he has always stressed for me to tell the truth."

Q. "Besides the truth, I'm talking about."

As if anything else were important.

Q. "Did Mr. Bugliosi ever tell you that some of your statements were wrong, or some of your answers were not logical, or did not make sense?"

A. "No, I told him; he never told me."

Q. "The fact that you were pregnant, wasn't that the reason that you stayed outside [the Tate residence] instead of going inside to participate?"

A. "Whether I was pregnant or not, I would never have killed anybody."

Shinn gave up after only an hour and a half. Linda's testimony remained unshaken.

With a heavy, ponderous shuffle, Irving Kanarek approached the witness stand. His demeanor was deceiving. There was no relaxing when Kanarek was cross-examining; at any moment he might blurt out something objectionable. There was also no anticipating him; he'd suddenly skip from one subject to another with no hint of a connecting link. Many of his questions were so complex that even he lost the thought, and had to have the court reporter read them back to him.

It was excruciatingly tiring listening to him. It was also very important that I do so, since, unlike the two attorneys who preceded him, Kanarek scored points. He brought out, for example, that when Linda returned to California to reclaim Tanya, she told the social worker that she'd left the state on August 6 or 7—which, had this been true, would have been *before* the Tate-LaBianca murders occurred. If accurate, this meant that Linda had fabricated all of her testimony regarding those murders. And if she had lied to the social worker to get her daughter back, Kanarek implied, she could very well lie to this Court to get her own freedom.

But mostly he rambled and droned on and on, tiring the spectators as well as the witness. Many of the reporters "wrote off" Kanarek early in the proceedings. Given a choice of defense attorneys, they quoted Fitzgerald, whose questions were better phrased. But it was Kanarek, in the midst of his verbosity, who was scoring.

He was also beginning to get to Linda. At the end of the day—her sixth on the stand—she looked a little fatigued and her answers were less sharp. No one knew how many days of this lay ahead, since Kanarek, unlike the other attorneys, consistently avoided answering Older's questions about the estimated length of his cross-examination.

On my way home that night I was again thankful the jury had been sequestered. You could see the headlines on every newsstand. The car radio had periodic updates.

Hughes: "I am guilty of contempt for uttering a dirty word, but Nixon has the contempt of the world to face." Fitzgerald: "It is very discouraging when the world's single most important person comes out against you." The most reported quote was that of Manson, who had passed a statement to the press via one of the defense attorneys. Mimicking Nixon's remarks, it was unusually short and to the point: "Here's a man who is accused of murdering hundreds of thousands in Vietnam who is accusing me of being guilty of eight murders."

The next day in chambers Kanarek charged the President with conspiracy. "The District Attorney of Los Angeles County is running for attorney general of California. I say it without being able to prove it, that Evelle Younger and the President got together to do this."

If this was so, Kanarek said, "he shouldn't be President of the United States."

THE COURT "That will have to be decided in some other proceeding, Mr. Kanarek. Let's stay with the issues here . . . I am satisfied there has been no exposure of any of these jurors to anything the press may have said . . . I see no reason for taking any further action at this time."

Kanarek resumed his cross-examination. On direct, Linda had stated that she had taken some fifty LSD "trips." Kanarek now asked her to describe what had happened on trip number 23.

BUGLIOSI "I object to that question as being ridiculous, Your Honor."

Though there is no such objection in the rule books, I felt there should be. Apparently Judge Older felt similarly, as he sustained the objection. As well as others when I objected that a question had been repeated "ad nauseam" or was "nonsensical."

Just after the noon recess Manson suddenly stood and, turning toward the jury box, held up a copy of the front page of the Los Angeles *Times*.

A bailiff grabbed it but not before Manson had shown the jury the huge black headline:

MANSON GUILTY, NIXON DECLARES

Older had the jury taken out. He then demanded to know which attorney, against his express orders, had brought a newspaper into court. There were several denials but no one confessed.

There was no question now that the jury would have to be voir dired. Each member was brought in separately and questioned by the judge under oath. Of the twelve jurors and six alternates, eleven were aware of the full headline; two saw only the words MANSON GUILTY; four only saw the paper or the name MANSON; and one, Mr. Zamora, didn't see anything: "I was looking at the clock at the time."

Each was also questioned as to his or her reaction. Mrs. McKenzie: "Well, my first thought was 'That's ridiculous.' " Mr. McBride: "I think if the President declared that, it was pretty stupid of him." Miss Mesmer: "No one does my thinking for me." Mr. Daut: "I didn't vote for Nixon in the first place."

After an extensive voir dire, all eighteen stated under oath that they had not been influenced by the headline and that they would consider only the evidence presented to them in court.

Knowing something about jurors, I was inclined to believe them, for a very simple reason. Jurors consider themselves privileged insiders. Day after day, they are a part of the courtroom drama. They hear the evidence. They, and they alone, determine its importance. They tend, very strongly, to think of themselves as the experts, those outside the courtroom the amateurs. As juror Dawson put it, he'd listened to every bit of the testimony; Nixon hadn't; "I don't believe Mr. Nixon knows *anything* about it."

My over-all feeling was that the jurors were annoyed with the President for attempting to usurp *their* role. It was quite possible that the statement might even have helped Manson, causing them to be even more determined that they, unlike the President, would give him every benefit of the doubt.

A number of national columnists stated that if Manson was convicted, his conviction would be reversed on appeal because of Nixon's statement. On the contrary, since it was Manson himself who brought the headline to the attention of the jury, this was "invited error," which simply means that a defendant cannot benefit from his own wrongdoing.

One aspect of this did concern me just a little. It was a subtler point. Although the headlines declared that Manson—not the girls—was guilty, it could be argued that as Manson's co-defendants the guilt "slopped over" onto them. Although I assumed this would be an issue they would raise on appeal, I felt fairly certain it would not constitute "reversible error." There are errors in every trial, but most do not warrant a reversal by the appellate courts. This might have, had not Older voir dired the jury and obtained their sworn statements that they would not be influenced by the incident.

Nor did the three female defendants exactly help their case when, the next day, they stood up and said in perfect unison: "Your Honor, the President said we are guilty, so why go on with the trial?"

Older had not given up his search for the culprit. Daye Shinn now admitted that just before court resumed he'd walked over to the file cabinet where the bailiff had placed the confiscated papers and had picked up several and brought them back to the counsel table. He'd intended to read the sports pages, he said, unaware that the front pages were also attached.

Declaring Shinn in direct contempt of Court, Older ordered him to spend three nights in the County Jail, commencing as soon as court adjourned. We were already past the usual adjournment time. Shinn asked for an hour to move his car and get a toothbrush, but Older denied the motion and Shinn was remanded into custody.

The next morning Shinn asked for a continuance. Being in a strange bed, and an even stranger place, he hadn't slept well the night before, and he didn't feel he could effectively defend his client.

These were not all of his troubles, Shinn admitted. "I

am now having marital problems, Your Honor. My wife thinks I am spending the night with some other woman. She doesn't read English. Now my dog won't even talk to me."

Declining comment on his domestic woes, Older suggested that Shinn catch a nap during the noon recess. Motion denied.

Irving Kanarek kept Linda Kasabian on the stand *seven days*. It was *cross*-examination in the most literal sense. For example: "Mrs. Kasabian, did you go to Spahn Ranch because you wanted to seek out fresh men, men that you had not had previous relations with?"

Unlike Fitzgerald and Shinn, Kanarek examined Linda's testimony regarding those two nights as if under a microscope. The problem with this, as far as the defense was concerned, was that some of her most damning statements were repeated two, three, even more times. Nor was Kanarek content to score a point and move on. Frequently he dwelt on a subject so long he negated his own argument. For example, Linda had testified that on the night of the Tate murders her mind was clear. She had also testified that after seeing the shooting of Parent she went into a state of shock. Kanarek did not stop at pointing out the seeming contradiction, but asked exactly when her state of shock ended.

A. "I don't know when it ended. I don't know if it ever ended."

Q. "Your mind was completely clear, is that right?"

A. "Yes."

Q. "You weren't under the influence of any drug, is that right?"

A. "No."

Q. "You weren't under the influence of anything, right?"

A. "I was under the influence of Charlie."

Although Linda remained responsive to the questions, it was obvious that Kanarek was wearing her down.

On August 7 we lost a juror and a witness.

Juror Walter Vitzelio was excused because both he and

his wife were in ill health. The ex-security guard was replaced, by lot, by one of the alternates, Larry Sheely, a telephone maintenance man.

That same day I learned that Randy Starr had died at the Veterans Administration Hospital of an "undetermined illness."

The former Spahn ranch hand and part-time stunt man had been prepared to identify the Tate-Sebring rope as identical with the one Manson had. Even more important, since Randy had given Manson the .22 caliber revolver, his testimony would have literally placed the gun in Manson's hand.

Though I had other witnesses who could testify to these key points, I was admittedly suspicious of Starr's sudden demise. Learning no autopsy had been performed, I ordered one. Starr, it was determined, had died of natural causes, from an ear infection.

KANAREK "Mrs. Kasabian, I show you this picture."

A. "*Oh, God!*" Linda turned her face away. It was the color photo of the very pregnant, and very dead, Sharon Tate.

This was the first time Linda had seen the photograph, and she was so shaken Older called a ten-minute recess.

There was no evidence whatsoever that Linda Kasabian had been inside the Tate residence or that she had seen Sharon Tate's body. Aaron and I therefore questioned Kanarek's showing her the photograph. Fitzgerald argued that it was entirely possible that Mrs. Kasabian had been inside both the Tate and LaBianca residences and had participated in all of the murders. Older ruled that Kanarek could show her the photo.

Kanarek then showed Linda the death photo of Voytek Frykowski.

A. "He is the man that I saw at the door."

KANAREK "Mrs. Kasabian, why are you crying right now?"

A. "Because I can't believe it. It is just—"

Q. "You can't believe what, Mrs. Kasabian?"

A. "That they could do that."

Q. "I see. Not that *you* could do that, but that *they* could do that?"

A. "I know I didn't do that."

Q. "You were in a state of shock, weren't you?"

A. "That's right."

Q. "Then how do you know?"

A. "Because I know. I do not have that kind of thing in me, to do such an animalistic thing."

Kanarek showed Linda the death photos of all five of the Tate victims as well as those of Rosemary and Leno LaBianca. He even insisted that she handle the leather thong that had bound Leno's wrists.

Perhaps Kanarek hoped that he would so unnerve Linda that she would make some damaging admission. Instead, he only succeeded in emphasizing that, in contrast to the other defendants, Linda Kasabian was a sensitive human being capable of being deeply disturbed by the hideousness of these acts.

Showing Linda the photos was a mistake. And the other defense attorneys soon realized this. Each time Kanarek held up a picture, then asked her to look closely at some minute detail, the jurors winced or squirmed uncomfortably in their chairs. Even Manson protested that Kanarek was acting on his own. And still Kanarek persisted.

Ronald Hughes approached me in the hall during a recess. "I want to apologize, Vince—"

"No apology necessary, Ron. It was a 'heat of the moment' remark. I'm only sorry that Older found you in contempt."

"No, I don't mean that," Hughes said. "What I did was a hell of a lot worse. I was the one who suggested that Irving Kanarek become Manson's attorney."

On Monday, August 10, 1970, the People petitioned the Court for immunity for Linda Kasabian. Though Judge Older signed the petition the same day, it was not until the thirteenth that he formally dropped all charges against her and she was released. She had been in custody since December 3, 1969. Unlike Manson, Atkins, Krenwinkel, and

Van Houten, she had been in solitary confinement the whole time.

My wife, Gail, was worried. "What if she goes back on her testimony, Vince? Susan Atkins did; Mary Brunner did. Now that she has immunity—"

"Honey, I have confidence in Linda," I told her.

I did, yet in the back of my mind was the question: Where would the People's case be if that confidence was misplaced?

The next day Manson passed Linda a long handwritten letter. It seemed, at first, mostly nonsensical. Only on looking closer did one notice that key phrases had been marked with tiny check marks. Extracted, spelling errors intact, they read:

"Love can never stop if it's love . . . The joke is over. Look at the end and begin again . . . Just give yourself to your love & give your love to be free . . . If you were not saying what your saying there would be no tryle . . . Don't lose your love its only there for you . . . Why do you think they killed JC? Answer: Cause he was a Devil & bad. No one liked him . . . Don't let anyone have this or they will find a way to use it against me . . . This trile of Man's Son will only show the world that each man judges himself."

Coming just after she had been granted immunity, the message could only have one meaning: Manson was attempting to woo Linda back into the Family, in hopes that once freed she would repudiate her testimony.

Her answer was to give the letter to me.

Though a number of people had seen Manson pass Linda the letter, Kanarek maintained that she had grabbed it out of his hand!

The most effective cross-examination of Linda Kasabian was surprisingly that of Ronald Hughes. Though this was his first trial, and he frequently made procedural mistakes, Hughes was familiar with the hippie subculture, having been a part of it. He knew about drugs, mysticism, karma, auras, vibrations, and when he questioned Linda about these things, he made her look just a little odd, just a wee bit zingy. He had her admitting that she believed in ESP, that there were times at Spahn when she actually felt she was a witch.

Q. "Do you feel that you are controlled by Mr. Manson's vibrations?"

A. "Possibly."

Q. "Did he put off a lot of vibes?"

A. "Sure, he's doing it right now."

HUGHES "May the record reflect, Your Honor, that Mr. Manson is merely sitting here."

KANAREK "He doesn't seem to be vibrating."

Hughes asked Linda so many questions about drugs that, had an unknowing spectator walked into court, he would have assumed Linda was on trial for possession. Yet Linda's alert replies in themselves disproved the charge that LSD had destroyed her mind.

Q. "Now, Mrs. Kasabian, you testified that you thought Mr. Manson was Jesus Christ. Did you ever feel that anybody else was Jesus Christ?"

A. "The biblical Jesus Christ."

Q. "When did you stop thinking that Mr. Manson was Jesus Christ?"

A. "The night at the Tate residence."

Though I felt confident the jury was impressed with Linda, I was pleased to hear an independent evaluation. Hughes requested that the Court appoint psychiatrists to examine Linda. Older replied: "I find no basis for a psychiatric examination in this case. She appears to be perfectly lucid and articulate. I find no evidence of aberration of any kind insofar as her ability to recall, to relate. In all respects she has been remarkably articulate and responsive. The motion will be denied."

Hughes ended his cross-examination of Linda very effectively:

Q. "You have testified that you have had trips on marijuana, hash, THC, morning-glory seeds, psilocybin, LSD, mescaline, peyote, methedrine, and Romilar, is that right?"

A. "Yes."

Q. "And in the last year you have had the following

major delusions: You have believed that Charles Manson is Jesus Christ, is that right?"

A. "Yes."

Q. "And you believed yourself to be a witch?"

A. "Yes."

HUGHES "Your Honor, I have no further questions at this time."

The basic purpose of redirect examination is to rehabilitate the witness. Linda needed little rehabilitating, other than being allowed to explain more fully replies which the defense had cut off. For example, I brought out that Linda meant "state of shock" figuratively, not medically, and that she was very much aware of what was going on.

On redirect the prosecution can also explore areas first opened on cross-examination. Since the theft of the $5,000 had come out on cross, I was able to bring in the mitigating circumstances: that after stealing the money, Linda had turned it over to the Family and that she neither saw it again nor benefited from it.

Not until the re-direct was I able to bring out why Linda had fled Spahn Ranch without Tanya.

The delay in getting this in was actually beneficial, I felt, for by this time the jury knew Linda Kasabian well enough to accept her explanation.

Direct. Cross. Redirect. Recross. Re-redirect. Re-recross. Just before noon on Wednesday, August 19, Linda Kasabian finally stepped down from the stand. She had been up there seventeen days—longer than most trials. Though the defense had been given a twenty-page summary of all my interviews with her, as well as copies of all her letters to me, *not once* had she been impeached with a prior inconsistent statement. I was very proud of her; if ever there was a star witness for the prosecution, Linda Kasabian was it.

Following the completion of her testimony, she flew back to New Hampshire for a reunion with her two children. For Linda, however, the ordeal was not yet over. Kanarek asked that she be subject to recall by the defense, and she would also have to testify when Watson was brought to trial.

Randy Starr was not the only witness the People lost during August.

Still afflicted with wanderlust, Robert Kasabian and Charles Melton had gone to Hawaii. I asked Linda's attorney, Gary Fleischman, if he could locate them, but he said they were off on some uncharted island, meditating in a cave, and there was no way to reach them. I'd wanted Melton especially, to testify to Tex's remark, "Maybe Charlie will let me grow a beard someday."

The loss of the other witness was a far greater blow to the prosecution. Saladin Nader, the actor whose life Linda had saved the night the LaBiancas were killed, had moved out of his apartment. He'd told friends he was going to Europe, but left no forwarding address. Although I requested the LaBianca detectives to try to locate him through the Lebanese Consulate and the Immigration Service, they were unsuccessful. I then asked them to interview his former landlady, Mrs. Eleanor Lally, who could at least testify that during August 1969 the actor had occupied Apartment 501, 1101 Ocean Front Walk, Venice. But with Nader's disappearance, we lost the only witness who could even partially corroborate Linda Kasabian's story of that second night.

On August 18, however, we found a witness—one of the most important yet to appear.

Over seven months after I had first tried to get Watkins and Poston to persuade him to come in for an interview, Juan Flynn decided he was ready to talk.

Fearful that he would become a prosecution witness, the Family had launched a campaign of harassment against the tall, lanky Panamanian cowboy that included threatening letters, hang-up phone calls, and cars racing past his trailer in the night, their occupants oinking or shouting "Pig!" All this had made Juan mad—mad enough to contact LASO, who in turn called LAPD.

Since I was in court, Sartuchi interviewed Flynn that afternoon at Parker Center. It was a short interview; transcribed, it ran to only sixteen pages, but it contained one very startling disclosure.

SARTUCHI "When did you first become aware of the

fact that Charles Manson was being charged with the crimes that he is presently on trial for?"

FLYNN "I became aware of the crimes that he is being charged with when he admitted to me of the killings that were taking place . . ."

In his broken English, Flynn was saying that Manson had admitted the murders to him!

Q. "Was there any conversation about the LaBiancas, or was that all at the same time, or what?"

A. "Well, I don't know if it was at the same time, but he led me to believe—he told me that he was the main cause for these murders to be committed."

Q. "Did he say anything more than that?"

A. "He admitted—he boasted—of thirty-five lives taken in a period of two days."

When LAPD brought him to my office, I hadn't yet talked to Sartuchi or heard the interview tape, so when in interviewing Flynn I learned of Manson's very incriminating admission, it came as a complete surprise.

In questioning Juan, I established that the conversation had taken place in the kitchen at Spahn Ranch, two to four days after the news of the Tate murders broke on TV. Juan had just sat down to lunch when Manson came in and, with his right hand, brushed his left shoulder—apparently a signal that the others were to get out, since they immediately did. Aware that something was up, but not what, Juan started to eat.

(Ever since the arrival of the Family at Spahn Ranch, Manson had been trying to get the six-foot-five cowboy to join them. Manson had told Flynn: "I will get you a big gold bracelet and put diamonds on it and you can be my head zombie." There were other enticements. When first offered the same bait as the other males, Juan had sampled it eagerly, to his regret. "That damn case of clap just wouldn't go away," Juan told me, "not for three, four months." Though he had remained at Spahn, Juan had refused to be anybody's zombie, let alone little Charlie's. Of late, however, Manson had become more insistent.)

Suddenly Manson grabbed Juan by the hair, yanked his head back, and, putting a knife to his throat, said,

"You son of a bitch, don't you know I'm the one who's doing all of these killings?"

Even though Manson had not mentioned the Tate-LaBianca murders by name, his admission was a tremendously powerful piece of evidence.*

The razor-sharp blade still on Juan's throat, Manson asked, "Are you going to come with me or do I have to kill you?"

Juan replied, "I am eating and I am right here, you know."

Manson put the knife on the table. "O.K.," he said. "You kill me."

Resuming eating, Juan said, "I don't want to do that, you know."

Looking very agitated, Manson told him. "Helter Skelter is coming down and we've got to go to the desert." He then gave Juan a choice: he could oppose him or join him. If he wanted to join him, Charlie said, "go down to the waterfall and make love to my girls."

(Manson's "my girls" was in itself a powerful piece of evidence.)

Juan told Charlie that the next time he wanted to contract a nine-month case of syphilis or gonorrhea, he'd let him know.

It was at this point that Manson boasted of killing thirty-five people in two days. Juan considered it just that, a boast, and I was inclined to agree. If there had been more than seven Manson-ordered murders during that two-day period, I was sure that at some point in the investigation we would have found evidence of them. Too, as far as the immediate trial was concerned, the latter statement was useless, as it was obviously inadmissible as evidence.

Eventually Manson picked up the knife and walked out.

*Legally, Manson's statement was an admission rather than a confession.

An admission is a statement by a defendant which is not a complete acknowledgment of guilt, but which tends to prove guilt when considered with the rest of the evidence.

A confession is a statement by a defendant which discloses his intentional participation in the criminal act for which he is on trial and which discloses his guilt for that crime.

And Juan suddenly realized he didn't have much appetite left.

I talked to Juan over four hours that night. Manson's admission was not the only surprise. Manson had told Juan in June or July 1969, while Juan, Bruce Davis, and Clem were standing on the boardwalk at Spahn, "Well, I have come down to it. The only way to get Helter Skelter going is for me to go down there and show the black man how to do it, by killing a whole bunch of those fuckin' pigs."

Among Flynn's other revelations: Manson had threatened to kill him several times, once shooting at him with the .22 Longhorn revolver; on several occasions Manson had suggested that Juan kill various people; and Flynn had not only seen the group leave Spahn on probably the same night the LaBiancas were killed; Sadie had told him, just before they left, "We're going to get some fucking pigs."

Suddenly Juan Flynn became one of the prosecution's most important witnesses. The problem now was protecting him until he took the stand. Throughout our interview Juan had been extremely nervous; he'd tense at the slightest noise in the hall. He admitted that, because of his fear, he hadn't had a full night's sleep in months. He asked me if there was any way he could be locked up until it came time for him to testify.

I called LAPD and requested that Juan be put in either jail or a hospital. I didn't care which, just so long as he was off the streets.

Bemused by this unusual turnabout, Sartuchi, when he picked up Juan, asked him what he wanted to be arrested for. Well, Juan said, thinking a bit, he wanted to confess to drinking a beer in the desert a couple of months ago. Since he was in a National Park, that was against the law. Flynn was arrested and booked on that charge.

Juan remained in jail just long enough to decide he didn't like it one bit. After three or four days he tried to contact me. Unable to reach me right away, he called Spahn Ranch and left a message for one of the ranch hands to come down and bail him out. The Family intercepted the message, and sent Irving Kanarek instead.

Kanarek paid Juan's bail and bought him breakfast. He instructed Juan, "Don't talk to anyone."

When Juan had finished eating, Kanarek told him that he had already called Squeaky and the girls and that they were on their way over to pick him up. Hearing this, Juan split. Though he remained in hiding, he called in periodically, to assure me that he was still all right and that when the time came he would be there to testify.

Although it would never be mentioned in the trial, Juan had a special reason for testifying. Shorty Shea had been his best friend.

August 19-September 6, 1970

After Kasabian left the stand, I called a series of witnesses whose detailed testimony either supported or corroborated her account. These included: Tim Ireland, counselor at the girls' school down the hill from the Tate residence, who heard the cries and screams; Rudolf Weber, who described the hosing incident and dropped one bombshell: the license-plate number; John Swartz, who confirmed that was the number on his car and who told how, on two different nigh's in the first part of August 1969, Manson had borrowed the vehicle without asking permission; Winifred Chapman, who described her arrival at 10050 Cielo Drive on the morning of August 9, 1969; Jim Asin, who called the police after Mrs. Chapman ran down Cielo screaming, "Murder, death, bodies, blood!"; the first LAPD officers to arrive at the scene—DeRosa, Whisenhunt, and Burbridge—who described their grisly find. Bit by bit, piece by piece, from Chapman's arrival to the examination of the cut phone wires by the telephone company representative, the scene was re-created. The horror seemed to linger in the courtroom even after the witnesses had left the stand.

Since Leslie Van Houten was not charged with the five

Tate murders, Hughes did not question any of these witnesses. He did, however, make an interesting motion. He asked that he and his client be permitted to absent themselves from the courtroom while those murders were discussed. Though the motion was denied, his attempt to separate his client from these events ran directly counter to Manson's collective defense, and I wondered how Charlie was reacting to it.

When McGann took the stand, I questioned him at some length as to what he had found at the Tate residence. The relevancy of many of the details—the pieces of gun grip, the dimensions and type of rope, the absence of shell casings, and so on—would become apparent to the jury later. I was especially interested in establishing that there was no evidence of ransacking or robbery. I also got in, ahead of the defense, that drugs had been found. And a pair of eyeglasses.

Anticipating the next witness, Los Angeles County Coroner Thomas Noguchi, Kanarek asked for a conference in chambers. He'd had a change of heart, Kanarek said. Though he'd earlier shown the death photos to Mrs. Kasabian, "I have thought about it, and I believe I was in error, Your Honor." Kanarek asked that the photos, particularly those which were in color, be excluded. Motion denied. The photos could be used for identification purposes. Older ruled; as to their admissibility as evidence, that motion would be heard at a later time.

Each time Kanarek tried such a tactic, I thought, surely he can't better this. And each time I found he not only could but did.

Although I had interviewed Dr. Noguchi several times, I had a last conference with him in my office before we went to court. The coroner, who had conducted Sharon Tate's autopsy as well as supervised those of the other four Tate victims, had a habit of holding back little surprises. There are enough of these in a trial without getting them from your own witnesses, so I asked him outright if there was anything he hadn't told me.

Well, one thing, he admitted. He hadn't mentioned it in the autopsy reports, but, after studying the abrasions on her left cheek, he had concluded, "Sharon Tate was hung."

This was not the cause of death, he said, and she had probably been suspended less than a minute, but he was convinced the abrasions were rope burns.

I revised my interrogation sheets to get this in.

Although almost all of Dr. Noguchi's testimony was important, several portions were especially so in terms of corroborating Linda Kasabian.

Noguchi testified that many of the stab wounds penetrated bones; Linda had testified that Patricia Krenwinkel had complained that her hand hurt from her knife striking bones.

Linda testified that the two knives she'd thrown out the car window had about the same blade length, estimating, with her hands, an approximate length of between 5½ and 6½ inches. Dr. Noguchi testified that many of the wounds were a full 5 inches in depth. This was not only close to Linda's approximation, it also emphasized the extreme viciousness of the assaults.

Linda estimated the blade width at about 1 inch. Dr. Noguchi said the wounds were caused by a blade with a width of between 1 and 1½ inches.

Linda estimated the thickness as maybe two or three times that of an ordinary kitchen knife. Dr. Noguchi said the thickness varied from ⅛ to ½ inch, which corresponded to Linda's approximation.

Linda—who, on Manson's instructions, had several times honed knives similar to these while at Spahn Ranch—testified that the knives were sharpened on both sides, on one side all the way back to the hilt, on the other at least an inch back from the tip. Dr. Noguchi testified that about two-thirds of the wounds had been made by a blade or blades that had been sharpened on both sides for a distance of about 1½ to 2 inches, one side then flattening out while the other remained keen.*

*The other one-third of the wounds, Noguchi said, could have been made by a single-edged blade—but he didn't rule out the possibility that even these might have been made by a double-edged weapon, the unsharpened portion blunting the wound pattern so it appeared, on the surface, that a single-edged blade had been used.

As I'd later argue to the jury, Linda's description of those two knives—their thickness, width, length, even the fine point of the double-edged blade—was strong evidence that the two knives she was talking about were the same knives Dr. Noguchi had described.

In his cross-examination of Noguchi, Kanarek not only repeatedly referred to the victims' "passing away," he spoke of Abigail Folger running to her "place of repose." It was beginning to sound like a guided tour of Forest Lawn.

The idiocy of all this was not lost on Manson. He complained; "Your Honor, this lawyer is not doing what I am asking him to do, not even by a small margin ... He is not my attorney, he is your attorney. I would like to dismiss this man and get another attorney."

I was not sure whether Manson was serious or not. Even if he wasn't, it was still a good tactical move. Charlie was in effect telling the jury, "Don't judge me by what this man says or does."

Kanarek then questioned Noguchi about each of Miss Folger's twenty-eight stab wounds. His purpose, as he admitted at the bench, was to establish "the culpability of Linda Kasabian." Had she run for help, he suggested, perhaps Miss Folger might still be alive.

There were several problems with this. At least for the purpose of the questioning, Kanarek was in effect admitting Linda's presence at the scene. He was also stressing, over and over and over again, the involvement of Patricia Krenwinkel. There was nothing unethical about this: Kanarek's client was Manson. What was surprising was that Krenwinkel's own attorney, Paul Fitzgerald, didn't object more often.

Aaron spotted the basic fallacy of all this. "Your Honor, had Dr. Christiaan Barnard been present with an operating room already set up to operate on the victim, the wound to the aorta would still have been fatal."

Later, while the jury was out, Older asked Manson if he still desired to replace Kanarek. By this time Charlie had changed his mind. During the discussion Manson made an interesting observation as to his own feelings on the progress of the trial thus far: "We did pretty good at the first of it. Then we kind of lost control when the testimony started."

Although Channel 7 newscaster Al Wiman had actually been the first to spot the clothing the TV crew found, we called cameraman King Baggot to the stand instead. Had we used Wiman as a witness, he wouldn't have been able to cover any portion of the trial for his station. Before Baggot was sworn, the judge and attorneys conferred with him at the bench, to make sure there was no mention of the fact that Susan Atkins' confession had led them to the clothing. Thus, when Baggot testified, the jury got the impression that the TV crew just made a lucky guess.

After Baggot identified the various items of apparel, we called Joe Granado of SID. Joe was to testify to the blood samples he had taken.

Joe wasn't on the stand very long. He'd forgotten his notes and had to go get them. Fortunately, we had another witness ready, Helen Tabbe, the deputy at Sybil Brand who had obtained the sample of Susan Atkins' hair.

Although I liked Joe as a person, as a witness he left much to be desired. He appeared very disorganized; couldn't pronounce many of the technical terms of his trade; often gave vague, inconclusive answers. Granado's failure to take samples from many of the spots, as well as his failure to run subtypes on many of the samples he had taken, didn't exactly add to his impressiveness. I was particularly concerned about his having taken so few samples from the two pools of blood outside the front door ("I took a random sampling; then I assumed the rest of it was the same") and his failure to test the blood on the bushes next to the porch ("At the time, I guess, I assumed all of the blood was of similar origin"). My concern here was that those samples he had taken matched in type and subtype the blood of Sharon Tate and Jay Sebring, although there was no evidence that either had run out the front door. While I could argue to the jury that the killers, or Frykowski himself, had tracked out the blood, I could foresee the defense using this to cast doubt on Linda's story, so I asked Joe: "You don't know if the random sampling is representative of the blood type of the whole area here?"

A. "That is correct. I would have had to scoop everything up."

Granado also testified to finding the Buck knife in the chair and the clock radio in Parent's car. Unfortunately, someone at LAPD had apparently been playing the radio, as the dial no longer read 12:15 A.M., and I had to bring out that this occurred after Granado observed the time setting.

Shortly after the trial Joe Granado left LAPD to join the FBI.

Denied access to the courtroom, the Family began a vigil outside the Hall of Justice, at the corner of Temple and Broadway. "I'm waiting for my father to get out of jail," Sandy told reporters as she knelt on the sidewalk next to one of the busiest intersections in the city of Los Angeles. "We will remain here," Squeaky told TV interviewers, as traffic slowed and people gawked, "until all our brothers and sisters are set free." In interviews the girls referred to the trial as "the second crucifixion of Christ."

At night they slept in the bushes next to the building. When the police stopped that, they moved their sleeping bags into a white van which they parked nearby. By day they knelt or sat on the sidewalk, granted interviews, tried to convert the curious young. It was easy to tell the hard-core Mansonites from the transient camp followers. Each of the former had an X carved on his or her forehead. Each also wore a sheathed hunting knife. Since the knives were in plain view, they couldn't be arrested for carrying concealed weapons. The police did bust them several times for loitering, but after a warning, or at most a few days in jail, they were back, and after a time the police left them alone.

Nearby city and county office buildings provided restroom facilities. Also public phones, where, at certain prearranged times, one of the girls would await check-in calls from other Family members, including those wanted by the police. Several sob sisters who were covering the trial wrote largely sympathetic stories about their innocent, fresh, wholesome good looks and their devotion. They also often gave them money. Whether it was used for food or other purposes is not known. We did know the Family was adding to its hidden caches of arms and ammunition. The Family was against hunting animals, and it was a safe guess that they were stockpiling for something other than self-protection.

The deaths of her mother and stepfather had caused Susan Struthers to have a nervous breakdown. Though she was slowly recovering, we called Frank Struthers to the stand to identify photographs of Leno and Rosemary LaBianca and to describe what he'd found on returning home that Sunday night. Shown the wallet found in the Standard station, Frank positively identified it, and the watch in the change compartment, as his mother's. On questioning by Aaron, Frank also testified that he had been unable to find anything else missing from the residence.

Ruth Sivick testified to feeding the LaBianca dogs on Saturday afternoon. No, she saw no bloody words on the refrigerator door. Yes, she had opened and closed the door, to get the food for the dogs.

News vendor John Fokianos, who testified to talking to Rosemary and Leno between 1 and 2 A.M. that Sunday, was followed by Hollywood Division officers Rodriquez and Cline, who described their arrival and discoveries at the crime scene. Cline testified to the bloody writings. Galindo, the first of the homicide officers to arrive, gave a detailed description of the premises, also stating: "I found no signs of ransacking. I found many items of value," which he then enumerated. Detective Broda testified to seeing, just prior to the autopsy of Leno LaBianca, the knife protruding from his throat, which, because of the pillowcase over the victim's head, the other officers had missed.

This brought us to Deputy Medical Examiner David Katsuyama. And a host of problems.

According to the first LaBianca investigative report, "The bread knife recovered from [Leno LaBianca's] throat appeared to be the weapon used in both homicides."

There was absolutely no scientific basis for this, since Katsuyama, who conducted both autopsies, had failed to measure most of the victims' wounds.

However, since the knife belonged to the LaBiancas, if this was let stand the defense could maintain that the killers had gone to the residence unarmed; ergo, they did not intend to commit murder. While a killing committed during the commission of a robbery is still first degree murder, this could affect whether the defendants escaped the death penalty. More important, it negated our whole theory of the case, which was that Manson, and Manson alone, had a motive for these murders, and that that motive was not robbery—a motive thousands of people could have—but to ignite Helter Skelter.

Shortly after I received the LaBianca reports, I ordered scale blowups of the autopsy photos, and asked Katsuyama to measure the length and thickness of the wounds. Initially I presumed there was no way to determine their depth, which would indicate the minimum length of the blade; however, in going over the coroner's original diagrams, I discovered that two of Rosemary LaBianca's wounds had been probed, one to the depth of 5 inches, the other 5½ inches, while two of Leno LaBianca's wounds were 5½ inches deep.

After many, many requests, Katsuyama finally measured the photos. I then compared his measurements with those of the bread knife. They came out as follows:

Length of blade of bread knife: 4⅞ inches.

Depth of deepest measurable wound: 5½ inches.

Thickness of blade of bread knife: just under 1/16 inch.

Thickness of thickest wound: 3/16 inch.

Width of blade of bread knife: from ⅜ to 1 3/16 inch.

Width of widest wound: 1¼ inches.

There was no way, I concluded, that the LaBiancas' bread knife could have caused all the wounds. Length, width, thickness—in each the dimensions of the bread knife were smaller than the wounds themselves. Therefore the killers must have brought their own knives.

Recalling, however, how Katsuyama had confused a leather thong for electrical cord before the grand jury, I showed him the two sets of figures and—questioning him in much the same manner as I would in court—asked him: Had he formed an opinion as to whether the bread knife found in Leno LaBianca's throat could have made all of the wounds? Yes, he had, Katsuyama replied. What was his opinion? Yes, it could have.

Suppressing a groan, I asked him to compare the figures again.

This time he concluded there was no way the LaBianca knife could have made all those wounds.

To be doubly safe, the day I was to call him to the stand I interviewed him again in my office. Again he decided the knife could have made the wounds, then again he changed his mind.

"Doctor," I told him, "I'm not trying to coach you. If it's your professional opinion that all the wounds were made by the bread knife, fine. But the figures that you yourself gave me indicate that the bread knife couldn't possibly have caused all the wounds. Now, which is it? Only don't tell me one thing now and something different on the stand. You've got to make up your mind."

Even though he stuck to his last reply, I had more than a few apprehensive moments when it came time to question him in court. However, he testified: "These dimensions [of the bread knife] are much smaller than many of the wounds which I previously described."

Q. "So it's your opinion that this bread knife, which was removed from Mr. LaBianca's throat, could not have caused many of the other wounds, is that correct?"

A. "Yes, it is."

Rosemary LaBianca, Katsuyama also testified, had been stabbed forty-one times, sixteen of which wounds, mostly in her back and buttocks, having been made after she had died. Under questioning, Katsuyama explained that after death the heart stops pumping blood to the rest of the body, therefore postmortem wounds are distinguishable by their lighter color.

This was *very* important testimony, since Leslie Van Houten told Dianne Lake that she had stabbed someone who was already dead.

Though Dr. Katsuyama had come through on direct, I

was worried about the cross-examination. In his initial report the deputy coroner had the LaBiancas dying on the afternoon of Sunday, August 10—a dozen hours after their deaths actually occurred. This not only contradicted Linda's account of the events of that second night, it gave the defense an excellent opportunity to go alibi. Conceivably, they could call numerous people who would testify, truthfully, that while horseback riding at Spahn Ranch that Sunday afternoon they had seen Manson, Watson, Krenwinkel, Van Houten, Atkins, Grogan, and Kasabian.

I not only hadn't asked Katsuyama about the estimated time of death on direct, I hadn't even asked Noguchi this on the Tate murders, because—though I knew his testimony would have supported Linda's—I didn't want the jury to wonder why I asked Noguchi and not Katsuyama.

Since Fitzgerald led off the cross-examination, he always had first chance to explode any bombs in the defense arsenal, and this was certainly a big one. But he only said, "No questions, Your Honor." As, to my amazement, did Shinn, Kanarek, and Hughes.

I could think of only one possible explanation for this: though they had received all these reports through discovery, none of the four had realized their importance.

Susan Atkins had a stomach-ache. Though a fairly minor occurrence, in this instance it led to Aaron Stovitz' being yanked off the Tate-LaBianca case.

Four court days were lost when Susan Atkins complained of stomach pains which the doctors who examined and tested her said "did not exist." After sending the jury out, Judge Older called Susan to the stand, where she dramatically enumerated her ailments. Unimpressed, and convinced, "she is now putting on an act," Older brought the jury back in and resumed the trial. As he was leaving the courtroom, a reporter asked Aaron what he thought of Susan's testimony. He replied, "It was a performance worthy of Sarah Bernhardt."

The next morning Aaron was ordered to appear in District Attorney Younger's office.

After the *Rolling Stone* interview, Younger had told

Aaron: "No more interviews." Being somewhat easygoing by nature, Aaron had trouble complying with the edict. Once, when Younger was in San Francisco, he'd turned on the radio to hear Aaron commenting on some aspect of the day's courtroom proceedings. Though Aaron's comments were not in violation of the gag order, on his return to L.A. Younger warned Aaron, "One more interview and you're off the case."

I accompanied Aaron to Younger's office. There was no way Aaron's comment could be called an interview, I argued. It was simply a passing remark. All of us had made many such during the trial.* But Younger autocratically declared, "No, I've made up my mind. Stovitz, you're off the case."

I felt very badly about this. In my opinion, it was completely unfair. But in this case there was no appeal.

Since I had prepared the case and examined most of the witnesses, Aaron's removal did not affect this portion of the trial. We had agreed, however, that we would share the arguments to the jury, each of which would last several days. Having to handle them all myself added a tremendous burden to the load I was already carrying; in terms of time alone it meant another two hours of preparation each night, when I was already putting in four or five. Although two young deputy DAs, Donald Musich and Steven Kay, had been assigned to replace Aaron, neither was familiar enough with the case to handle either the questioning or the arguments.

Ironically, Steve Kay had once dated Family member Sandra Good, the pair, both of whom had grown up in San Diego, having gone on a date arranged by their mothers.

Sergeants Boen and Dolan of the Latent Prints Section of SID came across as the experts they were. Latents, exemplars, lift cards, smudges, fragmentary ridges, nonconductive surfaces, points of identity—by the time the two

*Although for diplomatic reasons I didn't mention it, Younger, who was currently running for attorney general of California on the Republican ticket, had himself called several press conferences during the trial, much to the displeasure of Judge Older.

officers had finished, the jury had been given a mini-course in fingerprint identification.

Boen described how he had lifted the latent prints found at the Tate residence, particularly focusing on the latent found on the outside of the front door and the latent on the inside of the left French door in Sharon Tate's bedroom.

Using diagrams and greatly magnified photographs I'd ordered prepared, Dolan indicated eighteen points of identity between the print lifted from the front door of the Tate residence and the right ring finger on the Watson exemplar and seventeen points of identity between the print lifted from the door of the master bedroom and the left little finger on the Krenwinkel exemplar. LAPD, he testified, requires only ten points of identity to establish a positive identification.

After Dolan had testified that there has never been a reported case of two separate persons having an identical fingerprint, or of any single person having two matching prints, I brought out, through him, that in 70 percent of the crimes investigated by LAPD's fingerprint men not a single readable print belonging to anyone is obtained. Therefore, I could later argue to the jury, the fact that none of Susan Atkins' prints were found inside the Tate residence did not mean she had not been there, since the absence of a clear, readable print is more common than uncommon.*

No print belonging to Manson, Krenwinkel, or Van Houten had been found at the LaBianca residence. Anticipating that the defense would argue this proved that none of them had been there, I asked Dolan about the handle of the fork found protruding from Leno LaBianca's stomach. It was ivory, he said, a surface which readily lends itself to latent prints. I then asked him: "Did you secure

*I could have broken this down further. A print matching that of a defendant is obtained at only 3 percent of the crime scenes visited by LAPD. Therefore 97 percent of the time they don't find a matching print. 97 percent is a powerful statistic when introduced in a case where none of the defendant's prints are found. My reason for not mentioning it in this case was obvious: LAPD had found not one but two matching prints at 10050 Cielo Drive.

anything at all from that fork, a smudge, a trace, a fragmentary fingerprint, anything at all?"

A. "No, sir, there was not so much as a slight smudge on it; in fact it gave the impression to me"—Kanarek objected, but Older let Dolan finish—"it gave the impression to me that the handle of that particular fork had been wiped." Later, Dolan testified, he'd run a test: he'd grasped the fork with his fingers, then dusted it, "and found fragmentary ridges."

Although Mrs. Sivick had opened and closed the refrigerator door about 6 P.M. on the night of the murders, Dolan had found "not a smudge" on the chrome handle or enamel surface of the door. However, in examining the door, he testified, he did find "wipe-type marks."

Also important were the locations of the Krenwinkel and Watson latents at the Tate residence. That Krenwinkel's print had been found on the inside of the door which led from Sharon Tate's bedroom outside to the pool not only proved that Patricia Krenwinkel had been inside the residence, together with other evidence it indicated that she had probably chased Abigail Folger out this door. Blood spots inside the house, on the door itself, and outside the door were determined to be B-MN, Abigail Folger's type and subtype.* Therefore finding Krenwinkel's print here was completely consistent with Linda Kasabian's testimony that she saw Abigail running from this general direction chased by the knife-wielding Krenwinkel.

Even more conclusive was the position of the Watson print. Although Boen testified that it was on the outside of the front door, he'd also said that it was six to eight inches above the handle, near the edge, the tip of the finger pointing *downward*. As I illustrated to the jury, to leave the print where he did, Watson would have to be *inside* the Tate residence coming out. To make the print had he been outside, he would have had to twist his arm in a very uncomfortable and extremely unnatural direction. (Using the right ring finger and trying it both ways on a door, the reader will see what I mean.)

*Although Parent and Frykowski also had B-MN, there was no evidence Parent ever entered the Tate residence, while there was evidence that Frykowski had run out the front door.

The logical assumption was that Watson left his print while chasing Frykowski, Krenwinkel while in pursuit of Folger.

These were the strong points of the fingerprint testimony. There was one weak spot. Anticipating that the defense would try to make the most of those unidentified latents—twenty-five of the fifty found at the Tate residence, six of the twenty-five found at the LaBianca residence—I brought this out myself. But with several possible explanations. Since, as Dolan testified, no person has two matching fingerprints, it was possible the twenty-five unmatched Tate latents could have been made by as few as three persons, while the six at the LaBiancas' could even have been made by one person. Moreover, I established through Dolan that latent fingerprints can have a long life; under ideal conditions those inside a residence may last for several months. I could afford to point this out, since I'd already established that the two prints I was most concerned about, Krenwinkel's and Watson's, were on surfaces Winifred Chapman had recently washed.

I expected Fitzgerald to hit hardest on that one weak spot. Instead, he attacked Dolan where he was least vulnerable: his expertise. Earlier, I'd brought out that Dolan had been in the Latent Prints Section of SID for seven years, while assigned there conducting over 8,000 fingerprint investigations and comparing in excess of 500,000 latent fingerprints. Fitzgerald now asked Dolan: "Correct me if my mathematics are incorrect, Sergeant, but you testified you went to the scene of 8,000 crimes. If you went to one a day, and worked an average of 200 days a year, you would have been doing this for forty years?"

A. "I would have to figure that out on a piece of paper."

Q. "Assuming that you went to one crime scene per day—is that a fair statement, that you went to one crime scene per day, Sergeant?"

A. "No, sir."

Q. "How many crime scenes did you go to per day?"

A. "Anywhere, for two or three years there, between fifteen and twenty."

Q. "A day?"

A. "Yes, sir."

Fitzgerald had been knocked on his rump. Instead of getting up, dusting himself off, and moving onto safer territory, he set himself up for another pratfall by trying to attack the statistics. Had he done his homework (and, since a fingerprint was the only physical evidence linking his client to the murders, there was no excuse whatsoever for his not doing so) he would have learned, as the jury now did, that since 1940 SID had kept detailed records indicating exactly how many calls each officer made, the number of readable latents he obtained, and the number of times a suspect is thus identified.

Kanarek, in his cross-examination of Dolan, tried to imply that in using benzidine to test for blood, Granado could have destroyed some of the prints at the LaBianca residence. Unfortunately for Kanarek, Dolan noted that he had arrived at the LaBianca residence *before* Granado did.

Though Kanarek did less well with Dolan than some of the other prosecution witnesses, this didn't mean I could relax my guard. At any moment he was apt to do something like the following:

KANAREK "Your Honor, in view of the fact that the Los Angeles Police Department did not even choose to compare Linda Kasabian's fingerprints—"

BUGLIOSI "How do you know that, Mr. Kanarek?"

KANAREK "—I have no further questions of this witness."

THE COURT "Your comment is out of order."

BUGLIOSI "Would Your Honor admonish the jury to disregard that gratuitous remark of Mr. Kanarek's?"

Older did so.

Hughes' cross was brief and to the point. Had the witness compared a fingerprint exemplar of Leslie Van Houten with the latents found at the LaBianca residence? Yes. And none of those prints matched the prints of Leslie Van Houten, is that correct? Yes, sir. No further questions.

Hughes was learning, fast.

Apparently believing Kanarek was really on to something, Fitzgerald reopened his cross examination to ask:

"Now, did you have occasion to compare the latent fingerprints obtained at the Tate residence and the latent fingerprints obtained at the LaBianca residence against an exemplar of one Linda Kasabian?"

A. "Yes, sir, I did."

Q. "What was the result of that comparison?"

A. "Linda Kasabian's prints were not found at either scene."

FITZGERALD "Thank you."

As much as possible, I tried to avoid embarrassing LAPD. It wasn't always possible. Earlier, for example, I'd had to bring in Sergeant DeRosa's pushing the gate-control button, so the jury wouldn't wonder why there was no testimony regarding that particular print. In my direct examination of eleven-year-old Steven Weiss, I stuck to his finding the .22 caliber revolver on September 1, 1969, and did not go into the subsequent events. However, Fitzgerald, on cross, brought out that although an officer had recovered the gun that same day, it was December 16, 1969, before LAPD Homicide claimed the weapon—after Steven's father called and told them they already had the gun they were looking for. Fitzgerald also brought out how, after Steven had taken care not to eradicate any prints, the officer who picked up the gun had done so literally, putting his hands all over it.

I felt sorry for the next witness. The spectators had barely stopped laughing when officer Watson of the Valley Services Division of LAPD took the stand to testify that he was the officer who recovered the gun.

Officer Watson's testimony was essential, however, for he not only identified the gun—bringing out that it was missing its right-hand grip and had a bent barrel and broken trigger guard—he also testified that it contained two live rounds and seven empty shell casings.

Sergeant Calkins then testified that on December 16, 1969, he had driven from Park Center to the Valley Services Division to pick up the .22 caliber revolver.

On cross, Fitzgerald brought out that between September 3 and 5, 1969, LAPD had sent out some three-hundred gun flyers—containing a photograph and detailed description of the type of revolver they were looking for—to different police agencies in the United States and Canada.

Lest the jury begin wondering why LAPD hadn't recovered the gun from the Valley Services Division immediately after the flyers went out, I was forced to ask Calkins, on redirect: "Did you ever send a flyer to the Valley Services Division of the Los Angeles Police Department in Van Nuys?"

A. "Not to my knowledge, sir."

To avoid further embarrassment to LAPD, I didn't ask how close the Valley Services Division was to the Tate residence.

September 7-10, 1970

Because of the State Bar Convention, court recessed for three days. I spent them working on my arguments, and worrying about a telephone call I'd received.

When court reconvened on the tenth, I made the following statement in chambers:

"One of our witnesses, Barbara Hoyt, has left her parents' home. I don't have all the details, but the mother said Barbara received a threat on her life, that if she testified at this trial she would be killed and so will her family.

"I know two things. I know the threat did not come from the prosecution and it did not come from an aunt I have that lives in Minnesota.

"I think the most reasonable inference is it came from the defense.

"I'm bringing this out because I want the defense attorneys and their clients to know that we are going to prosecute whoever is responsible for subornation of perjury. Not only will we prosecute, when our witnesses take the stand I will do my best to bring out, in front of the jury, that they received threats on their lives. It is relevant.

"I suggest the defendants tell their friends this."

When we returned to the courtroom, I had to leave such concerns behind and focus completely on the evidence we were presenting. It was crucial. Piece by piece we were trying to link the gun to Spahn Ranch and Charles Manson.

On Friday, before our long adjournment, Sergeant Lee of the Firearms and Explosives Unit of SID positively identified the Sebring bullet as having been fired from the gun. Lee also stated that while the other bullets recovered from the Tate scene lacked sufficient stria to make a positive identification, he found no markings or characteristics which would rule out the possibility that they too were fired from the same gun.

When I attempted to question Lee about still another link in this chain, the shell casings we had found at Spahn Ranch, Fitzgerald asked to approach the bench. It was the defense's contention, he said, that the shell casings were the product of an illegal search, and therefore inadmissible.

"Anticipating that just such an objection might be raised," I told the Court, "I obtained George Spahn's permission on tape. Sergeant Calkins should have it," I said. "He was there with me."

Only Calkins didn't have the tape. And now, nearly a week later, he still hadn't found it. Finally, I called Calkins to the stand to testify that we had obtained Spahn's permission. Cross-examined by Kanarek, Calkins denied that the tape had "disappeared" or was "lost"; he just hadn't been able to locate it, he said.

Older finally ruled the search valid, and Lee testified that when examined under a comparison microscope the shell casing he'd test-fired from the gun and fifteen of the shell casings he'd found at Spahn Ranch had identical firing pin compression marks.

Stria, lands, grooves, firing pin marks: after hours of highly technical testimony, and more than a hundred objections, most of them by Irving Kanarek, we had placed the Tate murder gun at Spahn Ranch.

Although he had agreed to testify, Thomas Walleman, aka T. J., was a reluctant witness. He'd never completely broken with the Family. He'd drift away, drift back. He seemed attracted by the easy life style, repelled by the memory of the night he saw Manson shoot Bernard Crowe.

Though I knew I couldn't get the shooting itself in during the guilt trial, I did question T. J. as to the events immediately prior to it. He recalled how, after receiving a telephone call, Manson borrowed Swartz' '59 Ford, got a revolver, then, with T. J. accompanying him, drove to an apartment house on Franklin Avenue in Hollywood. After stopping the car, Manson handed T. J. the revolver and told him to put it in his belt.

Q. "Then you both entered the apartment, is that correct?"

A. "Yes."

This was as far as I could go. I then showed T. J. the .22 caliber Hi Standard revolver and asked: "Have you ever seen that particular revolver before?"

A. "I don't think so. It looks like it, but I don't know for sure, you know."

T. J. was hedging. I wasn't about to let him get away with it. Under further questioning, he admitted that this gun differed from the gun he had seen that night in only one particular: half the grip was missing.

Q. "Now, your first statement, I believe, was to the effect that you didn't think this was the revolver, and then you said it looked like it."

A. "I mean, I don't know *for sure* whether it was the revolver, but *it looks like the revolver*. There are a lot of those made."

I wasn't worried about that little qualification, for Lomax of Hi Standard had already testified that this model was relatively uncommon.

Though qualified, T. J.'s testimony was dramatic, as he was the first witness to connect Manson and the gun.

LAPD contacted me that night. Barbara Hoyt was in a hospital in Honolulu. Someone had given her what was believed to be a lethal dose of LSD. Fortunately, she had been rushed to the hospital in time.

I did not learn many of the details until I talked to Barbara.

After fleeing Barker Ranch, the pretty seventeen-year-old had returned home. Though she had cooperated with us, Barbara was extremely reluctant to testify, and when she was contacted by the Manson girls on the afternoon of September 5 and offered a free vacation in Hawaii in lieu of testifying, she'd accepted.

Among the Family members who'd helped persuade her were Squeaky, Gypsy, Ouisch, and Clem.

Barbara spent that night at Spahn Ranch. The next day Clem drove Barbara and Ouisch to one of the Family hideouts, a house in North Hollywood which was being rented by one of the newer Family members, Dennis Rice.*

Rice took the pair to the airport, bought them tickets, and gave them fifty dollars in cash plus some credit cards, including, not inappropriately, a TWA "Getaway" card. Using assumed names, the two girls flew to Honolulu, where they booked the penthouse suite of the Hilton Hawaiian Village Hotel. Barbara saw little of the islands, however, since Ouisch, sure the police would be looking for Barbara, insisted they remain in the suite.

While there, the pair, who had been close friends, had several long talks. Ouisch told Barbara, "We all have to go through Helter Skelter. If we don't do it in our heads, we'll have to do it physically. If you don't die in your head, you'll die when it comes down." Ouisch also confided that Linda Kasabian was not long for this world; at the most, she had six months to live.

At approximately the same time each morning, Ouisch made a long-distance call. (The number was that of a pay

*Rice, thirty-one, had a rap sheet that went back to 1958 and, in common with Clem, had been convicted of offenses ranging from narcotics possession to indecent exposure. He was currently on probation for assaulting a police officer. Though new to the Family, he became one of its most hard-core members.

phone in North Hollywood, three blocks from the Rice residence. At least one of these calls was to Squeaky, the unofficial leader of the Family in Manson's absence.)

Just after the call on the ninth, Ouisch's manner suddenly changed. "She became very serious and looked at me kind of strangely," Barbara said. Ouisch told Barbara that she had to go back to California, but that Barbara was to remain in Hawaii. She called and made a reservation on the 1:15 flight to Los Angeles that afternoon.

They caught a cab to the airport, arriving just before noon. Ouisch said she wasn't hungry, but suggested that Barbara eat something. They went into a restaurant, and Barbara ordered a hamburger. When it arrived, Ouisch took it and went outside, telling Barbara to pay the check.

There was a line at the cash register, and for several minutes Barbara lost sight of Ouisch.

When she came out, Ouisch gave her the hamburger, and Barbara ate it while they were waiting for Ouisch's flight. Just before she was to board, Ouisch remarked, "Imagine what it would be like if that hamburger had ten tabs of acid in it." Barbara's response was, "Wow!" She had never heard of anyone taking more than one tab of LSD, Barbara later said, and the thought was kind of frightening.

After Ouisch left, Barbara began feeling high. She tried to take a bus to the beach but became so sick she had to get off. Panicked, she then started running, and ran and ran and ran until she collapsed.

A social worker, Byron Galloway, saw the young girl sprawled on a curb near the Salvation Army headquarters. Fortuitously, Galloway was employed at the State Hospital, his specialty drug cases. Realizing that the girl was extremely ill, he rushed her to Queen's Medical Center, where her condition was diagnosed as acute psychosis, drug-induced. The doctor who examined her was able to get her name and her Los Angeles address, but the rest made little sense: according to the hospital records, "Patient said, 'Call Mr. Bogliogi and tell him I won't be able to testify today in the Sharon Tate trial.'"

After giving her emergency treatment, the hospital called the police and Barbara's parents. Her father flew to

Hawaii and was able to bring her back to Los Angeles with him the next day.

On receiving the first fragmentary report, I told LAPD I wanted the persons involved charged with attempted murder.

Since Barbara was a witness in the Tate case, the investigation was given to Tate detectives Calkins and McGann.

September 11-17, 1970

Though I knew Danny DeCarlo was afraid of Manson, the motorcyclist did a good job of disguising it while on the stand. When Charlie and the girls smiled at "Donkey Dan," he grinned right back.

I was concerned that DeCarlo might qualify his answers, as he had in the Beausoleil trial. After only a few minutes of testimony, however, my concern suddenly shifted from DeCarlo to Older. When I tried to establish the Manson-Watson relationship through DeCarlo, Older repeatedly sustained the defense objections. He also sustained objections to Manson's dinnertime conversations when he discussed his philosophy about blacks and whites.

Back in chambers Older made two remarks which totally stunned me. He asked, "What is the relevance of whether or not Manson was the leader?" And he wanted an offer of proof as to the relevance of Helter Skelter! It was as if Older hadn't even been present during the trial thus far.

That I was more than a little disturbed at his stance came across in my reply: "The offer of proof is that he used to say that he wanted to turn blacks against whites. Of course, this is only the motive for these murders. That is all it is. Other than that, it is not much else."

I noted: "The prosecution is alleging Mr. Manson *ordered* these murders. It was his philosophy *that led up to* these murders. The motive for these murders was *to ignite Helter Skelter*. I think it is so obviously admissible that I am at a loss for words."

THE COURT "I would suggest this to you, Mr. Bugliosi. Over the noon hour give some careful thought as to what you contend your proof is going to show. Now, I realize that part of it may have to come in through one witness and part through another. This is not unusual. But so far I can't see any connection between what Mr. Manson believed about blacks and whites in the abstract and any motive."

I sweated through that noon hour. Unless I could establish Manson's domination of the other defendants, I wouldn't be able to convince the jury they had killed on his instructions. And if Older foreclosed me from bringing in Manson's beliefs about the black-white war from DeCarlo, when my heavyweight witnesses on this—Jakobson, Poston, and Watkins—were still to come, then we were in deep trouble.

I returned to chambers armed with citations of authority as to both the admissibility and the relevance of the testimony. Yet even after a long, impassioned plea, it appeared that I had not changed Older's mind. He still couldn't see, for instance, the relevance of Watson's subservience to Manson, or why I was trying to bring out, through DeCarlo, that Tex had an easygoing, rather weak personality. The relevance, of course, was that if I didn't establish both, the jury could very well infer that it was Watson, not Manson, who had ordered these murders.

BUGLIOSI "I think the Court can tell the relevancy by the fact the defense counsel are on their hind legs trying to keep it out."

KANAREK "I think the heart of what we have here is this, that Mr. Bugliosi has lost his cool, because he has a monomania about convicting Mr. Manson."

BUGLIOSI "He is charged with seven murders, and I am going to be tenacious on this . . . I intend to go back with these witnesses and find out who Tex Watson was other than a name, Your Honor."

THE COURT "I am not going to stop you from *trying*, Mr. Bugliosi."

On returning to court, I asked DeCarlo exactly the same question I had asked hours earlier: "What was your impression of Tex Watson's general demeanor?"

KANAREK "Your Honor, I will object to that as calling for a conclusion."

BUGLIOSI "*People* vs. *Zollner*, Your Honor."

I so anticipated Older saying "Sustained" that I almost thought I was imagining it when he said, "Overruled. You may answer."

DECARLO "He was happy-go-lucky. He was a nice guy. I liked Tex. He didn't have no temper or anything that I could see. He never said much."

Glancing back, I saw both Don Musich and Steve Kay staring in openmouthed disbelief. Moments ago in chambers Older had objected to my whole line of inquiry. He'd now completely reversed himself. Going as fast as I could through the questioning, before he again changed his mind, I brought out that whenever Charlie told Tex to do anything, Tex did it.

That Older had gone along with us on the domination issue didn't mean that he saw the relevance of Helter Skelter. My fingers were crossed when I asked: "Do you recall Mr. Manson saying anything about blacks and whites? Black people and white people?"

Stunned and perturbed, Kanarek objected: "It is the same question that he was asking previously!"

THE COURT "Overruled. You may answer."

A. "He didn't like black people."

DeCarlo testified that Manson wanted to see the blacks go to war with the police and the white establishment, both of whom he referred to as "pigs"; that Charlie had told him that the pigs "ought to have their throats cut and be hung up by their feet"; and that he had heard Manson use the term Helter Skelter many, many times. Through all this Kanarek objected repeatedly, often in the midst of DeCarlo's replies. Older told him: "You are interrupting, Mr. Kanarek. I have warned you several times today. I warn you now for the last time."

KANAREK "I don't wish to make unnecessary objections, Your Honor."

THE COURT "Don't you? Then cease from doing it."

Within minutes, however, Kanarek was doing it again, and Older called him to the bench. Very angrily, Older told Kanarek: "You seem to have some sort of physical infirmity or mental disability that causes you to interrupt and disrupt testimony. No matter how many times I warn you, you seem to do it repeatedly, again and again and again . . . You are trying to disrupt the testimony of this witness. It is perfectly clear. Now, I have gone as far as I am going to go with you, Mr. Kanarek."

Kanarek complained, "I am trying to conscientiously follow your orders."

THE COURT "No, no, I am afraid your explanation won't go. I have heard too much from you. I am very familiar with your tactics, and I am not going to put up with it any longer." Older found Kanarek in contempt of Court and, at the conclusion of the day's testimony, sentenced him to spend the weekend in the County Jail.

Danny DeCarlo had never really understood Helter Skelter, or cared to. As he admitted to me, his major interests while at Spahn were "booze and broads." He couldn't see how his testimony about this black-white stuff really hurt Charlie, and he testified to it freely and without qualification. But when it came to the physical evidence—the knives, the rope, the gun—he saw the link and pulled back, not much, but just enough to weaken his identifications.

In interviewing Danny, I'd learned a great many things which were not on the LAPD tapes. For example, he recalled that in early August 1969, Gypsy had purchased ten or twelve Buck knives, which had been passed out to various Family members at Spahn. The knives, according to DeCarlo, were about 6 inches in length, 1 inch in width, ⅛ inch in thickness—very close to the dimensions provided by Kasabian and Noguchi. In going through the sheriff's reports of the August 16 raid, I found that a large number of weapons had been seized (including a submachine gun in a violin case) but not a single Buck knife.

The logical presumption, I'd later argue to the jury, was that after the murders the rest of the Buck knives had been ditched.

I intended to call Sergeant Gleason from LASO to testify that no knives were found in the raid. First, however, I wanted Danny to testify to the purchase. He did, but he qualified it somewhat. When I asked him who bought the Buck knives, he replied: "I'm not sure. I think Gypsy did, I'm not sure."

When it came to the Tate-Sebring rope, DeCarlo testified it was "similar" to the rope Manson had purchased at the Jack Frost store. I persisted: "Does it appear to be different in any fashion?"

A. "No."

DeCarlo had told me that Charlie preferred knives and swords to guns because "in the desert guns could be heard for a long distance." I asked DeCarlo if, among the guns at Spahn Ranch, Manson had a special favorite. Yeah, DeCarlo said, a Hi Standard .22 caliber Buntline revolver. I showed him the gun and asked him: "Have you ever seen this revolver before?"

A. "I saw one similar to it."

Q. "Does it appear to differ in any fashion?"

A. "The trigger guard is broken."

Other than that?

A. "I can't be sure."

Q. "Why can't you be sure?"

A. "I don't know. I don't know the serial number of it. I am not sure that is it."

DeCarlo had cleaned, cared for, and shot the gun. He had an extensive background in weapons. The model was unusual. And he had made a drawing of it for LAPD even before he was told that such a gun had been used in the Tate homicides. (I'd already introduced the drawing for identification purposes, over Kanarek's objection that it was "hearsay.") If anyone should have been able to make a positive identification of that revolver, it was Danny DeCarlo. He didn't do so, I suspected, because he was afraid to.

Though he was a shade weaker on the stand than in our interviews, I did succeed in getting a tremendous amount of evidence in through DeCarlo. Though court was interrupted for another three-day recess, DeCarlo's direct took less than a day and a half of actual court time. I completed it on September 17.

That morning Manson passed word through Fitzgerald and Shinn that he wanted to see me in the lockup during the noon recess. Kanarek was not present, though the other two attorneys were.

I asked Manson what he wanted to talk to me about.

"I just wanted you to know that I didn't have anything to do with the attempted murder of Barbara Hoyt," Manson said.

"I don't know whether you ordered it or they did it on their own," I replied, "but you know, and I know, that in either case they did it because they thought it would please you."

Manson wanted to rap, but I cut him off. "I'm not really in the mood to talk to you, Charlie. Maybe, if you have enough guts to take the stand, we'll talk then."

I asked McGann what was happening on the "Honolulu hamburger case," as the papers had dubbed the Hoyt murder attempt. McGann said he and Calkins hadn't been able to come up with any evidence.

I asked Phil Sartuchi of the LaBianca team to take over. Phil efficiently turned in a detailed report, with information on the airline tickets, credit cards, long-distance calls, and so forth. It was December, however, before the case was taken to the grand jury. In the interim, Ouisch, Squeaky, Clem, Gypsy, and Rice remained at large. I'd often see them with the other Family members at the corner of Temple and Broadway.

On cross-examination Fitzgerald asked DeCarlo: "Is it not true that Mr. Manson indicated to you that he actually loved the black people?"

Danny replied: "Yeah. There was one time he said that."

On redirect I asked DeCarlo about that single conversation. Charlie had told him he loved the blacks, he said, "for having the guts to fight against the police."

Shinn brought out that DeCarlo was aware of, and more than passingly interested in, the $25,000 reward, thereby establishing that he had a reason to fabricate his testimony. Kanarek pursued the subject in detail in his cross. He also dwelt at length on DeCarlo's fondness for weapons. Earlier DeCarlo had testified that he loved guns; would he describe that love? Kanarek asked.

DeCarlo's reply brought down the house. "Well, I love them more than I do my old lady."

It was easy to see where Kanarek was heading: he was trying to establish that it was DeCarlo, not Manson, who was responsible for all the weapons being at Spahn Ranch.

Kanarek switched subjects. Wasn't it true, he asked DeCarlo, that "during the entire time you were at the ranch you were smashed?"

A. "I sure was."

Q. "Were you so smashed that on many occasions you had to be carried to bed?"

A. "I made it a few times myself."

Kanarek hit hard on DeCarlo's drinking, also his vagueness as to dates and times. How could he remember one particular Saturday night, for example, and not another night?

"Well, that particular night," DeCarlo responded, "Gypsy got mad at me because I wouldn't take my boots off when I made love to her."

Q. "The only thing that is really pinpointed in your mind, that you really remember, is that you had a lot of sex, right?"

A "Well, even some of that I can't remember."

Kanarek had scored some points. He brought out that DeCarlo had testified on an earlier occasion (during the Beausoleil trial) that while at Spahn he was smashed 99 percent of the time. The defense could now argue that DeCarlo was so inebriated that he couldn't perceive what was going on, much less recall specific conversations. Unfortunately for the defense, Fitzgerald unintentionally undermined this argument by asking DeCarlo to define the difference between "drunk" and "smashed."

A. "My version of 'drunk' is when I'm out to lunch on the ground. 'Smashed' is just when I'm walking around loaded."

September 18, 1970

That afternoon we had a surprise visitor in court—Charles "Tex" Watson.

After a nine-month delay that would necessitate trying him separately, Watson had finally been returned to California on September 11, after U.S. Supreme Court Justice Hugo Black refused to grant him a further stay of extradition. Sergeants Sartuchi and Gutierrez, who accompanied Watson on the flight, said he spoke little, mostly staring vacantly into space. He had lost about thirty pounds during his confinement, most of it during the last two months, when it became obvious his return to Los Angeles was imminent.

Fitzgerald had asked that Watson be brought into court, to see if DeCarlo could identify him.

Realizing that Fitzgerald was making a *very* serious mistake, Kanarek objected, strenuously, but Older granted the removal order.

The jury was still out when Watson entered the courtroom. Though he smiled slightly at the three female defendants, who grinned and blew him kisses, he seemed oblivious to Manson's presence. By the time the jury came in, Watson was already seated and appeared just another spectator.

FITZGERALD "Mr. DeCarlo, you previously testified that a man by the name of Tex Watson was present at Spahn Ranch during the period of time that you were there in 1969, is that correct?"

A. "Yeah."

Q. "Do you recognize Mr. Watson in this courtroom?"

A. "Yeah. Right over there." Danny pointed to where Tex was sitting. Obviously curious, the jury strained to see the man they had heard so much about.

FITZGERALD "Could I have this gentleman identify himself for the Court, Your Honor?"

THE COURT "Will you please stand and state your name."

Watson stood, after being motioned to his feet by one of the bailiffs, but he remained mute.

Fitzgerald's mistake was obvious the moment Watson got up. One look and the jury knew that Charles "Tex" Watson was not the type to order Charles Manson to do anything, much less instigate seven murders on his own. He looked closer to twenty than twenty-five. Short hair, blue blazer, gray slacks, tie. Instead of the wild-eyed monster depicted in the April 1969 mug shot (when Watson had been on drugs), he appeared to be a typical clean-cut college kid.

Offstage, Watson could be made to seem the heavy. Having once seen him, the jury would never think this again.

Since our first meeting in Independence, I had remained on speaking terms with Sandy and Squeaky. Occasionally one or both would drop in at my office to chat. I usually made time for such visits, in part because I was still attempting to understand why they (and the three female defendants) had joined the Family, but also because I was remotely hopeful that if another murder was planned, one or the other might alert me. Neither, I was sure, would go to the police, and I wanted to leave at least one channel of communication open.

I'd had more hopes for Sandy than Squeaky. The latter was on a power trip—acting as Manson's unofficial spokesman, running the Family in his absence—and it seemed unlikely she would do anything to jeopardize her status. Sandy, however, had gone against Manson's wishes on several occasions, I knew; they were minor rebellions (when her baby was due, for example, she had gone to a hospital, rather than have it delivered by the Family), but they indicated that maybe, behind the pat phrases, I'd touch something responsively human.

On her first visit to my office, about two months earlier, we'd talked about the Family credo: Sandy had maintained it was peace; I'd maintained it was murder, and had asked how she could stomach this.

"People are being murdered every day in Vietnam," she'd countered.

"Assuming for the sake of argument that the deaths in Vietnam are murders," I responded, "how does this justify murdering seven more people?"

As she tried to come up with an answer, I told her, "Sandy, if you really believe in peace and love, I want you to prove it. The next time murder is in the wind at Spahn Ranch, I want you to remember that other people like to live just as much as you do. And, as another human being, I want you to do everything possible to prevent it from happening. Do you understand what I mean?"

She quietly replied, "Yes."

I'd hoped she really meant that. That naïve hope vanished when, in talking to Barbara Hoyt, I learned that Sandy had been one of the Family members who had persuaded her to go to Hawaii.

As I left court on the afternoon of the eighteenth, Sandy and two male followers approached me.

"Sandy, I'm very, very disappointed in you," I told her. "You were at Spahn when Barbara's murder was planned. There's no question in my mind that you knew what was going to happen. Yet, though Barbara was your friend, you said nothing, did nothing. Why?"

She didn't reply, but stared at me as if in a trance. For a moment I thought she hadn't heard me, that she was stoned on drugs, but then, very slowly and deliberately, she reached down and began playing with the sheath knife that she wore at her waist. That was her answer.

Disgusted, I turned and walked away. Looking back, however, I saw that Sandy and the two boys were following me. I stopped, they stopped. When I started walking again, they followed, Sandy still fingering the knife.

Gradually they were closing the distance between us. Deciding it was better to face trouble than have my back to it, I turned and walked back to them.

"Listen, you God damn bitch, and listen good," I told her. "I don't know for sure whether you were or weren't involved in the actual attempt to murder Barbara, but if you were, I'm going to do everything in my power to see that you end up in jail!" I then looked at the two males and told them if they followed me one more time, I was going to deck them on the spot.

I then turned and walked off. This time they didn't follow me.

My reaction was, I felt, exceptionally mild, considering the circumstances.

Kanarek felt otherwise. When court reconvened on Monday, the twenty-first, he filed a motion asking that I be held in contempt for interfering with a defense witness. He also asked that I be arrested for violating Section 415 of the Penal Code, charging that I had made obscene remarks in the presence of a female.

September 21-26, 1970

Finding nothing in Sandra Good's declaration "that in my opinion constitutes contemptuous conduct on the part of Mr. Bugliosi," Judge Older dismissed Kanarek's several motions. Again Manson asked to see me in the lockup during the noon recess. He hoped I wasn't taking all this—the attempted murder, the knife incident, the trial—personally.

"No, Charlie," I told him, "I was assigned to this case; I didn't ask for it; this is my job."

By now it should be obvious to me, Manson said, that the girls were acting on their own, that nobody was dominating them. When I raised a skeptical eyebrow, Manson said, "Look, Bugliosi, if I had all the power and control that you say I have, I could simply say, 'Brenda, go get Bugliosi,' and that would be it."

It was interesting, I thought, that Manson should single out Brenda McCann, t/n Nancy Pitman, as his chief assassin.

Later I'd have good reason to recall Manson's remarks.

Nothing personal. But immediately after this, the middle-of-the-night hang-up calls began. They'd continue even after we changed our unlisted number. And several times when I left the Hall of Justice at night, I was followed by various Family members, including Sandy. Only the first time disturbed me. Gail and the kids were circling the block in our car, and I was afraid they would be identified or the license number spotted. When I pretended not to see her, Gail quickly sized up the situation and drove around until I was able to shake my "followers," though, as she later admitted to me, she was far less cool than she appeared.

Though concerned with the safety of my family, I didn't take any of this very seriously until one afternoon when, apparently enraged at the domination testimony that was coming in, Manson told a bailiff, "I'm going to have Bugliosi and the judge killed."

By telling a bailiff this, Manson was making sure we got the message. Older was already under protection. The next day the District Attorney's Office assigned me a bodyguard for the duration of the trial. Additional precautions were taken, which, since they're probably used in protecting others, needn't be enumerated, though one might be noted. In order to prevent a repetition of the events at 10050 Cielo Drive, a walkie-talkie was installed in our home, which provided instant communication with the nearest police station, in case the telephone wires were cut.

Though Older and I were the only trial principals who had bodyguards, it was no secret that several, if not all, of the defense attorneys were frightened of the Family. Daye Shinn, I was told by one of his fellows, kept a loaded gun in each room of his house, in case of an unannounced visitation. What precautions, if any, Kanarek took I never learned, though Manson often assigned him top spot on his kill list. According to another defense attorney, Manson threatened numerous times to kill Kanarek; it was only fair, Manson supposedly said, since Kanarek was killing him in court.

Manson, at one point, had Fitzgerald draw up papers for Kanarek's dismissal. According to Paul, who told the story to me, Kanarek literally got down on his knees and, with tears in his eyes, begged Manson not to fire him. Manson relented and, though they continued to disagree, Kanarek remained on the case.

Each week a member of the Los Angeles Board of Supervisors issued a press release itemizing trial costs to date. Yet even with Kanarek's multitudinous objections, many of which called for lengthy conferences, we were covering a tremendous amount of testimony each day. A veteran court reporter said he'd never seen anything like it in twenty-odd years.

Thus far, Judge Older had done a remarkable job of holding Kanarek in check. Had he granted even half the "evidentiary hearings" Kanarek was always calling for, the ten-year estimate might have become a reality. Instead, each time Kanarek made the request, Older said, "Put your motion in writing with supporting citations." Because of the time involved, Kanarek rarely took the trouble.

For our part, although I'd originally planned to call some hundred witnesses, I'd cut that number down to about eighty. In a case of this magnitude and complexity this was a remarkably low number. Some days saw as many as a half dozen witnesses taking the stand. Whenever possible, I'd use a single witness for several purposes. In addition to his other testimony, for example, I asked DeCarlo the names and approximate ages of each of the Family members, so it would be apparent to the jury that Manson, being older than all of them, was not likely to have played a subservient role.

When I called sheriff's deputy William Gleason to testify that when Spahn Ranch was raided on August 16 not one Buck knife was found, Kanarek, seeing the implication of this, objected, and Older sustained the objection.

I'd almost given up getting this in when Fitzgerald, apparently thinking the absence of such knives was a plus for the defense, asked on cross-examination: "Did you find any Buck knives at the Spahn Ranch on the date of August the sixteenth, 1969?"

A. "No, sir."

The Family's attempt to silence Barbara Hoyt backfired. Once a reluctant witness, she was now very willing to testify.

Barbara not only confirmed Linda's story of the TV incident; she recalled that the previous night, the night of the Tate murders, Sadie called her on the field phone at the back house, asking her to bring three sets of dark clothing to the front of the ranch. When she arrived, Manson told her, "They already left."

Barbara's story was both support for Linda Kasabian's testimony and powerful evidence of Manson's involvement, and, though unsuccessful, Kanarek fought hard to keep it out.

I was not able to bring out the Myers Ranch conversation until after a full half day of argument in chambers, and then, as I'd anticipated, I could only get in part of it.

One afternoon in early September 1969, Barbara had been napping in the bedroom at Myers Ranch when she awoke to hear Sadie and Ouisch talking in the kitchen. Apparently thinking Barbara was still asleep, Sadie told Ouisch that Sharon Tate had been the last to die because, to quote Sadie, "She had to watch the others die."

I got this in, finally. What I couldn't get in, because of *Aranda*, was the rest of the conversation: Barbara had also heard Sadie tell Ouisch that Abigail Folger had escaped and run out of the house; that Katie had caught up with her on the lawn; and that Abigail had struggled so much that Katie had to call for help from Tex, who ran over and stabbed Abigail.

In chambers, Shinn argued that he should be allowed to question Barbara about this. Older, as well as the other defense attorneys, strongly disagreed. By "Arandizing" the conversation—omitting all reference to her co-defendants—this put the onus for all five murders on Susan, Shinn complained, adding, "But other people were there too, Your Honor."

BUGLIOSI "They were, Daye?"

Inadvertently, Shinn had admitted that Susan Atkins was present at the Tate murder scene. Fortunately for both attorney and client, this dialogue took place in chambers and not in open court.

As with the other ex-Family members, I was able to bring in through Barbara numerous examples of Manson's domination, as well as a number of Manson's conversations about Helter Skelter. The one thing I couldn't get in was the Family's attempt to prevent Barbara Hoyt from testifying.

During his cross-examination of Barbara, Kanarek attacked her for everything from her morals to her eyesight.

Aware that Barbara had very poor vision, Kanarek had her take off her glasses, then he moved around the courtroom, asking how many fingers he had up.

Q. "How many can you see now?"

A. "Three."

KANAREK "May the record reflect she said three and I have two up clearly, Your Honor."

THE COURT "I thought I saw your thumb."

Kanarek finally proved Barbara had bad eyesight. The issue, however, wasn't her sight but her hearing: she didn't claim to have seen Sadie and Ouisch in the kitchen at Myers Ranch, only to have heard them.

Kanarek also asked Barbara: "Have you been in any mental hospital for the last couple of years?"

Ordinarily I would have objected to such a question, but not this time, for Kanarek had just opened wide the door through which I could, on redirect, bring in the murder attempt.

Redirect is limited to the issues raised on cross-examination. For example, on redirect I had Barbara approximate the distance between the bedroom and the kitchen at Myers Ranch, then conducted a hearing experiment. She passed with no trouble.

Asking to approach the bench, I argued that since Kanarek had implied that Barbara Hoyt was in a mental hospital for an extended period of time, I had the right to bring out that she was in a mental ward only overnight and that it was not because of a mental problem. Older agreed, with one limitation: I couldn't ask who gave her the LSD.

Once I'd brought out the circumstances of her hospitalization, I asked: "Did you take this overdose voluntarily?"

A. "No."

Q. "Was it given to you by someone else?"

A. "Yes."

Q. "Were you near death?"

KANAREK "Calls for a conclusion, Your Honor."

THE COURT "Sustained."

It was good enough. I was sure the jury could put two and two together.

On Saturday, September 26, 1970, an era came to an end. A raging fire swept Southern California. Whipped by eighty-mile-an-hour winds, a wall of flame as high as sixty feet charred over 100,000 acres. Burned in the inferno was all of Spahn's Movie Ranch.

As the ranch hands tried to save the horses, the Manson girls, their faces illuminated by the light of the conflagration, danced and clapped their hands, crying out happily, *"Helter Skelter is coming down! Helter Skelter is coming down!"*

September 27-October 5, 1970

Juan Flynn, who described his job at Spahn Ranch as "manure shoveler," seemed to enjoy himself on the stand. Of all the witnesses, however, the lanky Panamanian cowboy was the only one who openly showed animosity to Manson. When Charlie tried to stare him down, Juan glared back.

After positively identifying the revolver, Juan remarked, "And Mr. Manson on one occasion fired this gun, you know, in my direction, you see, because I was walking with a girl on the other side of the creek."

It was difficult to stop Juan once he got started. The girl had come to Spahn Ranch to ride horses; she'd ignored Manson but went off down the creek with amorous-minded Juan. Charlie was so miffed he'd fired several shots in their direction.

Kanarek succeeded in having all this, except Juan's seeing Manson fire the revolver, struck.

He also tried, but failed, to keep out the two most important pieces of evidence Juan Flynn had to offer.

One night in early August 1969, Juan had been watching TV in the trailer when Sadie came in, dressed in black. "Where are you going?" Juan asked. "We're going to get some fucking pigs," Sadie replied. When she left, Juan looked out the window and saw her get into Johnny Swartz' old yellow Ford. Charlie, Clem, Tex, Linda, and Leslie got in also.

According to Juan, the incident had occurred after dark, about 8 or 9 P.M., and, though he wasn't able to pinpoint the date, he said it was about a week before the August 16 raid. The logical inference was that he was describing the night the LaBiancas were killed.

Juan's story was important both as evidence and as independent corroboration of Linda Kasabian's testimony. Not only did the time, participants, vehicle, and color of Susan Atkins' clothing coincide, Juan also noticed that Manson was driving.

Juan then testified to the kitchen conversation which occurred "a day or so" later, when, putting a knife to his throat, Manson told him, "You son of a bitch, don't you know I'm the one who's doing all of these killings?"

The newsmen rushed for the door.

MANSON ADMITTED MURDERS,
SPAHN RANCH COWBOY CLAIMS

Kanarek's objections kept out another piece of extremely damaging evidence.

One night in June or July 1969, Manson, Juan, and three male Family members were driving through Chatsworth when Charlie stopped in front of a "rich house" and instructed Juan to go in and tie up the people. When he'd finished, Manson said, he was to open the door and, to quote Manson, "We'll come in and cut the motherfucking pigs up." Juan had said, "No thanks."

This was in effect a dress rehearsal for the Tate-LaBianca murders. But ruling that "the prejudicial effect far outweighs the probative value," Older wouldn't permit me to question Juan about this.

I was also unable, for the same reason, to get in a comment Manson made to Juan: "Adolf Hitler had the best answer to everything."

That answer, of course, was murder, but, owing to Kanarek's objections, neither of these two incidents was heard by the jury or ever made public.

On cross-examination Fitzgerald brought out an interesting anomaly. Even after Manson had allegedly threatened him, not once but several times, Juan still stuck around. After the raid he'd even accompanied the Family to Death Valley, remaining with them a couple of weeks before splitting to join Crockett, Poston, and Watkins.

That had puzzled me too. One possible explanation was that, as Juan testified, at first he had thought Manson was "bullshitting" about the murders, that "nobody in their right mind is going to kill somebody and then boast about it." Also, Juan was easygoing and slow to anger. Probably more important, Juan was an independent cuss; like Paul Crockett, who didn't leave Death Valley until long after Manson threatened to kill him, he didn't like to be intimidated.

Kanarek picked up on Fitzgerald's discovery. "Now, Mr. Flynn, were you scared to be at the Myers Ranch with Mr. Manson?"

A. "Well, I was aware and precautious."

Q. "Just answer the question, Mr. Flynn. I understand you are an actor, but would you just answer the question please."

A. "Well, I liked it there, you know, because I wanted to think nice things, you know. But every time I walked around the corner, well, that seemed to be the main subject, you know, about how many times they could do me in. Then, finally, I just left."

Q. "Now, Mr. Flynn, will you tell me how you were aware and precautious? How did you protect yourself?"

A. "Well, I just protected myself by leaving."

Kanarek brought out that when Flynn was interviewed by Sartuchi he'd said nothing about Manson putting a knife to his throat. "You were holding that back, is that it, Mr. Flynn, to spring on us in this courtroom, is that right?"

A. "No, I told the officers about this before, you see."

Ignoring Flynn's response, Kanarek said: "You mean, Mr. Flynn, that you made it up for the purposes of this courtroom, is that correct, Mr. Flynn?"

Kanarek was charging that Flynn had recently fabricated his testimony. I made a note of this, though as yet unaware how important this bit of dialogue would soon be.

After focusing on all the things I had brought out which were not in the Sartuchi interview, Kanarek asked Juan when he first mentioned the knife incident to anyone.

A. "Well, there was some officers in Shoshone, you see, and I talked to them." Flynn, however, couldn't recall their names.

Kanarek strongly implied, several times, that Flynn was fictionalizing his story. Juan didn't take kindly to being called a liar. You could see his temper rising.

Intent on proving that Flynn was testifying so he could further his movie career (Juan had had bit parts in several Westerns), Kanarek asked: "You recognize, do you not, that there is lots of publicity in this case against Mr. Manson, right?"

A. "Well, it is the type of publicity that I wouldn't want, you big catfish."

The Court "On that note, Mr. Kanarek, we will adjourn."

After court I questioned Juan about the Shoshone interview. He thought one of the officers was from the California Highway Patrol, but he wasn't sure. That evening I called the DA's Office in Independence and learned that the man who had interviewed Juan was a CHP officer named Dave Steuber. Late that night I finally located him in Fresno, California. Yes, he'd interviewed Flynn, as well as Crockett, Poston, and Watkins, on December 19, 1969.

He'd taped the whole conversation, which had lasted over nine hours. Yes, he still had the original tapes.

I checked my calendar. I guessed Flynn would be on the stand another day or two. Could Steuber be in L.A. in three days with the tapes and prepared to testify? Sure, Steuber said.

Steuber then told me something I found absolutely incredible. He had already made a copy of the tapes and given it to LAPD. On *December 29, 1969.* Later I learned the identity of the LAPD detective to whom the tapes had been given. The officer (since deceased) recalled receiving the tapes but admitted he hadn't played them. He thought he had given them to someone, but couldn't remember to whom. All he knew was that he no longer had them.

Perhaps it was because the interview was so long, nine hours. Or perhaps, it being the holiday season, in the confusion they were mislaid. Neither explanation, however, erases the unpleasant fact that as early as December 1969 the Los Angeles Police Department had a taped interview containing a statement in which Manson implied that he was responsible for the Tate-LaBianca murders, and as far as can be determined, no one even bothered to book it into evidence, much less play it.

Ordinarily there would have been no way I could introduce the Steuber tape into evidence at the trial, for you cannot use a previously consistent statement to bolster a witness's testimony. However, there is an exception to that rule: such evidence is admissible if the opposing side contends the witness's testimony was recently fabricated and the prior consistent statement was made before the declarant had any reason to fabricate. When Kanarek asked, "You mean, Mr. Flynn, that you made it up for the purposes of this courtroom, is that correct, Mr. Flynn?" he was charging recent fabrication, and opening the door for me to bring the prior consistent statement in.

A lot of doors were opened on cross-examination, but at first the biggest did not look like a door at all. The defense had made much of the fact that Juan did not tell his story to the authorities until long after the events occurred. With this opening, I argued, I should be allowed to bring out the reason why: he was in fear of his life.

Responding to Kanarek's objection, Older said: "You can't go into all of these things on cross and expect the other side to do nothing about them, Mr. Kanarek. You can't paint them in a corner and say they can't work their way out."

Juan was permitted to testify that he didn't go to the police because "I didn't think it was safe for me to do that, you see. I got a couple of threat notes . . ."

Actually, Juan had received three such notes, all handed him by Family members, the last as late as two weeks ago, when Squeaky and Larry Jones had discovered that Juan was living in John Swartz' trailer in Canoga Park. Arguing against their admission, Fitzgerald made an interesting statement: "My life has been threatened three times, and I haven't come forward and talked about it."

Bugliosi "Has the prosecution threatened you?"

Fitzgerald "No, I am not saying that." He didn't elaborate.

Older ruled that Juan could testify to the notes, though not the identities of the persons who gave them to him. Juan also testified to the hang-up calls, the cars that raced past in the night, their occupants oinking and screaming, "Motherfucker!" and "Pig!"

I asked him: "And you considered these threats, is that correct?"

A. "Well, they sounded, you know, pretty strong to me."

Q. "Are those among the reasons why you didn't want to come downtown and talk?"

A. "Well, this was one of the reasons, yes."

Q. "Because of fear of your life?"

A. "Yes."

When I asked about the other reasons, Juan described how Manson, Clem, and Tex had creepy-crawled Crockett's cabin at Barker Ranch.

All of this came in because the defense so gratuitously opened the door on cross.

Because Kanarek had questioned Juan about Manson's "programming" of Family members, I was able to bring in a conversation Manson had with Juan in which he explained that he had to "unprogram" his followers to remove the programming placed upon them by their parents, schools, churches, and society. To get rid of the ego, Manson told him, you had to obliterate "all the wants that you had . . . give up your mother and father . . . all the inhibitions . . . just blank yourself out."

Since Manson's techniques differed depending on whether his subject was male or female, I asked what Manson had said about unprogramming the girls. I didn't anticipate that Juan would go into the detail he did.

A. "Well, he says, you know, to get rid of the inhibitions, you know, you could just take a couple of girls and, you know, have them lay down, you know, and have them eat each other, or for me to take a girl up in the hills, you know, and just lie back and let her suck my dick all day long . . ."

KANAREK "Your Honor, Your Honor! May we approach the bench, Your Honor?"

Earlier one of the alternate jurors had written Judge Older a letter complaining about the sexual explicitness of some of the testimony. I didn't look at him, but I suspected he must be having apoplexy. As I passed the counsel table on the way to the bench, I told Manson, "Don't worry, Charlie, I'm keeping all the bad stuff out."

Older struck the entire answer as nonresponsive.

I asked Juan: "Did Mr. Manson discuss with you—*without going into what he said, Juan*—plans that he had to 'unprogram' the people in the Family?" When he replied "Yes," I let it go at that.

What Manson never explained to his Family was that in the process of unprogramming them, he was reprogramming them to be his abject slaves.

Throughout his cross-examination Kanarek had implied, as he had with many of the earlier witnesses, that Juan had been coached by me. I thought Kanarek was going to do this again, for the umpteenth time, when on recross he started: "Mr. Flynn, when a question is asked of you that you think may not help the prosecution in this case—"

BUGLIOSI "Oh, stop arguing."

KANAREK "Your Honor, he's interrupting!"

BUGLIOSI "Be quiet."

THE COURT "Mr. Bugliosi, now, I'm not going to warn you again, sir."

BUGLIOSI "What's he doing, Your Honor? He's accusing me of something and I don't like it."

THE COURT "Approach the bench."

BUGLIOSI "I am not going to take it. I've had it up to here."

My indignation was as much a matter of trial tactics as anything else. If I let Kanarek get away with the same trick time after time, the jury might assume there was some truth to his charges. At the bench I told Older: "I'm not going to be accused of a serious offense by this guy day in and day out."

THE COURT "That's absurd. You interrupted Mr. Kanarek. You made outrageous statements in front of the jury . . . I find you in direct contempt of Court, and I fine you fifty dollars."

To the amusement of the clerk, I had to call my wife to come down and pay the fine. Later the deputy DAs in the office put up a buck each for a "Bugliosi Defense Fund" and reimbursed her.

As with the earlier citation of Hughes, I felt if I was in contempt of anyone, it was Kanarek, not the Court. The following day, for the record, I responded to the contempt, noting among other things that "in the future I would ask the Court to please consider two obvious points: this is a hotly contested trial and tempers become a little frayed; and also take into consideration what Mr. Kanarek is doing which incites a response on my part."

With my citation, we now had a perfect score: every attorney involved in the trial had been either cited for contempt or threatened with it.

The defense tried their best to ridicule Juan's fear of Manson.

Hughes brought out that since Manson was locked up, it was hardly likely he could hurt anyone; did Mr. Flynn actually expect the jury to believe that he was afraid of Mr. Manson?

Juan might have been speaking for all the prosecution

witnesses when he answered: "Well, not of Mr. Manson himself, but the *reach* that he has, you know."

By now I could see the pattern. The more damaging the testimony, the more chance Manson would create a disturbance, thereby assuring that he—and not the evidence itself—would get the day's headlines. Juan Flynn's testimony was hurting him badly. Several times while Flynn was on the stand, Older had to order Manson and the girls removed because of their outbursts. When it happened again, on October 2, Manson turned to the spectators and said: "Look at yourselves. Where are you going? You're going to destruction, that's where you're going." He then smiled a very odd little smile, and added, "*It's your Judgment Day, not mine.*"

Again the girls parroted Manson, and Older ordered all four removed.

Kanarek was livid. I'd just showed the judge the transcript pages where Kanarek accused Flynn of lying. Older ruled: "There is no question: there was an implied, if not express, charge of recent fabrication." Highway patrolman Dave Steuber would be permitted to play that portion of the taped interview dealing with Manson's incriminating admission.*

After establishing the circumstances of the interview, Steuber set up the tape recorder and began playing the tape at the point where the statement had begun. There is something about such physical evidence that deeply impresses a jury. Again, in words very similar to those they had heard him use when he was on the stand, the jurors heard Juan say: "Then he was looking at me real funny ... And then he grabbed me by the hair like that, and he put a knife by my throat ... And then he says, 'Don't you know I'm the one who is doing all the killings?' "

*Steuber had been investigating a stolen auto report, not murder, when he talked to Flynn, Poston, Crockett, and Watkins in Shoshone. However, realizing the importance of their story, he had spent over nine hours quizzing them on their knowledge of Manson and his Family. After the trial I wrote a letter to the California Highway Patrol, commending Steuber for the excellent job he had done.

Monday, October 5, 1970. Bailiff Bill Murray later said he had a very strong feeling that something was going to happen. You get a kind of sixth sense dealing with prisoners day after day, he said, noting that when he brought Manson into the lockup he was acting very tense and edgy.

Although they had made no assurances that they would conduct themselves properly, Older gave the defendants still another chance, permitting them to return to the courtroom.

The testimony was dull, undramatic. There was, at this point, no clue as to its importance, though I had a feeling Charlie just might suspect what I was up to. Through a series of witnesses, I was laying the groundwork for destroying Manson's anticipated alibi.

LASO detective Paul Whiteley had just finished testifying, and the defense attorneys had declined to cross-examine him, when Manson asked: "May I examine him, Your Honor?"

THE COURT "No, you may not."

MANSON "You are going to use this courtroom to kill me?"

Older told the witness he could step down. Manson asked the question a second time, adding, "I am going to fight for my life one way or another. You should let me do it with words."

THE COURT "If you don't stop, I will have to have you removed."

MANSON "I will have *you* removed if you don't stop. *I have a little system of my own.*"

Not until Manson made that very startling admission did I realize that this time he wasn't playacting but deadly serious.

THE COURT "Call your next witness."

BUGLIOSI "Sergeant Gutierrez."

MANSON *"Do you think I'm kidding?"*

It happened in less time than it takes to describe it. With a pencil clutched in his right hand, Manson suddenly leaped over the counsel table in the direction of Judge Older. He landed just a few feet from the bench, falling on one knee. As he was struggling to his feet, bailiff Bill

Murray leaped too, landing on Manson's back. Two other deputies quickly joined in and, after a brief struggle, Manson's arms were pinned. As he was being propelled to the lockup, Manson screamed at Older: *"In the name of Christian justice, someone should cut your head off!"*

Adding to the bedlam, Atkins, Krenwinkel, and Van Houten stood and began chanting something in Latin. Older, much less disturbed than I would have expected, gave them not one but several chances to stop, then ordered them removed also.

According to the bailiffs, Manson continued to fight even after he had been taken into the lockup, and it took four men to put cuffs on him.

Fitzgerald asked if counsel might approach the bench. For the record, Judge Older described exactly how he had viewed the incident. Fitzgerald asked if he might inquire as to the judge's state of mind.

THE COURT "He looked like he was coming for me."

FITZGERALD "I was afraid of that, and although—"

THE COURT "If he had taken one more step, I would have done something to defend myself."

Because of the judge's state of mind, Fitzgerald said, he felt it incumbent upon him to move for a mistrial. Hughes, Shinn, and Kanarek joined. Older replied: "It isn't going to be that easy, Mr. Fitzgerald . . . They are not going to profit from their own wrong . . . Denied."

Out of curiosity, after court Murray measured the distance of Manson's leap: ten feet.

Murray wasn't too surprised. Manson had very powerful leg and arm muscles. He was constantly exercising in the lockup. Asked why, he once told a bailiff: "I'm toughening myself up for the desert."

Murray tried to re-create his own leap. Without that sudden shot of adrenaline, he couldn't even jump up on the counsel table.

Though Judge Older instructed the jury to "disregard what you saw and what you have heard here this morning," I knew that as long as they lived they'd never forget it.

All the masks had been dropped. They'd seen the real face of Charles Manson.

From a reliable source, I learned that after the incident Judge Older began wearing a .38 caliber revolver under his robes, both in court and in chambers.

Judgment Day. Echoing Manson, the girls waiting outside on the corner spoke of it in conspiratorial whispers. "Wait till Judgment Day. That's when Helter Skelter will really come down."

Judgment Day. What was it? A plan to break out Manson? An orgy of retribution?

As important was the question of when. The day the jury returned their verdict of "Not guilty" or "Guilty"? Or, if the latter, the day the same jury decided "Life" or "Death"? Or perhaps the day of sentencing itself? Or might it even be tomorrow?

Judgment Day. We began to hear those words more and more often. Without explanation. As yet unaware that the first phase of Judgment Day had already begun, with the theft, from Camp Pendleton Marine Base, of a case of hand grenades.

October 6-31, 1970

Some weeks earlier, on returning to my office after court, I'd found a phone message from attorney Robert Steinberg, who was now representing Virginia Graham.

On the advice of her previous attorney, Virginia Graham had withheld some information. Steinberg had urged her to give this information to me. "Specifically," the phone message read, "Susan Atkins laid out detailed plans to Miss Graham concerning other planned murders, including the murders of Frank Sinatra and Elizabeth Taylor."

Since I was very busy, I arranged to have one of the co-prosecutors, Steve Kay, interview her.

According to Virginia, a few days after Susan Atkins

told her about the Hinman, Tate, and LaBianca murders—probably on November 8 or 9, 1969—Susan had walked over to Virginia's bed at Sybil Brand and begun leafing through a movie magazine. It reminded her, Susan said, abcut some other murders she had been planning.

She had decided to kill Elizabeth Taylor and Richard Burton, Susan matter-of-factly stated. She was going to heat a knife red-hot and put it against the side of Elizabeth Taylor's face. This was more or less to leave her mark. Then she'd carve the words "helter skelter" on her forehead. After which, she was going to gouge her eyes out—Charlie had shown her how—and—

Virginia interrupted to ask what Richard Burton was supposed to be doing during all this.

Oh, both would be tied up, Susan said. Only this time the rope would be around their necks and their feet, so they couldn't get away "like the others."

Then, Susan continued, she would castrate Burton, placing his penis, as well as Elizabeth Taylor's eyes, in a bottle. "And dig this, would you!" Susan laughed. "And then I'd mail it to Eddie Fisher!"

As for Tom Jones, another of her intended victims, she planned to force him to have sex with her, at knife point, and then, just as he was climaxing, she would slit his throat.

Steve McQueen was also on the list. Before Susan could explain what she had in mind for McQueen, Virginia interrupted, saying, "Sadie, you can't just walk up to these people and kill them!"

That would be no problem, Susan said. It was easy to find out where they lived. Then she'd simply creepy-crawl them, "just like I did to Tate."

She had something choice for Frank Sinatra, Susan continued. She knew that Frank liked girls. She'd just walk up to his door and knock. Her friends, she said, would be waiting outside. Once inside, they'd hang Sinatra upside down, then, while his own music was playing, skin him alive. After which they'd make purses out of the skin and sell them to hippie shops, "so everyone would have a little piece of Frank."

She had come to the conclusion, Susan said, that the

victims had to be people of importance, so the whole world would know.

Shortly after this, Virginia terminated the conversation with Susan. When asked by Steve Kay why she hadn't come forward with the story before this, Virginia explained that it was just so insane that she didn't think anyone would believe her. Even her former attorney had advised her to say nothing about it.

Were these Sadie's own plans, or Charlie's? Knowing as much as I did about Susan Atkins, I doubted if all this came from her. Though I had no proof, it was a reasonable inference that she had probably picked up these ideas from Manson.

In any case, it didn't matter. Reading a transcript of the taped interview, I knew I'd never be able to introduce any of this in evidence: legally, its relevance to the Tate-LaBianca murders was negligible, and whatever limited relevance it did have would be outweighed by its extremely prejudicial effect.

Though Virginia Graham's statement was useless as evidence, a copy of it was made available to each of the defense attorneys under discovery.

It would soon make its own kind of legal history.

Although it was Ronnie Howard who first went to the police, I called Virginia Graham to the stand first, since Susan had initially confessed to her.

Her testimony was unusually dramatic, since this was the first time the jury had heard what had happened inside the Tate residence.

Since their testimony was only against Susan Atkins, only Shinn cross-examined Graham and Howard. His attack was less on their statements than their backgrounds. He brought out, for example, sixteen different aliases Ronnie Howard had used. He also asked her if she made a lot of money as a prostitute.

Asking him to approach the bench, Older said, "You know the rules, Mr. Shinn. Don't give me that wide-eyed innocent stare and pretend you don't know what I am talking about."

SHINN "Does Your Honor mean I cannot ask a person their occupation?"

The prosecution had made no "deals" with either Virginia Graham or Ronnie Howard. Howard had been acquitted on the forgery charge, while Graham had served out her full sentence at Corona. In both cases, however, Shinn did bring up the reward. When he asked Ronnie if she knew about the $25,000, she bluntly answered: "I think I am entitled to it."

On redirect I asked each: "Are you aware that testifying in court is not a prerequisite to collecting the money?" Objection. Sustained. But the point was made.

The letters Susan Atkins had written to her former cellmates, Ronnie Howard, Jo Stevenson, and Kitt Fletcher, were very incriminating. Although I was prepared to call a handwriting expert to testify to their authenticity, Shinn, in order to save time, stipulated that Susan had written them. However, before they could be introduced in evidence, we had to "Arandize" them, excising any references to Atkins' co-defendants. This was done in chambers, outside the presence of the jury.

Kanarek fought to exclude almost every line. Disgusted at his constant objections, Fitzgerald complained to Older: "I don't have the rest of my life to spend here." Older, equally disgusted, told Kanarek: "I would suggest that you use a little more discretion and not try to clutter up the record with motions, objections, and statements which any ten-year-old child can see are either nonsense or totally irrelevant . . ."

Yet time and again Kanarek pointed out subtleties the other defense attorneys missed. For example, Susan had written Ronnie: "When I first heard you were the informer I wanted to slit your throat. Then I snapped that I was the real informer and it was my throat I wanted to cut."

You don't "inform" on yourself, Kanarek argued; you "confess." This implied that other people were involved.

After nineteen pages of argument, much of it very sophisticated, we finally edited this particular section to read: "When I first heard you were the informer I wanted to slit your throat. Then I snapped that it was my throat I wanted to cut."

Kanarek wanted the line "Love Love Love" excluded from the Stevenson letter because "it refers to Manson."

THE COURT "It sounds more like Gertrude Stein."

Since the "Love" references were among the few favorable things in Susan's letters, Shinn fought to retain them, remarking, "What do you want to do, make a killer out of her?"

LIZ, SINATRA ON SLAY LIST

The Los Angeles *Herald Examiner* broke the story on October 9, in an exclusive article bearing the by-line of reporter William Farr. Learning the night before that the story was going to appear, Judge Older again ordered the windows of the jury bus covered so the jurors couldn't see the headlines on corner newsstands.

Farr's article contained direct quotes from the Virginia Graham statement, which we had turned over to the defense on discovery.

Questioned in chambers, Farr declined to identify his source or sources. After observing that under California law he could not order the reporter to do so, Older excused Farr.

It was obvious that one or more persons had violated the gag order. Older, however, did not press the issue, and there, it appeared, the matter rested. There was no indication at this time that the issue would eventually become a *cause célèbre* and result in the jailing of Farr.

Gregg Jakobson was an impressive and very important witness. I had the tall, modishly dressed talent scout testify in detail to his many conversations with Manson, during which they discussed Helter Skelter, the Beatles, Revelation 9, and Manson's curious attitude toward death.

Shahrokh Hatami followed Jakobson to the stand, to

testify to his confrontation with Manson at 10050 Cielo Drive on the afternoon of March 23, 1969. For the first time the jury, and the public, learned that Sharon Tate had seen the man who later ordered her murder.

In Rudi Altobelli, Kanarek finally met his match. On direct examination the owner of 10050 Cielo Drive testified to his first encounter with Manson at Dennis Wilson's home, and then, in considerable detail, he described Manson's appearance at the guest house the evening before he and Sharon left for Rome.

Extremely antagonistic because Altobelli had refused him permission to visit 10050 Cielo Drive, Kanarek asked: "Now, presently, the premises on Cielo Drive where you live are quite secure, is that correct?"

A. "I hope so."

Q. "Do you remember having a conversation with me when I tried to get into your fortress out there?"

A. "I remember your insinuations or threats."

Q. "What were my insinuations or threats?"

A. "That 'We will take care of you, Mr. Altobelli,' 'We will see about you, Mr. Altobelli,' 'We will get the court up at your house and have the trial at your house, Mr. Altobelli.' "

Altobelli had told Kanarek that if the Court ordered it, he would be glad to comply. "Otherwise, no. It is a home. It is not going to be a tourist attraction or a freak show."

Q. "Do you respect our courts of law, Mr. Altobelli?"

A. "I think more than you, Mr. Kanarek."

Despite defense objections, I had succeeded in getting in perhaps 95 percent of the testimony I'd hoped to elicit through Jakobson, Hatami, and Altobelli.

With the next witness, I suddenly found myself in deep trouble.

Charles Koenig took the stand to testify to finding Rosemary LaBianca's wallet in the women's rest room of the Standard station in Sylmar where he worked. He described how, on lifting the top of the toilet tank, he'd seen the wallet wedged above the mechanism, just above the waterline.

Kanarek cross-examined Koenig at great length about

the toilet, causing more than a few snickers among spectators and press. Then I suddenly realized what he was getting at.

Kanarek asked Koenig if there was a standard procedure in connection with servicing the toilets in the rest room.

Koenig replied that the Standard station operating manual required that the rest room be cleaned every hour. The bluing agent, which is kept in the tank of the toilet, Koenig further testified, had to be replaced "whenever it ran out."

How often was that? Kanarek asked.

As "lead man," or boss of the station, Koenig had not personally cleaned the rest rooms, but rather had delegated the task to others. Therefore I was able to object to this and similar questions as calling for a conclusion on Koenig's part.

Fortunately, court then recessed for the day.

Immediately afterward I called LAPD with an urgent request. I wanted the detectives to locate and interview every person who had worked in this particular station between August 10, 1969 (the date Linda Kasabian testified she left the wallet there) and December 10, 1969 (the date Koenig found it). And I wanted them interviewed before Kanarek could get to them, fearing that he might put words in their mouths. I told the officers: "Tell them, 'Forget what the Standard station operating manual says you should do; forget too what your employer might say if he found you didn't follow the instructions to the letter. Just answer truthfully: Did you personally, at any time during your employment, change the bluing agent in that toilet?' "

To replace the bluing agent, you had to lift the top off the tank. Had anyone done so, he would have immediately seen the wallet. If Kanarek could come up with just one employee who claimed to have replaced the bluing agent during that four-month period, the defense could forcefully contend that the wallet had been "planted," not only destroying Linda Kasabian's credibility as to all of her testimony, but implying that the prosecution was trying to frame Manson.

LAPD located some, but not all, of the former employees. (None had ever changed the bluing agent.) Fortunately, Kanarek apparently had no better luck.

Hughes had only a few questions for Koenig, but they were devastating.

Q. "Now, Sylmar is predominantly a white area, is it not?"

A. "Yeah, I guess so."

Q. "Sylmar is not a black ghetto, is it?"

A. "No."

According to Linda, Manson had wanted a black to find the wallet and use the credit cards, so blacks would be blamed for the murders. My whole theory of the motive was based on this premise. Why, then, had Manson left the wallet in a white area?

In point of fact, the freeway exit Manson had taken was immediately north of Pacoima, the black ghetto of the San Fernando Valley. I tried to get this in through Koenig, but defense objections kept it out, and I later had to call Sergeant Patchett to so testify.

With a single witness, a service-station attendant, the defense—specifically Kanarek and Hughes—had almost knocked two huge holes in the prosecution's case.

By now I had narrowed down my opponents. Fitzgerald made a good appearance but rarely scored. Shinn was likable. For his first trial Hughes was doing damn well. But it was Irving Kanarek, whom most members of the press considered the trial's buffoon, who was scoring nearly all the points. Time and again Kanarek succeeded in keeping out important evidence.

For example, when Stephanie Schram took the stand, Kanarek objected to her testimony regarding the "murder school" Manson had conducted at Barker Ranch, and Older sustained Kanarek's objection. Though I disagreed with Older's ruling, there was no way I could get around it.

On direct Stephanie had testified that she and Manson returned to Spahn Ranch from San Diego in a cream-colored van on the afternoon of Friday, August 8. On cross-examination Fitzgerald asked her: "Could you be mistaken one day?" This indicated to me that Manson might still be planning to go alibi, so on redirect I brought in the traffic ticket they had been given the previous day. With the August 8 arrest report on Brunner and Good, which contained the license number of the same van, I was now ready to demolish Charlie if the defense claimed he wasn't even in Southern California at the time of the murders.

Yet I had no way of knowing whether Manson might have his own surprise bombshell, which he was waiting to explode.

As it happened, he had.

Sergeant Gutierrez, on the "HELTER SKELTER" door. DeWayne Wolfer, on the sound tests he'd conducted at the Tate residence. Jerrold Friedman, on the last telephone call Steven Parent made. Roseanne Walker, on Atkins' remarks about the eyeglasses. Harold True, on Manson's visits to the house next to the LaBianca residence. Sergeant McKellar, on Krenwinkel's attempts to avoid recognition just prior to her arrest in Mobile, Alabama. Bits and pieces, but cumulative. And eventually, I hoped, convincing.

Only a few prosecution witnesses remained. And I still didn't know what the defense would be. Although the prosecution had to give the defense a list of all our witnesses, the defense had no such obligation. Earlier Fitzgerald had told the press that he intended to call thirty witnesses, among them such celebrities as Mama Cass, John Phillips, and Beatle John Lennon, the latter to testify as to how he interpreted his own song lyrics. But that, and the rumors that Manson himself planned to testify, were the only clues to the defense. And even Manson's testifying was an iffy thing. In my talks with Charlie, he seemed to vacillate. Maybe I'll testify. Maybe I won't. I continued to goad him, but was worried that perhaps I'd overplayed my hand.

The defendants hadn't been in court since Manson's attack on the judge. The day Terry Melcher was to testify, however, Older permitted their return. Not wanting to face Manson, Terry asked me, "Can't I go back in the lockup and testify through the speaker?"

Of all the prosecution witnesses, Melcher was the most

frightened of Manson. His fear was so great, he told me, that he had been under psychiatric treatment and had employed a full-time bodyguard since December 1969.

"Terry, they weren't after you that night," I tried to reassure him. "Manson knew you were no longer living there."

Melcher was so nervous, however, that he had to be given a tranquilizer before taking the stand. Though he came over somewhat weaker than in our interviews, when he finished his testimony, he told me, with evident relief, that Manson had smiled at him, therefore he couldn't be too unhappy with what he'd said.

Kanarek, probably at Manson's request, did not question Melcher. Hughes brought out that when Wilson and Manson drove Terry to the gate of 10050 Cielo Drive that night, they probably saw him push the button. The defense could now argue that if Manson was familiar with the gate-operating device, it would be unlikely he'd have the killers climb over the fence, as Linda claimed they had.

By this time I had proof that *both* Watson and Manson had been to 10050 Cielo Drive on a *number* of occasions before the murders. But the jury would never hear it.

Some months earlier I'd learned that after Terry Melcher had moved out of the residence, but before the Polanskis had moved in, Gregg Jakobson had arranged for a Dean Moorehouse to stay there for a brief period. During this time Tex Watson had visited Moorehouse at least three, and possibly as many as six, times. In a private conversation with Fitzgerald, I told him this and he replied that he already knew it.

Though I intended to introduce this evidence during the Watson trial, I didn't want to bring it in during the current proceedings, and I was hoping that Fitzgerald wouldn't either, since it emphasized the Watson rather than the Manson link.

Though I suspected that Manson had visited there also during the same period, I had no proof of this until the trial was well under way, when I learned from the best possible source that Manson had been to 10050 Cielo Drive "on five or six occasions." My source was Manson himself, who admitted this to me during one of our rap sessions. Manson denied, however, having been in the house itself. He and Tex went up there, he said, to race dune buggies up and down the hills.

But I couldn't use this information against Manson, because, as he well knew, all of my conversations with him were at his insistance and he was never advised of his constitutional rights.

It was a decidedly curious situation. Although Manson had vowed to kill me, he still asked to see me periodically—to rap.

Equally curious were our conversations. Manson told me, for example, that he personally believed in law and order. There should be "rigid control" by the authorities, he said. It didn't matter what the law was—right and wrong being relative—but it should be strictly enforced by whoever had the power. And public opinion should be suppressed, because part of the people wanted one thing, part another.

"In other words, your solution would be a dictatorship," I remarked.

"Yes."

He had a simple solution to the crime problem, Manson told me. Empty the prisons and banish all the criminals to the desert. But first brand their foreheads with X's, so if they ever appeared in the cities they could be identified and shot on sight.

"Do I need two guesses as to who's going to be in charge of them in the desert, Charlie?"

"No." He grinned.

On another occasion, Manson told me that he had just written to President Nixon, asking him to turn over the reins of power to him. If I was interested, I could be his vice-president. I was a brilliant prosecutor, he said, a master with words, and, "You're right on about a lot of things."

"What things, Charlie? Helter Skelter, the way the murders came down, your philosophy on life and death?"

Manson smiled and declined to answer.

"We both know you ordered these murders," I told him.

"Bugliosi, it's the Beatles, the music they're putting out.

They're talking about war. These kids listen to this music and pick up the message, it's subliminal."

"You were along on the night of the LaBianca murders."

"I went out a lot of nights."

Never a direct denial. I couldn't wait to get him on the stand.

Manson told me that he liked prison, though he liked the desert, the sun, and women better. I told him he'd never been inside the green room at San Quentin before.

He wasn't afraid of death, Manson responded. Death was only a thought. He'd faced death before, many times, in both this and past lives.

I asked him if, when he shot Crowe, he'd intended to kill him.

"Sure," he replied, adding, "I could kill everyone without blinking an eye." When I asked why, he said, "Because you've been killing me for years." Pressed as to whether all this killing bothered him, Manson replied that he had no conscience, that everything was only a thought. Only he, and he alone, was on top of his thought, in complete control, unprogrammed by anyone or anything.

"When it comes down around your ears, you'd better believe I'll be on top of my thought," Manson said. "I will know what I am doing. I will know *exactly* what I am doing."

Manson frequently interrupted the testimony of Brooks Poston and Paul Watkins with asides. Kanarek's interruptions were so continuous that Older, calling him to the bench, angrily told him: "You are trying to disrupt the testimony with frivolous, lengthy, involved, silly objections. You have done it time and again during this trial . . . I have studied you very carefully, Mr. Kanarek. I know exactly what you are doing. I have had to find you in contempt twice before for doing the same thing. I won't hesitate to do it again."

It was all too obvious, to both Kanarek and Manson, that Poston and Watkins were impressively strong witnesses. Step by step they traced the evolution of Helter Skelter, not intellectually, as Jakobson understood it, but as onetime true believers, members of the Family who had watched a vague concept slowly materialize into terrifying reality.

The cross-examination didn't shake their testimony in the slightest; rather, it elicited more details. When Kanarek questioned Poston, for example, he accidentally brought out a good domination example: "When Charlie would be around, things would be like when a schoolteacher comes back to class."

Hughes asked Poston: "Did you feel you were under Mr. Manson's hypnotic spell?"

A. "No, I did not think that Charlie had a hypnotic spell."

Q. "Did you feel he had some power?"

A. "I felt he was Jesus Christ. That is power enough for me."

Looking back on his time with Manson, Poston said: "I learned a lot from Charlie, but it doesn't seem that he was making all those people free." Watkins observed: "Charlie was always preaching love. Charlie had no idea what love was. Charlie was so far from love it wasn't even funny. *Death is Charlie's trip*. It really is."

Since his extradition to California, Charles "Tex" Watson had been behaving peculiarly. At first he spoke little, then stopped speaking entirely. The prisoners in his cell block signed a petition complaining of the unsanitary condition of his cell. For hours he'd stare off into space, then inexplicably hurl himself against his cell wall. Placed in restraints, he stopped eating and, even though force-fed, his weight dropped to 110 pounds.

Though there was evidence that he was faking at least part of his symptoms, his attorney, Sam Bubrick, asked the Court to appoint three psychiatrists to examine him. Their conclusions differed but they agreed on one point: Watson was rapidly reverting to a fetal state, which, unless immediately treated, could be fatal. Acting on the basis of their examination, on October 29 Judge Dell ruled Watson was at present incompetent to stand trial and ordered him committed to Atascadero State Hospital.

Manson asked to see me during the recess.

"Vince," Manson pleaded through the lockup door, "give me just half an hour with Tex. I'm positive I can cure him."

"I'm sorry, Charlie," I told him. "I can't afford to take that chance. If you cured him, then everyone *would* believe you were Jesus Christ."

November 1-19, 1970

The day before Watson was committed to Atascadero, two court-appointed psychiatrists found seventeen-year-old Dianne Lake competent to testify.

Following her release from Patton, Dianne had received some good news: Inyo County investigator Jack Gardiner and his wife, who had befriended Dianne after her arrest in the Barker raid, had been appointed her foster parents. She would live with them and their children until she finished high school.

Because of *Aranda*, there were some things the jury never heard—for example, that Tex had told Leslie to stab Rosemary LaBianca and, later, to wipe fingerprints off everything they had touched—since Katie had related these things to Dianne, and any reference by Katie to her co-defendants had to be excised.

Dianne could testify to what Leslie had told her she had done; however, the problem here was that Leslie never told Dianne *whom* she had stabbed. She said she had stabbed someone who was already dead; that this occurred near Griffith Park; and that there was a boat outside. From these facts I hoped the jury would conclude that she was talking about the LaBiancas. Dianne also testified that one morning in August Leslie had come into the back house at Spahn and proceeded to burn a purse, a credit card, and her own clothing, keeping only a sack of coins, which the girls divided and spent on food. Dianne, however, was unable to pinpoint the exact date, and though I hoped the jury would surmise this had occurred the morning after the LaBiancas were killed, there was no proof that this was so.

Since this was the only evidence, independent of Linda Kasabian's testimony, which I had linking Leslie Van Houten to the LaBianca homicides, it hurt, and badly, when Hughes on cross brought out that Dianne wasn't sure whether Leslie had told her about the boat or whether she had read about it in the newspapers.

Hughes also focused on a number of minor discrepancies in her previous statements (she'd told Sartuchi the coins were in the purse, while she'd told me they were in a plastic bag), and what could have been one very big bombshell. On direct Dianne had said that she, Little Patty, and Sandra Good, "I believe," had divided the money.

If Sandy was present, this couldn't have been August 10, the morning after the LaBianca murders, since Sandra Good, along with Mary Brunner, was still in custody. However, questioned further, Dianne said Sandy "might not have been there."

In his cross-examination Kanarek brought out that Sergeant Gutierrez had threatened Dianne with the gas chamber. Fitzgerald also came up with a prior inconsistent statement: Dianne had told the grand jury that she was in Inyo County, rather than at Spahn Ranch, on August 8 and 9.

On redirect I asked Dianne: "Why did you lie to the grand jury?"

A. "Because I was afraid that I would be killed by members of the Family if I told the truth. And Charlie asked me not to—he told me not to say anything to anybody who had the power of authority."

On November 4, Sergeant Gutierrez, in search of a cup of coffee, had wandered into the jury room where the female defendants stayed during recesses.

He found a yellow legal pad with the name Patricia Krenwinkel on it. Among the notes and doodlings, Katie had written the words "healter-skelter" three times—misspelling that first word exactly the same way it had been misspelled on the LaBianca refrigerator door.

Older would not permit me to introduce it in evidence, however. I felt he was 100 percent wrong about this: it was unquestionably circumstantial evidence; it had relevance; and it was admissible. But Older ruled otherwise.

Older also gave me a scare when I attempted to introduce Krenwinkel's refusal to make a printing exemplar. Older agreed it was admissible, but he felt Krenwinkel should be given another chance to comply, and ordered her to do so.

The problem here was that this time Krenwinkel just might, on the advice of counsel, make the exemplar, and if she did, I knew there would be real problems.

Katie refused—on the instructions of Paul Fitzgerald!

What Fitzgerald apparently did not realize was that it would be extremely difficult, if not impossible, for LAPD to match the two printing samples. And had LAPD failed to do so, by law Patricia Krenwinkel would have to be acquitted of the LaBianca murders. Her refusal to give an exemplar was the only speck of independent evidence I had supporting Kasabian's testimony regarding Krenwinkel's involvement in these crimes.

Krenwinkel had been given an excellent chance to "beat the rap." To this day I still don't understand why her attorney instructed her as he did and so lost her that chance.

The People's last two witnesses, Drs. Blake Skrdla and Harold Deering, were the psychiatrists who had examined Dianne. On both direct and redirect examination, I elicited testimony from them to the effect that, although a powerful drug, LSD does not impair memory, nor is there any demonstrable medical evidence that it causes brain damage. This was important, since the defense attorneys had contended that the minds of various prosecution witnesses, in particular Linda and Dianne, had been so "blown" by LSD that they could not distinguish fantasy from reality.

Skrdla testified that people on LSD *can* tell the difference between the real and the unreal; in fact, they often have a heightened awareness. Skrdla further stated that LSD causes illusions rather than hallucinations—in other words, that which is seen is actually there, only the perception of it is changed. This surprised a lot of people, since LSD is called a hallucinogenic drug.

When Watkins was on the stand, I personally brought out that although he was only twenty, Paul had taken LSD between 150 and 200 times. Yet, as the jury undoubtedly observed, he was one of the brightest and most articulate of the prosecution witnesses. Skrdla also testified: "I have seen individuals who have taken it several hundred times and show no outward sign of any emotional disturbance while they are not on the drug."

Fitzgerald asked Skrdla: "Would LSD in large doses over a period of time make someone sort of a zombie, or would it destroy rational thought processes?"

If, as I suspected, Fitzgerald was trying to lay the foundation for a defense based on this premise, that foundation collapsed when Skrdla replied: "I have not seen this, counsel."

Dr. Deering was the People's last witness. He finished testifying on Friday, November 13. Most of Monday, the sixteenth, was spent introducing the People's exhibits into evidence. There were 320 of these, and Kanarek objected to every one, from the gun to the scale map of the Tate premises. His strongest objections were to the color death photos. Responding, I argued: "I grant the Court that these photographs are gruesome, there is no question about it, but if in fact the defendants are the ones who committed these murders, which the prosecution of course is alleging, they are the ones who are responsible for the gruesomeness and the ghastliness. It is their handiwork. The jury is entitled to look at that handiwork."

Judge Older agreed, and they were admitted into evidence.

One exhibit never made it into evidence. As mentioned earlier, a number of white dog hairs had been found on the discarded clothing the killers wore the night of the

Tate murders. Shown them, Winifred Chapman told me they looked like the hair of Sharon's dog. When I requested that they be brought over from LAPD, however, I got only excuses. Finally, I learned that while walking across the street to the Hall of Justice, one of the Tate detectives had dropped and broken the vial containing the hairs. He had been able to recover only one. Realizing that the expression "grasping at hairs" would be all too appropriate in this case, I decided against introducing that single hair into evidence.

At 4:27 P.M. that Monday—exactly twenty-two weeks after the start of the trial, and two days short of a year after my assignment to the case—I told the Court: "Your Honor, the People of the State of California rest."

Court was recessed until Thursday, November 19, at which time each of the defense attorneys argued the standard motions to dismiss.

Back in December 1969 a great many attorneys predicted that when we reached this point Manson would have to be acquitted because of insufficiency of evidence.

I doubted if any lawyer in the country felt that way now, including the attorneys for the defense.

Older denied all the motions.

THE COURT "Are you ready to proceed with the defense?"

FITZGERALD "Yes, Your Honor."

THE COURT "You may call your first witness, Mr. Fitzgerald."

FITZGERALD "Thank you, Your Honor. The defendants rest."

Nearly everyone in the courtroom was caught completely off guard. For several minutes even Judge Older seemed too stunned to speak. The ultimate legal issue at a criminal trial is not the defendant's guilt or innocence, as most people believe. The issue is whether or not the prosecution has met its legal burden of proving the guilt of the defendant beyond a reasonable doubt and to a moral certainty.* The defense obviously, but unexpectedly, had decided to avoid cross-examination and to rely on the argument that we hadn't proved the guilt of Manson and his co-defendants beyond a reasonable doubt and, hence, they were entitled to not-guilty verdicts.

The biggest surprise, however, was still to come.

*In American criminal jurisprudence, the term "Not Guilty" is not totally synonymous with innocence. "Not Guilty" is a legal finding by the jury that the prosecution hasn't proven its case. A "Not Guilty" verdict based on the insufficiency of the evidence can result from either of two states of mind on the part of the jury: that they believe the defendant is innocent and did not commit the crime charged, *or*, although they tend to believe he did commit the crime, the prosecution's case was not sufficiently strong to convince them of his guilt beyond a reasonable doubt and to a moral certainty.

Part 7

MURDER IN THE WIND

"You could feel something in the air, you know. You could feel something in the air."

Juan Flynn

"Snitches, and other enemies, will be taken care of."

Sandra Good

"Before his disappearance, Ronald Hughes, the missing defense attorney in the Tate-LaBianca murder trial, confided to close friends that he was in fear of Manson."

Los Angeles *Times*

November 19-December 20, 1970

Fitzgerald said the defense had rested. But the three female defendants now shouted that they wanted to testify.

Calling counsel into chambers, Judge Older demanded to know exactly what was going on.

There had been a split between the defense attorneys and their clients, Fitzgerald said. The girls wanted to testify; their attorneys opposed this, and wanted to rest their case.

Only after an hour of intense discussion did the real reason for the split come out, in an off-the-record admission by Fitzgerald:

Sadie, Katie, and Leslie wanted to take the stand and testify that they had planned and committed the murders—and that Manson was not involved!

Charlie had tried to explode his bombshell, but the attorneys for the girls had managed to defuse it, at least temporarily. Standing up against Manson for the first time, Ronald Hughes observed: "I refuse to take part in any proceeding where I am forced to push a client out the window."

The legal problems thus created were immense, but basically they came down to the question of which took precedence: the right to effective counsel or the right to testify. Worried that whichever course Older took might be reversible error on appeal, I suggested he take the matter to the State Supreme Court for a decision. Older, however, decided that even though the attorneys had rested, and had advised their clients not to take the stand, the right to testify "supersedes any and all other rights." The girls would be permitted to take the stand.

Older asked Manson if he also wished to testify. "No," he replied, then, after a moment's hesitation, added, "That is, not at this time anyway."

On returning to open court, Kanarek made a motion to sever Manson so he could be tried separately.

Charlie was now attempting to abandon ship, while letting the girls sink. After denying the motion, Older had the jury brought in and Susan Atkins took the stand and was sworn. Daye Shinn, however, refused to question her, stating that if he asked the questions she'd prepared, they would incriminate her.*

This created a whole new problem. Returning to chambers, Older remarked: "It is becoming perfectly clear that this entire maneuver by the defense is simply one . . . to wreck the trial . . . I do not intend to permit this to happen."

Still in chambers, and outside the presence of the jury, Susan Atkins told Judge Older that she wanted to testify to "the way it happened. The way I *saw* it happen."

THE COURT "You are subjecting yourself to the extreme risk of convicting yourself out of your own mouth, do you understand that?"

ATKINS "I understand that." She added that if she was convicted, "let them convict me on the truth. I do not wish to be convicted on a pack of lies taken out of context and just scattered every which way. Because, Mr. Bugliosi, your foundation is just crumbling. I have watched it crumble. You have been a sly, sneaky fox."

BUGLIOSI "Why do you want to put it back together for me, Sadie, if it is crumbling? You should be happy. You can go back to Barker Ranch if it is crumbling. Why do you want to take the stand to help me?"

Shinn said he would ask to be relieved as counsel if Older ordered him to question his client. Fitzgerald replied similarly, adding, "As far as I am concerned, it would be sort of aiding and abetting a suicide."

The matter was unresolved when court recessed for the day.

The following day Manson surprised everyone by saying that he too wanted to testify. In fact, he wanted to go on the stand before the others. Because of possible *Aranda*

*Shinn's remarks, in themselves incriminating, were later stricken from the record.

problems, however, it was decided that Manson should first testify outside the presence of the jury.

Manson was sworn. Rather than have Kanarek question him, he requested and received permission to make a statement.

He spoke for over an hour. He began almost apologetically, at first speaking so low that the spectators in the crowded courtroom had to lean forward to hear. But after a few minutes the voice changed, grew stronger, more animated, and, as I'd already discovered in my conversations with him, when this happened his face seemed to change too. Manson the nobody. Manson the martyr. Manson the teacher. Manson the prophet. He became all these, and more, the metamorphosis often occurring in midsentence, his face a light show of shifting emotions until it was not one face but a kaleidoscope of different faces, each real, but only for the moment.

He rambled, he digressed, he repeated himself, but there *was* something hypnotic about the whole performance. In his own strange way he was trying to weave a spell, not unlike the ones he had cast over his impressionable followers.

MANSON "There has been a lot of charges and a lot of things said about me and brought against the co-defendants in this case, of which a lot could be cleared up and clarified . . .

"I never went to school, so I never growed up to read and write too good, so I have stayed in jail and I have stayed stupid, and I have stayed a child while I have watched your world grow up, and then I look at the things that you do and I don't understand . . .

"You eat meat and you kill things that are better than you are, and then you say how bad, and even killers, your children are. *You* made your children what they are . . .

"These children that come at you with knives, they are your children. You taught them. I didn't teach them. I just tried to help them stand up.

"Most of the people at the ranch that you call the Family were just people that you did not want, people that were alongside the road, that their parents had kicked out, that did not want to go to Juvenile Hall. So I did the best I could and I took them up on my garbage dump and I told them this: that in love there is no wrong . . .

"I told them that anything they do for their brothers and sisters is good if they do it with a good thought . . .

"I was working at cleaning up my house, something that Nixon should have been doing. He should have been on the side of the road, picking up his children, but he wasn't. He was in the White House, sending them off to war . . .

"I don't understand you, but I don't try. I don't try to judge nobody. I know that the only person I can judge is me . . . But I know this: that in your hearts and your own souls, you are as much responsible for the Vietnam war as I am for killing these people . . .

"I can't judge any of you. I have no malice against you and no ribbons for you. But I think that it is high time that you all start looking at yourselves, and judging the lie that you live in.

"I can't dislike you, but I will say this to you: you haven't got long before you are all going to kill yourselves, because you are all crazy. And you can project it back at me . . . but I am only what lives inside each and every one of you.

"My father is the jailhouse. My father is your system . . . I am only what you made me. I am only a reflection of you.

"I have ate out of your garbage cans to stay out of jail. I have wore your second-hand clothes . . . I have done my best to get along in your world and now you want to kill me, and I look at you, and then I say to myself, You want to kill *me?* Ha! I'm already dead, have been all my life. I've spent twenty-three years in tombs that you built.

"Sometimes I think about giving it back to you; sometimes I think about just jumping on you and letting you shoot me . . . If I could, I would jerk this microphone off and beat your brains out with it, because that is what you deserve, that is what you deserve . . .

"If I could get angry at you, I would try to kill every one of you. If that's guilt, I accept it . . .

"These children, everything they done, they done for the love of their brother . . .

"If I showed them that I would do anything for my brother—including giving my life for my brother on the battlefield—and then they pick up their banner, and they go off and do what they do, that is not my responsibility. I don't tell people what to do . . .

"These children [indicating the female defendants] were finding themselves. What they did, if they did whatever they did, is up to them. They will have to explain that to you . . .

"It's all your fear. You look for something to project it on, and you pick out a little old scroungy nobody that eats out of a garbage can, and that nobody wants, that was kicked out of the penitentiary, that has been dragged through every hellhole that you can think of, and you drag him and put him in a courtroom.

"You expect to break me? Impossible! You broke me years ago. You killed me years ago . . ."

Older asked Manson if he had anything further to say.

MANSON "I have killed no one and I have ordered no one to be killed.

"I may have implied on several different occasions to several different people that I may have been Jesus Christ, but I haven't decided yet what I am or who I am."

Some called him Christ, Manson said. In prison his name was a number. Some now want a sadistic fiend, and so they see him as that. So be it. Guilty. Not guilty. They are only words. "You can do anything you want with me, but you cannot touch me because I am only my love . . . If you put me in the penitentiary, that means nothing because you kicked me out of the last one. I didn't ask to get released. I liked it in there because I like myself."

Telling Manson, "You seem to be getting far afield," Older asked him to stick to the issues.

MANSON "The issues? . . . Mr. Bugliosi is a hard-driving prosecutor, polished education, a master of words, semantics. He is a genius. He has got everything that every lawyer would want to have except one thing: a case. He doesn't have a case. Were I allowed to defend myself, I could have proven this to you . . .

"The evidence in this case is a gun. There was a gun that laid around the ranch. It belonged to everybody. Anybody could have picked that gun up and done anything they wanted to do with it. I don't deny having that gun. That gun has been in my possession many times.

"Like the rope was there." Sure he'd bought the rope, Manson admitted, 150 feet of it, "because you need rope on a ranch."

The clothes? "It is really convenient that Mr. Baggot found those clothes. I imagine he got a little taste of money for that."

The bloodstains? "Well, they are not exactly bloodstains. They are benzidine reaction."

The leather thong? "How many people have ever worn moccasins with leather thongs?"

The photos of the seven bodies, 169 stab wounds? "They put the hideous bodies on display and they imply: If he gets out, see what will happen to you."

Helter Skelter? "It means confusion, literally. It doesn't mean any war with anyone. It doesn't mean that some people are going to kill other people ... Helter Skelter is confusion. Confusion is coming down around you fast. If you can't see the confusion coming down around you fast, you can call it what you wish."

Conspiracy? "Is it a conspiracy that the music is telling the youth to rise up against the establishment because the establishment is rapidly destroying things? Is that a conspiracy?

"The music speaks to you every day, but you are too deaf, dumb, and blind to even listen to the music ...

"It is not my conspiracy. It is not my music. I hear what it relates. It says 'Rise,' it says 'Kill.'

"Why blame it on me? I didn't write the music."

About the witnesses. "For example, Danny DeCarlo. He said that I hate black men, and he said that we thought alike ... But actually all I ever did with Danny DeCarlo or any other human being was reflect him back at himself. If he said he did not like the black man, I would say 'O.K.' So consequently he would drink another beer and walk off and say 'Charlie thinks like I do.'

"But actually he does not know how Charlie thinks because Charlie has never projected himself.

"I don't think like you people. You people put importance on your lives. Well, my life has never been important to anyone . . ."

Linda Kasabian. She only testified against him because she saw him as her father and she never liked her father. "So she gets on the stand and she says when she looked in that man's eyes that was dying, she knew that it was *my* fault. She knew it was my fault because she couldn't face death. And if she can't face death, that is not my fault. I can face death. I have all the time. In the penitentiary you live with it, with constant fear of death, because it is a violent world in there, and you have to be on your toes constantly."

Dianne Lake. She wanted attention. She would make trouble, cause accidents to get it. She wanted a father to punish her. "So as any father would do, I conditioned her mind with pain to keep her from burning the ranch down."

Yes, he was a father to the young girls and boys in the Family. But a father only in the sense that he taught them "not to be weak and not to lean on me." Paul Watkins wanted a father. "I told him: 'To be a man, boy, you have to stand up and be your own father.' So he goes off to the desert and finds a father image in Paul Crockett."

Yes, he put a knife to Juan Flynn's throat. Yes, he told him he felt responsible for all of these killings. "I do feel some responsibility. I feel a responsibility for the pollution. I feel a responsibility for the whole thing."

He didn't deny that he had told Brooks Poston to get a knife and go kill the sheriff of Shoshone. "I don't know the sheriff of Shoshone. I am not saying that I didn't say it, but if I said it, at the time I may have thought it was a good idea.

"To be honest with you, I don't recall ever saying 'Get a knife and a change of clothes and go do what Tex says.' Or I don't recall saying 'Get a knife and go kill the sheriff.'

"In fact, it makes me mad when someone kills snakes or dogs or cats or horses. I don't even like to eat meat—that is how much I am against killing . . .

"I haven't got any guilt about anything because I have never been able to see any wrong . . . I have always said:

Do what your love tells you, and I do what my love tells me . . . Is it *my* fault that your children do what *you* do?

"*What about your children?*" Manson asked angrily, rising slightly in the witness chair as if he were about to spring forward and attack everyone in the courtroom. "*You say there are just a few?*

"There are many, many more, coming in the same direction.

"They are running in the streets—and they are coming right at you!"

I had only a few questions for Manson, none of which came from the notebooks I'd kept.

Q. "You say you are already dead, is that right, Charlie?"

A. "Dead in your mind or dead in my mind?"

Q. "Define it any way you want to."

A. "As any child will tell you, dead is when you are no more. It is just when you are not there. If you weren't there, you would be dead."

Q. "How long have you been dead?"

Manson evaded a direct reply.

Q. "To be precise about it, you think you have been dead for close to 2,000 years, don't you?"

A. "Mr. Bugliosi, 2,000 years is relative to the second we live in."

Q. "Suffice it to say, Department 104 is a long way from Calvary, isn't that true?"

Manson had testified that all he wanted was to take his children and return to the desert. After I reminded him that "the only people who can set you free so that you can go back to the desert are the twelve jurors in this case," and noting that, though he had testified for over an hour, "the jury in this case never heard a single, solitary word you said," I posed one final question: "Mr. Manson, are you willing to testify in front of the jury and tell them the same things that you have testified to here in open court today?"

Kanarek objected. Older sustained the objection, and I concluded my cross.

To my surprise, Older later asked me why I hadn't seriously cross-examined Manson. I'd thought the reason was obvious. I had nothing to gain, since the jury wasn't present. I had lots and lots of questions for Charlie, several notebooks full, *if* he took the stand in the presence of the jury, but in the meantime I had no intention of giving him a dry run.

However, when Older asked Manson if he now wished to testify before the jury, Charlie replied, "I have already relieved all the pressure I had."

As Manson left the stand and passed the counsel table, I overheard him tell the three girls: "You don't have to testify now."

The big question: what did he mean by "now"? I strongly suspected that Manson hadn't given up but was only biding his time.

After the defense had introduced their exhibits, Judge Older recessed court for ten days to give the attorneys time to prepare their jury instructions and arguments.

This being his first trial, Ron Hughes had never argued before a jury before, or participated in drawing up the instructions which the judge would give the jury just before they began their deliberations. He was obviously looking forward to it, however. He confided to TV newscaster Stan Atkinson that he was convinced he could win an acquittal for Leslie Van Houten.

He wouldn't even get the chance to try.

When court resumed on Monday, November 30, Ronald Hughes was absent.

Quizzed by Older, none of the other defense attorneys knew where he was. Fitzgerald said that he had last talked to Ron on Thursday or Friday, and that he sounded O.K. at that time. Hughes often spent his weekends camping at Sespe Hot Springs, a rugged terrain some 130 miles northwest of Los Angeles. There had been floods in the area the past weekend. It was possible that Hughes had been stranded there.

The next day we learned that Hughes had gone to Sespe on Friday with two teen-agers, James Forsher and Lauren Elder, in Miss Elder's Volkswagen. The pair—who were questioned but not held—said that when it began raining, they had decided to return to L.A., but Hughes had decided to stay over until Sunday. When the two tried to leave, however, their auto became mired down, and they were forced to abandon it and hike out.

Three other youths had seen Hughes on the morning of the following day, Saturday the twenty-eighth. He was alone at the time and on high ground, well away from the flood area. Chatting with them briefly, he appeared neither ill nor in any danger. Polygraphed, the three were found to have no additional knowledge and they were not held. Since Forsher and Elder had last seen Hughes a day earlier, they apparently were not polygraphed and their story was taken at face value.

Owing to the continued bad weather, it was two days before the Ventura Sheriff's Office could get up a helicopter to search the area. In the meantime, rumors abounded. One was to the effect that Hughes had deliberately skipped, either to avoid argument or to sabotage the trial. Knowing Ron, I seriously doubted if this was true. I became convinced it wasn't when reporters visited the place where Hughes lived.

He slept on a mattress in a garage behind the home of a friend. According to reporters, the place was a mess—one remarked that he wouldn't even let his dog sleep there. But on the wall of the garage, neatly framed and carefully hung, was Ronald Hughes' bar certificate.

Although there were numerous reports that a man fitting Hughes' description had been seen in various places—boarding a bus in Reno, driving on the San Bernardino freeway, drinking at a bar in Baja—none checked out. On December 2, Judge Older told Leslie Van Houten that he felt a co-counsel should be brought in to represent her during Hughes' absence. Leslie said she would refuse any other attorney.

On December 3, after consulting with Paul Fitzgerald, Older appointed Maxwell Keith co-counsel for Leslie.

A quiet, somewhat shy man in his mid-forties, whose conservative clothing and courtroom manner were in sharp contrast to those of Hughes, Keith had an excellent reputation in the legal community. Those who knew him well described him as conscientious, totally ethical, and completely professional, and it was clear from the start that he would be representing his client and not Manson.

Sensing this, Manson asked to have all the defense attorneys dismissed ("They aren't our lawyers; they won't listen to us") so he and the girls could represent themselves. He also demanded that the case be reopened so they could put on a defense. They had twenty-one witnesses waiting to testify, he said. Both requests were denied.

Keith had his work laid out for him. Before he could prepare his argument, he had to familiarize himself with 152 volumes of transcript, over 18,000 pages.

Though Older granted a delay until he could do so, he told all counsel: "We will continue to meet every day at 9 A.M. until further notice."

Older obviously wanted to count heads.

Several days earlier Steve Kay had overheard Manson tell the girls, "Watch Paul; I think he's up to something." I made sure Fitzgerald learned of the conversation. One missing attorney was one more than enough.

Neither the air search nor a subsequent ground search of the Sespe area yielded any trace of Hughes. The abandoned Volkswagen was found, with a batch of court transcripts inside, but other papers Hughes was known to have had, including a secret psychiatric report on Leslie Van Houten, were missing.

On December 6, Paul Fitzgerald told reporters, "I think Ron is dead." On December 7, an all-points bulletin was issued for Hughes, LASO admitting, "This is something you do when you have no other leads." On December 8, Judge Older went to the Ambassador Hotel to inform the jury of the reason for the delay. He also told them: "It appears fairly certain that you will be sequestered over the Christmas holidays." They took it much better than expected. On December 12, the search for Ronald Hughes was suspended.

The most persistent rumor was that Hughes had been murdered by the Family. There was, at this time, no evidence of this. But there was more than ample cause for speculation.

Though once little more than an errand boy for Manson, during the course of the trial Hughes had grown increasingly independent, until the two had finally split over whether there should be a defense—Hughes strongly opposing his client's taking the stand to absolve Charlie. I also heard from several sources, including Paul Fitzgerald, that Hughes was afraid of Manson. It was possible that he showed this fear, which, in Manson's case, was like waving a red flag before a bull. Fear turned Charlie on.

There could have been several reasons for his murder, if it was that. It may have been done to intimidate the other defense attorneys into letting Manson put on a defense during the penalty trial (one was so shaken by Hughes' disappearance that he went on a bender which ended in his arrest for drunken driving). Equally likely, it could have been a tactic to delay the trial—with the hope that it would result in a mistrial, or set the stage for a reversal on appeal.

Speculation, nothing more. Except for one odd, perhaps unrelated, incident. On December 2, four days after Hughes was last seen alive, fugitives Bruce Davis and Nancy Pitman, aka Brenda McCann, voluntarily surrendered to the police. Two of the Family's most hard-core members, Pitman had been missing for several weeks after failing to appear for sentencing on a forgery charge, while Davis—who had been involved in both the Hinman and Shea murders, who had picked up the gun with which Zero had "committed suicide" but had somehow left no prints, and who was the chief suspect in the slaying of two young Scientology students*—had evaded capture for over seven months.

Maybe it was just the proximity in time that linked the two events in my mind: Hughes' disappearance; Davis' and Pitman's surprise surrender. But I couldn't shake the feeling that in some way the two incidents might be related.

*These murders will be discussed in a later chapter.

On December 18—three days before the Tate-LaBianca trial reconvened—the Los Angeles County grand jury indicted Steve Grogan, aka Clem; Lynette Fromme, aka Squeaky; Ruth Ann Moorehouse, aka Ouisch; Catherine Share, aka Gypsy; and Dennis Rice on charges of conspiracy to prevent and dissuade a witness (Barbara Hoyt) from attending a trial. Three other charges, including conspiracy to commit murder, were dismissed by Judge Choate on a 995 motion by the defense.

Although we had presumed—as I suspected the involved Family members had also—that an overdose of LSD could be fatal, we learned from medical experts that there was no known case of anyone's dying from this cause. There were many cases, however, where LSD had resulted in death from misperception of surroundings: for example, a person, convinced he could fly, stepping out the window of a tall building. I thought of Barbara, running through the traffic in downtown Honolulu. That she hadn't been killed was no fault of the Family. The result, however, was that, despite the best efforts of the LaBianca detectives, the DA's Office had a very weak case.

Pending trial, four of the five were released on bail. They immediately returned to the corner outside the Hall of Justice, where they would remain, on and off, during most of the remainder of the trial. Since Ouisch, who had given Barbara the LSD-laden hamburger, was nearly nine months pregnant, Judge Choate released her on her own recognizance. She promptly fled the state.

Nancy Pitman, who had been arrested with Davis, was freed on the forgery charge. She was rearrested a few weeks later while trying to pass Manson a tab of LSD in the visitors' room at the County Jail. After serving thirty days, she was again freed, to rejoin the group on the corner and, subsequently, to become involved in still another murder.

December 21, 1970-January 25, 1971

When court reconvened, the four defendants created a disturbance—Manson throwing a paper clip at the judge, the girls accusing him of "doing away with Hughes"—all obviously planned actions to garner the day's headlines.

Older ordered the four removed. As Sadie was being escorted out, she passed behind me. Though I didn't see what happened, I felt it: she knocked over an exhibit board, hitting me on the back of the head. Those who witnessed the incident said it appeared she was lunging for the Buck knife, which was on a nearby table. Thereafter the knife was kept well out of the reach of the defendants.

Maxwell Keith then told the Court that though he now felt himself familiar with the evidence, from having read the transcripts and other documents, he was not at all sure he could effectively represent his client, since he had not been present when the witnesses testified and therefore could not judge their demeanor or credibility. On this basis, he requested a mistrial.

Though Keith argued persuasively, Judge Older denied the motion, observing that every day attorneys argue cases in appellate courts without having been present during the actual trials.

Once this and several other motions were out of the way, it was time for the People's opening argument.*

During the guilt phase of a trial in California, the prosecution delivers an opening argument, which is followed by the opening argument of the defense, and, last, a closing argument (or final summation) by the prosecution. Thus the People have the last word during the guilt trial.

*This is entirely separate from the opening statement, which is delivered at the start of the trial.

During the penalty trial, if there is one, each side gives two arguments, with the defense being allowed to argue last.

I had spent several hundred hours preparing my opening argument for the guilt trial, starting even before the beginning of the trial itself. The result was contained in some 400 handwritten pages. But by this time I knew their contents so well I didn't even need to read them, but only glanced at them periodically.

I began by discussing in depth, with charts and other aids, the points of law the jury would have to consider: murder, conspiracy, and so on. The instructions which the judge would give the jury are printed, formal statements of law that use nebulous, abstract terms that often even lawyers don't understand. Moreover, the judge does not tell the jury how these rules of law apply to the facts of the case. Thus, in the jury's mind, the rules are floating lazily in the air with no thread connecting them to anything tangible. In each case I try, I make it a point to supply that link, by the liberal use of common-sense examples, by translating legalese into words and thoughts the jury will understand, and by literally tying those rules to the evidence.

After I had done this, I got into the principal part of my opening argument, summarizing the testimony of each witness, often quoting verbatim the words he had used on the stand, interrelating this testimony with the other evidence, and drawing inferences from it. Though the presentation took three days, it was a tight, cohesive package, and by the time I had finished I felt confident that I had established, beyond all doubt, Manson's control, his motives, his involvement, and the involvement of Watson, Atkins, Krenwinkel, and Van Houten.

Apparently it got to Charlie. At the end of my opening statement, he had tried to bribe deputy Maupin to free him. The night after I completed the first day of my opening argument, he tried to break out of jail.

Though the incident was officially denied by LASO, one of the deputies told me the details. Despite daily searches of both his person and his cell, Manson had managed to obtain an incredibly long piece of string, at the end of which he had attached a small weight. By some unknown means or manner—for the area was supposedly under constant surveillance—he had got the string across the walkway in front of his cell and out a window, where it reached a full ten stories to the ground. One or more confederates then attached the contraband. However, something must have happened which prevented Manson from pulling it up, for when a deputy came around the corner of the Hall of Justice the next morning he spotted the string and its cargo: a lid of marijuana and a hacksaw blade.

Accepting a promise that they would behave, Judge Older permitted the three female defendants to return to court the next afternoon. Manson, who said he had no desire to return, remained in the lockup, listening to the proceedings from there.

I had just resumed my argument when Leslie created a disturbance. Sadie and Katie followed suit, and each of the three was again ordered removed. This time Sadie was led in front of the lectern where I was standing. Suddenly, without warning, she kicked one of the female deputies in the leg, then grabbed some of my notes, tearing them in half. Grabbing them back, I involuntarily muttered, beneath my breath, "You little bitch!"

Though provoked, I regretted losing my cool.

The next day the Long Beach *Independent* bore the following front-page headline:

MANSON PROSECUTOR
TAKES SWING AT SUSAN

According to reporter Mary Neiswender: "The chaos was capped by the chief prosecutor swearing at and attempting to slug one of the defendants ... Bugliosi slapped the girl's hand, grabbed his notes and then swung at her shouting, 'You little bitch!' "

In common with everyone else in the courtroom, Judge Older saw the incident somewhat differently. Describing it for the record, he branded the charge that I was struggling with Susan "absolutely false. There was no struggle between Mr. Bugliosi and anybody. What happened was [she] walked by the rostrum and grabbed the notes off the rostrum."

While I'd like to say this was the only inaccurate press coverage during the trial, unfortunately the accounts of several reporters—including a representative of one of the wire services, whose reports appeared in papers all over the country—were often so error-filled that reading them gave one the feeling that the reporters had been attending another trial. On the other hand, such reporters as John Kendall of the Los Angeles *Times* and Bill Farr of the Los Angeles *Herald Examiner* did an excellent job, often catching little nuances even the attorneys missed.

After Krenwinkel had been removed, Judge Older called counsel to the bench and said that he had had it. "It is perfectly obvious to the Court that after lo, these many months, the defendants are operating in concert with each other ... I don't think any American court is required to subject itself to this kind of nonsense day after day when it is perfectly obvious that the defendants are using it as a stage for some kind of performance ..." Older then stated that the defendants would not be permitted to return to court during the remainder of the guilt trial.

I had hoped to finish my argument before court recessed for the Christmas holiday, but Kanarek's multitudinous objections prevented my doing so.

The feelings of the jurors at being sequestered over Christmas were exemplified by one who hung up the hotel menu and wrote "BAH, HUMBUG" across it. Though they were permitted family visits, and special parties had been arranged at the Ambassador, it was for most a miserable time. None had anticipated being away from home this long. Many were worried whether they would still have their jobs when the trial ended. And no one, including the judge, would even venture a guess when that might be.

On weekends both jurors and alternates—always accompanied by two male and two female deputies—had taken trips to such places as Disneyland, the movie studios, the San Diego Zoo, many probably seeing more of

Southern California than they had in the whole of their lives. They had dinner at restaurants all over Los Angeles. They went bowling, swimming, even nightclubbing. But this was only partial compensation for their long ordeal.

To keep up morale, the bailiffs exhibited considerable ingenuity. For example, though the trial was perhaps the most widely publicized in history, there were days when most of the action took place in chambers and newsmen could find little to report. At such times bailiff Bill Murray often cut huge sections out of the newspapers, just to make the jurors think they were still in the headlines.

But the strain was getting to them. Older people for the most part, they were set in their ways. Inevitably, arguments broke out, factions developed. One temperamental male juror slapped bailiff Ann Orr one night when, against his wishes, she changed channels on the communal TV. Often Murray and Orr sat up to 4 or 5 A.M., listening to a juror's complaints. As we neared the end of the guilt trial, I began worrying not about the evidence but about the personal disagreements the jurors might be carrying into the jury room with them when they began their deliberations.

It only takes one person to hang up a jury.

I concluded my opening argument on Monday, December 28, by telling the jury what I thought the defense's case would be, thereby lessening the psychological impact of the defense attorneys' arguments.

"The defense will probably argue that there is no conspiracy . . . They will tell you that the Helter Skelter motive is absurd, ridiculous, unbelievable . . . They will tell you that the interpretation of the Beatles' songs by Manson was normal . . . They will tell you that Linda is insane with LSD; that she made up her story to be granted immunity; that Linda's testimony as an accomplice has not been corroborated . . . Probably they will tell you the reason why they never put on a defense is because the prosecution never proved their case . . . They will tell you that Charles Manson is not a killer; he wouldn't harm a flea.

"They will tell you that Charlie was not the leader of the Family; he never ordered these murders . . . They will tell you that this has been a case of circumstantial evidence—as if there is something wrong with circumstantial evidence—completely disregarding the direct evidence by the way of Linda's testimony.

"Out of 18,000 pages of transcript, they will come up here and there with a slight discrepancy between the testimony of one witness and another witness, which of course has to be expected, but they will tell you this means that the People's witnesses are liars."

I then asked the jury as intelligent men and women to conscientiously evaluate the evidence in this case, applying common sense and reason, and thereby reach a just and fair verdict.

"Under the law of this state and nation these defendants are entitled to have their day in court. They got that.

"They are also entitled to have a fair trial by an impartial jury. They also got that.

"That is all that they are entitled to!

"Since they committed these seven senseless murders, the People of the State of California are entitled to a guilty verdict."

Toward the opening of his argument for Patricia Krenwinkel, Paul Fitzgerald said, "If we set out to rebut every witness the prosecution put on that stand we would be here until 1974," unthinkingly emphasizing the strength of the People's case, as well as the defense's inability to answer it.

Fitzgerald's argument was very disappointing. Not only were there many things he could have argued but didn't, he repeatedly misstated the evidence. He said that Sebring was hanged; that all the victims had been stabbed to death; that Tim Ireland heard Parent scream. He referred to Sharon as "Mary Polanski"; he had the killers entering the Tate residence through a bedroom window; he confused how many times Frykowski had been stabbed and struck. He said Linda testified to five knives rather than three; he had Linda driving on the second night when Manson was, and vice versa; he had a deputy who wasn't even present arresting Manson during the Spahn raid; and so on.

The prosecution stressed "murder, murder, murder," Fitzgerald said. "Actually, you have to decide whether it is a murder." The first thing the jury should decide, he continued, is "what crimes, if any, were committed."

"Now, a .22 caliber pistol, it strikes me, is a classically inefficient way to kill somebody . . ."

"It obviously does not make sense to hang anybody . . ."

"If you were a mastermind criminal, if you had absolute power over the minds and bodies of bootlicking slaves, as they were referred to, would you send women out to do a man's job? . . . Women, ladies and gentlemen, are life-givers. They make love, they get pregnant, they deliver babies. They are life-givers, not takers away. Women are adverse to violence . . ."

Only a small portion of Fitzgerald's argument was devoted to the evidence against his client. And rebuttal it was not.

He said that "there is doubt as to whether or not that fingerprint [found at the Tate residence] belongs to Patricia Krenwinkel." Even presuming it did, he said, "It is entirely conceivable, possible, and reasonable that Patricia Krenwinkel was at that house as an invited guest or a friend."

Some friend!

As for Krenwinkel's so-called confession to Dianne Lake, that she dragged Abigail Folger from the bedroom to the living room, that wasn't a confession at all, Fitzgerald said. She didn't say when this occurred or where. Maybe it took place in San Francisco in 1967.

Fitzgerald did spend a great deal of time trying to destroy the credibility of Linda Kasabian. In my argument I had remarked: "Linda Kasabian was on that witness stand, ladies and gentlemen, for eighteen days—an extraordinarily long period of time for any witness to testify in any case. I think you will agree with me that during those eighteen days Linda Kasabian and the truth were companions." Fitzgerald challenged this. But he was unable to cite a single discrepancy in her account.

However, the greater portion of his argument dealt with the case against Charles Manson. All the testimony regarding Manson's philosophy proved, Fitzgerald said, was "that he is some sort of right-wing hippie." Manson, Manson, Manson.

Fitzgerald ended his argument with a long, impassioned plea—not for his client, Patricia Krenwinkel, but for Charles Manson. There was, he concluded, insufficient evidence against Manson.

Not once did he say that there was insufficient evidence against Patricia Krenwinkel.

Nor did he even ask the jury to come back with a not guilty verdict for his client!

Daye Shinn had prepared a chart listing all the witnesses who testified against his client, Susan Atkins. He said he would rebut each.

"The first one on the list is Linda Kasabian, and I believe Mr. Fitzgerald has adequately covered Miss Kasabian's testimony."

He then skimmed over the criminal records of DeCarlo, Howard, Graham, and Walker.

On Danny DeCarlo: "How would you like to have him for your son-in-law? How would you like to have him meet your daughters?"

On Virginia Graham: "How would you like to invite her to your house for Christmas? You would have to hide the silverware.

"Mr. Bugliosi is laughing. At least I did not put him to sleep."

Shinn's entire argument took only 38 pages of transcript.

Irving Kanarek, who followed Shinn, consumed 1,182.

For the most part, Kanarek ignored my argument against Manson. Remaining on the offense rather than taking the defense, he pounded home two names—Tex, Linda. Who was it Linda Kasabian first slept with at Spahn Ranch? Stole the $5,000 for? Accompanied to the Tate residence? Charles "Tex" Watson. The most logical explanation for these murders was the simplest, Kanarek said. "Love of a girl for a boy."

As for his client, Kanarek portrayed him as a peaceful man whose only sin, if he had one, was that he preached and practiced love. "Now the people who brought these charges, they want to get Charles Manson, for some ungodly reason, which I think is related to Manson's life style."

Though many of his statements seemed to me to be too ridiculous for comment, I took many notes during Kanarek's argument. For he also planted little doubts, which, unless rebutted, could grow into bigger ones when the jury began its deliberations.

If the purpose was to start a black-white war, why did it stop the second night? Why wasn't there a third night, and a fourth? . . . Why didn't the prosecution bring in Nader, and the policemen on the beach, and the man whose life Linda *claimed* to have saved? . . . Are we to believe that by means of a wallet found in a toilet tank Mr. Manson intended to start a race war? . . . If Tex pushed Parent's car up the driveway, why weren't his prints found on it?

Several times Kanarek referred to the trial as a "circus," a remark to which Judge Older reacted very strongly. He also reacted, this time without my prompting, to Kanarek's charge that the prosecution had suppressed evidence. "There is no evidence in this case that anyone has suppressed anything," Older said.

At the end of Kanarek's second day of argument, Judge Older told him that he was putting the jury to sleep. "Now, I am not going to tell you how to make an argument," Older said at the bench, "but I would suggest to you that you may not be doing your client the utmost amount of good by prolonging it unduly . . ."

He went on for a third day, and a fourth.

On the fifth day the jury sent a note to the bailiff, requesting NoDoz for themselves and sleeping pills for Mr. Kanarek.

On the sixth day Older warned Kanarek, "You are abusing your right to argue just as you have abused practically every other right you have in this case . . . There is a point, Mr. Kanarek, at which argument is no longer argument but a filibuster . . . Yours is reaching that point."

Kanarek went on another full day before bringing his

argument to an end with the statement: "Charles Manson is not guilty of *any* crime."

Several times during Kanarek's argument Manson had interrupted with remarks from the lockup. Once he shouted, loud enough for the jury to hear, "Why don't you sit down? You're just making things worse."

During one of the noon recesses Manson asked to see me. I'd turned down several earlier requests, with the comment that I'd talk to him when he took the stand, but this time I decided to see what he wanted.

I was glad I did, as it was one of the most informative conversations we had—Manson telling me exactly how he felt about his three female co-defendants.

Manson wanted to clear up a couple of wrong impressions. One was Fitzgerald's reference to him as a "right-wing hippie." Though I personally thought the description had some validity, Manson felt otherwise. He'd never thought of himself as a hippie, he said. "Hippies don't like the establishment so they back off and form their own establishment. They're no better than the others."

He also didn't want me to think that Sadie, Katie, and Leslie were the best he could do. "I've screwed girls that would make these three look like boys," he said.

For some reason it was important to Manson that I believe this, and he re-emphasized it, adding, "I'm a very selfish guy. I don't give a fuck for these girls. I'm only out for myself."

"Have you ever told them that, Charlie?" I asked.

"Sure. Ask them."

"Then why would they do what they're doing for you? Why would they be willing to follow you anywhere—even to the gas chamber at San Quentin?"

"Because I tell them the truth," Manson replied. "Other guys bullshit them and say 'I love you and only you' and all that baloney. I'm honest with them. I tell them I'm the most selfish guy in the world. And I am."

Yet he was always saying that he would die for his brother, I reminded him. Wasn't that a contradiction?

"No, because that's selfish too," he responded. "He's not going to die for me unless I'm willing to die for him."

I had the strong feeling that Manson was leveling with me. Sadie, Katie, and Leslie were willing to murder, even give their own lives, for Charlie. And Charlie personally couldn't have cared less about them.

Though he wasn't even present when the witnesses testified, Maxwell Keith, arguing for Leslie Van Houten, delivered the best of the four defense arguments. He also did what no other defense attorney had dared do during the entire trial. He put the hat on Charles Manson—albeit with a ten-foot pole.

"The record discloses over and over again that all of these girls at the ranch believed Manson was God, really believed it.

"The record discloses that the girls obeyed his commands without any conscious questioning at all.

"If you believe the prosecution theory that these female defendants and Mr. Watson were extensions of Mr. Manson—his additional arms and legs as it were—if you believe that they were mindless robots, they cannot be guilty of premeditated murder." To commit first degree murder, Keith argued, you must have malice aforethought and you must think and plan. "And these people did not have minds to make up . . . Each of the minds of these girls and Mr. Watson were totally controlled by someone else."

As for Leslie herself, Keith argued that even if she did all the things the prosecution contended, she still had committed no crime.

"At best, if you want to believe Dianne Lake, the evidence shows that she was there.

"At best, it shows that she did something after the commission of these homicides that wasn't very nice.

"And at best, it showed that she wiped some fingerprints off after the commission of these homicides, which does not make her an aider and abetter.

"As repugnant as you may feel this is, nobody in the world can be guilty of murder or conspiracy to commit murder who stabs somebody after they are already dead. I'm sure that desecrating somebody that is dead is a crime in this state, but she is not charged with that."

This case, Keith concluded, must be decided on the basis of the evidence, and "on the basis of the evidence, ladies and gentlemen, I say to you: You must acquit Leslie Van Houten."

I began my final summation (closing argument) on January 13.

In my opinion, final summation is very often the most important part of the trial, since it's the last, final word to the jury. Again, several hundred hours had gone into the preparation. I began by meeting head on each of the defense contentions. In this way I hoped to dispose of any questions or lingering doubts that otherwise might distract the jury during the last phase of my argument, during which I summarize, as affirmatively as I can, the highlights and strengths of my case.

Taking on each of the defense attorneys in turn, I cited twenty-four misstatements of either the law or the testimony in Fitzgerald's presentation. As for his suggestion that if Manson ordered these murders he would have sent men rather than women, I asked, "Is Mr. Fitzgerald suggesting that Katie, Sadie, and Leslie were inadequate to do the job? Isn't Mr. Fitzgerald satisfied with their handiwork?" Fitzgerald had also contended that perhaps Linda planted the bloody clothing a few days before it was found. I reminded the jury that Linda was returned to California on December 2, in custody, and that the clothing was found on December 15. "Apparently Mr. Fitzgerald wants you to believe that one night between these dates Linda snuck out of her room at Sybil Brand, rounded up some clothing, put some blood on them, hitchhiked out to Benedict Canyon Road, threw the clothing over the side of the hill, then hitchhiked back to the jail and snuck back into her room."

Fitzgerald had likened the circumstantial evidence in this case to a chain, saying that if one link were missing the chain was broken. I, instead, likened it to a rope, each strand of which is a fact, and "as we add strands we add strength to that rope, until it is strong enough to bind these defendants to justice."

Shinn had raised very few points that needed rebutting. Kanarek had raised a great many, and I took them on one by one. A few samples:

Kanarek had asked why the prosecution didn't have the defendants try on the seven articles of clothing to see if they fitted. I reversed this, asking why, if they didn't fit, the defense didn't illustrate this to the jury.

As for the absence of Watson's prints on Parent's vehicle, I reminded them of Dolan's testimony that 70 percent of the times LAPD goes to a crime scene no readable prints are found. I also noted that in moving his hand, it was very likely Watson had created an unreadable smudge.

When I lacked the answer to a question, I frankly admitted it. But usually I offered at least one and often several possibilities. Whom did the glasses belong to? Frankly, we didn't know. But we did know, from Sadie's statement to Roseanne Walker, that they did not belong to the killers. Why was there no blood on the Buck knife found in the chair? Kanarek had raised this point. It was a good one. We had no answer. We could speculate, however, that Sadie had lost the knife before she stabbed Voytek and Sharon, possibly while she was in the process of tying up Voytek, and that at some later point she borrowed another knife from Katie or Tex. "Much more important than what knife she used was the fact that she confessed stabbing both of the victims to Virginia Graham and Ronnie Howard."

The whole thrust of Irving Kanarek's seven-day argument, I told the jury, was that the prosecution had framed its case against his client, Charles Manson.

"In other words, ladies and gentlemen," I observed, "there are seven brutal murders, so the police and the District Attorney got together and said, 'Let's prosecute some hippie for these murders, someone whose life style we don't like. Just about any hippie will do,' and we just arbitrarily picked on poor Charles Manson.

"Charles Manson is not a defendant in this trial because he is some long-haired vagabond who made love to young girls and was a virulent dissenter.

"He is on trial because he is a vicious, diabolical murderer who gave the order that caused seven human beings to end up in the cold earth. That is why he is on trial."

I also hit, and hard, Kanarek's claim that the prosecution was responsible for the excessive length of the trial. The jury had missed both Christmas and New Year's at home, and I didn't want them entering the jury chambers resenting the prosecution for this.

"Irving Kanarek, the Toscanini of tedium, is accusing the prosecution of tying up this court for over six months. You folks are the best witnesses. Every single, solitary witness that the prosecution called to the stand was asked brief questions, directly to the point. The witnesses were on that stand day after day after day on cross-examination, not on direct examination."

As for Maxwell Keith, he did "everything possible for his client, Leslie Van Houten," I observed. "He gave his best. Unfortunately for Mr. Keith, he had no facts and no law to support him. Mr. Keith, if you look at his argument very closely, never really disputed that Linda Kasabian and Dianne Lake told the truth. Basically, his position was that even if Leslie did the things Linda and Dianne said she did, she is still not guilty of anything.

"I wonder if Max would concede that she is at least guilty of trespassing?"

KEITH "I will."

Max's response surprised me. He was in effect admitting that Leslie had been in the LaBianca residence.

Even if Rosemary LaBianca was dead when Leslie stabbed her, I told the jury, she was guilty of first degree murder as both a co-conspirator and an aider and abetter. If a person is present at the scene of a crime, offering moral support, that constitutes aiding and abetting. But Leslie went far beyond this, stabbing, wiping prints, and so forth.

Also, we had only Leslie's word for it that Rosemary was dead when she stabbed her. "Only thirteen of Rosemary's forty-one stab wounds were post-mortem. What about the other twenty-eight?"

Yes, Tex, Sadie, Katie, and Leslie were robots, zombies, automatons. No question about it. But only in the sense that they were totally subservient and obsequious and servile to Charles Manson. Only in that sense. "This does not mean that they did not want to do what Charles Manson told them to do and weren't very willing participants in these murders. To the contrary, all the evidence goes the other way. There is no evidence that any of these defendants objected to Charles Manson about these two horrendous nights of murder.

"Only Linda Kasabian, down in Venice, said: 'Charlie, I am not you. I can't kill.' "

The others not only didn't complain, I noted, they laughed when the Tate murders were described on TV; Leslie told Dianne that stabbing was fun, that the more she stabbed the more she enjoyed it; while Sadie told Virginia and Ronnie that it was better than a sexual climax.

"The fact that these three female defendants obeyed Charles Manson and did whatever he told them to do does not immunize them from a conviction of first degree murder. It offers no insulation, no protection whatsoever. If it did, then hired killers or trigger men for the Mafia would have a built-in defense for murder. All they would have to say is: 'Well, I did what my boss told me to do.' "

Mr. Keith also "suggested that Watson and the three girls had some type of mental disability which prevented them from deliberating and premeditating, even prevented them from having malice aforethought." The problem with this, I told the jury, was that the defense never introduced any evidence of insanity or diminished capacity; on the contrary, I reminded the jury, Fitzgerald described the girls as "bright, intuitive, perceptive, well educated," while the evidence itself showed "these defendants were thinking very, very clearly on these two nights of murder."

Cutting telephone wires, instructing Linda to listen for sounds, hosing blood off their bodies, disposing of their clothing and weapons, wiping prints—"their conduct clearly and unequivocally shows that on both nights they knew exactly what they were doing, that they intended to kill, they did kill, and they did everything possible to avoid detection.

"They were not suffering, ladies and gentlemen, from any diminished mental capacity. They were suffering from a diminished heart, a diminished soul."

Still up to his old tricks, Kanarek had constantly interrupted my argument with frivolous objections. Even after another contempt citation and a $100 fine, Kanarek persisted. Calling counsel to the bench, Judge Older stated: "I have come to the regretful conclusion during the course of the trial that Mr. Kanarek appears to be totally without scruples, ethics, and professional responsibility so far as the trial of this lawsuit is concerned, and I want the record to clearly reflect that."

KANAREK "May I be sworn?"

THE COURT "Mr. Kanarek, I wouldn't believe you if you were."

With the defense arguments out of the way, I spent an entire afternoon reviewing the eyewitness testimony of Linda Kasabian. Among the instructions Judge Older was going to give the jury was one regarding the testimony of an accomplice. Both Fitzgerald and Kanarek had read the start of it: "The testimony of an accomplice ought to be viewed with distrust." They stopped there, however. I read the jury the rest: "This does not mean that you may arbitrarily disregard such testimony, but you should give it the weight to which you find it to be entitled after examining it with care and caution in the light of all the evidence in this case."

I then took the evidence of other witnesses, totally independent of Linda Kasabian, and showed how it confirmed or supported her testimony. Linda testified that Watson shot Parent four times. Dr. Noguchi testified that Parent was shot four times. Linda testified that Parent slumped over toward the passenger side. The police photographs show Parent slumped over toward the passenger side. Linda testified that Watson slit the screen horizontally. Officer Whisenhunt testified that the screen was slit horizontally. For the night of the Tate murders alone, I noted forty-five instances where other evidence confirmed Linda's account.

I concluded: "Ladies and gentlemen, the fingerprint evidence, the firearms evidence, the confessions, and all of the other evidence would convince the world's leading skeptic that Linda Kasabian was telling the truth."

I then cited every single piece of evidence against each of the defendants, starting with the girls and ending with Manson himself. I also noted that there were 238 references in the transcript to Manson's domination over the daily lives of his Family and his co-defendants. The inference that he must have also been dominating and directing them on the two nights of murder was unmistakable, I pointed out.

Thinking back over those many months, I remembered how difficult it had been to come up with even a few.

Helter Skelter. During the trial the evidence of this had come in piece by piece, from the mouths of many witnesses. I assembled those pieces now, in one devastating package. Very forcefully, and I felt convincingly, I proved that Helter Skelter was the motive for these murders, and that that motive belonged to Charles Manson and Charles Manson alone. I argued that when the words "Helter Skelter" were found printed in blood, it was like finding Manson's fingerprints at the scene.

We were nearly finished now. Within a few hours the jury would begin its deliberations. I ended my summation on a very powerful note.

"Charles Manson, ladies and gentlemen, said that he had the power to give life. On the nights of the Tate-LaBianca murders, he thought he had the concomitant right to take human life.

"He never had the right, but he did it anyway.

"On the hot summer night of August the eighth, 1969, Charles Manson, the Mephistophelean guru who raped and bastardized the minds of all those who gave themselves so totally to him, sent out from the fires of hell at Spahn Ranch three heartless, bloodthirsty robots and—unfortunately for him—one human being, the little hippie girl Linda Kasabian.

"The photographs of the victims show how very well Watson, Atkins, and Krenwinkel carried out their master Charles Manson's mission of murder . . .

"What resulted was perhaps the most inhuman, nightmarish, horror-filled hour of savage murder and human slaughter in the recorded annals of crime. As the helpless, defenseless victims begged and screamed out into the night for their lives, their lifeblood gushed out of their bodies, forming rivers of gore.

"If they could have, I am sure that Watson, Atkins, and

Krenwinkel would gladly have swum in that river of blood, and with orgasmic ecstasy on their faces. Susan Atkins, the vampira, actually tasted Sharon Tate's blood . . .

"The very next night, Leslie Van Houten joined the group of murderers, and it was poor Leno and Rosemary LaBianca who were brutally butchered to death to satisfy Charles Manson's homicidal madness . . .

"The prosecution put on a monumental amount of evidence against these defendants, much of it scientific, all of it conclusively proving that these defendants committed these murders.

"Based on the evidence that came from that witness stand, not only isn't there any reasonable doubt of their guilt, which is our only burden, there is absolutely no doubt whatsoever of their guilt . . .

"Ladies and gentlemen, the prosecution did its job in gathering and presenting the evidence. The witnesses did their job by taking that witness stand and testifying under oath. Now you are the last link in the chain of justice.

"I respectfully ask that after your deliberations you come back into this courtroom with the following verdict." I then read in full the verdict the People wished.

I came now to the end of my argument, what the newspapers would call the "roll call of the dead." After each name I paused, so the jurors could recall the person.

"Ladies and gentlemen of the jury," I quietly began, "Sharon Tate . . . Abigail Folger . . . Voytek Frykowski . . . Jay Sebring . . . Steven Parent . . . Leno LaBianca . . . Rosemary LaBianca . . . are not here with us now in this courtroom, *but from their graves they cry out for justice.* Justice can only be served by coming back to this courtroom with a verdict of guilty."

Gathering up my notes, I thanked the jury for the patience and attention they had shown throughout the proceedings. It had been a very, very long trial, I noted, and an immense imposition on their personal and private lives. "You have been an exemplary jury. The plaintiff at this trial is the People of the State of California. I have all the confidence in the world that you will not let them down."

After the noon recess, Judge Older instructed the jury. At 3:20 P.M., on Friday, January 15, 1971—exactly seven months after the start of the trial—the jury filed out to begin their deliberations.

The jury deliberated all day Saturday, then took Sunday off. On Monday they sent out two requests: that they be given a phonograph so they could play the Beatles' White Album, which, though introduced in evidence and much discussed, had never been played in court; and that they be permitted to visit the Tate and LaBianca residences.

After lengthy conferences with counsel, Older granted the first request but denied the second. Though admitting that, not having been to either of the death scenes, he too was naturally curious, the judge decided such visits would be tantamount to reopening the case, complete to the recalling of witnesses, cross-examination, and so on.

On Tuesday the jury asked to have Susan Atkins' letters to her former cellmates reread to them. This was done. Probably unprecedented in a case of this magnitude and complexity, at no time did the jury request that any of the actual testimony be reread. I could only surmise they were relying on the extensive notes each had taken throughout the trial.

Wednesday, Thursday, Friday—no further messages were received from the jury. Long before the end of the week the New York *Times* was reporting that the jury had been out too long, that it appeared they were deadlocked.

I wasn't bothered by this. I'd already told the press that I didn't expect them to come back for four or five days at the very minimum, and I wouldn't have been surprised had they stayed out a week and a half.

Nor did I worry about our having proven our case.

What did worry me was human nature.

Twelve individuals, from completely different backgrounds, had been locked up together longer than any jury in history. I thought a great deal about those twelve persons. One juror had let it be known that he intended to write a book about his experiences, and some of the other jurors were apprehensive about how they might be portrayed. The same juror also wanted to be elected foreman, and when he wasn't even in the running, was so piqued that for a day or two he wouldn't eat with the others.* Would he—or any of the other eleven—hang up the jury because of some personal animosity or slight? I didn't know.

Both Tubick and Roseland had daughters about the same age as Sadie, Katie, and Leslie. Would this affect their decision, and if so, how? Again I didn't know.

It was rumored, largely on the basis of glances they had exchanged in court, that the youngest member of the jury, William McBride II, had become slightly enamored of defendant Leslie Van Houten. It was unsubstantiated gossip, yet in the long hours the press waited for some word from the jury room, reporters made bets on whether McBride would vote second degree for Leslie, or perhaps even acquittal.

Immediately after my assignment to the case, I'd requested as much information as was available on the background of Charles Manson. Like much of the evidence, it came in piecemeal. Not until after the People had rested their case did I finally receive the records covering the seven months Manson spent at the National Training School for Boys in Washington, D.C. I found most of the information already familiar, with one startling exception.

If true, it could very well be the seed which—nurtured with hate, fear, and love—flowered into Manson's monstrous, grotesque obsession with the black-white revolution.

Manson had been sent to the institution in March 1951, when he was sixteen years old. In his admission summary, which was drawn up after he had been interviewed, there was a section on family background. The first two sentences read: "Father: unknown. He is alleged to have been a colored cook by the name of Scott, with whom the boy's mother had been promiscuous at the time of pregnancy."

Was Manson's father *black?* Reading through the rest

*Alva Dawson, the ex-deputy sheriff, and Herman Tubick, the mortician, had tied. A coin was tossed, and Tubick was made foreman. A deeply religious man, who began and ended each day of deliberations with silent prayer, Tubick had been a stabilizing influence during the long sequestration.

of the records, I found two similar statements, though no additional details.

There were several possible explanations for the inclusion of this statement in Manson's records. The first was that it was totally erroneous: some bureaucratic snafu of which Manson himself may even have been unaware. Another possibility was that Manson had lied about this in his interviews, though I couldn't imagine any conceivable benefit he would derive, particularly in a reform school located in the South. It was also possible that it was true.

There was one further possibility, and in a sense it was even more important than whether the information was true or false. Did young Charles Manson *believe* it to be true? If so, this would go a long way toward explaining the genesis of his bizarre philosophy, in which the blacks finally triumph over the whites but eventually have to hand over the reins of power to Manson himself.

I knew only one thing for sure. Even had I received this information earlier, I wouldn't have used it. It was much too inflammatory. I did decide, however, to ask Manson himself about it, if I got the chance.

I was in bed with the flu when, at 10:15 A.M. on Monday, January 25, court clerk Gene Darrow telephoned and said, "Just got the word. The jury has reached a verdict. Judge Older wants to see all the attorneys in his chambers as soon as they can get here."

The Hall of Justice resembled a fortress, as it had since the jury went out. A secret court order had been issued that same day, which began: "Due to intelligence reports indicating a possible attempt to disrupt proceedings on what has been described as 'Judgment Day,' additional security measures will be implemented . . ." There followed twenty-seven pages of detailed instructions. The entire Hall of Justice had been sealed, anyone entering the building for whatever reason being given a personal effects and body search. I now had three bodyguards, the judge a like number.

The reason for this intensive security was never made public. From a source close to the Family, LASO had heard what they initially believed to be an incredible tale.

While working at Camp Pendleton Marine Base, one of Manson's followers had stolen a case of hand grenades. These were to be smuggled into court on "Judgment Day" and used to free Manson.

Again, we didn't know precisely what the Family meant by Judgment Day. But by this time we did know that at least a part of the story was true. A Family member *had* been working in the arms depot at Pendleton, and after he quit, a case of hand grenades *was* missing.

By 11:15 all counsel were in chambers. Before bringing the jury in, Judge Older said he wanted to discuss the penalty trial.

California has a bifurcated trial system. The first phase, which we had just completed, was the guilt trial. If any of the defendants were convicted, a penalty trial would follow, in which the same jury would determine the penalty for the offense. In this case we had requested first degree murder verdicts against all the defendants. If the jury returned such verdicts, there were only two possible penalties: life imprisonment or death.

The penalty trial is, in most cases, very short.

After conferring with counsel, Judge Older decided that if there was a penalty phase, it would commence in three days. Older also said he had decided to seal the courtroom until after the verdicts were read and all the jurors polled. Once the jurors and the defendants had been removed, the press would be allowed out, and then the spectators.

The girls were brought in first. Though they had usually worn fairly colorful clothing during the trial, apparently there hadn't been time for them to change, as all were wearing drab jail dresses. They seemed in good spirits, however, and were giggling and whispering. On being brought in, Manson winked at them and they winked back. Charlie was wearing a white shirt and blue scarf, and sporting a new, neatly trimmed goatee. Another face, for judgment day.

Single file, the jurors entered the jury box, taking their assigned seats, just as they had hundreds of times before. Only this time was different, and the spectators searched the twelve faces for clues. Perhaps the most common of all courtroom myths is that a jury won't look at the accused if they have reached a guilty verdict. This is rarely true. None held Manson's gaze when he stared at them, but then neither did they quickly look away. All you could really read in their faces was a tired tenseness.

THE COURT "All jurors and alternates are present. All counsel but Mr. Hughes are present. The defendants are present. Mr. Tubick, has the jury reached a verdict?"

TUBICK "Yes, Your Honor, we have."

THE COURT "Will you hand the verdict forms to the bailiff."

Foreman Tubick handed them to Bill Murray, who in turn gave them to Judge Older. As he scanned them, saying nothing, Sadie, Leslie, and Katie fell silent and Manson nervously fingered his goatee.

THE COURT "The clerk will read the verdicts."

CLERK "In the Superior Court of the State of California, in and for the County of Los Angeles, the People of the State of California vs. Charles Manson, Patricia Krenwinkel, Susan Atkins, and Leslie Van Houten, Case No. A–253,156. Department 104."

Darrow paused before reading the first of the twenty-seven separate verdicts. It seemed minutes but was probably only seconds. Everyone sat as if frozen, waiting.

"We, the jury in the above-entitled action, find the defendant, Charles Manson, *guilty* of the crime of murder of Abigail Folger in violation of section 187, Penal Code of California, a felony, as charged in Count I of the Indictment, and we further find it to be murder of the first degree."

Glancing at Manson, I noticed that, though his face was impassive, his hands were shaking. The girls displayed no emotion whatsoever.

The jury had deliberated for forty-two hours and forty minutes, over a nine-day period, a remarkably short time for such a long and complicated trial. The reading of the verdicts took thirty-eight minutes.

The People had obtained the verdicts they had requested against Charles Manson, Patricia Krenwinkel, and Susan Atkins: each had been found guilty of one count of conspiracy to commit murder and seven counts of murder in the first degree.

The People had also obtained the verdicts requested against Leslie Van Houten: she had been found guilty of one count of conspiracy to commit murder and two counts of murder in the first degree.

I later learned that although McBride had suggested the possibility of a lesser finding against Leslie Van Houten, when it came time to vote there was only one ballot and it was unanimous.

While the individual jurors were being polled, Leslie turned to Katie and said, "Look at the jury; don't they look sad?" She was right, they did. Obviously it had been a very rough ordeal.

As the jury was being taken out, Manson suddenly yelled at Older: "We are still not allowed to put on a defense? You won't outlive that, old man!"

Kanarek seemed strangely unmoved by the verdict. Though Fitzgerald told the press, "We expected the worst from the start," he appeared thoroughly shaken. Outside court, he told reporters, "We felt we lost the case when we lost our change of venue motion. We had a hostile and antagonistic jury. The defendants had the same chance Sam Sheppard had in Cleveland—none." Fitzgerald further stated that had the trial been held anywhere but in Los Angeles, he was sure they would have won acquittals for all the defendants.

"I don't believe that for one minute," I told the press. "It is just weeping on the part of the defense. The jury was not only fair, they based their verdict solely and exclusively on the evidence that came from that witness stand."

"Yes," I responded to the most frequently asked question, "we will seek the death penalty against all four defendants."

The Manson girls on the corner outside the Hall of Justice first heard the news over the radio. They too were strangely calm. Though Brenda told newsmen, "There's a revolution coming, very soon," and Sandy said, "You are next, all of you," these were Manson's words, delivered in court months before, which they had been mouthing ever since. There were no tears, no outward display of emotion. It was as if they really didn't care. Yet I knew this wasn't true.

Watching the interview later on TV, I surmised that perhaps they had conditioned themselves to expect the worst.

In retrospect, another possibility emerges. Once the lowest of the low in the Manson hierarchy, good only for sex, procreation, and serving men, the girls had now become his chief apostles, the keepers of the faith. Now Charlie was dependent on them. It appears quite likely that they were undisturbed by the verdict because they were already formulating a plan which, if all went well, could set not only Manson but all the other Family members free.

Part 8

FIRES IN YOUR CITIES

"Mr. and Mrs. America—you are wrong.
I am not the King of the Jews nor am
I a hippie cult leader. I am what you
have made of me and the mad dog devil
killer fiend leper is a reflection of
your society . . . Whatever the outcome of
this madness that you call a fair trial
or Christian justice, you can know
this: In my mind's eye my thoughts
light fires in your cities."

Statement issued by
Charles Manson after
his conviction for the
Tate-LaBianca murders

January 26-March 17, 1971

During the penalty trial the sole issue for the jury to decide was whether the defendants should receive life imprisonment or the death penalty. Considerations like mitigating circumstances, background, remorse, and the possibility of rehabilitation were therefore now relevant.

To avoid prolonging the trial and risk alienating the jury, I called only two witnesses: officer Thomas Drynan and Bernard "Lotsapoppa" Crowe.

Drynan testified that when he arrested Susan Atkins outside Stayton, Oregon, in 1966, she was carrying a .25 caliber pistol. "I asked Miss Atkins what she intended to do with the gun," Drynan recalled, "and she told me that if she had the opportunity she would have shot and killed me."

Drynan's testimony proved that even before Susan Atkins met Charles Manson she had murder in her heart.

On cross-examination Shinn asked Drynan about the .25 caliber pistol.

Q. "The size is very small—it looks like a toy gun—is that correct?"

A. "Well, not to me."

Crowe described how, on the night of July 1, 1969, Manson had shot him in the stomach and left him for dead. The importance of Crowe's testimony was that it proved that Manson was quite capable of committing murder on his own.

On February 1, I rested the People's case. That afternoon the defense called their first witnesses: Katie's parents, Joseph and Dorothy Krenwinkel.

Joseph Krenwinkel described his daughter as an "exceedingly normal child, very obedient." She was a Bluebird, Camp Fire Girl, and Job's daughter, and belonged to the Audubon Society.

FITZGERALD "Was she gentle with animals?"

MR. KRENWINKEL "Very much so."

Patricia had sung in the church choir, Mr. Krenwinkel testified. Though she was not an exceptional student, she received good grades in the classes she liked. She had attended one semester of college, at Spring Hill College, a Jesuit school in Mobile, Alabama, before returning to Los Angeles, where she shared an apartment with her half sister.

The Krenwinkels had divorced when Patricia was seventeen. According to Joseph Krenwinkel, there was no bitterness; he and his wife had parted, and remained, friends.

Yet just a year later, when Patricia was eighteen, she had abandoned her family and job to join Manson.

Dorothy Krenwinkel said of her daughter, "She would rather hurt herself than harm any living thing."

FITZGERALD "Did you love your daughter?"

A. "I did love my daughter; I will always love my daughter; and no one will ever convince me she did anything terrible or horrible."

FITZGERALD "Thank you."

BUGLIOSI "No questions, Your Honor."

Fitzgerald wanted to introduce into evidence a number of letters Patricia Krenwinkel had written to various persons, including her father and a favorite priest at Spring Hill.

All were hearsay and clearly inadmissible. All I would have needed to do was object. But I didn't. Though aware that they would appeal to the sympathies of the jury, I felt that justice should prevail over technicalities. The issue now was whether this girl should be sentenced to death. And this was an issue for the jury to decide, not me. I felt that in reaching that extremely serious decision, they should have any information even remotely relevant.

Fitzgerald was both relieved and very grateful when I let them come in.

Keith handled the direct examination of Jane Van Houten, Leslie's mother. Keith later told me that although Leslie's father didn't want to testify, he was behind Leslie 100 percent. Although, like the Krenwinkels, the Van

Houtens were divorced, they too had stuck by their daughter.

According to Mrs. Van Houten, "Leslie was what you would call a feisty little child, fun to be with. She had a wonderful sense of humor." Born in the Los Angeles suburb of Altadena, she had an older brother and a younger brother and sister, the latter Korean orphans whom the Van Houtens had adopted.

When Leslie was fourteen, her parents separated and divorced. "I think it hurt her very much," Mrs. Van Houten testified. That same year Leslie fell in love with an older youth, Bobby Mackey; became pregnant; had an abortion; and took LSD for the first time. After that she dropped acid at least once and often two or three times a week.*

During her freshman and sophomore years at Monrovia High School, Leslie was one of the homecoming princesses. She tried out again her junior year, but this time she didn't make it. Bitter over the rejection, she ran away with Mackey to Haight-Ashbury. The scene there frightened her, however, and she returned home to finish high school and to complete a year of secretarial training. Mackey, in the meantime, had begun studying with a yoga group. In an attempt to continue their relationship, Leslie joined also, giving up both drugs and sex. Her good intentions were short-lived; within a few months she broke with both Mackey and the group.

Mrs. Van Houten did not testify to the period which followed; possibly she knew little if anything about it. From interviews I'd learned that Leslie went full spectrum. The one-time yoga renunciate was now anxious to "try anything," be it drugs or answering sex-partner ads in the Los Angeles *Free Press*. A long-time friend stopped dating her because she had become "too kinky."

For a few months Leslie lived in a commune in Northern California. During this period she met Bobby Beausoleil, who had his own wandering "family," consisting of Gypsy and a girl named Gail. Leslie became a part

*Patricia Krenwinkel had also taken LSD before meeting Manson. Very obese in her early teens, she began using diet pills at fourteen or fifteen, then tried reds, mescaline, and LSD, provided by her half sister Charlene, now deceased, who was a heroin addict.

of the *ménage à quatre*. Gail, however, was jealous, and the arguments became near constant. First Gypsy split, moving to Spahn Ranch. Then, shortly after, Leslie followed, also joining Manson. She was nineteen.

About this time Leslie called her mother and told her that she had decided to drop out and that she wouldn't be hearing from her again. She didn't, until Leslie's arrest.

Keith asked Mrs. Van Houten: "How do you feel about your daughter now?"

A. "I love Leslie very much."

Q. "As much as you always have?"

A. "More."

As the parents testified, one realized that they too were victims, just as were the relatives of the deceased.

Calling the defendants' parents first was a bad tactical error on the part of the defense. Their testimony and plight evoked sympathy from everyone in the courtroom. They should have been called at the very end of the defense's case, just before the jury went out to deliberate. As it was, by the time the other witnesses had testified, they were almost forgotten.

Shinn called no witnesses on behalf of Susan Atkins. Her father, Shinn told me, had refused to have anything more to do with her. All he wanted, he said, was to get his hands on Manson.

A reporter from the Los Angeles *Times* had located Charles Manson's mother in a city in the Pacific Northwest. Remarried and living under another name, she claimed Charles' tales of childhood deprivation were fictions, adding, "He was a spoiled, pampered child."

Kanarek did not use her as a witness. Instead, he called Samuel Barrett, Manson's parole officer.

Barrett was a most unimpressive witness. He thought he first met Manson "about 1956, around that"; he couldn't remember whether Manson was on probation or parole; he stated that since he was responsible for 150 persons, he couldn't be expected to recall everything about each one.

Repeatedly, Barrett minimized the seriousness of the various charges against Manson prior to the murders. The reason he did this was obvious: otherwise, one might wonder why he hadn't revoked Manson's parole. One still did wonder. Manson associated with ex-cons, known narcotics users, and minor girls. He failed to report his whereabouts, made few attempts to obtain employment, repeatedly lied regarding his activities. During the first six months of 1969 alone, he had been charged, among other things, with grand theft auto, narcotics possession, rape, contributing to the delinquency of a minor. There was more than ample reason for parole revocation.

During a recess one of the reporters approached me in the hall. "God, Vince," he exclaimed, "did it ever occur to you that if Barrett had revoked Manson's parole in, say, April of 1969, Sharon and the others would probably still be alive today?"

I declined comment, citing the gag order as an excuse. But it had occurred to me. I had thought about it a great deal.

On direct, Barrett had testified that there was nothing in Manson's prison records to indicate that he was a behavioral risk. Over Kanarek's objections, on cross-examination I had him examine the folder on Manson's attempted escape from federal custody in 1957.

The parade of perjurers began with little Squeaky.

Lynette Alice Fromme, twenty-two, testified that she was from an upper-middle-class background, her father an aeronautical engineer. When she was seventeen, she said, her father kicked her out of the house. "And I was in Venice, sitting down on a curb crying, when a man walked up and said, 'Your father kicked you out of the house, did he?'

"And that was Charlie."

Squeaky placed great importance on the fact that she had met Manson before any of the other girls, excepting only Mary Brunner.

In questioning her about the Family, Fitzgerald asked: "Did you have a leader?"

A. "No, we were riding on the wind."

No leader, but—

"Charlie is our father in that he would—he would point out things to us."

Charlie was just like everyone else, but—

"I would crawl off in a corner and be reading a book, and he would pass me and tell me what it said in the book ... And also he knew our thoughts ... He was always happy, always ... He would go into the bathroom sometimes to comb his hair, and there would be a whole crowd of people in there watching him because he had so much fun."

Squeaky had trouble denying the teachings of her lord and master. When Fitzgerald tried to minimize the importance of the Beatles' White Album, she replied, "There is a lot in that album, there is a lot." Although she claimed, "I never heard Charlie utter the words 'helter skelter,' " she went on to say that "it is a matter of evolution and balance" and "the black people are coming to the top, as it should be."

Obviously these were not the answers Fitzgerald wanted, and apparently he betrayed his reaction.

FROMME "How come you're making those faces?"

FITZGERALD "I'm sorry, continue."

Calling counsel to the bench, Judge Older said, "She can only harm the defendants doing what she is doing."

I explained to Older, "If the Court is wondering why I am not objecting, it is because I feel that her testimony is helpful to the prosecution."

So helpful, in fact, that there was little need for cross-examination. Among the questions I had intended to ask her, for example, was one Kanarek now asked: "Did you think that Charles Manson was Jesus Christ?"

Squeaky hesitated a moment before answering. Would she be the apostle who denied Jesus? Apparently she decided she would not, for she replied: "I think that the Christians in the caves and in the woods were a lot of kids just living and being without guilt, without shame, being able to take off their clothes and lay in the sun ... And I see Jesus Christ as a man who came from a woman who did not know who the father of her baby was."

Squeaky was the least untruthful of the Family members who testified. Yet she was so damaging to the defense that thereafter Fitzgerald let the other defense attorneys call the witnesses.

Keith called Brenda McCann, t/n Nancy Laura Pitman, nineteen. Though not unattractive, Brenda came across as a tough, vicious little girl, filled with hostility that was just waiting to erupt.

Her father "designed the guidance controls of missiles over in the Pentagon," she said. He also kicked her out of the house when she was sixteen, she claimed. The dropout from Hollywood High School asserted there was no such thing as a Family, and Charlie "was not a leader at all. It was more like Charlie followed us around and took care of us."

But, as with Squeaky and the girls who would follow her, it was obvious that Brenda's world revolved around a single axis. He was nobody special but "Charlie would sit down and all the animals would gather round him, donkeys and coyotes and things . . . And one time he reached down and petted a rattlesnake."

Questioned by Kanarek, Brenda testified that Linda "would take LSD every day . . . took speed . . . Linda loved Tex very much . . . Linda followed Tex everywhere . . ."

On cross-examination I asked Brenda: "Would you give up your life for Charles Manson if he asked you to?"

A. "Many times he has given you his life."

Q. "Just answer the question, Brenda."

A. "Yes, I would."

Q. "Would you lie on the stand for Charles Manson?"

A. "No, I would tell the truth on the stand."

Q. "So you would die for him, but not lie for him?"

A. "That's right."

Q. "Do you feel that lying under oath is a more serious matter than dying, Brenda?"

A. "I don't take dying all that seriously myself."

All these witnesses were extremely antagonistic toward their real families. Sandra Good, for example, claimed that her father, a San Diego stockbroker, had disowned her, neglecting to mention that this was only after he had sent her thousands of dollars and was threatened by Manson if he didn't give her more.

Manson had severed their umbilical cords while fastening one of his own. And throughout their testimony it showed. Even more than Squeaky and Brenda, Sandy rhapsodized on Manson's "magical powers." She told the story of how Charlie had breathed on a dead bird and brought it back to life. "I believe his voice could shatter this building if he so desired ... Once he yelled and a window broke."

It was not until the penalty trial that the jury learned of the vigil of the Family members on the corner of Temple and Broadway. Rather movingly, Sandy testified to life there. "You can hardly see the sky most of the time for the smog. They are always digging; every day there is a new project going; something is always under construction. They are always ripping out something and putting something in, usually of a concrete nature. It is insane out there. It's madness, and the more I am out there the more I feel this X. I am X'd out of it."

After I'd declined to cross-examine Sandy, she very angrily asked, "Why didn't you ask me any questions?"

"Because you said nothing which hurt the People's case, Sandy," I replied. "In fact, you helped it."

I had anticipated that Sandy would testify that Manson wasn't even at Spahn Ranch at the time the murders had occurred. When she didn't, I knew the defense had decided to abandon the idea of using an alibi defense. Which meant they had something else in mind. But what?

Manson and the three female defendants had been allowed to return to court during the penalty phase. They were much quieter now, far more subdued, as if it had finally got through to them that this "play," as Krenwinkel had characterized it, might cost them their lives. While Squeaky and the other Manson girls testified, their mentor looked thoughtful and pulled on his goatee, as if to say: They're telling it like it is.

The female witnesses wore their best clothes for the occasion. It was obvious that they were both proud and happy to be up there helping Charlie.

The jurors shared a common expression—incredulity. Few even bothered to take notes. I suspected that all of them were mulling over the astonishing contrast. On the stand the girls talked of love, music, and babies. Yet while the love and the music and the babies were going on, this same group was going out and butchering human beings. And to them, amazingly enough, there was no inconsistency, no conflict between love and murder!

By February 4, I was fairly sure, from the questions Kanarek had been asking the witnesses, that Manson was not going to take the stand. This was my biggest disappointment during the entire trial, that I wouldn't have the chance to break Charlie on cross-examination.

That same day our office learned that Charles "Tex" Watson had been returned to Los Angeles and ruled competent to stand trial.

Only three days after his transfer to Atascadero, Watson had begun eating regular meals. Within a month, one of the psychiatrists who examined him wrote: "There is no evidence of abnormal behavior at the present time except his silence, which is purposeful and with reason." Another later noted: "Psychological testing gave a scatter pattern of responses inconsistent with any recognized form of mental illness . . ." In short, Tex was faking it. All this information would be useful, I knew, if Tex tried to plead insanity during his trial, which was now scheduled to follow the current proceedings.

Catherine Share, aka Gypsy, was the defense's most effective liar. She was also, at twenty-eight, the oldest female member of the Family. And, of all its members, she had the most unusual background.

She was born in Paris in 1942, her father a Hungarian violinist, her mother a German-Jewish refugee. Both parents, members of the French underground, committed suicide during the war. At eight, she was adopted and brought to the United States by an American family. Her adoptive mother, who was suffering from cancer, committed suicide when Catherine was sixteen. Her adoptive father, a psychologist, was blind. She cared for him until he remarried, at which time she left home.

A graduate of Hollywood High School, she had attended college for three years; married; divorced a year later. A violin virtuoso since childhood, with an unusually beautiful singing voice, she had obtained work in a number of movies. It was on the set of one, in Topanga Canyon, that she became involved with Bobby Beausoleil, who had a minor role. About two months later Beausoleil introduced her to Charles Manson. Though it was, on her part, love at first sight, she continued traveling with the Beausoleil menage for another six months, before splitting for Spahn Ranch. Although she was an avowed Communist when she joined the Family, Manson soon convinced her that his dogma was ordained. "Of all the girls," Paul Watkins had told me, "Gypsy was most in love with Charlie."

She was also the most eloquent in his defense. But, though brighter and more articulate than most of the others, she too occasionally slipped up.

"We are all facing the same sentence," she told the jury. "We are all in a gas chamber right here in L.A., a slow-acting one. The air is going away from us in every city. There is going to be no more air, and no more water, and the food is dying. They are poisoning you. The food you are eating is poisoning you. There is going to be no more earth, no more trees. Man, especially white man, is killing this earth.

"But those aren't Charles Manson's thoughts, those are my thoughts," she quickly added.

During her first day on the stand Gypsy dropped no bombshells. She did try to rebut various parts of the trial testimony. She said that Leslie often went out and stole things, to explain away the back-house incident. She claimed that it was Linda who suggested stealing the $5,000. She also said that Linda didn't want Tanya, and had dumped her on the Family.

It was not until her second day on the stand, on *redirect* by Kanarek, and immediately after Kanarek had asked to approach the witness and speak to her privately, that Gypsy suddenly came up with an alternative motive—one that was designed to clear Manson of any involvement in the murders.

Gypsy claimed that it was Linda Kasabian, not Charles Manson, who had masterminded the Tate-LaBianca murders! Linda was in love with Bobby Beausoleil, Gypsy said. When Bobby was arrested for the Hinman murder,

Linda proposed that the girls commit other murders which were similar to the Hinman slaying, in the belief that the police would connect the crimes and, realizing that Beausoleil was in custody when these other murders occurred, set him free.

The "copycat" motive was in itself not a surprise. In fact, Aaron Stovitz had suggested it as one of several possible motives in his interview with the reporters from *Rolling Stone*. There was only one thing wrong with it. It wasn't true. But in an attempt to clear Manson and to cast doubt on the Helter Skelter motive, the defense witnesses, starting with Gypsy, now began manufacturing their own bogus evidence.

The scenario they had so belatedly fashioned was as transparent as it was self-serving.

Gypsy claimed that on the afternoon of August 8, 1969, Linda explained the plan to her and asked her if she wanted to go along. Horrified, Gypsy instead fled to the mountains. When she returned, the murders had already occurred and Linda was gone.

Gypsy further testified that Bobby Beausoleil was innocent of the Hinman murder; all he had done was drive a car belonging to Hinman. And Manson wasn't involved either. The Hinman murder had been committed by Linda, Sadie, and *Leslie!*

Maxwell Keith quickly objected. At the bench he told Judge Older: "It sounds to me like this girl is leading up to testimony of an admission by my client to her participation in the Hinman, Tate, and LaBianca murders. This is outrageous!"

THE COURT "I don't know if Mr. Kanarek has the faintest idea of what he wants to do."

FITZGERALD "I am afraid so."

KANAREK "I know exactly."

Keith observed: "I talked to this witness yesterday at the County Jail about her testimony. It was sort of innocuous testimony regarding Leslie. And all of a sudden, boom, we are being bombed out of the courtroom."

On cross-examination I asked: "Isn't it true, Gypsy, that what you are trying to do is clear Charles Manson at the expense of Leslie and Sadie?"

A. "I wouldn't say that. No, it isn't true."

To destroy her credibility, I then impeached Gypsy with a number of inconsistent statements she had previously made. Only then did I return to the bogus motive.

Gypsy had testified that immediately after hearing of the Tate-LaBianca murders, she was sure that Linda, Leslie, and Sadie were involved.

I asked her: "If in your mind Linda, Sadie, and Leslie were somehow involved in the Tate-LaBianca murders, and Mr. Manson was innocent and had nothing to do with it, why haven't you come forward before today to tell the authorities about this conversation you had with Linda?"

A. "I didn't want anything to do with it. I don't believe in coming to you at all."

Earlier on cross-examination Gypsy had admitted that she loved Manson, that she would willingly die for him. After reminding her of these statements, I said: "All right, and you believe he had nothing to do with these murders, right?"

A. "Right."

Q. "And yet you let him stay in jail all these months without coming forward with this valuable information?"

Gypsy evaded a straight reply.

Q. "When was the first time that you told anyone about this infamous conversation that you had with Linda when she asked you to go out and murder someone?"

A. "Right here."

Q. "Today?"

A. "Uh-huh."

Q. "So today on the witness stand was the first time that you decided to release all this valuable information, is that right?"

A. "That's right."

I had her. I could now argue to the jury that here's Manson, being tried for seven counts of murder, and there's Gypsy, out on the corner of Temple and Broadway twenty-four hours a day since the start of the trial, a girl who loves Manson and would give her life for him, but who waits until well into the penalty trial, and on redirect at that, before she decides to tell anyone what she knows.

At 6:01 A.M. on February 9, 1971, a monster earthquake shook most of Southern California. Measuring 6.5 on the Richter scale, it claimed sixty-five lives and caused millions of dollars' worth of damage.

I awoke thinking the Family was trying to break into our house.

The jurors awoke to find water cascading on them from broken pipes above their rooms.

The girls on the corner told reporters Charlie had caused the quake.

Despite the disaster, court resumed at the usual time that morning, with Susan Atkins taking the stand to trigger an earthquake of her own.

Daye Shinn's first question of his client was: "Susan, were you personally involved in the Tate and LaBianca homicides?"

Susan, who was wearing a dark jumper and a white blouse, and looking very little-girlish, calmly replied, "Yes."

Although by this time all counsel knew that the three girls intended to take the stand and "confess," Fitzgerald having mentioned it in chambers nearly a week before, the jury and spectators were stunned. They looked at each other as if disbelieving what they had heard.

Shinn then took Susan through her background: her early religious years ("I sang in the church choir"); the death of her mother from cancer ("I couldn't understand why she died, and it hurt me"); her loss of faith; her problems with her father ("My father kept telling me, 'You're going downhill,' so I just went downhill"); her experiences as a topless dancer in San Francisco; her explanation for why she was carrying a gun when arrested in Oregon ("I was afraid of snakes"); and her introduction to drugs, Haight-Ashbury, and her first fateful meeting with Charles Manson.

Returning to the crimes, she testified: "This whole thing started when I killed Gary Hinman, because he was going to hurt my love . . ."

Judge Older called the noon recess. Before leaving the stand, Susan turned toward me and said, "Look at it, Mr. Bugliosi. Your whole thing, man, is just gone, your whole motive. It is so silly. So dumb."

That afternoon, Sadie recited the newly revised version of how the Hinman murder went down. According to Susan, when Manson arrived at the Hinman residence, to persuade Gary to sign over the pink slip on a car they had already purchased, Gary drew a gun on him. As Manson fled, Gary tried to shoot him in the back. "I had no choice. He was going to hurt my love. I had my knife on me and I ran at him and I killed him . . . Bobby was taken to jail for something that I did."

The holes in her story were a mile wide. I noted them for my cross-examination.

After the arrest of Beausoleil, Susan testified, Linda proposed committing copycat murders. ". . . and she told me to get a knife and a change of clothes . . . she said these people in Beverly Hills had burned her for $1,000 for some new drug, MDA . . ."

Before leaving Spahn Ranch, Susan said, "Linda gave me some LSD, and she gave Tex some STP . . . Linda issued all the directions that night . . . No one told Charlie where we were going or what we were going to do . . . Linda had been there before, so she knew where to go . . . Tex went crazy, shot Parent . . . Linda went inside the house . . . Linda gave me her knife." At this point in her narrative, Daye Shinn opened the blade of the Buck knife and started to hand the knife to Susan.

THE COURT "Put that knife back the way it was!"

SHINN "I only wanted to get the dimensions, Your Honor."

Susan skipped ahead in her narrative. She was holding Sharon Tate and "Tex came back and he looked at her and he said, 'Kill her.' And I killed her . . . And I just stabbed her and she fell, and I stabbed her again. I don't know how many times I stabbed her . . ." Sharon begged for the life of her baby, and "I told her, 'Shut up. I don't want to hear it.' "

Though Susan's words were horrifyingly chilling, her expression for the most part remained simple, even childlike.

There was only one way to describe the contrast: it was incredibly obscene.

In discussing the Hinman murder, Susan had placed Leslie Van Houten at the murder scene. There had never been any evidence whatsoever that Leslie was involved in the Hinman murder.

In discussing the night the LaBiancas were killed, Susan made some additional changes in the cast of characters. Manson didn't go along, she said. Linda drove; Tex creepy-crawled the LaBianca residence; Linda instructed Tex, Katie, and Leslie what to do; Linda suggested killing the actor in Venice. And when they returned to Spahn Ranch, "Charlie was there sleeping."

Just as improbable was another of her fictional embellishments. She had implicated Manson in her conversation with me and in her testimony before the grand jury, she claimed, because I had promised her that if she did so I would personally see that none of the defendants, including Manson, would receive the death penalty.

The best refutation of this was that she had implicated Manson on the tape she made with Caballero, days before our first meeting.

Describing that meeting, Sadie said, "Bugliosi walked in. I think he was dressed similar to the way he is dressed now, gray suit, vest."

Q. "This was way back in 1969, right?"

A. "Right. He looked a lot younger then."

We'd all gone through a lot in the last fourteen months.

Shinn then began questioning Susan about Shorty! I asked to approach the bench.

BUGLIOSI "Your Honor, I can't believe what is going on here. He is talking about Shorty Shea now!" Turning to Daye, I said, "You are hurting yourself if you bring in other murders, and you are hurting the co-defendants." Older agreed and cautioned Shinn to be extremely careful.

I was worried that if Shinn continued, the case might be reversed on appeal. What conceivable rationale could there be for having your client take the stand and confess to a murder with which she isn't even charged?

Fitzgerald took over the direct. He asked Susan why the Tate victims were killed.

A. "Because I believed it was right to get my brother out of jail. And I still believe it was right."

Q. "Miss Atkins, were any of these people killed as a result of any personal hate or animosity that you had toward them?"

A. "No."

Q. "Did you have any feeling toward them at all, any emotional feeling toward any of these people—Sharon Tate, Voytek Frykowski, Abigail Folger, Jay Sebring, Steven Parent?"

A. "I didn't know any of them. How could I have felt any emotion without knowing them?"

Fitzgerald asked Susan if she considered these mercy killings.

A. "No. As a matter of fact, I believe I told Sharon Tate I didn't have any mercy for her."

Susan went on to explain that she knew what she was doing "was right when I was doing it." She knew this because, when you do the right thing, "it feels good."

Q. "How could it be right to kill somebody?"

A. "How could it not be right when it is done with love?"

Q. "Did you ever feel any remorse?"

A. "Remorse? For doing what was right to me?"

Q. "Did you ever feel sorry?"

A. "Sorry for doing what was right to me? I have no guilt in me."

Fitzgerald looked beaten. By bringing out her total lack of remorse, he had made it impossible for the defense to persuasively argue that she was capable of rehabilitation.

We had reached a strange situation. Suddenly, in the penalty phase, long after the jury had found the four defendants guilty, I was in a sense having to prove Manson's guilt all over again.

If I cross-examined too strenuously, it would appear that I did not feel that we had proven our case. If I eschewed cross-examination, there was the possibility of leaving a lingering doubt as to guilt, which, when it came time for their deliberations, could influence the jury's vote on penalty. Therefore I had to proceed very carefully, as if trying to walk between raindrops.

The defense, and specifically Irving Kanarek, had tried

to plant such a doubt by providing an alternative to Helter Skelter—the copycat motive. Though I felt the testimony on this was thoroughly unconvincing, this didn't mean I could sit back and presume the jury would feel as I did.

As an explanation for why she was lying to save him, it was important that I conclusively prove to the jury Susan Atkins' total commitment to Manson. At the start of my cross-examination I asked her: "Sadie, do you believe Charles Manson is the second coming of Christ?"

A. "Vince, I have seen Christ in so many people in the last four or five years, it is hard for me to say which one exactly is the second coming of Christ."

I repeated the question.

A. "I have thought about it. I have thought about it quite a bit . . . I have entertained the thought that he was Christ, yes . . . I don't know. Could be. If he is, wow, my goodness!"

After confronting her with her letter to Ronnie Howard, in which she stated, "If you can believe in the second coming of Christ, M is he who has come to save," I asked her: "Even now on the witness stand, Sadie, you think that maybe Charles Manson, the man over there who is playing with his hair, might be Jesus Christ?"

A. "Maybe. I will leave it at that. Maybe yes. Maybe no."

I persisted until Susan admitted: "He represented a God to me that was so beautiful that I'd do anything for him."

Q. "Even commit murder?" I asked instantly.

A. "I'd do anything for God."

Q. "Including murder?" I pressed.

A. "That's right. If I believed it was right."

Q. "And you murdered the five people at the Tate residence for your God, Manson, didn't you?"

Susan paused, then said: "I murdered them for my God Bobby Beausoleil."

Q. "Oh, so you have two Gods?"

Evasively she replied: "There is only one God and God is in all."

Since Susan had now testified to these matters, the prosecution was able to use her prior inconsistent statements—including her grand jury testimony—for impeachment purposes.

On cross-examination I had Susan repeat the alleged reasons why they went to the Tate residence. Once she'd restated the copycat nonsense, I hit her with her statements regarding Helter Skelter's being the motive—made to me, to the grand jury, and in the Howard letter.

I also brought out that she had told me, and the grand jury, that Manson had ordered the seven Tate-LaBianca murders; that Charlie had directed all their activities the second night; and that none of them had been on drugs either night.

I then led her back through her scenario of the Hinman, Tate, and LaBianca murders, step by step, knowing she would slip up, which she did, repeatedly.

For example, I asked: "Where was Charles Manson when you stabbed Gary Hinman to death?"

A. "He left. He left right after he cut Gary's ear." Having inadvertently admitted this, she quickly added that she had tried to sew up Hinman's ear.

I then took her back again: Hinman drew a gun on Manson; Manson ran; Hinman started to shoot Manson; to protect her love, she stabbed Hinman to death. Just when, I asked, did she have time to play Florence Nightingale?

Susan further claimed that she didn't tell Manson that she had killed Hinman until after their arrest in the Barker raid. In other words, though she had lived with Manson from July to October 1969, she hadn't got around to mentioning this? "That's right." Why? "Because he never asked."

She hadn't even told him she committed the Tate and LaBianca murders, she claimed. Nor, until two days ago, had she told anyone that Linda Kasabian masterminded the murders.

Q. "Between August 9, 1969, and February 9, 1971, how come you never told anyone that Linda was behind these murders?"

A. "Because I didn't. It's that simple."

Q. "Did you tell *anyone* in the Family that you committed all these murders?"

A. "No."

Q. "If you told outsiders like Ronnie Howard and Virginia Graham, how come you didn't tell members of your own Family, Sadie?"

A. "Nothing needed to be said. What I did was what I did with those people, and that is what I did."

Q. "Just one of those things, seven dead bodies?"

A. "No big thing."

I paused to let this incredible statement sink in before asking: "So killing seven people is just business as usual, no big deal, is that right, Sadie?"

A. "It wasn't at the time. It was just there to do."

I asked her how she felt about the victims. She responded, "They didn't even look like people ... I didn't relate to Sharon Tate as being anything but a store mannequin."

Q. "You have never heard a store mannequin talk, have you, Sadie?"

A. "No, sir. But she just sounded like an IBM machine ... She kept begging and pleading and pleading and begging, and I got sick of listening to her, so I stabbed her."

Q. "And the more she screamed, the more you stabbed, Sadie?"

A. "Yes. So?"

Q. "And you looked at her and you said, 'Look, bitch, I have no mercy for you.' Is that right, Sadie?"

A. "That's right. That's what I said then."

BUGLIOSI "No further questions."

On Tuesday, February 16, after lengthy discussions in chambers, Judge Older told the jury that he had decided to end the sequestration.

Their surprise and elation were obvious. They had been locked up for over eight months, the longest sequestration of any jury in American history.

Though I remained worried about possible harassment from the Family, most of the other reasons for the sequestration—such as mention of the Hinman murder, Susan Atkins' confession in the Los Angeles *Times*, her grand jury testimony, and so on—no longer existed, since the jury heard this evidence when Sadie and the others took the stand.

It was almost as if we had a new jury. When the twelve entered the box the next day, there were smiles on all their faces. I couldn't remember when I'd last seen them smiling.

The smiles would not remain there long. Patricia Krenwinkel now took the stand, to confess her part in the Tate and LaBianca homicides.

An even more improbable witness than Susan Atkins, her testimony regarding the copycat motive was vague, nebulous, and almost devoid of supporting detail. The point in her taking the stand was to take the focus off Manson. Instead, like the other Family members who had preceded her, she repeatedly highlighted his importance. For example, describing life at Spahn Ranch, she said: "We were just like wood nymphs and wood creatures. We would run through the woods with flowers in our hair, and Charlie would have a small flute . . ."

On the murder of Abigail Folger: "And I had a knife in my hands, and she took off running, and she ran—she ran out through the back door, one I never even touched, I mean, nobody got fingerprints because I never touched that door . . . and I stabbed her and kept stabbing her."

Q. "What did you feel after you stabbed her?"

A. "Nothing—I mean, like what is there to describe? It was just there, and it's like it was right."

On the murder of Rosemary LaBianca: According to Katie, she and Leslie took Rosemary LaBianca into the bedroom and were looking through the dresses in her closet when, hearing Leno scream, Rosemary grabbed a lamp and swung at them.

On the mutilation of Leno LaBianca: After murdering Rosemary, Katie remembered seeing Leno lying on the floor in the living room. She flashed, "You won't be sending your son off to war," and "I guess I put WAR on the man's chest. And then I guess I had a fork in my hands, and I put it in his stomach . . . and I went and wrote on the walls . . ."

On cross-examination I asked her: "When you were on

top of Abigail Folger, plunging your knife into her body, was she screaming?"

A. "Yes."

Q. "And the more she screamed, the more you stabbed?"

A. "I guess."

Q. "Did it bother you when she screamed for her life?"

A. "No."

Katie testified that when she stabbed Abigail she was really stabbing herself. My next question was rhetorical. "But you didn't bleed at all, did you, Katie; just Abigail did, isn't that right?"

The defense was contending, through these witnesses, that the words POLITICAL PIGGY (Hinman), PIG (Tate), and DEATH TO PIGS (LaBianca) were the clues which the killers felt would cause the police to link the three crimes. But when I'd asked Sadie why she'd written POLITICAL PIGGY on the wall of the Hinman residence in the first place, she had no satisfactory answer. Nor could she tell me why, if these were to be copycat murders, she'd only written PIG and not POLITICAL PIGGY at Tate. Nor was Katie now able to give a convincing explanation as to why she'd written HEALTER SKELTER on the LaBiancas' refrigerator door.

It was obvious that Maxwell Keith wasn't buying the copycat motive either. On redirect he asked Katie: "The homicides at the Tate residence and the LaBianca residence had nothing to do, did they, with trying to get Bobby Beausoleil out of jail?"

A. "Well, it's hard to explain. It was just a thought, and the thought came to be."

Judge Older was becoming increasingly irritated with Kanarek. Repeatedly, he warned him that if he persisted in asking inadmissible questions, he would find him in contempt for the fifth time. Nor was he very happy with Daye Shinn. Shinn had been observed passing a note from a spectator to Susan Atkins. The week before, the girls on the corner had been seen reading court transcripts which had Shinn's name on them. Confronted with this by Older, Shinn explained: "They borrowed them to look at them."

THE COURT "I beg your pardon? Are you familiar with the publicity order in this case?"

Shinn admitted that he was.

THE COURT "It appears to me, Mr. Shinn, that you are not paying the slightest attention to the publicity order, and you haven't been for some time. I have felt, in my own mind, for a long, long time, that the leak—and there is a leak—is you."

Maxwell Keith very reluctantly called his client, Leslie Van Houten, to the stand. After taking her through her background, Keith asked to approach the bench. He told Older that his client was going to involve herself in the Hinman murder. He had discussed this with her for "hours and hours" but to no avail.

Once she began reciting her tale, the transparency of her fictions became obvious. According to Leslie, Mary Brunner was never at the Hinman residence, while both Charles Manson and Bobby Beausoleil left before the actual killing took place. It was Sadie, she said, who killed Gary.

Though implicating herself in the Hinman murder, at least by her presence, Leslie did try to provide some mitigating circumstances for her involvement in the LaBianca murders. She claimed she knew nothing about the Tate murders and that when she went along the next night she had no idea where they were going or what they were going to do. The murder of Rosemary LaBianca was made to seem almost like self-defense. Only after Rosemary swung at her with the lamp did she "take one of the knives and Patricia had a knife, and we started stabbing and cutting up the lady."

Q. "Up to that time, did you have any intention of hurting anybody?"

A. "No."

Q. "Did you stab her after she appeared to be dead, Les?"

A. "I don't know if it was before or after she was dead, but I stabbed her . . . I don't know if she was dead. She was lying there on the floor."

Q. "Had you stabbed her at all before you saw her lying on the floor?"

A. "I don't remember."

Leslie's forgetting such things was almost as improbable as her claim that she hadn't mentioned the murders to Manson until they were in the desert.

Very carefully, Keith tried to establish that Leslie had remorse for her acts.

Q. "Leslie, do you feel sorrow or shame or a sense of guilt for having participated in the death of Mrs. LaBianca?"

A. [Pause]

Q. "Let me go one by one. Do you feel sorrowful about it; sorry; unhappy?"

You could almost feel the chill in the courtroom when Leslie answered: "Sorry is only a five-letter word. It can't bring back anything."

Q. "I am trying, Leslie, to discover how you feel about it."

A. "What can I feel? It has happened. She is gone."

Q. "Do you wish that it hadn't happened?"

A. "I never wish anything to be done over another way. That is a foolish thought. It never will happen that way. You can't undo something that is done."

Q. "Do you feel as if you wanted to cry for what happened?"

A. "Cry? For her death? If I cry for death, it is for death itself. She is not the only person who has died."

Q. "Do you think about it from time to time?"

A. "Only when I am in the courtroom."

Through most of the trial Leslie Van Houten had maintained her innocent-little-girl act. She'd dropped it now, the jury seeing for the first time how cold and unfeeling she really was.

Another aspect of her real nature surfaced when Kanarek examined her. Angry and impatient at some of his questions, she snapped back hostile, sarcastic replies. With each spurt of venom, you could see the jurors drawing back, looking at her as if anew. Whatever sympathy she may have generated earlier was gone now. Even McBride no longer met her eyes.

Leslie Van Houten had been found guilty of two homicides. I felt she deserved the death penalty for her very willing participation in those acts. But I didn't want the jury to vote death on the basis of a crime she didn't even commit. I told her attorney, Maxwell Keith, that I was willing to stipulate that Leslie was not at the Hinman residence. "I mean, the jury is apt to think she was, and hold it against your client, and I don't think that is right."

Also, during cross-examination I asked: "Did you tell anyone—prior to your testimony on the witness stand—that it was you who was along with Sadie and Bobby Beausoleil at Gary Hinman's house?"

A. "I told Patricia about it."

Q. "Actually it was Mary Brunner who was inside the residence, not you, isn't that correct?"

A. "That is what you say."

Although I was attempting to exonerate Leslie of any complicity in the Gary Hinman murder, I did the opposite when it came to the murder of Rosemary LaBianca. By the time I'd finished my cross-examination on this, Leslie had admitted that Rosemary might still have been alive when she stabbed her; and that she not only stabbed her in the buttocks and possibly the neck, but "I could have done a couple on the back." (As I'd later remind the jury, many of the back wounds were not post-mortem, while one, which severed Rosemary LaBianca's spine, would have been in and of itself fatal.)

As with Sadie and Katie, I emphasized the improbabilities in her copycat tale. For example, though she had testified that she was "hopelessly in love" with Bobby Beausoleil, and became aware that these murders had been committed in an attempt to free him, I brought out that she hadn't even offered to testify in either of his trials, when her story, had it been true, could have resulted in his release.

At this point I decided to go on a fishing expedition. Though I had no definite knowledge that this was so, I strongly suspected that Leslie had told her first attorney, Marvin Part, the true story of these murders. I did know that Part had recorded her story and, though I never heard the tape, I recalled Part almost begging the judge to listen to it.

BUGLIOSI "Isn't it true, Leslie, that before the trial started you told someone that Charles Manson ordered these murders?"

A. "I had a court-appointed attorney, Marvin Part, who was insistent on the fact that I was—"

Keith interrupted her, objecting that we were getting into the area of privileged communications. I noted to Judge Older that Leslie herself had mentioned Part by name and that she had the right to waive the privilege. Kanarek also objected, well aware of what I was hoping to bring out.

VAN HOUTEN "Mr. Kanarek, will you shut up so I can answer his question? . . . I had a court-appointed attorney by the name of Marvin Part. He had a lot of different thoughts, which were all his own, on how to get me off. He said he was going to make some tape recordings, and he told me the gist of what he wanted me to say. And I said it."

Q. "What did you tell Mr. Part?"

A. "I don't remember. It was a long time ago."

I asked her if she told Part that Manson had ordered these murders.

A. "Sure I told him that."

Did she tell Part that Manson was along the second night, and that when they stopped on Waverly Drive, Manson got out and entered the LaBianca house?

After a number of evasive replies, Leslie angrily answered: "Sure I told him that!"

THE COURT "We will take our recess at this time—"

VAN HOUTEN "Mr. Bugliosi, you are an evil man!"

Each of the Family witnesses denied that Manson hated blacks. But in the light of what I'd recently learned, several put it in a very curious way. When Fitzgerald asked Squeaky: "Did he love the black man or did he hate him?" she had replied: "He loved them. He is his father—the black man is Charlie's father." Gypsy had testified: "First of all, Charlie spent nearly all of his life in jail. So he got to know the black people very, very well.

In fact, I mean, they were like his father, you know." Leslie had said something very similar, adding: "If Charlie hated black people he would hate himself."

During a recess I asked Manson, "Charlie, was your father black?"

"*What?*" He seemed startled by the question, yet whether because it was such a crazy idea or because I'd found out something he didn't want known I couldn't tell. There was nothing evasive about his eventual response, however; he emphatically denied it.

He seemed to be telling the truth. Yet I wondered. I still do.

The next witness was no stranger to the stand. Brought back from New Hampshire at the request of Irving Kanarek, Linda Kasabian was again sworn. Fitzgerald, Keith, and Shinn had opposed calling her; Kanarek should have listened to their advice, as Linda again came over so well that I didn't even cross-examine her. None of her previous testimony was shaken in the slightest.

Linda, her husband, and their two children were living together on a small farm in New Hampshire. The footloose Bob Kasabian had turned out to be a pillar of strength, and I was pleased to hear that their marriage now seemed to be working.

Ruth Ann Moorehouse, aka Ouisch, age twenty, who'd once told Danny DeCarlo she couldn't wait to get her first pig, repeated the now familiar refrain: "Charlie was no leader." But "the rattlesnakes liked him, he could play with them" and "he could change old men into young men."

Adding a few more fictional touches to the copycat motive, Ouisch claimed that Bobby Beausoleil was the father of Linda Kasabian's second child.

I asked her: "You would do anything to help Charles Manson and these three female defendants, wouldn't you, Ouisch?"

When she evaded a direct reply, I asked: "You would even murder for them, wouldn't you?"

A. "I could not take a life."

Q. "All right, let's talk about that, Ouisch. Do you know a girl by the name of Barbara Hoyt?"

On the advice of her attorney, Ouisch refused to answer any questions about the Hoyt murder attempt. By law, when a witness refuses to be cross-examined, that witness's entire testimony can be stricken. This was done in Ouisch's case.

Easily the weirdest of all the witnesses was Steve Grogan, aka Clem, age nineteen. He spoke of the "engrams" on his brain; answered questions about his father by talking about his mother; and claimed that the real leader of the Family was not Manson but Pooh Bear, Mary Brunner's child by Manson.

Kanarek complained, at the bench, that Older was smiling at Grogan's replies. Older responded: "I find nothing whatsoever funny about this witness, I can assure you ... Why you would want to call him is beyond my comprehension, but that is up to you ... No jury will ever believe this witness, I promise you that."

The youth who beheaded Shorty Shea appeared to be a complete idiot. He grinned incessantly, made funny faces, and played with his beard even more than Manson. Yet it was more than partly role playing, as several of his very careful replies indicated.

Clem recalled accompanying Linda, Leslie, Sadie, Tex, and Katie one night in a car; he claimed that Linda had given them all LSD first; and he insisted that Manson was not along. But he was very careful not to say that this was the night of the LaBianca murders, to avoid implicating himself.

Many of his responses were almost exact quotations from Manson. For example, when I asked him, "When did you join the Family, Clem?" he replied, "When I was born of white skin."

I also asked him, since it had been brought out on the direct examination, about his arrest in the Barker raid. What had he been charged with? I inquired.

A. "I was arrested on a breach of promise."

Q. "Breach of promise? Some girl you made a promise to, Clem, or what?"

A. "It was a promise to return a truck on a certain date."

Q. "Oh, I get it. Sometimes that is called 'grand theft auto,' too, isn't it, Clem?"

The defense called their next witness: Vincent T. Bugliosi. At the bench Fitzgerald admitted that this was an unusual situation: "On the other hand, in this case Mr. Bugliosi has been an investigator as well as a prosecutor."

Daye Shinn questioned me about my interview with Susan Atkins and her testimony before the grand jury. Why did I feel Susan hadn't told the grand jury the whole truth? he asked. I enumerated the reasons, noting, among other things, my belief that she had stabbed Sharon Tate.

Q. "How did you come to that conclusion?"

A. "She admitted it on the witness stand, Mr. Shinn, for one thing. Also, she told Ronnie Howard and Virginia Graham that she stabbed Sharon Tate."

Shinn was trying to reinstate the "deal" in which the DA's Office agreed not to seek the death penalty against Susan if she testified truthfully. As Older told him at the bench: "Susan Atkins took the stand in this case under oath and testified that she was lying at the grand jury. If there'd been any agreement, that in itself would have been enough to negate it."

Keith asked me if I had either heard the tape Leslie made with Part or discussed its contents with him. I replied that I had not. Kanarek's cross-examination went so far afield that Judge Older finally terminated it.

Others who took the stand in succeeding days included Aaron Stovitz; Evelle Younger, former Los Angeles District Attorney and now California State Attorney General; attorneys Paul Caruso and Richard Caballero; and promoter Lawrence Schiller. Every aspect of the December 4, 1969, agreement; the taping of Atkins' account; the selling of her story; her grand jury testimony; and her firing of Caballero the day after her meeting with Manson was discussed. Shinn's most strenuous cross-examination of the entire trial took place when he had Schiller on the stand: Shinn wanted to know exactly how much Susan's story had earned and in which bank accounts every penny was. Shinn was to receive Susan's share for representing her.

During my cross-examination of these witnesses, I scored a number of significant points. I brought out through Caruso, for example, that during the December 4, 1969, meeting he had stated that Susan Atkins probably wouldn't testify at the trial "because of her fear of Manson."

Kanarek, however, scored one of the biggest points—for the prosecution. In questioning Caballero, Atkins' former attorney, he asked: "What did [Susan Atkins] tell you about the language written in blood at these three homes?"

CABALLERO "I told you not to ask me that question, Irving."

Apparently convinced that Caballero was hiding something favorable to his client, Kanarek repeated the question.

Caballero sighed and said: "She told me that Charles Manson had wanted to bring on Helter Skelter and it wasn't happening fast enough, and the use of the word 'pig' was for the purpose of making them think that Negroes were committing these crimes, because the Panthers and people like that are the ones that used the name 'pig' to mean the establishment, and that was the whole purpose of it, that Helter Skelter wasn't happening fast enough, and Charlie was going to bring on the ruination of the world, and this is why all the murders were committed.

"I asked you not to ask me these questions, Mr. Kanarek."

Having failed abysmally in their attempt to sell the copycat motive, the defense now switched to a new tactic. They called a number of psychiatrists to the stand, hoping to establish that LSD had affected the minds of the three female defendants to the extent that they were not responsible for their acts.

It was not a real defense, but it could be made to seem a mitigating circumstance which, unless thoroughly rebutted, might tip the scales in favor of life imprisonment.

Their first witness, Dr. Andre Tweed, professed to be an expert on LSD, but almost all of his testimony was contrary to that of acknowledged experts in the field.

Tweed claimed he knew of one case where a youth while under LSD heard voices which told him to kill his mother and his grandmother, and he did just that. On the basis of this single, unidentified case, Tweed concluded that "people may perform homicidal acts while under the influence of LSD." It was also his opinion, he said, that LSD probably caused brain damage.

On cross-examination I brought out that Dr. Tweed had only talked to Patricia Krenwinkel for two hours. He had not read the trial transcripts or interviewed any of her friends or relatives. He had never done any controlled research in the field of LSD, had only lectured once on the subject, and had written no papers on it. When I asked him why he considered himself an expert, he rather loftily replied: "What is an expert but what the beholder thinks he is from his experience? Many people consider me an expert, so I have accustomed myself to assuming that I am."

Q. "Do you consider Dr. Thomas Ungerleider of UCLA an expert in LSD?"

A. "Yes, I do."

Q. "More than yourself?"

A. "I am not in a position to judge that. I will leave that to others."

Q. "Do you consider Dr. Duke Fisher of UCLA an expert in the field of LSD?"

A. "Yes."

I then brought out that the two men had written a paper entitled "The Problems of LSD in Emotional Disorders," in which they concluded that "there is no scientific demonstrable evidence of organic brain damage caused by LSD."

Tweed now had to admit that was correct, as far as present evidence went.

On December 24, 1969, Patricia Krenwinkel had been examined by a Mobile, Alabama, psychiatrist, a Dr. Claude Brown. Since Tweed had based his conclusions in part on Brown's report, I was given a copy of it just prior to my cross-examination.

It was a bombshell, as my next question to Dr. Tweed indicated:

Q. "In forming your opinions with respect to Patricia Krenwinkel, did you take into consideration that she told Dr. Brown that on the night of the Tate murders Charles Manson told her to go along with Tex Watson?"

After numerous objections and lengthy conferences at the bench, Dr. Tweed admitted that he had considered this. Still later, Patricia Krenwinkel was recalled to the stand, where, though she denied the truth of the statement, she admitted that she had told Dr. Brown that this was so.

We now had a perfect score. Manson had called Sadie, Katie, and Leslie to the stand in an attempt to exonerate him. Instead, I had now proven that each of the three had previously told others that Manson was behind these murders.

There were other surprises in the Brown report. Krenwinkel also told the doctor that she had fled to Mobile "because she was afraid of Manson finding her and killing her";* that on the day of the Tate murders she was coming *off* an acid trip and wasn't on any drugs that night; and that following the murders "she was always fearful that they would be arrested for what they had done, but 'Charlie said nobody could touch us.' "

This latter statement proved that Katie was well aware of the consequences of her acts.

This was important, since it was obvious from their questions that the defense attorneys were trying to imply that the three female defendants were insane at the time they committed these murders.

Under California law an insanity plea must be entered *before* the start of the trial. A separate sanity phase is then held, after the guilt trial. The defense, however, had

*Although harmful to Manson, this could only be helpful to Fitzgerald's client, Patricia Krenwinkel. However, it was not Fitzgerald who brought this out but Keith, after Fitzgerald had concluded his examination.

not entered such a plea at the proper time. Therefore, in one sense, the question of whether the defendants were sane or insane was irrelevant, since this was not an issue which the jury would have to decide. In another sense, however, it was crucial. If the defense could cause the jury to doubt the sanity of the defendants, this could strongly influence their vote on the penalty they were to pay.

Suddenly I was not only having to prove Manson's guilt all over again, I was also having to prove that the girls were legally sane.

In most states, including California, the legal test of insanity is the M'Naghten Rule. Among other things, M'Naghten provides that if a defendant, as a result of mental disease or defect, does not realize that what he did was wrong, then he is legally insane. It is not enough, however, that he personally believe his acts were not wrong. Were this so, every man would be a law unto himself. For instance, a man could rape a dozen women, say, "I don't think it's wrong to rape," and therefore evade criminal punishment. The clincher is whether he knows that society thinks his actions are wrong. If he does, then he cannot be legally insane. And deliberate acts to avoid detection—such as cutting telephone wires, eradicating prints, changing identities, disposing of incriminating evidence—constitute circumstantial evidence that the defendant knows society views his acts as wrong.

Earlier Dr. Tweed had testified that Patricia Krenwinkel didn't believe these murders were wrong. I now asked him on cross: "In your opinion, when Patricia Krenwinkel was committing these murders, did she believe that society thought it was wrong to do what she was doing?"

A. "I believe so."

BUGLIOSI "No further questions."

On March 4, Manson trimmed his beard to a neat fork and completely shaved his head, because, he told newsmen, "I am the Devil and the Devil always has a bald head."

Interestingly enough, this time the three female defendants did not follow Manson's example. Nor, when he occasionally acted up in court, did they parrot him, as they had in the guilt trial. Obviously it had got across to them, albeit belatedly, that such antics only proved Manson's domination.

While denying that LSD can cause brain damage, the next witness, psychiatrist Keith Ditman, testified that the drug can have a detrimental effect on a person's personality. He also stated that a person using LSD is more susceptible to the influence of a second party, and that Leslie's use of the drug, *plus* Manson's influence over her, could have been significant factors in causing her to participate in a homicide.

VAN HOUTEN "This is all such a big lie. I was influenced by the war in Vietnam and TV."

On cross-examination I got Ditman to concede that not all people react the same to LSD, that it depends upon the personality structure of the person ingesting the drug. I then brought out that Ditman had never examined Leslie; therefore, not knowing what her personality structure was, he couldn't say what effect, if any, LSD had on her mental state.

Nor, turning this around, not having examined her, could he say for certain whether she did or did not have inherent homicidal tendencies.

Keith, on redirect, asked Ditman: "What is meant by inherent homicidal tendencies?"

A. "That a person has, let's say, more than the average human being, a killer instinct . . ."

Q. "Psychiatrically speaking, do some people have greater killer instincts than others, in your opinion?"

A. "Well, some people have a more covert and overt hostility and aggression. In that sense, they are *more capable* of committing crimes of violence, such as murder."

Dr. Ditman had just articulated one of the chief points of the final argument I was preparing to give at the close of the penalty phase.

Dr. Joel Fort, the almost legendary "hippie doctor of the Haight," didn't look the part. The founder of the National Center for Solving Social and Health Problems was fortyish, dressed conservatively, talked quietly, didn't have long hair (in fact he was bald). Angered by his testimony, Manson shouted, "If he ever seen a hippie, it was in the street while he was driving by in his car."

Manson's anger had good cause. Even on direct, Dr. Fort was more helpful to the prosecution than the defense. The author of one book on drugs and co-author of eleven others, Dr. Fort stated that "a drug by itself does not perform a magical transformation—there are many other factors."

On cross-examination I brought out one. Fort said: "It was my feeling [after examining Leslie Van Houten] that Mr. Manson's influence played a very significant role in the commission of the murders."

Another very crucial point came out on cross. To negate the defense's new argument that the girls were on LSD during the murders, and therefore less responsible for their acts, I asked Fort: "Isn't it true, Doctor, that people under the influence of LSD do not tend to be violent?"

A. "That is true."

Still attacking the prosecution's theory of Manson's domination, Kanarek asked Fort: "Now, do you know of any cases where someone has—I mean, other than in the Frankenstein type of picture—do you know where someone has sat down and programmed people to go out, let's say, and commit armed robberies, burglaries, assaults? Do you know of any such instances?"

A. "Yes. In one sense, that is what we do when we program soldiers in a war ... The Army uses a peer group technique and the patriotic ideals that are instilled in citizens of a particular country to bring about this pattern of behavior."

Dr. Fort was typical of many persons who, though opposed to capital punishment in principle, felt that these murders were so savage and senseless, so totally lacking in mitigating circumstances, that justice demanded that these persons be sentenced to death. I learned this in a conversation with him in the hall outside court, in which he stated that he was extremely unhappy that he had been called to testify for the defense in this case. Greatly concerned about the stain the Manson Family had cast on all young people, Dr. Fort offered to testify for the prosecution when I brought Charles "Tex" Watson to trial, an offer which I later accepted.

It was in just such a hallway interview that I discovered how potentially damaging to the defense their next witness could be. Learning that Keith intended to call Dr. Joel Simon Hochman during the afternoon session, I cut my lunch hour short so I could spend a half hour interviewing the psychiatrist.

To my amazement, I learned that Maxwell Keith hadn't even interviewed his own witness. He was calling him to the stand "cold." Had he talked to him for just five minutes, Keith would never have called Hochman. For the doctor, who *had* interviewed Leslie, felt that the use of LSD wasn't an important influence on her; rather, he felt there was something very seriously wrong with Leslie Van Houten.

In his testimony and the psychiatric report he wrote following the examination, Dr. Hochman called Leslie Van Houten "a spoiled little princess" who was unable "to suffer frustration and delay of gratification." From childhood on, she'd had extreme difficulties with impulse control. When she didn't get her way, she went into rages; for example, beating her adopted sister with a shoe.

"From a position of over-all perspective," Hochman noted, "it is quite clear that Leslie Van Houten was a psychologically loaded gun which went off as a consequence of the complex intermeshing of highly unlikely and bizarre circumstances."

Hochman confirmed something I had long suspected. Of the three female defendants, Leslie Van Houten was the least committed to Charles Manson. "She listened to [Manson's] talk of philosophy, but it wasn't her trip." Nor could she "get that into Charlie sexually, and that bothered her a lot. 'I couldn't get it on with Charlie like I could with Bobby,' she said . . ." According to Hochman, Leslie was obsessed with beauty. "Bobby was beautiful, Charles was not, physically. Charles was short. That is something that always turned me off."

Yet she killed at his command.

Keith asked Hochman: "Doctor, did you ask her

whether or not Mr. Manson, during her association with him, had any influence over her in her thought process and in her conduct and activity?"

A. "She denies it. But I don't buy that."

Q. "Why don't you buy that?"

A. "Well, I don't understand why she would stay on the scene that long if there was nothing there for her, on some unconscious basis."

As I'd observe in my final argument, many came to Spahn Ranch but only a few stayed; those who did, did so because they found the blackhearted medicine Manson was peddling very palatable.

According to Hochman, in talking to him Leslie professed "a kind of primitive Christianity, love for the world, acceptance of all things. And I asked her, 'Well, professing that, how can it be you would murder someone?' She said, 'Well that was something inside of me too.' "

Maxwell Keith should have stopped right there. Instead, he asked Hochman: "How do you interpret that?"

A. "I think it's rather realistic. I think that in reality it *was* something inside of her, despite her chronic denial of the emotional aspects of herself, that a rage was there."

Nor did Keith leave it at that. He now asked: "When you say a rage was there, what do you mean by that?"

A. "In my opinion it would take a rage, an emotional reaction to kill someone. I think it is unquestionable that that feeling was inside of her."

Q. "Bearing in mind that she had never seen or heard of Mrs. LaBianca, in your opinion there was some hate in her when this occurred?"

A. "Well, I think it would make it easier for her not to know Mrs. LaBianca ... It is hard to kill someone that you have good feelings towards. I don't think there was anything specific about Mrs. LaBianca.

"Let me make myself clear: Mrs. LaBianca was an object, a blank screen upon which Leslie projected her feelings, much as a patient projects his feelings on an analyst whom he doesn't know ... feelings towards her mother, her father, toward the establishment ...

"I think she was a very angry girl for a long time, a

very alienated girl for a long time, and the anger and rage was associated with that."

Hochman was articulating one of the main points of my final summation: namely, that Leslie, Sadie, Katie, and Tex had a hostility and rage within them that pre-existed Charles Manson. They were different from Linda Kasabian, Paul Watkins, Brooks Poston, Juan Flynn, and T. J. When Manson asked them to kill for him, each said no.

Tex Watson, Susan Atkins, Patricia Krenwinkel, and Leslie Van Houten said yes.

So there had to be something special about these people that caused them to kill. Some kind of inner flaw. Apart from Charlie.

Though he had badly damaged his own case, Keith had tried to put the hat on Manson. Fitzgerald, in his examination of Hochman, did just the opposite. He sought to minimize the importance of Manson's influence over Leslie. Asking Hochman what Manson's influence actually was, he received this reply: "His ideas, his presence, the role he played in his relationship to her, served to reinforce a lot of her feelings and attitudes. It served to reinforce and give her a way of continuing her general social alienation, her alienation from the establishment."

Q. "So, really, all you are saying is that (A) Manson could possibly have had some influence, and (B), if he did have some influence, it would only contribute to the lowering of her restraints on her impulsiveness, is that correct?"

A. "Yes."

Q. "So any influence Manson had on Leslie Van Houten, in terms of your professional opinion, is tenuous at best, is that correct?"*

A. "Let me give you another example that may make it clearer ... Suppose someone comes in and says, 'Let's

*There was no meaningful dichotomy between Leslie Van Houten and Fitzgerald's client, Patricia Krenwinkel. Both young girls had joined the Family, submitted to Manson's domination, and ultimately murdered for him. In trying to establish that Manson was not responsible for causing Leslie to kill, Fitzgerald was at the same time establishing that Manson wasn't responsible for Katie's killing either. Hochman's reply badly hurt not only Leslie but Katie and Sadie as well.

eat the whole apple pie.' Obviously your temptation is stimulated by the suggestion, but your final decision on whether or not to eat the whole pie or just one piece comes out of you. So the other person is influential, but is not a final arbiter or decider of that situation . . .

"Someone can tell you to shoot someone, but your decision to do that comes from inside you."

Kanarek, when his turn came, picked up the scent. "And so you are telling us then, in layman's language, that when someone takes a knife and stabs, the decision to do that is a personal decision?"

A. "In the ultimate analysis it is."

Q. "It is a personal decision of the person who does the stabbing?"

A. "Yes."

Ironically, Kanarek and I were now on the same side. Both of us were seeking to prove that, even independent of Manson, these girls had murder within them.

Manson was very impressed by Hochman and at first wanted to be interviewed by him. I was relieved, however, when he later abandoned the idea. I wasn't greatly worried about Manson conning Hochman. But even if Hochman didn't buy Manson's story, Kanarek would make sure he repeated it on the stand. Thus, using Hochman as a conduit, Manson could get almost everything he wanted before the jury, without being subject to my cross-examination.

Hochman found in all three girls "much evidence in their history of early alienation, of early antisocial or deviant behavior." Even before joining the Family, Leslie had more emotional problems than the average person. Sadie actively sought to be everything her father warned her not to be. "She thinks now, in retrospect," Hochman noted, "that even without Charles Manson she would have ended up in jail for manslaughter or assault with a deadly weapon." Katie first had sex at fifteen. She never saw the boy again, and she suffered tremendous guilt because of the experience. Manson eradicated that guilt. He also, in letting her join the Family, gave her the acceptance she desperately craved.

Of the three, Hochman felt Sadie had a little more remorse than the other two—she often talked of wishing her life were over. Yet he also noted, "One is struck by the absence of a conventional sense of morality or conscience in this girl." And he testified, "She does not seem to manifest any evidence of discomfort or anxiety about her present circumstances, or her conviction and possible death sentence. On the contrary, she seemed to manifest a remarkable peacefulness and self-acceptance in her present state."

According to Hochman, all three girls denied "any sense of guilt whatever about anything." And he felt that intellectually they actually believed there is no right or wrong, that morality is a relative thing. "However, I, as a psychiatrist, know that you cannot rationally do away with the feelings that exist on the irrational, unconscious level. You cannot tell yourself that killing is O.K. intellectually when you have grown up all your life feeling that killing is wrong."

In short, Hochman believed that as human beings the girls felt some guilt deep down inside, even though they consciously suppressed it.

Keith asked Hochman: "In your opinion, Doctor, would Leslie be susceptible or respond to intensive therapy?"

A. "Possibly."

Q. "In other words, you don't feel that she is such a lost soul that she could never be rehabilitated?"

A. "No, I don't think she is *that* lost a soul, no."

To a psychiatrist, no one is beyond redemption. This is essential, standard testimony. Yet only one of the defense attorneys, Maxwell Keith, asked the question, and then only on redirect.

Earlier I'd brought out that Hochman had only the word of the girls that they were on LSD either night. I now asked him: "Have you ever read a reported case in the literature of LSD of any individual who committed murder while under the influence of LSD?"

A. "No. Suicide, but not murder."

As I'd later ask the jury, could Watson, Atkins, Krenwinkel, and Van Houten, *all four*, be exceptions?

A large portion of Hochman's testimony had dealt with the mental states of the three girls. Susan Atkins was suffering from a diagnosable condition, he said: an early childhood deprivation syndrome which had resulted in a hysterical personality type.

This was not legal insanity as defined by M'Naghten.

Leslie Van Houten was an immature, unusually impulsive person, who tended to act spontaneously without reflection.

Nor was this legal insanity as defined by M'Naghten.

In his report on Krenwinkel, Dr. Claude Brown, the Mobile psychiatrist, had stated that "at the time I saw Miss Krenwinkel, she showed a schizophrenic reaction." He added, however, that "I do not state with any certainty that this psychosis existed at the time of the alleged murders."

Schizophrenia *may* be legal insanity as defined by M'Naghten. But Dr. Brown's opinion was qualified, and when Fitzgerald asked Dr. Hochman if, on the basis of his examination of Krenwinkel, he agreed that she was, or had been, schizophrenic, Hochman replied, "I would say no."

It remained to bring these points across to the jury, in terms they could easily understand.

On recross-examination I had Hochman define the word "psychotic." He replied that it meant "a loss of contact with reality."

I then asked him: "At the present time, Doctor, do you feel any of these three female defendants are psychotic?"

A. "No."

Q. "In your opinion, do you feel that any of these three female defendants have ever been psychotic?"

A. "No."

BUGLIOSI "May I approach the witness, Your Honor? I want to ask the witness a question privately."

THE COURT "Yes, you may."

I had already questioned Dr. Hochman once about this. But I wanted to be absolutely certain of his reply. Once I had received it, I returned to the counsel table and asked him a number of unrelated questions, so the jury wouldn't know what we had been talking about. I then gradually worked up to the big one.

Q. "The term 'insanity,' Doctor, you are familiar with that term, of course?"

A. "Yes."

Q. "Basically, you define the word 'insanity' to be the layman's synonym for 'psychotic'?"

A. "I would say that the word 'insanity' is used generally to mean 'psychotic.' "

Q. "Then, from a psychiatric standpoint, I take it that in your opinion none of these three female defendants are presently insane nor have they ever been insane, is that correct?"

A. "That is correct."

As far as the psychiatric testimony was concerned, with Hochman's reply the ball game was over.

The defense called only three more witnesses during the penalty trial, all hard-core Family members. Each was on the stand only a short time, but their testimony, particularly that of the first witness, was as shocking as anything that had gone before.

Catherine Gillies, whose grandmother owned Myers Ranch, parroted the Family line: Charlie never led anyone; there was never any talk of a race war; these murders were committed to free Bobby Beausoleil.

Coldly, matter-of-factly, the twenty-one-year-old girl testified that on the night of the LaBianca murders, "I followed Katie to the car, and I asked if I could go with her. Linda, Leslie, and Sadie were all in the car. And they said that they had plenty of people to do what they were going to do, and that I didn't need to go."

On direct examination by Kanarek, Cathy stated: "You know, I am willing to kill for a brother, we all are."

Q. "What do you mean by that?"

A. "In other words, to get a brother out of jail, I would kill. I would have killed that night except I did not go ..."

Q. "What prevented you from going with them, if anything?"

A. "Just the fact that they didn't need me."

Apparently Fitzgerald hoped to soften the harshness of her reply when he asked her: "Have you killed anybody to get someone out of jail?"

With a strange little smile, Cathy turned her head and, looking directly at the jury, replied: "Not yet."

Cathy had testified on direct examination that Katie had told her about the Tate-LaBianca murders. On cross-examination I asked her: "When Katie told you that they had murdered these people, did this disturb you at all?"

A. "Actually it had very little effect on me because I knew why they had done it."

Q. "So it didn't upset you?"

A. "No, it definitely didn't upset me."

Q. "You didn't decide that you would rather not continue living with murderers?"

A. "Obviously not."

Q. "Were you upset that you didn't get to go along with them?"

A. "I wanted to go."

Mary Brunner, first member of the Manson Family, claimed that the police had told her that she would be charged with murder if she did not implicate Manson in the Hinman slaying. She now repudiated this testimony and further denied even being at the Hinman residence.

Keith brought out that Mary Brunner had testified both in the second trial of Bobby Beausoleil and before the Hinman grand jury, and neither time did she say anything about Leslie Van Houten being present when Hinman was killed.

I had no questions for her. The point was made.

Brenda McCann was recalled to the stand, to testify that on the nights of the Tate and LaBianca murders she had seen Manson sleeping with Stephanie Schram in Devil's Canyon.

The groundwork for my cross-examination of Brenda had been laid fifteen months before. I impeached her with her testimony before the grand jury, when she stated that she couldn't remember where she, or Manson, was on either night.

Brenda was the last witness. She completed her testimony on Tuesday, March 16, 1971. That afternoon, after a number of delays—Kanarek, for example, refused to stipulate that Gary Hinman was dead—the defense rested. Wednesday we worked on the jury instructions, and on Thursday the trial entered its final stage. All that now remained were the arguments, the deliberations, and the verdict.

March 18-29, 1971

My opening argument in the penalty trial was brief, lasting less than ten minutes. As with all my arguments during the trial, Manson decided to sit this one out, in the lockup. The psychology behind this was obvious: he didn't want the jury focusing on him when I discussed him.

I began by saying: "I am not going to address myself to the frantic effort by the three female defendants and the defense witnesses to make it look like Charles Manson wasn't involved in these murders. I am sure all of you clearly saw that they were lying on that witness stand to do what they could for their God, Charles Manson.

"Well, Charles Manson has already been convicted. He has already been convicted of seven counts of first degree murder and one count of conspiracy to commit murder.

"The difficulty in your decision, as I see it, is not whether these defendants deserve the death penalty, ladies and gentlemen. In view of the incredibly savage, barbaric, and inhuman murders they committed, the death penalty is the only proper verdict." I then stated the very heart of my argument: *"If this case were not a proper case for the imposition of the death penalty, no case ever would be.* In view of what they did, life imprisonment would be the greatest gift, the greatest charity, the greatest handout, as it were, ever given.

"The difficulty in your decision, as I see it, is whether you will have the fortitude to return verdicts of death against all four defendants."

The defense attorneys, I anticipated, would beg for their clients' lives. This was not only commendable, I told the jury, it was also understandable, just as it was understandable that they "argued during the guilt phase that their clients were not involved in these murders, even though during the penalty phase the three female defendants took the stand and said: 'Yes, we were involved.'"

There was absolutely no reason for these defendants to viciously and inhumanly snuff out the lives of these seven human beings, I noted. There were *no* mitigating circumstances.

"These defendants are not human beings, ladies and gentlemen. Human beings have a heart and a soul. No one with a heart and a soul could have done what these defendants did to these seven victims.

"These defendants are human monsters, human mutations.

"There is only one proper ending to the Tate-LaBianca murder trial," I concluded, "verdicts of death for all four defendants."

Kanarek stipulated, at the start of his argument, that "Mr. Manson is not all good." However, he continued, "Mr. Manson is innocent of these matters that are before us."

Why was he on trial then? Kanarek returned to his two favorite themes: "Mr. Manson has had quite a share of troubles because of the fact that he likes girls." And he was only brought to trial "so someone in the District Attorney's Office can have a gold star and say, 'I got Charles Manson.'"

Kanarek's argument stretched over three days. It was occasionally ridiculous, as when he said, "We can perform a public service for the United States of America by giving these people life, because if there is a revolution, this is the kind of thing that could spark it." It was sometimes unintentionally funny, as when he stated that, unlike Patricia Krenwinkel and Leslie Van Houten, "Charles Manson has no family to come here to testify." But mostly he tried to plant little seeds of doubt.

Why, if Susan Atkins lied on the stand to absolve Manson, would she have implicated him in the Hinman murder? Wasn't the fact that Manson himself shot Crowe, to protect the people at Spahn Ranch, evidence that he didn't need to order others to act for him? If these girls were lying about Manson's non-involvement in the murders, wouldn't they have also lied and said they had sorrow and remorse?

Kanarek only briefly mentioned the copycat motive; he didn't even try to argue it. Instead, he suggested still another alternative motive. "But for the fact that at least some of these people [supposedly referring to the Tate victims] were engaged in a narcotic episode of some type, these events would not have taken place."

Daye Shinn, who argued next, fastened on Dr. Hochman's statement that he believed these girls had subconscious if not conscious remorse.

As for Susan, "She is still young," Shinn argued. "She is only twenty-two years old. I believe there is still a hope of rehabilitating her . . . Maybe someday she may be rehabilitated to the extent that she may finally realize what she has done was not right. I believe that she deserves the chance, an opportunity, so that maybe someday she may be released and live the rest of her life out of prison."

This was very bad strategy on Shinn's part, implying that if Susan Atkins was given life imprisonment she might someday be released on parole. By law, the prosecution can't argue this, it is so prejudicial to the defendant.

Of the four defense attorneys, Maxwell Keith gave the best opening argument. He was also the only one who really attempted to rebut my contentions.

"Mr. Bugliosi tells you that if the death penalty is not appropriate in this case, it would never be appropriate. Well, I wonder if it ever is appropriate?

"Mr. Bugliosi read to you at the close of his argument on the guilt phase the roll call of the dead. Let me read to you now, ladies and gentlemen, the roll call of the living dead: Leslie, Sadie, Katie, Squeaky, Brenda, Ouisch, Sandy, Cathy, Gypsy, Tex, Clem, Mary, Snake, and no doubt many more. These lives, and the lives of these three young girls in particular, have been so damaged that it is possible, in some cases, their destruction is beyond repair. I hope not, but it is possible."

Leslie Van Houten, he strongly argued, was capable of rehabilitation. She should be studied, not killed. "I am not asking you to forgive her, although to forgive is divine. I am asking you to give her the chance to redeem herself. She deserves to live. What she did was not done by the real Leslie. Let the Leslie of today die—she will, slowly and maybe painfully. And let the Leslie as she once was live again."

Nowhere in Paul Fitzgerald's argument, which followed, did he state, or even imply, that Manson was responsible for what had happened to Patricia Krenwinkel.

"Patricia Krenwinkel is twenty-three years old," Fitzgerald observed. "With 365 days in the year, there are approximately 8,400 days in 23 years, and approximately 200,000 hours in her lifetime.

"The perpetration of these offenses took at best approximately three hours.

"Is she to be judged solely on what occurred during three of 200,000 hours?"

Just before court commenced on March 23, I walked over to the water cooler. Manson, in the nearby lockup, called out to me, rather loudly, "If I get the death penalty, there is going to be a lot of bloodletting. Because I am not going to take it."

Both the court clerk and Steve Kay overheard the remark. Kay intemperately rushed out of the courtroom and repeated it to the press. Learning of this, I asked the reporters not to print it. The *Herald Examiner* wouldn't agree, and it broke the story with a banner headline:

MANSON DEATH THREAT

Warns of Terror
If Doomed to Die

Before this, however, Judge Older, made aware of what had happened, decided that rather than wait to the close of arguments, he would sequester the jury immediately.

In my final argument I rebutted point by point the earlier defense contentions. For example, the defense had claimed that Linda got her story from listening to the Susan Atkins tapes. Why would Linda need to listen to the tapes, I asked, when she was present both nights?

Kanarek had told the jury that if they returned death penalty verdicts, they would be killers. This was a very heavy argument. As support, he cited the Fifth Commandment: "Thou shalt not kill."

In answer, I told the jury that most biblical scholars and theologians interpret the original language to mean: "Thou shalt not commit murder," which is exactly how it appears in the New English Bible, dated 1970.

The Ten Commandments appear in Exodus, chapter 20, I noted. What Kanarek did not mention, I observed, is that the very next chapter authorizes the death penalty. Exodus 21, verse 12, reads: "Whoever strikes a man a mortal blow must be put to death," while verse 14 of the same chapter reads: "When a man kills another, after maliciously scheming to do so, you must take him even from my altar and put him to death."

Kanarek argued that there was no domination. In addition to all the evidence during the guilt trial, I observed, during the penalty trial, "When Atkins, Krenwinkel, and Van Houten played the part of the sacrificial lamb and admitted their participation in these murders, and then lied on that witness stand and said that Manson wasn't involved, the fact that they were willing to lie on that witness stand just proves, all the more, Manson's domination over them ..." As for the other Family witnesses, Squeaky, Sandy, and the others, "All of them sounded like a broken record on that witness stand. They all have the same thought; they use the same language; each one was a carbon copy of the other. They are all still totally subservient and subject to Charles Manson. They are his X'd-out slaves."

I came now to the copycat motive. My objective was to completely demolish it, yet not dwell on it so long that it would seem that I was giving it credence.

"It is really laughable, ladies and gentlemen," I began, "the way the three female defendants and the defense witnesses sought to take the hat off Charles Manson.

"They had to come up with a motive for these murders other than Helter Skelter. Why? Because no less than ten witnesses during the guilt trial had irrevocably connected Manson with Helter Skelter, so they certainly could not say from that witness stand that the motive for these murders was Helter Skelter. If they said that, they would be saying, 'Yes, Charles Manson masterminded these murders.' So they came up with the copycat motive.

"I could give you between twenty and thirty reasons why it's obvious that this nonsensical story of the defense was fabricated out of whole cloth, but I won't take up your time with it, and I am not going to insult your intelligence." I did point out a few:

Linda Kasabian testified during the penalty trial that she had never heard anyone discuss committing these murders to free Bobby Beausoleil.

Gary Hinman was stabbed not more than four times. Voytek Frykowski was stabbed fifty-one times, Rosemary LaBianca forty-one times, Leno LaBianca twenty-six times. Rather a great difference, if these were copycat slayings.

And, if these murders were to be carbon copies, why weren't the words "political piggy" used at the Tate and LaBianca residences? And why no bloody paw print at the latter two houses?

The most powerful evidence demolishing this ridiculous motive, I noted, was that as early as February 1969, "long before there was any Hinman murder to copy, long before there were any words 'political piggy' to copy, Manson told Brooks Poston and other Family members—including all of his co-defendants—that, quoting Poston: 'He said a group of real blacks would come out of the ghettos and do an atrocious crime in the richer sections of Los Angeles and other cities. They would do an atrocious murder with stabbing, killing, cutting bodies to pieces, smearing blood on the walls, writing 'pigs' on the walls.'

"Writing 'pigs' on the walls," I repeated.

"So writing 'pig' at the Tate and LaBianca residences was simply a part of Manson's blueprint for starting Helter Skelter, not an effort to copy the Hinman murder.

"Incidentally," I observed, "Mr. Kanarek never did try to explain to you why the words 'helter skelter' were printed in blood on the refrigerator door at the LaBianca residence. What does Helter Skelter have to do with freeing Bobby Beausoleil or an alleged $1,000 MDA burn at the Tate residence? Absolutely nothing, that's what. The words 'helter skelter' were found printed in blood on the LaBianca refrigerator door because all of the evidence at this trial shows beyond all doubt that Helter Skelter was the principal reason for these savage murders.

"Yes," I admitted, "there is a connection between the Hinman murder and the Tate-LaBianca murders. But it was not this silly Bobby Beausoleil nonsense. Here is the connection. Mr. Manson not only ordered the Tate-LaBianca murders, he also ordered the Hinman murder. That is the connection."

As for Susan Atkins' claim that Linda Kasabian masterminded these murders, I noted that not until the penalty phase did she say anything about this, and then "all of a sudden Linda Kasabian is Charles Manson."

I noted some of the reasons why this was preposterous, among them the ridiculousness of the docile, subservient Linda taking over the leadership of the Family in just one month. "Only one person ordered these murders, ladies and gentlemen, and his initials are CM. He also has an aka: JC. And he is in that lockup right now listening to me . . ."

The most preposterous thing about all this was that supposedly for one and a half years both Sadie and Gypsy kept this secret in their perjurous bosoms. They not only didn't tell the other members of the Family, they didn't even tell Manson's attorney, though both testified they loved and would willingly die for Charlie.

"And why didn't they tell him about this motive? Because it didn't exist. It was recently fabricated."

As for Manson's alibi, that he was with Stephanie Schram in Devil's Canyon on both of these nights, "Isn't it strange that all of Mr. Manson's X'd-out slaves have testified to this during the penalty trial, and the very person, Stephanie Schram, whom they claim Manson was with, testified that Manson was not with her?"

I then addressed myself to the issue of whether the four defendants should receive the death penalty.

The strongest argument that can be made in support of capital punishment is, I feel, deterrence—that it may save additional lives. Unfortunately, under California law the prosecution could not argue deterrence, only retribution.

"These weren't typical murders, ladies and gentlemen. This was a one-sided war where unspeakable atrocities were committed. If all of these defendants don't receive the death penalty, the typical first-degree murderer only deserves ten days in the County Jail."

As for Fitzgerald's contention that killing these defendants would not bring the seven victims back to life, "If we were to accept that line of reasoning, no one would ever be punished for any crime, since punishing a person does not remove the fact that the crime was committed." For example, "Don't punish a man for arson because the punishment is not going to rebuild the building."

In California, if a defendant is seventeen years of age or younger, he or she cannot be sentenced to death. Though Fitzgerald repeatedly called the three female defendants "children," I reminded the jury that Leslie was twenty-one, Susan twenty-two, Katie twenty-three. "They are adults by any standard, and completely responsible for their acts."

In regard to the defense contention that the three female defendants were insane, I reminded the jury that Dr. Hochman, the only psychiatrist to examine all three, said they are not and have never been insane.

Dr. Hochman testified that we are all capable of killing, I noted. "He did not say that we are all capable of murder. There is a vast difference between killing—as in justifiable homicide, self-defense, or defense of others—and murder. And no one can convince me, ladies and gentlemen, that all of us are capable of murdering strangers for no reason whatsoever like these three female defendants did.

"It takes a special type of person to do what they did. It takes a person who places no value on the life of a fellow human being.

"True, Watson, Atkins, Krenwinkel, and Van Houten committed these murders because Charles Manson told them to, but they would never have committed these murders in a million years if they did not already have murder in their guts, in their system. Manson merely told them to do what they were already capable of doing."

Moreover, there was no evidence that Manson *forced* Watson and the girls to murder for him. "In fact, the inference is that they wanted to go along. That seemed to be the general feeling in the Family. Witness the statement of Cathy Gillies. Witness Susan Atkins' telling Juan Flynn, 'We're going to get some fucking pigs.' Does that sound like someone who is being forced to go out?"

Manson ordered the murders, but Watson and the three girls personally committed them "because they wanted to. Make no mistake about that. If they did not want to murder these victims, *all they had to do was not do it.*"

I examined now the backgrounds of the three girls. Like the other female members of the Family, they had "one common denominator among them. It was obvious that each of them had a revulsion, an antipathy, a seething feeling of disgust for society, for their own parents." Each of the three girls had dropped out of society before even meeting Charles Manson; each had taken LSD and other drugs before meeting Manson; and each had rejected her real family before meeting Manson.

Looking right at juror Jean Roseland, who had two teen-age daughters, I said, "Don't confuse them with the girl-next-door type. These three female defendants had repudiated and renounced their very families and society before they ever met Charles Manson.

"In fact, it was precisely because they had contemptuously disavowed and rejected their families and society that they ended up with Charles Manson. That is the very reason.

"Manson was simply the catalyst, the moving force that

translated their preexisting disgust and hatred for society and human beings into violence."

I anticipated an argument that I felt Maxwell Keith might give. "The thought certainly may enter your mind that as wicked and as vicious as these three female defendants are, by comparison to Charles Manson they are nowhere as wicked and vicious as he is; therefore, let's give Manson the death penalty and these three female defendants life imprisonment.

"The only problem with that type of approach is that these female defendants are given credit, as it were, because of Manson's extreme wickedness and viciousness. Under that type of reasoning, if Adolf Hitler were Charles Manson's co-defendant, Manson should receive life imprisonment because of the indescribably evil Adolf Hitler." Rather than compare the three female defendants with Manson, I told the jury, they should evaluate the conduct of *each* of the defendants and determine whether it warranted the imposition of the death penalty. I then went into the acts of each, starting with Manson, enumerating one by one the reasons they deserved death rather than life.

One question the jury would surely ask, I noted, was: Why no remorse? The answer was simple: "Manson and his co-defendants like to kill human beings. That is why they have no remorse. As Paul Watkins testified, 'Death is Charlie's trip.' "

I came to the end of my argument.

"Now the defense attorneys want you to give these defendants a break. Did these defendants give the seven victims in this case a break?

"Now the defense attorneys want you to give their clients another chance. Did these defendants give the seven victims in this case any chance at all?

"Now the defense attorneys want you to have mercy on their clients. Did these defendants have any mercy at all on the seven victims in this case when they begged and pleaded for their lives?"

I then reminded the jurors that nine months earlier, during voir dire, each had told me he would be willing to vote death if he felt this was a proper case. I reiterated:

"If the death penalty is to mean anything in the State of California, other than two empty words, this is a proper case."

I concluded: "On behalf of the People of the State of California, I can't thank you enough for the enormous public service you have rendered as jurors in this very long, historic trial."

That night after dinner I said to Gail, "There must be *something* I have to do tonight." But there wasn't. For a year and a half, seven days a week, I had been totally immersed in the case. Now all I could do was listen to the closing arguments of the defense attorneys and wait until the jury reached its verdict.

Kanarek began by implying that perhaps I had poisoned the glass of water on the lectern and ended, more than a day later, by reading chapter after chapter from the New Testament.

"Now, this being the Easter season, there is an analogy here between Mr. Manson—this may sound at first blush to be ridiculous, and we are not suggesting that Mr. Manson is the deity or Christlike or anything like that—*but how can we know?"*

Judge Older, who had several times warned Kanarek that he had exhausted all relevant rebuttal, finally brought his sermon to an end at the point of resurrection.

Shinn spent his time attacking the DA's Office and in particular me: "Miss Atkins was drowning without friends . . . and she saw Mr. Bugliosi with an oar. She said: Oh, here comes help now. Miss Atkins reached out for that oar. And what do you think Mr. Bugliosi did? He hit her over the head with the oar."

Keith delivered a strong argument against the death penalty itself. Before this, however, he said: "Now strangely, or perhaps not so strangely, I accepted wholeheartedly certain areas of Mr. Bugliosi's argument.

"I accept his exposition to you that Mr. Manson dominated these girls and ordered the homicides.

"I accept that the 'free Bobby Beausoleil' motive is nonsense.

"I accept his telling you that you shouldn't hold the Hinman murder against Leslie.

"I accept his argument that Leslie's testimony and the testimony of the other girls in this case shows Mr. Manson's domination and influence still persists and is all-pervasive."

To deny these things, Keith said, would be to deny the evidence. Thus Keith became the first, and only, defense attorney to accuse Manson of these murders.

Keith, however, said that he did not agree that any of the defendants should receive the death penalty, not even Charles Manson. For in his opinion, Keith said, "Mr. Manson is insane," and in instilling his thoughts into the minds of the three female defendants he had also infected them with his madness.

Keith concluded: "Give Leslie the chance for redemption, to which she is entitled. Remember, Linda Kasabian cut the umbilical cord, in Mr. Bugliosi's words, that tied her to Manson and his Family. Give Leslie the chance to do the same. Give her life. I thank you."

Fitzgerald read a short argument, at the end of which he began describing in detail how the three female defendants would be executed in the gas chamber at San Quentin Prison if the jury returned verdicts of death. This was improper argument, and I objected. When we approached the bench, Paul literally begged Judge Older to let him proceed. "This is extremely important! I can't impress on the Court how important it is!" Because he was so desperate, I decided to back off, agreeing not to object if he would describe this as a hypothetical situation—"Imagine that this is happening"—and not as fact. He did so, after which Judge Older instructed the jury. They left the courtroom at 5:25 P.M. on Friday, March 26, 1971.

While I felt confident that the jury would return a death penalty verdict against Charles Manson, I was less sure when it came to the girls. Only four females had been executed in California history, none of them as young as the defendants.

I had anticipated that the jury would be out at least four days. When I received the call Monday afternoon, after only two days, I knew there could be only one verdict. It was too fast for anything else. Their actual deliberations, I later learned, had taken only ten hours.

Again under extraordinary security precautions, the jury was brought back into the courtroom, at 4:24 P.M. on Monday, March 29, with their verdicts.

Manson and the girls had been brought into the courtroom earlier—the three female defendants now, when it was too late to influence the jury, having shaved their heads also—but before the clerk could read the first verdict, Manson yelled, "I don't see how you can get by with this without letting me put on some kind of defense ... You people have no authority over me ... Half of you in here ain't as good as I am ..." and Older ordered him removed.

Manson's no-defense claim was nonsense. It was obvious that the defense he intended to put on during the guilt phase had been delivered in toto during the penalty phase. The jury's reaction to it was now being delivered, in a courtroom jammed with spectators and press.

The clerk read the first verdict: "We, the jury in the above-entitled action, having found the defendant Charles Manson guilty of murder in the first degree as charged in Count I of the Indictment, do now fix the penalty as death."

KRENWINKEL "You have just judged yourselves."

ATKINS "Better lock your doors and watch your own kids."

VAN HOUTEN "Your whole system is a game. You blind, stupid people. Your children will turn against you."

Judge Older had the three girls removed. They too listened over the loudspeaker as the clerk fixed the penalty for all four defendants as death on all counts.

Judge Older left the bench to shake hands with each juror. "If it were within the power of a trial judge to award a medal of honor to jurors," he told them, "believe me, I would bestow an award on each of you."

For the first time the jurors could speak to the press about their ordeal.

Jury foreman Herman Tubick told reporters that the jury was convinced "the motive was Helter Skelter." Mrs. Thelma McKenzie said the jury had "certainly tried" to find point upon which they could sentence the female defendants to a verdict less severe, "but we couldn't." William McBride remarked: "I felt sympathy for the women but sympathy can't interfere with justice. What they did deserves the death penalty." Marie Mesmer said she felt more pity for Susan Atkins than for the other two girls, because of her background, but that she was shocked when all three showed no signs of remorse. As for Manson, she said: "I wanted to protect society. I think Manson is a very dangerous influence." Jean Roseland, mother of three teenagers, two of them girls, said the most terrible part of the whole trial was Leslie Van Houten "looking at me with those big brown eyes." Mrs. Roseland was convinced Manson's power to manipulate others came not from within himself but "from the voids within the minds and souls of his followers."

Later *Life* ran an article entitled "The Manson Jury: End of a Long Ordeal."

Ironically, there appeared in the same issue an article entitled "Paul McCartney on the Beatles Breakup."

That there had been irreconcilable troubles within the group became apparent, McCartney said, while they were making the White Album.

Colonel Paul Tate was reported to have said, regarding the death sentence verdicts: "That's what we wanted. That's what we expected. But there's no jubilation in something like this, no sense of satisfaction. It's more a feeling that justice has been done. Naturally I wanted the death penalty. They took my daughter and my grandchild."

Mrs. Tate told reporters that she didn't believe any human being should have the power to take a life, that that was up to God.

Roman Polanski declined comment, as did the other relatives of the victims whom the media contacted.

Sandy, Cathy, and the other girls on the corner had threatened to burn themselves to death with gasoline if any of the four were given death sentences. They didn't carry out their threat, though all did later shave their heads.

On learning of the decision, Sandy looked into the TV cameras and screamed: *"Death? That's what you're all going to get!"*

With the exception of the sentencing, the trial was over. It had been the longest murder trial in American history, lasting nine and a half months; the most expensive, costing approximately $1 million; and the most highly publicized; while the jury had been sequestered 225 days, longer than any jury before it. The trial transcript alone ran to 209 volumes, 31,716 pages, approximately eight million words, a mini-library.

For almost everyone, the ordeal was not only long but expensive. A number of the jurors, anticipating that they would be paid by their employers, now found themselves either unpaid or without jobs. Mrs. Roseland, for example, claimed that TWA did not honor a verbal agreement to keep her on salary until the end of the trial, and estimated she lost about $2,700 in back pay. TWA denied there was any such agreement. There were several such denials.

The financial sacrifice on the part of the defense attorneys was enormous. Fitzgerald said: "It's just really wiped me out." He told a reporter that he had lost about $30,000 in income and incurred $10,000 in trial expenses. He had been forced to sell his stereo and other possessions, and had spent $5,000 which he didn't have. Six-times-married Daye Shinn said: "I'm behind in my house payments and child support and my alimonies." Shinn had received $19,000 in royalties from the Atkins book, he said, but he claimed that about $16,000 of it went back to the Manson Family. Kanarek refused to discuss his financial situation. Another of the defense attorneys did tell me, however, that at one point during the trial Manson had ordered Shinn to give Kanarek $5,000 from the Atkins account, to help defray his expenses, but how much more he received, if any, is unknown. Keith, who received a fee from the county, since he was court-appointed, admitted his private practice had gone downhill and that he didn't expect to gain any new clients as a result of the publicity.

The trial cost another attorney his life.

In the avalanche of stories on the Manson verdict, one small item which appeared that same day went almost unnoticed.

The Ventura County Sheriff's Office reported that they had found a body believed to be that of the missing defense attorney, Ronald Hughes. The badly decomposed corpse had been found face down, wedged between two boulders, in Sespe Creek, miles from where Hughes had last been seen alive.

Two fishermen had discovered the body early Saturday but didn't report it until Sunday night, because "we didn't want to spoil our fishing trip."

The cause of death was at this time unknown. Through our office, I ordered an immediate autopsy.

April 19, 1971

Judge Older had set Monday, April 19, 1971 as the date of sentencing.

There was speculation that Older might decide on his own to reduce at least some of the verdicts from death to life. In a previous case Older had done this for a defendant who had poured gasoline on two beds where four children were sleeping, killing one of them. However, I personally felt that since Older had complimented the jurors, he wouldn't turn right around and set aside their verdict.

On the nineteenth the Court heard, and rejected, a number of defense motions, including those for a new trial. Judge Older then asked the defendants if they had anything to say. Only Manson did.

Charlie's left hand was trembling and he seemed near tears. Very meekly, with a quivering voice, he said: "I accept this court as my father. I have always done my best in my life to uphold the laws of my father, and I accept my father's judgment."

THE COURT "After nine and a half months of trial, all of the superlatives had been used, all of the hyperbole has been indulged in, and all that remains are the bare, stark facts of seven senseless murders, seven people whose lives were snuffed out by total strangers . . .

"I have carefully looked, in considering this action, for mitigating circumstances, and I have been unable to find any . . .

"It is my considered judgment that not only is the death penalty appropriate, but it is almost compelled by the circumstances. I must agree with the prosecutor that if this is not a proper case for the death penalty, what would be?"

Speaking to Manson, Judge Older said: "The Department of Corrections is ordered to deliver you to the custody of the Warden of the State Prison of the State of California at San Quentin to be by him put to death in the manner prescribed by law of the State of California."

There was at this time no Death Row for women. A special isolation wing was being constructed at the California Institute for Women at Frontera, and Atkins, Krenwinkel, and Van Houten were sent there to await execution.

It was anticipated that the appeals would take at least two and possibly as long as five years.

In actuality, their fate would be decided in less than one.

After the sentencing, I didn't anticipate ever seeing Charles Manson again. But I'd see him twice more, the last time under very peculiar circumstances.

Epilogue

A SHARED MADNESS

"A more comprehensive description of her condition will necessitate further study. But at this time we might suggest the possibility that she may be suffering from a condition of *folie à famille*, a kind of shared madness within a group situation."

Dr. Joel Hochman,
in his psychiatric
report on Susan Atkins

"I lived with Charlie for one year straight and on and off for two years. I know Charlie. I know him inside and out. I became Charlie. Everything I once was, was Charlie. There was nothing left of me anymore. And all of the people in the Family, there's nothing left of them anymore, they're all Charlie too."*

Paul Watkins

"We are what you have made us. We were brought up on your TV. We were brought up watching 'Gunsmoke,' 'Have Gun Will Travel,' 'FBI,' 'Combat.' 'Combat' was my favorite show. I never missed 'Combat.' "*

Brenda

*From the Robert Hendrickson documentary film, *Manson*.

"Whatever is necessary, you do it. When somebody needs to be killed, there's no wrong. You do it, and then you move on. And you pick up a child and you move him to the desert. You pick up as many children as you can and you kill whoever gets in your way. That is us."*

Sandy

"If you find an apple that has a little spot on it, you cut out that spot."

Squeaky

"You just better hope I never get out."

Bobby Beausoleil

*From the Robert Hendrickson documentary film, *Manson.*

A Shared Madness

Although Manson and the girls had been convicted, the trials, and the murders, were not yet over.

For their part in the attempted murder of prosecution witness Barbara Hoyt, four of the five defendants served only ninety days in the County Jail, while the fifth escaped punishment entirely.

Although I was not assigned to the case, I questioned the way it was handled. Because it was felt that the evidence against the defendants was weak, and because of the expense of flying in witnesses from Hawaii, the DA's Office, LAPD, and the defense attorneys agreed to a "deal." In return for the defendants pleading "no contest" to one count of conspiracy to dissuade a witness from testifying, the prosecutor made a motion to reduce the charge from a felony to a misdemeanor. Judge Stephen Stothers granted the motion, and on April 16, 1971, he sentenced four of the five defendants—Lynette Fromme, aka Squeaky; Steve Grogan, aka Clem; Catherine Share, aka Gypsy; and Dennis Rice—to ninety days in the County Jail. Since they had already served fifteen days, they were back on the streets in seventy-five days.

The fifth defendant, Ruth Ann Moorehouse, aka Ouisch, the girl who actually gave Barbara Hoyt the LSD-laden hamburger, got off scot-free. When it came time for sentencing, she failed to appear. Although a bench warrant was issued for her arrest and she was known to be living in Carson City, Nevada, the DA's Office decided it wasn't worth the trouble to extradite her.

Of the five, three would later be involved in other murders, some attempted, some successful.

Charles "Tex" Watson went on trial in August 1971. A good portion of my preparation took place not in a law library but in a medical library, since I was relatively sure that Watson was going to plead not guilty by reason of insanity and put on a psychiatric defense.

The trial had three possible phases——guilt, sanity, and penalty—each of which presented its own special problems.

Even though defense attorney Sam Bubrick told me that Watson intended to take the stand and confess, I knew I still had to present a strong case during the guilt phase, since it was a safe bet that Watson's testimony would be self-serving. Too, I had to prove (by evidence such as Watson's instructing Linda to steal the $5,000) that although Watson was dominated by Manson, he still had enough independence to make him legally responsible for his acts. One of the key issues during the guilt trial, then, was whether Watson was suffering from diminished mental capacity at the time of the murders. If he was, and it was of such a nature that it prevented him from deliberating and premeditating, the jury would have to find the chief Tate-LaBianca killer guilty of second rather than first degree murder.

If convicted of any degree of criminal homicide, then there would be a sanity trial, in which the sole issue would be whether Watson was sane or insane at the time of the murders. I anticipated, and quite rightly, that the defense would call a number of prominent psychiatrists (eight were called), many of whom would testify that in their opinion Watson was insane. Therefore I'd not only have to subject their testimony to withering cross-examination, I'd also have to present an abundance of evidence showing that Watson was in full command of his mental faculties at the time of the murders and that he was well aware that in the eyes of society what he was doing was wrong. In short, I had to prove that he wasn't legally insane. Such evidence as his cutting of the telephone wires, his telling Linda to wipe the knives of fingerprints, his manner when talking to Rudolf Weber, and his using an alias when questioned by the authorities in Death Valley a few weeks after the murders thus became extremely important to proving my case, in that all were circumstantial evidence of a consciousness of wrongdoing and guilt on Watson's part.

If Watson was convicted of first degree murder and also found sane, then the jury would have to decide the ultimate question: whether he was to be given life or death. And this meant I would again face many of the same problems I had with the girls in the penalty phase of the earlier trial.

Still another problem was Watson's demeanor. In an obvious attempt to project a college-boy image, Watson dressed very conservatively in court—short hair, shirt and tie, blue blazer, slacks. But he still looked strange. His eyes were glassy, and never seemed to focus. He reacted not at all to the damning testimony of such witnesses as Linda Kasabian, Paul Watkins, Brooks Poston, and Dianne Lake. And his mouth was always slightly gaping, giving him the appearance of being mentally retarded.

Taking the stand on direct examination by the defense, Tex played the part of Manson's abject slave. He admitted shooting or stabbing six of the Tate-LaBianca victims, but denied stabbing Sharon Tate. And everything which showed either premeditation or deliberation he put on Manson or the girls.

My cross-examination so shook Tex that he often forgot he was supposed to be playing the idiot. By the time I'd finished, it was obvious to the jury that he was in complete command of his mental faculties and probably always had been. I also got him to admit that he had stabbed Sharon Tate too; that he didn't think of the victims as people but as "just blobs"; that he had told Dr. Joel Fort that the people at the Tate residence "were running around like chickens with their heads cut off," and that when he said this he had smiled; and I tore to shreds his story that he was simply an unthinking zombie programmed by Charles Manson, as well as cast considerable doubt on his claim that he now felt remorse for what he had done.

Watson's testimony cleared up some mysteries:

Contrary to the findings of LAPD evidence-expert DeWayne Wolfer, Watson identified the pair of red wire cutters found in Manson's dune buggy as the pair he had used to cut the Tate telephone wires that night.

Also revealed for the first time were Manson's exact instructions to Watson on the night of the murders at 10050 Cielo Drive. Watson testified: "Charlie called me over behind a car . . . and handed me a gun and a knife. He said for me to take the gun and knife and go up to where Terry Melcher used to live. He said to kill everybody in the house as gruesome as I could. I believe he said something about movie stars living there."

And Watson admitted that when he entered the LaBianca residence, he was already armed with a knife.

My greatest difficulty during the entire Watson trial came not from the evidence, the defense attorneys, or the defense witnesses, but from the judge, Adolph Alexander, who was a personal friend of defense attorney Sam Bubrick.

Alexander not only repeatedly favored the defense in his rulings, he went far beyond that. During voir dire he remarked: "Many of *us* are opposed to the death penalty." When prosecution witnesses were testifying, he gave them incredulous, unbelieving looks; when defense witnesses took the stand, he industriously took notes. All this was done right in front of the jury. He also frequently cross-examined the prosecution witnesses. Finally, I'd had it. Asking to approach the bench, I reminded Alexander that this was a jury trial, not a court trial, and that I was immensely concerned that by cross-examining the prosecution witnesses he was giving the jury the impression that he didn't believe the witnesses, and since a judge has substantial stature in the eyes of a jury, this could be extremely harmful to the People. I suggested that if he wanted to have certain questions asked, he write them out and give them to the defense attorneys to ask.

Thereafter Alexander cut down on his cross-examination of the prosecution witnesses. However, he still continued to amaze me. When the jury went out to deliberate, he didn't even have the exhibits sent back to the jury room—a virtually automatic act——until after I had demanded that he do so. And once, in chambers and off the record, he referred to the defendant as "poor Tex."

Also off the record was a remark I made to him toward the end of the trial: "You're the biggest single obstacle to my obtaining a conviction of first degree murder in this case."

Despite the problems presented by Judge Alexander, on October 12, 1971, the jury found Watson guilty of seven counts of first degree murder and one count of conspiracy to commit murder. That I had effectively destroyed the testimony of the defense psychiatrists on cross-examination was borne out by the fact that on October 19 it took the jury only two and a half hours to decide that Watson was sane. And on October 21, after remaining out only six hours, they returned with a verdict of death.

The trial had lasted two and a half months and cost a quarter of a million dollars. It also added another forty volumes, 5,916 pages, to the mini-library on the Tate-La-Bianca murders.

Although Judge Alexander thanked the jury for the conscientious job they had done, he remarked, on the day he sentenced Watson, "If I had tried this case without a jury, I possibly would have arrived at a different verdict."

In still other proceedings, Susan Atkins pleaded guilty to the murder of Gary Hinman and was given life imprisonment. In sentencing her, Judge Raymond Choate called her "a danger to any community," who should spend "her entire life in custody."

The defense obtained separate trials for Charles Manson, Bruce Davis, and Steve Grogan on the combined Hinman-Shea murder charges. Despite the fact that the body of Donald "Shorty" Shea hadn't been found (and hasn't to this day), prosecutors Burt Katz, Anthony Manzella, and Steven Kay succeeded in the difficult task of obtaining guilty verdicts against each of the defendants on all of the counts. Verdicts of life imprisonment were returned for Manson and Davis. The Grogan jury voted death, but when it came time for sentencing—two days before Christmas 1971—Judge James Kolts, commenting that "Grogan was too stupid and too hopped up on drugs to decide anything on his own," and declaring that it was really Manson "who decided who lived or died," reduced the sentence to life imprisonment.

During voir dire in his trial, Manson, angered by the judge's refusal to let him represent himself, told the Court: "I enter a plea of guilty. I chopped off Shorty's head." The judge refused to accept the plea, and the next day Manson withdrew it. During another angry outburst, Manson turned to the press and said, "I've told my people to start killing you."

Again Manson was represented by Irving Kanarek. With Irving, he knew it would be a long trial, postponing his trip to San Quentin's Death Row.

Through all the trials, the Manson girls continued their vigil on the corner of Temple and Broadway. Literally in the shadow of the Hall of Justice, in view of the thousands of people who passed that corner every day, they fashioned a bizarre plot to free all the imprisoned Manson Family members.

In late July of 1971 my co-author learned from a Family member in the San Francisco Bay Area that the Family was planning to break out Manson sometime within the next month. Though he was not told how they intended to accomplish this, he was given some additional details: the Family was stockpiling arms and ammunition; they had secretly rented a house in South Los Angeles and were hiding an escaped convict there; and with Manson's escape "Helter Skelter will really start; the revolution will be on."

Wishful thinking? I wasn't sure, and passed the information along to LAPD. When I did, I learned that among the witnesses Manson had called in the Hinman-Shea trial was a Folsom convict named Kenneth Como, also known by the colorful aka Jesse James. Though it hadn't been publicized, when brought to Los Angeles less than a week before, Como had managed to escape from the Hall of Records. LAPD doubted, however, that he was still in the area. As for the Manson escape, they had heard rumors also, but nothing definite. They were inclined to doubt the tale.

On schedule, less than a month later, the Manson Family made their attempt.

Shortly after closing time on the night of Saturday, August 21, 1971, six armed robbers entered the Western Surplus Store in the Los Angeles suburb of Hawthorne. While one kept a shotgun on the female clerk and two customers, the others began carrying rifles, shotguns, and pistols to a van parked in the alley outside. They had collected about 140 guns when they spotted the first police car. LAPD, alerted by a silent alarm, had already sealed off the alley.

The robbers came out shooting. In the ten-minute gun battle that followed, the van was riddled with over fifty bullets, and some twenty bullets crashed into the black-and-whites. Surprisingly, no one was killed, though three of the suspects received slight wounds.

All six robbers were Manson Family members. Apprehended were Mary Brunner, twenty-seven, first member of the Family; Catherine Share, aka Gypsy, twenty-nine, and Dennis Rice, thirty-two, both recently freed after serving ninety-day sentences for their part in the attempted silencing of Barbara Hoyt; Lawrence Bailey, aka Larry Jones, twenty-three, who was present the night the Tate killers left Spahn; and escaped convict Kenneth Como, thirty-three. Another Family member, Charles Lovett, nineteen, got away during the gun fight but was subsequently apprehended.

After their arrest it was learned that the same group was also responsible for the robbery of a Covina beer distributorship on August 13, which netted them $2,600.

The police surmised that through the robberies the group intended to get enough guns and ammunition to stage a San Rafael-type commando raid on the courthouse. Steve Grogan had called Manson as a witness in his trial. It was believed that the day Manson appeared in court the Family intended to storm the Hall of Justice, breaking out both.

Actually, the real plan was far more spectacular. And, given the right circumstances and enough public pressure, it just *might* have worked.

Although never made public before this, according to a Family member who was privy to the planning of the Hawthorne robbery, the real plan was as follows:

Using the stolen weapons, the Family was going to hijack a 747 and kill one passenger every hour until Manson and all the other imprisoned Family members were released.

Extraordinary security measures were taken during the trial of the Hawthorne robbery defendants, in part because the defense had called as witnesses what Judge Arthur Alarcon labeled "the biggest collection of murderers in Los Angeles County at one time." Twelve convicted killers, including Manson, Beausoleil, Atkins, Krenwinkel, Van Houten, Grogan, and Davis, took the stand. Their presence in one place made everyone a little nervous. Especially since by this time the Family had discovered that the Hall of Justice was not escapeproof.

In the early-morning hours of October 20, 1971, Kenneth Como hacksawed his way through the bars of his thirteenth-floor cell, climbed down to the eighth floor on a rope made of bed sheets, kicked in a window in the courtroom of Department 104 (where just a few months earlier I'd prosecuted Manson and his three female co-defendants), then left the building by way of the stairs. Sandra Good picked up Como in the Family van. Though Sandy later smashed up the van and was arrested, Como managed to elude capture for seven hours. Also arrested—but subsequently released, there being no positive proof that they had aided and abetted the escape—were Squeaky, Brenda, Kitty, and two other Family members.

No attempt was made to break out Manson during the Hawthorne trial. However, two of the jurors had to be replaced by alternates after receiving telephone threats that they would be killed if they voted for conviction. The calls were linked to an unidentified female Family member.

Although Gypsy and Rice had previously been given only ninety days for their part in the attempted murder of a prosecution witness, they and their co-defendants found that the courts take shooting at police officers a little more seriously. All were charged with two counts of armed robbery. Rice pleaded guilty and was sent to state prison. The others were convicted on both counts and given the following sentences: Lovett, two consecutive five-year-to-life terms; Share, ten years to life; Como, fifteen years to life; Brunner and Bailey, twenty years to life.

Sandra Good was subsequently tried for aiding and abetting an escape. Her attorney, the one and only Irving Kanarek, claimed she had been kidnapped by Como. The jury didn't buy it, and Sandy was given six months in jail.

The day Como escaped, Kanarek, appearing in Judge Raymond Choate's court, claimed in his patented way: "I allege with no proof at this particular time that this escape was deliberately allowed to take place."

Judge Choate asked Kanarek if he could explain why Como was forced to climb down a rope from the thirteenth to the eighth floor.

"That makes it look good, Your Honor," Kanarek explained.

While Manson was still on trial for the Hinman-Shea murders, I dropped into the courtroom one day. It was a welcome relief to be a spectator for a change.

Manson, who had recently taken to wearing a black storm trooper's uniform in court, spotted me and sent a message by the bailiff that he wanted to speak to me. There were a few things I wanted to ask him about also, so I stayed over after court recessed. Sitting in the prisoner's dock in the courtroom, we talked from 4:30 P.M. to nearly 6 P.M. None of the talk concerned the current charges against him. Mostly we discussed his philosophy. I was especially interested in learning the evolution of some of his ideas, and questioned him at length about his relationship with Scientology and with the satanic cult known as The Process, or the Church of the Final Judgement.

Manson had wanted to speak to me, he said, because he wanted me to know "I don't have no hard feelings." He told me that I had done "a fantastic, remarkable job" in convicting him, and he said, "You gave me a fair trial, like you promised." He was not bitter about the result, however, because to him "prison has always been my home; I didn't want to leave it the last time and you're only sending me back there." There were regular meals, not great, but better than the garbage at Spahn Ranch.

And since you don't have to work if you don't want to, he'd have plenty of time to play his guitar.

"That may be, Charlie, but you don't have any women there," I said.

"I don't need broads," he replied. "Every woman I ever had, *she* asked *me* to make love to her. I never asked them. I can do without them." There was plenty of sex in prison, he said.

Although Manson again claimed that the Beatles' music and LSD were responsible for the Tate-LaBianca murders, he admitted that he had known they were going to happen, "because I even knew what the mice were doing at Spahn Ranch." He then added, "So I said to them: 'Here, do you want this rope? Do you want this gun?' And later I told them not to tell anyone about what happened."

Though careful never to do so in open court, in our private conversations Manson often referred to blacks as "niggers." He claimed he didn't dislike them. "I don't hate anyone," he said, "but I know they hate me."

Returning to the familiar theme of Helter Skelter, I asked him when he thought the black man was going to take over.

"I may have put a clog in them," he replied.

"You mean the trial alerted whitey?"

His reply was a simple, and sad, "Yeah."

Our conversation took place on June 14, 1971. The following day one of the attorneys complained, and Judge Choate conducted an evidentiary hearing in open court. I testified to the gist of our conversation, noting that Manson had asked to speak to me, and not vice versa, and that the current charges were not discussed. There was nothing unethical about this, I observed. Moreover, I'd told Kanarek that Manson wanted to talk to me, but Kanarek had merely walked away.

The bailiff, Rusty Burrell, who had sat in on the conversation, staying overtime because he found it interesting, supported my account. As did Manson himself.

MANSON "The version the man [indicating me] gave was right on. I am almost sure Mr. Kanarek knew that I had asked to see him. I had wanted to speak to this man for the last year, and it was my request that motivated it."

As for the hearing itself, Manson said: "Your Honor, I don't think this is fair at all. You know, this was my mistake."

Agreeing, and ruling that there had been no impropriety involved, Judge Choate brought the hearing to an end.

The irony of all this was not lost on the press, which reported, with some incredulity, that Manson had taken the stand to defend the man who had convicted him of seven murders!

My interest in the sources of Manson's beliefs stretched back to my assignment to the case. Some of those sources have been mentioned earlier. Others, though inadmissible as evidence in the trial, have more than a passing interest, if only as clues to the genesis of such a sick obsession.

I knew, from Gregg Jakobson and others, that Manson was an eclectic, a borrower of ideas. I knew too, both from his prison records and from my conversations with him, that Manson's involvement with Scientology had been more than a passing fad. Manson told me, as he had Paul Watkins, that he had reached the highest stage, "theta clear," and no longer had any connection with or need for Scientology. I was inclined to accept at least the latter portion of his claim. In my rather extensive investigation, I found no evidence of any kind that Manson was involved with Scientology after his release from prison in 1967.* By this time, he had gone on to do his own thing.

What effect, if any, Scientology had on Manson's mental state cannot be measured. Undoubtedly he picked up from his "auditing" sessions in prison some knowledge of mind control, as well as some techniques which he later put to use in programming his followers.

Manson's link with The Process, or the Church of the

*One of Manson's chief disciples, Bruce Davis, was very closely involved with Scientology for a time, working in its London headquarters from about November or December of 1968 to April of 1969. According to a Scientology spokesman, Davis was kicked out of the organization for his drug use. He returned to the Manson Family and Spahn Ranch in time to participate in the Hinman and Shea slayings.

Final Judgement, is more tenuous, yet considerably more fascinating. The leader of the satanic cult is one Robert Moore, whose cult name is Robert DeGrimston. Himself a former disciple of Scientology founder L. Ron Hubbard, Moore broke with Scientology about 1963 to form his own group, after apparently attaining a high position in the London headquarters. He and his followers later traveled to various parts of the world, including Mexico and the United States, and for at least several months, and possibly longer, he lived in San Francisco. He also reportedly participated in a seminar at the Esalen Institute in Big Sur, though whether this coincided with any of Manson's visits there is unknown.

One of DeGrimston's most fervent disciples is one Victor Wild, a young leather goods manufacturer whose Process name is Brother Ely.

Up until December of 1967, Victor Wild's residence, and the San Francisco headquarters for The Process, was 407 Cole Street, in Haight-Ashbury.

From about April through July 1967, Charles Manson and his still fledgling Family lived just two blocks away, at 636 Cole. In view of Manson's curiosity, it appears very likely that he at least investigated the satanists, and there is fairly persuasive evidence that he "borrowed" some of their teachings.

In one of our conversations during the Tate-LaBianca trial, I asked Manson if he knew Robert Moore, or Robert DeGrimston. He denied knowing DeGrimston, but said he had met Moore. "You're looking at him," Manson told me. "Moore and I are one and the same." I took this to mean that he felt they thought alike.

Not long after this I was visited by two representatives of The Process, a Father John and a Brother Matthew. Having heard that I was asking questions about the group, they had been sent from their Cambridge, Massachusetts, headquarters to assure me that Manson and Moore had never met and that Moore was opposed to violence. They also left me a stack of Process literature. The following day the names "Father John" and "Brother Matthew" appeared on Manson's visitor's list. What they discussed is unknown. All I know is that in my last conversation with Manson, Charlie became evasive when I questioned him about The Process.

In 1968 and 1969, The Process launched a major recruiting drivc in the United States. They were in Los Angeles in May and June of 1968 and for at least several months in the fall of 1969, returning to England in about October, after claiming to have converted some two hundred American hippies to their sect. Manson was in Los Angeles during both periods. It is possible that there may have been some contact with Manson and/or his group, but I found no evidence of this. I'm inclined to think that Manson's contact with the group probably occurred in San Francisco in 1967, as indicated, at a time when his philosophy was still being formulated. I believe there was at least some contact, in view of the many parallels between Manson's teachings and those of The Process, as revealed in their literature.

Both preached an imminent, violent Armageddon, in which all but the chosen few would be destroyed. Both found the basis for this in the Book of Revelation. Both conceived that the motorcycle gangs, such as Hell's Angels, would be the troops of the last days. And both actively sought to solicit them to their side.

The three great gods of the universe, according to The Process, were Jehovah, Lucifer, and Satan, with Christ the ultimate unifier who reconciles all three. Manson had a simpler duality; he was known to his followers as both Satan and Christ.

Both preached the Second Coming of Christ, a not unusual belief, except in their interpretation of it. According to a Process pamphlet: "Through Love, Christ and Satan have destroyed their enmity and come together for the End: Christ to Judge, Satan to execute the Judgement." When Christ returned this time, Manson said, it would be the Romans, i.e., the establishment, who went up on the cross.

Manson's attiude toward fear was so curious I felt it to be almost unique. At least I felt that until reading in a special issue of *The Process* magazine devoted to fear:

"Fear is beneficial . . . Fear is the catalyst of action. It is the energiser, the weapon built into the game in the beginning, enabling a being to create an effect upon himself, to spur himself on to new heights and to brush aside the bitterness of failure." Though the wording differs, this is almost exactly what Manson preached.

Manson spoke frequently of the bottomless pit, The Process of the bottomless void.

Within the organization, The Process was called (at least until 1969) "the family," while its members were known as brothers, sisters, mothers, fathers.

The symbol of The Process is similar, though not identical, to the swastika Manson carved on his forehead.

Among the precepts of The Process which parallel Manson's own: "The Time of the End is now . . . The Ultimate Sin is to kill an animal . . . Christ said love your enemy. Christ's enemy was Satan. Love Christ and Satan . . . The Lamb and the Goat must come together. Pure Love descended from the Pinnacle of Heaven, united with Pure Hatred raised from the depths of Hell."

One former Process member, being interrogated by LAPD in connection with two motorcycle gang slayings (neither of which was connected with The Process), said of the cult, "They don't like anybody that they can't indoctrinate or anybody that is not with them. They are just totally against what they call the 'gray forces,' the rich establishment or the Negroes—"

Q. "Why don't they like Negroes?"

A. "I don't know. They just don't."

Q. "They have a natural hate for the Negro?"

A. "They have a natural hate but they would also like to use the Negro as a whole to begin some kind of militant thing . . . They are really good at picking out angry people."

This was merely the opinion of one disaffiliated member, and may well not be the official position of The Process itself, but the similarities to Manson's own philosophy are still chilling.

These are only some of the parallels I found. They are enough to convince me, at least, that even if Manson himself may never have been a member of The Process, he borrowed heavily from the satanic cult.*

Nor are these the only connections between the Manson Family and satanists.

Bobby Beausoleil was for a time closely associated with filmmaker Kenneth Anger, who was himself deeply involved in both the motorcycle gang mystique and the occult. Beausoleil starred in Anger's film *Lucifer Rising*, playing the part of Lucifer. This was before he ever met Manson.

In his psychiatric report on Susan Atkins, Dr. Joel Hochman wrote of a portion of her San Francisco period, apparently sometime in 1967 or 1968, before she too met Manson: "At this time she entered into what she now calls her Satanic period. She became involved with Anton LaVey, the Satanist.† She took a part in a commercial production of a witch's sabbath, and recalls the opening night when she took LSD. She was supposed to lie down in a coffin during the act, and lay down in it while hallucinating. She stated that she didn't want to come out, and consequently the curtain was 15 minutes late. She stated that she felt alive and everything else in the ugly world was dead. Subsequently, she stayed on her 'Satanic trip' [for] approximately eight months . . ."

During the Tate-LaBianca trial, Patricia Krenwinkel doodled. Her two favorite subjects, according to bailiff Bill Murray, were Devil's heads and the Mendes Goat, both satanist symbols.

Before he killed him, Charles "Tex" Watson told Voytek Frykowski: "I am the Devil and I'm here to do the Devil's business."

An apparently important influence on Manson, in both precept and example, was a dead man: Adolf Hitler. Manson looked up to Hitler and spoke of him often. He told his followers that "Hitler had the best answer to ev-

*There is at least one precept Manson did not borrow from the group: unmarried adherents are expected to remain chaste.

†LaVey, founder of the San Francisco–based First Church of Satan, is known, by those knowledgeable in such matters, more as a spectacular showman than as a demonic satanist. He has stated numerous times that he condemns violence and ritual sacrifice.

erything" and that he was "a tuned-in guy who leveled the karma of the Jews." Manson saw himself as no less a historical figure, a leader who would not only reverse the karma of the blacks but level all but his own Aryan race—his all-white, all-American Family.

There were both surface and substantive parallels between Hitler and Manson.

Both were vegetarians; both were little men; both suffered deep wounds in their youth, the psychological scars at least contributing to, if not causing, their deep hatred for society; both suffered the stigma of illegitimacy, in Manson's case because he himself was a bastard, in Hitler's because his father was.

Both were vagrant wanderers; both were frustrated, and rejected, artists; both liked animals more than people; both were deeply engrossed in the occult; both had others commit their murders for them.

Both were racists; yet there is some evidence that both also believed they carried the blood of the very people they despised. Many historians believe that Hitler was secretly obsessed with the fear that he had a Jewish ancestor. If Manson's prison records are correct, he may have believed his father was black.

Both surrounded themselves with bootlicking slaves; both sought out the weaknesses of others, and used them; both programmed their followers through repetition, repeating the same phrases over and over; both realized and exploited the psychological impact of fear.

Both had a favorite epithet for those they hated: Hitler's was "*Schweinehund*," Manson's was "pigs."

Both had eyes which their followers described as "hypnotic"; beyond that, however, both had a presence, a charisma, and a tremendous amount of personal persuasive power. Generals went to Hitler intent on convincing him that his military plans were insane; they left true believers. Dean Moorehouse went to Spahn Ranch to kill Manson for stealing his daughter, Ruth Ann; he ended up on his knees worshiping him.

Both had an incredible ability to influence others.

Both Manson's and Hitler's followers were able to explain away the monstrous acts their leaders committed by retreating into philosophical abstractions.

Probably the single most important influence on Hitler was Nietzsche. Manson told Jakobson that he had read Nietzsche. Whether true or not—Manson read with difficulty and Nietzsche is not easy reading—both Manson and Hitler believed in the three basic tenets of Nietzsche's philosophy: women are inferior to men; the white race is superior to all other races; it is not wrong to kill if the end is right.

And kill they both did. Both believed that mass murder was all right, even desirable, if it furthered the attainment of some grand plan. Each had such a plan; each had his own grandiose obsession: Hitler's was the Third Reich, Manson's was Helter Skelter.

At some point parallels become more than coincidence. How much of this was conscious borrowing on Manson's part, how much unconscious emulation, is unknown. I do believe that if Manson had had the opportunity, he would have become another Hitler. I can't conceive of his stopping short of murdering huge masses of people.

Some mysteries remain. One is the exact number of murders committed by members of the Manson Family.

Manson bragged to Juan Flynn that he had committed thirty-five murders. When Juan first told me this, I was inclined to doubt that it was anything more than sick boasting on Charlie's part. There is now evidence, however, that even if this wasn't true *then*, the total to date may be very close to, and may even exceed, Manson's estimate.

In November 1969, Susan Atkins told Ronnie Howard, "There are eleven murders that they will never solve." Leslie Van Houten used the same number in her interrogation by Mike McGann, while Ouisch told Barbara Hoyt that she knew of ten people the Family had killed "besides Sharon."

Susan told Virginia Graham that, in addition to the eight Hinman-Tate-LaBianca slayings, "there's more—and more before." One was undoubtedly Shea. Another was probably the "Black Panther" (Bernard Crowe), whom Susan, like Manson himself, erroneously believed dead.

Susan may have been referring to Crowe when, in the tape she made with Caballero, she said that the .22 caliber Longhorn revolver used in the Tate homicides had been used in "other killings," though on the tape this was clearly plural, not singular.

Susan also told Virginia, "There's also three people out in the desert that they done in." According to Virginia, Susan "just said it very nonchalant like, mentioning no names." When Steve Zabriske tried unsuccessfully to convince Portland police that a Charlie and a Clem were involved in both the Tate and the LaBianca murders, he also said that Ed Bailey had told him that he had seen this Charlie shoot a man in the head. The murder had occurred in Death Valley, according to Bailey, and the gun was a .45 caliber automatic. When interrogated by LAPD in May 1970, Bailey, t/n Edward Arthur Bailey, denied this. However, another source, who was for a time close to the Family, claims he heard "there are supposed to be two boys and a girl buried about eight feet deep behind Barker Ranch."

No bodies have ever been found. But then the body of Donald "Shorty" Shea has never been found either.

On October 13, 1968, two women, Clida Delaney and Nancy Warren, were beaten, then strangled to death with leather thongs a few miles south of Ukiah, California. Several members of the Manson Family were in the area at the time. Two days later Manson suddenly moved the whole Family from Spahn to Barker ranch. The Mendocino County Sheriff's Office believed there might be a link. But a belief is not evidence.

At about 3:30 A.M. on December 30, 1968, seventeen-year-old Marina Habe, daughter of writer Hans Habe, was abducted outside the West Hollywood home of her mother as she was returning home from a date. Her body was found on New Year's Day, off Mulholland near Bowmont Drive. Cause of death: multiple stab wounds in the neck and chest.

It has been rumored, but never confirmed, that the victim was acquainted with one or more members of the Family. Though most of his followers were at Barker Ranch, Manson was apparently in Los Angeles on December 30, returning to Barker the following day. Though several persons, including KNXT newscaster Carl George, believed there was a connection, nothing definite has been established, and the murder remains unsolved.

On the night of May 27, 1969, Darwin Orell Scott was hacked to death in his Ashland, Kentucky, apartment. The killing was so savage that the victim, who was stabbed nineteen times, was pinned to the floor with a butcher knife.

Sixty-four-year-old Darwin Scott was the brother of Colonel Scott, the man alleged to be Charles Manson's father.

In the spring of 1969 a motorcycle-riding guru from California who called himself "Preacher" appeared in the Ashland area with several female followers. Dispensing free LSD to local teen-agers, he attempted to set up a commune in an abandoned farmhouse near Huntington. He remained in the area until April, at which time vigilantes burned down the house and drove off the group, because, quoting the Ashland paper, "they didn't like hippies and didn't want any more around." At least four local residents later told reporters that Manson and Preacher were one and the same person. Despite their positive IDs, Manson's presence in California during at least part of this period is fairly well documented, and it would appear that he was in California on the day of Scott's murder.

On May 22, 1969, Manson telephoned his parole officer, Samuel Barrett, requesting permission to travel to Texas with the Beach Boys. Permission was withheld pending verification of Manson's employment with the group. In a letter dated May 27, the same day as Scott's murder, Manson said that the group had left without him and that he had moved from Death Valley back to Spahn Ranch. To categorize Barrett's control over Manson as minimal would be an exaggeration. Barrett did not again talk to Manson until June 18.

Barrett did not note the postmark on the letter. He did note that he didn't receive it until June 3, seven days after it was supposedly written. It is possible that Manson was using the letter as an alibi; it is also possible that he sent one of his killers to murder Scott. But both possibilities are strictly conjecture. The murder of Darwin Scott also remains unsolved.

Early on the morning of July 17, 1969, sixteen-year-old Mark Walts left his parents' home in Chatsworth and hitchhiked to the Santa Monica Pier to go fishing. His pole was later found on the pier. His body was found about 4 A.M. on July 18, off Topanga Canyon Boulevard a short distance from Mulholland. Young Walts' face and head were badly bruised and he had been shot three times in the chest by a .22 caliber weapon.

Though neither a ranch hand nor a Family member, Walts occasionally hung around Spahn Ranch. Although LASO sent investigators to Spahn, they were unable to uncover any evidence linking the killing to anyone there.

Walts' brother, however, called the ranch and told Manson, "I know you done my brother in, and I'm going to kill you." Though he didn't carry through, he obviously felt Manson was responsible.

When Danny DeCarlo had his marathon session with LAPD, he was asked: "What do you know about a sixteen-year-old boy that was shot?"

DeCarlo replied: "That had nothing to do with anybody up there. I'll tell you why, because they were just as shocked about it [as I was]. If they had done it they would have told me."

DeCarlo informed the officers about the brother's call. One asked: "Why do you think he suspected Charlie?" DeCarlo replied: "Because there aren't too many maniacs on the street that would just pull a gun on someone and blow their head off for no reason at all."

LAPD didn't pursue it further, since this was LASO's case. The murder remains unsolved.

In a period of one month—between July 27 and August 26, 1969—Charles Manson and his murderous Family slaughtered nine people: Gary Hinman, Steven Parent, Jay Sebring, Abigail Folger, Voytek Frykowski, Sharon Tate, Leno LaBianca, Rosemary LaBianca, and Donald Shea.

Though it is known that a number of female Family members were involved in the "cleanup" operation that followed Shea's murder, none has ever been tried as an accessory after the fact. Some are still on the streets today.

Manson's arrest on October 12, 1969, did not stop the murders.

As already mentioned, on November 5, 1969, John Philip Haught, aka Christopher Jesus, aka Zero, was shot to death in a beach house in Venice. The four Family members still present when the police arrived claimed he had killed himself while playing Russian roulette. Linda Baldwin, aka Little Patty, t/n Madaline Joan Cottage, said she had been lying on the bed next to him when it happened. The others—Bruce Davis; Susan Bartell, aka Country Sue; and Cathy Gillies—all told the officers they hadn't witnessed the act but had heard the shot.

At least one, and possibly all, lied.

During the penalty phase of the Tate-LaBianca trial, I asked Cathy: "You said that Zero shot himself. Who told you that? Certainly not Zero."

A. "Nobody had to tell me. I saw it happen."

Q. "Oh, you were present?"

A. "Yes."

Q. "Can you explain how it happened?"

A. "I was talking to him and he walked into the next room. Little Patty was lying on the bed. He sat down on the bed next to her. He reached over, grabbed the gun, and shot himself."

Q. "Just like that?"

A. "Yes."

Q. "Out of a clear blue sky?"

A. "Right out of a clear blue sky."

Three big questions remain: why was Zero playing Russian roulette with a fully loaded gun; why, if he took the gun out of the leather case, was the case clean of prints; and why, though Bruce Davis admitted picking up the gun, were neither his prints nor those of Zero on it?

About a week after the story of Manson's involvement in the Tate-LaBianca murders broke in the press, Los Angeles *Times* reporter Jerry Cohen was contacted by a man who claimed he had been present when Zero was shot.

Only Zero hadn't been playing Russian roulette; he had been murdered.

The man was about twenty-five, five feet eight, blond, of slight build. He refused to give Cohen his name. He was, he admitted, "scared to death."

Six or eight persons had been in the Venice pad that night, smoking hash. "It was one of the chicks that killed Zero," he told Cohen. But he wouldn't say which one, only that recently, at another Manson Family gathering, she had sat staring at him for three hours, all the while fingering her knife.

In questioning him, Cohen established that he had become involved with the Family after the Tate-LaBianca murders. He had never met Manson, he said, but he had heard from other Family members that there had been "many more murders than the police know of" and that "the Family is a whole lot larger than you think."

The youth wanted money to get to Marin County, in Northern California. Cohen gave him twenty-five dollars, implying there would be more if he returned to identify Zero's murderer. He never saw him again.

On November 16, 1969, the body of a young girl was found dumped over an embankment at Mulholland and Bowmont Drive near Laurel Canyon, in almost the same spot where Marina Habe's body was found. A brunette in her late teens, five feet nine, 115 pounds, she had been stabbed 157 times in the chest and throat. Ruby Pearl remembered seeing the girl with the Family at Spahn, and thought her name was "Sherry." Though the Manson girls traded aliases often, LASO was able to identify only one Sherry, Sherry Ann Cooper, aka Simi Valley Sherri. She had fled Barker Ranch at the same time as Barbara Hoyt and was, fortunately, still alive. The victim, who had been dead less than a day, became Jane Doe 59 in police files. Her identity is still unknown.

The proximity in time of her death to that of Zero suggests the possibility that she may have been present at the murder, then killed so she wouldn't talk. But this is strictly conjecture, and there is no evidence to support it. Her murder remains unsolved.

On November 21, 1969, the bodies of James Sharp, fifteen, and Doreen Gaul, nineteen, were found in an alley in downtown Los Angeles. The two teen-agers had been killed elsewhere, with a long-bladed knife or bayonet, then dumped there. Each had been stabbed over fifty times.

Ramparts Division Lieutenant Earl Deemer investigated the Sharp-Gaul murders, as did Los Angeles *Times* reporter Cohen. Although the two men felt there was a good possibility that a Family member was involved in the slayings, the murders remain unsolved.

Both James Sharp and Doreen Gaul were Scientologists, the latter a Scientology "clear" who had been residing in a Church of Scientology house. According to unconfirmed reports, Doreen Gaul was a former girl friend of Manson Family member Bruce Davis, himself an ex-Scientologist.

Davis' whereabouts at the times of the murders of Sharp, Gaul, and Jane Doe 59 are not known. He disappeared shortly after being questioned in connection with the death of Zero.

On December 1, 1969, Joel Dean Pugh, husband of Family member Sandy Good, was found with his throat slit in a London hotel room. As noted, local police ruled the death a suicide. On learning of Pugh's demise, Inyo County DA Frank Fowles made official inquiries, specifically asking Interpol to check visas to determine if one Bruce Davis was in England at the time.

Scotland Yard replied as follows: "It has been established that Davis is recorded as embarking at London airport for the United States of America on 25th April 1969 while holding United States passport 612 2568. At this time he gave his address as Dormer Cottage, Felbridge, Surrey. This address is owned by the Scientology Movement and houses followers of this organization.

"The local police are unable to give any information concerning Davis but they understand that he has visited our country more recently than April 1969. However, this is not borne out by our official records."

Davis did not reappear until February 1970, when he was picked up at Spahn Ranch, questioned briefly on the Inyo County grand theft auto charges, then released. After the grand jury indicted him for the Hinman murder, he vanished again, this time not surfacing until December 2, 1970, four days after the mysterious disappearance of Ronald Hughes. As mentioned, when he gave himself up he was accompanied by Family member Brenda McCann.

With three exceptions, these are all the known murders which have been proven, or are suspected to be, linked to the Manson Family. Are there more? I've discussed this with officers from LAPD and LASO, and we tend to think that there probably are, because these people liked to kill. But there is no hard evidence.

As for those three other murders, two of them occurred as late as 1972.

On November 8, 1972, a hiker near the Russian River resort community of Guerneville, in Northern California, saw a hand protruding from the ground. When police exhumed the body, it was found to be that of a young man wearing the dark-blue tunic of a Marine dress uniform. He had been shotgunned and decapitated.

The victim was subsequently identified as James T. Willett, twenty-six, a former Marine from Los Angeles County. This information appeared on radio and TV newscasts on Friday, November 10.

On Saturday, November 11, Stockton, California, police spotted Willett's station wagon parked in front of a house at 720 West Flora Street. When refused entry to the house, they broke in, arresting two men and two women and confiscating a number of pistols and shotguns.

Both women had Manson Family X's on their foreheads. They were Priscilla Cooper, twenty-one, and Nancy Pitman, aka Brenda McCann, twenty. A few minutes after police entered the residence, a third female called, asking to be picked up and given a ride to the house. The police obliged, and also arrested Lynette Fromme, aka Squeaky, twenty-four, ex-officio leader of the Family in Manson's absence.

The two men were Michael Monfort, twenty-four, and James Craig, thirty-three, both state prison escapees wanted for a number of armed robberies in various parts of California. Both had the letters "AB" tattooed on their left breasts. According to a spokesman for the state Department of Corrections, the initials stood for the Aryan Brotherhood, described as "a cult of white prison inmates, dedicated largely to racism but also involved in hoodlum activities, including murder contracts . . ."

While in the house, the police noticed freshly turned earth in the basement. After obtaining a search warrant, they began digging, and early the following morning exhumed the body of Lauren Willett, nineteen. She had been shot once in the head, her death occurring either late Friday night or early Saturday morning, not long after the identity of her slain husband was revealed on news broadcasts.

Questioned by the police, Priscilla Cooper claimed that Lauren Willett had killed herself "playing Russian roulette."

Although, like Zero, Mrs. Willett was not able to contradict this story, the Stockton police were far more skeptical than had been LASO. The three women and two men were charged with her murder.

They were scheduled to go on trial in May 1973. On April 2, however, four of the five surprised the Court by entering guilty pleas. Michael Monfort, who pleaded guilty to the murder of Lauren Willett, was sentenced to seven years to life in state prison. Superior Court Judge James Darrah also ordered consecutive terms of up to five years and two years for James Craig, who had pleaded guilty to being an accessory after the fact to murder and to possessing an illegal weapon, i.e., a sawed-off shotgun. Both girls also pleaded guilty to being an accessory after the fact, and both Priscilla Cooper and Nancy Pitman, aka Brenda, who Manson once indicated to me was his chief candidate for Family assassin, were sent to state prison for up to five years.

Still another Family member, Maria Alonzo, aka Crystal, twenty-one, arrested while trying to smuggle a switchblade knife into the Stockton jail, was subsequently released.

As was Squeaky. There being insufficient evidence to link Lynette Fromme to Lauren Willett's murder, the charges against her were dropped and she was freed, to again assume leadership of the Manson Family.

Monfort, and an accomplice, William Goucher, twenty-three, subsequently pleaded guilty to second degree murder in the death of James Willett, and were sent to state prison for five years to life. Craig, who pleaded guilty to being an accessory after the fact to the murder, was given another prison term of up to five years.

The motive for the two murders is not known. It is known that the Willetts had been associated with the Manson Family for at least a year, and possibly longer. Police surmised that Lauren Willett was killed after learning of the murder of her husband, to keep her from going to the police. As for the murder of James Willett, the official police theory is that Willett himself may have been about to inform about the robberies the group had committed.

There is another possibility. It may be that both James and Lauren Willett were killed because they knew too much about still another murder.

James and Lauren. Something about those first names seemed familiar. Then it connected. On November 27, 1970, a James Forsher and a Lauren Elder drove defense attorney Ronald Hughes to Sespe Hot Springs. After Hughes disappeared, the couple were questioned but not polygraphed, the police being satisfied that when they left the flooded area Hughes was still alive.

At first I thought "Elder" might be Lauren Willett's maiden name, but it wasn't. Nor, in checking the police reports and newspaper articles, was I able to find any description of Forsher and Elder. All I did find were their ages, both given as seventeen, and an address, from which I subsequently learned they had long since moved. All other efforts to track them down were unsuccessful.

It appears unlikely that James Forsher and James Willett were the same person: Willett would have been twenty-four in 1970, not seventeen. But Lauren is a decidedly uncommon name. And, nineteen in 1972, she would have been seventeen in 1970.

Coincidence? There had been far stranger ones in this case.

One thing is now known, however. If an admission by one of Manson's most hard-core followers is correct, Ronald Hughes *was* murdered by the Manson Family.

It was some weeks after the conclusion of the Tate-LaBianca trial before I received the autopsy report I'd requested from Ventura County. The identification, made through dental X-rays, was positive. The body was that of Ronald Hughes. Yet the rest of the autopsy report added little to the newspaper accounts. It noted: "The decedent was observed face down in a pool of water with the head and shoulder wedged under a large rock." One arm was almost completely severed at the shoulder, and there were large open areas in the chest and back. Other than this, "no outward evidence of violence was noted" while "no evidence of foul play [was] indicated by the X-rays." All this was qualified more than a little by the fact that the body was badly decomposed. As for the report's primary findings, there were none: "Nature of death: Undetermined. Cause of death: Undetermined."

The report did note that the stomach contained some evidence of "medication residue." But its exact composition—drugs, poison, whatever—was, like the nature and cause of death, left undetermined.

Completely dissatisfied with the report, I requested that our office conduct an investigation into the death of Hughes. The request was denied, it being decided that since there was no evidence of foul play, such an investigation was unnecessary.

There the matter remained, until very recently. While the Tate-LaBianca trial was still in progress, motion-picture director Laurence Merrick began work on a documentary on the Manson Family. The film, simply titled *Manson*, dealt only briefly with the murders and focused primarily on life at Spahn and Barker ranches. I narrated a few segments, and there were interviews with a number of Manson's followers. The movie was shown at the Venice Film Festival in 1972 and nominated for an Academy Award the following year. During its filming Merrick gained the confidence of the Manson girls. Sandra Good admitted, for example, on film, that when she and

Mary Brunner learned of the Tate murders, while still in the Los Angeles County Jail, "Mary said, 'Right on!' and I said, 'Wow, looks like we did it!' "

Off camera, and unrecorded, Sandy made a number of other admissions to Merrick. She told him, in the presence of one other witness, that to date the Family had killed "thirty-five to forty people." And that "Hughes was the first of the retaliation murders."

The trials did not write finis to the Manson saga. As Los Angeles *Times* reporter Dave Smith observed in *West* magazine: "To pull the curtain over the Manson case is to deny ourselves any possible hint of where the beast may come from next, and so remain afraid of things that go bump in the night, the way we were in August of 1969."

Mass murders have occurred throughout history. Since the Tate-LaBianca slayings, in California alone: labor contractor Juan Corona has been convicted of killing twenty-five migrant farm workers; John Linley Frazier slaughtered Dr. Victor Ohta, his wife, two of his sons, and his secretary, then dumped their bodies in the Ohta swimming pool; in a rampage that lasted several months, Herbert Mullin killed thirteen persons, ranging in age from three to seventy-three; Edmund Kemper III, ruled insane after slaying his grandmother and grandfather, was ruled sane and released, to later kill his mother, one of her friends, and six college coeds; and a possible total of seventeen murders has been attributed to two young ex-convict drifters.

With the exception of the latter pair, however, these were the work of loners, obviously deranged, if not legally insane, individuals, who *committed the murders by themselves.*

The Manson case was, and remains, unique. If, as Sandra Good claimed, the Family has to date committed thirty-five to forty murders, this may be near the U.S. record. Yet it is not the number of victims which makes the case intriguing and gives it its continuing fascination, but a number of other elements for which there is probably no collective parallel in the annals of American crime: the prominence of the victims; the months of speculation, conjecture, and pure fright before the killers were identified; the incredibly strange motive for the murders, to ignite a black-white Armageddon; the motivating nexus between the lyrics of the most famous rock group ever, the Beatles, and the crimes; and, behind it all, pulling the strings, a Mephistophelean guru who had the unique power to persuade *others to murder for him*, most of them young girls who went out and savagely murdered total strangers at his command, with relish and gusto, and with no evident signs of guilt or remorse—all these things combine to make Manson perhaps the most frightening mass murderer and these murders perhaps the most bizarre in American history.

How Manson gained control remains the most puzzling question of all.

During the Tate-LaBianca trials, the issue was not so much how he did this but proving that he did it. Yet in understanding the whole Manson phenomenon, the *how* is extremely important.

We have some of the answers.

During the course of his wanderings Manson probably encountered thousands of persons. Most chose not to follow him, either because they sensed that he was a very dangerous man or because they did not respond to the sick philosophy he preached.

Those who did join him were not, as noted, the typical girl or boy next door. Charles Manson was not a Pied Piper who suddenly appeared on the basketball court at Texas State, handed Charles Watson a tab of LSD, then led him into a life of crime. Watson had quit college with only a year to go, gone to California, immersed himself in the selling as well as the using of drugs, before he ever met Charles Manson. Not just Watson but nearly every other member of the Family had dropped out before meeting Manson. Nearly all had within them a deep-seated hostility toward society and everything it stood for which pre-existed their meeting Manson.

Those who chose to go with him did so, Dr. Joel Hochman testified, for reasons "which lie within the individuals themselves." In short, there was a need, and Manson seemed to fulfill it. But it was a double process of selection. For Manson decided who stayed. Obviously he did not want anyone who he felt would challenge his authority, cause dissension in the group, or question his dogma. They chose, and Manson chose, and the result was the Family. Those who gravitated to Spahn Ranch and stayed did so because basically they thought and felt alike. This was his raw material.

In shaping that material into a band of cold-blooded assassins who were willing to vent, for him, his enormous hostility toward society, Manson employed a variety of techniques.

He sensed, and capitalized on, their needs. As Gregg Jakobson observed, "Charlie was a man of a thousand faces" who "related to all human beings on their level of need." His ability to "psych out" people was so great that many of his disciples felt he could read their minds.

I doubt seriously if there was any "magic" in this. Having had many, many years to study human nature in prison, and being the sophisticated con man that he is, Manson probably realized that there are certain problems that nearly every human being is beset with. I strongly suspect that his "magical powers" were nothing more, and nothing less, than the ability to utter basic truisms to the right person at the right time. For example, any girl, if she is a runaway, has probably had problems with her father, while anyone who came to Spahn Ranch was searching for something. Manson made it a point to find out what that something was, and supply at least a semblance of it, whether it was a father surrogate, a Christ figure, a need for acceptance and belonging, or a leader in leaderless times.

Drugs were another of his tools. As brought out in the psychiatric testimony during the trials, LSD was not a causal agent but a catalyst. Manson used it very effectively, to make his followers more suggestible, to implant ideas, to extract "agreements." As Paul Watkins told me, Charlie always took a smaller dose of LSD than the others, so he would remain in command.

He used repetition. By constantly preaching and lecturing to his subjects on an almost daily basis, he gradually and systematically erased many of their inhibitions. As

Manson himself once remarked in court: "You can convince anybody of anything if you just push it at them all of the time. They may not believe it 100 percent, but they will still draw opinions from it, especially if they have no other information to draw their opinions from."

Therein lies still another of the keys he used: in addition to repetition, he used isolation. There were no newspapers at Spahn Ranch, no clocks. Cut off from the rest of society, he created in this timeless land a tight little society of his own, with its own value system. It was holistic, complete, and totally at odds with the world outside.

He used sex. Realizing that most people have sexual hangups, he taught, by both precept and example, that in sex there is no wrong, thereby eradicating both their inhibitions and their guilt.

But there was more than sex. There was also love, a great deal of love. To overlook this would be to miss one of the strongest bonds that existed among them. The love grew out of their sharing, their communal problems and pleasures, their relationship with Charlie. They were a real family in almost every sense of that word, a sociological unit complete to brothers, sisters, substitute mothers, linked by the domination of an all-knowing, all-powerful patriarch. Cooking, washing dishes, cleaning, sewing—all the chores they had hated at home they now did willingly, because they pleased Charlie.

He used fear, very, very effectively. Whether he picked up this technique in prison or later is not known, but it was one of his most effective tools for controlling others. It may also have been something more. As Stanford University professor Philip Zimbardo, a long-time student of crime and its effects, noted in a *Newsweek* article: "By raising the level of fear around you, your own fear seems more normal and socially acceptable." Manson's own fear bordered on paranoia.

He taught them that life was a game, a "magical mystery tour." One day they would be pirates with cutlasses, slashing at anyone who dared board their imaginary ship; the next they'd change costumes and identities and become Indians stalking cowboys; or devils and witches casting spells. A game. But there was always a pattern behind it:

them versus us. Dr. Hochman testified: "I think that historically the easiest way to program someone into murdering is to convince them that they are alien, that they are them and we are us, and that they are different from us."

Krauts. Japs. Gooks. Pigs.

With the frequent name changing and role playing, Manson created his own band of schizophrenics. Little Susan Atkins, who sang in the church choir and nursed her mother while she was dying of cancer, couldn't be held responsible for what Sadie Mae Glutz had done.

He brought to the surface their latent hatred, their inherent penchant for sadistic violence, focusing it on a common enemy, the establishment. He depersonalized the victims by making them symbols. It is easier to stab a symbol than a person.

He taught his followers a completely amoral philosophy, which provided complete justification for their acts. If everything is right, then nothing can be wrong. If nothing is real, and all of life is a game, then there need be no regret.

If they needed something that couldn't be found in the garbage bins or communal clothing pile, they stole it. Step by step. Panhandling, petty theft, prostitution, burglaries, armed robberies, and, last of all, for no motive of gain but because it was Charlie's will, and Charlie's will is Man's Son, the final step, the ultimate act of defiance of the establishment, the most positive proof of their total commitment—murder.

Comedians punned that "the family that slays together stays together." But behind the grim jest there was truth. Knowing they had violated the strictest of all commandments created a bond not less but more binding in that it was *their* secret.

He used religion. Not only did he find support for much of his philosophy in the Bible, he often implied that he was the Second Coming of Christ. He had his twelve apostles, several times over; not one but two Judases, Sadie and Linda; his retreat to the desert, Barker Ranch; and his trial, in the Hall of Justice.

He also used music, in part because he was a frustrated

musician but also because he must have known it was the one thing that could get through to more young people than any other.

He used his own superior intelligence. He was not only older than his followers, he was brighter, more articulate and savvy, far more clever and insidious. With his prison background, his ever adaptable line of con, plus a pimp's knowledge of how to manipulate others, he had little trouble convincing his naïve, impressionable followers that it was not they but society which was sick. This too was exactly what they wanted to hear.

All of these factors contributed to Manson's control over others. But when you add them all up, do they equal murder without remorse? Maybe, but I tend to think that there is something more, some missing link that enabled him to so rape and bastardize the minds of his followers that they would go against the most ingrained of all commandments, Thou shalt not kill, and willingly, even eagerly, murder at his command.

It may be something in his charismatic, enigmatic personality, some intangible quality or power that no one has yet been able to isolate and identify. It may be something he learned from others. Whatever it is, I believe Manson has full knowledge of the formula he used. And it worries me that we do not. For the frightening legacy of the Manson case is that it could happen again.

I believe Charles Manson is unique. He is certainly one of the most fascinating criminals in American history, and it appears unlikely that there will ever be another mass murderer quite like him. But it does not take a prophet to see at least some of the potentials of his madness in the world today. Whenever people unquestioningly turn over their minds to authoritarian figures to do with as they please—whether it be in a satanic cult or some of the more fanatic offshoots of the Jesus Movement, in the right wing or the far left, or in the mind-bending cults of the new sensitivity—those potentials exist. One hopes that none of these groups will spawn other Charles Mansons. But it would be naïve to suggest that the chilling possibility does not exist.

There are some happy endings to the Manson story. And some not so happy.

Both Barbara Hoyt and Dianne Lake returned to and graduated from high school, with apparently few if any permanent scars from their time with Manson. Barbara is now studying to be a nurse.

Stephanie Schram has her own dog-grooming shop. Paul Watkins and Brooks Poston formed their own combo and appear at various clubs in the Inyo County area. Their songs were good enough to be used as background music in the Robert Hendrickson documentary film on Manson.

After the fire George Spahn sold his ranch to an investment firm, which planned to turn it into a dude ranch for German visitors to the United States. He's since purchased another ranch, near Klamath Falls, Oregon, and Ruby Pearl is running it for him.

I haven't heard from Juan Flynn recently, but I'm not worried about him. Juan was always able to take care of himself. Though I last saw him in my office, for some reason I visualize him on a big white horse, his pretty girl friend behind him holding on for dear life as they gallop off into the sunset. Which, I suspect, is Juan's own image of himself.

Since the murder of his wife, Roman Polanski has produced several motion pictures, including a new version of *Macbeth*. Critics noticed in his interpretation disturbing parallels to the Tate murders. Polanski himself posed for an *Esquire* interview, holding aloft a shiny knife, and, according to the press, he has recently moved back to Los Angeles, into a home not far from 10050 Cielo Drive.

Polanski's attorney, working in conjunction with LAPD, divided the $25,000 reward as follows: Ronnie Howard and Virginia Graham each received $12,000, while Steven Weiss, the young boy who found the .22 caliber murder weapon, received $1,000.

Neither Danny DeCarlo nor Alan Springer was around to share in the reward. Shortly before the Watson trial, Danny skipped bail on the federal gun charge and fled to Canada; his exact whereabouts are unknown. According to LAPD, biker Al Springer simply "vanished." It is not known whether he is alive or dead.

Ronnie Howard tried working as a cocktail waitress but found it difficult to hold a job. Everywhere she went, she said, she was identified as the "Manson case snitch." Several times she was beaten up on her way home from work, and one night someone fired a bullet through the living-room window of her apartment, missing her head by inches. The would-be assailant was never identified. The next day she told reporters: "I should have kept my mouth shut in the first place."

Virginia Graham had a job as a receptionist in a legal office and seemed well on the way to rehabilitation, when she jumped parole. As this is written, she is still a fugitive.

Seven months after reporter Bill Farr declined to tell Judge Older who gave him the Virginia Graham statement regarding the "celebrity murders" the Manson Family had planned, Judge Older called Farr back into court and ordered him to either do so or be found in contempt.

Under California law the confidentiality of a reporter's news source is protected. However, since the Tate-LaBianca trial, Farr had left the Los Angeles *Herald Examiner* and was now working in a press secretary job. Older said that since he was no longer a reporter he was no longer protected by the law.

Farr argued—and I feel quite persuasively—that if Older's order was permitted to stand, both the news media and the public would suffer, since, if not guaranteed anonymity, many persons would decide not to provide essential information to the press. On both constitutional grounds and his own personal convictions, Farr declined to identify his sources. He did state, on the advice of his attorneys, that he had obtained copies of the Graham statement from two lawyers and another person subject to the gag order. But he declined to name them.

Under orders from Judge Older, defense attorneys Daye Shinn, Irving Kanarek, and Paul Fitzgerald, and prosecutors Steven Kay, Donald Musich, and I all took the stand. All six denied under oath giving the statement to Farr. All I know is that I didn't give Farr the statement.

Judge Older held Farr in civil contempt and sentenced

him to an indefinite jail term. He later served forty-eight days in the Los Angeles County Jail before being freed by an order by U.S. Supreme Court Justice William O. Douglas pending the outcome of a new appeal.

Had Farr been cited for criminal contempt and given consecutive sentences, the maximum penalty would have been sixty-five days in jail and a fine of $6,500. But Older cited him for civil contempt, and gave him an indefinite sentence, which could mean that if Older remains adamant, and the higher courts rule against Farr, he could remain in jail for as long as fifteen years, until fifty-five-year-old Charles Older reaches seventy, the mandatory age of retirement!

Many, though not all, of the hard-core Manson Family members are now serving time in various penal institutions. Other Family members split to follow new leaders. Cathy Gillies, according to the last information I received, was a "mom" with one of the motorcycle gangs. Still others continue to make headlines. Maria Alonzo, aka Crystal, who was released shortly after the Stockton murder, was arrested in March 1974 and charged with allegedly plotting to kidnap a foreign consul general in an attempt to secure the release of two prisoners in the Los Angeles County Jail. As this is written, she has yet to be brought to trail.

For a time there was a spate of books, plays, and motion pictures which, if not glorifying Manson, depicted him in a not wholly unfavorable light. And, for a time, it looked as if a Manson cult was emerging. Not only were there buttons reading "FREE THE MANSON FOUR," that cancerous growth known as the Family again began growing. When interviewed, the new converts—who had never had any personal contact with Manson—looked and talked exactly like Squeaky, Sandy, and the others, giving rise to the very disturbing possibility that Manson's madness might be communicable. But the strange phase quickly passed, and there is little left of the Manson Family now, though little Squeaky, chief cheerleader of the Manson cause, is still keeping the faith.

Although undisputed leader of the Family while Charlie

is in absentia, and presumably involved in the planning of their activities, and though arrested more than a dozen times on charges ranging from robbery to murder, she has only been convicted a few times, and always on minor charges. Moreover, not long ago she found a champion in, of all places, the District Attorney's Office in Los Angeles.

One of the young deputy DAs, William Melcher, first became acquainted with Squeaky while the group was holding its vigil on the corner of Temple and Broadway. For Christmas 1970, Melcher's wife baked cookies for the Manson girls, and a friendship developed. Not long after Squeaky was released on the Stockton murder charge, she was rearrested as a suspect in a Granada Hills armed robbery. Convinced they had the wrong person, Melcher successfully proved this to the police and she was freed. Clearing her was, Melcher told the Los Angeles *Times*, "my greatest satisfaction in three years as a prosecutor." Noting that the group had "a lot of ill-feeling about the police and courts, I wanted them to know that justice also works on their side of the street." Someday he would like to write a book on the girls, Melcher added. "I'd like to write not an exposé of the tragedy and violence, which I do not condone, but a book about the beauty I've seen in that group—their opposition to war, their truthfulness and their generosity."

The fate of Charles Manson, Charles Watson, Susan Atkins, Patricia Krenwinkel, Leslie Van Houten, and Robert Beausoleil was decided on February 18, 1972. That day the California State Supreme Court announced that it had voted 6-1 to abolish the death penalty in the state of California. The opinion was based on Article I, Section 6, of the State Constitution, which forbids "cruel or unusual punishment."*

*In June 1972 the United States Supreme Court ruled, in a 5-4 decision, that the death penalty, if imposed in an arbitrary fashion with the jury being given absolute discretion and no guidelines, constituted "cruel and unusual punishment" in violation of the Eighth Amendment to the U.S. Constitution.

Although a number of states, including California, have since passed laws restoring the death penalty and making it mandatory for certain crimes, including mass murders, at the time this is writ-

The sentences of the 107 persons awaiting execution in California were automatically reduced to life imprisonment.

Manson, in Los Angeles as a defense witness in the Bruce Davis trial, grinned broadly on hearing the news.

In California a person sentenced to life imprisonment is eligible to apply for parole in seven years.

By August 1972 the last prisoners had left California's Death Rows, most to be transferred to the "yards," or general inmate population, of various state penal institutions. Although at this writing Atkins, Krenwinkel, and Van Houten remain in the special security unit constructed for them at the California Institute for Women at Frontera, it is likely that in time they will join the general population also.

In his psychiatric report on Patricia Krenwinkel, Dr. Joel Hochman said that of the three girls Katie had the most tenuous hold on reality. It was his opinion that if she were ever separated from the others and the Manson mystique, it was quite possible she would lose even that, and lapse into complete psychosis.

With regard to Leslie Van Houten, who of the three girls was least committed to Manson, yet still murdered for him, I fear that she may grow harder and tougher; I have very little hope for her eventual rehabilitation.

Writing of Susan Atkins, Los Angeles *Times* reporter Dave Smith expressed something which I had long felt. "Watching her behavior—bold and actressy in court, cute and mincing when making eye-play with someone, a little haunted when no one pays attention—I get the feeling that one day she might start screaming, and simply never stop."

As for the other convicted Manson Family killers—Charles Watson; Robert Beausoleil; Steve Grogan, aka Clem; and Bruce Davis—all are now in the general inmate

---

ten the United States Supreme Court has yet to rule on their constitutionality.

Even if the California law is let stand, it would not affect the Manson Family killers, since the new statute is not retroactive.

population. Tex is no longer playing insane and has a girl friend who visits him regularly. Bobby received a certain amount of national attention when he was interviewed by Truman Capote during a TV documentary on American prisons. Not long afterward his jaw was broken and his hand dislocated in a brawl in the yard of San Quentin. The fight was the result of a power struggle over the leadership of the Aryan Brotherhood, with which Beausoleil had become affiliated. The AB, which is believed responsible for more than a dozen fatal stabbings in various California prisons in the last few years, is the successor to several earlier groups, including a neo-Nazi organization. Its total membership is not known, but it is believed to have about two hundred hard-core inmate followers, and it espouses many of the same racial principles that Charles Manson did. The legacy lives on.

Of all the Manson Family killers, only their leader merits special handling. In October 1972, Charles Manson was transferred to the maximum security adjustment center at Folsom Prison in Northern California. Described as "a prison within a prison," it provides special housing for "problem inmates" who cannot be safely controlled in the general prison population. With the transfer Manson lost not only all of the special privileges afforded those awaiting execution, he also lost his regular inmate privileges, because of his "hostile and belligerent attitude."

"Prison is my home, the only home I ever had," Manson often said. In 1967 he begged the authorities not to release him. Had anyone heeded his warning, this book need never have been written, and perhaps thirty-five to forty people now dead might still be alive.

In convicting him, Manson said, I was only sending him home. Only this time it won't be the same. Observed San Quentin warden Louis Nelson, before Manson was transferred to Folsom: "It would be dangerous to put a guy like Manson into the main population, because in the eyes of other inmates he didn't commit first-class crimes. He was convicted of killing a pregnant woman, and that sort of thing doesn't allow him to rank very high in the prison social structure. It's like being a child molester. Guys like that are going to do hard time wherever they are."

Too, like Sirhan Sirhan, convicted slayer of Senator Robert Kennedy, his notoriety is his own worst enemy. For as long as he remains in prison, Manson will be looking over his shoulder, aware that any con hoping to make a reputation need only put a shiv in his back.

That Manson, Watson, Beausoleil, Davis, Grogan, Atkins, Van Houten, and Krenwinkel will be eligible for parole in 1978 does not mean that they will get it, only that this is the earliest date they will be eligible to apply. The average incarceration in California for first degree murder is ten and a half to eleven years. Because of the hideous nature of their crimes and the total absence of mitigating circumstances, my guess is that all will serve longer periods: the girls fifteen to twenty years, the men—with the exception of Manson himself—a like number.

As for the leader of the Family, my guess is that he will remain in prison for at least twenty-five years, and quite possibly the rest of his life.

In mid-October of 1973 some thirty prisoners in California's toughest lockup, Folsom Prison's 4-A adjustment center, staged what was described by the San Francisco *Chronicle* as a "peaceful protest" against prison conditions.

The man who used and championed fear did not participate. According to the *Chronicle* story: "Mass murderer Charles Manson is among the inmates in 4-A, although prison spokesmen say he is not involved in this demonstration. Manson has been threatened by other inmates in the past, and authorities say he seldom ventures out of his cell for fear of being attacked."

Index

ABOUT THE AUTHOR

VINCENT T. BUGLIOSI received his law degree in 1964 from UCLA law school, where he was president of his graduating class. In his eight-year career as a prosecutor for the Los Angeles District Attorney's Office, he tried close to 1,000 felony and misdemeanor court and jury trials. Of 106 felony jury trials, he lost but one case. His most famous trial was, of course, the Manson case, which became the basis of his best-selling book *Helter Skelter.* But even before the Manson case, in the television series "The D.A.," actor Robert Conrad patterened his starring role after Bugliosi. His most recent nonfiction book, *Till Death Us Do Part,* was also a bestseller and he has recently had his first novel (co-written with Ken Hurwitz) *Shadow of Cain,* published in hardcover. He lives with his wife, Gail, and children, Wendy and Vince, Jr., in Los Angeles, where he is in private practice.

Also available in Arrow

MINDLESS MURDERS

John Dunning

Twenty Chilling True Stories

A murder without motive is the most chilling crime of all. And the twenty seemingly pointless murders described here are all the more horrifying because every one is true.

The dissected body found still partly deep-frozen in the park, the corpse cooked through in the sauna, the murder of an elderly woman from Black Mamba venom – these are just some of the extraordinary cases discribed in *Mindless Murders*.

'John Dunning has the journalist's eye for the gruesome, for human oddity, and for sheer dramatic tension'
Colin Wilson

STRANGE DEATHS

John Dunning

A chilling connection of terrifying murders

Fifteen true stories of the most shocking and unusual murders of this century, each one retold in frighteningly accurate detail by an outstanding historian of crime. Stories that are guaranteed to send shivers of terror down your spine.

THE ONE THAT GOT AWAY

Chris Ryan

The true hero of the *Bravo Two Zero* mission tells his own story

The SAS mission conducted behind Iraqi lines is one of the most famous stories of courage and survival in modern warfare. Of the eight members of the SAS regiment who set off, only one escaped capture. This is his story.

'You have personally made SAS history'
General Sir Peter de la Billiere

'It's a thrill-a-minute story of terror, hardship, heroism, bravery and sheer guts'
The Sun

'Raw and brutal'
Daily Express

'Chris Ryan's *The One That Got Away* must rank with the great escape stories of modern military history'
Soldier Magazine

'Chris Ryan is tough. More than just tough, he has a strength of spirit which has proved unbreakable'
Evening Chronicle

SLEEPERS

Lorenzo Carcaterra

An unforgettable true story of friendship, loyalty and revenge

Lorenzo, Michael, John and Tommy shared everything – the laughter and the bruises of an impoverished childhood on New York's violent West Side. Until one of their pranks misfired and they were sent to reformatory school.

Twelve months of systematic mental, physical and sexual abuse left the boys transformed for ever.

Eleven years later, one of them has become a journalist, one a lawyer – and the other two killers for the mob. In a chance encounter they came face to face with one of their torturers and shot him dead in front of several witnesses. The trial that followed brought the four friends together again in one last, audacious stand – and a courtroom climax as gripping as any John Grisham novel.

'Undeniably powerful, an enormously affecting and intensely human story'
The Washington Post

'Fabulous, unbelievably good'
Entertainment Weekly

'A brilliant, troubling, important book'
Jonathan Kellerman

A CIVIL ACTION

Jonathan Harr

'Whether in truth or in fiction I have never read a more compelling chronicle of litigation.'
John Grisham

A Civil Action is the story of a young lawyer's battle to win compensation from two of America's industrial giants on behalf of the families whose lives were wrecked by alleged toxic poisioning of their town well. The case became one of the most monumental in American legal history and nearly led to the lawyer's ruin.

At the beginning of the 1980s, Jan Schlichtmann was one of Boston's most successful malpractice lawyers. Then against his better judgement and the advice of his associates, he took on the case of the Woburn families. It took nine years in which Schlichtmann risked every dollar he had ever made and every ounce of sanity he could muster as he struggled to beat the opposition's lawyers.

A Civil Action reads like a courtroom drama, but everything in it is true, meticulously researched by a journalist who came to live the case almost as a participant. It gives an insight into American law and lawyers like no other book every written.

'Riveting'
Spectator

'A suspenseful narrative full of intellectual surprises and bold-faced characters . . . an outstanding work of journalism'
Time

MY DARK PLACES

James Ellroy

America's greatest crime novelist turns to non-fiction, and the 38-year-old mystery of his mother's murder.

On the night of 21 June 1958, Geneva Hilliker Ellroy left her home in El Monte, California. She was found strangled the next day. Her ten-year-old son James had been away for the weekend and returned to their house to hear the news.

Jean's murderer was never found, but her death had an enduring legacy on her son who spent his early adult life as a wino, petty burglar and derelict. Only later, through his obsession with crime fiction, triggered by his mother's murder, did Ellroy begin to delve into his past.

Shortly after the publication of his ground-breaking novel *White Jazz* Ellroy determined to solve the crime, with the detectives who worked on the case. The result is one of the few classics of crime non-fiction and autobiography to appear in the last decades, a hypnotic trip to America's underbelly and one man's tortured soul.

'The outstanding crime-writer of his generation'
Peter Gutteridge, *Independent*

'One of the most popular fiction writers in America, whose best books take their readers to the darkest places of the human condition – a Tinseltown Dostoyevsky'
Time Out

WHITE JAZZ

James Ellroy

Los Angeles, 1958: a city on the make. A boom town at the edge of a new era ripe for plunder.

Lieutenant Dave Klein: in turn a lawyer, bagman, slum landlord, mob killer. Klein stands at the centre of a complex web of plots where violence and death will intersect.

'A vivid enthralling read . . . James Ellroy is the outstanding American crime-writer of his generation'
Peter Gutteridge, Independent

'At last, the final part of James Ellroy's LA Quartet is available. With it, he has completed a climb to the very pinnacle of crime writing. Names like Robert B Parker, George V Higgins and Elmore Leonard certainly don't pale into significance, but they don't shine so brightly any more. *White Jazz* is without doubt his best yet'
Marcin Miller, City Limits

'Recent novels by the likes of Carl Hiaasen, Andrew Vachss and George V Higgins . . . James Ellroy . . . may be the exception. He seems in less danger of burnout than of going supernova'
John Williams, New Statesman and Society

THE BIG NOWHERE

James Ellroy

1950s Los Angeles: The City of Angels has becom the city of the Angel of Death.

Communist witchhunts and insanely violent killings are terrorising the community. Three men are plunged into a maelstrom of violence and deceit when their lives become inextricably linked as each one confronts his own personal darkness . . .

'Ellroy is a unique voice in American fiction'
Jonathan Kellarman

'Epic, obsessively imagined history.'
The Face

' Like Hammett and Chandler, but Ellroy adds layers they never dared. One of the most compelling crime novels in a long time'
Philadelphia Enquirer

THE BLACK DAHLIA

James Ellroy

A chilling novel based on, Hollywood's most notorious murder case.

Los Angeles, 10th January 1947: a beautiful young woman walked into the night and met her horrific destiny.

Five days later, her tortured body was found drained of blood and cut in half. The newspapers called her 'The Black Dahlia'. Two cops are caught up in the investigation and embark on a hellish journey that takes tem to the core of the dead girl's twisted life . . .

'One if those rare, brilliantly written books you want to press on other people'
Time Out

'A wonderful tale of ambition, insanity, passion and deceit'
Publishers Weekly